The Taxation of Petroleum and Minerals

There are few areas of economic policy-making in which the returns to good decisions are so high – and the punishment of bad decisions so cruel – as in the management of natural resource wealth. Rich endowments of oil, gas and minerals have set some countries on courses of sustained and robust prosperity; but they have left others riddled with corruption and persistent poverty, with little of lasting value to show for squandered wealth. And amongst the most important of these decisions are those relating to the tax treatment of oil, gas and minerals.

This book provides a comprehensive and accessible account of the main issues – drawing lessons from theory, describing the main features of current practice in each of these areas, and addressing the practicalities of administration – in taxing these resources. What share of the proceeds from the extraction of these resources should governments take? How can investors be given the assurances in relation to tax treatment they require if they are to be willing to invest billions of dollars in projects that will last decades? To what extent, and how, should government's tax take be sensitive to commodity prices? How can governments evaluate alternative possible tax regimes? Can, and should, auctions play a greater role in these sectors? What is the experience with, and potential of, innovative forms of corporate taxation in this area? Should government participate directly in exploration and extraction? These and many other key questions receive thorough attention.

The contributions in this book – by widely-respected experts drawn from the international institutions, academe and the private sector – provide a guide to past experiences and current thinking, as well as some new ideas on profits tax design, that is not only readable, but detailed enough to inform practical decision-making and to bring researchers to the frontiers of the topic. This book will be of interest to economics postgraduates and researchers working on resource issues, as well as professionals working on taxation of oil, gas and minerals/mining.

Philip Daniel is Deputy Head, Tax Policy Division, in the Fiscal Affairs Department of the International Monetary Fund. **Michael Keen** is Assistant Director in the Fiscal Affairs Department of the International Monetary Fund, where he was previously head of the Tax Policy and Tax Coordination divisions. **Charles McPherson** is Technical Assistance Adviser in the Fiscal Affairs Department of the International Monetary Fund with particular responsibilities for fiscal and financial policies in resource rich countries.

The Taxation of Petroleum and Minerals

Principles, problems and practice

Edited by **Philip Daniel,
Michael Keen and
Charles McPherson**

LONDON AND NEW YORK

First published 2010
by Routledge
2 Park Square, Milton Park, Abingdon, Oxon OX14 4RN

Simultaneously published in the USA and Canada
by Routledge
270 Madison Avenue, New York, NY 10016

Routledge is an imprint of the Taylor & Francis Group, an informa business

Typeset in Times by Wearset Ltd, Boldon, Tyne and Wear
Printed and bound in Great Britain by Antony Rowe Ltd,
Chippenham, Wiltshire

British Library Cataloguing in Publication Data
A catalogue record for this book is available from the British Library

Library of Congress Cataloging in Publication Data
The taxation of petroleum and minerals: principles, problems and practice/
edited by Philip Daniel, Michael Keen and Charles McPherson.
p. cm.
Includes bibliographical references and index.
Petroleum–Taxation. 2. Mines and mineral resources–Taxation. 3. Mining leases. I. Daniel, Philip. II. Keen, Michael. III. McPherson, Charles P., 1944–

HD9560.8.A1T39 2010
336.2'66553–dc22

2009047902

ISBN13: 978-0-415-56921-7 (hbk)
ISBN13: 978-0-415-78138-1 (pbk)
ISBN13: 978-0-203-85108-1 (ebk)

Contents

List of figures	vii
List of tables	ix
Notes on contributors	xi
Preface	xiv
DOMINIQUE STRAUSS-KAHN	

1 Introduction 1
PHILIP DANIEL, MICHAEL KEEN, AND CHARLES McPHERSON

**PART I
Conceptual overview** 11

2 Theoretical perspectives on resource tax design 13
ROBIN BOADWAY AND MICHAEL KEEN

3 Principles of resource taxation for low-income countries 75
PAUL COLLIER

**PART II
Sectoral experiences and issues** 87

4 Petroleum fiscal regimes: evolution and challenges 89
CAROLE NAKHLE

5 International mineral taxation: experience and issues 122
LINDSAY HOGAN AND BRENTON GOLDSWORTHY

6 Natural gas: experience and issues 163
GRAHAM KELLAS

PART III
Special topics 185

7 **Evaluating fiscal regimes for resource projects: an example from oil development** 187
PHILIP DANIEL, BRENTON GOLDSWORTHY,
WOJCIECH MALISZEWSKI, DIEGO MESA PUYO,
AND ALISTAIR WATSON

8 **Resource rent taxes: a re-appraisal** 241
BRYAN C. LAND

9 **State participation in the natural resource sectors: evolution, issues and outlook** 263
CHARLES McPHERSON

10 **How best to auction natural resources** 289
PETER CRAMTON

PART IV
Implementation 317

11 **Resource tax administration: the implications of alternative policy choices** 319
JACK CALDER

12 **Resource tax administration: functions, procedures and institutions** 340
JACK CALDER

13 **International tax issues for the resources sector** 378
PETER MULLINS

PART V
Stability and credibility 403

14 **Contractual assurances of fiscal stability** 405
PHILIP DANIEL AND EMIL M. SUNLEY

15 **Time consistency in petroleum taxation: lessons from Norway** 425
PETTER OSMUNDSEN

Index 445

Figures

2.1	Resource price movements	20
4.1	Evolution of the UKCS petroleum fiscal regime and oil price	110
5.1	Mineral prices	124
5.2	Illustrative economic rent in the minerals industry (supernormal profit or excess profit)	136
5.3	Illustrative industry impact of a Brown tax, risk neutral investors	137
5.4	Illustrative industry impact of an ad valorem royalty, risk neutral investors	140
5.5	Illustrative industry impact of a mixed system, risk neutral investors	143
6.1	Global natural gas supply 2000–2020	164
6.2	Global LNG supply 2000–2020	164
6.3	Global natural gas reserves and consumption	165
6.4	Natural gas value chain	166
6.5	Schematic examples of segmented and integrated LNG projects	168
6.6	Upstream vs midstream taxation	169
6.7	Total government take under different transfer pricing policies	170
6.8	Australia's residual price methodology to establish transfer prices in LNG projects	171
6.9	Total country take under different transfer pricing policies	172
6.10	Oil vs gas prices	177
6.11	Oil field vs gas field production profiles	178
7.1	Uncertainty in prices and price forecasts	188
7.2	WEO oil price projection (as of February 2009)	205
7.3	Time path of gross revenues and government revenues under "current terms"	209
7.4	AETR over a range of pre-tax cash flows discounted at 15 percent	211
7.5	R-factor and cumulative IRR to the investor for the deep water oil project	212
7.6	Government revenues: alternative package vs "current terms"	213
7.7	Government share of total benefits over a range of pre-tax IRR	216
7.8	Cumulative probabilities of post-tax NPV, discounted at 15 percent	219

7.9	AETR and breakeven price	221
8.1	Resource rent	245
8.2	Rent potential of a hypothetical resource base	246
8.3	Progressive and regressive fiscal regimes	246
9.1	Competing budgetary allocations in Nigeria, FYs 2005–2007	270
9.2	Tax revenues and equity returns	271
9.3	Government take from oil and mining projects compared	272
9.4	Impact of project delays on state revenues, Angola	273
12.1	Separation of roles	367

Tables

2.1	Receipts from hydrocarbons and minerals in percent of government revenue	18
4.1	Angola's profit oil splits	107
5.1	World exports for selected mineral commodities, 2006	123
5.2	Mining corporate income tax rates	128
5.3	Fiscal instruments	130
5.4	Key results for illustrative resource projects	146–147
5.5	Summary of mineral taxation in selected developed countries	150–153
5.6	Summary of mineral taxation in selected other countries	154–159
7.1	Evaluation criteria and indicators	204
7.2	Project examples	205
7.3	Simulated "current terms"	207
7.4	Summary results for the "current terms"	208
7.5	Alternative package	210
7.6	AETR, breakeven price, and METR	214
7.7	Mean government NPV, CV, and early share of total benefits	217
7.8	Mean expected post-tax IRR and CV	218
7.9	Comparator countries for analysis	220
7.10	Index of revenue stability and yield, with expected risk index	222
7.11	Mean expected post-tax IRR, CV, and probability of returns below 15 percent	223
7.12	Prospectivity gap	224
7.13	Summary of fiscal regimes	230–231
7.14	AETR, breakeven price and METR, at various discount rates	232–233
7.15	Government NPV, CV and early share of total benefits	233–234
7.16	Mean expected post-tax IRR, CV, and probability of returns below 10 and 20 percent	235
8.1	Some examples of resource rent taxes	243
8.2	The basic calculation of a resource rent tax	248
8.3	Comparison of resource rent tax with other taxes on profits	250
8.4	Details of resource rent taxes in selected countries	259
9.1	State participation in petroleum-rich countries	265
9.2	State participation in minerals-rich countries	266

x   *Tables*

10.1 Alternative auction approaches   313
13.1 International tax systems for dividends received by corporate
      taxpayers, 2008   385

Contributors

Robin Boadway is David Chadwick Smith Chair in Economics at Queen's University in Canada. He is President of the International Institute of Public Finance and past Editor of the *Journal of Public Economics*.

Jack Calder is a freelance oil tax administration consultant. He previously worked for the UK Inland Revenue, latterly as a Deputy Director of the Oil Taxation Office.

Paul Collier is Professor of Economics and Director of the Centre for the Study of African Economies at Oxford University, and former Director of Development Research at the World Bank. He is the author of many influential articles and books, including the best-selling *The Bottom Billion*.

Peter Cramton is Professor of Economics at the University of Maryland. Since 1983, he has conducted research on auction theory and practice. On the practical side, he is Chairman of Market Design Inc., an economics consultancy focusing on the design of auction markets.

Philip Daniel is Deputy Division Chief, Tax Policy, in the Fiscal Affairs Department of the International Monetary Fund. He formerly held posts at the Universities of Cambridge and Sussex (UK), and at the Commonwealth Secretariat. As a consultant, he advised many governments on commercial negotiations and policies for extractive industries.

Brenton Goldsworthy is an Economist in the Fiscal Affairs Department of the International Monetary Fund. He was formerly a Manager in the Macroeconomic Group in the Australian Treasury.

Lindsay Hogan is a Senior Economist in the Energy, Minerals and Trade Branch of the Australian Bureau of Agricultural and Resource Economics, where she works on international and domestic energy and minerals issues, and a range of natural resource management issues including water, fisheries and forestry.

Michael Keen is an Assistant Director in the Fiscal Affairs Department of the International Monetary Fund. He was formerly Professor of Economics at the University of Essex and President of the International Institute of Public Finance.

Graham Kellas is a Vice President in Wood Mackenzie's consulting group and specializes in the analysis of fiscal regimes. He has advised several governments on appropriate fiscal policies and is principal author of Wood Mackenzie's fiscal benchmarking studies. He previously worked with Petroconsultants, two exploration companies and with Professor Alex Kemp at Aberdeen University.

Bryan C. Land is a Senior Oil, Gas and Mining Specialist in the Oil, Gas and Mining Policy and Operations Unit of the World Bank. He was formerly a Special Advisor (Economic) and Head of the Economic and Legal Section in the Commonwealth Secretariat.

Charles McPherson is a Technical Assistance Advisor, Tax Policy, in the Fiscal Affairs Department of the International Monetary Fund. Before coming to the IMF, he was Senior Advisor and Manager, Oil and Gas Policy, at the World Bank. He previously worked at two major oil companies, focusing primarily on the negotiation of international government agreements.

Wojciech Maliszewski is an Economist in the European Department in the International Monetary Fund. He was formerly a Researcher in the Center for Social and Economic Research CASE in Warsaw and holds a PhD from the London School of Economics.

Peter Mullins is a Senior Tax Counsel with the Australian Tax Office (ATO). He was previously a Senior Economist with the International Monetary Fund, and prior to that held a number of senior positions in the Australian Treasury and ATO.

Carole Nakhle is an Associate Lecturer at the Surrey Energy Economics Centre, University of Surrey, UK, where she previously acted as energy research fellow for three years. She is also special parliamentary advisor in the House of Lords, UK, and formerly of StatoilHydro.

Petter Osmundsen is Professor of Petroleum Economics at the Department of Industrial Economics, the University of Stavanger. He was formerly Associate Professor of Economics at the Norwegian School of Economics and Business Administration.

Diego Mesa Puyo is an Economist at PricewaterhouseCoopers Canada. Between 2007 and 2009 he was a member of the Fiscal Analysis of Resource Industries team in the Fiscal Affairs Department of the International Monetary Fund. He was also a graduate intern in the United Nations Economic Commission for Latin America and the Caribbean.

Emil M. Sunley served at the IMF as an Assistant Director in the Fiscal Affairs Department, prior to that, he was a tax director at Deloitte & Touche, Deputy Assistant Secretary for Tax Policy at the U.S. Treasury, and a senior fellow at the Brookings Institution.

Alistair Watson is a Technical Assistance Advisor, Tax Policy, in the Fiscal Affairs Department of the International Monetary Fund. He was previously a freelance consultant specializing in fiscal regime analysis and negotiation for the petroleum and mining industry.

Preface

There are few areas of economic policymaking in which the returns to good decisions are so high – and the punishment of bad decisions so cruel – as in the management of natural resource wealth. Rich endowments of oil, gas and minerals have set some countries on courses of sustained and robust prosperity; but they have left many others riddled with corruption and persistent poverty, with little of lasting value to show for squandered wealth.

Realizing the potential value of natural resources is a challenge for several areas of economic policy. Macroeconomic policy needs to be sensitive to the potential impact on the non-resource part of the economy; budgetary arrangements need to accommodate the extreme volatility of commodity prices and ensure fair sharing of the benefits of resource wealth across the generations; and governance structures need to assure transparency of, and accountability for, the financial flows associated with them. Not least – indeed in many ways underlining all these other concerns – is the concern that this book addresses: fiscal arrangements need to ensure that governments take a share of the financial benefits (and costs) associated with natural resource exploitation that recognizes their ownership rights without adversely impacting the exploration and investment without which they have no value.

The International Monetary Fund has for many years paid close attention to the special challenges faced by resource-rich countries. Those relating to macroeconomic and budgetary management have long figured in our surveillance work and lending arrangements, and we continue to champion initiatives towards greater transparency in the extractive industries. And in our technical dialogues with resource-rich countries, the design of fiscal regimes has also been a central topic – an especially lively and active one in the last few years of high, and, more especially, volatile, commodity prices.

This book is one way in which the Fund seeks to take forward and promote such dialogue. The chapters were first presented at a conference on the topic organized by the Fund in September 2008, with generous support from the governments of Norway, the United Kingdom and Germany. The wide and lively participation that this attracted confirmed the growing interest in these issues, and the importance of both experience-sharing and analytical work in addressing them.

The purpose of the book is thus to provide policymakers, practitioners, civil society, academics and others working on the taxation of oil, gas, and minerals with a comprehensive but accessible account of the core issues in the area – which range from the conceptual to the very practical. There can be no complete answers, of course. But in drawing on an impressive array of the most respected and experienced experts in the area, we hope that this book will prove a useful guide for those struggling with the difficult but critical tasks of designing and implementing fiscal regimes in resource-rich economies.

Dominique Strauss-Kahn
Managing Director
International Monetary Fund

1 Introduction

Philip Daniel, Michael Keen, and
Charles McPherson

What this book is about

There is big money in oil, gas, and minerals – big not only in absolute terms but also, and more importantly, relative to the overall size of many resource-endowed countries. Upfront investment costs are commonly huge, as are the potential rewards (and losses). How all this gets shared between the governments that control access to the resources and those who discover and exploit them – that is, how these resources are taxed – can have a powerful impact on the economic and political fate of resource-rich countries.

But it is not only the sheer magnitude of the sums at stake that motivates this book: that in itself need not pose intellectual or practical challenges qualitatively different from those studied in the wider public finance literature. The principal motivation lies rather in distinct challenges for tax design and implementation that are posed by inherent characteristics of the sector: heavy sunk costs and long production periods (making the certainty and credibility of tax policies critical for investors), pervasive uncertainty (technological and economic), the volatility of commodity prices, the prospect of substantial earnings in excess of the minimum required by investors, and the ultimate exhaustibility of deposits. All but the last of these are present in other activities too. But in the resource sector they are center-stage rather than – as in most of the literature on business taxation – minor players. It is the conjunction of massive practical importance and distinctive conceptual and practical difficulty that is at the heart of this book.

Specifically, this book aims to provide an exhaustive account – accessible and useful to all those with more than a passing interest in the topic, whether practical or more academic – of core issues that arise in designing and implementing fiscal regimes for oil, gas, and mineral taxation, the focus being on taxation in the countries where the resources lie, not necessarily those in which they are ultimately used. The concept of a "fiscal regime" here includes not only literal taxes – compulsory unrequited payments to government – but also, for instance, production sharing, royalties, state participation, contract fees, output pricing constraints, and the like, together with tax administration. (Quite often, as in the title of the book, we use "taxation" as synonymous with fiscal regimes in this wider sense). Reflecting the focus of most the work of the IMF in resource tax issues, some but by no means all of the chapters give special attention to the particular circumstances of resource-rich lower-income countries (which face, for instance, quite different challenges in administering resource taxes).[1]

As a guide to reading, this introduction provides a taster of each of the chapters.

What the chapters are about

The book is divided into five parts, though each chapter is intended to be self-contained: so they can be dipped into in any order.

Part I sets out key conceptual issues and ideas, providing a framework for many of the more applied contributions that follow.

Robin Boadway and Michael Keen review key concepts and issues in resource tax design, setting out a conceptual framework for many of the more applied contributions in this book. They bring to the central challenges of resource taxation a perspective drawn from the wider public finance tradition, pointing out that literatures on resource taxation, on the one hand, and on general business and commodity taxation, on the other, have evolved largely distinct from each other, with much for each strand to learn from the other. They examine various forms of potentially neutral rent tax – including not only the resource rent tax, familiar to resource practitioners, but also the "allowance for corporate equity" scheme that developed from analysis of distortions inherent in the conventional corporate income tax rather than from any special concern with natural resource issues.

Boadway and Keen also devote substantial attention to the issue of progressivity in resource taxation. They find that progressivity is likely to be unappealing for many low income countries in the presence of uncertainty. On the other hand, the strongest case for progressive resource tax arrangements in lower income countries may well be in dealing with the politics of time consistency, and determining the optimal degree of progressivity is likely to involve trading this off against the associated costs of risk-bearing.

Boadway and Keen accept that royalties will often have an important role in a resource tax regime, but emphasize that sole reliance on them risks creating costly distortions. Recognition that revenues may be easier for the tax authorities to monitor than costs suggests that royalties might be combined with rent taxes to exploit the advantages of both. They might also be combined with auctions in which the rate of rent taxation (and/or royalty) becomes a bid variable, not just an initial cash bonus bid. Ultimately, they conclude, it will seldom be optimal to rely on a single tax instrument, because of the range of challenges that governments face in designing their resource tax regimes: the preferred time path of revenues, problems of time consistency and asymmetric information, administrative capacity, and political economy pressures.

The chapter by Paul Collier, which developed from a lunchtime address given at the conference from which this book grew, aims to provoke debate over points sometimes taken as conventional wisdom in resource taxation and revenue management matters. His core theme is that economic principles for taxing resource extraction imply that the way in which natural resources are harnessed for society should differ considerably as between, say, Australia, Canada, and Norway on the one hand and Angola, Chad, and Timor-Leste on the other.

Collier stresses four distinctive features of the resource challenge in low-income countries: (i) the discovery process is more important (Africa, for example, is relatively underexplored); (ii) institutions are less robust, so the credibility of government commitments is impaired; (iii) both consumption and capital are scarce, with the rate of return on scarce capital likely to be high; and (iv) governments are usually at a particularly severe informational disadvantage vis-à-vis resource companies. He deploys these features to challenge common prescriptions in favor of integrated budgets,[2] use of the permanent income hypothesis as a guideline for absorption, and the application of excess profits taxes. He argues for a wider separation of exploration from extraction, more frequent use of auctions, royalties geared to observable variables (such as prices), and adjustment of exploration to the pace of absorption of investment. He concludes by observing that earmarking of revenues, and assembly of infrastructure packages linked to resource development (common in China's relations with Africa, for example) can serve as valuable "commitment technologies" to support positive development outcomes from resource wealth. Some of these are indeed quite radical departures from current recommendations, and are likely to receive closer attention in the coming years.

The second part of the book turns to the particularities of practice and experience in the three sectors with which it is concerned: oil, minerals, and gas,

One of the central issues in the oil sector, reviewed by Carole Nakhle, is the choice between tax and royalty (or "concessionary") regimes and contractual regimes. She points out the possibility of deploying equivalent fiscal outcomes under either type, and then explores the evolution and characteristics of each, subdividing the contractual regimes into those of a production-sharing type (where produced oil and gas are shared) and those of a service contract type (where a cash fee is paid, even if geared to project results). Tax and royalty systems prevail in OECD countries, service contracts dominate where there are national restrictions on private participation in petroleum production, while production sharing has spread to much of the developing world – especially to Africa and south east Asia, but not to Latin America.

Nakhle finds that the choice between concessionary or contractual regimes has little impact on outcomes for core fiscal regime issues: the structure of the fiscal regime itself, the impact of price volatility, ownership and control, fiscal stability, or the sharing of risks. These issues remain equally difficult under either legal form – and equally capable of resolution. The choice of legal form comes down to factors of political economy and national institutions. In all cases, Nakhle sees potential for oil and gas producing countries to establish investment frameworks (including fiscal regimes) that respect their national sovereignty, and yet engage the finance and expertise which the international oil industry can provide.

Lindsay Hogan and Brenton Goldsworthy blend a survey of fiscal regimes for minerals with an approach to evaluating the component fiscal instruments. They find wide variation in fiscal systems among countries and over time. Mining fiscal regimes have tended to be unstable, and to respond sharply to price developments or to prevalent political trends (such as that towards state ownership of mines from the 1950s onwards, and privatizations after 1980). Production sharing and other contractual forms of fiscal regime have not taken hold in mining – the reason for this not being entirely clear, and perhaps meriting closer study – so Hogan and Goldsworthy focus on the key mineral taxation devices that prevail in most of the world: royalties, corporate income tax, and rent-based taxes.

Using the "certainty equivalent approach,"[3] they evaluate the three main instruments, alone and in combination, in terms of their effects on neutrality, revenue yield, and investors' assessment of risk under differing assumptions about attitude to risk. Rent or profit-based taxes tend to rank highly on neutrality, while output-based instruments (royalties) tend to rank highly in terms of moderating government risk, and administration and compliance criteria.

Graham Kellas addresses the special case of fiscal regimes for natural gas projects. Although gas has many economic properties in common with oil, and is frequently produced in association with oil, the problems of bringing gas to market and of pricing it are significantly different. Commercialization of gas requires a chain of operations "from drill bit to burner tip" that includes upstream production, pipeline transportation, processing or liquefaction, transportation again (for example, on LNG (liquefied natural gas) tankers), distribution or regasification (if liquid), and final sale to end user as fuel, electric power, or an industrial input. At each stage there may be arm's length prices or transfer prices, and rents may arise. Fiscal regime design for gas is therefore complex, and may have to be adapted to the commercial structure of individual projects. Kellas points out that individual project arrangements are common (outside the United States, where a spot market supported by a national pipeline system exists, and perhaps north-west Europe, similarly interconnected).

Kellas explores the commercial structure of different project types, making a key distinction between "segmented" projects where transfer prices must be established at each stage of the chain, and "integrated" projects where only the final price of gas (usually LNG) matters. Since petroleum fiscal regimes usually apply to upstream production in a segmented structure, and normal corporate income taxation will apply to other stages, the transfer price from the field delivery point is critical to the fiscal outcome. Kellas considers other complications too, including the higher costs of delivering gas and the historical tendency for markets to undervalue its calorific content (heating value) relative to that of oil. He argues that government policies on gas pricing, equity participation, and on fiscal terms must be developed simultaneously if governments are to extract a significant share of rents from the production of natural gas.

Part III of the book addresses a range of special topics whose importance spans the sectors of interest.

Philip Daniel, Brenton Goldsworthy, Wojciech Maliszewski, Diego Mesa Puyo, and Alistair Watson (Daniel *et al.*) address the key question, critical for well-informed resource tax policy: How can one evaluate and compare alternative fiscal regimes for resource projects? In answering this, they present results from the Fiscal Analysis of Resource Industries (FARI) project undertaken in the Fiscal Affairs Department of the IMF. They use the example of an oil field development, but also show how the analysis can be extended to the exploration decision. After outlining criteria for evaluating resource taxation systems, they derive indicators that can be used in a practical project modeling framework to assess the regime against those criteria. Although much of their approach draws from standard procedures used by practitioners in the evaluation of petroleum projects and fiscal regimes for resources, following Boadway and Keen they try to relate these procedures to concepts employed in wider analysis of tax systems and their incentive effects.

Daniel *et al.* illustrate the application of the criteria and indicators using a simulation for "Mozambique." They do not replicate any particular contract or field for that country, but use Mozambique's model exploration and production concession contract with bid or negotiated parameters (which are not specified in that model) added by the authors. The circumstances of a country such as Mozambique recur elsewhere: one major petroleum project is already operating, there are further discoveries but, as yet, no further development decisions, and exploration interest is significant but possibly not sufficient to permit an auction process to work properly. After considering fiscal regime issues and impacts for their "Mozambique" case, Daniel *et al.* locate the possible outcome in international comparisons. As with all such exercises, they caution that these have limitations and need to be carefully interpreted, taking account of things they do not show. An investment decision in any country will be determined by much more than a mechanical comparison of the effect of a fiscal regime on investor returns, simulating an identical field across a number of different country regimes.

Bryan Land re-appraises the benefit of resource rent taxes to host governments in the light recent commodity price swings. His focus is on non-royalty devices for extracting resource rent, usually meaning a tax on net cash flows levied only after the project has generated a minimum acceptable return to capital. As Land notes, a resource rent tax (RRT) of this type has had both proponents, who regard it as an indispensable part of the resource tax armory, and detractors, who consider RRT inappropriate and/or unworkable.

After a survey of both design principles and experience in implementation of RRT, Land concludes that there is a place for such a tax device in making fiscal regimes more responsive to uncertain outcomes. In practice, RRT has only been used in combination with other devices (usually royalty and income tax). The RRT can be less distorting than other levies aimed at rent capture. RRT can, however, present administrative challenges in countries with poor tax administration capacity – though no more so than the regular corporate income tax. Land concludes that the benefits of RRT depend on the government's discount rate and risk preference: a government will have to be willing to accept back-loading of fiscal take, and a procyclical pattern of resource tax revenues.

Charles McPherson considers state participation in resource industries, drawing on case studies from both mining and petroleum jurisdictions, and countries at varied stages of economic development and institutional strength. He finds that state participation is not only durable – having been a key feature of sector development for about 50 years – but also shows signs of revival following the commodity price surge that peaked in 2008. He defines state participation broadly: from 100 percent equity participation, through partial or carried equity arrangements, to equity participation without financial obligation. He outlines the evolution of these forms, beginning with the founding of national oil companies in Argentina and Mexico, and identifying the 1970s as the time of greatest extension of state participation. Noting that the fiscal effect of each form of state participation can be replicated by a tax, he goes on to identify the noneconomic objectives, as well as the commercial and fiscal objectives, that commonly underpin state participation, and may, in many cases, be more important than strictly commercial and fiscal objectives.

McPherson then explores the systemic issues arising from state participation: governance problems; challenges for macroeconomic management; funding of developments; commercial efficiency; conflicts of interest; sector responsibilities and institutional capacity. He finds positive recent policy responses to some of these challenges, especially as a result of the global movement in support of greater transparency and accountability in natural resource sectors. In particular, he points to improved clarity on roles and responsibilities of government agencies and national resource companies.

Against a background of rapidly increasing interest in auctions as a means of allocating exploration and extraction rights for natural resources, Peter Cramton surveys the arguments for this approach and the possible means of conducting auctions. Auctions allocate and price scarce resources in settings of uncertainty. They are a competitive, formal, and transparent method of assignment. Cramton argues that a primary advantage of an auction is its tendency to assign lots (of rights to explore and extract) to those best able to use them. A well-designed auction can perform well with respect to both efficiency and revenues – although there are subtleties in auction design which can affect their efficiency.

In stressing that auction design matters, Cramton advocates three initial steps: (i) establish the objectives of the auction (he assumes this will usually be revenue maximization, but in any case stresses that there must be a clear and unambiguous way to translate bids into winners and terms); (ii) define the product – specify what is being sold; for oil, gas, and minerals this means the terms of the license or contract, including the biddable terms, and the geographic scope of the lots; and (iii) specify the auction process well in advance of the tender – the bottleneck is usually the administrative process, rather than technical auction design and implementation. He goes on to examine the role of bidder preferences, and then alternative forms of auction. The best auction format will depend on the particular setting, especially the structure of bidder preferences and the degree of competition. Cramton reviews a number of developing country experiences with oil and gas auctions, but cautions that research on the use and impact of natural resource auctions is not well-advanced (compared with the study of auctions, for example, of the spectrum for wireless telephony).

Practical issues of implementation are the focus of Part IV. It begins with two chapters by Jack Calder on the administration of fiscal regimes for the resource sector – a topic of great concern in many lower income countries, but which has received very little attention from practitioners.

The first of Calder's chapters addresses the interaction between tax policy and tax administration for natural resource sectors. Its organizing theme is a challenge to the widespread view that poor tax administration capacity rules out a progressive profit-based regime: first, it is possible simply and quickly to acquire administrative capacity by contracting out (he cites the case of Angola), at a small cost in relation to the large resource revenues at stake; second, a range of policy actions can be taken within a profits-based regime to simplify administration. He points out that, moreover, supposedly "simpler" levies, such as royalties, are not always as simple as they seem, and are made complex by rate differentiation, exemptions and conditions, and discretionary provisions.

Calder considers constraints on policy simplification, such as tax stability agreements, but argues that changes to the administrative framework are often easily accomplished despite such agreements. "[Companies] have no interest in the stability of unpredictable and inconsistent tax administration," where the changes improve it. He argues for separation of tax administration from resource management functions (an implicit criticism of production-sharing regimes), and also for a clear role for administrators in tax policy formulation.

Jack Calder's second chapter deals with the detailed functions, procedures, and institutions of resource tax administration. He stresses the importance of sound "routine" administration, especially of proper accounting for resource taxes, and argues that shortcomings ought to be straightforward to fix. Among "nonroutine" tasks, Calder examines valuation of output, tax audit, dispute resolution, and appeals; each of these varies according to the type of regime chosen. Turning then to institutions, he addresses relations among the different agencies that may have responsibilities in the resource sector, and the internal organization of the tax administration. He emphasizes that the administrative capacity actually required for resource tax administration can be exaggerated – there are very large returns to very small investments. Calder then turns to the transparency agenda in tax administration, including the clarity of roles and responsibilities, public availability of information, and assurances of integrity. Finally, he considers the politics of tax administration reform, and the possible role of technical assistance. Overall, Calder's view of administrative possibilities is optimistic; there are lessons to learn, but good practice can be found in surprising places. In some respects, indeed, administration should actually be easier in relation to resources than in other sectors.

Many resource firms operating in the resource sector, especially in developing countries, are likely to be foreign multinational firms. Peter Mullins takes up the international tax issues that consequently arise. While a country's domestic resource tax regime is important, its revenue-raising capacity and its attractiveness to investors can be enhanced or undermined by tax rules that apply to international transactions. In particular, Mullins points to the need to ensure that revenue is not unnecessarily eroded through aggressive tax planning.

Mullins guides us through recent international developments in corporate income taxation, taking up the theme from Boadway and Keen that thinking on resource taxation and general business taxation have tended to evolve independently of each other. Developments in business taxation may affect a country's attractiveness to investors, the way an investment in a resource project is best structured, and also the revenue yield for government. Resource-rich countries will want to ensure their right to tax rents yet limit the potential for double taxation of profits derived by multinational firms. Mullins examines transfer pricing and thin capitalization problems, advance pricing agreements and the potential pitfalls and uses of double taxation agreements. He sees scope for regional cooperation and information exchange.

The last part of the book deals with the issue of stability and credibility in resource taxation, which the heavy sunk costs and long duration of oil, gas, and mineral projects make such a concern for investors.

Philip Daniel and Emil Sunley explore contractual assurances of fiscal stability. They observe two general forms of a fiscal stability assurance to investors in resource contracts: the "frozen law" formulation, and the "agree-to-negotiate" formulation. They identify a number of practical difficulties with both forms: the locked-in benefits may be unsustainably generous; problems may arise in determining just what the fiscal laws were when the agreement was signed; when the agreement follows the agree-to-negotiate formulation, on the other hand, the offsetting change that would be appropriate under one set of assumptions about relevant economic circumstances may be too generous, or not generous enough, under a different set of assumptions. Finally, many fiscal stability clauses are asymmetric, protecting the investor from adverse changes but passing on changes that are beneficial.

With country examples, Daniel and Sunley outline a possible political economy of fiscal stability assurances, by analogy with other institutional devices designed to promote wider fiscal discipline. The assurances may indicate a "commitment" to the particular investor by government to abide by fiscal terms, but, alternatively, they may be a "signal" to other investors that government is serious, or even a "smokescreen" permitting use of devices not covered by the assurance when adherence to its terms becomes too costly. Daniel and Sunley note that there are few examples where a fiscal stability clause has been invoked in arbitration or court proceedings. For an investor, the real benefit of a fiscal stability clause may be to sow the seed of doubt in the host government that it might be invoked, and thereby promote appropriate behavior. Fiscal stability clauses do not necessarily prevent contract renegotiation, where fiscal regimes in place do not respond flexibly to substantial changes in circumstances.

Petter Osmundsen argues that Norway has dealt with the time consistency problem by building credibility as a reasonable tax collector, with the government initially tailoring the tax rates imposed on its oil sector to economic, geological, and technical conditions, and gradually changing the regime into a neutral and stable tax system. At a core conceptual level, he applies game theoretic models on commitment and time consistency to oil and gas taxation, and identifies special conditions in this industry which complicate a credible commitment. He finds that Norway's specific evolution of tax policy was important in arriving at the present fixed and unchanging system. In particular, it was important that the Norwegian government sought to secure the development of a substantial number of new fields, creating a disciplinary effect on the taxation of existing fields. He does not argue that the Norwegian example is applicable in all circumstances, and sets out conditions under which it does work. Osmundsen does nevertheless conclude that petroleum taxation should be shaped in a long-term perspective, with the emphasis on credibility and predictability.

Acknowledgments

This book grew from a conference on resource taxation at the International Monetary Fund in September 2008, made possible by generous support from the Oil for Development Program of the Norwegian Development Agency (NORAD), the UK Department for International Development and the German Technical Cooperation Service (GTZ). The African Development Bank and the International Finance Corporation also supported participation in the event from lower income countries. Norway's Oil for Development Program also directly supported the production of this book. We greatly appreciate this generous support and encouragement.

Brenton Goldsworthy, a contributor to this book, made a major contribution to the organization of the conference. We also thank Heidi Canelas for her diligent and enthusiastic preparation of the manuscript, and Patti Lou for guiding us through the process.

Notes

1 The book is long but does not cover everything. Issues of fiscal federalism in resource-rich economies are discussed in Ahmad and Mottu (2003), Brosio (2006) and McLure (2003); and challenges of macroeconomic management in resource-rich economies in several contributions to Davis, Ossowski and Fedelino (2003) and by Venables and van der Ploeg (2009). Transparency issues, a major and topical concern, appear in several of the chapters below but have been separately treated by the IMF in its *Guide on Resource Revenue Transparency* (2007). The book also deals only with exhaustible resources (renewable ones, such as forestry and fishery, raising distinct issues of maintaining the resource stock). Given the focus on extracting countries and upstream taxation, it does not address issues of final product pricing, from the difficulties raised by continuing subsidization of fuel consumption in some countries to the importance of crafting proper carbon pricing as a core instrument for addressing climate changes: a recent discussion of the former is in Coady *et al.* (2010) and the latter are addressed from a fiscal perspective in IMF (2008).

10 *P. Daniel* et al.

2 "Integrated budgets" means the channeling of all revenues for expenditure through a single consolidated budget, with as little earmarking as possible.
3 The certainty equivalent expected value to a risk-averse investor of a risky project being the project's expected net present value at a risk-free discount rate, less a risk premium compensating for the project risk.

References

Ahmad, Ehtisham and Eric Mottu (2003), "Oil Revenue Assignments: Country Experiences and Issues," in Jeffrey M. Davis, Rolando Ossowski and Annalisa Fedelino (eds.), *Fiscal Policy Formulation and Implementation in Oil Producing Countries*, pp. 216–242 (Washington DC: International Monetary Fund).

Brosio, Giorgio (2006), "The Assignment of Revenue from Natural Resources," in Ehtisham Ahmad and Giorgio Brosio, *Handbook of Fiscal Federalism*, pp. 431–458 (Cheltenham: Edward Elgar).

Coady, David, Robert Gillingham, Rolando Ossowski, John M. Piotrowski, Shamsuddin Tareq, and Justin Tyson (2010), "Petroleum Product Subsidies: Costly, Inequitable and on the Rise," IMF Staff Position note 2010/05.

Davis, Jeffrey M., Rolando Ossowski, and Annalisa Fedelino (eds.) (2003), "Fiscal Policy Formulation and Implementation in Oil Producing Countries" (Washington DC: International Monetary Fund).

International Monetary Fund (2008), "The Fiscal Implications of Climate Change," Fiscal Affairs Department, available at: www.imf.org/external/np/pp/eng/2008/022208.pdf (Washington DC).

International Monetary Fund (2007), *Guide on Resource Revenue Transparency*. Fiscal Affairs Department, available at: www.imf.org/external/np/fad/trans/guide.htm.

McLure, Charles (2003), "The Assignment of Oil Tax Revenue," in Jeffrey M. Davis, Rolando Ossowski, and Annalisa Fedelino (eds.), *Fiscal Policy Formulation and Implementation in Oil Producing Countries*, pp. 204–215 (Washington DC: International Monetary Fund).

Venables, Anthony and Frederick van der Ploeg (2009), "Harnessing Windfall Revenues: Optimal Policies for Resource-Rich Developing Economies," Oxford Centre for the Analysis of Resource Rich Economics, Research paper no. 2008-09.

Part I
Conceptual overview

2 Theoretical perspectives on resource tax design

Robin Boadway and Michael Keen

1 Introduction

Natural resources are a large part of the wealth of many countries, and the way in which their potential contribution to government revenues is managed can have a powerful impact – for good or ill – on their prosperity and economic development. The challenges to good tax design, however, are formidable, both in the technicalities of dealing with the distinctive features of resource activities and in coping with the interplay between the interests of powerful stakeholders.

The purpose of this chapter is to review the most central of these challenges, bringing to bear a perspective drawn from the wider public finance tradition. To a large extent, the literatures on resource taxation in particular and on business and commodity taxation more generally have evolved largely distinct from one another, and indeed the same is true in terms of policy formation. This is surprising and unfortunate. Many of the challenges faced in the resource sector are not qualitatively unique but arise in any business activity; it is just that they loom especially large in relation to resources. The resource tax literature has consequently delved into some issues (how uncertainty can shape the impact of taxation on investors' incentives, for instance) more deeply than has the wider public finance literature. On other issues (such as the design of rent taxes), it has perhaps not fully absorbed advances, theoretical and practical, in wider understanding of the essential issues and possibilities. Part of the purpose here is to bring the mainstream and specialist perspectives closer together. In doing so, the chapter is also intended to provide a conceptual framework for many of the more applied contributions in later chapters of the book.

The coverage is broad, having in mind oil, gas, and mining activities. Specialist treatments are commonly provided for each, reflecting differences in their practical features and associated traditions of tax design.[1] Their considerable analytical similarities as non-renewable resources, however, warrant a unified conceptual treatment: for brevity, the paper uses the term 'resource' to refer to all three.[2] Also for brevity, the term 'tax' is used in a broad sense to include payments to governments (such as royalties associated with the right to exploit deposits owned by the state, or equity participation) that are not taxes in the formal sense of being unrequited, but are compulsory nevertheless.

The coverage is also broad in terms of the design issues addressed. One, however, is given particular emphasis, running through much of the discussion. This is the question of whether or not resource tax regimes should incorporate some element of progressivity, in the broad sense (rarely defined more precisely) of implying an average tax rate that rises with the realized profitability of the underlying project. This naturally rises to special prominence in public discussions in times of high resource prices, but more fundamentally goes to the heart of many of the basic questions of credibility, risk-sharing and efficiency that arise in designing efficient tax regimes for the sector.

The focus of the chapter is limited, nevertheless. For the most part, the design problem considered is that of the country in which the resource deposits lie; we do not consider the pricing of final sales (the benchmark instead being one in which resources trade at world prices); governance issues are largely set aside; and so too are environmental considerations. This precludes significant policy problems: resource importing countries could choose to levy windfall taxes on rents earned on imports, for instance, or (perhaps in pursuit of energy security objectives) to impose tariffs; fuel subsidies remain a pressing concern in many countries; governance is a prevalent concern in the sector, whose nature and extent could depend on the tax regime in place; and environmental concerns are particularly prominent in the resource sector at both the local level and, for fossil fuels, through the global public bad of climate change. All these concerns could have powerful implications for efficient tax design, and are neglected here only because the issues that remain merit separate treatment.

The chapter first reviews key features of the resource sector that shape the tax design problem, and the extent (or not) of their uniqueness. Section 3 then examines some of the key instruments that are or might be deployed, and how their combined impact may be measured. Some of the central challenges for tax design emerging from the features highlighted in Section 2 are considered in Section 4. Section 5 concludes.

There is some algebra – but it is not in the main text, and can be skipped.

2 What's special about resources?

The resource sector has a number of features that make its taxation not only especially important for many countries but also particularly challenging – though in some respects, as will be seen, it is more straightforward to tax than are many others. Most of these features, it will be argued, are not in themselves unique to resources. What is distinctive is their sheer scale. This section reviews these features, postponing until later discussion of the challenges for the tax design that they pose.

A High sunk costs, long production periods

Discovering, developing, exploiting, and closing a mine or oil field can cost hundreds of millions of dollars, and take decades. In mining, for instance, it is not uncommon for 50 years or so to pass between exploration and rehabilitation. Moreover, the associated expenses are to a large degree incurred early in the life of the project, often prior to the generation of any cash flow, and are then sunk, in the sense they have little if any alternative use. An offshore oil platform may be moved to other fields, for instance, but money spent looking for oil fields (successfully or not) is gone. While significant sunk costs are incurred in other lines of business too – in developing power plants, for example, or in undertaking R&D (analogous to exploration spending) on pharmaceuticals – their pervasiveness and magnitude in resource activities put them at the heart of the problem of sectoral tax design.

The importance of these features is that they pose a fundamental problem of *time consistency*. While a resource project is still in the design stage, the prospective tax base is highly sensitive to the anticipated tax regime: if investors feel it will be too onerous, they can simply not undertake the project. Once they have incurred the sunk costs, however, investors have little choice: so long as they can cover their variable costs, production is more profitable than ceasing operations, making the tax base relatively insensitive to tax design. The government thus has an incentive to offer relatively generous treatment at the planning stage (the tax base then being relatively elastic), but much less generous treatment once it is in place (the tax base then being relatively inelastic): the 'obsolescing bargain' of the resource literature. The importance of this is that it creates a potential inefficiency: the forward-looking investor will recognize the changed incentive that the government will face ex post, and so may be reluctant to invest even if promised generous treatment: they see all too clearly the incentive that the government will have to renege. All this may leave investors reluctant to invest: the 'hold up' problem.

The problem does not arise from any duplicity or ill will on the part of either the government or investors: it simply reflects the general principle of efficient tax design that tax rates be set in inverse relation to the elasticity of the underlying tax base. The fundamental difficulty is simply the inability of the government to commit in advance to apply the scheme that it would be optimal to impose at the outset: a promise alone may not be credible, since investors know that the incentives even of a wholly benevolent government will change once the investment is made. While this incentive to renege on promised tax arrangements arises whenever investors incur sunk costs, the temptation will naturally tend be greater the more profitable an investment proves. Events in Zambia, Ecuador, and Venezuela during 2008, for example, show that pressures can be especially strong at times of high resource prices.

B The prospect of substantial rents

Economic rent is the amount by which the payment received in return for some action – bringing to market a barrel of oil, for instance – exceeds the minimum required for it to be undertaken. The attraction of such rents for tax design is clear: they can be taxed at up to (just less than) 100 percent without causing any change of behavior, providing the economist's ideal of a non-distorting tax. And this appeal on efficiency grounds – which is conceptually distinct from any notion of fairness based on the government's legal or moral claim to ownership of the resource – is reinforced on equity grounds (at least from a national perspective) if those rents would otherwise accrue to foreigners. Equally clear, most recently with the spectacular run-up in commodity prices to the latter part of 2008, is the potential magnitude of these rents in the resource sector. Rent extraction is thus a primary concern in designing resource tax regimes.

The resource sector is by no means the only one in which rents may be present. In a competitive world, they can arise only if there is some factor of production that is in fixed supply (for if there were not, new firms would enter at lower prices and eliminate the rent). In the resource context, the fixity of resource endowments – not just over infinite time but over the fewer years and decades needed to bring new sources online – and the diverse quality of deposits create evident scope for the existence of such rents.[3] In other sectors, rents may arise from fixed factors in the form of protected intellectual property rights, superior management, better locations, as well as from barriers to competition. Again, it is the sheer scale and potential persistence of such rents that mark out the resource sector.

Care always needs to be taken in operationalizing the notion of rents to include all the relevant costs of the actions at issue: failing to do so means that a tax on 'rents' will actually distort decisions. This is not an easy task. It requires, for instance, making appropriate allowance for any risk premium in the cost of capital faced by resource companies and for any part of the return to shareholders that may represent incentive payments to managerial skill. In the resource context, two particular issues loom large.

First, one of the costs of extracting some resource this period is the revenue foregone by the consequent inability to extract it in the future: this is sometimes referred to as 'Hotelling rent.'[4] Importantly, however, while these period-specific costs do affect the optimal time profile of resource extraction (as discussed below), they do not affect the rent optimally accumulated over the full lifetime of a project: a firm may incur some opportunity cost today by restricting output so as to be able to extract more tomorrow, but when tomorrow comes it derives an offsetting benefit. Thus – despite its prominence in the resource literature – the taxation of rents over a project's life does not require any measurement of Hotelling rent, or even any use or understanding of the concept.

Second is the importance of the notion of 'quasi-rents,' meaning rents whose existence derives from a previous outlay of sunk costs. Following Garnaut and Clunies Ross (1983), a resource project's life might be divided into three phases: exploration, development, and extraction. (One could add fourth and fifth phases, those of processing the extracted ore and of cleanup and shutdown of the mine, though these would not affect the current discussion). The first two phases will involve substantial investment costs, and in the case of exploration some uncertainty about the size of resource deposit found. At the end of the first phase, exploration costs are sunk and uncertainty about the size of the deposit is substantially resolved. The present value of subsequent expected revenues less development and extraction costs is the quasi-rent from the known deposit. Again, after the second phase development costs have been incurred, there will be a quasi-rent associated with future expected revenues less extraction costs. An integrated firm will operate so as to maximize its quasi-rents in each phase less its initial outlay, and in so doing will also maximize its overall rents ex ante. By the same token, if different firms are involved in the three phases, overall rent maximization will be achieved if resource property rights are properly priced in going from one phase to another. Thus, the value of a resource discovered by an exploration firm could in principle be sold to a developing firm at a price reflecting expected future quasi-rents.

A resource tax system that aims to be efficient should tax full rents, not quasi-rents. This may be difficult to do if tax is applied only at the extraction stage, since by then only successful resource discoveries will be pursued. The full cost of resource exploitation includes the costs of unsuccessful exploration expenditures as well, and unless these are somehow treated as deductible costs for tax purposes, exploration will be inefficiently low. (The time consistency problem discussed above is precisely the temptation to tax away such quasi-rents). Suppose, for example, that exploration costing $10 million has a 10 percent chance of discovering deposits that can be sold for $160 million (and extracted costlessly), and 90 percent chance of finding nothing. In the event of success, the quasi-rents of $160 million cannot be fully taxed away if exploration is to be profitable. Clearly it would not be enough simply to allow exploration costs as a deduction in the event of success, and levy tax of $150 million, since the possibility of failure means that expected return to exploration would then be negative. The most that can be taken in tax in the event that the project succeeds is $60 million: the investor then stands a 10 percent chance of earning $90 million after tax and exploration costs that just offsets the 90 percent chance of simply losing $10 million.[5] It is this $60 million that represents rent viewed over the full lifetime of the project, and which the objective of efficient rent taxation should lead policy makers to focus on.

All this points to a resource tax system that recognizes all phases of resource production. The treatment of exploration costs, in particular, is critical – just as the treatment of R&D expenses more generally can be critical to efficient support of innovation.

The prospect of large, persistent rents also creates well-known problems of rent-seeking and corruption: these, however, are not the focus of attention here.[6]

C Tax revenue can be substantial and a primary benefit to the host country

Reflecting the substantial rents to be earned, government revenue from resource activities can be sizable not only absolutely but also as a share of all such revenue: Table 2.1 documents this for selected resource-rich countries. Access to a relatively efficient revenue source of this kind potentially strengthens the fiscal

Table 2.1 Receipts from hydrocarbons and minerals in percent of government revenue (average 2000–2007, selected countries)*

Hydrocarbons		Minerals**	
Algeria	72	Botswana (diamonds)	44
Angola	76	Chile (copper)	12
Azerbaijan	59	Guinea (bauxite/alumina)	19
Bahrain	74	Jordan (phosphates)	1
Bolivia	24	Liberia (iron ore, gold)	8
Cameroon	27	Mongolia (copper, gold)	9
Chad	27	Namibia (diamonds)	8
Colombia	10	Peru (Gold, copper, silver)	5
Congo, Republic of	73	Sierra Leone (diamonds, bauxite)	1
Ecuador	25	South Africa (gold, platinum)	2
Equatorial Guinea	77		
Gabon	10		
Indonesia	26		
Iran	65		
Iraq	97		
Kazakhstan	27		
Kuwait	79		
Libya	77		
Mauritania	11		
Mexico	34		
Nigeria	78		
Norway	26		
Oman	83		
Papua New Guinea	21		
Qatar	68		
Russia	22		
São Tomé and Principe	35		
Saudi Arabia	72		
Sudan	50		
Syrian Arab Republic	39		
Timor Leste	70		
Trinidad and Tobago	38		
Turkmenistan	46		
United Arab Emirates	69		
Venezuela	48		
Vietnam	31		
Yemen	72		

Source: IMF staff calculations.

Notes
* Revenue (taken from the *World Economic Outlook*) is 'General government, total revenue and grants' when available (which is in most cases), and 'Central government, total revenue and grants' otherwise.
** Principal minerals in brackets.

position, allowing reduced borrowing, increased spending and/or less reliance on more distorting taxes. One would expect, for example, that resource-rich countries would take the benefit in part by making less use of presumably less efficient non-resource tax instruments; Bornhorst *et al.* (2009) find that this has indeed been the case for a panel of oil-rich countries.

The importance of resource revenues, especially when concentrated within countries on relatively few fields, has another implication: more systematically than in other areas, tax design is de facto a matter of negotiation between government and investor (and/or of frequent changes to the general regime), rather than of designing some system that is then simply applied uniformly to all. While there may be merits in terms of transparency, and perhaps fairness and credibility too, in having tax rules set an arms-length from the circumstances of particular projects and investors, in practice – and especially for countries with only a few large sources – this will simply not happen.

Tax revenue may not be the only economic gain from resource projects. Foreign investment is often seen as conveying substantial external benefits to host economies – beyond, that is, the domestic share in the financial returns it yields – in terms, notably, of easing unemployment and developing human capital. Resource investments, however, are highly capital intensive, so that associated employment (especially in upstream activities) can be quite modest, and also relatively low-skilled. Joint ventures are in large part seen as a way to encourage transfer of higher level skills, though there is little evidence on how successfully this has been achieved: the continued dominance of firms based in developed countries suggests perhaps that success has been limited. While encouraging (which does not necessarily mean subsidizing) industrial linkages beyond resource enclaves can clearly be useful, spillovers, in this sense, may be quite limited. And of course they are in some respects adverse, with the risk of significant environmental damage both from the inescapable footprint of extraction activities and accidental oil spills and other damage.

Combined with the prevalence of foreign ownership, and the sheer scale of government receipts, all this means that tax revenue is likely to be not simply a side-benefit of resource extraction but the core benefit itself. Not entirely unique to resources – much the same is true, for example, of the offshore banking that many developing countries have tried to attract – this makes proper tax design in the host country still more important.

D Uncertainty

Resource projects are subject to considerable uncertainty at all stages, from exploration through development to extraction and closure. Once again, the same is true in many sectors, not least those (like chemicals) that are intensive in R&D. But the inherent uncertainties and longevity of the production period exacerbate the extent of the challenges.

Geology poses its own uncertainties: How much of the resource will be present, in what quality, how accessibly, and by means of what perhaps as yet undeveloped technology? For multinationals operating a portfolio of projects, or countries endowed with many deposits these idiosyncratic risks may pose little difficulty, as failure in some places is offset by success elsewhere. For countries with just a few possible deposits, however, the uncertainty poses real problems.

Price uncertainty poses more systemic difficulties, not being naturally diversified in the same way. And the uncertainty and volatility of output prices[7] is indeed one of the most marked features of the sector. Figure 2.1 illustrates, showing the prices of crude oil, copper and uranium over the last 40 years (20 for uranium). The roller-coaster of the last decade or so epitomizes the difficulty. From around $15 per barrel at the end of 1998, for example, the price of crude oil rose to $112 by the summer of 2008 before falling to $60 at year end. Copper prices also rose to a peak at around the same time, before a marked fall, as did other mineral prices. Developments in the uranium price were spectacular, rising from under $10 per pound at the start of the decade to more than $120 at end 2007, before tumbling to $64 at the end of 2008.

These large and in many cases rapid price movements translate into considerable uncertainty and variability in the aggregate rents obtained over the lifetime of a project, and the distinct possibility that total rents will turn out to be negative – with powerful implications for decision-making, and the way in which tax design can affect it. They also strongly impact public debate on the tax treatment of resource activities: widespread talk of windfall taxes and contract renegotiation around mid-2008, for instance, had evaporated by year-end.

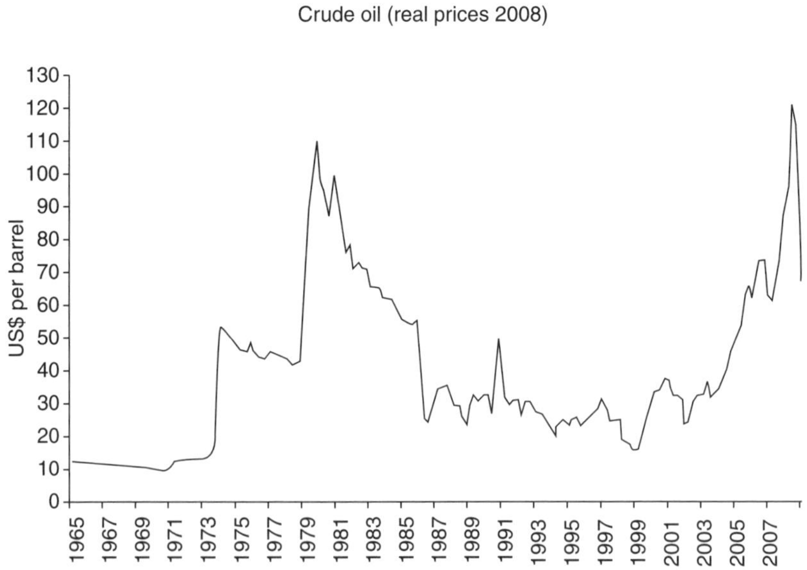

Crude oil (real prices 2008)

Figure 2.1 Resource price movements.

Note
Simple average of Dated Brent, West Texas Intermediate, and the Dubai Fateh, US$ per barrel.

Copper (real prices 2008)

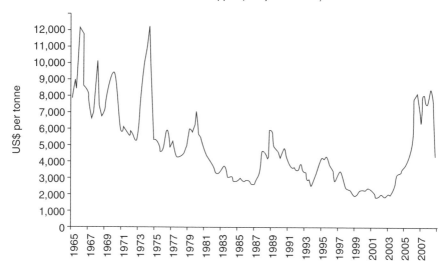

Note
Copper, grade A cathode, LME spot price, CIF European ports, US$ per metric tonne.

Uranium (real prices 2008)

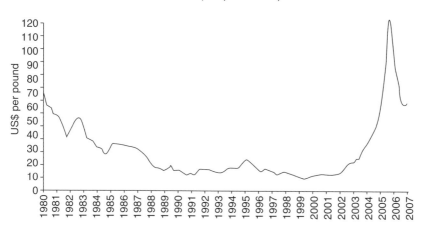

Note
Uranium, u308 restricted price, Nuexco exchange spot, US$ per pound.

Figure 2.1 continued

In addition to these uncertainties inherent in the economics of resource extraction, there are also many policy uncertainties, some reflecting the time consistency problem stressed above, some arising from wider political risks in dealing with potentially unstable regimes, and others reflecting specific policy uncertainties, not least, for oil and other fossil fuels, in relation to evolving policies towards climate change.

Resource activities can entail particular risks for workers and entire communities. With resources often located in remote areas, communities growing up around them may be one-firm towns, exposing workers and their families to risks that they find hard to diversify away. Governments are often left to assume some responsibility for the hardship felt by resource-dependent communities that fall on tough times.

E International considerations

Reflecting the relative scarcity of the technical and managerial skills needed, the development and exploitation of natural resources is commonly undertaken primarily by foreign-owned firms, albeit often in conjunction with state-owned companies (especially in the oil sector) or in joint ventures with domestically-owned companies. Once more this is not unique to the sector, but is so pervasive as to make it especially important for resource tax design. It has several implications.

The most obvious is that since more than one jurisdiction will typically seek to tax any resource project, investors and each government concerned must look to the combined impact of all these taxes, not just those in any single country. This in turn has a number of consequences.

One is that the effective rate of taxation on any project depends not only on the tax system in the host country, but also on tax rules in the home country of the investing firm, the countries in which owners of the investing firm reside, and, perhaps, any countries through which income is routed. It is conventional to focus only on the host country tax system in evaluating tax impacts on projects, but taxation in these other countries can also have a powerful impact on revenues, profitability, and behavior. Of particular importance is the treatment in home countries asserting the right to tax income that has been earned and taxed abroad. Standard corporate and withholding tax payments will generally be creditable against home country liability in such countries, for instance, but royalties will not; and explicit rent taxes may be creditable only if explicit provision for this is made for this in double tax agreements.

Awareness of the interactions between the various tax systems can in turn impact proper tax design. The impact of a host country rent tax on incentives to invest, for instance, depends critically on whether or not such tax payments are available as a credit against the liability of the foreign-owned firm in its home country. And if host countries – which have, de facto and de jure, the first right to tax activities undertaken in their jurisdiction – fail to fully tax the rents on some resource activity, the home government may seek to do so instead. The international nature of resource companies' operations also creates particular opportunities for tax avoidance, and corresponding challenges for national tax administrations – often an inherently unequal contest, given the expertise and funds available to large multinationals relative to domestic tax administrations even in relatively advanced economies. In some respects, these challenges are actually easier in the resource sector than in others. In particular, resources themselves often have well-established world prices that can be used to monitor transfer pricing arrangements within multinationals.[8] This is especially so in relation to oil. But it is not always the case: spot prices for natural gas are limited, for instance (as stressed by Kellas in Chapter 6 of this book). Moreover, even when resource prices are observable there remain other avoidance opportunities, notably through using financial arrangements to shift taxable income from high and to low tax jurisdictions. These and other technical aspects of international tax rules as they affect the resource sector are not, however, pursued further here: a full treatment is given by Mullins in Chapter 13.[9]

The prevalence of foreign ownership may also affect host countries' incentives in tax setting: after-tax profits accruing to foreigners are presumably less valuable socially than are receipts accruing to domestic citizens. They may thus be given relatively little weight in tax design.

There is another aspect of the international nature of the resource business that is more puzzling. Host countries evidently care very much how their tax systems compare with others, and are often concerned not to offer regimes that are substantially more onerous. Quite why this is so, however, is by no means obvious. It is clear enough, for instance, why a country wishing to attract a car factory or the research headquarters of a large software company would not wish to find others offering more attractive tax regimes: the factory or research center might be established elsewhere instead. But a company cannot choose to exploit a gold deposit located in one country by building a mine in another. Resource deposits, however, are specific to a particular location, so that standard tax theory would suggest that any associated rents can be taxed at up to 100 percent without jeopardizing the existence of the project. The puzzle, to which we return below, is to explain why tax competition is as strong in relation to resources as casual inspection suggests it to be.

F Asymmetric information

Policy makers will generally be less well-informed of the geological and commercial circumstances at all stages of particular resource projects than are those who undertake the exploration, development, and extraction. These asymmetries of information make rent extraction potentially far more difficult than would otherwise be the case, since operators, knowing that it may increase their tax charge, have no direct interest in sharing their superior information with government. They are likely to have an interest in understating the likely stock of the resource, and overstating the difficulty of its extraction. And, even short of outright evasion, they may have a range of devices for understating measured profits in the host country once activity is underway, for example through transfer pricing and similar profit-shifting of the type discussed above.

Asymmetries of information of this kind are far from unique to the resource sector, and indeed without them tax design and implementation would be a largely trivial problem (since liability could be directly tied, without risk of distortion, to underlying features determining ability to pay). Policy makers can to some degree mitigate the asymmetry in resource activities by undertaking their own geological surveys and using consultancy services of those with industry-specific expertise. But asymmetries are likely to remain, and to be especially marked in lower income countries that find themselves with limited domestic capacity to match against large and long-established multinationals. The same is true in other sectors too, of course – such as in relation to financial institutions – but the challenges are again so fundamental to resource activities as to merit special attention.

G Market power

Most analyses of resource taxation assume that host governments and investors behave competitively, in the sense of taking the world price of the resource concerned as given. But this may not always be so. Host governments may be able to exercise appreciable control over the flow of some resources into the world markets, whether collectively (the most familiar example being OPEC) or, in some cases, individually: the ten largest oil producing countries, for example, account for around 60 percent of world production, and South Africa holds nearly 90 percent of the world's reserves of platinum. Companies may also exercise significant market power: the Potash Corporation of Saskatchewan, for example, produces over 20 percent of the world's potash. Such market power can have several implications.

First, it can change the incentives for tax-setting in both host countries and resource-importing ones. A country that can deploy a rent tax, for instance, would not benefit (in revenue terms) by taxing exports if its production does not affect world prices: because of the distortion that the export tax creates – causing less to be produced than could profitably be sold at world prices – the revenue consequently raised would be less than the rent foregone. If it can affect world prices, however, then some taxation of exports would generally be desirable as a means of raising that world price.[10] By the same token, resource importers have an incentive to impose a tariff if by doing so they can reduce its world price. These incentives for strategic tax-setting are made more complex by the exhaustible nature of natural resources, discussed below, but the broad insights remain: Karp and Newbery (1992), for instance, find that on this account oil importing countries have an incentive to impose substantial tariffs.

Not least, market power may also provide an additional source of rents for governments to seek to tax. It can also change the impact of standard tax instruments. A royalty imposed on all sales by a group of imperfectly competitive extracting firms, for instance, could cause their profits to *increase*: this is because it would serve, in effect, as a device for achieving a coordinated output reduction that they are unable to achieve by any credible agreement amongst themselves (see, for instance, Stern (1987)).

H Project basis

Less commonly remarked, but quite unusual by wider standards, is the possibility and practice of taxing resource sector activities on a project rather than a company basis. One does not think, for example, of taxing a soft drink company separately on its various production plants, or an accounting firm differentially on the profits earned from its various offices. There are exceptions, of course: special incentives are sometimes provided for large projects, and restrictions on company grouping for the corporate income tax are in a broad sense analogous to ring-fencing arrangements in resource taxation. But the nature of resource activities – the inability to switch deposits between projects – lends itself to a project-based approach to tax design and evaluation not found systematically in other areas. Otto *et al.* (2006) argue that mine-by-mine royalty-setting has become less common. Nevertheless, differentiation across projects continues to be found – between onshore and offshore oil projects, for instance and, inherently, in the use of auctioning – and remains an option in a wide range of circumstances.

I Exhaustibility

None of the features above is entirely unique to the resource sector. What is unique to non-renewable resources with which we are concerned, is, by definition, the finiteness of potential production. The point should not be taken entirely literally: new resource deposits are discovered,[11] the extent to which deposits are exploited is itself a choice variable, and for many resources known stocks are so large that finiteness is not an immediate concern. (Current coal stocks, for example, are enough for several hundred years, at current usage rates). Nevertheless, the basic distinctive feature remains, and applies both in aggregate and to particular projects: more extraction now means less potential extraction later.

This has profound implications for the economics of resource extraction. Four are particularly relevant for tax design (details being spelt out in Box 2.1):

- The marginal cost to which the marginal benefit from extraction is optimally equated in each period reflects not only the current production cost but the opportunity cost in terms of future extraction foregone (this being the (marginal) Hotelling rent discussed above).
- A resource stock should be depleted in such a way that the shadow price of the resource (that is, the value of an additional unit of the resource stock) rises at the discount rate less a term reflecting the extent to which extraction becomes more costly as the stock declines. The reason for this is simply that deferring extraction will be worthwhile whenever this leads to a gain in future welfare, including through any reduction in future extraction costs, that outweighs the discounting of that future benefit.
- As a (very) special case of the previous point, if extraction is costless the price of the resource should rise at the rate of discount: the 'Hotelling rule.'
- A higher discount rate is expected (though the point is not theoretically clear-cut) to lead to faster extraction, the intuition being that it increases the financial return from extracting resources early and investing the proceeds.

Empirically, there is substantial evidence that the evolution of resource prices and valuations is not well-described by the simple model that underlies these results: see for example, Krautkraemer (1999), where possible reasons for this (such as the importance of new discoveries) are also discussed. Nevertheless, these relations capture inescapable trade-offs that arise in exploiting established resource stocks and which, as will be seen below, bear on important aspects of tax design.

Box 2.1 The economics of resource extraction – some key results

Denote by $V(S)$ the maximized value of some objective function – whether that of a policy maker, or of a private investor – conditional on a current resource stock of S, and reflecting the expectation of optimal decision making at all future dates. With extraction of q giving rise to current benefits of $B(q)$ and costs of $C(q, S)$ (so that, for instance, C is decreasing in S if extraction becomes more costly as the stock is exhausted), this maximized value is defined recursively as

$$V(S_t) = \max_{q_t}\left\{ B(q_t) - C(q_t, S_t) + \frac{1}{1+r} E_t[V(S_{t+1})] \right\}, \tag{1.1}$$

the discount rate being r and the expectation (conditional on information at time t) reflecting potential future uncertainties, for instance in resource prices. (When B is simply revenue from sales of the resource, V corresponds to quasi-rent, costs sunk in discovering the stock and readying for its extraction being taken as given). With extraction reducing the available stock (and, by assumption, no new discoveries), so that $S_{t+1} = S_t - q_t$, optimal extraction in period t requires (if positive) that

$$B'(q_t) = C_q(q_t, S_t) + \frac{1}{1+r} E_t[V'(S_{t+1})], \tag{1.2}$$

(and is zero if $B(q) < C(q, s_t)$ for all q), with derivatives being denoted by primes for functions of a single variable and subscripts for functions of several. This gives the first result highlighted in the text. Tighter implications for the optimal extraction path follow from differentiating in (1.1) with respect to S_t and rearranging to find

$$\frac{E_t[V'(S_{t+1})] - V'(S_t)}{V'(S_t)} = r + \frac{(1+r)C_S(q_t, S_t)}{V'(S_t)}, \tag{1.3}$$

which gives the second. The third follows on taking the special case in which the marginal benefit from extraction is equal to the price of the resource, p_t (either because the resource is all consumed domestically or, perhaps more plausibly, because the only concern is the net profit earned from the project and the price is fixed on world markets)[12] and extraction is costless.

The implications of the conditions in (1.2) and (1.3) for current extraction are hard to see, since both involve all future decisions through the marginal valuation term

$E[V'(S_{t+1})]$. Combining the two, this can be eliminated to find[13] that along the optimum

$$\frac{E_t[(B'(q_{t+1})-C_q(q_{t+1},S_{t+1})]-\{B'(q_t)-C_q(q_t,S_t)\}}{B'(q_t)-C_q(q_t,S_t)} = r + \frac{E_t[C_S(q_{t+1},S_{t+1})]}{B'(q_t)-C_q(q_t,S_t)}, (1.4)$$

so that the net marginal benefit from extraction is expected to rise at the rate of interest plus a term reflecting the effect of stock depletion on production costs. To see how an increase in the interest rate is likely to affect extraction rates, note first that, with the same total stock of the resource to be exhausted, the extraction paths under a high and a lower interest rate will at some date cross. With q_t, say, the same under both paths (and assuming that $C_S = 0$), it follows from (1.4), given the concavity of net benefit, that q_{t+1} is lower at the higher interest rate; which means – the fourth point in the text – that extraction is more rapid.

3 Tax instruments and their effects

This section reviews the main tax (and tax-like) instruments that are or might be deployed in the resource sector, and some of the issues that arise in assessing their likely impact on resource operations and government revenue.

A Key tax instruments for the resource sector

Reflecting the complexities of governments' objectives and the accumulation of considerable ingenuity in responding to the fiscal challenges posed by the special features of mining and petroleum operations, a wide range of tax instruments is found in the sector, with single projects commonly subject to multiple charges. An exhaustive listing of such taxes would be tedious; the aim here is simply to outline some of the principal design choices that each raises.

Royalties

While the term has come to be used increasing imprecisely,[14] the essential idea of a royalty – also (though now less commonly) referred to as a severance tax – is that of a charge (whether specific or ad valorem) levied directly on the extraction of the resource itself. Such charges are commonly given a legalistic justification, as payment to the resource owner, usually the state (which, outside the United States, almost always has legal title to the resource itself), for the right to take ownership of its property. For this reason, royalties are commonly recorded in the fiscal accounts as non-tax revenues. From the perspective of the investor, of course, it makes little difference whether a payment is called a royalty or a tax: the economic impact is the same. In terms of policy design too, whether one thinks of a royalty as akin to a user fee or as an explicit tax, the determination of its proper level and time path reduces to the same question in optimal pricing.

Royalties can significantly affect extraction decisions (and, through the anticipation of such effects, and their impact on profitability, decisions on exploration and development too). Importantly, this effect of royalties depends not only their current level but on their future levels too: the alternative to extracting now and paying today's royalty is to extract later and pay tomorrow's. What matters is thus not the level of today's royalty, but whether it is higher or lower than the present value of tomorrow's.[15] The extraction path is entirely unaffected, for instance, if (and only if) the royalty per unit of output rises at the investor's discount rate: for then the present value of the tax payable when some unit of the resource is extracted is the same whenever that extraction takes place.[16] In effect, the tax then functions as a non-distorting charge on the quasi-rents earned by existing projects. Few royalties are specified to grow in this way, however, so that the extraction path may be affected. For instance, for a royalty charged as a specific amount (that is, a fixed and unchanging amount per unit of the resource), the incentive is to defer extraction, since the present value charge is lower the later extraction occurs.[17] On the other hand, a royalty charged as an ad valorem amount (that is, as a proportion of sales receipts) will tend to accelerate extraction if the resource price is expected to increase at a pace above the interest rate.

A more commonly expressed concern with royalties is that they may lead to premature closure of operations: social optimality requires that extraction cease once price no longer covers marginal extraction costs, but private operators faced with a royalty will instead end operations when price ceases to cover extraction cost *plus* the royalty. How significant such effects have been in practice is unclear, as Otto *et al.* (2006) note: many mining laws contain provisions, discretionary or otherwise, for royalties to be waived or deferred if they would make extraction unprofitable.

The impact on closure decisions will also depend on the effective incidence of the tax. While the analysis above presumes a single price-taking producer, a royalty levied on all sales of some resource might lead not to a reduction in the price received by the producer but an increase in that paid by the consumer. In this case the main challenge to continued production may come rather from the development of alterative technologies. A prime instance of this is in relation to fossil fuels. The incidence of a uniform carbon tax might then fall largely on consumers, with little impact on extraction paths but potentially significant effects in fostering the development of alternative technologies (Sinn (2008), Strand (2008)).

A further potentially important efficiency loss from royalties arises because they apply only at the extraction phase of resource production. At best, they constitute imperfect taxes on the quasi-rents from successful deposits and take no account of the sunk costs of exploration and site development. Quite apart from whether they tax quasi-rents efficiently (that is, without distorting the path of extraction), they will discourage exploration and development since their base is not the entire rent. By the same token, they discourage risky projects by taxing only successful outcomes.

Royalties are not quite ubiquitous in practice – Chile and South Africa, for example, have long had no conventional mining royalties (though they have royalties that are partially profit-related), and nor has Denmark for oil and gas production or the UK (since 2002) for oil – but are very widely applied to resource activities. Their precise form, however, can vary considerably, and hence so too might their impact:

- Ad valorem and specific royalties – even if initially equal in monetary value – can imply different time paths of extraction, as just noted.
- The precise base can also differ: the royalty might be based on the value of ore at the minehead, for example, or on the net smelter return (the value of the processed or refined product net of processing costs), or on the value of exports after 'netback' for transport and other costs. Otto *et al.* (2006) give an example in which (non-profit related) royalties at rates varying between 2.75 and 3.45 percent can imply the same total tax take, depending on exactly how the base is defined.
- These differences can also have behavioral consequences. For instance, a specific tax (rare, in practice, outside industrial minerals) on the refined product can distort decisions as to which grade of the resource to extract (because tax paid will be higher for richer ores) when, for instance, one on the crude ore does not (because then tax paid is independent of ore quality).[18]
- Royalty structures can display a wide range of non-linearities: they may increase with the amount extracted and/or the world price of the resource (in the latter case, for example, tending to encourage extraction when prices are expected to increase rapidly), and in some cases have been structured to decrease over time, eventually vanishing.
- Royalties may be levied at the same rate on a range of minerals, or differentiated across them. There is evidently some, perhaps modest, administrative merit in the simplicity of uniform structures – and perhaps political advantage too, in protecting against special pleading. The case for differentiation is less clear. If the royalty on some resource were intended to exercise power in world market, the appropriate rate would vary with demand and supply characteristics, which would be likely to differ across resources. But that is rarely the purpose. If they are serving to bring forward tax payments, the rate might appropriately vary with the time profile of output and profits, and the proper differentiation would likely vary as much across deposits as across minerals. The most persuasive argument for differentiation – rationalizing perhaps the higher royalty rate often applied to diamonds – is that the royalty is serving as a rent extraction device. But the scope for distortions makes it a poorly targeted one: if effective rent taxation is in place, the case for differential royalty rates is correspondingly weakened.
- Stretching normal usage of the term, royalties may also be profit-based, in the sense of being levied on revenue less some elements of cost: the ad

valorem royalty rate might depend for instance, on the ratio of revenue to sales. Such taxes may apply either in isolation or as part of hybrid in which they are combined with simple output-based schemes, with the latter in effect operating as a minimum tax creditable against the former. Profit-based royalties are perhaps most usefully regarded simply as profit taxes, discussed separately below.

What then might be the proper role of royalties – focusing here on the very simplest form, of charges related to output or its value (and abstracting from quality effects) – in a well-constructed resource tax system?

In some circumstances, royalties may have an essentially corrective role in encouraging efficient utilization. This will be the case, for example if investors discount at an inappropriate rate. If they use too high a discount rate, for example, and so tend to extract too quickly, this can be offset by imposing a royalty that decreases (in present value) sufficiently rapidly.

More subtly, but perhaps no less plausibly, a role for royalties also emerges if – as is almost invariably the case – the extractor has unlimited rights to extract the resource over some finite contract period (and receives no payment for the resource remaining at the end of the period for which it enjoys extraction rights).[19] Attaching no value to any of the resource left in the ground at the end of its contract, the firm will tend to extract too rapidly. In the final period, most clearly, it will simply extract up to the point at which the resource price just covers marginal extraction cost; but this, recalling the first bullet before Box 2.1, implies excessively fast extraction since it ignores the opportunity cost in terms of future extraction foregone. More generally, given the cost advantage of smoothing production, one would expect extraction to be more than socially optimal throughout the period of the contract, with the extent of this inefficiency rising – because the enterprise cares less about future extraction opportunities foregone – as the end of the contract period approaches.[20] Correcting this, to ensure an efficient extraction path, requires that the investor face a charge for each unit of extraction equal to the amount by which their marginal valuation of the remaining stock falls short of the appropriate social marginal valuation – which is likely to mean a royalty that increases over time as the end of the contract approaches.[21] The strength of this argument for the use of royalties clearly depends, however, on the length of the investor's horizon. If it has full title to the entire deposit (or can sell the remaining stock when its contract expires) then it will itself recognize the opportunity cost of current extraction, and no corrective charge is needed to ensure that it fully internalizes this in its own extraction decisions.

In practice, the principal rationale of simple royalties is a pragmatic one, reflecting three potential advantages to the government over profit-based taxes. First, royalties may be relatively easy to implement. Oil and gas production, for instance, is readily measured by equipment at the wellhead. Measuring the amount or value of other minerals extracted, however, can be less than entirely straightforward. Nevertheless, royalties may be less susceptible to the implementation difficulties that asymmetric information can cause, for example, for rent taxes – a point pursued further in Section 4 below. Second, royalties yield revenue from the very start of production. Of course, earlier revenues for the government entail higher upfront payments by producers. Such a pattern of revenue flows may be rationalized if governments discount the future more heavily than do producers, an issue also taken up later. It may have political advantages too, in ensuring that foreign-owned projects do not produce without paying at least something to the fisc. Third, royalties may provide a more stable and predictable tax base. But royalties have important disadvantages, too, not only in the potential distortion of extraction decisions but also – through being levied only at extraction stage, with no offset for exploration and development costs – in potentially bearing discouragingly heavily on quasi-rents.

Rent taxes

The term 'rent tax' is often used quite loosely in the resource literature. Many taxes will bear in part on rents: export taxes can have this effect, for instance, and this can even be the case, as noted above, of royalties. Resource taxes are often tailored, moreover, in an ad hoc but explicit way intended to reflect the likely extent of rents: by, for instance, charging a higher rate of corporate income tax on onshore than offshore operations. Here, however, we use the term more precisely, to refer to any tax that is intended to extract only rents.

The case for rent taxes reflect three attributes of exhaustible resources, their relative fixity in supply, at least once discovered (generating Hotelling rent), the differing qualities of deposits (generating 'Ricardian rent,')[22] and the notion that somehow property rights to a nation's resources are at least partly owned collectively. One way of exercising these property rights in an efficient way is to rely on the private sector to find, develop, extract, process, and market resources and then to tax the rents that accrue. So long as the tax base accurately reflects rents – and assuming perfect certainty for the moment – any tax bearing only on rents, whether proportional, progressive or degressive – will leave private decisions unaffected.[23] Uncertainty, however, significantly complicates matters, as will be seen.

In thinking about the design of taxes on rents, it is useful to consider in turn the tax base and the level and structure of tax rates applied to it.

THE CHOICE OF BASE

One way to think about rents is in terms of the conventional notion of economic profit over some interval, say of one year. Economic profit earned during a year is the difference between revenues and imputed costs over that period, all on an accruals basis. In the case of revenues, this is simply accounts receivable. Costs are more difficult. For current costs (materials, rents, labor, ...), accounts payable are used. For costs associated with assets, the imputed costs are those associated with holding or using the asset for a year, rather than the costs of acquiring the assets initially. These imputed costs include financing costs (such as interest paid on debt and the required return to equity finance), depreciation or depletion due to use, and capital losses over the period. An annual tax system levied at a constant marginal rate, whose base is economic profits thus defined, would be neutral (that is, would leave investors' decisions unaffected). Intuitively, firms maximize the present value of their economic profits, so a proportional tax would simply reduce the objective function proportionately, leaving optimal choice unchanged.

Standard corporate taxes, however, are not taxes on economic profits, and nor are they intended to be. To the extent that they allow interest on debt to be deducted but not the cost of equity financing, they approximate a tax on a firm's equity income, both normal returns to equity and any pure profits or rents. More important, some of the elements that constitute imputed costs are very difficult to measure. For depreciable assets, the rate of depreciation over the year will not be easily observed given the absence of market prices for capital in use. This may not be so much a problem for depletable resources whose use can be readily measured. Greater problems are posed by intangible assets, which, in the case of resource firms, include the value of information learned by exploration expenditures and all long-term assets that have no physical substance, such as development drilling. This makes an economic profit tax base virtually impossible to implement.

Happily, there exist viable alternatives whose tax bases are equivalent to economic profits not period-by-period but rather in present value over the full lifetime of a project. Prominent amongst these are:

- An *R-based cash flow tax* (Meade, 1978), commonly referred to in the resource literature as a *Brown Tax* (Brown, 1948). This is one charged simply on the producer's cash flow, which in the case of goods-producing firms, consists of all real (as opposed to financial) transactions on a cash basis. The base is thus all revenue from the sale of output less all cash outlays for purchases of all inputs, both capital and current. No deduction is allowed for interest or other financial costs: with all investment expenditure immediately expensed, doing so would amount to giving a double deduction. The supplementary charge on petroleum activity in the UK, for example, is in effect an R-based cash flow tax. Note that under a pure R-based cash flow or Brown tax, negative cash flows would give rise to negative tax liabilities that would be fully refunded immediately. Indeed the resource literature generally takes immediate refunding on tax losses as inherent in the Brown tax, and for brevity we shall follow this usage.
- An *S-based cash flow tax*, also proposed by Meade (1978), is a charge on net distributions to shareholders (dividends less new equity). This includes in the base financial as well as real cash transactions, and so is intended to capture rents from financial services (less of a concern for resource firms).
- An *Allowance for Corporate Equity* (ACE) tax base allows firms to deduct not only interest payments on debt but also a notional return on their equity,

with the retained earnings element of equity calculated for this purpose using the same depreciation rate as that used to calculate taxable profits. There is now quite extensive experience with the ACE (which is reviewed in Klemm (2007)): Belgium currently operates such a system, as for some time did Croatia, while Italy has employed, and Brazil still does, variants.

- A *Resource Rent Tax* (RRT), as proposed by Garnaut and Clunies Ross (1975, 1983), taxes cash flows once their value, cumulated at an appropriately chosen interest rate (this choice being discussed below), becomes positive.[24] Such a scheme is equivalent to a Brown tax with losses not generating refunds but instead carried forward at this same interest rate (provided that, in each case, there is sufficient positive cash flow by the end of the project life to cover losses, or the tax value of any unrelieved losses is fully refunded at the end of the project life – an important consideration that is also discussed below).

Nor are these the only possible forms of rent tax. Indeed all are special cases of a general class of cash flow equivalent tax schemes, for which the present value of the base is equal to the present value of cash flows. The first part of Box 2.2 describes a class of such present value-equivalent rent taxes, the defining feature being that in each year cash outlays (costs) are added to an account and the firm deducts against tax some fraction of that account, say α_t – different schemes corresponding to different choices of time path for α – along with an interest deduction consisting of the firm's discount rate times the size of the account. Thus cash outlays that are not immediately deducted are carried forward with interest so that the present value of deductions from a given expenditure equals that of the expenditure itself. Hence all such taxes ultimately tax the present value of cash flows, that is, rents. Importantly, the time profile of α_t can be chosen arbitrarily, different choices differing only in the time path of tax payments they imply.[25] This means, for example, that the neutrality of an ACE does not require that depreciation for tax purposes match the true decline in the value of productive assets: 'excessive' depreciation in one period means a reduction in the account carried forward, and consequent increase in future taxes, that in present value has an exactly offsetting effect. In this way these and all other members of this class of rent taxes avoid the difficulty of measuring depreciation that, as noted above, arises under an accruals-based income tax.

Another set of equivalencies is instructive. Of the schemes just described, the Brown tax and RRT both allow full deduction of current outlays. In this respect they are members of another general class of schemes, differing in the fraction of cumulated net cash flows that are brought into tax. As shown in the second part of Box 2.2, provided that interest is paid on untaxed cumulated net cash flows at the firm's discount rate, all such schemes are also equivalent in present value to a tax on rents.

Box 2.2 Present value-equivalent rent taxes

A wide range of tax structures are equivalent, in present value, to a tax on rents.

Outlays not necessarily immediately deductible

Suppose all cash outlays in year t, denoted C_t, are added to an account that will gradually be deductible in the future. Let the size of that account in year t be denoted A_t, this being the cumulative sum of past outlays that have not yet been written off. Suppose that in year t a proportion α_t of accumulated outlays A_t are written off. The account thus evolves according to $\Delta A_t = C_t - \alpha_t A_t$, where α_t can vary from year to year. Let the tax base in year t be $R_t - (\alpha_t + r)A_t$, where R_t represents cash revenues and r is the firm's nominal discount rate (assumed constant for simplicity). The present value of the tax base thus defined will be the same as the present value of cash flows themselves, since, using the expression for ΔA_t,

$$\sum_{t=0}^{T} (R_t - (\alpha_t + r)A_t)(1+r)^{-t} = \sum_{t=0}^{T} (R_t - C_t + \Delta A_t - rA_t)(1+r)^{-t} = \sum_{t=0}^{T} (R_t - C_t)(1+r)^{-t}.$$

(assuming $A_0 = 0$). In effect, non-deducted cash outlays are carried forward at the rate of discount so that their present value remains unchanged. The value of α_t each year is completely flexible and can be chosen to generate any time pattern for the tax base. The only additional information required to apply this cash-flow-equivalent tax base is the firm's discount rate r.

Tax schemes in this class can be thought of as alternative forms of ACE, differing in the effective rate of depreciation. The Brown tax corresponds to the extreme case of immediate expensing, so that $\alpha_t = 1$. An economic profits tax base would set α_t to the true economic depreciation rate of the firm's assets, which is hard to do. In each case, applying a constant proportional tax to the base would be neutral provided that any negative tax liabilities are either fully refunded or carried forward indefinitely with interest (a point discussed further in the text below). A cash flow tax can also be made progressive while maintaining neutrality (under perfect certainty) if the tax rate in each year is increasing in cash flows (rents) accumulated up to that year.

Cash flow-based taxes

There is another (intersecting) class of schemes that are also equivalent to rent taxes in present value, but are based on net cash flows and do not rest on any notion of depreciation. To describe these, denote by B_t the cumulative cash flow, compounded at the discount rate r, that has yet to be taxed, and σ_t the proportion of cumulative cash flows that are added to the tax base in period t. Then B_t evolves according to $\Delta B_t = R_t - C_t - \sigma_t B_t + rB_t$. The tax base in period t is $\sigma_t B_t$, so that the present value of the tax base is:

$$\sum_{t} \sigma_t B_t (1+r)^{-t} = \sum_{t} (R_t - C_t - \Delta B_t + rB_t)(1+r)^{-t} = \sum_{t} (R_t - C_t)(1+r)^{-t}$$

Note the following equivalences:

- If $\sigma_t = 1$, the scheme is the Brown tax, with base $\sigma_t B_t = B_t = R_t - C_t$.

- If $\sigma_t = 0$ for $B_t < 0$ and $\sigma_t = 1$ otherwise, the scheme gives the RRT base. Note that this requires choosing an appropriate discount rate r, which the Brown tax does not require.

The key difference between the Brown and RRT bases is the timing of the tax bases: the former presumes immediate loss offsetting, the latter does not.

Note that for the RRT to be fully equivalent to a cash-flow tax in present value terms, negative cumulative cash flows B_t remaining at the end of the project's life must be extinguished. That is, σ_t must then be set to unity. This will be particularly relevant if there are clean-up costs associated with closing down.

More generally, any time profile of tax liabilities can be generated by appropriate choice of a time path of σ_t.

The important differences between these present value-flow equivalent rent taxes is in the time pattern of tax base, and hence of tax payments, that they imply. What then might be the preference of the government over different time profiles? Or might firms themselves be allowed to choose the tax parameters that fix the evolution of the tax base? Note that while the firm should be indifferent across all such schemes – since all imply the same present value of the base, calculated at its own discount rate – the government will value them differently in so far as it has a different discount rate.

In many developing countries, the government may discount the future more heavily than investors (as discussed in Section 4 below). If there were no restrictions on the timing of tax liabilities, it would then prefer them to be paid entirely upfront, such as by a fixed fee (for example, a signature bid) obtained through auction. Suppose however that the tax base cannot exceed cumulated cash flows and nor can tax payments be negative. In this case, it can be shown – the proof is in Appendix I – that the best among all possible cash flow-based rent taxes is precisely the RRT. Crucially, however, there are other forms of rent tax – members of the first class of schemes in Box 2.2 – which involve earlier receipt of revenue. One such is the ACE, which yields revenue as soon as revenues exceed depreciation and the required return on capital, which is likely to be well before the date at which they recover, with interest, the full cost of their initial investment.

Also important to stress is that all these schemes, other than the Brown tax, involve using the firm's discount rate to carry forward either costs not yet deducted or cash flows not yet taxed. How to treat such generalized losses is especially important for resource projects, since cash flows are typically negative in the (many) early years, then increase and (if all goes well) become positive in later years, before possibly falling off as resources become more difficult to extract and shutdown costs arise. Given tax authorities' evident reluctance to pay refunds to firms making losses, as the Brown tax requires, the alternative – if neutrality is to be retained – is for the government to pay interest on losses carried forward. This too is rarely done in practice for the regular corporate income tax (though Croatia did so, for example), but the proper procedure in a world of perfect certainty – as has so far has been assumed – is in principle straightforward: the firms' discount rate will be the risk-free rate, and it is this that should be used in the schemes set out above. Setting any other rate would destroy the neutrality property of the tax: too low a rate would be expected to lead to under-investment (tax being charged even when no rents are earned), and too high a rate to over-investment.[26]

Uncertainty, however – so central a feature of resource activity – substantially complicates matters, raising two issues. One is the appropriate discount rate for the calibration of schemes of the kind described above; the other is the tax treatment of projects that fail to yield positive rents (which, in a world of perfect certainty, would never be undertaken). The two are closely related.

The question here is deeper than that of how to treat losses that may occur in any single period: as just discussed, these can arise even in a world of perfect certainty. The difficulty, rather, is that in an uncertain world taxing projects that do earn positive rent over their lifetime without providing some tax relief for those that do not creates an asymmetry which results in expected tax rates exceeding the statutory rate. Taxing rents only in good outcomes can destroy the neutrality of a rent tax. Suppose, for example, that a project stands equal chances of earning rent of $20 million and a loss of $10 million, so that expected rent is $5 million: in the absence of tax, the project is thus attractive to investors. But if rents in the event of success are taxed at, say, 60 percent, the expectation is of an after-tax loss of $1 million, and it will not be undertaken.[27]

A central insight into these design challenges posed by uncertainty – the choice of discount rate and treatment of projects earning negative lifetime rents – is provided by a result of Bond and Devereux (1995, 2003). They show, for a class of cash flow-equivalent taxes, that if tax is fully refundable in the event that the firm ceases operations – corresponding in the resource context to projects that fail to earn a positive lifetime rent – then it is the risk-free-rate that should be used in order to preserve neutrality. Intuitively, if the firm is perfectly certain that it will achieve full loss offset in the future then it will value the corresponding tax refunds at the risk-free rate; carrying losses forward at the risk-free rate thus assures their equivalence in present value to immediate refund. Identifying a risk-free rate in practice is problematic, of course. But this result is nevertheless of considerable practical importance for designing any of the present-value equivalent rent taxes described above (other than the Brown tax, which involves no carrying forward), since it implies that the proper interest rate need not be tailored to the differing circumstances of different firms or projects. Garnaut and Clunies Ross (1983) argue, for instance, that the 'supply price of investment' is likely to vary across firms and projects, so that applying a single threshold rate under an RRT must lead to the kind of inefficiency noted above, a disadvantage not shared by the Brown tax. But this argument has much less force in light of the Bond–Devereux result that discounting in a cash flow-equivalent tax system should be at a risk-free rate, since this would in principle be the same for all firms and projects.

Sovereign risk, however, provides an important caveat to the Bond–Devereux argument. If commitment or other problems mean that the investor is not perfectly sure that cumulated tax credits will be made good, at an unchanging tax rate, they will wish to take account of that in the discount rate applied in valuing future tax reliefs. Applying a risk-free rate to carry-forwards will be insufficient to compensate the firm for waiting: from the perspective of the firm, the expected tax base will exceed expected rents, and investment will be discouraged.

In terms of practicability, any of these present value-equivalent rent taxes would seem much easier to implement than a tax on annual economic profit.[28] They either dispense altogether with the need to specify depreciation rates, for instance, or make the rate irrelevant; and the cumulation that they typically involve does not, in principle, require record-keeping over long periods, since all relevant past information is summarized in an account carried forward from the previous period. Nevertheless, these rent taxes are not without their difficulty. Unlike an annual tax on economic profit, for instance, they are neutral only if they are expected to be levied at a constant rate over time: if not, firms will have an incentive to alter their real decisions so that the annual base is lower in years when the tax rate is lower.[29] Thus a present value-equivalent rent tax is neutral only if firms believe the government is committed to a constant tax rate into the future, which may be hard for the government to do credibly given the volatility of resource prices. These taxes are also not entirely avoidance-proof (though the same is also true of standard income taxes). For example, the distinction between labor income and profits may be opaque for owner-managed firms, and vertically-integrated resource firms may be able to reduce their liability by using transfer pricing on intra-firm transactions for upstream use to deflate their resource revenues.[30] The implications of these and other opportunities for firms to exploit their superior information to understate the base of a rent tax are discussed in Section 4.

Designing and implementing rent taxes is thus not straightforward. What is important to recognize, however, is that there are many ways in which one can set about doing this: the choice is much wider than that between a Brown tax and an RRT: an ACE, for example, avoids both the refunds associated with the former and the delay in government receipts associated with the latter. Indeed there has been increasing practical interest in rent taxation design in relation to business activities in general, much of it focused on the ACE or similar schemes. The present is a time of experimentation in the structure of the corporate income tax, and many of these experiments have been in the direction of targeting the tax more directly on rents.[31]

TAX RATES AND THE PURSUIT OF PROGRESSIVITY

There is relatively little discussion in the literature of the appropriate rate at which rent taxes should be set, as Lund (2009) stresses. No doubt this is largely because efficiency concerns give the simple prescription of taxing rents as heavily as possible. The issue then becomes that of identifying features that prevent their being taxed at (close to) 100 percent. One such is the importance of distinguishing rents from quasi-rents, as discussed above, and avoiding taxing the latter so heavily as to discourage future exploration and development. This suggests, interestingly, that quasi-rents at the extraction stage will be taxed more heavily in countries that face either very high or very low chances of future discovery: in the former case, there is little need to moderate tax charged in order to provide relief for unsuccessful exploration; in the latter, the prospect of discouraging future exploration is of little concern. A second potential consideration is a perceived need to broadly match the tax treatment available in other countries, and a third is the possibility that asymmetries of information may prevent perfect implementation of rent taxes: both of these issues are considered in Section 4.

Putting aside then the simple prescription of taxing all rents at 100 percent, the issue also arises as to the appropriate rate structure for a tax on rents. The simplest tax is a constant proportional one, with the same rate applying in all years. All cash flow-equivalent tax systems will be in this case be neutral: a proportional tax on cash flows in all periods is equivalent to a proportional tax on the present value of rents. Such a tax remains nondistorting, moreover, in the presence of uncertainty, so long as investors are risk-neutral[32] (meaning that they look only to their expected return, not to the full distribution of possible outcomes).[33]

The suggestion is sometimes made, however, to subject the cumulative rents V to some tax $T(V)$ that is progressive in the sense that the average tax rate $T(V)/V$ increases with V. There are many ways in which this could be done.[34] The best known and most influential proposal for progressive taxation of lifetime project earnings in the resource context, is that of Garnaut and Clunies Ross (1975), who envisage a progressive variant of the simple RRT described above. This adds to the single threshold rate of return a second (and maybe more) higher rate above which some additional tax applies. The wide range of rent taxes characterized in Box 2.2 – other than the Brown tax, which involves no cumulation – could be made progressive in essentially the same way. The essential idea was pioneered (for petroleum) in Papua New Guinea. Land (1995) lists nine countries as having such schemes; several more have adopted one since.

While there is thus no difficulty of principle in levying a progressive rent tax, it is not obvious why one might want to do so. There is generally no compelling equity reason, since – even in so far as they accrue to domestic residents (fairness among foreigners presumably being of no concern) – a claim to high rents is neither necessary nor sufficient for high income at personal level. A more subtle rationale, offered by Garnaut and Clunies Ross (1983), is that the use of multiple threshold rates, accompanied by a lower starting marginal tax rate (and with subsequently higher marginal rates recouping any consequent revenue loss), may mitigate the risk of distorting decisions by applying a single but wrongly chosen threshold rate. The stronger, however, is the case for using a risk-free rate in the basic RRT, discussed above, the less force this consideration has. An alternative rationale for some progressivity may be found in political economy considerations: this is pursued later.

Against any benefits of progressivity, in any case, must be weighed a clear disadvantage. This is that – unlike a proportional tax – in the presence of uncertainty a progressive tax is distortionary even if investors are risk-neutral. With an increasing marginal tax rate, rents in favorable states of nature will bear a higher tax than those in unfavorable states, so discriminating against risky investments (as Garnaut and Clunies Ross (1979) themselves stress).[35] Given, too, the additional burden of administration and compliance implied – and leaving aside potential political economy considerations taken up in Section 4 – there is room for doubt as to whether there are any real advantages from taxing cumulative rents progressively.

Sector-specific profit taxes

Resource operations may also be subject to charges that are based on some notion of profit but without such a set of allowances as to make the tax one on rents. These are commonly designed, moreover, to be progressive in a sense that the rate applied to such profits increases with their level.

This is the case for several of the 'profit-based royalty' schemes referred to above. Otto *et al.* (2006) give the example, for instance, of a scheme in Ghana by which the royalty rate is piecewise linear, with a marginal rate that increases with the ratio of the operating margin to sales. This, it is easily seen, is simply equivalent to a progressive tax on operating profit.

The scheme long applied to gold mining operations in South Africa is also a member of this class of schemes,[36] but with a continuously varying marginal tax rate and applying only on earnings in excess of some (within-period) return. The impact of such arrangements can sometimes be opaque: the South African scheme, for instance, is equivalent (for a taxpaying operation) to a proportional tax on profits combined with a subsidy to extraction.

Production sharing

Under production sharing agreements (PSAs) – commonplace in oil and gas, though less so in mining (and described in detail by Nakhle in Chapter 4)) – the share of 'profit oil' (the profit that remains after 'cost oil' has been taken to cover the contractors' cost) corresponds to a proportionate tax on profits. (Or rather, and the difference may matter, to a tax on whatever 'profit' is defined to be for this purpose: if borrowing costs are not to be covered from cost oil, for example, and investment spending is immediately covered, the charge on profit oil is in effect an R-based cash flow tax). Indeed the similarity between government profit oil and explicit taxation is sometimes recognized by providing for the former to cover the contractors' liability to corporate tax.

Other features of PSAs also replicate possible tax arrangements. Limits on the recovery of cost oil, for instance – allowing only up to some percent of cost to be met from sales proceeds – function in effect as an implicit royalty.

Equity participation

Government may also take direct ownership in resource activities (beyond its ownership of the resource itself), especially at the development stage. This can and does take a variety of forms, in each case – short of a fully paid-up equity share on commercial terms – being equivalent to some tax arrangement in terms of the payments to and from government that it implies: a comprehensive account is in Daniel (1995). For example:

* If the government simply acquires and maintains an equity holding free of charge,[37] it in effect levies a dividend tax at a rate equal to its proportional holding.[38]
* Under carried interest arrangements, the state acquires equity from its allocated share of profits, this payment being inclusive of an interest charge. Since this arrangement has positive net present value to the government only to the extent that the rate of return ultimately earned on its equity exceeds the interest rate charged on its contribution, this is equivalent[39] to an RRT on returns in excess of that interest rate.

These and other revenue equivalences for PSAs and equity participation do not imply, of course, that these equivalences are complete. This is so not only in terms of the impact of state participation on the efficiency and transparency of government operations but also in more narrow revenue terms. An ownership stake may allow the government to exert direct (perhaps implicit) influence on the extent of tax avoidance activities, for example, and help overcome problems of asymmetric information that may constrain fully arms-length tax design. Government equity participation (even on commercial terms) might also improve efficiency by mitigating political risk: to the extent that the government has a stake in ownership, its temptation to confiscate rents ex post recedes (Garnaut and Clunies Ross, 1983). As discussed by McPherson in Chapter 9, however, there can be severe downsides to having state companies act as fiscal agents.

Auctions[40]

Auctions serve two distinct roles as elements of resource taxation regimes. They allocate rights to exploit natural resources among potential producers, and they generate revenues ex ante for the state. Arguably, the former is at least as important as the latter, given that revenues can be raised by other and complementary methods. These two elements – efficiency and revenue-raising – are also preoccupations of auction theory and design.

Producers to exploit natural resources can be selected in various ways.[41] Simple rationing schemes (such as first-come-first-served) might be used, as in the case where prospectors can freely stake claims in large geographical areas. There is no guarantee that the most efficient exploration producers will emerge in this case. Still, once discoveries are made, those making them can maximize rents by selling rights to exploit the deposit to more efficient producers. More relevant is the case in which substantial property tracts must be assigned to larger, vertically integrated producers. In this case, simple rationing schemes might be expected to lead to inefficient outcomes. A more sophisticated mechanism is for the government to allocate rights on the basis of technically supported applications: so-called 'beauty contests.' Provided governments are sufficiently well-informed to choose among applicants, and are free from capture, political influence and corruption – these are big 'ifs' – more efficient producers can be sorted out from less efficient ones. To the extent that applications for resource rights contain monetary bids and are made independently by several producers, they are effectively like either bonus bid auctions or royalty rate auctions (depending on whether the bid consists of a single sum for the right to extract or a payment per unit of extraction). Using auctions explicitly has the advantage that in addition to selecting producers, they also generate revenues. Well-designed auctions should in the right circumstances both select producers efficiently and generate the most revenue for the government.

Auctions can be conducted in a variety of ways. The 'revenue equivalence' theorem of auction theory shows that the leading candidates are in some circumstances equivalent – but, as Cramton (2009) makes clear, the conditions required are stringent. What form of auction maximizes the governments expected revenue then depends on such considerations as the nature of bidders' preferences and the characteristics of the objects being auctioned.

The preferences reflected in auctions will be of the 'common-value' type if the value of a natural resource deposit is independent of others held, though different producers may have different information about that value depending on what they have learned from prior technical investigation. More generally, however, the value of one block may be affected by owning others, given complementariness or substitutability in exploration or exploitation. In these circumstances, as Cramton (2009) outlines, ascending auctions (that is, those in which successive bids must be increasing in value) that simultaneously involve many blocks allow for 'price discovery' in the sense of enabling bidders to learn something about the information others might have, and allows for inter-linkages between packages of blocks of resources. But ascending auctions can have disadvantages. Observation of bids might lead to opportunities for signaling that allow firms to collude.[42] This problem can be avoided by a sealed bid procedure, though at the cost of eliminating information transmission altogether. More generally, there may be too few participants in auctions because of the costs of entry and the knowledge that the chances of winning might be low for less efficient bidders. And the winner's curse (the tendency to bid cautiously when the true value of the item is uncertain, given the danger that the winner has over-estimated its value) can lead to understatement of expected values.

Importantly, many of the potential problems with alternative auction mechanisms may well result in too little revenue being generated for the government rather than in the wrong producers being chosen. So long as the government is able to obtain revenue ex post by other taxation measures (credibly committed to prior to the auction), revenue shortfalls from auctions can be less important than selecting the most efficient producers who will generate the highest future rents. This points too to the importance of selecting the bid variables: including an element of royalty bids – or bids on profit tax rates – can provide some assurance against unduly low bonus bids. Such structuring may also help overcome what may have been a significant obstacle to the use of auctions in many developing countries (they remain particularly rare in relation to minerals): the possibility that bonus bids will be depressed by the government's inability to commit not to levy additional charges in the future.

Beyond the auction mechanism itself, a number of details are important to auction design. The objects to be auctioned must be defined. Given that resource properties may cover large areas, these may be divided into blocks of chosen sizes. A larger block size will internalize more information from exploration, but might also limit the number of participants in the auction because of scale. The terms of the property rights must be specified including the time horizon, as well as obligations with respect to environmental costs and disposal of waste after the resource is exhausted. There may be contractual obligations imposed on the government as well, such as the provision of infrastructure, the regulatory regime, and even the future tax regime. Indeed, this might be one potential way of enhancing commitment and thereby mitigating the time-consistency problem. However, it would be difficult to make commitment absolute, since one cannot preclude government legislation overriding tax rate obligations.

Other sector-specific charges

Resource operations may also be subject to a range of charges not applied more generally. These may include:

- Bonuses paid to the government at various stages in project development, such as on signature of contracts or licenses, discovery, or when production reaches some level – serving in part to bring forward revenue receipts and shift risk to the contractor. These can be for substantial amounts: Nakhle (in Chapter 4) cites a signature bonus of $1 billion per block of 4,100 km^2 in Angola.
- Export taxes, which can serve a variety of purposes: as a blunt alternative to income taxation when administrative weaknesses mean that this cannot be imposed directly; to restrict the world supply, and hence raise the world price, of resources for which the country has a considerable market share; and/or to encourage domestic processing activities. These have become less important over the years, in part reflecting greater use of better-targeted tax instruments and, perhaps, increased skepticism as to the effectiveness of tax incentives for domestic processing.
- Charges closer to user fees or corrective taxes, such as rental payments for surface rights needed for extraction, or the taxation implicit in requirements to set aside reserves to cover eventual shut down costs.

- The requirement (perhaps implicit) to provide infrastructure.[43] This is tantamount to earmarking tax revenues, which can create costly inflexibility in the allocation of public spending. The potential advantage of earmarking, on the other hand – stressed by Collier (2010, Chapter 3) in discussing recent experiences in Africa, and formalized by Brett and Keen (2000) – is that it can limit politicians' ability to divert revenue to their own purposes (though they may also prove adept in turning spending to their own interests).

Standard taxes, as applied to the resource sector

Resource companies will typically also be subject to taxes of general applicability, though some special issues arise (even leaving aside the international tax aspects discussed in Chapter 13 by Mullins (2010)).

CORPORATE INCOME TAX

The corporate income tax (CIT) applied to businesses in general is commonly also applied to resource firms in particular, though often with particular provisions relating to the tax base.

One such – a project-based approach along the lines raised at the outset – is the potential *ring-fencing* of operations that are analogous to the restrictions on grouping for CIT purposes but applied at project rather than company level. These restrictions in effect expand the tax base by limiting the use that can be made of losses (an especially important concern in the resource sector given the heavy upfront investment and long lead times). They may also have some merit in easing barriers to new entry that might otherwise arise from the ability of established firms to set off the losses at start-up against earnings from established activities. Efficiency, however, argues against ring-fencing: as stressed above, failure to provide relief for losses – especially in a sector marked by such large costs and long pre-production periods as are resources – runs the risk of creating serious distortions. Thus the better response to any entry barriers is to improve loss-offset arrangements, not limit them. Nevertheless, ring-fencing is likely to appeal to cash-strapped governments, even though they may also be vulnerable to transfer pricing and other profit shifting devices.

Another is the possibility of providing *depletion allowances* reflecting (sometimes in a rough-and-ready way) the reduction in the value of resource stocks implied by their extraction – analogous to depreciation allowances for produced assets. That analogy also stresses that, just as depreciation allowances acknowledge spending to acquire assets, so depletion allowances are appropriate within the logic of an annual income tax only to the extent that payment has been made for the right to extract, and that payment has not already been deductible from taxes: otherwise, allowing depletion is in effect a subsidy to extraction, equivalent to a negative royalty.[44] And in a cash flow framework, expenditure on acquiring such rights would simply be expensed, like any other investment, with no subsequent tax recognition needed.

The impact of other taxes may also depend on their treatment under the CIT. One set of issues concerns the availability of foreign tax credits, which, as discussed by Mullins (2010) in Chapter 13, typically calls for sequencing tax charges so as to maximize, within a given total tax payment, corporate tax liability (crediting the CIT against others rather than vice versa). Interactions with the CIT can also be important when the various taxes accrue to different jurisdictions. Allowing royalties to be deductible against the corporate tax (reflecting the perception of them as in effect a cost of production), for instance, is structurally irrelevant in that the same level of aggregate payment could be achieved if they were not deductible simply by setting the royalty at an appropriately lower rate.[45] If, however – as in Canada, for instance – the royalty accrues to provinces but CIT in large part to the federal government, the incentives in tax-setting can be quite different: provinces have an incentive to set higher royalty rates than they otherwise would, since the cost to the taxpayer of any additional revenues this raises is in part offset by a reduction in federal CIT revenue.

Resource activities may also be differentially treated in terms of the CIT rate applied, a higher rate being a simple but blunt device for rent extraction, as stressed by Garnaut and Clunies Ross (1983). Egypt, Mexico, Norway, and the United Kingdom, for example, apply a differentially high rate of CIT to some resource activities.[46] The principal downside to this – other than the CIT generally not being precisely targeted as a rent tax – is the risk of profit-shifting created by any differentiation in statutory CIT rates.[47]

IMPORT DUTIES

Where tariffs on imported equipment might be problematic – and the trend to lower tariff rates over the last 20 years or so has made this less common than formerly – arrangements are often made to exempt large resource projects. There is indeed good reason for this. Since there is rarely domestic production of these capital goods to protect, the main purpose that such tariffs can serve is simple revenue-raising; but while they succeed in doing so early in a project's lifetime (even before royalties are payable), the same can be achieved by other devices, such as bonus payments, that can be better tailored to the likely overall return to the project.

VAT

Intended as a tax on final domestic consumption, the VAT should in principle have little impact on resource operations, which are commonly largely for export. But that export-orientation itself, combined with heavy upfront costs and long lead times, pose particular problems: with little if any output VAT on domestic sales, relief for VAT charged on inputs cannot be obtained by crediting it against that liability but must come from refunds paid by the domestic tax authorities. And many developing countries have found it hard to pay such refunds in a timely manner[48] – in which case the input VAT 'sticks', raising input costs and serving as an implicit export tax.

The best response is of course to improve the operation of the refund system. Short of that, however, one possibility is to zero-rate purchases by resource operations, at least in their early years (when the problem is most acute, though it is likely to remain throughout the project lifetime). Applied to both domestic purchases and imports, this preserves trade neutrality, but zero-rating 'indirect exporters' in this way creates further problems in the need to ensure that zero-rated supplies are not then inappropriately also made to the domestic market. In many cases the zero-rating (or, what achieves the same effect, deferral of tax due on import until the first regular inland payment)[49] is for this reason restricted to imports and – to avoid an unacceptable pro-import bias – to large capital goods unlikely to be produced domestically. This still leaves the risk of de facto input taxation, however, on other items, such as the purchase of services.

B *Effective tax rates and the evaluation of resource tax regimes*

Understanding the impact of these various tax instruments on government revenues and on firms' profitability and decision-making is not straightforward: details of tax base matter as much, if not more, than rates; and, as with royalties, there can be complex intertemporal dimensions to consider. These difficulties are compounded when several taxes are applied, with the interactions between them then playing a potentially important role (the impact of royalty payments, for example, being dampened if they are deductible against profits-based taxation). To evaluate and compare alternative resource tax regimes, much effort has gone into developing notions of 'effective' tax rates, intended to provide simple summary indicators of likely tax impacts on resource activities. Daniel *et al.* (2010) provide in Chapter 7 an exhaustive account and illustration of these methods: here we simply review some the over-arching conceptual issues.

The desire to evaluate and compare tax regimes arises outside the resource sector, of course, and there is a well-established methodology for effective rate calculations with non-resource industries in mind. To a large degree, however, these two lines of work on effective tax rates have developed independently, to the detriment of each: the resource tax literature has been perhaps less rigorous in basing effective rate measures on fully formulated views of firms' optimization decisions, and the wider public finance approach has to a large degree neglected the features that loom large in the resource sector but are also present more widely, such as long gestation periods before initial investment payoff, pervasive uncertainty – and the possibility that projects will simply never be profitable.

There are broadly two types of forward-looking effective tax rate:[50]

- **The average effective tax rate** (AETR) is simply the proportion of the present value of the income generated by some hypothetical project that is taken in tax[51] – it is what resource economists tend to call the 'tax take' – and unity minus the AETR is the proportion of the present value of income that accrues to the company. Importantly, the AETR can be calculated at various points in a project's lifetime: the most common is after discovery has been made, though it is conceptually straightforward (as described in Chapter 7 by Daniel *et al.* (2010)) to calculate an effective tax rate prior to exploration. Some aspects of detail in these calculations are less than clear-cut. One issue is the choice of discount rate (which may differ, of course, when the tax take is viewed from perspective of government and of company); a point discussed further in Section 4 below. This is closely related to wider questions related to the treatment of uncertainty. One approach, dispensing altogether with the attempt to provide a single summary statistic, is to describe the distribution of the present value of tax payments – or key aspects of it, such as the probability of failing to meet some particular rate of return – as it varies with the resource price or other underlying source of uncertainty.[52]

- *Marginal effective tax rates* (METRs) are intended to capture the extent to which the tax system distorts firms' decision making by in effect raising the marginal cost of various actions. They measure the proportion of the pre-tax return on an activity which leaves the firm just breaking even that goes to the government, so capturing the size of the tax distortion to that decision. Three dimensions of behavior in the resource sector are of particular interest in this respect: spending on exploration; capital investment in developing identified deposits (sinking mines, putting oil rigs in place, and so on); and extraction. In each case, embedding in a simple extension of the model of firm decisions set out in Box 2.1 a fairly detailed description of the tax system of interest enables one to derive tax wedges that describe the extent to which the tax system raises the marginal cost (given the company's optimal response) of exploring, investing and extracting: Box 2.3 elaborates.[53] Amongst these METRs, the non-resource literature has focused almost exclusively on that on investment, the other dimensions of decision making being less paramount in other industries; in the resource sector, however, this is arguably one of the less important dimensions, with limited opportunities for substitution between capital and other factors in developing deposits, and those capital requirements then largely dictated by the extent of the resource believed to be available. Although less familiar, the notion of an METR for exploration is straightforward, capturing the extent to which the marginal cost of the exploration that companies will undertake falls short (or exceeds) the expected return from the discovery of new sources (suggesting that a greater (or lesser) level of spending on exploration would be appropriate): in the absence of taxation, the two would be equated. The METR on extraction is more subtle, reflecting the intertemporal considerations discussed earlier.

Box 2.3 Marginal effective tax rates on resource activities

Extending the framework of Box 2.1 to allow for the use of capital K in production, generated by investment I that depreciates at a rate δ, and for exploration spending of e to generate (perhaps stochastically) discoveries of $D(e)$, the firm's value function becomes

$$V(S_t, K_t) = \max_{q_t, I_t} \left\{ p_t q_t - C(q_t, K_t, S_t) - e_t - I_t - T(q_t, e_t, \{I\}) \right.$$

$$\left. + \frac{1}{1+r} E[V(S_t + D(e_t) - q_t, (1-\delta)K_t + I_t)] \right\}$$

where $T(.)$ describes tax payable, which depends on the details of the tax system (the term $\{I\}$ indicating that depreciation allowances generally depend on the past history of investment).

The firm's choice of extraction q, investment I and exploration e generates three necessary conditions; combining these with the impact of the resource and capital stocks on the valuation function, the corresponding METRs (the formalities are omitted here) summarize the wedge between the value of the marginal benefit from each of these decisions before and after tax:

- In the case of investment, the marginal benefit is the pre-tax rate of return on capital, which in equilibrium equals the net-of-depreciation user cost of capital. The METR is then the pre-tax rate of return on capital less the required after-tax rate of return on savings (conventionally expressed as an ad valorem rate by dividing by the pre-tax return on capital).
- For extraction, the notion of an METR is more complex (and rarely applied in practice), since, as is evident from Box 2.1 and the later discussion of royalties, extraction this period is potentially affected by not only current taxes but all future taxes too. One approach would be to characterize tax impacts in terms of their effect on the equilibrium path of net current benefits from extraction. Recalling footnote 15, for example, if only a specific royalty at rate θ is in place, the METR would be $(1 + r)\theta_t - \theta_{t+1}$: a positive METR then means that the royalty is increasing in present value, creating an incentive to bring extraction forward.
- The METR on exploration is the pre-tax marginal value of resource discoveries less the pre-tax cost, where the former will reflect taxes paid once production has begun, and the latter the tax treatment of exploration expenses.

The AETR and the METR on investment are related, as[54]

$$AETR = \tau + \zeta.METR$$

where τ is the rate of CIT and ζ the ratio of the net return on the marginal investment to the average pre-tax return.

The AETR and METRs are conceptually quite distinct, and can take quite different numerical values.[55] A rent tax of the type described above, for instance, has no impact on firms' decisions, so that each of the three METRs will be zero. The AETR, however, reflecting the revenue raised, will then be equal to the rate at which the rent tax is levied. And it is perfectly possible, for instance, for a tax system to be marked by negative METRs (reflecting the generosity of allowances) but a positive AETR (reflecting tax raised on infra-marginal profit).

The reason for an interest in METRs is clear: they indicate how the tax system is likely to affect key dimensions of project design. For the most part, however, the resource tax literature has focused more on AETRs than METRs. The reason for this merits some thought.

In non-resource contexts, the significance of the AETR is commonly seen as in affecting in which jurisdiction a company will choose to locate some foot-loose investment – a factory, say, or a distribution center. Countries will thus naturally be concerned that their AETR not be too far above those offered by their competitors. In the resource context, however, the underlying source of rents – the deposit itself – is not mobile across countries, and conventional theory would suggest that such rents can indeed be taxed at up to 100 percent without fear of driving investment abroad. Clearly it is important here to distinguish between the AETR calculated conditional on discovery (in which case it is quasi-rents that are being taxed, and as stressed earlier these cannot be taxed too heavily without discouraging exploration) or prior to exploration (in which case it is less obvious why 100 percent rent taxation should not be feasible). The basic point, remains, however, that the immobility of the underlying source of rents – potential resources in the ground – makes it less obvious than in non-resource contexts why countries should care how their tax take compares with that offered in other countries. Indeed one might expect their concern to be with ensuring that their tax take is *higher* than that available elsewhere, for reassurance that they extract at least as much rent as do others. In some cases, and not least in times of high resource prices, that does indeed seem to be their concern. In others, however, the concern appears on the contrary to be that the tax take not be too high relative to others, so that countries appear to be engaging in tax competition of the kind that has become familiar in non-resource contexts. Quite why such tax competition should occur in relation to what appear to be location-specific rents, however, is far from clear. This puzzle is taken up in Section 4 below.

A final point. While distinct, the concepts of AETR and the METR on investment are formally related, with an important implication for the progressivity issue. The formalities are in Box 2.3, but the intuition is simple. Suppose that the METR is negative: this can quite plausibly be (and often is) the case for debt-financed investments in assets receiving accelerated depreciation, since then the cost of the investment is effectively deducted more than once. For a project that earns only a modest return, the AETR will be somewhat less than the statutory tax rate because of this marginal tax subsidy. For a project that earns an extremely high return, on the other hand, the AETR will be close to the statutory rate: if resource prices were infinitely high, to take an extreme example, the CIT base would be essentially revenue, which is also then essentially rent. The implication is that in such circumstances the AETR increases with the rate of return on the underlying project (so long as the METR is positive). Even without any progressivity built into the structure of the statutory rate schedule – the same rate applies to all levels of taxable profit – a standard CIT *is* then progressive in the sense that the term is commonly used in the resource literature.

4 Challenges in designing resource tax regimes

The features of the resource sector set out in Section 2 – many of them applying also to other activities, but writ very large for resources – pose a range of challenges for tax design. This section considers how they might be addressed.

A Discount rates and their implications

For such long-lived projects as are commonplace in the resource sector, the discount rates applied by government and investor – and differences between them – can play a critical role.

For investors, the discount rate applied to expected cash flows can be taken to be a (tax-adjusted) cost of capital reflecting the risks associated with the project and, importantly, the extent to which these are diversified across the company's entire range of activities (not, unlike national governments, simply those within any country): companies holding a portfolio of licenses are to some extent self-insured against the risks they face in terms of the extent, quality, and accessibility of any single source. In principle, too, companies' discount rates should reflect the opportunities for their ultimate shareholders to diversify risk within a wider portfolio of assets. On the other hand, their discount rates will reflect any political risk they perceive from the inability of the host government to commit to existing or announced tax and other policies.

The somewhat different considerations that arise for governments are examined in Box 2.4. These suggest, broadly speaking, that governments are likely to have relatively low discount rates when they attach a high weight to the well-being of future generations, have relatively high income and slow prospective growth, are not strongly risk-averse and are able to diversify away the risks associated with resource extraction. For many developing countries, especially those heavily dependent on the resource sector – even more so if there are just a few projects – some or all of these conditions are unlikely to hold, pointing to a relatively high discount rate. All this, moreover, relates to the discount rate that a fully benevolent government would apply. In practice, policy makers also face political risk in terms of their own longevity in office. This in itself will likely cause them to discount future returns more heavily, implying the pursuit of policies that are inefficient from a wider social perspective.

Box 2.4 The government's discount rate

Suppose that for each unit of an asset costing P purchased today (period 1) the government can obtain an uncertain return of X tomorrow (period 2), and evaluates this decision in terms of maximizing expected utility

$$U(Y_1 - aP) + \frac{1}{1+\rho} E[U(Y_2 + aX)] \tag{4.1}$$

where a denotes the number of units of the risky asset bought, Y_t is (exogenous) income in period t (so that the argument of each function is consumption at the corresponding date) and ρ is the rate which future utility is discounted.

From the first order condition for the choice of a, the value placed on the asset is then approximately:

$$P \approx \frac{E[X]}{1 + \rho + RRA(C_1)E[G] - \text{cov}[U'(C_2)X]} \tag{4.2}$$

where $\text{cov}(w,z) \equiv (E[wz] - E[w]E[z])/E[w]E[z]$ is a normalized covariance, $G \equiv (E[C_2] - C_1)/C_1$ is the expected growth in consumption, and $RRA(C) \equiv -U''(C) C/U'(C)$ is the coefficient of relative risk aversion (defined to be positive).[56] The certainty-equivalent discount rate used to value the asset thus has four components:

- The rate of pure time preference, ρ. This is essentially an ethical parameter, and the appropriate value has long been contentious. The Stern Review (2007) on climate change, for instance, follows a long tradition in setting this to zero on the grounds that it is improper to attach less weight to the well-being of future generations than to our own; others point that this is not how governments appear to behave, and is also ethically questionable: one alternative, for instance, is to maximize the well-being of the least well-off generation – which is likely to be the current one.
- The degree of curvature of the marginal utility function. This is as described by the coefficient of relative risk aversion, though (since this term also applies under perfect certainty) here it is capturing the extent to which the consumption of future generations is discounted because they enjoy higher consumption: the stronger the curvature, the more heavily future returns are discounted.
- The anticipated growth rate: faster growth implies less weight attached to future consumption, since that is associated (to an extent that depends on the curvature of marginal utility) with lower marginal utility of future consumption.
- The covariance between returns to the project and the marginal utility of consumption. This will be more negative – and the discount rate consequently higher – the more important returns to the project are to the aggregate economy (since then a low return is associated with low consumption and hence a high marginal utility). While there may be some opportunities for risk reduction through such devices as hedging, these operate only over periods that are quite short relative to project lifetimes. Attitudes to risk enter this final component too, with higher risk aversion, and hence a more sensitive marginal utility of income, again pointing to a higher discount rate.

The levels of the discount rates applied by government and investor can affect, for example, their rankings of alternative projects. Perhaps even more important for policy design, however, are differences between them. And here, for the reasons just given, the best working assumption is likely to be that in many lower income countries governments are likely to discount more heavily than many investors.

Differing discount rates matter, it should be stressed, even in the absence of uncertainty. Most fundamentally, they create scope for intertemporal trade between government and investor. If investors have a lower discount rate than the government, for instance, then by bringing forward their payments during the life of the project they can confer a benefit on the government – unable, perhaps, to borrow against future receipts – that the latter will be willing to pay for by lowering future payments so much that the present value of returns to the investor, evaluated at its own discount rate, will rise. This in turn may affect optimal instrument choice. In the circumstances just described, for instance, both parties could gain – commitment problems aside – by levying an up-front fee (such as a signature bonus) rather than taxing ex post rents. Different discount rates may also rationalize deploying distorting tax instruments. They imply for instance[57] that the extraction path which maximizes the present value of rents for one party will typically not maximize it for the other. If the investor has a lower discount rate than the government, for instance, then it will tend to extract resources too slowly from the perspective of a government that attaches value to those rents (perhaps because it is taxing them). It will then wish to speed up extraction, which (recalling the discussion in Section 3.A) it can do by setting a royalty that increases in present value over time.

B Risk sharing

Alternative tax schemes imply different allocations between government and investor of the underlying risk associated with a project, creating scope for mutually beneficial trading of that risk between them. Both can gain by exploiting differences in attitude towards risk, with the party better able to bear more risk willing to do so in return for a higher expected return that the other is willing to pay.

To see what uncertainty might imply for optimal tax design, it is useful to abstract from the intertemporal dimension (for the moment) by supposing that project returns all accrue at a single future date and – also putting the time consistency issue aside – that the government can credibly commit to any state-contingent tax policy: that is, can announce, and will rightly be expected to implement, any schedule that prescribes some tax liability contingent on the outcome of the project (thought of, for simplicity, as simply the realization of an uncertain resource price). This tax schedule could take any shape: it might be progressive, with a higher average tax rate the more successful the project; or it could be regressive. Suppose too that the tax system itself is non-distorting, in the sense that it has no impact on the design of or payoffs to the project.

There is no uniquely optimal tax schedule in this setting, but some potential candidates will be inefficient in the sense that both parties could gain by instead adopting a different one. Box 2.5 characterizes the set of schedules that are Pareto-efficient in the sense of leaving no such room for mutual improvement.

Box 2.5 Progressivity and risk-sharing

Denote by $p(s)$ the return to the project in state s and by $\tau(s)$ the corresponding state contingent average tax rate. Pareto efficiency then requires that the government maximize its own expected utility subject to providing some given level of expected utility to the investors, the Lagrangean for this being

$$\sum_s \pi(s)U_G[p(s)\tau(s)] + \lambda \sum_s U_I[(1-\tau(s))p(s)]\pi(s) \tag{5.1}$$

where $\pi(s)$ denotes the probability of state s occurring and the utility functions of government and investor are indicated by subscripts G and I. Taking the necessary conditions for this to define τ as a function of p, the optimal average tax rate can be shown to vary with profitability as[58]

$$\tau'(p) = (RRA_I - RRA_G)/\Omega \tag{5.2}$$

where RRA_j denotes the relative risk aversion of party $j = G, I$ and $\Omega \equiv -[U_G''/U_G') + (U_I''/U_I')]p^2(>0)$ (all evaluated at the solution).

If, to take one extreme, the government is risk-neutral (so that $RRA_G = 0$), efficiency requires that $\tau' = 1$, so that the after-tax receipts of the investor be the same whatever the before-tax return, so that government bears all the risk; and the opposite is true if it is the investor that is risk-neutral. More generally, whether Pareto-efficient risk-sharing requires a progressive or regressive tax system thus depends on the relative risk aversion of the two parties. Assuming constant relative risk aversion, for definiteness, efficiency requires progressive rent taxation if and only if the government is less risk-averse than the investor.

The conclusion is straightforward: efficiency requires that risk be borne more heavily by whichever party is less risk-averse.[59] If firms are risk-neutral, for instance, then efficient risk-sharing requires that they receive all the uncertain return in exchange for payment of some fixed fee to the government. Pursuing that logic, efficient risk-sharing requires a progressive tax schedule if, and only if, the government has lower (relative) risk aversion than the investor. For the reasons above, the presumption must be that risk-sharing considerations argue against progressivity in many lower income countries.

The temporal dimension of uncertainty, reflected in the discussion of discounting above, can also have a critical impact on instrument choice. As discussed above, risk-averse governments will have higher discount rates, all else equal, and so will prefer to get tax revenue sooner. This is best done, in principle, by intertemporal trade that does not dissipate the potential return to the project by tax-induced distortions: by auctioning, for example. If, however, credibility or other considerations prevent this being done, the (first-order) benefit from retiming tax revenue through the use of distorting instruments may offset the (second-order) loss that the induced inefficiency implies. Royalties, in particular, are commonly rationalized on these grounds: the government collects some revenue, including in the early days of the project, even if that project ultimately proves unsuccessful.

In this logic, the royalty functions akin to a minimum tax, which is a feature of the regular tax system in many countries (intended also as protection against transfer-pricing and other forms of profit-shifting). These minimum taxes are often specified as some fraction of turnover, and so are precisely analogous to an ad valorem royalty. This rationale suggests, however, that the royalty should be creditable against any profits-based tax (rather than, as is normally the case, deductible).

C Responding to information asymmetries

Policy makers labor under the potential difficulty of being less well-informed on the geological and commercial circumstances of resource projects than are those to whom they entrust their implementation. One response is for governments to undertake the projects themselves, and indeed this remains commonplace in oil activities. The experience with state-run operations, however, has been less than entirely happy, as discussed in Chapter 9 by McPherson (2010), in part because asymmetries of information re-emerge to contaminate relations between national resource companies and other parts of government and wider society. Another possibility is the use of auctions (discussed briefly above and at more length in Chapter 10 by Cramton (2010)), a key purpose of which is precisely to elicit information from firms bidding for resource rights. Well-designed auctions that induce competitive bidding and information sharing can be relatively simple to administer, transparent and influence-resistant. At the same time, if there are few potential bidders or if the terms and conditions attached to property rights are complex and negotiable, the government might be tempted to adopt more discretionary contractual approaches to assigning property rights. Alternatively, the government might wish to tailor the tax instruments at its disposal so as to limit the damage that lingering asymmetries information can do to the pursuit of its core policy objectives.

Suppose, for instance, that some projects are of two possible types, with either low or high costs for any given level of extraction. Firms know what type their project is. But the government – whose objective, assume, is simply to maximize its tax revenue – does not, and cannot rely on firms to self-report their profitability correctly. It can though observe (only) the level of extraction and the price at which the resource is sold: so it cannot implement a profit-based tax, but only a royalty (perhaps at a rate that varies with the level of output) and a fixed fee. Optimal policy, given that the government cannot tell directly whether the project has low or high costs, involves deploying both.

More precisely, it involves offering a choice between two tax packages: one with no royalty but a relatively high fee, the other a royalty but a relatively low fee. The reasoning behind this is spelt out in Box 2.6, but the essential intuition is straightforward. At any given royalty rate, extraction will be greater for the low than for the high cost project: firms are thus more anxious to avoid paying them when costs are low, and to do so will be willing to pay a larger fixed fee. While the royalty distorts the extraction level for the high cost project, the inefficiency this creates is more than offset by the ability to discourage low cost projects from masquerading as high cost ones, and hence to extract greater rent from them without jeopardizing the revenue from high cost projects.

One other feature of the optimal tax package should be noted: it leaves the low cost project earning strictly positive rents. This is because any tax package that is intended to ensure that high cost producers break even must imply that low cost producers earn strictly positive profit, since they can always pretend to be high cost and (actually being more efficient than high cost producers) earn strictly positive rents by doing so. In the presence of asymmetric information, firms may enjoy informational rents that cannot efficiently be taxed away.

Box 2.6 Optimal tax design with asymmetric information – more intuition

Suppose that the government starts by deploying only a single fixed fee F. To maximize revenue, it will set this as high as is possible without making the high cost project unprofitable. Note that extraction will then be greater if the project is low cost than if it is high: $q^1 > q^2$, say.

Now suppose the government offers firms a choice: they can either produce output q^1 and continue to pay only the fixed fee, or they can produce the lesser amount q^2 and pay a small royalty $d\theta > 0$ together with a fee slightly reduced by $dF < 0$, where these have been calibrated to have no effect on the after-tax profit of a high cost project initially producing q^2: that is, $q^2 d\theta + dF = 0$. The change in the tax paid by this high cost project is then $q^2 d\theta + \theta dq^2 + dF = 0$, and so, since there is initially no royalty, is also zero. A firm with a low cost project now has a choice: it can remain at q^1 as before, or it can choose the royalty regime. Denoting the optimal level of output in that latter case by $\hat{q}^1$, it would then pay tax of $\hat{q}^1 d\theta + F + dF$. Comparing this with its initial tax payment of F, the implied change in tax payments is $d\theta(\hat{q}^1 - q^2)$; which, since the low cost project will produce more than the high at any royalty rate, is strictly positive. Adding to this the reduction in pretax profits implied by the distortion of its output level if this option is chosen, the low cost project strictly prefers the option of producing q^1 and paying no royalty. But the government can exploit that strict preference by requiring that a slightly higher fee be paid if q^1 is produced. By offering these different $\{\theta, F\}$ packages, the government can thus increase its revenue.

The process cannot continue indefinitely, since when the initial royalty is strictly positive a perturbation of this kind that leaves after-tax profits of the high tax project unchanged will reduce tax revenue (as a consequence of the reduction in output). Nor can it be optimal to impose a royalty on the low cost project: if a positive royalty were set, slightly lowering it would increase pre-tax profit, and this could be extracted by setting a somewhat higher differential fee, without making it attractive for the low cost project to masquerade as high cost.

The tax design problem becomes still more complicated if production extends over several periods. Under the scheme just described, for instance, firms effectively reveal whether the project is high or low cost by the tax package they choose. If tax rules could be reset thereafter – and (as is plausible) costs were correlated, so that a project that had low costs in one period will also have low costs in the next – then low cost projects would have an incentive not to reveal themselves as such in order to avoid heavier taxation in the future. Osmundsen (1998) shows that in this case optimal policy, assuming (perhaps heroically, given the time consistency problem) that the government is fully able to commit, again requires offering a menu of royalties and fixed charges but with the former now depending not only on current output but also on output in previous periods.[60]

The solutions to the optimal tax design problem in these (relatively simple) cases are evidently complex: even in the one-shot problem, for instance, the royalty is nonlinear in output. They do stress, however, the potential value of deploying royalties as part of the response to problems of asymmetric information: while distorting extraction decisions they can provide an indirect way of ensuring that more profitable projects pay more tax. This remains so even when the government cannot implement a nonlinear royalty, but must apply the same rate at all output levels (and so must also offer only a single license fee). It can be shown that it will indeed then be optimal to set a positive royalty rate: this means setting a lower fee than would otherwise be the case in order for the high cost project to go ahead, but the consequent revenue loss is more than offset by the revenue gained from applying the royalty to the high level of output that will remain optimal for the low cost project.

The potential usefulness of royalties is amplified the greater are the difficulties of accurately measuring costs, as, not least, when firms are adept at shifting taxable income to lower-tax jurisdictions. Indeed, recognition that revenues may be easier for the tax authorities to monitor than costs suggests that royalties might be combined with rent taxes to exploit the advantages of both. To the extent that firms can overstate their costs for profit tax purposes, they will have an incentive to undertake excessive expenditures. This can be countered by a royalty that applies only on revenues. Box 2.7 presents a stylized example to illustrate the point, showing how a royalty can correct the inefficiency associated with overstatement of costs for tax purposes and lead to efficient rent extraction. In that simple example, a royalty can be used to tax away revenue in the same proportion as the firm understates costs, leaving an undistorted measure of rents as the base for the rent tax proper.

But the merits of royalties as a response to informational problems should not be overstated. They are not without their own implementation difficulties (as discussed in Chapter 11 by Calder (2010a), and in Otto *et al.* (2006)). Conversely, the difficulty of observing business costs is a pervasive problem that does not preclude governments operating business income taxes more generally. And explicit rent taxes may in some respects be even simpler to implement (as discussed in Chapter 12 by Calder (2010b) and Chapter 8 by Land): they do not require the accurate measurement of depreciation, for instance. Thus countries with relatively strong administrations, such as Norway and the UK, have felt able to dispense with royalties in their oil tax regimes. Even where administration is weak, royalties are best seen as an adjunct to, not a substitute for, effective profit tax regimes.

Box 2.7 Royalties and rent taxes to alleviate asymmetric information

Suppose a resource firm incurs a cost of K in the first period to generate a quantity of resource $q(K)$ with certainty in the second period, where $q' > 0 > q''$. The resource sells for a price p and costs $C(q(K))$ to extract. The government imposes an ad valorem royalty at the rate θ on revenues and a tax on reported rents at the rate τ. Revenues can be perfectly observed by the government, whereas firms can over-report costs with limited chances of being caught. Suppose that the firm reports costs that are simply some multiple $\lambda(\tau) \geq 1$ of its true costs, with λ', $\lambda'' \geq 0$ (the higher the tax rate, the greater the incentive to overstate costs); the same overstatement applies to both initial costs and extraction costs.

The firm chooses K to maximize the present value of its after-tax rents:

$$\pi = -K(1-\tau\lambda(t)) + \frac{(1-\theta-\tau)pq(K)-(1-\tau\lambda(\tau))C(q(K))}{1+r} \tag{7.1}$$

the first-order condition for which can be written

$$((1-\theta-\tau)p-(1-\tau\lambda)C')q' = (1-\tau\lambda)(1+r) \cdot \tag{7.2}$$

From this, investment $K(\theta, \tau)$ can be shown to be decreasing in the royalty rate θ and (at zero royalty and for $\lambda > 1$) increasing in the rent tax rate: the royalty evidently discourages production, whereas the over-statement of costs means that the rent tax effectively acts as marginal subsidy to investment.

Indeed in this simple example the inefficiency can be eliminated entirely by setting the two instruments so that $\theta = (\lambda - 1)\tau$. After-tax rents in (7.1) then become

$$\pi = (1-\tau\lambda)\left(-I + \frac{pq-C}{1+r}\right) \tag{7.3}$$

so that the system becomes equivalent to a tax on rents at the rate $\tau\lambda$. By combining royalties and a rent tax set at appropriate levels, the government can then effectively choose the proportion of rents to extract from the firm.

D Dealing with time consistency

A government's inability to commit to its future tax treatment of resource projects can hurt both itself and investors. In principle, it ultimately restricts attention to tax policies that are 'time consistent,' in the sense that the government will find them optimal to implement ex post given that investors' behavior is predicated on it indeed behaving in such ways (so that investors are not surprised, and the government always acts in its own best interests). The problem this creates is that such policies are generally inferior, for all concerned, to those that could be achieved if the government could commit. Suppose, for example, that the government is unlimited in its revenue needs and so, ex post, will want to extract all the return from any successful project. The only time consistent equilibrium then has no private investment: investors rightly expect that their quasi-rents would be expropriated if the project succeeds, and so do not invest. Both sides would be better off if the government could credibly promise to tax away only part of the returns from the project.

Less extreme views of the government's preferences lead to less extreme out-comes. If the government values not only tax revenue but also (and strongly enough) after-tax profits accruing to the investor, then – an example of this will be discussed further below – it will typically not expropriate all quasi-rents once investment had been sunk. Some investment may thus continue to be made, but at a reduced level. The basic difficulty thus remains: investment will be too low relative to the fully efficient outcome that would be obtained if the government could commit.

There may be circumstances – as with the very high oil and mineral prices of mid 2008, perhaps – in which outcomes are so extraordinary, relative to what might have been conceived when tax arrangements were entered into, that some renegotiation is seen even by investors as generally reasonable. And countries with a strong reputation for good governance may be able to change tax rules frequently without very marked damage to investors' confidence: the UK, for instance, has altered the taxation of North Sea oil activities very frequently, without disturbing investors too dramatically. Nevertheless, the potential bene-fits of achieving credibility in resource taxation are substantial. A key question is thus how governments might do so, or at least, what kind of tax design time con-sistency may require of them. There are a number of possibilities.

One is to provide an up-front cash subsidy to investments, or equivalently make negative tax liabilities arising from initial investment cash expenditures fully refundable[61] (as Norway now does for exploration spending, for instance). This may be appropriate where countries have strong fiscal positions and low discount rates relative to potential investors (as perhaps in Norway) or, at the opposite extreme, for countries with such poor reputation and modest prospects that investment is otherwise completely blocked. But the disadvantages are evident: most countries are looking to obtain revenue in the early days of a project, not to give it away.

A second possibility, when interactions with investors are repeated over time – perhaps reflecting knowledge of rich deposit possibilities and a consequent expec-tation of a continued flow of developments (as in the Norwegian case, as stressed by Osmundsen (2010) in Chapter 15) – is for the government to seek to acquire a reputation for keeping its word. This can be supported by investors adopting a pun-ishment strategy: refusing to invest at all for several years, for example, once com-mitments have been violated. In such circumstances, if the government has a sufficiently low discount rate it may prefer to honor its word rather than take the short-term benefit of setting a higher tax than promised. But circumstances may not always be favorable to such an outcome. The necessary coordination and commitment amongst investors may be lacking, and governments can turn over quickly. For post-conflict countries, not least, establishing a good reputation, and providing assurance to investors that conflict will not re-erupt, is likely to take some time. And some countries have only limited likely reserves – in some cases just one major development, in others reserves that are expected to be exhausted relatively soon – so that the risk of deterring future investments may have little force.

Governments can also seek to provide some form of legal assurance on future tax policy: a government cannot bind its successors, but it can try to restrict their room for maneuver. Guarantees might be provided in the constitution, though in some countries constitutional amendments are fairly commonplace, and as Osmundsen (2010) notes in Chapter 15, the time required to change constitutions may be modest relative to project lifetimes. International investment agreements, with the force of treaty, commonly provide for at least reasonable compensation in the event of expropriation.[62] Violating these may be especially costly, given the wider signal that would send, but the protection is only against the most extreme outcomes. More targeted, and quite common, is the inclusion of fiscal stability clauses in sectoral laws or specific agreements. A range of issues that arise in designing their precise terms – whether for instance a premium should be charged in return for such stability assurances – are discussed by Daniel and Sunley (2010) in Chapter 14. They also stress, however, that politics can nevertheless exert significant pressures for the effective abrogation of such agreements; if not explicitly, then through significant encouragement of private companies to renegotiate the terms of their agreements 'voluntarily.'

It may also be that some features of tax design can be exploited to ease the difficulties created by the inability to commit. Is it the case, in particular, that schemes with some degree of progressivity – the average tax being higher at higher rates of ex post return – are helpful in this context, in the sense that both investors and government can fare better than they would if progressivity were precluded?

It may be that time consistent tax schemes are indeed progressive. Appendix II gives an example of this, in which a government attaches some constant marginal value to tax revenue and a positive but decreasing marginal value to realized after-tax profits. In this case, it will indeed impose a progressive tax on quasi-rents: it leaves them entirely untaxed if low enough (profits then having more value than tax revenue) but at an increasing rate above that (leaving investors with the level of after-tax profits that has the same marginal value as tax revenue). This result is certainly special – time consistency would require a regressive schedule, for instance, if the value attached to profits were constant and that to tax revenue decreasing – but suggestive nonetheless.

Intuition suggests, moreover, that progressive rate schedules may have particular appeal in terms of political economy, being more robust against political pressures in the event of high return outcomes than are proportional schemes. This indeed has become part of folk wisdom – at least for some folk – in this area.[63] Box 2.8 sets out a simple political economy model in which this indeed turns out to be the case, so long as domestic electors are sufficiently risk-averse. This latter feature contrasts interestingly with the earlier arguments on dealing with uncertainty itself. The conclusion there was that if, as is in many cases plausible, host governments are relatively risk-averse, progressive taxation is unappealing. The political economy of time consistency, however, suggests the exact opposite: it is where risk aversion is high that progressivity is desirable. The model is highly stylized, but makes the point that the strongest case for progressive resource tax arrangements in lower income countries may well be in dealing with the politics of time consistency, and that determining the optimal degree of progressivity is likely to involve trading this off against the associated costs of risk-bearing.

One other point is worth noting. This is that the weakness of tax administration in many countries may in itself mitigate the time consistency problem: if host authorities are simply not capable of levying heavy taxes on ex post rents – perhaps because they have very little ability to monitor profit-shifting arrangements – then investors have little to fear. In some contexts, it may for this reason even be optimal for governments to deliberately underdevelop their administrative capacity: in effect, a weak administration can itself serve as a commitment device (Boadway and Keen (1998)). The point should not be over-stated, given the extreme weakness of tax administrations in many lower income countries (and, in any event, threats of non-renewal of licenses and the like can be effective even without a strong tax administration). Nevertheless, the reality is that weakness of tax administration serves to some degree as a commitment device.

Box 2.8 Politics and progressivity in resource taxation

Suppose an incumbent government knows it will face re-election after the state-contingent return to some project, $p(s)$, has become known and – free to set whatever tax rate it then chooses – it has announced that it will tax these at rate $\tau(s)$ and distributed the proceeds equally across all voters, yielding each welfare of $U[\tau(s) \, p(s)]$ (the number of electors being normalized at unity). Its opponent will be a 'populist' party that will instead tax away and share out all returns, so yielding each voter $U[p(s)]$. Voters do not necessarily vote for the party offering the higher payout, however, since they also have ideological preferences between the two, described by a parameter ϕ distributed across the voter population, independent of the state realized and having (without loss of generality) mean zero. Thus voter j will vote for the populist party in state s if and only if

$$U(p) \geq U(\tau p) + \varphi_j . \tag{8.1}$$

The incumbent party wishes to remain in office, reflecting some non-monetary 'ego-rents' from which it derives value. Suppose too, however, that if it diverges from its pre-announced tax policy it will suffer some form of punishment, perhaps in the form of reduced future investment.

　　The incumbent can achieve both these objectives – be re-elected and keep its promises – if it announces a state-contingent tax schedule such that, for every s, the median voter supports its re-election. This requires the schedule to be such that, for all s,

$$U(p(s)) = U(\tau(p(s))p(s)) + \varphi_{median} \qquad (8.2)$$

which is consistent with setting a tax rate of less than 100 percent so long as the median voter has an ideological preference for the incumbent. More precisely, it is shown in Appendix III to require that $\tau'(p(s))$ be strictly positive at all s – meaning a progressive schedule – if and only if $RRA(\tau(p(s))p(s)) > 1$, so that the voters' relative risk aversion at all outcomes is greater than unity.

E International tax competition and coordination

As noted earlier, it is easy to explain why a country seeking to attract a new car factory might want to offer an AETR that is not too far above those available elsewhere, or, similarly, why it may not wish its statutory rate of CIT to be far above those elsewhere, given the opportunities for profit-shifting this can create. With countries shaping their tax policies in this way, the international corporate tax competition that now appears underway – reflected by a substantial fall in both statutory rates and AETRs – comes as no surprise. But it is far from obvious why a country considering a new resource development should have the same concern with the AETR: the car factory could be located elsewhere, but the resource deposit cannot. Resolving this puzzle – why countries might be concerned at having a higher resource AETR than elsewhere – is more than an intellectual curiosity: it may affect, for example, the case for international coordination in resource taxation.

This question has received little attention. Part of the answer, no doubt, is that similar transfer pricing issues arise as in other sectors, not only with the standard CIT but also in relation to such sector-specific taxes as royalties. Difficulties can also arise with smuggling if, for example, export tax rates differ across countries or – a case in which the resource itself is effectively mobile – when border-crossing deposits can be exploited from more than one jurisdiction. But the concern seems to be deeper than that.

One possibility is that production is limited by the scarcity of some input other than the resource itself, which countries must therefore compete to attract. Osmundsen (2005) – perhaps the only paper to address this issue – suggests that this might be managerial or technical capacity. Or the constraint might be in the finance available to resource firms. In so far as the shadow value of such constraints is not properly accounted for as a cost in AETR calculations, governments would need to offer packages that leave an after-tax return adequate to attract these factors. A difficulty with this line of explanation, however, is that – at least if entry is not blocked – one would expect high rewards to expand the supply of these scarce factors, at least in the medium term, just as one would expect a shortage of oil rigs to lead to an increase in their price.

Other explanations might focus on imperfections of competition, not only in terms of entry barriers limiting the supply of scarce inputs but also in restricting output supply so as to raise the world price of the resource at issue. A company that is large in the world market for some resource, for instance, might choose not to develop now all available deposits, even if that would be profitable at the current price, because it recognizes that doing so would cause the price to fall: it might choose to open only one of two possible gold mines, for instance, with the two host governments then having an incentive to offer the more attractive tax terms. But the practical importance of such considerations – and again, new entry should ultimately constrain such behavior – is unclear.

A third possibility is related to the time consistency issue: in seeking to acquire a reputation conducive to potential investors, countries may seek to benchmark their own systems relative to those available elsewhere. It may be, for instance, that credibility is enhanced by offering to new projects terms comparable to those that have proved acceptable to governments and investors alike elsewhere.

If countries do indeed compete in the resource tax regimes they offer, it could be that by doing so they ultimately derive no benefit but, to the contrary, simply cause each other mutual damage. If, for instance, they compete to attract some factor, such as managerial capacity, that is scarce in the aggregate but mobile between them, it could be that tax rates end up inefficiently low: acting collectively, countries could raise revenue relatively efficiently from a relatively inelastic base, but by to failing to coordinate their policies they dissipate this opportunity, and so must resort to less efficient tax instruments or forego worthwhile spending. A case can then be made for international or regional coordination to limit such tax competition, and there has been some interest in this in the resource context: WAEMU (West African Economic and Monetary Union), for example, has adopted a mining code[64] that in specifying some tax benefits – including a three year tax holiday from the start of production – may serve to limit members' ability to compete by offering still stronger tax incentives. There has been discussion too of adopting common limits on tax benefits (including an avoidance of tax holidays) in the South Africa Development Community.[65] There is a large literature focused on the desirability or otherwise of such agreements intended to limit downward tax competition: on whether such coordination remains desirable, for instance, when policy makers may spend some part of tax revenues unwisely or corruptly, on whether coordination by a subset of countries can worsen their position by exposing them to more aggressive competition from third countries, and on the implications of alternative forms of coordination. Many of these generic considerations[66] are as relevant to the resource sector as to any other.

But there are differences. One is that since the reasons for any tax competition are less fully understood, so too the case for coordination is less clear: if downward pressure on tax rates reflects imperfections in market competition, for example, coordination is likely to be inferior to reducing those imperfections. Another potential concern is the time consistency issue raised above. Indeed in this respect the stronger case could perhaps be made for coordination intended to impose common *maximum* rates – achieving commitment by international agreement – not minima.

The usual arguments for international coordination of business tax policies have as yet had relatively little impact on practical policy. It is important to recognize, however, that they do not evidently apply with equal force, or in the same way, in relation to resources.

5 Concluding remarks

It is conventional to stress that no single resource tax regime will suit all countries and circumstances. That is undoubtedly so. Low income countries may reasonably be supposed to discount the future more heavily than others, for instance, and so to be more impatient to receive revenues relatively early in projects' lifetimes. They may also be less willing to bear risk than the large multinationals with which they deal, and be more constrained in terms of administrative capacity. These considerations may point to heavier reliance on royalties than elsewhere. Geology also matters: a country with a single large deposit may face greater time consistency problems than those with strong prospects of continued discovery. While country characteristics must thus shape practical policy advice, theory does provide some fairly specific guidance.

One lesson is that it will typically not be optimal to rely on a single tax instrument, whether auction, royalty, rent tax, or other. This is less because of multiple objectives – we have seen for instance that it may be optimal to use both royalties and fixed fees when the aim is simply to maximize revenues – than because of the range of challenges that governments face in crafting their resource tax regimes: shaping the preferred time path of revenues, dealing with problems of time consistency and asymmetric information, fitting the regime to their administrative capacity, and responding to political economy pressures. The discussion above points to a range of considerations that should inform the design of resource tax regimes to address these challenges. Amongst these:

- There is no easy solution to the fundamental time consistency problem, but building in some marked degree of sensitivity of tax payments to underlying profitability may help ease political economy pressures to renege on initial agreements. This might ideally take the form of an explicit rent tax, so as to minimize consequent distortions, though there may be a case for sensitivity to short-term prices rather than long-run rents since political pressures may arise at times of high resource prices even if rents remain moderate.
- Auctions – widely used in oil and gas operations, though not (yet) for minerals – have considerable potential appeal as a response (arguably the best response) to problems of asymmetric information, and (when the government's discount rate is relatively high) as a way of ensuring that substantial revenue is received early in the project lifetime. Their effectiveness may be less, however, where time consistency is perceived as a significant problem: participants will then bid less than they otherwise would in the expectation of an additional subsequent burden if the project proves highly successful. One way to mitigate

this may be by combining the auction with a non-distorting rent tax: while the latter will reduce the amounts bid, to the extent that it eases the time consistency problem it will also reduce the discount for sovereign risk.

- Much emphasis is often placed on the potential for royalties to distort producers' decisions on exploration and development, the pace of resource extraction and the closure of operations. There are circumstances, however, in which some such distortion of private decisions actually enhances social efficiency. One is that in which operators do not have proper incentives to leave resources in the ground at the end of their contract period: in this case, a royalty that increases as the terminal date of the contract approaches can in principle serve a useful corrective role (though it seems they are rarely used in this way in practice). Perhaps more fundamentally, royalties may also have a distinct role to play in responding to informational asymmetries: they can be used to counteract the tendency towards the overstatement of costs under a rent tax, and – though the point appears as yet to have had little impact on practice – can be combined with other instruments, such as a fixed fee, to enable liability to be differentiated across project and firm type in a way that raises more revenue than could either instrument on its own. What does seem clear is that while royalties will often have a proper role in resource regime, sole reliance on them risks creating costly distortions.

- While the resource literature has focused on the particular resource rent tax (RRT) of Garnaut and Clunies Ross (1975, 1979, 1983), there are many other forms of tax (indeed, infinitely many) that – in the absence of informational asymmetries, and with proper carry forward arrangements (including in relation to exploration expenses, especially on unsuccessful projects) – are nondistorting. A potential weakness of the RRT within this class of taxes, and one that seems to be keenly felt in practice, is that revenue accrues to the government only relatively (perhaps very) late in the project's life, once cumulated rents are positive. There are other rent taxes, equivalent to the RRT in present value, that yield revenue earlier (by not giving immediate relief for all cash outlays). One such, for instance, is the Allowance for Corporate Equity (ACE), under which all financing costs (including a notional return on equity) are deducted, along with depreciation (calculated at an essentially arbitrary rate). The ACE and other such schemes have attracted increased attention in recent years as potentially desirable reforms of the general corporate income tax. They may have particular appeal for resource activities too.

Appendix I Optimality of the RRT among cash flow-based rent taxes

Continuing the notation of Box 2.2, taking B_t as given, consider the effects of a small change in σ_t combined with such a change in σ_{t+1} as to leave B_{t+2} unchanged. Noting that B evolves as

$$B_{t+1} = R_t - C_t + (1 - \sigma_t + r)B_t \tag{A1.1}$$

this implies that

$$dB_{t+1} = -B_t d\sigma_t \tag{A1.2}$$

$$dB_{t+2} = 0 = -B_{t+1} d\sigma_{t+1} + (1 - \sigma_{t+1} + r) dB_{t+1}. \tag{A1.3}$$

The present value of government revenue evaluated at the discount rate ψ (which may differ from r) is proportional (the tax rate is taken as given) to $\Sigma_s \sigma_s B_s (1 + \psi)^{-s}$. The revenue effect of the perturbation is thus (after post-multiplying by $(1 + \psi)^{t+1}$) proportional to:

$$B_t d\sigma_t (1 + \psi) + B_{t+1} d\sigma_{t+1} + \sigma_{t+1} dB_{t+1} \tag{A1.4}$$

$$= B_t d\sigma_t (1 + \psi) + (1 - \sigma_{t+1} + r) dB_{t+1} + \sigma_{t+1} dB_{t+1} \tag{A1.5}$$

$$= (\psi - r) B_t d\sigma_t \tag{A1.6}$$

where (A1.5) substitutes for $B_{t+1} d\sigma_{t+1}$ from (A1.3), and (A1.6) for dB_{t+1} from (A1.2). From (A1.6), if $\psi > r$ then it is optimal to raise (lower) σ_t whenever B_t is positive (negative). Supposing that σ_t must lie between zero and one, the result follows.

Appendix II Time consistency with less than full ex post taxation – an example

Suppose that an investment of K yields a return of $sp(K)$ in state s, which occurs with probability $f(s)$, with s non-negative in all states (since projects can be shut down if they fail to cover variable costs), and $p(K)$ strictly increasing and strictly concave in K. The efficient level of investment (assuming risk-neutrality) is then that which maximizes $W(K) \equiv \int_0^\infty sp(K)f(s) - K$, the necessary condition for this being

$$W'(K) = p'(K) \int_0^\infty sf(s)ds - 1 = 0 \tag{A2.1}$$

which simply says that investment is chosen such that its expected marginal product equals its marginal cost (unity). Suppose now that the government announces the tax rate $\tau(s)$ once the investment decision has been made and the state of nature revealed, and does so to maximize the sum of tax revenue and some strictly concave function υ of after-tax profit:

$$\tau sp(K) + \upsilon[(1 - \tau)sp(K) - K]. \tag{A2.2}$$

Suppose that the government cannot make negative tax payments, and define γ to be the level of profit at which it is just indifferent, at the margin, between tax revenue and private profit: that is, $\upsilon'(\gamma) = 1$. It is then straightforward to see that it will set a tax rate of zero if pre-tax profits $sp(K) - K$ are less than γ, and for higher levels of profit will set τ so that after-tax profits are exactly γ. This latter implies that

$$\tau(s,K) = 1 - \left(\frac{\gamma + K}{sp(K)} \right) \tag{A2.3}$$

which is increasing in sp. The tax schedule is thus progressive: the tax rate is zero below some level of pre-tax profit, above which it is charged at an increasing average and marginal rate.

Anticipating such ex post taxation, the firm chooses K to maximize its net profit

$$\int_0^{\eta(K)} \{sp(K) - K\} f(s)ds + (1 - F(\eta(K)))\gamma \tag{A2.4}$$

where $\eta(K)$, implicitly defined by

$$\eta(K)p(K) - K = \gamma, \tag{A2.5}$$

is the level of the shock at which tax becomes payable, and $F(s)$ is the cumulative distribution function of s. The firm's necessary condition is thus

$$\int_0^{\eta(K)} \{sp'(K) - 1\} f(s)ds = 0 \tag{A2.6}$$

(the terms through the integrand in the first term of (A2.4) and the second term canceling by (A2.5)). Note that since p is strictly increasing, this implies that

$$\eta(K)p'(K) - 1 > 0 \tag{A2.7}$$

so long as $F(\eta) > 0$. At the level of investment defined by (A2.6), (A2.1) implies that

$$W'(K) = \int_{\eta(K)}^{\infty} \{sp'(K) - 1\} f(s)ds$$

$$\geq \{\eta(K)p'(K) - 1\} \{1 - F(\eta(K))\}$$

which, from (A2.7), is strictly positive if there is some possibility that the government would impose a tax if the efficient level of investment is undertaken (so that $F(\eta) < 1$). There will then be under-investment in the sense that $W'(K) > 0$.

This example is special. If, for instance, the government attaches constant weight to after-tax profits but decreasing weight to tax revenue, then the time consistent tax scheme is regressive: it fully taxes quasi-rents below some critical level, above which it applies a decreasing tax rate. Investment, however, would again be inefficiently low.

Appendix III Conditions for a progressive rent tax in political equilibrium

Differentiating (8.2) with respect to p gives:

$$U'(p) = U'(\tau p)\{\tau + p\tau'\} \tag{A3.1}$$

so that $\tau'(p) = F(\tau)/pU'(\tau p)$, where $F(\tau) \equiv U'(p) - \tau U'(\tau p)$. Since $F(1) = 0$, to establish that $\tau'(p) > 0$ it thus suffices to show that $F'(\tau) < 0$. Differentiating gives

$$F'(\tau) = -U'(\tau p) - \tau p U''(\tau p) = -U'\left(1 + \frac{\tau p U''}{U'}\right) = -U'(1 - R) \tag{A3.2}$$

and the result follows.

Acknowledgments

We are grateful to Bob Conrad, Philip Daniel, Michael Devereux, Martin Grote, Charles McPherson, Petter Osmundsen, Kevin Roberts, Emil Sunley, and Jean-François Wen for helpful comments and suggestions, and to Diego Mesa Puyo for excellent research assistance. Views expressed here should not be attributed to the International Monetary Fund, its Executive Board, or its management.

Notes

1 The chapters by Hogan and Goldsworthy (2010; Chapter 5), Nakhle (2010; Chapter 4), and Kellas (2010; Chapter 6) focus respectively on minerals, oil and gas. See also Sunley *et al.* (2003) on oil and gas, and Baunsgaard (2001) and Otto *et al.* (2006) on mining.
2 Renewable resources, such as timber and fisheries, raise quite different resource management (and hence also fiscal) issues.
3 Diagrammatic treatments of the nature of resource rents are in Garnaut and Clunies Ross (1983) and Otto *et al.* (2006).
4 Following the classic treatment of these issues in Hotelling (1931).
5 Similarly, the largest tax that could be imposed ex ante (before the outcome of exploration is known), without expected profits becoming negative, is $6 million, just offsetting expected pre-tax earnings of $(0.1) \times (160 - 10) - (0.9) \times 10$ million.
6 See, for instance, McPherson and MacSearraigh (2007).
7 There is input price uncertainty too, which to some degree parallels that of output prices: key inputs in minerals production, for instance, include chemicals whose price in turn reflects minerals prices, and supplies of specialist equipment, such as oil rigs, may be relatively fixed in the short term.
8 In Chapters 11 and 12, Calder (2010a, b) discusses these and other challenges in administering taxes on the resource sector.

9 See also Clark (1995).

10 The same logic applies within federations when one state exports some resource to others: taxation of those exports may not be constitutionally permissible, but production taxation can serve a similar purpose – as, for instance, with the severance tax on West Virginia coal sold for power generation in other states.

11 Krautkraemer (1999) notes, for instance, that petroleum reserves increased by more than 10 years of current consumption between 1972 and 1990 even though annual consumption increased very substantially.

12 Whether extraction will be faster or slower than in this competitive case when the producer has monopoly power – so that marginal benefit in Box 2.1 becomes downward-sloping marginal revenue – is theoretically indeterminate: see Stiglitz (1976).

13 This follows on taking the expectation at time t of the necessary condition (1.2) for extraction at time $t + 1$, combining it with that condition for time t and using too the time t expectation of the expected change in marginal valuations between $t + 1$ and $t + 2$ implied by (1.3).

14 The definition of 'royalty' in Otto *et al.* (2006), for example, is extremely broad, including anything that is called a royalty.

15 To see this, note that for a competitive producer (for whom the marginal benefit of extraction is simply the resource price), payment of royalties θ_t and θ_{t+1} (adding to costs by these amounts) changes the necessary condition (1.4) to

$$\frac{\Delta E[p - C_q]}{p - C_q} = r + (\theta_{t+1} - (1+r)\theta_t)$$

(it being assumed for simplicity that $C_s = 0$).

16 This observation is due to Burness (1976). The argument here ignores the potential impact of royalties on the shutdown decision, discussed in the next paragraph.

17 This effect arises it should be noted, even if the specific royalty is indexed to the general price level.

18 Conrad and Hool (1991).

19 Approval of production plans is often required – potentially an implicit royalty – but rarely exercised, it seems (in the activities at issue in this paper), in the direction of preserving future stocks.

20 This assumes that it is not optimal, from the owner's perspective, to entirely exhaust the resource within the contract period. If it is, then (supposing private and social discount rates to coincide) there is no inefficiency from the truncation of the contractor's horizon.

21 Suppose, for instance (assuming perfect certainty, for simplicity) that the profit-maximizing operator plans not to fully extract the resource during the contract period. Then it will act as if the resource were not exhaustible – the shadow value V' in Box 2.1 will be zero at all times – and so will simply extract so as to set the net marginal benefit $B' - C_q$ to zero in each period. From the wider social perspective, however, exhaustibility does matter, and (1.4) shows that net marginal benefit should increase at the rate of interest (also assuming, for simplicity, that costs are unaffected by the remaining stock). There is thus a corrective role for using royalties to slow extraction by driving pre-tax marginal costs increasingly below marginal benefit; and this, by the argument above, requires a royalty that increases (in present value) over time. (If, on the other hand, the operator chooses to fully extract the resource strictly within the contract period, there is – absent such considerations as a divergence between private and social discount rates – no inefficiency).

22 As demonstrated in, for instance, Otto *et al.* (2006).

23 Denote rents over the full lifetime of the project, which may depend on some choice a made by the investor, by $V(a)$. Then for any tax function T for which average and

marginal rates are everywhere less than unity, the value of a that maximizes after-tax rents $V(a) - T[V(a)]$ is the same as that which maximizes pre-tax rents.

24 The literature often uses the term resource rent tax quite loosely, to refer to schemes that in some broad sense are targeted on rent extraction. It is used here more precisely, to refer to the specific Garnaut–Clunies Ross scheme.

25 There are other ways in which the time profile of government receipts from rents may be varied. If there is a reasonably competitive system for auctioning rights to resource exploration and development, for instance, changes in the tax rate (capitalized in the price bidders will be willing to pay) effectively change the balance between ex post and ex ante rent collection by the government.

26 A simple example illustrates. Consider a project with an initial investment outlay of a that generates a constant stream of cash flows for the life of the project. Let the present value of those cash flows to the firm be some concave function $v(a)$, so that project rents are $v(a) - a$. If the tax is based on rent calculated using a discount rate different from the firm's, then (taking the simple case in which future cash flows are the same in each period) the present value of tax liabilities can be written $T(\mu v(a) - a)$, where μ is greater (or less) than one as the discount rate is lower (or higher) than the firm's discount rate. (The potential non-linearity of T allows for the possibility of progressivity, discussed further below). Maximizing after-tax rents $v(a) - a - T(\mu v(a) - a)$ then leads to less (more) investment than in the absence of tax as μ is higher (lower) than unity; that is, as the discount rate used in calibrating the tax system is lower (higher) than the firm's.

27 Ball and Bowers (1983) pursue the nature of this distortion further for an RRT bearing only on positive rents, noting that it is equivalent to a call option taken by the government on the wealth created by a resource project, with exercise price equal to the cumulative investment in it. The analogy implies, for instance, that just as the value of an option increases with the riskiness of the underlying asset so the government's expected tax claim – and hence the discouragement to investment – is greater, all else equal, for riskier projects.

28 Calder (2010), in Chapters 11 and 12, and Land (2010), in Chapter 8, discuss implementation issues more fully.

29 See Sandmo (1979).

30 More generally, this raises the issue of what should be the limits of resource activities for the purposes of taxing rents. To eliminate such transfer pricing possibilities, these need to extend at least to the processing stage given that different qualities of resource will fetch different values up to that stage.

31 Tilton (2004, p.146) argues that 'rarely do those advocating the taxation of mining rents extend their proposal to other rents.' To the contrary, much of the focus of recent corporate tax reform has been focused precisely on achieving more effective rent taxation: see, for example, Auerbach et al. (2008).

32 Maximizing the expected value of after-tax profit $(1 - t)E[V(a)]$ requires maximizing the expected value of pre-tax profit $E[V(a)]$, and so leads to the same decisions as in the absence of tax.

33 Risk-neutrality is assumed throughout the discussion of uncertainty in the text (perhaps reflecting effective diversification by investors). This is a significant assumption. For a risk-averse investor, for example, a proportional tax, with full loss offset, makes riskier assets strictly *more* attractive since it unambiguously reduces the dispersion of possible outcomes. The qualifications that risk aversion implies for the discussion below are qualitatively straightforward.

34 Angola, for instance, levies an annual tax that increases with the realized internal rate of return.

35 To see this, suppose that in the absence of tax one project generates perfectly certain rents of $\bar{V}$ while a second has a stochastic return V with expected value of $\bar{V}$. By Jensen's inequality, if T is convex, $E[V - T(V)] < E[V] - T(E[V])$; for convex T,

progressive taxation thus changes indifference between the two projects into a strict preference for the safer one.

36 This scheme (which dates back to 1918 and is also used by Botswana, Uganda and Zambia (in varying forms), and, until recently, in Namibia) charges tax on profits at a rate T that depends on the ratio of taxable income from mining to mining revenues (in percent), m, according to

$$T(m) = \max\left\{0, \tau\left(1 - \frac{\rho}{m}\right)\right\}$$

where τ and ρ are parameters: the latter is the rate of return above which tax is payable (earnings below this are in the tax-free 'tunnel') and the former is the tax rate towards which tax payable increases as m rises. The claim in the next sentence follows on noting that, writing $m = \pi/R$, where π denotes taxable profit and R revenue, this becomes

$$T(m)\pi = \max\left\{0, \tau\pi - \rho R\right\}.$$

37 The common term 'free equity' can be something of a misnomer, as Conrad *et al.* (1990) note: the government, after all, contributes the resource itself.

38 If it were to subscribe at cost to new equity issues, the equivalence would be with an S-based cash flow tax.

39 Here, as in other of these equivalencies, it is assumed that there are no other taxes in place; with a corporate income tax also imposed, for example, the implicit base will differ from that of an RRT.

40 The treatment of auctions here is brief: see Cramton (2010), Chapter 10.

41 It is assumed here that property rights are defined and enforced. If not, a form of tragedy of the commons occurs, with, at a minimum, a tendency to overspend on exploration and, at worst, conflict over the exploitation of discovered resource deposits: see Collier and Venables (2008).

42 Klemperer (2004).

43 Daniel (1995) explores the analogy between spending requirements of this type and explicit tax measures.

44 Ad valorem or specific, depending on whether the allowance is related to the value or the volume of extraction: see Conrad and Hool (1981). The Technical Committee on Business Taxation in Canada (Department of Finance, 1998) documented that excessive deductions for resource depletion resulted in marginal effective tax rates substantially lower in resource industries than in other industries.

45 With an ad valorem royalty at rate θ deductible against a CIT levied at rate τ, the effective marginal tax rate on an additional dollar of sales is $\tau + \theta - \tau\theta$; which is exactly as it would be if there no deductibility but the royalty rate were instead $(1 - \tau)\theta$.

46 Norway applies a special rate of 50 percent in addition to the standard 28 percent, while (since 2007) the UK has levied CIT on the continental shelf at 30 percent rather than the standard 28 percent. Both countries provide some uplift for capital expenditures – that is, allow deduction of more than 100 percent – against this higher corporate tax rate.

47 Interestingly, there is some evidence that resource-rich countries tend to levy higher general rates of CIT than do others: Keen and Mansour (2008) suggest this to be the case, for instance, in sub-Saharan Africa. This is as one would expect if resource rents were relatively immobile and there were a commitment to uniform CIT treatment across sectors.

48 Ebrill *et al.* (2001) and Harrison and Krelove (2005) discuss the refund problem and possible solutions.
49 So that tax becomes due not at import but at precisely the same time as an offsetting credit can be claimed.
50 'Forward looking' effective tax rates are those based on projections of future profits and interest rates. 'Backward looking' effective rates are based on realized profits and tax payments for firms and industries. (On the latter, see Feldstein *et al.* (1983)).
51 This differs somewhat from the widely-cited formulation of the AETR in Devereux and Griffith (2003), who – as they discuss in detail – prefer to calibrate the AETR by using the pre-tax return, rather than rents, in the denominator (to avoid the complications that arise in handling marginal projects, for which rent is zero).
52 An early application is in Conrad *et al.* (1990).
53 The original formulation is in Boadway *et al.* (1987). A recent application – focusing in particular on the time to build between discovery and extraction – is in Mintz (2009).
54 A proof is in the Appendix of Thakur *et al.* (2003).
55 It should be stressed too that the calculated AETRs and METRs rest on a host of assumptions – on how investments are financed, for instance, and (for the AETR) the assumed rate of return – and so should not be interpreted as having definitive precision.
56 Rewriting the first order condition as $P = E[U'(C_2)X]/(1 + \rho)U'(C_1)$, equation (4.2) follows on using the approximations $E[U'(C_2)] \approx U'(C_1)(1 - RRA(C_1)G)$ and $(1 + \rho)/(1 + cov)(1 - RRAG) \approx 1 + \rho - cov + RRAG$.
57 Recalling (1.4) in Box 2.1.
58 The necessary conditions for the choice of the $\tau(s)$ imply that for all states s' and s

$$\frac{U'_G[p(s')\tau(s')]}{U'_G[p(s)\tau(s)]} = \frac{U'_I[(1-\tau(s'))p(s')]}{U'_I[(1-\tau(s))p(s)]} ,$$

the prime indicating differentiation. Taking this to define $\tau(s')$ as a function of $p(s')$, the result follows.
59 A full treatment of this issue is in Leland (1984), though focusing there on the marginal rate of tax (the higher this is, the more risk is borne by government) and on progressivity in the sense of an increasing marginal tax rate rather than, as here, an increasing average rate.
60 Osmundsen (2010) discusses these results further in Chapter 15.
61 Doyle and van Wijnbergen (1994) show how tax holidays and subsidies can result from a sequential bargaining framework between a host government and multinational in the absence of commitment. Vigneault (1996) finds that time-consistent tax rates can increase over time.
62 Chapter 11 of the North American Free Trade Agreement being an example, where expropriation is defined to include taking 'a measure tantamount to nationalization or expropriation of an investment.'
63 Nellor and Robinson (1984) provide an early account of the time consistency issue in resource taxation that pays explicit attention to political economy aspects. Assuming that investors perceive some arbitrary link between ex post profitability and the likelihood of their being expropriated, they conclude that there will be some relationship between realized cash flows and the average tax paid, but derive no sharp conclusions on its nature.
64 Règlement 18/2003/CM/UEMOA.
65 United Nations Economic Commission for Africa (2004).
66 Reviewed for example by Wilson (1999) and Keen (2008).

References

Auerbach, Alan J., Michael P. Devereux, and Helen Simpson (2008), 'Taxing Corporate Income.' Background Paper for the Mirrlees Review, *Reforming the Tax System for the 21st Century*.

Ball, Ray and John Bowers (1983), 'Distortions Created by Taxes which are Options on Value Creation: The Australian Resources Rent Tax Proposal,' *Australian Journal of Management*, Vol. 8, pp. 1–14.

Baunsgaard, Thomas (2001), 'A Primer on Mineral Taxation,' IMF Working Paper 01/139 (Washington DC: International Monetary Fund).

Boadway, Robin, Neil Bruce, Ken McKenzie, and Jack Mintz (1987), 'Marginal Effective Tax Rates for Capital in the Canadian Mining Industry,' *Canadian Journal of Economics*, Vol. 20, pp. 1–16.

Boadway, Robin and Michael Keen (1998), 'Evasion and Time Consistency in the Taxation of Capital Income,' *International Economic Review*, Vol. 39, pp. 461–476.

Bond, Stephen R. and Michael P. Devereux (1995), 'On the Design of a Neutral Business Tax under Uncertainty,' *Journal of Public Economics*, Vol. 58, pp. 57–71.

—— (2003), 'Generalised R-Based and S-Based Taxes Under Uncertainty,' *Journal of Public Economics*, Vol. 87, pp. 1291–1311.

Bornhorst, Fabian, Sanjeev Gupta, and John Thornton (2009), 'Natural Resource Endowments and the Domestic Revenue Effort,' *European Journal of Political Economy*, Vol. 25, pp. 439–446.

Brett, Craig and Michael Keen (2000), 'Political Uncertainty and the Earmarking of Environmental Taxes,' *Journal of Public Economics*, Vol. 75, pp. 315–340.

Brown, E. Cary (1948), 'Business-Income Taxation and Investment Incentives,' in *Income, Employment and Public Policy: Essay in Honor of Alvin H. Hansen* (New York: Norton).

Burness, H. S. (1976), 'On Taxation of Nonreplenishable Natural Resources,' *Journal of Environmental Economics and Management*, Vol. 3, pp. 289–311.

Calder, Jack (2010a), 'Administrative Challenges From Resource Tax Policy,' in Philip Daniel, Michael Keen, and Charles McPherson (eds.) *The Taxation of Petroleum and Minerals: Principles, Problems and Practice.*

—— (2010b), 'Resource tax administration: Functions, Processes and Institutions,' in Philip Daniel, Michael Keen and Charles McPherson (eds.) *The Taxation of Petroleum and Minerals: Principles, Problems and Practice.*

Clark, Graham R. (1995), 'International Considerations of Resource Taxation,' in James Otto (ed.), *The Taxation of Mineral Enterprises*, pp. 47–61 (London: Graham & Trotman).

Collier, Paul (2010), 'Principles of Resource Taxation for Low income Economies,' in Philip Daniel, Michael Keen and Charles McPherson (eds.) *The Taxation of Petroleum and Minerals: Principles, Problems and Practice.*

—— and Anthony J. Venables (2008), 'Managing The Exploitation of Natural Assets: Lessons for Low Income Countries,' Research Paper No. 2008–11, Oxford Centre for the Analysis of Resource Rich Economics, University of Oxford.

Conrad, Robert and Bryce Hool (1981), 'Resource Taxation with Heterogeneous Quality and Endogenous Reserves,' *Journal of Public Economics*, Vol. 16, pp. 17–33.

Conrad, Robert, Zmarak Shalizi, and Janet Syme (1990), 'Issues in Evaluating Tax and Payments Arrangements for Publicly Owned Minerals,' Public Economics Department Working Paper WPS 496 (Washington DC: World Bank).

Cramton, Peter (2007), 'How Best to Auction Oil Rights,' in Macartan Humphreys, Jeffrey D. Sachs, and Joseph E. Stiglitz (eds.), *Escaping the Resource Curse*, Ch. 5, pp. 114–151 (New York: Columbia University Press).

Daniel, Philip (1995), 'Evaluating State Participation in Mineral Projects: Equity, Infrastructure and Taxation,' in James Otto (ed.) *The Taxation of Mineral Enterprises*, pp. 165–187 (London: Graham & Trotman).

—— and Emil Sunley (2010), 'Contractual Assurances of Fiscal Stability,' in Philip Daniel, Michael Keen, and Charles McPherson (eds.) *The Taxation of Petroleum and Minerals: Principles, Problems and Practice.*

——, Brenton Goldsworthy, Wojciech Maliszewski, Diego Mesa Puyo and Alistair Watson (2010), 'Evaluating Fiscal Regimes for Resource Projects,' in Philip Daniel, Michael Keen, and Charles McPherson (eds.) *The Taxation of Petroleum and Minerals: Principles, Problems and Practice.*

Department of Finance (1998), *Report of the Technical Committee on Business Taxation*, Department of Finance (Ottawa, Canada).

Devereux, Michael and Rachel Griffith (2003), 'Evaluating Tax Policy for Location Decisions,' *International Tax and Public Finance*, Vol. 10, pp. 107–126.

Doyle, Chris and Sweder van Wijnbergen (1994), 'Taxation of Foreign Multinationals: A Sequential Bargaining Approach to Tax Holidays,' *International Tax and Public Finance*, Vol. 1, pp. 211–225.

Ebrill, Liam, Michael Keen, Jean-Paul Bodin, and Victoria Summers (2001), *The Modern VAT* (Washington DC: International Monetary Fund).

Feldstein, Martin, Louis Dicks-Mireaux, and James Poterba (1983), 'The Effective Tax Rate and the Pretax Rate of Return,' *Journal of Public Economics*, Vol. 21, pp. 129–158.

Garnaut, Ross and Anthony Clunies Ross (1975), 'Uncertainty, Risk Aversion and the Taxing of Natural Resource Projects,' *Economic Journal*, Vol. 85, pp. 272–287.

—— (1979), 'The Neutrality of the Resource Rent Tax,' *Economic Record*, Vol. 55, pp. 193–201.

—— (1983), *Taxation of Mineral Rents* (Oxford: Clarendon Press).

Harrison, Graham and Russell Krelove (2005), 'VAT Refunds: A Review of Country Experience,' IMF Working Paper 05/218 (Washington DC: International Monetary Fund).

Hogan, Lindsay and Brenton Goldsworthy (2010), 'Minerals Taxation: Experience and Issues,' in Philip Daniel, Michael Keen and Charles McPherson (eds.) *The Taxation of Petroleum and Minerals: Principles, Problems and Practice.*

Hotelling, Harold (1931), 'The Economics of Exhaustible Resources,' *Journal of Political Economy*, Vol. 39, pp. 137–175.

Karp, Larry, and David M. Newbery (1992), 'Dynamically Consistent Oil Import Tariffs,' *Canadian Journal of Economics*, Vol. 25, pp. 1–21.

Keen, Michael (2008), 'Tax Competition,' in Steven Durlauf and Lawrence Blume (eds.) *The New Palgrave Dictionary of Economics*, second edition (Macmillan, Basingstoke).

Keen, Michael and Mario Mansour (2008), 'Revenue Mobilization in Sub-Saharan Africa: Challenges from Globalization: Part I, Trade Liberalization; Part II, Corporate Taxation,' forthcoming in *Development Policy Review*.

Kellas, Graham (2010), 'The Taxation of Natural Gas Projects,' in Philip Daniel, Michael Keen and Charles McPherson (eds.) *The Taxation of Petroleum and Minerals: Principles, Problems and Practice.*

Klemm, Alexander (2007), 'Allowances for Corporate Equity in Practice,' *CESifo Economic Studies*, Vol. 53, pp. 229–262.

Klemperer, Paul D. (2004), *Auctions: Theory and Practice* (Princeton: University Press).

Krautkraemer, Jeffrey A. (1999), 'Nonrenewable Resource Scarcity,' *Journal of Economic Literature*, Vol. XXXVI, pp. 2065–2107.

Land, Bryan (1995), 'The Rate of Return Approach to Progressive Profit Sharing in Mining,' in James Otto (ed.) *The Taxation of Mineral Enterprises*, pp. 91–112 (London: Graham & Trotman).

—— (2010), 'Resource Rent Taxation: Theory and Experience,' in Philip Daniel, Michael Keen and Charles McPherson (eds.) *The Taxation of Petroleum and Minerals: Principles, Problems and Practice*.

Leland, Hayne E. (1984), 'Optimal Risk Sharing and the Leasing of Natural Resources,' *Quarterly Journal of Economics*, Vol. 92, pp. 413–437.

Lund, Diderik, (2009) 'Rent Taxation for Non-Renewable Resources,' *Annual Review of Resource Economics*, Vol. 1, pp. 287–308.

McPherson, Charles (2008), 'State Participation in the Natural Resource Sectors: Evolution, Issues and Outlook,' in Philip Daniel, Michael Keen, and Charles McPherson (eds.) *The Taxation of Petroleum and Minerals: Principles, Problems and Practice*.

—— and Stephen MacSearraigh (2007), 'Corruption in the Petroleum Sector,' in J. Edgardo Campos and Sanjay Pradhan (eds.) *The Many Faces of Corruption* (Washington DC World Bank).

Meade, James E. (1978), '*The Structure and Reform of Direct Taxation*,' Report of a Committee chaired by Professor J. E. Meade (London: George Allen & Unwin).

Mintz, Jack (2009), 'Measuring Effective Tax Rates for Oil and Gas in Canada,' mimeo, University of Calgary.

Mullins, Peter (2010), 'International Tax Issues for the Resources Sector,' in Philip Daniel, Michael Keen, and Charles McPherson (eds.) *The Taxation of Petroleum and Minerals: Principles, Problems and Practice*.

Nakhle, Carole (2010), 'Petroleum Fiscal Regimes: The Debate Continues,' in Philip Daniel, Michael Keen, and Charles McPherson (eds.) *The Taxation of Petroleum and Minerals: Principles, Problems and Practice*.

Nellor, David and Marc S. Robinson (1984), 'Binding Future Governments: Tax Contracts and Resource Development,' UCLA Working Paper No. 297.

Osmundsen, Petter (1998), 'Dynamic Taxation of Non-Renewable Natural Resources Under Asymmetric Information About Reserves,' *Canadian Journal of Economics*, Vol. 31, pp. 933–951.

—— (2005), 'Optimal Petroleum Taxation – Subject to Mobility and Information Constraints,' in S. Glomsrød and P. Osmundsen (eds.) *Petroleum Industry Regulation within Stable States: Recent Economic Analysis of Incentives in Petroleum Production and Wealth Management* (Ashgate: Studies in Environmental and Natural Resource Economics).

—— (2010), 'Time Consistency in Petroleum Taxation: Lessons from Norway,' in Philip Daniel, Michael Keen, and Charles McPherson (eds.) *The Taxation of Petroleum and Minerals: Principles, Problems and Practice*.

Otto, James, Craig Andrews, Fred Cawood, Michael Doggett, Pietro Guj, Frank Stermole, John Stermole, and John Tilton (2006), *Mining Royalties* (Washington DC: World Bank).

Sandmo, Agnar (1979), 'A Note on the Neutrality of the Cash Flow Corporate Tax,' *Economic Letters*, Vol. 4, pp. 173–176.

Sinn, Hans-Werner 2008, 'Public Policies Against Global Warming: A Supply Side Approach,' *International Tax and Public Finance*, Vol. 15, pp. 360–394.

Stern, Nicholas (1987), 'The Effects of Taxation, Price Control and Government Contracts in Oligopoly and Monopolistic Competition,' *Journal of Public Economics*, Vol. 32, pp. 133–158.

Stern, Nicholas and others (2007), *The Economics of Climate Change* (Cambridge: Cambridge University Press).

Stiglitz, Joseph E. (1976), 'Monopoly and the Rate of Extraction of Exhaustible Resources,' *American Economic Review*, Vol. 66, pp. 651–661.

Strand, Jon, (2008), 'Importer and Producer Petroleum Taxation: A Geo-Political Model,' IMF Working Paper No. 08/35 (Washington DC: International Monetary Fund).

Sunley, Emil, Thomas Baunsgaard, and Dominique Simard (2003), 'Revenue from the Oil and Gas Sector: Issues and Country experience,' in J. M. Davis, R. Ossowski, and A. Fedelino (eds.), *Fiscal Policy Formulation and Implementation in Oil-Producing Countries*, pp. 153–183 (Washington DC: International Monetary Fund).

Thakur, Subhash, Michael Keen, Balazs Horváth, and Valerie Cerra (2003), *Can the Bumblebee Keep Flying? An Assessment of the Swedish Welfare State* (Washington DC: International Monetary Fund).

Tilton, John E. (2004), 'Determining the Optimal Tax on Mining,' *Natural Resources Forum*, Vol. 28, pp. 144–149.

United Nations Economic Commission for Africa (2004), *Harmonization of Mining Policies, Standards, Legislative and Regulatory Frameworks in Southern Africa.*

Vigneault, Marianne (1996), 'Commitment and the Time Structure of Taxation of Foreign Direct Investment,' *International Tax and Public Finance*, Vol. 3, pp. 479–494.

Wilson, John D. (1999), 'Theories of Tax Competition,' *National Tax Journal*, Vol. 52, pp. 269–304.

3 Principles of resource taxation for low-income countries

Paul Collier

1 Introduction

The taxation of extractable natural resources poses complex design problems – and indeed the chapters of this book address many of these in detail. These complexities arise because natural resources are not akin to most other economic activity: their distinctive features make government central. In low-income countries the problems that are generic to the taxation of natural resources in all contexts are compounded by important additional features which make the solutions appropriate for a high-income country inapplicable.

The chapters in this volume largely focus on this distinctive low-income context. To date, most of the work on tax design has been for high-income countries, and I will try to set out why the distinctive features of low-income countries change the policies that are appropriate. The new website www.naturalresourcecharter.org complements both this chapter and this book in setting out for resource-rich low-income societies the entire decision chain involved in harnessing natural assets for transformative development. However, as a preliminary it may be helpful to set out the four generic features of natural resource extraction that make it distinctive from normal economic activity. These are that the ownership of natural assets is rightly vested in citizens; that extraction is a process of asset depletion rather than merely production; that investment in extraction requires high sunk costs and long periods of payback; and that the prices of depleting assets are volatile. Since the rents from extraction belong, in their entirety, to citizens, the government as their agent needs a tax regime which captures these rents, over and above the standard taxation of profits. If the tax system does not discriminate between rents and returns to other factors of production then it is sure to be misdesigned. In practice, this implies that the taxation of resource extraction is likely to look quite different from that of most other economic activities. Because resource extraction is depleting an asset it is not sustainable, and so the savings rate out of these revenues should be higher than that out of ordinary taxation. Finally, because prices are volatile, rents and profits will also be volatile.

In Section 2A lays out the distinctive features of low-income resource-rich countries. Section 3A suggests how these features make the policies that are conventional in high-income resource-rich countries inappropriate. Section 4A sketches what more appropriate policies might look like, although it should be evident that to do this thoroughly is an undertaking well beyond the scale of this brief chapter.

2 Four distinctive features of low-income countries

A Discovery is key

The first distinctive feature of low-income countries is that the discovery process is likely to be far more important than in the high-income resource-rich countries. A snapshot of discovered natural assets for the year 2000 assembled by the World Bank brings this out. In the OECD the average square kilometre possesses known sub-soil assets to the value of $125,000, whereas the figure for Africa is only $25,000. Since both land masses are enormous such a large difference is unlikely to reflect differences in luck: the original endowments of sub-soil assets were probably not very different. Further, since the OECD has been depleting its natural assets for far longer than Africa, a reasonable expectation is that Africa has more sub-soil assets remaining than the OECD. Of course, even in the OECD by no means all natural assets have yet been discovered: discovery is costly so there is little incentive to prove reserves that will not be exploited for decades, and as the technology of discovery improves more becomes economic. The implication is that a large majority of Africa's natural assets remain undiscovered. The predominant reason for this is presumably that the incentive regime is less conducive to discovery. This is supported by the substantially lower density of drilling in the major sedentary basins of Africa compared to those in the OECD. Since Africa has radically less invested capital, physical and human, than most other regions, its successful management of its extensive undiscovered natural assets is both absolutely and relatively far more important: the design of an appropriate tax regime for resource extraction is a first-order issue.

B Commitment problems

The second distinctive feature of low-income countries is that their institutions are less robust. They lack the sanctity of time, and any particular institution is likely to be less well-defended because other institutions are weak or missing, and because there are fewer supports from the neighbourhood. If institutions are not robust then the credibility of government commitments is impaired: even if everything is currently satisfactory it is less likely to stay that way. There is only a limited amount that a government can do to reduce doubts about the future and so it is necessary to recognize the consequences of the limited credibility of commitments. There are two respects in which this is particularly pertinent in respect of natural resources.

The first is that the extraction process typically requires massive initial investment which need not then be renewed. In this respect the time profile of investment in the extractive industries is highly distinctive. For example, in manufacturing it is likely that investment gradually builds up over the decades, so that a wise government knows that should it attempt to expropriate accumulated investment through heavy taxation it will kill the valuable process of future investment. In contrast, investment in resource extraction faces a *time-consistency* problem: the initial investment is so large relative to all future investment that once made it is rational for the government to confiscate it. Fearing such an eventuality the extraction company decides not to make the investment in the first place and the government, despite being worse off than if it could credibly commit not to impose such taxation, is unable to do so.[1]

The second respect in which the lack of a commitment technology matters is that the government may find it difficult or even impossible to commit not to spend all the revenues from asset depletion on consumption. Yet the inability to make such a commitment may imply that it is wiser to leave the assets unexploited until the commitment problem has been overcome.

C Capital and consumption scarcity

The third respect in which low-income countries are distinctive is that both consumption and capital are scarce. As the economy gradually converges with richer ones the marginal value of consumption will fall, but the society is unable to borrow for consumption now as much as would be appropriate because it is rationed in capital markets. Similarly, the rate of return on capital is likely to be high because capital is so scarce.

D Asymmetric information

The final distinctive respect of low-income countries is that their governments are likely to be a severe informational disadvantage vis-à-vis resource extraction companies. Governments are not able to recruit civil servants with the requisite specialist knowledge, due both to a shortage of nationals and the inability of government pay-scales to match private rewards. Specialist information can be purchased on the global market and is typically well worthwhile, but because it is expensive and hires non-nationals, many governments do not buy enough of it.

3 Principles appropriate only for high-income countries

I now set out three conventional principles and explain why they are only appropriate in the context of high income countries.

A Integrated budgets

The principle of an integrated budget is Fiscal Economics 101. The advantage of pooling all revenues without any prior earmarking is evident: it enables the marginal benefit of public spending to be equated across all components of spending, and it enables flexible responses to unanticipated circumstances which change the relative values of the components. These are powerful arguments, not to be dismissed lightly.

However, they presuppose a context in which the government is able to function extremely well. In particular, the preservation of flexibility, which is the great achievement of an integrated budget, comes at no cost. Yet in other contexts the case for commitment technologies is now fully accepted in both academic and policy circles. In particular, the independence of central banks has, over the past three decades, become a standard commitment technology against inflation. In resource-rich low-income countries the key need for a commitment technology is not monetary but fiscal, and the key fiscal issue to be addressed is the replacement of depleting natural assets with other assets, real and financial. Where it is possible, the equivalent of a constitutionally independent central bank might be a fiscal constitution. Essentially, what such a constitutional provision would need to do would be to ring-fence a substantial part of the revenues from natural resources from expenditure on consumption. However, as discussed below, it will normally be appropriate to spend savings on domestic investment, and so the Future Generations Fund model in which revenues do not even reach the budget is not appropriate. Rather, the revenues need to be earmarked for investment. As discussed below, this still leaves an important role for periodic accumulation of foreign financial assets, but the role is essentially to buy time, putting a brake upon the rate of increase in domestic investment until the capacity to invest is enhanced.

Why might such a fiscal commitment technology be necessary? The clear answer is that there are strong day-to-day political pressures for subverting resource revenues from investment into public consumption. The interest of the future is at best only fitfully represented in the political market place. A far-sighted Finance Minister, acting in the long-term national interest, would indeed want to create commitment technologies for defending the future against the potent special interests of the consumption lobbies. In the OECD societies political institutions and the sophistication of electorates may have evolved to the stage at which such commitment technologies are unnecessary. In the resource-rich, low-income societies this is clearly not the case.

Such institutions for earmarking some revenues to savings and ultimately to investment are only in their infancy and have suffered from substantial design flaws. The *College* in Chad attempted to ring-fence resource revenues but earmarked them not for investment but for particular social uses. These social priorities were rapidly weakened by the government. The Nigerian Fiscal Responsibility Bill attempted to earmark a proportion of oil revenues for savings, but initially ran foul of constitutional requirements to share revenues with the state governments. In general, earmarking a substantial proportion of resource revenues for asset accumulation curtails a degree of flexibility, which is undesirable. The need for a commitment technology, however, overrides concerns about the loss of flexibility. Nevertheless, as earmarking becomes more specific as to which assets should be accumulated, it increasingly contravenes the valid principles of an integrated budget.

B Permanent income and future generation funds

If the government and firms of a country can borrow on world capital markets at an interest rate very close to that at which they can lend, then the country will already be developed. In particular, it will have borrowed sufficient to drive down the rate of return on domestic investment to the world interest rate. As Ploeg and Venables (2008) argue, this is the condition necessary for the permanent income hypothesis to be the appropriate guide for policy. With this condition fulfilled, on the discovery of a natural resource consumption would leap to a permanently sustainable level and as natural assets were depleted they would be offset by the accumulation of foreign financial assets. Note that even in this scenario the discovery would be followed by an initial phase of borrowing: consumption should leap on the discovery while revenues will take time to come through.

Manifestly, this is not the context for a low-income country. Such countries are not able to access world capital markets sufficiently to finance the massive investment needed to drive down the return on domestic capital to world levels: they are capital-scarce. This has two important corollaries. First, because current generations are much poorer than future generations, some of the revenues should be consumed: the permanent income approach of consuming only the sustainable income from the natural assets no longer has a sound analytic foundation. In low-income countries the appropriate use of natural assets is *to accelerate the evolution towards* the eventual level of sustainable income, whereas under the Permanent Income Hypothesis (appropriate for a developed economy) it is *to raise that eventual level.* Second, because domestic rates of return are above world rates, such savings as are appropriate should gradually be directed into domestic investment rather than foreign financial assets. This needs at once to be qualified. As the pace of investment is increased the returns on investment fall below the returns on installed capital because of congestion and inefficiencies in the investment process. Hence, the pace of investment needs to be set by the capacity to absorb it efficiently. However, the accumulation of foreign financial assets is not the solution to this problem; it merely buys the time in which to address it. In these economies development is fundamentally about raising the capacity to invest productively. The process can be thought of as 'investing in investing.' It is an agenda for the real economy: improving bureaucratic procedures to design and implement public investment; enhancing the efficiency of the capital goods producing and distributing sectors; and increasing incentives for private investment. A policy of financial asset accumulation should not detract from this by weakening the sense of urgency. Nevertheless, it is often necessary to buy time. A classic instance of the consequences of attempting to ramp up investment ahead of the capacity to implement it efficiently was the Nigerian 'cement armada' of 1975. In this instance the uncoordinated and excessive purchase of cement encountered the bottleneck of limited port capacity and dissipated expenditures on investment in avoidably high costs.[2]

C Excess profits taxes

Natural resource extraction generates both normal profits and rents: the latter need to be captured by the government. Since both normal profits and rents are aggregated into reported profits, the first-best is to decompose reported profits into its two components, applying the normal corporate profits tax to normal profits and imposing a very high 'excess profits' tax on the rents. The alternative of a royalty payment on resource revenues, however, structured, is second-best because it cannot target the rents as precisely as the excess profits tax. For example, as full depletion approaches and extraction costs mount the company will choose not to extract those resources which incur a royalty in excess of the diminishing rents and so some rents will be left unexploited; other resources may be left unexploited.

The problem with any form of taxation is that information is costly and held asymmetrically: the company knows the true division between rents and profits but has no incentive to reveal it. On the contrary, where the government has little information the company has considerable scope for concealing profits altogether by reclassifying them into costs. While these problems are generic to all forms of taxation, they are far more acute with the taxation of resource rents.[3] Whereas tax rates on profits that result from capital and risk are typically around 25 percent, in principle the tax rate on excess profits should approach 100 percent. The incentives to cheat are thus radically greater, and the scope for cheating is increased by the co-existence of two conceptually distinct forms of profit. As a result, whereas within the OECD the first-best is unambiguously the right policy, in the context of small, low-income countries it is at least debatable. The choice in tax design therefore reduces to one between an excess profits tax that will be gamed by companies unless resources are spent to counter it, and a royalty which, though inefficient, may be harder to game because revenues are more observable than profits. In this situation it may no longer be possible to navigate by the simple principles which rank the excess profits tax as analytically superior to a royalty, and a good system may combine elements of both.[4]

4 Rethought principles

If the principles that are appropriate for a resource-rich country in the OECD are not appropriate for the typical resource-rich low-income country then policies should look different. Norway and Timor-Leste both have oil, but their policy responses should be different. How different should they be?

A The discovery process

Recall that the discovery process is far more important in low-income countries than in the OECD: there is much more to be discovered. However, at the discovery stage the lack of a credible commitment technology imposes compounded risks onto investment in prospecting. The company is uncertain both as to whether anything will be found, and what the eventual tax regime will be. A pre-commitment to a tax regime which is based on inadequate geological information will lack credibility. As a result, if the incentive for discovery is that the company will acquire extraction rights to whatever it discovers, the expected value of these rights will be heavily discounted by these uncertainties. Further, the rate of discount used by the typical resource extraction company is very high.

To the extent possible the government should not sell extraction rights until geological uncertainties have been reduced. The objective is not for the government itself to take on all the risk of prospecting, but to narrow likely outcomes to a sufficiently narrow range that contingent tax arrangements are regarded as credible. The government can collate and commission seismic data. Since the rate of return on private prospecting is typically high, these costs would be an appropriate use for aid: the donor is able to bear the risk, and the aid will on average have a high return.[5] This implies that the government should, to the extent possible, separate the prospecting process from the extraction process.

B Auctions for price discovery

Once the government has good geological information it can then auction the rights to extraction. The auction would essentially reveal the appropriate rate of taxation or royalty. The design of auctions is complex,[6] but they are the best way of tackling the acute asymmetry of information, and also, if properly supervised, of tackling the scope for corruption inherent in negotiated deals. Auctions are particularly appropriate where citizens are suspicious of government because, if verified by independent international scrutiny, they can enable a government to signal to its citizens that their suspicions are unwarranted.

There is likely to be a need for pre-screening of bidders. Typically the ideal number of bidders is around four: many more than this and no company invests enough in information to judge true value so that bids are liable to be opportunistic; much less than four and there is a risk of collusion. Since the exclusion of bidders is replete with opportunities for corruption this stage should also be subject to international verification.

C Geared royalties

If information is sufficiently asymmetric then a royalty may be the best option. In this case can we say anything about its design? It would need to be conditioned upon those observables which cannot readily be gamed, such as the price of the commodity and some basic features of geology. Since what can be observed depends upon the expenditure of the government upon monitoring, as monitoring is enhanced profits themselves become observable. Where, however, profits are not realistically observable, the royalty will generate less grounds for dispute the more it is anchored to those observables with clear consequences for profits. For example, in respect of the world price of the commodity, one feature that is at once apparent is that rents will be increasing more than proportionately in the price: there is some unobservable but positive price at which rents are zero. Hence, a (second-best) efficient royalty should be highly geared to the price of the commodity. The conventional practice of setting the royalty at a flat rate of 3 percent fails to satisfy this design rule.

D Pace exploration by absorption of investment

Above, I have discussed the need to pace investment by the rate at which it can be absorbed. What should be done with resource revenues that are substantially in excess of this level? The answer may well be that they are best not generated: resources can simply be left undiscovered. The advantage of leaving some resources undiscovered is that the economic pace of extraction of those resources that have been discovered, which is gradual, provides an automatic commitment mechanism. In contrast, resources accumulated in foreign financial assets can be no more robust than the constitutional provisions which protect them from rapid liquidation, and in low-income countries constitutional provisions have often proved to be fragile. However, building up financial assets has offsetting advantages: in particular it diversifies the asset portfolio away from dependence upon the commodity that is being extracted. Hence, the appropriate strategy is determined by a balance of risks. The risks that commodity prices will appreciate by less than the world interest rate can at least be estimated from the past history of prices; the risk that a future opportunistic regime will liquidate accumulated financial assets cannot be readily estimated but may reasonably be judged so substantial that it dwarfs the additional risk implied by the lack of portfolio diversification.

In this case, the rate of resource exploration should be matched to the ability of the economy to absorb domestic investment. Evidently, the latter is amenable to policy, and so augmenting the capacity to invest is a high priority.

E Borrowing, but only for appropriate uses and with appropriate signals

The conventional concession to the special conditions of low-income countries is to advise their governments not to borrow in anticipation of resource revenue. Indeed, the most conservative variant of this advice is to use all the resource revenues to accumulate foreign financial assets, and to increase consumption only by the rising income stream from these accumulating assets, this being the 'bird-in-hand' rule.

In practice, governments try to avoid the need for borrowing by advancing revenues through signature bonuses. For reasons discussed above, the true interest rate on signature bonuses is likely to be high (though lower than non-securitized borrowing which may well be prohibitive) and so they are a poor form of borrowing compared to loans from public agencies. Some borrowing can be appropriate and it would be useful if the international financial institutions developed financial instruments to support this need: for example, an International Bank for Reconstruction and Development window. However, the problems for the government are partly of prudence and partly of signalling to its own citizens.

Commodity prices are so volatile that the safe assignment of revenues to consumption is very low. For example, in the first quarter of 2008 when the current oil price was $115, based on its past volatility the 95 percent confidence interval for the forecast of the price in the first quarter of 2009 was in the very wide range $65–$200. Hence, the 'safe' revenue estimate would have been only around half the current price. Yet even this proved to be far from safe, the actual price being only around $43. The prudent approach to this extraordinary volatility is that borrowing for consumption should be kept to very low levels. However, borrowing to finance investment is far less risky. The government is not taking on a liability backed only by the highly uncertain future value of its natural assets: the borrowing is also backed by its new investment. The rationale for borrowing for investment is that the country can thereby get started on 'investing in investing' several years earlier than if it were to wait for the natural resource revenues to come on-stream.

Two types of governments would wish to borrow in anticipation of future resource revenues, the very good and the very bad. The very good government astutely recognizes that consumption now is much more valuable than consumption in the future because of current poverty. The very bad government simply wishes to plunder the future so as to enrich its members. Since citizens can be presumed to be well aware of the dangers of borrowing for plunder, the problem facing the very good government is to signal to its own citizens that it is indeed not of the plundering type. In the standard theory of signalling, the solution to this problem is for the good government to adopt a strategy that would not be imitated by the bad government: what might this be in the present instance? The most promising approach is for the spending from borrowing to be earmarked to uses which cannot directly benefit members of the government, but which clearly directly benefit ordinary citizens. An example of such expenditures is a bursary paid directly to school children. By linking the borrowing to such a use the good government reveals its type.

F An application: China in Africa

How might these rethought principles affect the assessment of what is surely the single most important new resource-related phenomenon: the deals being struck between China and various African governments for infrastructure in return for extraction rights?

On the conventional principles these deals are unambiguously undesirable. They are non-transparent, and instead of revenues flowing into the budget they are earmarked for a particular form of spending. On conventional principles the deals would be far better unbundled into an extraction contract, with revenues going into the budget, and then construction contracts financed by all or part of the public spending supported by the revenues.

How might the issue look differently given the issues raised above? First, the Chinese approach offers a new commitment technology: resources extracted are, with certainty, offset by the accumulation of a domestic asset. A wise Finance Minister may reasonably decide that this is much safer than letting the revenues flow transparently into the budget and then hoping to emerge triumphant from the subsequent political contest for spending. Second, the Chinese approach bypasses both the civil service and domestic construction companies and so relaxes the constraint upon domestic absorption of investment. Of course, this bypass may in some contexts be undesirable: it might be better to generate local employment in the construction sector even if this slows down the pace of investment.

These two advantages are real and substantial: in effect, the Chinese have innovated rather than merely undermined existing practices. The appropriate response is therefore to learn from the innovation and to improve upon it. It would, in fact, not be difficult to improve upon the current Chinese model. Its limitation is not that the extraction and construction contracts are bundled, but that China is currently a monopolist in this form of packaged contract. The appropriate response is therefore for other consortia of resource extraction companies, construction companies and donors to compete with China. Competition could then be fitted into the framework proposed above, namely auctions. Where a government determined that a packaged approach would be advantageous the auction would be conducted in terms of the amount of infrastructure provided for a predetermined set of extraction rights. Prior to the auction the government would set out a prioritized listing of desired infrastructure. The auction would reveal the best value: the bid that undertook to go furthest down the ranked list. Transparency would come about not through unbundling the contract, or insisting on its components being individually priced, but through the process by which the packaged contract was awarded. As with other auctions, bids would need to be screened for credibility. Additionally, there would need to be a specified and credible process for monitoring the quality and timeliness of infrastructure provided, including penalties for non-performance. Such matters are not trivial and may sometimes make the entire process so unsatisfactory that the unbundled approach is clearly superior. The ability to manage the process might be enhanced if an agency such as the World Bank provided loans available to winning consortia in return for standardized procedures and verification.

5 Conclusion

In this brief overview my purpose has been to highlight the implications of the profound differences between those resource-rich countries that are at OECD levels of income, and those that are impoverished. The economic principles for taxing resource extraction imply that the way in which natural assets are harnessed for society should differ considerably in Australia, Canada and Norway on the one hand, and in Angola, Chad and Timor-Leste on the other.

This point is important because to date virtually all the serious analysis has been conducted with reference to the OECD economies. Currently, those Finance Ministers from low-income countries who are most concerned to manage opportunities well look to the OECD models for guidance: for example, this is manifested in the application of what is often wrongly imagined to be the 'Norwegian model' to contexts which are wildly different from that of Norway. In recent years some 50 governments of resource-rich countries have approached the government of Norway for advice. Yet, as the government of Norway is careful to explain, there is no 'Norwegian model.' For example, the high-profile Sovereign Wealth Fund was not begun until some 30 years after natural resource revenues had started: until then they were deployed domestically.

It is one thing to criticize the inappropriate application of an OECD model, it is quite another to replace it with principles that are appropriate. In this paper I have merely sketched the outlines of what needs to be a substantial undertaking.

Notes

1 Several chapters in this book focus on this time consistency issue: Boadway and Keen (2010) review what theory has to say about possible responses, Daniel and Sunley (2010) focus on experience with one of these – fiscal stability agreements – and, an interesting illustration of the importance of strong institutions in this context, Osmundsen (2010) discusses how Norway has managed to achieve substantial credibility in its petroleum tax regime.
2 The appropriate use of resource revenues in low-income countries is discussed more fully in Collier *et al.*, 2010.
3 Experience with the design and implementation of rent and other resource taxes in low income countries are discussed elsewhere in this volume by Calder (2010) Land (2010).
4 See Boadway and Keen (2010) for a formalization.
5 This possibility was raised by a few commentators in response to earlier mineral price booms, see Garnaut and Clunies Ross (1983: 61).
6 Cramton (2010) provides a detailed treatment of auction design for the resource sector.

References

Boadway, Robin and Michael Keen (2010), 'Theoretical Perspectives on Resource Tax Design,' in Philip Daniel, Michael Keen, and Charles McPherson (eds.) *The Taxation of Petroleum and Minerals: Principles, Problems and Practice.*
Calder, Jack (2010), 'Resource Tax Administration,' in Philip Daniel, Michael Keen, and Charles McPherson (eds.) *The Taxation of Petroleum and Minerals: Principles, Problems and Practice.*
Collier, Paul, Rick van der Ploeg, Michael Spence, and Antony Venables (2009), *Managing Resource Revenues in Developing Economies*, IMF Staff Paper advance online publication, July 21, 2009. Available online at http://dx.doi.org/10.1057/imfsp.2006.16, doi: 10.1057/imfsp.2009.16. Last seen: March 2, 2010.
Cramton, Peter (2010), 'How Best to Auction Natural Resources,' in Philip Daniel, Michael Keen, and Charles McPherson (eds.) *The Taxation of Petroleum and Minerals: Principles, Problems and Practice.*
Daniel, Philip and Emil Sunley (2010), 'Contractual Assurances of Fiscal Stability,' in

Philip Daniel, Michael Keen, and Charles McPherson (eds.) *The Taxation of Petroleum and Minerals: Principles, Problems and Practice.*

Garnaut, Ross and Anthony Clunies Ross (1983), 'Taxation of Mineral Rents,' *The Economic Journal*, Vol. 94, pp. 427–428 (Oxford: Clarendon Press).

Land, Bryan (2010), 'Resource Rent Taxation: Theory and Experience,' in Philip Daniel, Michael Keen, and Charles McPherson (eds.) *The Taxation of Petroleum and Minerals: Principles, Problems and Practice.*

Osmundsen, Petter (2010), 'Time Consistency in Petroleum Taxation: Lessons from Norway,' in Philip Daniel, Michael Keen, and Charles McPherson (eds.) *The Taxation of Petroleum and Minerals: Principles, Problems and Practice.*

Ploeg, R. van der and Anthony J. Venables (2008), 'Harnessing Windfall Revenue in Developing Economies,' Discussion Paper No. 6954, CEPR (London, United Kingdom).

Part II

Sectoral experiences and issues

4 Petroleum fiscal regimes

Evolution and challenges

Carole Nakhle

1 Introduction

The central objective in designing petroleum[1] fiscal regimes is easily stated. It is to acquire for the state in whose legal territory the resources in question lie, a fair share of the wealth accruing from the extraction of that resource, whilst encouraging investors to ensure optimal economic recovery of the hydrocarbon resources. How to achieve this balance is a subject of enduring controversy.

Petroleum fiscal regimes, for the purpose of this chapter, encompass taxation, contractual framework, state participation[2] and bonus payments. Fiscal regimes are the principal system for sharing hydrocarbon wealth between host governments and investors. Both governments and oil companies want to secure 'fair' shares of the oil proceeds. The big problem resides with the vagueness surrounding the subjective concept of 'fairness.' Since there is no objective yardstick for sharing economic wealth between the various interests involved in petroleum activity, controversy and tensions will always prevail between investors and the host government.

These issues arise in almost all taxation policy activities. But in the case of oil and gas, they assume a special character and complexity. The petroleum investor has to invest in the country where the resource is found – unlike other sectors where a factory can be closed in one country and opened in another. And while it is true that the oil industry has a strongly international character, local influences, both external and internal to the industry itself can still be decisive in shaping the tax regime and in turn determining the overall attractiveness of the region. Of central relevance are the uncertainties associated with petroleum geology, the specific characteristics of individual oil fields and the investment returns. The costs of petroleum projects tend by their nature to be incurred up front. The time lags are considerable, often of many years and even decades, from the initial discovery of oil or gas reserves to the time of first production. Moreover, the imposition of petroleum taxes and the involvement of the private sector in oil activity tend to be accompanied by intense political debate, where myths and political dogmas can overshadow economic principles.

The design of fiscal regimes is a critical factor in shaping perceptions of an oil and gas basin's competitiveness. Exploration and development activities present delicate legal, technical, financial and political problems and any solution requires a balancing act between the respective interests of the producing countries and the oil companies. A trade-off is bound to exist, since both government and oil companies want to maximize own rewards. This can be achieved through the design of a competitive fiscal regime, which takes into consideration different stakeholders' interests and is attractive for investors in comparison with opportunities in other countries. The outcome is then mutually beneficial, with both the government and investors sharing the rewards and enjoying a more sustainable long-term relationship. If fiscal terms are too generous, government returns are weakened and this could plant the seeds for an adverse reaction towards investors. If the terms are too tough, the incentives to the oil companies to invest in exploration, development and production can be severely damaged with the result that investment flows to countries offering a more attractive fiscal regime.

Against this background, this chapter compares the main petroleum fiscal regimes that apply in oil and gas producing countries round the world. It also analyses the central issues surrounding petroleum taxation, from an economic perspective. In reality, it is difficult to generalize in the field of petroleum taxation because the political, social and economic drivers are country specific and constantly changing.

The remainder of this chapter proceeds as follows. Section 2 focuses on the different options that oil producing countries can choose from in terms of developing their oil and gas activity and the type of relationship, if any, they would want to develop with the private sector. That choice influences the fiscal arrangements that will be adopted. The section also analyses the economic and political dynamics of the different relationships between host governments and investors, which in turn have implications for the fiscal terms. Section 3 studies the controversial areas surrounding petroleum taxation. Supporting evidence is taken from different oil and gas producing countries, with a special focus on key developments over the last four decades. Section 4 provides concluding remarks.

2 Spectrum of policies and frameworks

In the case of minerals in the ground, and petroleum in particular, governments and state authorities in most countries are the legal owners of these resources and are therefore fully entitled to collect a revenue stream from what they own. This ownership status can be translated into policy in a variety of ways. The oil producing nations can opt for complete state ownership (or monopoly) at one extreme (such is the case in Saudi Arabia, Kuwait and Mexico) or permit total private enterprise operations at the other (as in the USA and the UK). Between the two extremes of pure state and pure private ownership a combination of the two is often found. Most oil producing countries fall within that spectrum, the norm being a pattern of involvement by the International Oil Companies (IOCs), in cooperation with the host country's National Oil Company (NOC) and within a clear framework of national control.

The policy that governments choose to develop their hydrocarbon resources has significant implications on the fiscal regime – its type, structure and terms.

A Strategic choices

The three main options that an oil producing country can select from are: 'go-it-alone strategy,' entire private ownership or IOC–NOC cooperation. Under the 'go-it-alone' strategy, the fiscal regime is almost irrelevant, since there are no private companies involved. Under entire private ownership, the norm is to apply concessionary regimes, as is the case in OECD countries, while under the hybrid strategy a wider selection of regimes is available, varying between concessionary, production sharing agreements and service contracts.

If the country chooses to develop its resources on its own, the government formulates and finances an adequate investment program itself and executes it through an NOC. Saudi Arabia is one of the very few countries to have adopted this 'go-it-alone strategy' – after many years of reliance on outside oil companies (the original Aramco).[3] Such a strategy requires the establishment of an NOC that is fully capable of taking the operations role in upstream asset development. Saudi Aramco has access to abundant resources domestically and is mainly focused on the self-sufficient development of those national resources. Similar NOCs exploit their resource base both as a means of supporting the national economy and as a tool to sustain their country's oil supplies.

However, other NOCs have not been as successful.[4] Normally, NOCs have to meet costly non-commercial national obligations that can hinder their ability to raise external capital and to compete at international levels. NOCs, for instance, can be coerced by governments to favour excessive employment and/or be forced to sell their petroleum products to domestic consumers at subsidized prices. These constraints hinder the national firms' ability to produce at a technically efficient level that maximizes the overall value that could be obtained from their oil resources. Consequently, there is under-investment in reserves, stagnation in capacity growth and an inability to maintain or grow the country's oil production capacity. Mexico's State oil company, Pemex (nationalized in 1938), has long been regarded as a critical source of income to the government; virtually all Pemex income is transferred to the state. In the light of the rapid decline in production, the company is facing serious financial pressure with a mounting debt, reaching $42.5 billion (as of 2008) and hindering its investment capabilities. To save Pemex from a deep financial and operational crisis, the Mexican Government has considered – despite strong public opposition – narrowly opening its oil and gas sectors to international players under the restrictive terms of risk service contracts (see Section 2B).

The second option is the other extreme, where the host nation encourages the IOCs to take the lead. In this model, the government creates the appropriate regulatory and fiscal frameworks for IOCs to make the necessary investments in their upstream sectors. This enables the state to avoid allocating much capital itself. The skills required at political and policy level in making this approach attractive and balanced should not be underestimated, but the core investment and operations are undertaken by international firms, both major IOCs and associated service providers, with an appropriate return-sharing framework. Concessionary regimes are normally found under this kind of arrangement.

Entire private ownership is pretty much exclusively confined to the OECD. Indeed most OECD countries follow this model, made easier by the fact that the IOCs are domiciled within OECD nations, hence appearing as 'national champions,' creating the benefits of substantial employment and repatriation of significant dividend flows. The UK Continental Shelf (UKCS) has had a successful oil and gas industry for more than 40 years. The industry is fully privatized – the British National Oil Company (BNOC) existed up until 1982 when it was successfully privatized as part of the government's aim of reducing the role of the state across the entire spectrum of the British economy. The UK Government came to the view that the industry would be more efficient without any state interference and that it could share in the rewards through the tax regime.

The US Gulf of Mexico (GoM) is also entirely owned and operated by IOCs (as is the entire petroleum industry in North America). Leading edge technology is continually being developed and deployed to extend commercial operations into ever deeper water and further into the waters of the Northern Arctic exposed to the seasonal pack ice. The Federal Government continues to earn substantial sums from lease sales (exceeding $178 billion from the Outer Continental Shelf). Sustained growth in production and development activity continues. Between 1992 and 2008, oil companies have drilled more than 2,100 wells at depths greater than 1,000 feet in the US gulf. In stark contrast, and over a similar period, Pemex has only drilled a handful of wells in the deepwater GoM.

The third alternative is to adopt a hybrid solution using NOC–IOC partnerships. This, in effect, is a combination of the other two options, where an active NOC joins forces with material and significant foreign capital and technical expertise to meet the investment needs of the country. Most oil and gas producing countries, outside the OECD, have adopted this approach (as in Egypt and Indonesia, for example) and some inside the OECD (such as Norway). This approach permits a variety of interfaces between the national and the international partners and allows for experiment and innovation. A wide range of petroleum fiscal arrangements is found under this model.

The IOC-host government/NOC interaction does not have to be reduced to a zero-sum game, where what one side wins the other loses. These two entities have different objectives, functions, capabilities, assets and tolerances for risk. In principle, each side possesses what the other side seeks: governments hold the below ground resources sought by IOCs, and IOCs control most of the technical, managerial, and project execution resources that governments need.

Under this third option, the government exercises control over the critical strategic investment decisions such as the exploration for and development of new oil and gas deposits. However, it does not need to interfere in the day-to-day running of the oil and gas fields or in the procurement strategy. This is because the state's tasks and skills differ from those required in day-to-day business operations. IOC investment creates space for state resources to be diverted to other priorities as well as providing access to early revenues. This hybrid solution can strike the right balance between national political objectives and the need to secure capital and expertise from the private sector. The state seeks to improve performance and delivery by concentrating on genuinely public services whilst leaving oil and gas operations as far as possible to the IOCs or private sector, within an appropriate and enabling regulatory framework.

State monopoly may weaken incentives to put in place an effective or efficient fiscal regime, which is less important for a state-owned organization as the money goes from one government pocket to another.

An exclusively private industry requires a well thought out regime balancing state and industry interests, but risks falling short on meeting non-fiscal aspirations. Some states believe that their equity participation provides a return in excess of what can be extracted by the tax system alone. The hybrid route may prove the most popular option as it provides opportunities to meet political imperatives of state control while benefiting from private sector technology and expertise.

Although oil producing countries can choose between those three options, they can reposition themselves over time as conditions, both external and internal to the oil and gas industry, evolve. Over time, NOCs may be partially or fully privatized. The same NOCs once confined to a purely domestic agenda may be given the freedom to invest overseas and trade assets in pursuit of business development and portfolio management ambitions. The list of private sector players may well increase over time as a deliberate policy ambition to increase activity levels. The type, structure and terms of the fiscal regimes can evolve and change accordingly.

B Fiscal arrangements

In the spread of varying relationships between governments and the oil industry, two basic and broad systems of granting rights to investors have developed over the years – the concessionary system and the contractual scheme. The concessionary system[5] originated with the very beginning of the petroleum industry (mid-1800s), and still predominates in OECD countries. The contractual system emerged a century later (mid-1950s), and has been typically favoured by developing countries. The UK, Brazil, Canada, US and Norway, for example, operate a concessionary regime, companies being entitled to the ownership of the oil extracted. By contrast, countries like Azerbaijan, Algeria, Nigeria and Angola[6] apply a contractual regime where the government retains the ownership of the petroleum produced – although private oil companies are entitled to ownership of part of the oil produced under one type of contractual regime, namely production sharing contracts (PSCs) or agreements (PSAs).

Some argue that in concessionary regimes, oil companies are in a much stronger position compared with the contractual systems, where the government exercises deeper control over the exploitation and production of the natural resource. But the reality which has emerged behind these different approaches suggests that they can be made equivalent not only in terms of control but also in terms of fiscal impact. Most probably, the hostile sentiment towards concessionary regimes dates back to the first half of the twentieth century, where governments in oil producing countries were perceived as being exploited by the oil majors. But it has to be recalled that it is not the principles of the regime per se that devalued government sovereignty at those early days of oil activity; it was a combination of different political, economic, social and legal conditions, which have changed dramatically since then.

Concessionary systems: evolution and basic characteristics

A concession is an agreement[7] between a government and a company that grants that company the exclusive right to explore for, develop, produce, transport and market petroleum resources at its own risk and expense within a fixed area for a specific amount of time (Blinn *et al.*, 1986). So long as they remain in the ground (or under the seabed) all such resources continue in most jurisdictions to be the property of the state (or Crown). The concession to the oil company is for the right or title to produce oil at the wellhead, along with the requirement to pay the appropriate royalties and taxes. The company is entitled to ownership of the oil so produced and is free to dispose of it, often subject to some form of obligation to supply to the local market. However, from early oil industry days, a much broader type of concession has also existed and is still used in the US, which assigns rights of ownership not just to the wellhead producer but to the discoverer of the oil reserves and the owners of the land under which they lie. Indeed, the US has long recognized private ownership of minerals below the ground, as long as they are not on Federal lands.

A striking example of this earlier pattern was the concession granted to W.K. D'Arcy by the Persian monarchy in 1901. This stretched over very large areas, covering the entire national territory, and with very long duration, up to 60 and 75 years. Similar 'long-lease' concessions were granted in earlier years (sometimes up to 99 years in Kuwait), providing exclusive ownership to certain IOCs of the reserves found in the area covered by the concession. In the UAE, a single onshore concession, granted in the 1930s, covers the whole of Abu Dhabi.

The financial benefits accruing to the host government under such arrangements were limited, consisting primarily of royalties based on the volume of production, at a flat rate rather than a percentage of the value of the oil produced. The concessionaire retained control over virtually all aspects of the operations, including the rate of exploration, the decision to bring new fields into exploitation, and the determination of production levels, among others. Furthermore, this type of early concession agreement did not provide for any possibility of renegotiation of the terms and conditions of the agreement, should a change of circumstances warrant it, and nor did it enable the government to participate in the ownership of the petroleum produced, thus leaving it with a passive role.

Such one-sided agreements were granted by comparatively inexperienced governments with sometimes little authority, often under foreign political dominance and not possessing a legal framework liable to govern such things as petroleum operations. Most importantly, competition was limited as the industry was dominated by a small number of global players. Those arrangements were bound to be called in question as the balance of power changed in favour of ruling authorities and governments.

After the Second World War, a second generation of concession agreements was developed, providing for a more active role for the host government and a corresponding decrease in the rights of IOCs. The concession areas began to be delineated as blocks, and the awarding of concessions restricted to a limited number of blocks. Modern concession agreements also entail provisions for the surrender of most of the original area (where a commitment to develop the area has not been made within a prescribed timescale), while the total duration of the concession tends to be far more tightly regulated. They can also include bonuses payable on signature of the agreement, on discovery of a petroleum field or on reaching certain levels of production. Those constraints have financial implications for the size and timing of fiscal revenues.

Nowadays, the usual way of taxing oil companies operating within concessionary regimes is via a combination of income tax, a special petroleum tax and royalty. That is why concessionary regimes are commonly known as 'Royalty/ Tax Systems.'

Gross royalty

Royalty can be a per-unit tax, which is a uniform fixed charge levied on a specified level of volume of production or an ad-valorem tax, which is a fixed charge levied on the value of the output (gross revenues). Royalty rates for oil are generally set in a range from 5 per cent to 25 per cent but most are nearer 10 per cent to 15 per cent of production. Natural gas is often assigned a lower rate than oil.

Royalty holds its attractions to host governments. Royalty is relatively simple to administer, predictable and provides an early revenue stream as soon as production starts. The optics of early revenues for the government minimizes the political risk of further intervention.

But as the royalty is not profit related, it may deter marginal projects that are profitable on a pre-tax basis from proceeding. The regressive nature of royalty – the lower is project profitability, the higher are royalty payments relative to profits – can cause operating income to become negative even when gross revenues exceed extraction costs, and consequently can lead to a premature abandonment of the field. Royalty directly reduces the quantities of reported production and booked reserves for companies (which analysts and media commentators take interest in as one of the performance indicators for IOCs in stock markets, although booked reserves are not directly linked to profitability), unlike other tax elements. For instance, a royalty of 15 per cent results in only 85 per cent of the reserves being booked under a Tax and Royalty regime (see section 3C).

In mature high cost basins such as the UK and Norway, royalty has been progressively eliminated. Some nations are more attached to a strong royalty tradition, particularly the US, where royalty rates in the US GoM have increased from 12.5 per cent to 16.66 per cent. Other countries have introduced a profit element in royalties by having them depend on the level of production (like China) or in some cases oil price. This is known as a sliding scale royalty, where the royalty rate is low when production or oil price is low and vice versa, thereby decreasing the possibility of negative cash flows when production or oil prices are low.

Royalty is normally allowable as a deduction against other taxes, such as field-based taxes (like the PRT in the UK) and income taxes.

Corporate income tax

Income tax systems usually consist of a basic, single rate structure, plus provisions for deduction of all costs items from the tax base, sometimes with supplementary levies and tax incentives. The overall level of corporate income tax rates varies considerably from country to country. In many countries the level is typically between 25 per cent and 35 per cent.

Most countries provide an incentive for exploration and development by allowing exploration costs to be recovered immediately and allowing accelerated recovery of development costs (tax depreciation), for example, over five years or less. Accelerated depreciation brings forward payback for the investor and reduces the latter's cumulative cash exposure. In addition to cost deductions, in many cases interest expenses and losses carried forward and/or back are commonly allowed in the computation of the tax liability. All forms of income tax allow relief for capital expenditure (at a varying pace), but extra reliefs are sometimes given to provide incentives to develop high cost 'marginal' projects. The UK has gone further than most and introduced 100 per cent depreciation in the year of expenditure. This ensures that no project will pay tax until payback has been secured – a uniquely attractive feature for investors.

The income tax regime for oil and gas companies is generally the same regime that applies to all corporate activities for all industries in the country in question. Though the rate may be higher and the range of qualifying cost deductions may differ (so that some ring-fencing is needed), the tax is levied at a corporate rather than oil field level, as such it is generally known as corporation tax or tax on corporate net income. Since income tax is a profit-based tax, it introduces fewer distortions compared to an over-reliance on revenue-based taxes.

Special petroleum tax

Many concessionary regimes also include a special petroleum tax, similar to a resource rent tax,[8] in order to capture a larger share of economic rent from oil production. The special tax is usually imposed along with the general corporate income tax but it is levied on a project or field basis rather than on aggregate company income. The tax is normally based on cash flow but is imposed only when cumulative cash flow is positive. Negative cash flows are carried forward and deducted from positive cash flows in later periods. The negative net cash flows may be uplifted by a minimum rate of return requirement and added to the next year's net cash flow. The uplift is often characterized as a proxy for financing costs. The accumulation process is continued until a positive net cash flow is generated. No special tax is payable until the firm has recovered its costs inclusive of a threshold rate of return which is compounded from year to year. Tax kicks in only when positive cash flows emerge, the project investment is recovered and a threshold return on the investment is made. If costs rise or oil prices fall, taxable profits change in sympathy, as does the special petroleum tax burden. Incremental investment opportunities may be attractive in fields with existing production and current taxable income. In this case, the investment will typically secure immediate or accelerated tax relief in comparison to a greenfield or standalone opportunity where there is a greater time lag between the investment and the tax relief. Also, if the investment is unproductive the tax relief is still available which cushions the impact on the investor.

Additional payments and measures[9]

Other payments can also be made to the government in oil producing countries where concessionary regimes apply. These include bonuses, which are lump sum payments made to the government (and are also common under contractual systems). They can be signature or lease bonus, payable upon signing the agreement with the government or award of a lease, discovery bonus, payable when a commercial discovery is made, or production bonus,[10] payable at an agreed amount (or bid)[11] upon the achievement of a stated level of daily production. Signature bonuses capture some of the anticipated resource value regardless of the success of exploration and production activities. Since the investment is made up-front, once paid, they have no further impact on the future economic decisions of the investor. The sums can be very large; they comprise a material proportion of overall government take, particularly if the acreage is unproductive. The discovery bonus is also a one-off fee. It is required after commercial discovery is declared and after the NOC has approved the IOCs development plan. Production bonuses, however, can be recurring. They are due when production reaches a certain level. They are normally on a sliding scale of production, therefore if daily production reaches a certain level the government takes a fixed sum, which increases if daily production reaches higher levels. Depending on the tax regime, bonuses may be deductible for income tax purposes.

Some countries ring-fence their oil and gas activities (usually under corporate income tax) whilst others ring-fence individual projects (usually under special petroleum tax). Ring-fencing imposes a limitation on deductions for tax purposes across different activities or projects undertaken by the same taxpayer. In other words, all costs associated with a given licence or field must be deducted from revenues generated within that field – not from other licences or fields. These rules matter for two main reasons. First, the absence of ring-fencing can postpone government tax receipts because a company that undertakes a series of projects is able to deduct exploration and development costs from each new project against the income of projects that are already generating taxable income. Second, as an oil and gas area matures, the absence of ring-fencing may discriminate against new entrants that have no income against which to deduct exploration or development expenditures. However, existing players are encouraged to sustain their investment given the availability of the tax shelter.

Contractual regimes: basic characteristics

During the second half of the twentieth century, and with the political developments round the world, the concessionary regime came to be regarded as incompatible with government sovereignty. Contractual regimes emerged as the result of efforts to modify the nature of the relationships between IOCs and host governments, and above all to find an alternative to the concessionary regime, allowing the host government, in theory, to exercise more control over both petroleum operations and the ownership of production.

Two types of contractual regimes apply: production sharing contracts (PSCs) and risk service contracts. The concept of the PSC was used firstly as early as the 1950s. But in their currently used form, PSCs in particular became popular in Indonesia in the 1960s. Risk service contracts first came into use in the late 1960s (Blinn *et al.*, 1986).

Under the typical contractual systems, the oil company is appointed by the government as a contractor for operations on a certain area. The title to the hydrocarbons remains with the state, and all production belongs to the government unless it is explicitly shared, while the IOC executes petroleum operations in accordance with the terms of the contract and operates at its own risk and expense under the control of the government. The IOC also provides all the financing and technology required for the operation.

The two parties agree that the contractor will meet the exploration and development costs in return for a share of production or a cash fee for this service, if production is successful.

- If the company receives a share of production (after the deduction of Government share), the system is known as a PSC – also known as a *production sharing agreement* (PSA) – which is a binding commercial contract between an investor – the IOC – and a state (or national oil company). A PSC defines the conditions for the exploration and development of natural resources from a specific area over a designated period of time. Under a PSC, as the company is rewarded in physical barrels, it therefore takes title to that share of petroleum extracted at the delivery point (export point from the contract area).
- If the IOC is paid a fee (often subject to taxes) for conducting production operations, the system is known as a *service contract*, also called a *risk service contract*. The latter is so called because the host government (or its

national oil company) hires the services of an international oil company and, in the case of commercial production from the contractual area, the oil company is paid in cash for its services without taking title to any petroleum extracted. A distinction is sometimes made between service contracts and risk service contracts. The former is simply based on defined compensation for a specific task, while the latter may involve additional risk being taken by the contractor for which a variable fee may be applicable.

While some service contracts are disguised PSCs, especially with regard to ownership of the resource, the main differences between the two contract forms are the remuneration of the contractor and the control over operations.

Production sharing contract

Over time PSCs have changed substantially, and they now take many different forms. One cannot refer, for instance, to a typical Asian or a typical Eastern European contract. Terms vary between one country and the other. But in its most basic form a PSC has four main properties. The IOC pays a royalty on gross production to the government, if applicable. After the royalty is deducted, the IOC is entitled to a predetermined share of production for cost recovery. The remainder of the production, so called profit oil, is then shared between government and IOC at a prespecified share. The contractor then has to pay income tax on its share of profit and cost oil combined, after deductions permitted under tax law. A few systems (Angola, Russia) have used profit oil alone as the base for income tax.

In contractual regimes (as with concessionary systems), the oil company bears all the costs and risks of exploration and development. It has no right to be paid in the event that discovery and development do not occur. However, if there is a discovery the company is allowed to recover the costs it has incurred, and this is known as *cost recovery* or *cost oil*. The investor typically may take oil for cost recovery up to a fixed proportion of total production from the project, known as the cost oil limit, as compensation for the cost of exploration and development. The oil that remains after the oil company has taken its cost oil is usually termed *profit oil*.

Cost recovery[12] is similar in concept to deductible expenses for tax purposes (including depreciation of capital assets) under the concessionary systems. It includes mainly unrecovered costs carried over from previous years, operating expenditures, capital expenditures, abandonment costs and some investment incentives. Financing cost or interest expense is generally not a recoverable cost, though unrecovered costs can often be rolled forward with an uplift in lieu of interest. Normally, a predetermined percentage of production is allocated on a yearly basis for cost recovery. However, in general there is a limit for cost recovery that typically ranges from 30 to 60 per cent of gross revenue, in other words, for any given period the maximum level of costs recovered is 60 per cent of revenue, although contracts with unlimited cost recovery are also in existence (see Indonesia, Bahrain and Algeria for instance). A fixed ceiling on cost oil ensures a minimum quantity of profit oil from which the state can secure up-front revenues as soon as production commences.

Many PSCs specify annual cost oil allowances either on a sliding scale or state that this variable is biddable or negotiable up to a certain maximum value. Full cost recovery occasionally comes with a time limit attached to it. The share of production set aside for cost oil may decline after, for instance, five years, in which case it works similarly to accelerated depreciation. Unrecovered costs in any year are sometimes but not generally carried forward with interest to sub-sequent years. Investment incentives (credits, uplift or allowances) may also be provided to allow the contractor to recover an additional percentage of capital costs through cost recovery. The more generous the cost recovery limit is, the longer it takes for the government to realize its take. There is usually a ring fence for cost recovery around the contract area or development area – costs associated with a particular block or licence must be recovered from revenues generated within that block or licence.

Royalties can also feature in PSC regimes but the same economic impact can be secured by having cost oil limits below 100 per cent, together with a minimum state profit oil share, which also ensure an early flow of revenues to the state.

The principle of cost recovery applies to both a PSC and in risk-service agreements. However, the basis of the contractor's remuneration after it has recovered its cost differs in type.

In a PSC, profit oil is divided between the host government and the company according to a pre-determined percentage negotiated in the contract. The split can be constant, or on a scale linked to cumulative or daily production rates, or there can be a progressive split linked to achieved project profitability, that is to rate of return (ROR) or R-factors. Under ROR systems, the effective government take increases as the project ROR increases. The government is guaranteed early revenues through the operation of the cost oil ceiling which ensures there is always a minimum quantity of profit oil to be shared between the investor and the state in each year. The elements determining the R-factor, or payback ratio, vary from one country to the other, but normally both revenue and cost (and in some cases interest) are included in the equation. The R-factor can be broadly defined as the ratio of cumulative net earnings (some countries use gross revenues) to cumulative total expenditures. The R-factor is calculated in each accounting period and once a threshold is reached, a new sharing rate will apply in the next accounting period. The objective of the ROR and R-factor is to link the sharing between the government and the contractor to profitability.[13] Over time these parameters will increase the government share of profit oil. However, in exceptional circumstances, if the ROR fell then this could lead to a fall in government's share of profit oil, but this would require a period of negative cash flows. It is theoretically possible for a substantial enhanced oil recovery (EOR) project to benefit from these circumstances if its associated investment is suffi-ciently large to generate negative cash flows for long enough for the ROR to fall and engender a reduction in the government share of profit oil. However, a period of negative cash flows later in the life of the field would normally result in the field ceasing production.

The contractor's share of profit oil is usually, but not always, taxable.[14] In many PSCs the government pays the contractor's income tax from its share of profit oil; these are called 'pay on behalf' PSCs. The precise legal provisions that give effect to these 'pay on behalf' regimes are important in the context of assessing the foreign tax credit position of IOCs which may give rise to additional tax liability in their home country if poorly constructed.

In some countries, the government has the option to purchase a certain portion of the contractor's share of production at a price lower than the market price: a provision known as the domestic market obligation (DMO). There can also be additional government take in form of bonus payments, whether signature bonus or production bonus. Most tax regimes allow for bonuses to be tax deductible, since they are a cost of doing business; the larger the tax relief for the bonuses offered in the contract, the greater the magnitude of the upfront bonus is likely to be. However they are typically not allowable for cost recovery under PSC rules, which ensures that the state receives more profit oil.

Box 4.1 Net cash flow under contractual systems

Determining the net cash flow under contractual systems is not as straightforward as under concessionary systems. There are several stages that must be determined:

First, net revenue is determined. This is the gross revenue less royalty, if applicable.

Second, cost oil is determined. This includes broadly the operating expenditures, depreciation of capital expenditures and any investment credit and uplift (and sometimes financing cost) investment credit applies only to facilities such as platforms, pipelines and processing equipment, while uplift applies to all capital costs. Uplift is essentially an alternative or a proxy for interest.

Third, the costs available for recovery are then compared to the cost oil limit, in order to determine the level of costs allowed for deduction at a particular period. For instance, if the cost recovery limit is 80 per cent, in a given period the maximum cost recovery that can be taken is 80 per cent of revenue. If costs exceed that limit, the difference between the actual value of costs and the allowed value is carried forward to a future period.

The following stage differs between a PSC and a service contract:

In a PSC, the difference between net revenue and cost oil determines the profit oil that will be shared between the contractor and the government, depending on the split rate. As such, the contractor's share can be expressed as in the following:

Contractor profit oil = Net revenue – Cost recovery – Government share

Finally, the contractor's profit oil can be subject to income tax. In this case, the contractor's profit oil plus cost oil minus allowable deductions can be considered as the taxable income under a concessionary system. In general, investment credits and uplifts are cost recoverable but not deductible for calculation of income tax (their cost recovery may form part of taxable income). The opposite is true for bonuses, which are not cost recoverable but are tax deductible.

Consequently, the contractor entitlement can be calculated as follows:

Contractor entitlement = Cost recovery
plus Investment credits
plus Contractor share of profit oil
less DMO
less Government tax
less Royalty (if applicable)

Government total share can be expressed as the sum of:

- Royalty (if applicable)
- Share of profit oil
- Bonus
- DMO
- Tax

In a service contract, the contractor entitlement includes its cost recovery (normally plus interest) and an agreed rate of return, as the remuneration fee. This sum, covering cost recovery, interest and the rate of return, is paid over a certain number of months in equal instalments. Once the contractor receives all its payment, that period is known as the 'handover date,' at which the foreign contractor hands over facilities to the government (or the national company) and as such it is no longer involved in the project. Consequently, up to the handover date, the contractor entitlement can be expressed as in the following:

Contractor entitlement = Cost recovery
plus Investment credits
plus Remuneration fee
less DMO
less Government tax
less Royalty (if applicable)

The government share in this case is any remaining profitability of the oil field, once the contractor received the remuneration for its service.

Risk service contracts

In the case of service contracts, the contractor carries out development work on behalf of the host country for a fee, although in exceptional circumstances the remuneration can itself be in the form of oil. The government allows the contractor to recover the costs associated with development of the hydrocarbon resources. The government pays the contractor a fee which is agreed up-front, and remuneration under a service contract is also usually determined using project performance indicators linked to actual production rates and based on pre-agreed capital budgets. All production belongs to the government. Since the contractor does not, strictly speaking, receive a share of production, terms such as production sharing and profit oil are not appropriate, even though the arithmetic will often carve out a share of revenue in the same fashion that a PSC shares production. The fixed fee remuneration – service fee – of the contractor can be subject to tax. It is analogous to taxable income in a concessionary system and profit oil in a PSC. The service contracts are also known as risk service contracts or risk contracts: the term risk is added because the oil company puts up all the capital and risks being exposed to cost overruns which, typically, it is unable to recover.

Over time, service contracts have taken many forms; *technical assistance contracts* and *buyback* are two variations.

TECHNICAL ASSISTANCE CONTRACTS (TAC) OR TECHNICAL SERVICE AGREEMENTS (TSA)

These contracts are often referred to as 'rehabilitation,' 'redevelopment' or 'enhanced oil recovery' projects. They are associated with existing fields of production and sometimes, but to EOR less often, abandoned fields. The contractor takes over operations including equipment and personnel if applicable. The assistance that includes capital provided by the contractor is principally based on special technical know-how. These arrangements are suitable for small companies as they provide low-risk situations with opportunities for a company to exploit technical expertise, and they are usually applied to marginal fields.

This kind of arrangement is more characteristic of countries where the State has substantial capital but seeks only expertise. It can be quite similar to those found in the oil service industry, where the contractor is paid a fee for performing a service, such as drilling, development or medium-risk exploration services. Hence they are suitable for service-providers. Furthermore, despite the reduced risks, cost and timing estimates as well as fiscal terms are critical. Many countries try to tighten the fiscal terms on EOR projects because of the reduced risk. However, these projects require careful screening as EOR can be very limited and costly in marginal, depleted fields. If fiscal terms are out of balance, no amount of technical expertise can salvage a project.

BUYBACK

Under a buyback agreement (where the government or NOC 'buys back' the project after a period by fulfilling the remuneration obligation to the contractor), the arrangements with foreign companies 'shall in no way entitle the companies to any claims on the crude oil.'[15] The scope of work to be carried out by the oil company is set in a development plan, which normally forms the basis of the technical bids for the project. The period of time from the effective date of the contract until final commissioning is referred to as the 'development phase,' which ends when all development operations have been completed by the contractor in accordance with the buyback contract, and all wells and facilities described in the development plan have been installed, commissioned, started up, tested and handed over to the national oil company. During development operations the contractor acts as the field operator under the control and direction of a joint management committee comprising a number of representatives from the contractor and the national oil company. During this period, the contractor funds all capital and non-capital expenditures and all operating costs incurred in the performance of development operations. After the successful completion of the development operations, operatorship of the field is transferred back to the national oil company for production operations, at the handover date. After that, the state is entitled to all the future net incomes. A government take[16] of 95–97 per cent is considered typical under such a risk service arrangement.

A buyback may offer the IOC an exploration contract which will not necessarily be converted into a development contract even if commercial discovery is declared. The agreements have a relatively short duration of between five and seven years. Capital cost ceilings can only be exceeded for new additional work approved by NOC. The extra expenditure is then added to the initial capital costs and repaid under the amortization period of the contract. The IOC receives its project expenditure plus a taxable fee. The latter is some percentage of total capital costs excluding finance charges and operating costs.

Generally, service contracts are not favoured by IOCs. They tend to attract relatively little in the way of investment capital as they simply offer, in the eyes of the investor, too little in the way of return for the deployment of resources required. Some countries are trying to address this perception by introducing performance incentives, such as a fee per barrel produced. This offers the contractor the opportunity to share in reservoir performance.

For many IOCs these sort of contract formulations are 'loss leaders' in the hope that the initial contract will facilitate a constructive relationship with the host country that will lead to a follow on long-term contract based on a PSC. However, very little evidence supporting this belief can be reported. In Kuwait, IOCs have over a period of years participated in a number of tightly defined small-scale technical assistance programmes with the expectation that this would lead to a substantive long-term role. The anticipated IOC participation has not been forthcoming, however, and the Kuwait petroleum sector is suffering from lack of investment and access to leading edge technology.

3 Key issues and controversies

It is often asked what model a country should adopt in developing the best regulatory and fiscal framework for the expansion of its oil production. Is there a stand out model from the dozen different regimes in operation around the world? The answer is that each country should follow its own model. It should build a robust framework uniquely suited to its own conditions, needs and aspirations. No two countries' conditions are the same. Attempts to export and replicate the fiscal regimes of one state in another can fail. But policy makers should certainly look closely at the experience of other countries and learn from both their successes and their failures.

The perfect fiscal regime has yet to be designed. The complexities and uncertainties of the real world are probably greater than any theoretical economic prescriptions. But there are some guiding axioms that can be followed. These are summarized below.

A The importance of fiscal design and structure

Judgements are sometimes made based on the type of fiscal regime in place and the tax rates imposed. But these are rather too simplistic considerations if fiscal comparisons do not assess country-specific geological, location or political risk factors.[17]

While concessionary regimes are often perceived to offer more attractive terms to private investors than contractual regimes – namely PSCs or risk-sharing contracts – a closer evaluation of various regimes round the world shows that concessionary regimes and PSCs can be designed in a way to generate similar economic outcomes. What matters is the ambition of the host government and the way the fiscal regime is structured to deliver these objectives. Very onerous fiscal terms can be found under concessionary regimes, such as Norway where government take reaches 78 per cent. Back in the 1980s, the UK government take reached nearly 90 per cent for a brief period. The difference between concessionary and PSCs is a political and legal rather than economic issue, as discussed further in Section 3C.

A more one-dimensional judgement is based on the apparent tax rates imposed. For instance a regime that imposes a corporate tax rate of 30 per cent is seen as generous compared to a regime that has 60 per cent corporate tax rate. But in practice three important points should be noted.

First, what matters is what governments want to achieve. A country may have low tax take for a number of reasons, namely, to attract more investment, to compensate for perceptions of high fiscal risk, high costs, small volumes, high geological risk, and basin maturity, or simply because of the belief in a low tax environment for business in general. The US GoM is an instructive example of how a stable and relatively low tax environment can encourage and sustain a significant level of activity, in particular, the development of technology to cope with extremes of water depths and ocean conditions. The fiscal regime was adjusted to the perceived prospectivity of the continental shelf. It can be argued that the level of investment flows and production from the US GoM deep water would not have transpired in a materially higher tax environment.

Although Russia's PSCs signed between 1994 and 1995 are used sometimes to illustrate the defects of PSCs, it is important to consider the aims of the Russian government and country conditions at that period. The main objective was to stimulate foreign investment in geographically isolated and technologically complex hydrocarbon projects as well as to boost oil and gas production, all in a low oil price environment. In fact, the 1990s witnessed the lowest levels of oil price in recent decades, reaching $10/bbl back in 1998. As the investment climate improved – namely more political stability and more favourable economic conditions (especially higher oil prices) – the Russian government leaned more towards securing higher share of revenues. This led the state to intervene and recast the PSC terms to ensure a better balance of reward between investors and the tax-levying authority. Most significantly, the state became a direct equity participant in the project.

Second, the conditions of the oil and gas region must be kept in perspective. A high level of government take may not be justified in cases of high-risk exploration and high-cost development, or for those areas with remaining modest petroleum potential, suffering the challenges of basin maturity as is the case in the UKCS. The cost of producing oil can overwhelm any price incentive. Large price incentives are needed to increase production while the costs of production are rising. In contrast, a country like Iraq, with world class resource base, can afford to impose high tax rates. High government takes are generally sustainable if the basin offers high volumetric potential and high returns; these are critical for large IOCs, which need to replace their production with new discoveries or field growth.

But it is important to maintain the delicate balance between ensuring an adequate share of revenues for tax-levying authority whilst simultaneously providing sufficient incentives to encourage investment. In examining the attractiveness of an oil or gas region, a prospective investor will take into account many factors, including: basin prospectivity and cost structure, volumetric potential (size of discoveries), access to infrastructure and opportunities, the fiscal terms and political risks. The balance of those factors will enable the investor to assess the basin competitiveness.

The Angolan petroleum fiscal regime is often regarded as a model that succeeded in establishing a balance between investors' and the state's interests. Some argue that Angolan PSCs have onerous components, including relatively low and fixed cost oil, as well as high income tax plus high signature bonuses to secure the initial concession. It should be remembered though that the signature bonus is a cost freely volunteered by the investor to win a competitive bid for the lease in question. Moreover, these elements are somewhat balanced by the absence of explicit royalties and an IRR-based sliding scale for profit oil (the higher the achieved rate of return, the higher the government share of profit oil). Very high prospectivity also underpins the fiscal structure; recent exploration success in Angola has been amongst the best of any offshore basin, with a number of large discoveries. Given this balance, Angola has clearly designed a fiscal regime that both encouraged a sustained high level of investment from IOCs and generated substantial revenues to the state. In 2007, Angola received in excess of $18 billion in revenues from the petroleum sector (including Sonangol), according to official figures from the Angolan ministry of finance. The authorities have also taken advantage of the competitive instincts of the IOCs by awarding licenses on the basis of the largest signature bonus.

Box 4.2 Angola petroleum fiscal terms

Angola is a long established petroleum province with exploration and production activities that can be traced back over 100 years. However, sustainable activity in the petroleum sector did not really get into gear until the 1980s, several years after independence and the end of the civil war. Initial efforts were focused on the onshore production and shallow water provinces and by 1990 production had reached nearly 500 thousand bbl/d (mbpd). However, the real success story for Angola is the deep water which was licensed in the early 1990s and has resulted in a series of world class discoveries. Many of these are now in or soon to enter production. As a result Angolan production is on steeply rising trend passing 1.7 million bbl/d in 2007 and expected to reach 2.5 million bbl/d by the early years of the next decade.

Sonangol has built a solid reputation in the oil industry both in Angola and abroad. This is a direct result of strong relationships with the wide range of oil companies which operate, or which have interests and investments, in Angola. As a signal of Sonangol's capability the company secured its first operated license in 2003. Most of Sonangol's exploration costs are carried by the IOCs and reimbursed with interest from its share of production.

The Angolan government encouraged inward investment from the IOCs by offering a stable and competitive fiscal regime based on production sharing contracts.

The fiscal terms for each PSC differ and are tailored to expected opportunities from each license area. Nevertheless there are many common features and similarities between contracts are greater than differences. Typical features are:

- No royalty
- Cost oil 50 per cent
- Uplift – 40 per cent of capex
- Depreciation 4 years straight line
- Profit oil splits are formulaically linked to an earned project rate of return. Typical IRR-based profit splits are given in Table 4.1. This became the basis of all licences awarded since 1991. Prior to this date the profit splits on PSCs were linked to cumulative production.
- Income tax 50 per cent

Table 4.1 Angola's profit oil splits

Rate of return (%)	State share (%)	Contractor share (%)
Nominal		
Less than 15	25	75
15–25	35	65
25–30	55	45
30–40	75	25
Over 40	85	15

> The benefit of this fiscal structure is that the government take automatically rises as the project profitability increases, either as a result of higher prices, higher reserves or lower costs. This aligns the requirements of investors, for downside protection and the needs of the state to capture the project upside. It is notable that countries such as Angola with such responsive or progressive fiscal terms have not needed to intervene to increase government take with higher prices. This happens automatically.

In a mature basin such as the UK large discoveries are highly unlikely and the basin's attraction has shifted from volume to value. The reduced average size of finds in the UKCS coupled with the relatively high costs of exploration and development have meant that there is an insufficient resource base to attract larger oil company investment in exploration, particularly when other international opportunities are in keen competition for funds.

Finally, the precise design and interaction of various taxes and other elements play an important role. Some regimes may have similar apparent structures and tax rates, but their impacts on oil projects' and companies' profitability and government take can be quite different. Several factors, such as tax reliefs and the process of calculating the tax base – or simply the way the fiscal model has been designed – can lead to significant differences among fiscal packages, while different structures and regimes can produce the same results in terms of revenue and tax take. Judgement about the effectiveness or strengths of a fiscal regime cannot be made simply by looking at the tax rate. The main indicator used to compare a fiscal regime in overall terms is the project government take defined as the net present value of total government revenues as a proportion of pre-tax revenues. Government revenues in this context include all taxes, royalties, profit oil and bonuses paid to the government.[18]

The UK, Australia and Norway have all adopted concessionary regimes. On the surface, a certain harmonization seems to exist between the three regimes. In each case, a royalty was imposed when the country first opened up for production but later the royalty element was progressively abolished and replaced by a profit-related regime. In all three regimes the income tax rate is now below 30 per cent. In the UK, however, a supplementary charge of 20 per cent was imposed in April 2002, calculated on the same base as the income tax except that no relief for interest expense is permitted. The income tax is the general tax that applies to all companies operating in the three countries respectively. Also, a special resource tax applies in the three countries – although in the UK it applies only on fields that received development consent before 1993. The rate in each country ranges between 40 and 50 per cent. The tax is based on deemed profitability after allowance for a threshold rate of return representing normal profits. Additionally, the three countries provide tax incentives and extra expenditure reliefs, which results in the taxes typically being paid only when net cash flow begins to turn positive.

Nevertheless, the economic outcomes in terms of government take differ because of the way the regimes are structured and designed, namely in the treatment of expenditures, abandonment costs and the interaction of various taxes. For instance, in the UK, no project pays any tax until payback is reached; this is a favourable arrangement for investors. In Australia, abandonment costs are not deductible expenses (but all costs plus annual uplift are recoverable before the special petroleum tax is payable). In terms of the special resource tax, in Norway, the special petroleum tax (SPT) is not deductible from the income tax base. In fact, the Norwegian SPT acts as an income tax with uplift; in Australia, the petroleum resource rent tax (PRRT) is rather a resource rent tax. As a result, the effective tax rates in the UK range from 50 per cent for new fields to 75 per cent for older ones. In contrast Norway has a static 78 per cent tax take across all classes of investment.

In assessing a fiscal regime, looking only at the level of tax rates can be very misleading. One cannot make judgements about the effectiveness or strengths of a fiscal regime, simply by looking at the tax rate. Several factors, such as fiscal reliefs and the process of calculating the tax base, can lead to significant differences among fiscal packages, while different structures and regimes can produce the same results in terms of revenue and tax 'take.' Furthermore, evaluating the impact of fiscal regimes on government take and the allocation of risk is a complex exercise: in Chapter 7, Daniel *et al.* consider the technical issues raised by such evaluations, and how they can be addressed.

B Oil price link and the lagged effect

The oil price moves in unpredictable cycle, and so do costs though these are correlated with price movements. Historically, periods of increasing oil prices result in tightening of fiscal terms (especially where the fiscal regime is not explicitly linked to oil price). The reaction to falling oil prices, however, tends to be slower and more erratic. On the upswing, governments are eager to capture a windfall; on the downswing, they are short of money and find cutting taxes unaffordable.

As oil prices recovered from their low levels in the 1990s and increased in the first eight years of the twenty-first century, several countries introduced tougher fiscal measures. In the UK, the Government imposed a 10 per cent supplementary charge in 2002, then doubled it in 2005 (see Figure 4.1). In the US (Alaska), allowances were removed from certain fields in 2005 and new progressive taxes introduced, resulting in three large tax increases within three years. Venezuela increased royalty for new fields under its 2002 hydrocarbon law and removed royalty incentives for heavy oil in 2004, then increased royalty rates in 2006. The Venezuela government went even further and introduced a compulsory transfer of equity from IOCs to PDVSA ensuring a minimum 50 per cent share for the national oil company. This was contested by some of the IOCs who remain in dispute with the government for appropriate compensation. Similarly, Bolivia increased royalty from 18 per cent to 50 per cent in 2005 while Ecuador introduced a 60 per cent windfall tax in 2006.

Following the oil price crash in 1986, many governments responded by reducing or even abolishing royalty rates and other 'regressive' fiscal terms in an

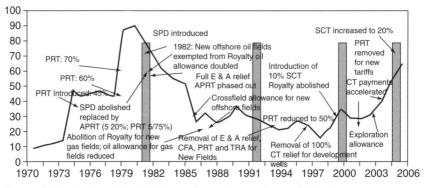

Figure 4.1 Evolution of the UKCS petroleum fiscal regime and oil price.

attempt to make the level of fiscal take more sensitive to project profitability than to revenues. But it can take many years for a country to reverse fiscal policies in order to attract new investment. After the oil price slump of 1998–1999, it took producing governments three to five years to implement new incentives for foreign oil investment. In Algeria, it took five years from the oil price collapse for a consensus to emerge on the need for reforms to the petroleum law, but by the time the changes came into effect in 2005, the oil price had rebounded to such an extent that the government reverted to more aggressive terms within a year.

Box 4.3 Evolution of the UK petroleum fiscal regime

The structure of the current fiscal regime was legislated through the Oil Taxation Act of 1975. Three main instruments applied:

- Royalty at 12.5 per cent.
- Petroleum revenue tax at 45 per cent. The tax base broadly equates to revenue receipts less the expenditure incurred in developing and operating the field. PRT offered three types of reliefs.

  - Uplift 35 per cent of capital expenditures
  - Oil allowance granting 250,000 tonnes for each 6 months to be exempt from PRT up to a cumulative maximum of 5 Mt
  - Safeguard introduced to limit the PRT liability in any chargeable period to 80 per cent of the amount by which gross profits exceed 15 per cent of cumulative expenditure

- CT at 52 per cent. Exploration costs fully deductible. Development costs were subject to various tax depreciation allowances. CT is the standard company tax on profits that applies to all companies operating in the UK. However, in the case of petroleum activity, there is a ring fence that prohibits the use of losses from other activities outside the ring fence to reduce the profits originating from within the UKCS ring fence. Losses and capital allowances inside the ring fence may be set against income arising outside the ring fence.

The changes in oil prices resulted in changes in fiscal terms:

- In 1978, the UK Government increased the PRT rate to 60 per cent, reduced the uplift allowance to 35 per cent and reduced the oil allowance from 1 Mt to 500,000 tonnes per year, with a maximum allowance of 5 Mt.
- In 1980, the PRT rate was raised to 70 per cent, thereby increasing the combined marginal rate to some 87 per cent. A new tax, supplementary petroleum duty (SPD), was introduced on a field by field basis by reference to 20 per cent of gross revenues less an oil allowance of 1 Mt per annum. SPD was payable on monthly basis.
- In 1983, SPD was replaced by advance petroleum revenue tax (APRT). Like SPD, APRT was imposed on gross revenues less an allowance of 1 Mt per year. The rate applied was 20 per cent and payments were to be made on monthly basis. However, unlike SPD, APRT was not a new tax but rather an instrument for accelerating the payment of PRT. It consisted of an advance payment of PRT that would be offset against the actual PRT payments due later in the life of a field. Additionally, the PRT rate was increased to 75 per cent, while royalty was abolished on fields receiving development consent after April 1982. The oil allowance against PRT was restored to 1 Mt per year for a maximum of ten years. In addition, a cross-field allowance was introduced with respect to PRT, permitting up to 10 per cent of the development costs of a new field to be offset against the PRT liabilities of another field.
- By the end of 1986, APRT was abolished and CT that applied on oil activity reduced to 35 per cent, though the desire to reduce the CT rate was driven by the broader requirements of UK industry as a whole, not just North Sea considerations.
- In 1993, PRT was reduced to 50 per cent on existing fields receiving development approval before April 1993 and abolished on all fields receiving development consent after that date.
- In 2002, a 10 per cent supplementary charge was applied on the same basis as normal CT, but there is no deduction for financing costs against the supplementary charge. Additionally, a 100 per cent capital investment allowance was introduced against both general corporation tax and the supplementary charge, instead of the 25 per cent allowance per annum declining balance previously available. Furthermore, royalty was abolished on older fields that had received development consent before 1983, in an attempt to encourage fuller exploitation of reserves from those fields.
- In 2005, in the light of rising oil prices, the UK Government doubled the supplementary charge to 20 per cent.

The UK offshore oil and gas industry is the highest taxed industry in the UK. As of 2006, fields developed since March 1993 are taxed at 50 per cent, liable for both CT at 30 per cent plus the supplementary charge at 20 per cent. The marginal tax rate rises to 75 per cent on fields developed prior to 1993, which are also liable for PRT at 50 per cent.

In general, during periods of low oil prices there is limited scope for higher taxation – indeed there is a necessity for a reversal of opportunistic tax increases to ensure that a competitive fiscal regime remains in place.

Cutting taxes is more difficult during recessions as governments' budgets are squeezed to assist troubled industrial sectors such as the banking sector and car industry and especially at a time where the oil industry is still seen as a significant tax payer. In the UK, over the period 2008/2009, the oil industry was the largest source of corporate tax revenue to the government. The loss of banking sector tax receipts was a major drawback; the sector contributed some 25 per cent of corporate tax revenues in recent years, but in 2008/2009 they claimed tax refunds on bad debts written off. This left the government even more reliant on the oil and gas sector.

In summary, price volatility strengthens the case for flexible and responsive fiscal regimes.

C *Ownership and control*[19]

The ownership of oil resources in the ground or under the seabed is more or less a closed and settled issue, where the government has asserted sovereign rights over the resources.[20] However, differences of view endure about the desirable degree of state 'ownership' in oil at the wellhead, and in the various stages of oil production and on the role private enterprise should play. Moreover, opinion about the amount of private involvement can vary over time, as pragmatic political imperatives to 'own' the entire oil industry process in a producing country clash with the realization that private sector skills are needed for exploration and production. Libya, Venezuela and Bolivia are examples to illustrating the strong sentiments surrounding this issue. In those countries, ownership of the entire production chain is often seen as reflecting government's sovereignty and power.

The perception still persists in some quarters that if a government allows private oil companies to operate in its oil and gas sector, it cedes control and loses sovereignty. Hence it is believed that the government renounces its sovereignty under both concessionary regimes and PSCs as IOCs are entitled to ownership of all or a proportion of the oil produced respectively. The government, however, is thought to maximize its control under a risk service agreement. A closer examination of regimes round the world proves that matters are less clear-cut. In fact, full public ownership could well mean loss of political control, poor accountability and the progressive transfer of direction and influence to unelected boards with their own powerful constituencies.

The question of ownership is mainly of legal and political significance. In economic terms, the key issue is how the underlying value from the barrel is shared between the state and investor. If the level of taxation on a barrel is, say 80 per cent, then the state receives the bulk of the value and it does not matter who technically owns or sells the barrel provided regulations are in place to ensure the barrels are sold at market value.

For private oil companies, potential ownership of the barrel at the delivery point is referred to as the ability to book reserves. The term 'book' means that the company in question has rights to take delivery of and sell the production in question to third parties and as a consequence is able to report these barrels as part of its aggregate reported production. Once reserves are booked they fall onto the balance sheet of an oil company as an increase in the asset base or replacement of produced assets. This is attractive for investors and can consequently increase shareholders' value, something most upstream oil and gas management see as significant at a strategic level when making investment decisions, hence their preference to book as many barrels as possible.

Concessionary regimes enable most of the production to be reported. The 'booking' of reserves under PSCs is actually the 'booking' of the oil to which the company will be entitled under cost-recovery and profit-oil sharing terms. Under risk service contracts it is rare for any production to be reported as company production. This partly explains why IOCs typically have a very clear preference for tax and royalty regimes or PSCs.

However, reported production is perhaps over simplistic as no two barrels are alike in terms of their underlying value; extraction costs vary widely as do the levels of taxation. Besides, ownership of the physical barrels should not be equated with control of the barrel. The latter can be devolved and policed through regulation, as is the case through the OECD, whilst value is controlled through the all important fiscal system.

Government control does not depend on the type of regime that is adopted. The North Sea, both the UK and the Norwegian continental shelves, is an example in which even when the ownership of the oil and gas production is granted to the private oil companies, the government maintains full control. In the North Sea, the industry operates under rigorous control. Not even a single well can be drilled in the British and Norwegian waters without government consent and approval of the development plans, including the production profile and other critical operational decisions. Investors require explicit government consent for a wide range of critical decisions and are required to comply with a lengthy list of regulatory requirements in respect of day-to-day oil field management and environmental protection.

Norway has one of the toughest fiscal regimes among countries that adopt concessionary regimes. The country also has a powerful state oil company (Statoil-Hydro, 70 per cent government owned), a petroleum fund worth more than $331 billion (2008), and a healthy private industry. In none of these examples, where concessionary regimes are applied, had the government lost control. In contrast, governments were in a strong position to successfully exploit the competitive instinct of the oil companies, and benefit from the deployment of IOCs resources to build successful oil and gas industries within a relatively short span of time.

It is rare for governments to intervene and reduce production unless due to an OPEC quota restriction (this is happening now in Angola). Governments usually want to maximize production and can push investors to invest in projects which offer poor returns. There are even threats to punish companies that under-invest, or to force a sale to a third party. Regardless the type of fiscal regime, the government can maintain control through the wider legal and regulatory framework.

D Fiscal stability[21]

Stability is an intangible yet crucial attribute of a fiscal regime; it is highly desirable but difficult to achieve, particularly given the very considerable volatility of oil prices. Perceptions of fiscal stability directly affect the confidence of investors in a host government's commitment to encouraging investment in the basin. Fiscal stability is important in the case of petroleum extraction activity, where long-term projects are the norm. New oil field developments take two to seven years to bring into production – often much longer if they are marginal or extensive appraisal is required – and may well be producing for 10–25 years.

Fiscal policies which focus on taxing rent at the peak of the each cycle whilst ignoring the pain of the troughs are unlikely to attract and sustain the interest of investors. Oil prices are volatile and it is futile to adjust fiscal policy to every micro movement in oil price. If a government introduces fiscal changes based on high oil prices, then it could be argued that they should consider the corollary – namely that they should reduce tax rates if oil prices fall. However, a wiser policy would be to accept that short-term fluctuations in oil prices should not be the basis for the application of fiscal changes.

Additionally, oil and gas projects have inherent levels of risk present at every stage, from exploration to abandonment. Unstable fiscal regimes negatively affect the confidence of investors in government policy: if a tax system changes frequently and unpredictably, it may seriously affect future development projects since it increases political risk and reduces the value placed by investors on future income streams. If the variation of taxes over project life can be minimized – that is, if the tax regime is stable – there is one less variable to worry the investor. One risk factor is either reduced or eliminated (see Section 3E on risk sharing below).

Stabilization clauses can give the legal comfort that fiscal stability is protected. In reality, most IOCs are often reluctant to invoke these mechanisms for fear of damaging their relationship and reputation with the host government.

If fiscal stability cannot be guaranteed, then investors have to live with the fiscal risk. This might be acceptable provided that the fiscal risk is compensated for by a lower level of government take. This is a characteristic witnessed in the UK where the regime is one of the most unstable in the world but the fiscal risk has over the long term been compensated for by competitive tax levels. In contrast, Norway offers a relatively stable regime, yet the reward is high marginal tax rate.[22] So investors face real choices – an unstable but low tax rate or a stable but high tax rate? Arguably oil companies should be happy to take fiscal risk in the same way that they accept oil price risk, geological risk, development risk and political risk. Shareholders and institutional investors can more effectively diversify the risk than oil companies. Attempts to lay the fiscal risk off in particular projects in exchange for very high tax levels may ultimately destroy shareholder value.

In reality, fiscal regimes cannot be expected to be set in stone. Circumstances are constantly changing in any basin. A certain degree of flexibility has to be allowed in any tax system if it is to respond to differing conditions, such as maturity, and to evolve as a result of major changes in the external environment. One of the clear problems of the oil industry is the lack of consistency in the messages it promotes when it comes to fiscal stability. The cynic would suggest that oil companies only want fiscal stability when they fear an increase in tax, while fiscal instability is welcomed if the prospect is for reductions in tax. Investors should recognize the inconsistency in this message and perhaps it will be better emphasize the competitiveness of a given fiscal regime instead. Such a position implicitly acknowledges the need for fiscal change provided the fiscal regime remains competitive. Clearly, an oil company would never advocate an increase in tax but perhaps would accept it if the economic circumstances and perceptions of excess 'rent' and returns demand it.

PSCs were originally devised to protect weak states from the IOCs. Today, however, PSCs are generally considered as protecting IOCs from the political risks associated with upstream investment in unstable and developing countries. By establishing the terms and conditions of exploration and development for the life of the project, PSCs are designed to protect foreign companies from risks such as arbitrary tax legislation, expropriation and unpredictable regulation. The most common response in contracts and agreements to sovereign risk is international arbitration. However, PSCs are not necessarily stable since one or even both signatories may want to renegotiate at some point in time. The inherent instability of contracts may result in some projects not being developed although they are economically attractive in general. The uncertainties over risk and reward-sharing prevent one or both parties from going ahead with the venture.

Emphasis on stability is equally important to governments. A tax system that has some level of predictability and reliability enables governments to know how much revenue will be collected and when. Stable government revenue clearly assists with reliable expenditure forecasting and budgeting.

E Risk sharing

Risk is present at all stages of an oil and gas project's life cycle. It can be geological (uncertainties with respect to structure and reservoir characteristics), exploratory (chance of failure), technical (reserves and cost estimation), economic (oil and gas prices), commercial (contractual, including third-party relationships) or political (regulatory and fiscal). Risk is not only limited to the exploration phase; 'only when the deposit is exhausted do you know precisely what the reserves were' (Andrews-Speed, 1998, p. 14).

There is no doubt that companies have the means to diversify certain levels of risks through, for instance, a large, worldwide portfolio, but every project has to offer the prospect of acceptable risked returns that cover the cost of capital. Given the wide range of countries that IOCs operate in and the equally diverse range of fiscal regimes that they find acceptable, investors have learnt to be pragmatic in terms of the fiscal burden they find acceptable. They naturally seek to secure the best terms they can, but this is a function of the competitive landscape and the opportunity cost of investing in better projects elsewhere. Strategic preferences differ from company to company and it certainly serves the interests of host governments to invite as many players as possible into a basin. A project that offers unacceptable returns to one company may well be acceptable to another. A regulatory framework that induces some investors to divest of assets with little activity also ensures that other companies who wish to invest have access to the opportunities and are not frustrated by unwilling investors.

The appetite of the investor depends not only on the level of tax, but also on the extent to which the government shares the project's risks. A popular construct is that in most fiscal regimes, be they a PSC or tax and royalty, with high levels of government take, the state is sharing in the project risk, by virtue of the fact that the investor gets a large tax deduction for his investment. In Norway, the marginal tax rate is 78 per cent. Therefore, if the investor invests US $100, then he gets a tax deduction of US $78, reducing his net exposure to US $22.

However, if the argument is taken to its logical conclusion then regimes with government take approaching 100 per cent should be the most attractive in eliminating risk as in these circumstances the state takes by implication nearly all the risk. In reality, the state permits relief for capital costs incurred but these are only of value if there is taxable income to relieve them against. Besides, in many cases it takes a number of years to secure the relief due to extended depreciation rules. For first-time investors, there will be no possibility of tax relief until the project commences production and generates taxable income. In these circumstances, all the exploration risk is borne by the investor: if there is no commercial discovery then the government will have taken no risk as the investor will have no income to shelter the expenditure. In contrast, if there is existing production from other projects then it will be possible to secure tax relief from failed exploration and development expenditure, assuming no ring-fencing. Countries like Norway have gone one step further and specifically reimburse tax relief (at a rate of 78 per cent) to all investors who are not in a tax paying position.

Under a PSC, the contract is signed (and signature bonuses paid) before the IOC has had the opportunity to explore the oilfield on offer. Only when oil is discovered and successfully developed can the IOC recover its exploration expenditures. Meanwhile, financial circumstances might change; borrowing can become more costly and prices can fall. That is why the IOC has a strong incentive to accelerate the exploration and development phases to secure an early return on up-front capital. The same is also true under a tax and royalty regime. The state, on the other hand, has no direct financial risk during the exploration phase but it has to monitor that the IOC complies with the work obligations specified in the contract (number of wells to be drilled, depth, technology, etc) and clearly wants any discoveries to be developed as quickly as possible (to boost government coffers). Since the IOC bears the entire exploration risk, it will need to ensure that the contract terms allow for sufficient rewards in the development phase of the project to remunerate these costs and risks. If the contract never enters into its production stage, the IOC will not be able to recover its exploration costs. If commerciality is declared and production begins, the IOC will want to recover its costs as early as possible.

During the development and production stage, apart from the reservoir risk, IOCs face additional uncertainties: the risk of cost increases, and price decreases. Higher costs can be recovered through the cost recovery mechanism and, in circumstances where uplift arrangements are in place, the impact of higher costs on project value and returns can be minimal to the investor but not to the host government. Governments like higher investment but dislike higher costs. Price risk refers to sudden significant changes in oil price. A low-price environment may result in the non-exploration of some oilfields, and the non-commerciality of existing operations. The level of price risk to the stakeholders (with the exception of risk service contracts where the government decides to take all the price risk) depends on the extent to which the contract is flexible to accommodate price changes. One of the consequences of the era of high prices and runaway costs[23] is a move towards revenue-based taxation which leaves the risk of cost increase with investors but links production tax and/or royalty rates to oil prices.

Risk service and buyback contracts work in a fundamentally different way. The investor normally has no price risk or volume exposure but is expected to take development cost exposure. This is asymmetric. Normally, higher oil prices result in higher development costs, hence under risk service contract the investor is exposed to cost inflation risk but gets no compensatory outcomes from the price upside or reservoir performance. This is an additional reason why most IOCs try to avoid risk service agreements. Such contracts seem to function best in respect of managing investment in existing and mature fields, where the investor is taking less risk (no exploration risk, little development risk, extensive subsurface database), rather than in new fields.

4 Conclusion

There is no fixed or universal solution to the ever-changing and evolving set of challenges which oil industry taxation presents. No two fiscal regimes are the same, indeed similar projects can be subject to different levels of government take within the same country if the fiscal regime has parameters determined by age of field. Also, fashions change and evolve about the preferred relationship which governments may wish to have with their oil and gas extraction sectors.

No single best oil tax regime exists. A country's tax regime is the product of balancing the need for an internationally competitive system with government policies that reflect the nation's specific priorities. As a result, oil-producing nations have implemented oil tax regimes that include a wide range of varying features to suit their individual conditions, political and social environments and oil price expectations. They can choose between concessionary regimes and contractual arrangements – the latter including PSCs and service contracts. Within the selected fiscal and contractual framework, governments have a wide range of options to pick from in designing the fiscal regime that best matches their own objectives and country conditions.

But, despite the diversity, there are some guiding economic principles that can be used when evaluating or designing a fiscal regime. And although each country has to design the fiscal regime that suits its own conditions and beliefs, it is important to learn from other countries' experience.

While one might expect to find tougher terms on contractual arrangements this is not necessarily the case. Concessionary arrangements can be just as tough, and while two concessionary regimes may have similar structures the tax rates applied within them can lead to major differences in outcome. The tax rate gives a poor guide to the underlying fiscal regimes, its strengths and effectiveness; fiscal reliefs and the way the tax base is calculated, lead to major differences between fiscal packages. Great care must be exercised in designing and maintaining a country's oil taxation regime. This is a dynamic process and the fiscal regime will need to evolve with the development and maturity of the basin and reflect competitive pressure in alternative hydrocarbon regions.

The importance of combining the vigor of competition and enterprise with the discipline of government approval and control is now recognized round the world. Involving IOCs allows not only the flow of investment and early revenues, it also frees up government resources to tackle other needs in the country. It can also be conducive to the transfer of technology and expertise. In countries where IOCs have no or only a limited role to play, the financial and other benefits accruing to the government are diluted by the need to find funds for investment. Payments of signature bonuses, for instance, are not applicable, as companies are unlikely to bid up-front large sums for what they believe are unattractive terms. As such, if it is early revenues governments are seeking to sustain their economies without overstretching their own budget, then service contracts may not be the best answer.

Oil and gas projects are by nature long-term, with much of the investment and costs being incurred up-front. A long-term partnership with a contractor may result in better overall field performance and much more value for the state than in the short-term approach. This is a major drawback of service contracts, as they normally last for nine years or less. Under a service contract, the IOCs interests are likely to be short-term. IOCs are bound to lack incentives to use new or proprietary technology or deploy their best people as the fixed fee and the short duration of the contract offer little upside or reward for superior performance. They tend to maximize output extraction in the first few years of the operation in order to recoup their investments within a scheduled time, without attention to an optimum recovery schedule over the reservoir's lifespan. Under buybacks, the contractor has even smaller incentive to reduce the long-term costs and improve efficiency, since the field is likely to be under the control of the government at the handover date. Iranian buybacks illustrate that problem. Iran has been suffering from declining production, low rate of recovery from existing fields and little wildcat exploration. However, in a situation where the contractors' involvement in a given project was, say, 15 or 20 years, they might be willing to use new and more expensive technology for longer-term gains.

There are no uniform solutions to the challenges of petroleum taxation. In reality, it does not have to be one regime or another. Countries offering different types of opportunities can opt for hybrid solutions. In the case of Iraq, for instance, a service contract could be applied to the large fields already in production, a production sharing contract to those in the development/exploration phase. Also, as experience in many OECD countries shows, a government does not need to own all the barrels in order to control. The latter can be well secured by a strong regulatory and fiscal framework. Transparency is equally important: the more transparent the means by which the government obtains revenues, the better informed the investors and the less the scope for manipulation and administrative discretion.

An oil producing country can work out its own destiny in sensible and practical ways which respect its own national sovereignty and yet call on the best qualities and expertise which the international oil industry can provide. The two are not mutually exclusive.

Notes

1 This chapter focuses more on oil than gas, but the fiscal principles studied apply equally to both hydrocarbons. For more detail on natural gas, see Kellas, Chapter 6.
2 Chapter 9 by McPherson provides more detail on state participation.
3 The original Aramco, the Arabian American Oil Company, became Saudi Aramco (Saudi Arabian Oil Company) in 1988, after the Saudi Government gradually acquired its participation interest in the company.
4 See McPherson, Chapter 9.
5 Sometimes know as a 'licensing system.'
6 Both Nigeria and Angola have older producing areas held under licences (concessions) that are not subject to PSAs.
7 It may simply be a standard licence, with no special agreement, but the licence will set out the rights and obligations of the parties that are not already enshrined in statute law.
8 For more detail, see Chapter 8 by Land.
9 Most or all found under contractual regimes as well; for instance, in Angola the bonus reached $1 billion per block of 4,100 km^2.
10 Production bonuses are not royalties. The former are fixed whereas the latter depend on field performance and oil price. Production bonus triggers vary – they can be linked to production rate or cumulative production.
11 Cramton provides a detailed treatment of auctions in Chapter 10.
12 Strictly, costs allowable for recovery out of cost oil.
13 ROR and R-factor have similar economic impacts but with a distinction that the R-factor does not take time value of money into account.
14 Payment of income tax is usually necessary to achieve foreign tax credit in the investor's home jurisdiction.
15 Barrows, 2000, p.105.
16 The net present value of the tax divided by the pre-tax net present value of the project. Also called 'average effective tax rate.'
17 Chapter 7 by Daniel *et al* gives more detail on evaluating resource tax regimes.
18 This is the same concept as the average effective tax rate (AETR) used in wider tax analysis. See Chapter 2 by Boadway and Keen or Chapter 7 by Daniel *et al.*
19 See Chapter 9 on state participation.

20 Situations in which fields span national jurisdictions, or boundaries are disputed, can cause difficulty.
21 This is discussed in more detail in Chapter 14 by Daniel and Sunley.
22 Chapter 15, by Osmundsen, discusses how Norway has acquired a reputation for fiscal stability.
23 Costs follow oil price with a lag. Higher oil prices mean more cash to invest, more investment stretches supply chain resources which then increase their profit margin to exploit skills and equipment shortages. The opposite happens when oil prices fall. The problem became accentuated between 2004 and 2008 as it coincided with global economic boom putting pressure on all commodities and skills availability.

References

Bindemann, Kirsten (1999), 'Production Sharing Analysis,' WPM No. 25, (Oxford: Oxford Institute for Energy Studies).

Blinn, Keith, Claude Duval and Honore Le Leuch (1986), 'International Petroleum Exploration and Exploitation Agreements,' Legal, Economic and Policy Aspects, Barrows Company Inc.

Boadway, Robin and Michael Keen (2010), 'Theoretical Perspectives On Resource Tax Design,' in Philip Daniel, Michael Keen and Charles McPherson (eds) *The Taxation of Petroleum and Minerals: Principles, Problems and Practice.*

Bond Stephen, Michael Devereux, and Michael Saunders (1987), *North Sea Taxation for the 1990s* (London: Institute for Fiscal Studies).

Cramton, Peter (2010), 'How Best to Auction Natural Resources,' in Philip Daniel, Michael Keen and Charles McPherson (eds) *The Taxation of Petroleum and Minerals: Principles, Problems and Practice.*

Crawson, Philip (2004), *Astride Mining: Issues and Policies for the Minerals Industry* (Mining Journal Books).

Daniel, Philip, Brenton Goldsworthy, Wojciech Maliszewski, Diego Mesa Puyo and Alistair Watson (2010), 'Evaluating Fiscal Regimes for Resource Projects,' in Philip Daniel, Michael Keen and Charles McPherson (eds) *The Taxation of Petroleum and Minerals: Principles, Problems and Practice.*

Daniel, Philip and Emil Sunley (2010), 'Contractual Assurances of Fiscal Stability,' in Philip Daniel, Michael Keen and Charles McPherson (eds) *The Taxation of Petroleum and Minerals: Principles, Problems and Practice.*

Dasgputa, Partha, and Joseph Stiglitz (1971), 'Differential Taxation, Public Production and Economic Efficiency,' *Review of Economic Studies*, Vol. 38, pp. 151–174.

Diamond, Peter and James Mirrlees (1971) 'Optimal Taxation and Public Production II: Tax Rules,' *American Economic Review*, Vol. 41, pp. 277–296.

Garnaut, Ross and Anthony Clunies Ross (1983), *Taxation of Mineral Rents* (New York: Oxford University Press).

—— (1975), 'Uncertainty, Risk Aversion and the Taxing of Natural Resource Projects,' *Economic Journal*, Vol. 85, pp. 272–287.

Heady, Christopher (1993), 'Optimal Taxation as a Guide to Tax Policy: A Survey,' *Fiscal Studies*, Vol. 14, pp. 15–41.

Johnston, Daniel (1998), *International Petroleum Fiscal Systems and Production Sharing Contracts* (PennWell Books).

Kellas, Graham (2010), 'Natural Gas: Experience and Issues,' in Philip Daniel, Michael Keen and Charles McPherson (eds) *The Taxation of Petroleum and Minerals: Principles, Problems and Practice.*

Kemp, Alex and Linda Stephens (1997), 'The UK Petroleum Fiscal System in Retrospect,' mimeo (Aberdeen: University of Aberdeen).

Land, Bryan (2010), 'Resource Rent Taxation—Theory and Experience,' in Philip Daniel, Michael Keen and Charles McPherson (eds) *The Taxation of Petroleum and Minerals: Principles, Problems and Practice.*

McPherson, Charles (2010), 'State Participation in the Natural Resources Sectors: Evolution, Issues and Outlook,' in Philip Daniel, Michael Keen and Charles McPherson (eds) *The Taxation of Petroleum and Minerals: Principles, Problems and Practice.*

—— and Keith Palmer (1984), 'New Approaches to Profit Sharing in Developing Countries,' *Oil and Gas Journal*, Vol. 119.

Mommer, Bernard (2001), *Fiscal Regimes and Oil Revenues in the UK, Alaska and Venezuela* (Oxford: Oxford Institute for Energy Studies).

—— (1996), *Bernard Mommer Defends Petroleum Royalty as an Efficient Rent-Collecting Device* (Oxford: Oxford Energy Forum).

Musgrave, Richard (1982), 'A Brief History of Fiscal Doctrine,' in *Handbook of Public Economics*, A. Auerbach and M. Feldstein (eds), Vol. 1, pp. 1–59 (Amsterdam: North Holland).

Nakhle Carole (2007), 'Do High Oil Prices Justify an Increase in Taxation in a Mature Oil Province? The Case of the UK Continental Shelf,' *Energy Policy*, Vol. 35, pp. 4305–4318.

—— (2008a), 'Iraq's Oil Future: Finding the Right Framework,' Surrey Energy Economics Centre, University of Surrey, United Kingdom (Washington DC: study sponsored by the International Tax and Investment Centre).

—— (2008b), *Petroleum Taxation: Sharing the Oil Wealth* (London: Routledge).

Petroleum Intelligence Weekly (2009), 'Price Slump Tests Mettle of Nationalists,' Energy Intelligence Group, Monday, January 26.

Samuelson, Paul (1986), 'Theory of Optimal Taxation,' *Journal of Public Economics*, Vol. 30, pp. 137–143.

Sarma, J.V.M. and Naresh, Gautam (2001), 'Mineral Taxation Around the World: Trends and Issues,' Asia-Pacific Tax Bulletin, pp. 2–10.

Smith, Ben (1999), 'The Impossibility of a Neutral Resource Rent Tax,' Faculty of Economics and Commerce, Working Paper No. 380, Australian National University.

Sunley, Emil, Thomas Baunsgaard and Dominique Simard (2002), 'Revenue from the Oil and Gas Sector: Issues and Country Experience,' in J.M. Davis, R. Ossowski, and A. Fedelino (eds) *Fiscal Policy Formulation and Implementation in Oil-Producing Countries*, pp. 153–183 (Washington DC: International Monetary Fund).

Tordo, Silvana (2007), 'Fiscal Systems for Hydrocarbons: Design Issues,' Working Paper No. 123 (Washington DC: World Bank).

Van Kooten, Gerrit Cornelis and Erwin H. Bulte (2001), *The Economics of Nature – Managing Biological Assets* (Oxford: Blackwell).

Watkins, Campbell (2001), 'Atlantic Petroleum Royalties: Fair Deal or Raw Deal,' *The AIMS Oil and Gas Papers*, Atlantic Institute for Market Studies (Halifax, Nova Scotia).

5 International mineral taxation

Experience and issues

Lindsay Hogan and Brenton Goldsworthy

1 Introduction

Minerals (other than petroleum) are an important source of export earnings and taxation revenue in a wide range of countries. For example, world exports of selected major mineral commodities were valued at US$448 billion in 2006 comprising coal (11 percent), ores and concentrates (24 percent) and metals (65 percent) (see Table 5.1). Nearly half of world exports of these commodities were sourced from developing economies: 60 percent for ores and concentrates, 46 percent for metals and 45 percent for coal. Mineral taxation revenue accounts for a significant share of total fiscal revenue in several countries: most notably, over the period 2000–2005, this share was 62.5 percent in Botswana, 17.9 percent in Papua New Guinea, 17.8 percent in Guinea, 9.4 percent in Chile, 8.2 percent in Mongolia and 5.9 percent in Namibia (IMF 2007).

In Chapter 2, Boadway and Keen (2009) present an extensive discussion of resource taxation issues, and the evaluation of resource tax regimes is discussed by Daniel *et al.* in Chapter 7 with particular reference to the oil industry. There are two main objectives in this chapter: first, to examine the international evolution of fiscal regimes in minerals and, second, to discuss key economic issues in mineral taxation using an approach complementary to that in Chapter 7. In particular, this chapter uses a simple economic framework – the certainty equivalent approach – to illuminate the implications of four key fiscal instruments for private risk assessments.

The structure of the chapter is as follows. In Section 2, the international evolution of fiscal regimes in minerals is discussed. In Section 3, criteria for assessing fiscal instruments are presented and, based on the approach taken in Baunsgaard (2001), an overview of the advantages and disadvantages of the most common mineral taxation options is provided. In Section 4, economic issues in the design of selected mineral taxation options are discussed further and a simplified graphical representation of these options is provided. In Section 5, simulations of some hypothetical resource projects are presented, based on the certainty equivalent approach to the assessment of risky projects, to illustrate some important implications of key mineral taxation options. Concluding comments are provided in Section 6.

Table 5.1 World exports for selected mineral commodities, 2006

	Developed economies		Developing economies		World
	Exports	Share of world	Exports	Share of world	
	US$b	%	US$b	%	US$b
Coal	27.3	55.4	22.0	44.6	49.3
Ores and concentrates					
Iron ore and concentrates	14.8	45.1	18.0	54.9	32.8
Copper ores and concentrates	6.3	19.7	25.6	80.3	31.8
Nickel ores and concentrates	4.0	52.6	3.6	47.4	7.5
Aluminium ores and concentrates[1]	7.6	60.6	4.9	39.4	12.6
Ores and concentrates of base metals, nes	10.6	46.2	12.3	53.8	22.9
Total of above	43.2	40.1	64.4	59.9	107.6
Metals					
Silver, platinum[2]	19.8	55.7	15.7	44.3	35.5
Copper	46.7	42.1	64.1	57.9	110.8
Nickel	13.8	62.9	8.1	37.1	21.9
Aluminium	65.2	65.2	34.9	34.8	100.1
Lead	2.0	53.9	1.7	46.1	3.8
Zinc	8.6	54.7	7.1	45.3	15.7
Tin	0.7	19.1	2.7	80.9	3.4
Total of above	156.7	53.8	134.5	46.2	291.2
Total of above	227.2	50.7	220.9	49.3	448.1

Source: United Nations Commodity Trade Statistics, *Yearbook 2006* (available at: http//comtrade. un.org/pb/).

Note
1 Including alumina.
2 Includes other metals of the platinum group.

2 Evolution of fiscal regimes for minerals

Fiscal regimes for minerals (and other resources) tend to differ from those found in other sectors due to the presence of resource rents and unusual risks. Resource rents represent surplus revenues from a deposit after the payment of all exploration, development and extraction costs, including an investor's risk-adjusted required return on investment.[1] Since rent is pure surplus, it can be taxed whilst upholding the core taxation principle of neutrality. Furthermore, governments aim to capture the resource rent, not least because minerals are typically owned by the state.

The unusual and substantial risks inherent in the mining sector need to be emphasized. These risks include, for example: a long exploration period with uncertain geological outcomes; a large significant outlay of development capital that is not transportable (i.e. becomes "sunk") once invested; uncertain future revenues due to very volatile and unpredictable mineral prices; a long period of production to reach break-event point, which exposes the investor to political and policy instability; and potentially significant environmental impacts requiring large costs to be incurred when the mine closes, and often during production to support affected local communities. These considerations motivate measures, such as accelerated depreciation and extended loss-carry forward limits, to hasten payback of initial outlays.

While rents and risks are also present in other sectors, their scale and characteristics (such as the rent being derived from minerals owned by the state) have led to special tax treatment of the sector, using a wide variety of fiscal instruments.[2] These instruments include royalties, resource rent taxes, windfall taxes, corporate income taxes and state ownership. Each has its advantages and disadvantages with respect to the impact on investor behavior, the degree of progressivity (i.e. extent to which the "government take" increases as a project's profitability increases), the sharing of risk between the government and investor, and the administrative and compliance costs. The characteristics of fiscal instruments are discussed in Section 3.

Mineral fiscal regimes vary widely between countries and minerals for a number of reasons. For example, the level of taxation is likely to vary with country risk.[3] This is because investors base their decisions on risk-adjusted rates of return, and the lower the country risk the higher the level of taxation consistent with a given project exceeding the minimum required return. The royalty rate and other instruments most directly targeted at rent are also likely to vary with the perceptions of the size of rent available.[4] This explains why high value minerals like diamonds and gold tend to attract a higher royalty rate.

The optimal mix of fiscal instruments will also vary depending on the country's preferences and capabilities. Some governments may prefer production-based

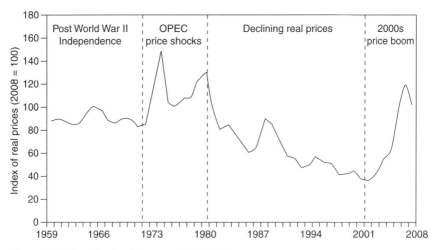

Figure 5.1 Mineral prices[1] (source: IMF WEO).

Note
1 Excludes oil (simple average of Aluminium, Copper, Gold, Iron Ore, Nickel, Tin, Uranium and Zinc).

instruments as they are easier to administer and provide earlier and more stable revenue. However, as this shifts more of the risk onto companies, governments will most likely need to accept a lower overall expected level of taxation.[5] Other countries might therefore prefer a more progressive regime that involves the government assuming more risk but also expecting to receive a higher take from profits. A summary of current arrangements for selected countries is provided in Appendix I.

In addition to variation between countries, a number of global trends can be identified over the past half century. These have tended to be punctuated by external events that shifted the balance of power between mineral producing countries and investors. This shift in power, which is evident in the evolution of mineral prices (Figure 5.1), can usefully be analyzed with reference to a number of distinct periods.[6] The experiences of Papua New Guinea, Chile and Zambia provide useful illustrations of these trends (Box 5.1).

Box 5.1 Selected country experiences

Chile – state participation, private competition, royalty rates

By the late 1960s, Chile's four principal copper mines were owned by US companies. Frustrated by low revenues, successive governments introduced measures to increase government participation in the mines via Codelco (a state owned enterprise). The mines were eventually nationalized after the socialist Salvador Allende won the 1971 election. After Pinochet's coup in 1973, the nationalized mines remained under Codelco's control but market-oriented reforms paved the way for new foreign investment. Chilean copper production grew rapidly but the taxes paid by private companies were comparatively low (Pizarro, 2004). In part, this reflected generous fiscal terms designed to attract new investment, including a zero royalty rate. Dissatisfaction over the private companies' contribution to revenue grew in line with rising copper prices. After a failed attempt to introduce a profit-based royalty in 2004, a sliding scale royalty (0–5 percent) based on sales became effective in 2006.

Papua New Guinea – renegotiation, additional profits tax

Bougainville Copper Limited (BCL) commenced commercial production at the Panguna mine in 1972. The mine was highly profitable and in 1974 the government sought to renegotiate terms. A revised agreement, which became effective in December of that year, eliminated various tax incentives, and introduced an additional profits tax under which the mine was subject to a marginal rate of 70 percent after it had earned a 15 percent rate of return on funds invested. An additional profits tax became an integral part of the fiscal regime for all mines, seen as a means of capturing a large share of any future rents, whilst still attracting investment by ensuring an adequate return to the investor. From the late 1980s successive governments made a number of changes, and in 2002, when real mineral prices were near record lows, the terms were revised once more with a view to making the sector more attractive to investors. Key changes included: abolishing the additional profits tax (which no company other than BCL is understood to have paid); relaxing ring-fencing rules; more attractive accelerated depreciation arrangements; and elimination of loss-carry forward time limits.

Zambia – state participation, privatization, renegotiation, windfall tax

After independence in 1964, President Kaunda nationalized the copper industry, and the Zambia Consolidated Copper Mines (ZCCM) conglomerate was created. The industry flourished, with rising copper prices and the mineral rights now accruing to the state (formerly benefiting the British South African Mining Company). However, a combination of falling prices and deteriorating mining infrastructure led to declining copper production and large deficits for ZCCM and the government. A market-reform orientated government led by President Chiluba privatized various operating divisions of ZCCM in 1997–2000.

The Mines and Minerals Act of 1995, which facilitated the privatization process, permitted the government to enter into "Development Agreements" under which fiscal terms could be negotiated on a mine-by-mine basis. Typical fiscal terms were generous (e.g. a royalty rate of 0.6 percent and a company income tax rate of 25 percent) and "locked" in by fiscal stability agreements. While successfully rejuvenating the copper industry, the government take was low and was considered unacceptable when copper prices rose unexpectedly. In 2008, the government controversially scrapped development agreements and introduced a new fiscal regime, which included a higher royalty rate (3 percent), a variable income tax and a windfall tax applied to the value of production with a sliding scale of rates triggered by the copper price. The windfall tax was repealed in 2009.

A Before World War II

The typical arrangement prior to World War II was for the government to grant concessions to corporations or investors to explore for and extract mineral resources. In return, the government received payments through mechanisms such as initial bonuses, royalties and land rental fees. Income taxes were less common in developing countries. Royalties, which provided the bulk of revenues, were levied on production at relatively low rates. For countries occupied by colonial powers, an implication of low taxes was that much of the rent flowed out of the country to corporations and investors in the colonial power.

B After World War II – independence

The shift to independence after World War II in much of the mineral-rich world led to an increased focus on a country's sovereignty over its natural resources. A central element of this was a desire for the home government to attain a larger share of resource rents. Against a background of reconstruction and a related rapid increase in demand for raw materials, the environment was ripe for an overhaul of existing mining arrangements in favor of mineral producing countries. The key developments were the following:

• *State ownership*. Many governments sought to increase state ownership and control over mineral assets through nationalization, equity participation or joint ventures. Nationalization began in Bolivia with tin mining in 1952 and later occurred in Chile (copper), Peru (iron ore, copper), Venezuela (iron ore), Zambia (copper), Democratic Republic of the Congo (formerly Zaire; copper), Ghana (gold), and Jamaica, Guyana and Suriname (bauxite). In addition to attaining a larger share of rents, a major driving force behind increased state ownership was the belief that greater control over mineral assets would lead to greater beneficial spillovers to the rest of the economy.[7]

• *Ad valorem royalties*. Royalties based on production value, and not simply volume, became increasingly common. The royalty was most often applied at a constant rate for a specified mineral. More recently, several jurisdictions have adopted sliding scales based on price, production, sales and even perceived cost of operation.[8] In developed countries with advanced tax administrations, there has been a recent shift toward profit-based royalties (most provinces in Canada, the Northern Territory in Australia, and Nevada in the United States). The shift from volume-based to value- and profit-based royalties represents an attempt to more accurately target rent.

• *Income tax*. In many countries, there was a shift from royalty to income tax as the major source of revenue. Investment incentives were – and still are – often incorporated into the income tax regime, most commonly through accelerated depreciation allowances, loss-carry forward provisions and, for exploration and mining companies, the full expensing of exploration costs.

• *Introduction of other payments*. Most developing countries introduced withholding taxes on dividends, interest and foreign-provided services. Withholding taxes are now commonly used, both to provide revenue and to counteract tax avoidance and evasion through, for example, use of related party debt and payment of contractors at non-market prices. Customs and excise duties, sales taxes and, more recently, value added taxes were also introduced, although many countries now provide exemptions to encourage investment and to ease the administrative burden from having mining companies in large VAT refund situations due to the zero rating on their exports.

C 1970s price shocks

In 1973–1974, oil prices quadrupled following a decision of the Organization of Petroleum Exporting Countries (OPEC) to restrict oil production. Many mineral prices also increased sharply around this time, albeit by a much smaller amount and partly influenced by independent factors.[9] These developments further encouraged mineral producing countries in their efforts to capture a higher share of the rent through taxation and nationalization. Papua New Guinea, followed by others, introduced special instruments designed to increase the government "take" in boom times. The specific form varied from country to country but most typical was a cash flow-based tax that increased the marginal rate of income tax for projects that earned more than a specified rate of return.[10] There was also a growing focus on using the fiscal regime to encourage local processing, such as by imposing export duties on raw materials.

D Declining real mineral prices: 1980s and 1990s

In the 1980s and 1990s, mineral prices declined in real terms. State-owned enter-prises, which often struggled to deliver the expected higher revenues in the boom years due to inefficient operations, became an even greater drain on government finances. Combined with a poor economic performance overall, a high debt burden, and the break-up of the Soviet Union which discredited central planning, mineral producers reconsidered the role of the state. Some began a process of privatizing their mining industry and confined government's role to one of regulation and investment promotion. Others commercialized state enterprises, lowered the level of state participation and placed greater emphasis on attracting private sector involve-ment. Countries that made substantive changes in this direction included Bolivia, Chile, the Democratic Republic of Congo, Ghana, Indonesia, Peru and Zambia.

Depressed prices discouraged mineral exploration and mine development. In an effort to promote activity in the sector and foreign direct investment more broadly, countries became increasingly concerned with how their level of mining and non-mining taxation compared with that of competitors. International competition prompted revised fiscal terms in a number of countries that, in general, involved lower rates. Mining corporate tax rates fell from an average of 50 percent to 30–40 percent (Kumar, 1995; non-mining rates fell similarly), royalty rates were lowered and reduced to zero in Chile,[11] and Indonesia, Papua New Guinea and Namibia (variable income tax) removed additional profits taxes. Table 5.2 illustrates the

Table 5.2 Mining corporate income tax rates

	1983	1991	2008
Australia	46	39	30
Canada[1]	38	29	22
Chile	50	35	35
Indonesia	45*	35	30
Mexico	42	35	28
Papua New Guinea	36.5*	35*	30
South Africa[2]	46–55†	50–69†	28
USA[1]	46	34	35
Zambia[3]	45	45	30*†

Source: *Mining Taxation: A Global Survey*, Coopers & Lybrand, Washington, DC, 1991 and 1983.

Notes
* denotes additional profits/windfall tax also applies.
† denotes a variable income tax formula.
1 Federal only.
2 High rate is maximum payable for gold under variable income tax formula. Low rate is non-gold, non-diamond flat rate. Diamond mining was subject to 52% in 1983 and 56% in 1991.
3 In 2008, a flat rate of 30% applies if the windfall tax based on price is payable, otherwise variable income tax applies with a minimum rate of 30%.

decline in corporate income taxes in select countries. At around the same time, pressures emerged to introduce or strengthen environmental, safety and community obligations, thereby increasing some non-fiscal costs.

E 2002–2008 price boom

In 2002 the trend decline in real mineral prices suddenly changed course with prices tripling over a five-year period, largely on account of rapid demand growth in China and other emerging market economies.[12] This prompted governments to reassess whether they were receiving a reasonable share of increased rents. Liberia introduced a resource rent tax, and Mongolia and Zambia introduced windfall taxes triggered by prices. Kazakhstan, Botswana and South Africa (gold) were percipient in having progressive arrangements in place prior to the boom. Among developed countries, the application of windfall taxes has been debated in the United States, United Kingdom and Australia, most commonly focused on the petroleum industry. As many mining companies are domiciled in these countries, the application of windfall taxes would capture rents otherwise taxable in the host countries.

During this period there has also been an increased emphasis on transparency, in recognition that weak governance has contributed to the persistence of poverty in resource-rich countries. The Extractive Industries Transparency Initiative (EITI), launched in 2002, attempts to strengthen governance through the verification and publication of company payments and government revenues from extractive industries. The EITI is gaining adherents among developing countries and mining companies operating within them.[13]

IMF (2007) provides a guide on resource revenue transparency containing a number of recommendations based on best practice. One encouraging development is that there is a movement away from negotiating fiscal terms on a mine-by-mine basis towards establishing terms applicable to all mining projects in general legislation.[14] In addition to being more transparent, this reduces administrative costs and probably the investor's perception of risk that the government will renege on the terms. Furthermore, the investor would invariably have more information than the government on the profitability of the project, placing them in a stronger negotiating position.

3 Criteria for assessing fiscal instruments

Baunsgaard (2001) evaluated several fiscal instruments in mineral taxation including: direct tax instruments (corporate income tax, progressive profit tax and the resource rent tax), indirect tax instruments (royalties, import duties and the value added tax) and non-tax instruments (fixed fees and bonus payments, production sharing and state equity). Using the ratings approach in Baunsgaard (2001), Table 5.3 provides an overview of the advantages and disadvantages of the most common fiscal instruments in the mining sector based on seven criteria: neutrality, stability, project risk, flexibility, fiscal loss, revenue delay and administration. These criteria

Table 5.3 Fiscal instruments

	Neutrality	Investor risk		Rent collection and government risk			Administration and compliance
		Stability	Project risk	Flexibility	Fiscal loss	Revenue delay	
Rent-based taxes							
Resource rent tax	+2	+8	+2	+3	-2	-3	-3
Excess profits tax	+1	+3	+2	+2	-1	-1	-2
Profit-based taxes							
Corporate income tax	-1	+1	0	+1	0	0	-1
Output-based royalties							
Profit-based royalty	-1	+1	0	+1	0	+1	-1
Ad valorem royalty	-2	0	-1	-1	+1	+2	+1
Graduated windfall tax	-2	+2	+1	0	0	0	+1
price-based							
Specific royalty	-3	-1	-2	-2	+2	+2	+2
State equity							
Paid equity	+3	+1	+3	+3	-3	-1	+3
Carried interest	+2	+3	0	+3	-2	-3	+1

Sources: Rating system based on Garnaut and Clunies Ross (1975) and Baunsgaard (2001).

Note

7 point scale -3 to +3, where +3 means that the instrument performs extremely well on the criterion and -3 signifies the opposite.

and the rationale for the assessments in the table are discussed below. It should be emphasized that the comparative assessment is broadly indicative and will vary according to the actual settings for the fiscal parameters including, for example, the tax and royalty rates. The fiscal instruments are defined in Box 5.2.

Although it is useful to look at the characteristics of each instrument in isolation, a regime will typically comprise multiple instruments in which case it is necessary to assess the tax system in its entirety.[15] For example, the international trend toward lower corporate income tax rates in recent decades may have implications for the design of other fiscal instruments to ensure that a reasonable share of the resource rent is collected by the government.

Box 5.2   Fiscal instruments

Rent-based taxes[16]

- *Brown tax* – named after Brown (1948), this is levied as a constant percentage of the annual net cash flow (the difference between total revenue and total costs) of a resource project with cash payments made to private investors in years of negative net cash flow. The Brown tax is a useful benchmark against which to assess other policy options, but is not considered to be a feasible policy option for implementation since it involves cash rebates to private investors.[17]
- *Resource rent tax* – rather than providing a cash rebate, negative net cash flows are accumulated at a threshold rate and offset against future profit. When this balance turns positive it becomes taxable at the rate of the resource rent tax. The resource rent tax was first proposed by Garnaut and Clunies Ross (1975) for natural resource projects in developing countries to enable more of the net economic benefits of these projects to accrue to the domestic economy.
- *Excess profits tax* – the government collects a percentage of a project's net cash flow when the investment payback ratio (the "R-factor") exceeds one. The R-factor is the ratio of cumulative receipts over cumulative costs (including the upfront investment). This method differs from the resource rent tax in that it does not take explicit account of the time value of money or the required return of the investor. No excess profits tax in the R-factor form has been applied to the mining sector.

Profit-based taxes and royalties

- *Corporate income tax* – typically an important part of the fiscal regime for all countries; a higher tax rate may be applied to mineral companies within the standard corporate income tax regime, and it may be designed to vary with taxable income (e.g. Botswana).
- *Profit-based royalty* – the government collects a percentage of a project's profit; typically based on some measure of accounting profit. This differs from the standard income tax in that it is levied on a given project rather than the corporation.

Output-based royalties

- *Ad valorem royalty* – the government collects a percentage of a project's value of production.
- *Graduated price-based windfall tax* – the government collects a percentage of a project's value of production with the tax rate on a sliding scale based on price (that is, a higher tax rate is triggered by a higher commodity price).
- *Specific royalty* – the government collects a charge per physical unit of production.

State equity

- *Paid equity* – the government becomes a joint venture partner in the project. Paid equity on commercial terms is analogous to a Brown tax where the tax rate is equal to the share of equity participation.
- *Carried interest* – the government acquires its equity share in the project from the production proceeds including an interest charge. Carried interest is analogous to a resource rent tax where the tax rate is equal to the equity share and the threshold rate of return is equal to the interest rate on the carry.

A Economic efficiency

Neutrality

A fiscal instrument is neutral if an action or project that is assessed to be financially viable in the absence of the fiscal instrument (that is, profitable or economic before tax) remains viable after the fiscal instrument is applied. Typically, the neutrality criterion is used to evaluate the extent to which fiscal instruments may have a negative impact on mineral exploration, development, production and closure decisions. In particular, some projects that are viable before tax may become unprofitable after a fiscal instrument is applied, resulting in efficiency losses.

Compared with output-based royalties, rent- and profit-based taxes and state equity instruments rank more highly under this criterion since the government take under these arrangements tends to vary with project profitability. Notably, there are differing degrees of efficiency within this group and the resource rent tax ranks more highly than profit-based taxes.

Investor risk

Investor risk is incorporated in the economic efficiency criterion since fiscal instruments may have a significant impact on private risk assessments and influence industry outcomes.

SOVEREIGN RISK (STABILITY)

Sovereign risk refers to the investor's assessment of the political or policy risks associated with a resource project. Changes in the fiscal settings over the life of a project may have a significant impact on the future profitability of the project. In particular, the risk of future adverse policy change may influence the initial decision to invest in the project: the higher the perceived risk, the higher the investor's risk premium (all else constant), and the lower the assessed viability of the project. Osmundsen provides in Chapter 15 a useful discussion of the issue of sovereign risk, or time consistency issues more broadly, in petroleum resource taxation with particular reference to developments in Norway.

Rent and profit-based taxes and state equity instruments rank more highly under this criterion since the government take tends to vary with project profitability so that the government may be less likely to adjust fiscal settings in response to major changes in market conditions. A major concern under output-based royalties is the risk of higher royalty rates during mining booms (including the risk of delay in reducing rates following the end of the boom). However, while royalties have a lower ranking, they too can contribute to fiscal regime stability by ensuring a politically popular payment whenever production occurs.

PROJECT RISK

Project risk refers to the investor's assessment of the market risks associated with a resource project. The choice of fiscal instrument may have significant implications for the investor's assessment of project risk and hence project viability. A fiscal instrument for which tax revenue is not responsive to changes in future market conditions results in greater variability in future possible outcomes for project profitability compared with an alternative fiscal instrument where the tax revenue varies with project profitability.

Rent and profit-based taxes and state equity instruments rank more highly under this criterion since the government take tends to vary with project profitability and both the investor and government share in the risks of adverse market outcomes.

B Rent collection and government risk

Rent collection – flexibility

Flexibility refers to the responsiveness of fiscal instruments to changes in future market conditions – that is, the capacity of fiscal instruments to collect a reasonable share of the resource rent over time under a range of future market outcomes (including both better and worse than expected outcomes).

Rent and profit-based taxes and state equity instruments rank more highly under this criterion since the government take tends to vary with project profitability.

Government risk

A major concern expressed by a wide range of governments is the risk associated with the magnitude and timing of mineral taxation revenue, specifically the risk of fiscal loss and revenue delay.

FISCAL LOSS

Fiscal loss refers to the situation where the government obtains a lower than expected return to the resource, particularly under adverse market outcomes. The paid equity instrument also exposes the government to the risk of project failure with losses including part or all of the equity. A fiscal instrument where tax revenue is not responsive to changes in future market conditions results in greater stability in tax revenue flows, reducing the risk of fiscal loss (but also not managing well the risk of fiscal gain).

Output-based instruments rank more highly under this criterion since the government receives royalty payments in all years in which production from the resource project is positive, including any in which losses may occur.

REVENUE DELAY

Revenue delay refers to the situation where the government does not start to collect tax revenue until some time after the project's production commencement date. Under a resource rent tax, for example, revenue collection is delayed until investors have received a specified threshold rate of return on their capital outlays.

Output-based instruments rank more highly under this criterion since royalty revenue is collected throughout the production phase of the project.

Dependence on minerals taxation revenue and stability of the revenue stream are significant issues, particularly in several developing economies. In Chapter 2, Boadway and Keen provide a useful discussion of the issue of government preferences for the timing of resource tax revenue.

C Administration and compliance costs

Administration and compliance costs refer, respectively, to the costs incurred by government in designing, implementing and monitoring compliance with a fiscal instrument and to the costs incurred by investors in complying with the fiscal instrument. In general, both types of cost associated with a fiscal instrument tend to be higher if the information requirements of the policy are higher. Ideally, information on project profitability is required for all fiscal instruments to determine appropriate fiscal settings. Output-based instruments tend to require less information that is more readily verified than is the case with rent- or profit-based instruments (which also require an assessment of expenditures). However, output-based instruments are also more likely to be adjusted over time as market conditions change, increasing administrative and compliance costs. Baunsgaard (2001) also includes international tax arrangements, particularly the availability of tax credits, as a criterion for evaluating fiscal instruments.

Output-based instruments tend to rank more highly under this criterion since the information requirements tend to be lower than for profit-based instruments. Rent-based taxes rank the lowest due to the additional calculations required but, as Land (2009) notes in Chapter 8, they are in some respects simpler than profit-based taxes in that capital investments are expensed in full so there is no need to worry about depreciation.

The Chapters by Calder (11 and 12), Land (8) and Mullins (13) provide useful discussions of resource tax administration issues, the last two focusing on issues related to resource rent taxation and international considerations, respectively. Netback pricing issues are discussed in Chapter 6 by Kellas. Otto *et al.* (2006) and IMF (2007) examine issues associated with administrative feasibility and resource revenue management in developing economies. Increasing transparency and ensuring that minerals taxation arrangements are part of the legal framework are important in increasing the efficiency of administrative processes and the effectiveness of policy assessments and outcomes. Increasing capacity through training and recruitment of quality audit staff is also critical.

4 More detailed assessment of selected mineral taxation options

A Resource rent – economic rationale for rent-based taxes

The economic rent in an economic activity is the excess profit or supernormal profit, and is equal to revenue less costs where costs include normal profit or a "normal" rate of return to capital. This normal rate of return, which is the minimum rate of return required to hold capital in the activity, has two components: a risk-free rate of return, and a risk premium that compensates risk averse (RA) private investors for the risks incurred in the activity (information on attitudes toward risk and the profitability assessments of risky projects is presented in Box 5.3).

The economic rationale for mineral taxation in addition to that applied to all industries is based on the scale of resource rent in the minerals industry. The concept of resource rent in the minerals industry applies over the longer term and takes into account the costs of the following distinct economic activities:

- *Exploration* – the cost of finding new mineral ore deposits.
- *New resource developments* – the cost of new resource developments based on mineral ore deposits that are known.
- *Production* – the cost of extracting resources from established mine sites (including abandonment costs such as mine site rehabilitation costs).

Resource rent in the mining sector may persist in the long run due to the quality or scarcity value of different ore deposits (these concepts are discussed by Boadway and Keen in more detail in Chapter 2). Resource rent is typically assumed to be equal to the economic rent in the minerals industry, although it is important to note that economic rent may be larger than the resource rent due to other factors such as managerial skills.

A graphical representation of the mineral industry's economic rent is provided in Figure 5.2 where, for simplicity, price is assumed to be determined on

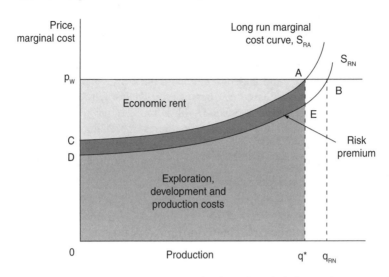

Figure 5.2 Illustrative economic rent in the minerals industry (supernormal profit or excess profit).

world markets at p_w. The long run industry supply curve, S_{RA}, is an annual representation of the long run marginal cost of exploration, development and production including a normal return to capital.[18] The equilibrium position for the industry occurs at point A, with production given by q^*. It would not be profitable for the industry to incur any additional costs by increasing production beyond this level and there would be unexploited profit opportunities if activity stopped at a lower level.

Total industry revenue is given by the area $0p_wAq^*$ (equal to the world price multiplied by output, or p_wq^*), total industry costs are given by the area under the supply curve, $0CAq^*$, and the economic rent is given by the area Cp_wA (total revenue less total costs).

To identify the industry's risk premium, Figure 5.2 explicitly includes the industry supply curve, S_{RN}, that would exist if private investors were risk neutral (RN). The equilibrium position for the risk neutral industry occurs at point B with output given by q_{RN}. The industry's risk premium (expressed as a value, not a rate of return to capital; see Box 5.3) is the difference between the two supply curves up to the industry output, q^*, and is given by the area ACDE. In the presence of risk and risk averse private investors, industry output is lower than would otherwise be the case since a number of marginal projects are assessed to be too risky to be undertaken given future possible outcomes relating to the geological, economic and policy environments.

B Rent-based taxes

Brown tax

Under the Brown tax, the government essentially acts as a silent partner in all resource projects. In years where net cash flow is negative – typically in the exploration and development stages of a resource project – the government pays the investor the Brown tax rate multiplied by the losses. In years where net cash flow is positive – typically in the production stage – the government receives the same fixed proportion of the profits.

If private investors are assumed to be risk neutral, the Brown tax is a neutral mineral taxation policy: in profitability assessments undertaken by private investors, the Brown tax reduces the expected profit of a project or modifies the expected loss, but it does not result in any switching between economic and uneconomic projects. A graphical representation of the Brown tax assuming risk neutral private investors is presented in Figure 5.3. Under the Brown tax, industry output is unchanged from the before-tax outcome of q_{RN} and the government collects a constant share of the economic rent (equal to the tax rate).

The Brown tax shares the risks of resource projects between risk averse private investors and the government (this is similar to the paid equity fiscal instrument which is an alternative to the Brown tax). With risk averse private investors, the risk premium is therefore reduced and it is possible that a project may switch from being uneconomic before tax to economic after tax. Industry output may therefore increase under a Brown tax (this implies that, in Figure 5.2, output would be larger than q^* but still less than q_{RN}; see Hogan (2007) for further discussion of this issue).

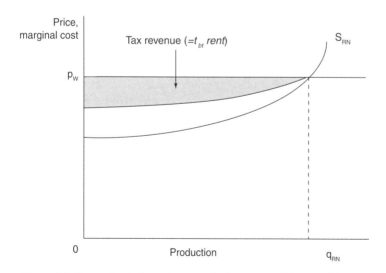

Figure 5.3 Illustrative industry impact of a Brown tax, risk neutral investors.

Resource rent tax

The resource rent tax is typically regarded as a practical alternative to the Brown tax since the government avoids the need to provide private investors with a cash rebate during years of negative net cash flow. The resource rent tax is only paid when a private investor achieves the threshold rate of return on the investment in the resource project. To achieve full loss offset in a resource rent tax while avoiding cash rebates, the main options are:

- *Transfers between projects within a company* – to allow companies to transfer the losses from failed projects to successful projects within the same group.
- *Transfers between companies* – for companies without successful projects against which to offset losses, to allow the sale of losses on failed projects to other companies with resource rent tax obligations.
- *Carry losses forward* – to allow companies to carry losses forward at a specified interest rate as an offset against future resource rent tax obligations from successful projects.

The transferability of losses between projects or between companies typically applies only to mineral operations within the same jurisdiction or country.

For risk neutral private investors, the threshold rate at which all losses are accumulated should clearly be set at the risk free interest rate (typically assumed to be the long-term government bond rate in developed economies).

For risk averse private investors, there are significant issues relating to the inclusion of a risk premium allowance in the threshold rate and the setting of the tax rate. If the threshold rate for a given project is set at the private investor's minimum rate of return (comprising the risk free interest rate plus an appropriate risk premium), the remaining net cash flow represents the economic rent of the project. If the economic rent and resource rent are equivalent, it is reasonable for the government to target the entire economic rent as a return to the mineral resource. If the economic rent exceeds the resource rent – that is, part of the rent represents a return to factors other than the mineral resource (such as a return to managerial skills or a technology leader) – it may be reasonable for the government to target less than the entire economic rent as a return to the mineral resource. There are also likely to be significant estimation errors in measuring rents.

The tax rate needs to be sufficiently below 100 percent to ensure that it does not seriously weaken efficiency incentives in the private sector (or encourage rent dissipating activities): this includes, for example, the risk of early mine closure, transfer pricing, "inflating" costs and lobbying government for tax breaks. A threshold rate that is below the minimum rate of return would compensate the government, at least to some extent, for a tax rate that is below 100 percent provided the project remains profitable for the private investor (that is, the certainty equivalent value of the project remains non-negative; see Box 5.3).

However, reducing the threshold rate may increase the possibility of some negative distortions to private investment decisions.

Lack of full loss offset in the resource rent tax is another consideration. For example, a resource rent tax that is levied only on successful resource projects fails to fully account for all revenues and costs in the minerals industry. A lower tax rate would compensate private investors for the lack of full loss offset. The original approach suggested by Garnaut and Clunies Ross (1975) was for the resource rent tax to apply to individual resource projects where, importantly, exploration activity in a failed lease area would be treated as a distinct resource project. They argued that a higher risk premium and/or lower tax rate than would otherwise apply would compensate industry for the lack of full loss offset.

Fane and Smith (1986) argued that the threshold rate should be set equal to the risk free interest rate (the long-term government bond rate) since, with full loss offset, the accumulated expenditures represent a perfectly certain reduction in future resource rent tax liabilities. They argued that an investor has the option of reducing current holdings of long-term government bonds to finance expenditure, foregoing the annual interest rate that would otherwise have accrued, to be compensated when the reduction in tax liabilities is triggered. Alternatively, if the company does not hold long-term government bonds, the expenditure may be financed through the release of corporate debentures with interest rates typically only marginally higher than the long-term government bond rate: this is analogous to a carried interest state equity approach (see Box 5.2). Fane and Smith (1986) further argued that the difficulties in making any actual tax proposal approximate the theoretical concept of a pure rent tax (or neutral tax) provide a justification for choosing a fairly low rate of rent tax. In practice, few systems incorporate full loss offset in which case some risk premium in the fiscal settings would be justified.

Developments in Australia's petroleum resource rent tax provide an indication of various issues associated with the implementation of a resource rent tax. The threshold rate of return in Australia's petroleum resource rent tax comprises a risk free rate of return and a risk premium. The original petroleum resource rent tax was introduced in Australia in the mid-1980s. An important modification to the petroleum resource rent tax was introduced in 1990 to allow companywide deductibility of exploration costs in recognition that typically a private investor may undertake exploration in a number of lease areas before a significant discovery is made that leads to petroleum field development and production. The threshold rate, which was relatively high to compensate private investors for the lack of full loss offset, was reduced. In 2005, exploration expenditure by established companies in specified frontier areas was provided with a 150 percent tax deduction in recognition of the relatively high risks associated with this activity (see Hogan (2003) for further information). A tax rate of 40 percent has applied in the petroleum resource rent tax since its inception.

Chapter 15 by Osmundsen discusses Norway's petroleum taxation system. This represents an alternative approach to the resource rent tax whereby the Brown tax is approximated using the corporate tax system.

C Output-based royalties

Ad valorem royalty (levied at a constant rate)

The ad valorem royalty is most often applied at a constant rate with the government collecting a constant percentage of the value of production from each resource project. From a government perspective, the main advantages of this ad valorem royalty are revenue stability – the risk of fiscal loss and revenue delay are reduced compared with rent-based taxes – and lower administration and compliance costs.

However, the ad valorem royalty reduces the expected revenue and hence expected profitability of a resource project. Some resource projects may therefore switch from being economic to uneconomic under the ad valorem royalty. These efficiency losses are illustrated in Figure 5.4 with industry output reduced from q_{RN} to q_{adv}. The ad valorem royalty is regressive since the share of the rent collected through the royalty is higher for lower profit resource projects: that is, compared with a rent-based tax, the ad valorem royalty tends to "overtax" low profit projects and "undertax" high profit projects.

For risk averse private investors, there are two important mechanisms whereby the ad valorem royalty influences the risk assessment. First, the royalty is paid in all years in which production is positive even if net cash flow is low or negative: that is, the ad valorem royalty is responsive to unexpected changes in price but not net cash flow. Second, sovereign risk tends to be a significant issue under this policy instrument since governments sometimes raise the ad valorem royalty rate during periods of high prices. The ad valorem royalty results in an increase in the private investor's risk premium, resulting in greater efficiency losses than would otherwise occur (see Hogan (2007) for further discussion of this issue).

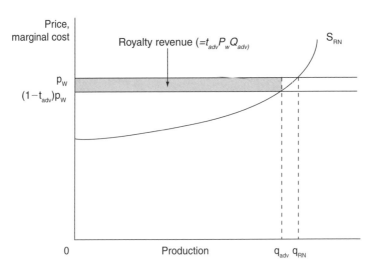

Figure 5.4 Illustrative industry impact of an ad valorem royalty, risk neutral investors.

Since mining is a dynamic process, the industry's supply curve may be interpreted as an annual snapshot of the industry's cost structure including a return to capital (alternatively, the supply curve may represent an industry position over a number of years). The industry's long run marginal cost curve may change over time in response to various factors. Importantly, technology adoption is an important process that places downward pressure on industry costs, while declining ore grade quality over time places upward pressure on industry costs (differences in ore grade quality result in the upward slope in the long run marginal cost curve; however, the mix of ore grades will change over time, particularly as high quality ore deposits are depleted). In a recent study, Topp *et al.* (2008) found these have been significant influences on productivity in Australia's mining sector. The basic ad valorem royalty is not responsive to changes in the industry's cost structure.

Other output-based royalties and taxes

OTHER AD VALOREM ROYALTIES AND TAXES

Variants of the basic ad valorem royalty have been adopted in both developed and developing economies to address, at least to some extent, the limitations of the basic instrument. These ad valorem royalties generally aim to reduce efficiency losses, increase the flexibility of the system and/or increase the share of rent collected through the royalty by introducing a sliding scale in the royalty rate. Ad valorem royalties and taxes incorporating a variable rate include:

- *Exemption for relatively small or low income mines* – adopted in several countries, a zero royalty rate applies to small or low income mines, including artisanal mines in some developing economies, to reduce the efficiency losses under the royalty.
- *Sliding scale based on sales or production* – sales or production is sometimes used in the sliding scale, with a higher royalty rate applying to larger resource projects. This attempts to proxy a rent-based tax on the argument that larger resource projects tend to be more profitable due to the presence of economies of scale. This system may also include an exemption for small mines.
- *Sliding scale based on cost* – of limited use in practice, this aims to reduce efficiency losses by applying a lower royalty rate to higher cost resource projects.
- *Sliding scale based on price* – a graduated price-based windfall tax where a higher tax rate applies to a higher price bracket. Adopted in some countries, particularly during the recent price boom, to increase the flexibility of the system: the focus for several governments was on increasing tax revenue during a period of relatively high commodity prices.

Efficiency losses may be reduced somewhat through these modified ad valorem royalties, although sovereign risk is likely to remain a significant issue. The government would be more likely to adjust the fiscal settings over time in response to future market changes under these royalties than under a rent-based tax. Under a graduated price-based windfall tax system, a particular focus for private investors would be to assess the risks to net cash flow during periods of relatively high commodity prices: for example, industry costs increased significantly during the recent commodity price boom. A further issue for such a system is the private investor's assessment of the government response to the risk of fiscal loss during periods of relatively low commodity prices.

Administration and compliance costs are likely to be higher under these arrangements than under the basic ad valorem royalty. An important issue relates to the additional complexity that is established in the policy framework through variable royalty rates. A sliding scale provides an economic incentive for mining companies to adopt strategies to avoid moving into a higher royalty bracket.

SPECIFIC ROYALTY

The specific or unit-based royalty is still utilized in most countries for low value, high volume minerals (for example, industrial minerals) and, in some cases, for a range of other minerals. The specific royalty is typically levied as a constant charge per physical unit of production for a specified mineral. For a given price, the specific royalty rate may be calibrated to collect the same amount per unit of output as under an ad valorem royalty. In this case, the impact on industry production is identical, for risk neutral investors, as that indicated in Figure 5.4 (the royalty revenue collected under a specific royalty, levied at t_{sp}, is $t_{sp}q_{sp}$ where $t_s = t_{adv}p_w$ and noting $q_{sp} = q_{adv}$). In practice, however, mineral prices change over time and the revenue collected under an ad valorem royalty will differ from that collected under a specific royalty (unless the latter is adjusted regularly).

The main advantage of the specific royalty is its relative administrative simplicity: this is the primary justification for its continued application to low value, high volume minerals that have low variation in grade quality across mines. The main disadvantage of the specific royalty is its lack of responsiveness to changes in price or net cash flow. The private investor's risk premium would be higher under the specific royalty compared with the ad valorem royalty, increasing the likelihood that an economic project would become uneconomic under the specific royalty.

D Mixed system: resource rent tax and ad valorem royalty

Introducing a sliding scale in the ad valorem royalty may address some of the disadvantages of the basic ad valorem royalty, but an alternative approach is to combine the basic ad valorem royalty with a resource rent tax (with royalty payments fully deductible under the resource rent tax). This mixed system is illustrated in Figure 5.5 under the assumption of risk neutral private investors: industry production is reduced from q_{RN} to q_{mix} (where, assuming a lower royalty rate, q_{mix} exceeds q_{adv} in Figure 5.4).

The aim in this mixed system would be to manage the government risks of fiscal loss and revenue delay through the ad valorem royalty – reducing effi-

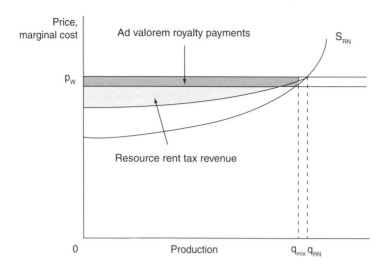

Figure 5.5 Illustrative industry impact of a mixed system, risk neutral investors.

ciency losses by applying a lower rate than in a stand alone system – while increasing the flexibility of the system through the resource rent tax: in particular, to provide a relatively efficient mechanism for rent collection from higher profit resource projects. Under this mixed system, the private investor's risk premium would be higher than under a stand alone resource rent tax but lower than under a stand alone ad valorem royalty.

Countries that have introduced rent-based taxes (e.g. Kazakhstan, Liberia) or profit-based royalties (e.g. many of the large mineral producing provinces in Canada) tend to adopt a mixed system by combining them with an ad valorem royalty.

5 Simulations of key mineral taxation options

The objective in this section is to provide simulations of hypothetical projects to illuminate the comparison between four key fiscal instruments. The certainty equivalent approach provides a simple economic framework that clarifies the roles of risk and attitudes toward risk in the private investor's profitability assessments. This approach is complementary to the evaluation of fiscal regimes for oil resource developments in Chapter 7 by Daniel *et al.*

In the certainty equivalent approach – discussed briefly in Box 5.3 – ex ante measures of project profitability, or economic rent, that are assumed to be used as decision rules by private investors are: the net present value (NPV), if the investment is risk free; the expected net present value (ENPV), if the investment is risky and the investor is risk neutral; and the certainty equivalent value (CEV) if the investment is risky and the investor, being risk averse, demands a risk premium (RP) as compensation for incurring risks (where CEV = ENPV − RP).

Box 5.3 Certainty equivalent approach for assessing project profitability

Mining is an inherently risky activity. The private investor's assessment of the profitability of a prospective resource project following successful exploration activity depends on risks in the geological, economic and policy setting over the life of the resource project and the attitude of the investor to incurring risks. In the assessment of risky projects using the certainty equivalent approach, it is assumed the investor is able to identify a range of possible outcomes reflecting significant sources of risk and assign (objective or subjective) probabilities to each of these outcomes.

It is useful to consider the profitability assessments for resource projects in three categories that vary according to the presence of risk and attitudes toward risk.

Risk free investment

A private investor ranks risk-free projects according to the net present value (NPV) since it is a measure of the return to the investment when future conditions are known with certainty. It is important to note that the net present value is the sum of the annual net cash flows over the duration of the project discounted at the risk-free interest rate (assumed to be the long-term government bond rate or LTBR). A project with a net present value that is greater than or equal to zero is assessed to be profitable since it indicates that the investment will achieve a return that is greater than or equal to the risk-free interest rate.

Risky investment

Risk neutral investors

A risk neutral investor is indifferent to the risk that an outcome may be either worse or better than expected, and so summarizes the profitability of a resource project by calculating the expected net present value (ENPV). The expected net present value is the probability weighted sum of the net present value of each possible outcome (where the net present value is calculated based on the risk-free interest rate, as in the previous case). A project with an expected net present value that is greater than or equal to zero is assessed to be profitable since it indicates that the investment is expected to achieve a return that is greater than or equal to the risk-free interest rate.

Risk averse investors

A risk averse investor is relatively more concerned about the risk of unexpected losses than the risk of unexpected gains. In the presence of risk, a risk averse investor summarizes the profitability of a resource project by calculating the certainty equivalent value (CEV). The certainty equivalent value is equal to the project's expected net present value (calculated using the risk-free interest rate, as above) less a risk premium (RP) that provides adequate compensation for the risks associated with the project (that is, $CEV = ENPV - RP$). A project with a certainty equivalent value that is greater than or equal to zero is assessed to be profitable. The certainty equivalent value of a project may be interpreted as the net present value of a risk-free project that is ranked equally with the risky project. The valuation of the risk premium may have an important influence on the assessment of project profitability.

A Project assumptions

The hypothetical projects we consider vary widely in size, with the value of production assumed to range from $5 million for project 1 to $250 million for project 5. The cost structure reflects the presence of economies of scale, whereby average operating costs are lower for larger projects: in the sensitivity analysis, capital costs are assumed to be 25 percent higher than in the base case. Production and operating costs are assumed to be constant during the production phase of each project. The mine life is assumed to be 20 years for project 5 and ten years for the other projects.

For simplicity, the resource price is the only source of risk. This price risk – usually considered to be a major source of risk in resource development projects – is introduced into the project simulations in a relatively simple way. There are assumed to be seven possible price outcomes over the development and production stages of the resource projects. For example, the probability that a price of $1,000 a tonne will occur is assumed to be 30 percent, while the price outcomes of $650 a tonne or $1,350 a tonne are each assumed to occur with a probability of 1 percent.

In the profitability assessments, risk averse private investors need to estimate the risk premium for each hypothetical resource project. The coefficient of relative risk aversion, R, is assumed to be 2 and the risk premium is given by the variance of the distribution of the net present values divided by the expected net present value (see Newbery and Stiglitz (1981, page 73 and related examples) for further information).

B Results

Before tax or royalty

The main simulation results are summarized in Table 5.4. Before tax, all five projects are profitable for both risk neutral and risk averse investors. For risk neutral investors, the expected net present value ranges from $8.9 million for the relatively small project 1 to $995 million for the relatively large project 5. For risk averse investors, the risk premium ranges from $2.3 million for project 1 to $52 million for project 5. As a consequence, the certainty equivalent value ranges from $6.5 million for project 1 to $943 million.

With higher capital costs, each of the five hypothetical resource projects remains profitable before tax, although project profitability is reduced (see the results for the sensitivity analysis at the bottom of Table 5.4). Under the higher capital cost assumption, the certainty equivalent value ranges from $3.3 million for project 1 to $817 million for project 5.

Rent-based taxes

The Brown tax, included as a benchmark fiscal instrument, is levied at a rate of 40 percent. For consistency, the resource rent tax is also levied at a rate of 40

Table 5.4 Key results for illustrative resource projects[1]

| | Before tax $m | Rent-based taxes | | | Output-based royalties | | | |
| | | Brown tax $m | Resource rent tax | | Ad valorem royalty | | Specific royalty | |
			5%[2] $m	10%[3] $m	10% $m	5% $m	$100/t $m	$50/t $m
Expected tax revenue								
Project 1	–	3.5	2.8	2.0	3.7	1.8	3.7	1.8
Project 2	–	18	16	12	18	9	18	9
Project 3	–	50	46	40	37	18	37	18
Project 4	–	130	124	113	74	37	74	37
Project 5	–	398	386	364	184	92	184	92
Project profitability assessments								
Risk neutral investors – expected net present value (ENPV)								
Project 1	8.9	5.3	6.1	6.9	5.2	7.0	5.2	7.0
Project 2	44	27	28	32	26	35	26	35
Project 3	125	75	79	85	89	107	89	107
Project 4	324	195	201	211	251	288	251	288
Project 5	995	597	609	631	811	903	811	903
Risk averse investors								
Risk premium (RP)								
Project 1	2.3	1.4	1.3	1.2	3.2	2.6	4.0	2.9
Project 2	12	7	7	6	16	13	20	15
Project 3	16	10	9	8	19	17	23	19
Project 4	25	15	15	13	27	26	33	29
Project 5	52	31	30	28	51	52	64	57

Certainty equivalent value (CEV = ENPV–RP)

	6.5	3.9	4.8	5.7	2.0	4.4	1.2	4.1
Project 1	6.5	3.9	4.8	5.7	2.0	4.4	1.2	4.1
Project 2	33	20	22	26	10	22	6	20
Project 3	109	65	70	77	70	90	65	88
Project 4	299	179	186	198	224	262	218	259
Project 5	943	566	578	603	759	851	747	846

Sensitivity analysis: certainty equivalent value under the higher capital cost assumption

	3.3	2.0	2.5	3.3	-3.2	0.6	-4.6	0.2
Project 1	3.3	2.0	2.5	3.3	-3.2	0.6	-4.6	0.2
Project 2	16	10	11	15	-16	3	-23	1
Project 3	81	49	53	64	39	61	33	58
Project 4	247	148	155	173	170	209	163	206
Project 5	817	490	503	540	631	724	617	718

Source: Hogan (2007).

Notes
1 In present value terms. See Box 5.3 for further information.
2 No risk premium in the threshold rate.
3 5% risk premium in the threshold rate.

percent. Two options are considered for the threshold rate in the resource rent tax: 5 percent (equal to the risk free interest rate) and 10 percent (equal to the risk free interest rate plus a risk premium of 5 percent). The tax rate and risk premium of 5 percent in threshold rate are consistent with the settings in the Australian Government's petroleum resource rent tax.

Under these rent-based taxes, the government tax take varies with project profitability. For example, under a resource rent tax with a threshold rate of 10 percent, the expected present value of tax revenue ranges from $2.0 million for project 1 to $364 million for project 5.

The private investor's risk premium is reduced compared with the before tax outcome reflecting the reduced dispersion of possible returns under these rent-based taxes. For example, under a resource rent tax with a threshold rate of 10 percent, the risk premium ranges from $1.2 million for project 1 to $28 million for project 5.

Reflecting the efficiency advantages of these fiscal instruments, all projects are assessed to be profitable under each of these rent-based taxes. For example, under a resource rent tax with a threshold rate of 10 percent, the certainty equivalent value ranges from $5.7 million for project 1 to $603 million for project 5. With higher capital costs, each of the five projects remains profitable under the rent-based taxes, although the certainty equivalent value is lower in each case: this contrasts with the results for output-based royalties where projects 1 and 2 become uneconomic or marginal (discussed further below).

Output-based royalties

The ad valorem royalty is levied at a rate of 10 or 5 percent (an ad valorem royalty rate of 10 percent applies to petroleum projects in most state and territory governments in Australia). The specific royalty is levied at a rate of $100 a tonne and $50 a tonne (this equates the royalty revenue under the ad valorem and specific royalties for the expected price of $1,000 a tonne).

Under output-based royalties levied at a constant rate, the government tax take varies with the value and/or volume of production and there is some tendency, depending on the royalty rate, for ad valorem and specific royalties to overtax low profit projects and undertax high profit projects. For example, under the 5 percent ad valorem royalty, the expected present value of tax revenue ranges from $1.8 million for project 1 to $92 million for project 5. Under a 10 percent ad valorem royalty, the government tax take increases to $3.7 million for project 1 and $184 million for project 5. It should be noted these are relatively simple numerical examples that do not take into account factors such as sovereign risk.

The risk premium under these output-based royalties is higher than under the rent-based taxes and, except for project 5 under the ad valorem royalties, is higher than the before tax outcome. For example, under the 5 percent ad valorem royalty, the risk premium ranges from $2.6 million for project 1 to $52 million for project 5. The ad valorem royalties have a negligible impact on the risk assessment of the highly profitable projects reflecting the relatively low government tax take.

All projects are assessed to be profitable under each of these output-based royalties for the base case assumptions. For example, under the 5 percent ad valorem royalty, the certainty equivalent value ranges from $4.4 million for project 1 to $851 million for project 5.

In contrast to the results for the rent-based taxes, with higher capital costs, projects 1 and 2 become unprofitable under the 10 percent ad valorem royalty and $100 a tonne specific royalty: that is, these projects switch from being economic before tax to uneconomic after the royalty. Production will then not occur and royalty revenue is zero under these options. Under the 5 percent ad valorem royalty and $50 a tonne specific royalty, the certainty equivalent value of projects 1 and 2 is reduced significantly, but remains positive in each case.

The project assumptions and results are discussed in further detail in Hogan (2007).

6 Conclusion

A complex system of mineral taxation arrangements currently apply in the world economy. Mineral taxation arrangements vary between countries, between jurisdictions within countries, between minerals and between projects. Progress has been achieved in several areas, enabling governments to obtain a return to the community from mineral extraction while reducing adverse impacts on the industry. For coal, metallic minerals and gemstones, output-based royalties and taxes mainly apply (in addition to the standard corporate income tax arrangements). However, profit-based royalties have been adopted in some developed economies, including most jurisdictions in Canada and a single jurisdiction in Australia (the Northern Territory) and the United States (Nevada). Rent or profit-based taxes have also recently been adopted in some developing economies including, for example, Kazakhstan and Liberia. Specific royalties mainly apply to high volume, low value non-metallic minerals, particularly construction materials.

This paper has discussed key economic issues in mineral taxation with some focus on the implications of fiscal instruments for the risk assessments of private investors. Rent or profit-based taxes and state equity instruments tend to rank highly on neutrality, investor risk and flexibility criteria, while output-based instruments tend to rank highly on government risk (fiscal loss and revenue delay) and administration and compliance criteria. An alternative approach is to combine an ad valorem royalty with a rent or profit-based fiscal instrument (with the former fully deductible against the latter): the ad valorem royalty would ensure a minimum return to the government, while the rent or profit-based tax can be a relatively efficient mechanism for rent collection from higher profit resource projects.

Appendix I Mineral taxation in selected countries

Table 5.5 Summary of mineral taxation in selected developed countries

Fiscal regime	Royalties	Corporate income tax	Additional minerals tax	Import duties	VAT	Withholding taxes Interest	Withholding taxes Dividend	State participation
Australia								
Western Australia	• Ores: 7.5% • Concentrates: 5.0% • Metals: 2.5% • Gold: 1.25–2.5% based on price • Export coal: 7.5% • Coal not exported: Specific royalty	Federal tax rate: 30% No separate state income tax.	nil	nil	The standard rate is 10%; exported minerals are GST free.	10% or as specified by tax treaty.	30% on unfranked dividends; varies (usually 15%) if there is a tax treaty.[1]	nil
Queensland	• Coal: 7% • Other minerals: Fixed rate option: 2.7%. Variable rate option: 1.5–4.5% based on price							
New South Wales	• Aluminium: AUD 0.35 per ton of bauxite • Industrial minerals: AUD 0.4 or 0.7 per ton • Coal: 4.7% ad valorem • Phosphate: AUD 0.7 per ton • Copper, Gold, Iron, Zinc: 4% of ex-mine value							

Northern Territory	• 18%, profit-based						
Canada British Columbia	• Minimum tax is 2% ad valorem (deductible against profit royalty) • 13% profit royalty • Losses can be carried forward under profit royalty	*British Columbia* 14.36% on net resource income; the 2% royalty on net proceeds can be deducted.	nil	Most minerals are exempt.	The standard GST rate is 7%; exported minerals are exempt.	25% is withheld on payments made to non-residents.	None in Ontario; n/a for others.
Northwest Territories	• 5–14% profit royalty (sliding scale) • No tax if income below CAN$10,000	*Federal* 22.12%, which includes the 28% statutory rate, 4% surtax and 7% resource rate reduction. Provincial royalty and mining taxes are not deductible from federal taxes.[2]					
Ontario	• 10% profit royalty • No tax if income above CAN$500,000 • Tax reductions for mines in remote regions						

continued

Table 5.5 continued

Fiscal regime	Royalties	Corporate income tax	Additional minerals tax	Import duties	VAT	Withholding taxes		State participation
						Interest	Dividend	
United States Arizona	• At least 2% ad valorem • Rate set by commissioner	*Federal* 15–35% rates. Foreign countries taxed on gross withholding basis. An additional branch profits tax of 30% (or as stated by tax treaty) applies on income of foreign companies from US sources.	nil	Vary by country and commodity.	nil	30% to non-treaty countries; 0–15% to treaty countries.	30% to non-treaty countries; 0–15% to treaty countries	n/a

Michigan	• 2.7% ad valorem (sliding scale)	*Arizona* 6.968%. Applies to taxable income that is assessed similarly to federal taxable income and adjusted for Arizona tax.
Nevada	• 2–5% profit royalty (sliding scale) • 5% if net proceeds above US$4 million	*Michigan* 4.95%[3] *Nevada* nil

Notes

1 If dividends paid out of profits have already been taxed at corporate tax rate, the company gets franking credits for the tax paid and may choose to use them.

2 Allowable deductions are costs directly related to operations, loss carry forwards, development and exploration costs, asset depreciation and accelerated depreciation allowance, resource allowance, reclamation contributions, and depletion allowance.

3 The New Michigan Business Tax. First $45,000 of tax base exempt. Plus, 0.8% of modified gross receipts (receipts less purchases from other firms) on receipts of $350,000 or more. A surcharge of 21.99% applies.

Table 5.6 Summary of mineral taxation in selected other countries

Fiscal regime	Royalties	Corporate income tax	Additional minerals tax	Import duties	Withholding taxes		State participation
					Interest	Dividend	
Africa							
Botswana	• Most minerals: 3% • Metals: 5% • Precious stones: 10%	Variable rate formula: 70–1500/Y where Y is the ratio of taxable income to gross income. 25% minimum tax.	nil	nil	15%	15%	nil
Ghana	• All minerals: 3–6% rate graduated on operating profit	25%	nil	nil	8%	8%	Minimum 10%
Malawi	• Most minerals: 3% (on gross value minus transport costs)	30%	10% RRT when after-tax cumulative cash flows exceeds 20%	nil	15% (non-resident, no double-taxation, agreement, under which withholding taxes are waived)	10% (no double-taxation agreement)	
Mozambique	• Coal and other minerals: 3% • Basic minerals: 5% • Semiprecious stones: 6% • Precious metals: 10% • Diamonds: 10%–12%	32%	nil	5 year exemption	20%	20%	nil

continued

Namibia	• Most minerals: 5% maximum • Uncut precious stones: 10%	37.5% non-diamond mining 55% diamond mining	nil	nil	nil	Residents are exempt; 10% for non-residents	nil
South Africa	• Variable rate depending on EBIT • Max rate for refined minerals 5%, for unrefined 7%	28% normal CIT Gold mining companies subject to variable income tax: a) $y = 34 - 170/x$ where company has elected not to pay the secondary tax on companies (STC), or b) $y = 43 - 215/x$ where company pays STC on companies; where x is the ratio of taxable income from gold mining to income from gold mining and y is tax rate.	nil	nil	nil	10% STC to be withdrawn in 2010	nil

Fiscal regime	Royalties	Corporate income tax	Additional minerals tax	Import duties	Withholding taxes		State participation
					Interest	Dividend	
Zambia	• Base metals, industrial minerals, and energy minerals, including copper: 3% • Precious stones and gemstones: 5%	variable according to the following formula: $30\% + 15\% \times (1 - 8\%/Y)$ when Y is the ratio of taxable income to gross income	nil (windfall tax introduced in 2008 was repealed in 2009)	nil	15%	Exempt	Varies: 10% is an indicative rate
Asia and Pacific							
China	• Aluminium, iron and zinc: Ad valorem + per unit charge • Copper: 2% + 0.4–30 • Gold: 4% + 0.4–30 • Industrial minerals: 2% + 0.5–20 CNY/tonne	25%[1]	nil	Exports are zero rated; imports of mining equipment are exempt.	10%	nil	nil
India	• Aluminium: 0.35% • Copper: 3.2% • Gold: 1.5% primary, 2.5% byproduct • Industrial minerals: 45–55 INR/tonne • Iron: 4–27 INR/tonne • Phosphate: 5% apatite, 5–11% rock • Zinc: 6.6%	30% residents 40% foreign 10% surtax residents 10% surcharge non-residents	nil	Inputs purchased and used in the manufacture of export goods will be refunded; exports are exempt.	2–7.5%	20%	17%	Government-owned companies account for 75% of the value of the country's mineral production.

Country								
Indonesia	• Aluminium, iron and phosphate: Unit based • Copper: 45–55 USD/tonne • Gold: 7.5% from placer, 2.5% otherwise • Industrial minerals: 0.14–0.16 USD/tonne	10% on first IDR 50m, 15% on next IDR 50m and 30% on balance.	nil	nil	Pre-production purchases of machinery and equipment are exempt; exports are zero rated	Residents exempt; 20% non-residents.	15% residents; 20% non-residents.	nil
Mongolia	• Most minerals: 5% • Domestically sold coal and other minerals: 2.5%	10% on taxable income up to MNT 3 billion, 25% on excess.	68% when copper price exceeds USD 2,600 per metric ton and gold exceeds USD 500 per troy ounce. Base is value of production.	5%	10%; exports are zero rated; goods supplied to mining companies are exempt.	20%	20%	Up to 50%
Philippines	• Most minerals: 2%	35%, to be reduced to 30% in 2009	nil	nil	Exports are zero rated; VAT on goods and services are exempt.	10% on residents 35% for non-residents or 15% if the non-resident foreign company's domicile country allows a deemed-paid tax credit of at least 20%.	20%	nil

continued

Table 5.6 continued

Fiscal regime	Royalties	Corporate income tax	Additional minerals tax	Import duties	Withholding taxes Interest	Dividend	State participation
Latin America							
Argentina	• Most minerals: 0–3%	35%	nil	nil	35% for residents non-residents are exempt	35% for residents 15.05% for non-residents	nil
Bolivia	• Gold: 4–7% depending on price • Gold from marginal deposits: 3–5% depending on price • Silver: 3–6% depending on price • Lead, tin and copper: 1–5% depending on price	25%	nil	nil	Residents exempt 12.5% for non-residents	Residents exempt 12.5% for non-residents	nil
Brazil	• Aluminium and phosphate: 3% • Copper, iron, zinc: 2% • Gold: 1% • Industrial minerals: 2%	34%[2]	nil	nil	15% on interest paid to non-residents	nil	nil

Chile	• Copper: 0.5–5% based on sales	35%	nil	10% (deductible)	4% if loan granted by foreign bank, 35% otherwise	35%	nil
Mexico	nil	28%	nil	nil	nil	nil	n/a
Peru	• Most minerals: 1–3%	30% +0.5% tax on total assets above DEN 1 million	nil	12%	30% non-treaty rate	4.1%	8% workers profit share based on net income before tax.
Venezuela	• Most minerals: 3–4%	34%	nil	0–10%	3–5%	nil	n/a

Notes
1 Companies operating in special economic zones benefit from a reduced tax ratio of 15%.
2 34% is total effective tax rate: 15% CIT, plus a 9% social security tax (non-deductible against corporate tax), and 10% surtax tax on income greater than BRL 240,000.

Acknowledgments

The authors wish to thank Craig Andrews for providing insightful discussant comments at the IMF conference in September 2008. The authors are also grateful to Michael Keen and Philip Daniel for providing very helpful comments and suggestions on earlier drafts of this chapter, and to Elsa Sze and Diego Mesa Puyo for excellent research assistance. The views expressed are those of the authors and should not be attributed to the International Monetary Fund.

Notes

1 Resource rent can be categorized into different types depending on how it is created. See Otto *et al.* (2004) for an explanation of the types relevant to the resource sector.
2 See Chapter 2 by Boadway and Keen.
3 Country risk is sometimes referred to as political risk, but may also encompass broader factors relating to the risk of operating in a specific country including, for example, political and legal stability.
4 Because royalties tend to be viewed as a payment for rights to minerals they typically accrue to the owner of the minerals. In the United States, unlike other jurisdictions, mineral rights belong to the owner of the surface rights of the land – private royalty systems may operate on private lands, although federal lands are also important in mineral production. In Australia and Canada, for example, the rights to onshore resources belong to the state and territory governments (although the Australian Government has jurisdiction over uranium resources in the Northern Territory).
5 When the government and investor have different time preferences and risk attitudes, there may be some scope for mutual benefit from changing the time and risk allocation between them.
6 Much of this discussion is based on material in Kumar (1995).
7 See McPherson's detailed discussion of the evolution of state participation in Chapter 9.
8 For example, in New South Wales in Australia, the ad valorem rate for coal varies for deep underground (5 percent and assessed to be the highest cost category), other underground (6 percent) and open cut (7 percent).
9 Gold, tin and zinc price rises were particularly sharp. The gold price was influenced by the end of the gold standard in the US in 1971, and the tin price by increased demand arising from the Vietnam War.
10 See Land's thorough discussion of such instruments in Chapter 8.
11 Greenland, Mexico, and Sweden also do not apply a royalty (Otto *et al.*, 2006).
12 Prices fell sharply in the second-half of 2008 due to the global financial crisis, although the prices of most minerals remain well above their lows. It remains to be seen what impact, if any, this latest development will have on mineral taxation.
13 29 developing countries are in the process of becoming EITI compliant. See http://eitransparency.org/ for further details.
14 Otto *et al.* (2006) report that the practice of setting a royalty on a mine-by-mine basis is becoming less frequent, although mine-specific arrangements still exist in several jurisdictions (for example, Olympic Dam and the Argyle diamond mine in Australia).
15 See Chapter 7 by Daniel *et al.* for a comprehensive evaluation for oil.
16 See Boadway and Keen's discussion of other rent-based taxes in Chapter 2.
17 Cash payments to investors under the Brown tax can be approximated in other rent or profit-based systems. For example, Norway's fiscal regime for petroleum can approxi-

mate a Brown Tax when companies have significant portfolios of projects, deducting expenditures from one against income from others – see Chapter 15 by Osmundsen for further information. The issue of full loss offset under a resource rent tax is discussed in section IV.
18 Fixed costs are for simplicity assumed in the figures that follow to be zero.

References

Banks, Glenn (2001), *Papua New Guinea Baseline Study*, Mining, "Minerals and Sustainable Development," No. 180 (Australia: University of New South Wales).

Baunsgaard, Thomas (2001), "A Primer on Mineral Taxation," IMF Working Paper No. 01/139 (Washington DC: International Monetary Fund).

Boadway, Robin and Michael Keen (2010), "Theoretical Perspectives on Resource Tax Design," in Philip Daniel, Michael Keen and Charles McPherson (eds.) *The Taxation of Petroleum and Minerals: Principles, Problems and Practice*.

Brown, Edgar (1948), "Business-Income Taxation and Investment Incentives," in *Income, Employment and Public Policy*, Essays in Honor of Alvin H. Hansen (Norton, New York).

Calder, Jack (2010a), "Administration Challenges from Resource Tax Policy," in Philip Daniel, Michael Keen and Charles McPherson (eds.) *The Taxation of Petroleum and Minerals: Principles, Problems and Practice*.

—— (2010b), "Resource Tax Administration: Functions, Processes and Institutions," in Philip Daniel, Michael Keen and Charles McPherson (eds.) *The Taxation of Petroleum and Minerals: Principles, Problems and Practice*.

Daniel, Philip (1995), "Evaluating State Participation in Mineral Projects: Equity, Infrastructure and Taxation," in James Otto (ed.) *Taxation of Mineral Enterprises* (London: Graham & Trotman).

——, Brenton Goldsworthy, Wojciech Maliszewski, Diego Mesa Puyo and Alistair Watson (2010), "Evaluating Fiscal Regimes for Resource Projects: An Example from Oil Development," in Philip Daniel, Michael Keen and Charles McPherson (eds.) *The Taxation of Petroleum and Minerals: Principles, Problems and Practice*.

Fane, George and Ben Smith (1986), "Resource Rent Tax," in C.D. Trengove (ed.) *Australian Energy Policy in the 1980s*, Centre of Policy Studies (Sydney: George Allen and Unwin).

Garnaut, Ross and Anthony Clunies Ross (1975), "Uncertainty, Risk Aversion and The Taxing of Natural Resource Projects," *Economic Journal*, Vol. 85, pp. 272–287.

Hogan, Lindsay (2003), *Australia's Petroleum Resource Rent Tax: An Economic Assessment of Fiscal Settings*, ABARE eReport 03.1, prepared for the Department of Industry, Tourism and Resources, Canberra, available at: www.abare.gov.au.

—— (2007), *Mineral Resource Taxation in Australia: An Economic Assessment of Policy Options*, ABARE Research Report 07.1, prepared for the Australian Government Department of Industry, Tourism and Resources, Canberra, available at: www.abare.gov.au.

International Monetary Fund (2007), *Guide on Resource Revenue Transparency*, Fiscal Affairs Department, available at: www.imf.org/external/pubs/cat/longres.cfm?sk=18349.0.

Kellas, Graham (2010), "Natural Gas: Experience and Issues," in Philip Daniel, Michael Keen and Charles McPherson (eds.) *The Taxation of Petroleum and Minerals: Principles, Problems and Practice*.

Kumar, Raj (1995), "Mine Taxation: The Evolution of Fiscal Regimes," in James Otto (ed.) *Taxation of Mineral Enterprises* (London: Graham & Trotman).

Land, Bryan (2010), "Resource Rent Tax: A Re-Appraisal," in Philip Daniel, Michael Keen and Charles McPherson (eds.) *The Taxation of Petroleum and Minerals: Principles, Problems and Practice*.

Lungu, John (2008), "The Politics of Reforming Zambia's Mining Tax Regime," presented at the Mine Watch Zambia Conference, September 19–20.

Lyday, Travis (2002), "The Mineral Industry of Papua New Guinea," in *US Geological Survey Minerals Yearbook*.

McPherson, Charles (2010), "State Participation in the Natural Resource Sectors: Evolution, Issues, and Outlook," in Philip Daniel, Michael Keen and Charles McPherson (eds.) *The Taxation of Petroleum and Minerals: Principles, Problems and Practice*.

Mullins, Peter (2010), "International Tax Issues for the Resources Sector," in Philip Daniel, Michael Keen and Charles McPherson (eds.) *The Taxation of Petroleum and Minerals: Principles, Problems and Practice*.

Newbery, David and Joseph Stiglitz (1981), *The Theory of Commodity Price Stabilization: A Study in the Economics of Risk* (Oxford: Clarendon Press).

Otto, James (2000), *Mining Taxation in Developing Countries* (Colorado: Colorado School of Mines).

——, Craig Andrews, Fred Cawood, Michael Doggett, Pietro, Guj, Frank Stermole, John Stermole and John Tilton (2006), *Mining Royalties: A Global Study of Their Impact on Investors, Government, and Civil Society* (Washington DC: World Bank).

Pizarrro, Rodrigo (2004), "The Establishment of Royalty in Chile," *Mining and Sustainable Development Series*, No. 2.

Topp, Vernon, Leo Soames, Dean Parham and Harry Bloch (2008), *Productivity in the Mining Industry: Measurement and Interpretation*, Productivity Commission Staff Working Paper, available at: www.pc.gov.au.

6 Natural gas

Experience and issues

Graham Kellas

1 Introduction

Sales of natural gas are growing significantly around the world. Who benefits from this production is, in large part, determined by the fiscal terms applicable in the various links of the gas value chain. Fiscal policies can influence the price received by producers and processors of gas as well as the extent and timing of the recovery of investment costs. Fiscal policies can also drive different operational and ownership structure of gas projects.

This chapter discusses the various issues that need to be considered by policymakers when designing an appropriate fiscal regime for the development of their natural gas resources.

While many aspects of the natural gas business are very similar to oil, there are some significant differences (which are discussed in Section 3D on petroleum economics) that result in a very different investor perspective on gas projects, compared to their oil equivalent. Moreover, in many countries the development of natural gas has occurred only recently whereas oil has been produced for many years. In particular, the export of gas, primarily via liquefied natuaral gas (LNG) schemes, has only really emerged in the last 15 years. These developments have generated a number of particular issues which fiscal policymakers need to address and these are also considered in this paper.

To put the fiscal policymakers' task into perspective the chapter starts with a description of the growing size of the natural gas business and how its 'value chain' is created. This introduces both the 'size of the prize' and some of the major issues involved in determining how this prize gets distributed between the different participants in the business, including government.

2 Background

A Natural gas: resources and demand

The supply of natural gas worldwide has increased by 25 per cent between 2000 and 2008 (from 80 trillion cubic feet per annum (Tcfpa) to 102 Tcfpa) and is expected to increase to over 140 Tcfpa by 2020, as illustrated in Figure 6.1. In

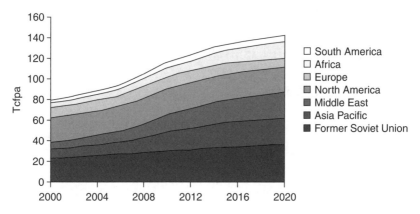

Figure 6.1 Global natural gas supply 2000–2020 (source: Wood Mackenzie (3Q 2008)).

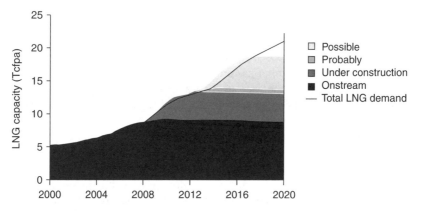

Figure 6.2 Global LNG supply 2000–2020 (source: Wood Mackenzie (3Q 2008)).

Note
1 Tcfpa = 21.3 mmtpa.

the same period the amount of gas volumes traded as LNG has doubled (from 5 Tcfpa to 10 Tcfpa and is expected to double again by 2020 (~20 Tcfpa) as shown in Figure 6.2, taking LNG's contribution to overall supply from 6 per cent in 2000 to 14 per cent in 2020.

Figure 6.3 illustrates the extent of the divergence between the regions which own the remaining gas resources and those which currently consume the most gas. Seventy per cent of remaining proven reserves is in the former Soviet Union and Middle East, which currently account for only 30 per cent of consumption. By contrast, Europe and North America make up nearly half of global current consumption but have only 8 per cent of remaining reserves. This picture may change if the perceived scale – and commerciality – of the recent shale gas discoveries in the US becomes proven.

The opportunity for new LNG projects to meet the growing dependence on imported gas in the main demand centres has stimulated the industry's appetite

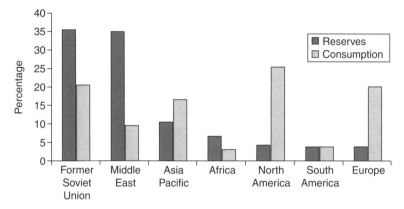

Figure 6.3 Global natural gas reserves and consumption (% world total) (source: Wood Mackenzie (3Q 2008)).

Note
US reserves source: BP Statistical Review of World Energy 2008.

for gas in resource-rich countries and companies are increasingly keen to acquire gas reserves. A major stumbling block for them is the fact that gas reserves remain largely under state control in many of these countries. The inability of domestic consumers to pay anything like the gas prices received in the developed countries has traditionally meant that local gas projects have largely been developed by governments, which have taken ownership of the gas reserves. The emergence of export markets for gas mean that governments are now keen for increased export revenues, but remain equally keen that abundant local gas supplies replace oil and other primary fuels in power generation and industrial projects and contribute to the expansion of these activities. To promote investment in domestic projects, therefore, some governments have begun to tie investor's rights to export gas with obligations to develop local gas projects.

The ability of governments and industry to meet growing domestic and export demand for natural gas is influenced by many factors such as exploration success, LNG marketing advantages, corporate positions and geopolitics – all of which are uncertain and subject to change. Where the parties can influence outcomes is in the design of an appropriate taxation policy to ensure risks are balanced by rewards along the value chain. The design of a suitable fiscal policy for natural gas presents government with a number of simultaneous policy issues, notably gas pricing and equity participation, and these are discussed in this chapter.

B Natural gas: value chain

Getting natural gas from the drill bit to burner tip involves a chain of operations, as illustrated in Figure 6.4. Depending on the ultimate consumer of the gas produced, natural gas extracted from a reservoir will:

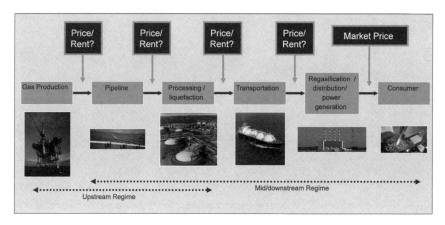

Figure 6.4 Natural gas value chain.

Note
Number of links in each chain depends on the project (e.g. gas may be sold directly to consumer after processing).

- be sent by pipeline to a processing plant or direct to the end user;
- be processed, which will likely include extraction of associated liquids and may also include liquefaction of the gas itself within an LNG or gas to liquids (GTL) project;
- be sent on to the market, either as dry gas to the end user or for secondary processing (e.g. power generation) or as liquids;
- be converted into the end product (e.g. electricity) or back into dry gas, if in liquid form (i.e. regasified); and
- finally, be sold to the end user.

The final market for the gas may be domestic, which is likely to have prices regulated by the government, or abroad. Fiscal policies and terms need to address all of these possibilities as the gas industry in any country may encompass the whole spectrum of gas utilisation projects and ownership combinations.

The owners of each link in the chain incur significant costs and expect to recover these costs, plus a share of the economic rent generated. Economic rent is defined as the product sale price less the costs of production, transportation and distribution, including a minimum return on capital employed, over the full cycle (i.e. lifetime) of a project. Each link also has to balance the inherent risks involved with the potential rewards. While the ultimate price may fluctuate, affecting all links of the chain, upstream producers encounter the most risks, including geological (exploration), reservoir and technology risks and will usually seek a proportionally higher share of the rewards as a result.

Depending on their attitude to market risks, the owners of any of the links in the chain may try and either protect or expose their operation to prevailing market prices. Risk-averse owners may charge a fixed fee (e.g. feedgas price, pipeline or plant processing tariff) while risk takers will seek as much of the final price as possible. Normally, the more risk-averse owners will accept a lower share of the overall economic rent generated in exchange for 'downside' protection.

Where the owners of each link are different, pricing agreements between links should be transparent and 'arm's length', although the complex, global relationships between buyers and sellers has raised the question of whether any transaction is truly 'arm's length'; this issue is discussed elsewhere in this volume. Where the owners of different links are the same and there is clearly no arm's length sale, then transfer and reference prices need to be established for fiscal purposes. These should reflect the different risks being assumed by the different links and prevailing market conditions. The alternative is to create a unique fiscal regime for the entire 'integrated' project.

In countries where gas industry infrastructure is not well developed and/or the gas project is particularly large, gas producers will often seek to have an economic interest in the full chain and participate in the ownership of the pipelines, processing facilities and transportation. They may even seek to buy the gas themselves for re-sale in another country. The main driver for this is normally control of the entire project, but it can also be driven by a desire to ensure that the company participates in any link of the chain which is generating the most economic rent. Most integrated projects are LNG export schemes but integrated domestic projects also exist, notably independent power projects (IPP), where gas producers own and operate the power generation plant and sell electricity into the local market.

If the ownership of links in the chain is different, it is regarded as 'segmented'. The upstream links tend to include production and transport of the gas to the processing plant. Variations include producers which sell the gas at the wellhead and gas fields which include gas processing in the production facilities. Midstream links tend to include the initial and secondary processing and transportation to the end user. Gas producers will sell their production either to a pipeline owner or processing plant, which then sells on to the next link, until reaching the end user. (See Figure 6.5 for examples of segmented and integrated LNG projects.)

In a segmented chain, negotiated agreements will usually dictate the market price and level of economic rent achieved in each link. North America, the UK and a small number of emerging markets in other consuming countries have established 'spot' markets where significant volumes are openly bought and sold and prices fluctuate on a daily basis. Elsewhere, natural gas is commonly sold under long-term contracts, with producers and midstream suppliers committing to supply certain volumes to buyers over a 20–year period for a price which will often be indexed to movements in competing energy products, such as fuel oil or coal.

Most sales contracts will include clauses designed to protect both the buyer (from upstream risks) and the seller (from market risks). Producers will commit to supplying a base volume in any period, often with a 'swing' factor, enabling the buyer to take significantly more in periods of high demand. In return, the

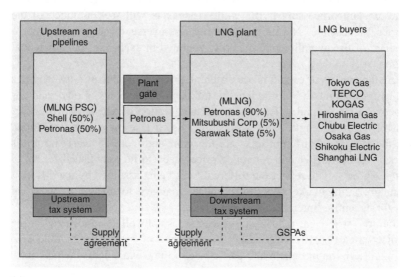

(a)

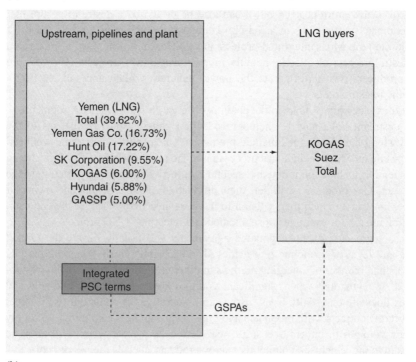

(b)

Figure 6.5 Schematic examples of segmented and integrated LNG projects: (a) Segmented taxation: Malaysian LNG; (b) Integrated taxation: Yemen LNG (source: Wood Mackenzie's LNG service).

buyers will commit to 'take or pay', which forces the buyer to pay for the base volumes even in periods of low demand. The pricing formula will also normally include provisions for fluctuations in the final market prices, substitute fuels (such as fuel oil and coal), currency exchange rates and other inflation measures. In many LNG contracts, price 'floors' and 'ceilings' are also agreed. Prevailing market conditions and resulting bargaining power, will heavily influence the final terms agreed in any gas sales agreement.

The government may own one or more links of the chain and dictate the level of economic rent to be captured by those links. For example, Algeria and Oman insist that most of the gas produced in the country, associated[1] with oil, is taken by the government which reimburses only the producers' costs. By contrast, the Indonesian government owns several LNG plants, which it operates on a tolling basis, recovering its own costs but enabling the remainder of the LNG price received to be passed to producers.

3 Natural gas taxation

A Upstream vs midstream taxation

The fiscal regimes for upstream and midstream operations are very different in most producing countries. Upstream production tends to be subject to more complex fiscal terms and can include bonuses, royalty, production sharing and windfall profits taxes, as well as corporate/petroleum income tax. Midstream operations, on the other hand, tend to be treated as general industrial projects and are subject only to standard corporate income tax. Major projects, such as green-field LNG plants, may even receive fiscal incentives such as temporary tax holidays.

The Malaysian LNG (MLNG) project highlights the differences between midstream and upstream taxation policies and the implications for other government policies, such as gas pricing and equity participation. Figure 6.6 illustrates the

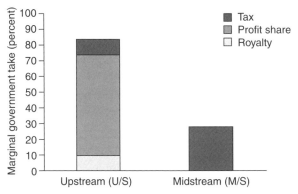

Figure 6.6 Upstream vs midstream taxation (Malaysia LNG) (source: Wood Mackenzie).

significant difference in the government take[1] from Malaysian upstream and midstream operations, where the total fiscal take is 83 per cent of upstream profits but only 28 per cent of midstream profits.

Petronas, the Malaysian national oil company (NOC), has a 50:50 joint venture with Shell in the upstream MLNG PSC. Petronas is also the purchaser of the gas at the plant gate, where it then sells the gas on to the LNG plant owners (at the same price as it pays for the gas). The price at the plant gate is usually referred to as the 'gas transfer price'. Petronas owns 90 per cent of the plant, which sells LNG to markets in North Asia.

The relationship between fiscal and gas pricing policies is critical. Figure 6.7 illustrates the difference between the total government take and investor profits from the project, under three different transfer pricing policies:

- Transfer price is established at the maximum price the midstream can pay (i.e. the plant's breakeven price).
- Transfer price is established at the minimum price the upstream can receive (i.e. the producer's breakeven price).
- Transfer price is established at the midpoint between upstream and midstream breakeven prices.

Figure 6.7 shows the distribution of the project's total profit, i.e. LNG price less the upstream and midstream costs.

The 'midstream breakeven' policy (which is comparable to the Indonesian policy of only reimbursing the LNG plant's costs) ensures that the upstream transfer/netback price is as high as possible. Figure 6.7 shows that, under these assumptions, this policy generates the highest level of overall government take because of the higher fiscal take from upstream operations.

The 'upstream breakeven' policy, which results in all of the economic rent residing in the midstream operation, is far less common. It is comparable to the

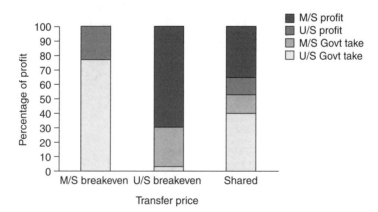

Figure 6.7 Total government take under different transfer pricing policies (source: Wood Mackenzie).

situation where upstream producers are deemed to have no rights to gas associated with oil production and deliver the gas to the government or midstream plant, with only costs reimbursed (e.g. Oman LNG) or recovered from oil revenues (e.g. Angola LNG). As a result of the lower tax rates applicable to the midstream operation, this generates the lowest overall government take of the different options.

The third alternative is that the difference between the two breakeven prices is shared between the upstream and midstream operations, either as a result of negotiation between the two parties or by government regulation. This results in a government take from the total project somewhere between the two extremes.

An example of this system is Australia's residual price mechanism (RPM), which is established for integrated LNG projects. (See Figure 6.8.) Australia levies a Petroleum Resource Rent Tax (PRRT) on upstream profits, but not on midstream operations. If there is no arm's-length agreement between the two operations, or a comparable local benchmark or price formula agreed in advance with government, then a proxy gas transfer price (GTP) needs to be established for purposes of calculating the PRRT payable by the upstream operation. Under the RPM, two prices are established:

- Cost-plus price.
- Netback price.

The RPM involves taking the average of the gap (or economic rent) between the cost-plus and netback prices for that operation. The cost-plus price represents the lowest price the upstream phase of a gas to liquids operation would sell its sales gas for; that is, the lowest price at which that operation would fully recover its costs of producing the sales gas. A gas transfer price below the cost-plus price means that it would be uneconomic to produce sales gas.

The netback price represents the highest price the midstream phase of a gas to liquids operation would pay for sales gas; that is, the highest price the operation

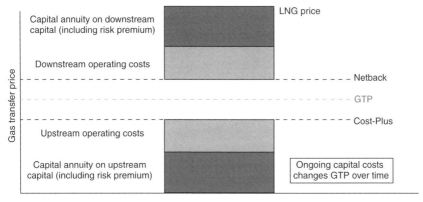

Figure 6.8 Australia's residual price methodology to establish transfer prices in LNG projects (source: Australian Government (Department of Resources, Energy and Tourism)).

could pay for sales gas and fully recover its costs of using the sales gas to produce LNG from the proceeds the operation obtains from selling LNG in the market place. A gas transfer price above the netback price means that it would be uneconomic to produce LNG.

In the cost-plus and netback calculations, capital costs incurred in the project pre-first gas are augmented using a capital allowance. Capital costs are uplifted by the long-term bond-rate plus a 'risk premium' of 7 per cent.

A feature of the RPM is that the transfer price tends to rise throughout the life of the project – a function of greater ongoing capital expenditure in the upstream phase of the project. This has the effect of gradually shifting more of the revenue to the upstream (higher tax) phase, and steadily increases the overall tax burden on the project.

As a general rule, therefore, the government will prefer to see the upstream transfer price as high as possible, when the upstream fiscal take is higher than from midstream operations. However, the government's equity interest in the chain's links can alter this perception. In the Malaysian LNG project example, the overall country take – i.e. the government take plus the NOC's equity inter-est – can be calculated and compared with the other companies' profit under the different pricing policies.

Figure 6.9 shows that the very high equity interest in the lower-taxed mid-stream operation results in a higher overall 'country take' when the lowest upstream transfer price is used than when the upstream transfer price is highest. As long as the government regards fiscal revenue and the NOC profits as similar sources of revenue, its attitude to transfer pricing can, therefore, be completely changed as a result of the difference in the NOC equity interest in the different links of the chain. Issues arise, however, when the NOC's profits begin to be diverted away from government coffers – for example, in the expansion of inter-national investments or in dividend payments following part-privatisation.

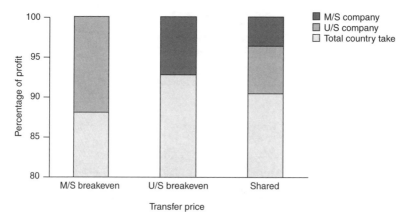

Figure 6.9 Total country take under different transfer pricing policies (source: Wood Mackenzie).

Thus, three policies relating to segmented natural gas projects need to be developed simultaneously:

i   Transfer pricing.
ii NOC equity in different links in the chain.
iii Upstream and midstream fiscal terms.

One route to resolving these simultaneous issues is to integrate the upstream and midstream operations into a single project with a specific fiscal regime. The NOC can take an equity interest in the entire project and there would be no need for an upstream transfer price as all fiscal considerations will be based on the final price received and all costs will be considered together.

B Integrated projects

Only projects which have a fiscal 'ring fence' around the entire project are truly integrated. If different tax systems apply to upstream and midstream, then, even with common ownership, the project is really 'segmented'. The existence of well-established upstream and midstream fiscal systems is one of the main stumbling blocks to integrating gas projects, as a new fiscal regime to apply only to the integrated project will need to overcome significant administrative and legal obstacles.

Another issue is that the gas supply needs to be dedicated wholly from fields or licence areas which are owned by the midstream participants. As soon as there is a divergence between the interests of the gas suppliers and the midstream operations, then transfer prices – and fiscal ring fences – need to be established, as discussed above. And one of the main attractions of integrated projects for government is the removal of concern about fair transfer prices being established.

Despite the difficulties inherent in establishing integrated projects, there are some notable examples:

*   *RasGas LNG (Qatar)*. The development of North Field gas is subject to a consolidated royalty/tax regime, based on the entire project revenues and costs.
*   *Yemen LNG*. All gas comes from the Block 18 PSC area and the PSC terms apply to gas production, valued at the Free on Board: (i.e. buyer pays for transportation (FoB)) LNG price with upstream and midstream costs included in cost recovery.
*   *Snøhvit LNG (Norway)*. Uniquely for Norway, all onshore (midstream) and offshore (upstream) operations in the Snøhvit project are treated as part of an offshore project and liable to offshore taxation, which allows all offshore operations to be consolidated for tax purposes. Onshore operations are only liable to a 28 per cent corporate tax while offshore operations are subject to an additional 50 per cent 'special tax'. Investors preferred the entire Snøhvit

LNG project to be treated as offshore rather than split between upstream and midstream because they could receive immediate tax relief at an effective 78 per cent rate from oil revenue, even though all future profits would be liable to tax at the 78 per cent rate. An additional fiscal incentive granted to the project was accelerated depreciation of capital costs (three years compared to standard six years schedule). These factors highlight the importance to investors of being able to recover capital costs as rapidly as possible, as this significantly improves the rate of return.

- *North West Shelf LNG (Australia).* Midstream costs are included in the upstream ring fence for royalty, excise and tax purposes. This is the only project offshore Australia which is liable to royalty and excise duty and not to the PRRT system described above.
- *Okpai IPP (Nigeria).* Power generation plant capital costs are consolidated with Eni JV's oil operations and attracts tax relief at the 85 per cent oil tax rate, with upstream gas profits (which are minimal) taxed at the standard corporate tax rate of 30 per cent.

Integrating the upstream and midstream operations within the same ring fence removes the need for government to regulate and/or monitor the gas transfer price to ensure fiscal fairness, but it still needs to ensure that the final product price is also reasonable. This issue is discussed further in Section 4 'Natural gas pricing and taxation'.

C Comparison of natural gas and oil taxation

The high levels of rent associated with oil production has resulted in many fiscal regimes for oil generating a very high level of government take from oil revenues. Some governments have used the existence of highly profitable oil projects to incentivise development of less attractive gas projects, particularly associated gas.[2] Gas which cannot be produced commercially must either be re-injected or flared. If the quantities of gas are large, re-injection can only be a temporary solution and gas flaring is universally discouraged (even if it still continues in some old facilities). Investors and government keen to progress development of oil then need to seek alternative solutions for the simultaneous development of the gas. Some examples of the resolution of this apparent stalemate can be found in:

- Nigeria: oil producers are currently allowed to include costs associated with the development of gas facilities in the capital cost pool for oil tax purposes and, therefore, receive tax relief at the Petroleum Profits Tax (PPT) rate of 85 per cent. Any operating profit from the gas sales (i.e. revenue less operating costs) is only liable to standard corporate income tax at 30 per cent. This enables producers to accept much lower gas prices than would be possible if the gas capital costs were not consolidated with oil.
- Angola: the NOC receives associated gas from certain deep water oil developments free of charge at the beach. In return the oil producers are allowed

to include the costs of the gas pipeline in their cost recovery pool, which attracts an uplift allowance and is included in the IRR-based oil production-sharing calculation, thus reducing the government's share of the oil profits.

• Algeria: in some projects, the investor is entitled to a share of the proceeds from sales of condensate and other associated liquids to recover costs and make a return, but all of the separated gas production is taken by the national oil company, Sonatrach.

Governments also often compensate for the less attractive economics of gas projects (see Section 3D 'Petroleum economics') by offering more attractive fiscal terms to gas producers, compared to oil. These can take several forms, but the most common are:

• lower royalty rates (e.g. Nigeria, Tunisia, Vietnam);
• higher cost-recovery ceilings and/or profit shares (e.g. Egypt, Indonesia, Malaysia);
• lower tax rates (e.g. Nigeria, Tunisia, Papua New Guinea); and
• exemption from certain oil taxes (e.g. Trinidad and Tobago (Supplementary Petroleum Tax)).

Just as gas can be a by-product of oil production, liquids may also be present in gas production streams (i.e. condensate or natural gas liquids (NGLs)). If the fiscal terms for oil and gas are differentiated, the treatment of condensate and other liquids produced in association with gas is an important issue for policy makers. On one hand, as condensate tends to command prices comparable to oil, it is logical for these revenues to be treated as oil revenue and subject to the same fiscal terms as oil. This is the practice followed in most countries.

On the other hand, treating the liquids revenue as gas revenue and subjecting these revenues to lower tax rates can significantly increase the economic viability of a gas project and enable the 'breakeven' gas price required to be much lower than if there were no associated liquids. If a very high level of tax is levied on the liquids revenue, however, this economic advantage is eroded for investors. This issue is most complex when the gas production is associated with oil production. With facilities already established for the export of oil, it makes sense to separate any liquids associated with gas production in the upstream facilities and export these using the oil infrastructure. It is then more difficult for investors to argue for preferential fiscal treatment for the condensate revenues.

The application of differentiated fiscal terms when oil and gas are produced together requires costs to be allocated to the different revenue streams. Many costs, particularly operating and maintenance costs, will be common to both operations and impossible to identify as pertaining to one or the other. In these situations, some form of cost allocation is required, which can be problematic and open to possible manipulation by investors to minimise the fiscal take. The most common approach is to allocate shared costs each year according to the proportion of total revenue generated by the project which is attributable to the different production streams.

In the few areas where domestic gas prices are not regulated and gas is sold in spot markets – primarily North America and the UK – fewer (if any) fiscal incentives are offered and the same fiscal regime applies to oil and gas production equally. This can create problems for investors if a significant divergence between oil and gas prices emerges in the spot markets. In a rising oil price environment, upstream costs tend to increase and most of these costs (e.g. drilling rig rates and fabrication rates for pipelines and production facilities) are the same for both gas and oil operations. But if gas prices do not rise as fast as oil, gas project economics will suffer in comparison.

There are a number of countries where fiscal terms have been agreed with investors for exploration and production of oil but contain no commercial terms for gas, such as many PSCs in West Africa. Investors who discover commercial quantities of gas may find that the government regards them as having no rights to the gas at all, and their involvement in the gas development will need to be gained, potentially in competition with other potential investors. In other situations, the oil investor may have the right to develop appropriate commercial terms with the government, but often the contract is silent as to the principles this should be based on.

Finally, an approach which can overcome many of the issues surrounding oil versus gas taxation is to develop fiscal terms which are linked to project profitability, such as profit sharing or tax rates linked to rate of return or 'R- factor' measures. These 'progressive' terms can apply to any individual project and will generate a high government take only from the most profitable projects. The arguments for and against the use of such fiscal regimes are made in more detail elsewhere in this volume.

D Petroleum economics: gas is not oil!

Upstream gas project economics are typically much less robust than oil for a number of reasons. First, consumers rarely pay the same for natural gas as the 'oil equivalent' price – primarily because oil production can be transported to energy markets more easily and is therefore in greater demand. Although some recent LNG purchases in Asia have been almost on a parity with oil prices and European and North American spot prices have occasionally resulted in parity pricing, normally gas prices are lower than the oil equivalent. Regulated prices in the domestic markets of developing countries will also tend to result in lower prices than for oil. Gas producers supplying export markets normally receive lower prices than oil, because of the additional liquefaction, transport and re-gasification costs. This is illustrated in Figure 6.10.

Given an FoB oil price of US$100/bbl (3Q 2008), the energy equivalent gas price is US$16.7/mmbtu (million British Thermal Units) (based on a bbl:mmbtu ratio of 1:6). However, FoB LNG prices will almost always be lower than this. Although some recent LNG sales agreements include parity

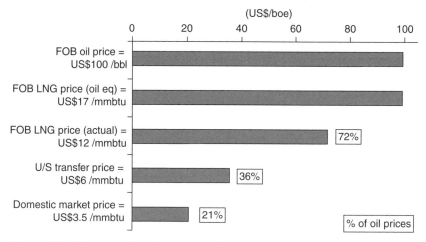

Figure 6.10 Oil vs gas prices (source: Wood Mackenzie).

Note
Numbers are hypothetical for illustrative purposes but based on some real LNG and domestic gas sales when oil was trading at US$100/bbl.

with oil prices for delivered LNG, there is still a discount for transportation to the market and re-gasification. Most existing sales contracts do not offer parity with oil, however, and for the purposes of this illustration, an indicative FoB LNG of US$12/mmbtu has been assumed – a 28 per cent discount on the oil equivalent price.

Before the producer receives its price, the midstream operation needs to recover its costs and make a return. Based on a US$12/mmbtu LNG price and assuming half of the price is passed upstream, the upstream gas price is US$6/mmbtu. This represents a 64 per cent discount to the oil equivalent price for the producer. Domestic sales prices in many developing countries are currently (3Q 2008) much lower than this. An indicative domestic price of US$3.5/mmbtu represents only 21 per cent of the oil equivalent price.

Gas is also more difficult to transport and generally incurs higher costs. However, even if gas production were sold at parity with oil and the costs were the same on an equivalent basis, gas project economics would still likely be less attractive than oil. This is because gas in most parts of the world is sold under long-term contracts, which imposes long, flat production profiles that reduce the present value of the production.

Figure 6.11 illustrates the difference in typical production profiles between oil and gas projects with the same reserves (100 million boe). Whereas the gas is produced over 20 years, the oil field would normally be depleted much faster, with a higher proportion of reserves produced in the early years. This has a significant impact on the present value of the production. In the example, discounting future production at 10 per cent p.a. provides a 'present value' of 73 per cent for the oil field but only 47 per cent for gas. In other words, even if prices and costs

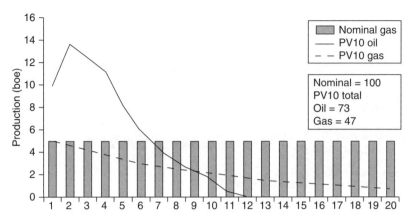

Figure 6.11 Oil field vs gas field production profiles (source: Wood Mackenzie).

are identical on an energy equivalent basis, gas production can be a third less valuable than oil production – unless the gas can be sold on spot markets and depleted as quickly as oil.

4 Natural gas pricing and taxation

A Final market and export prices

A major challenge for governments in the taxation of export projects is ensuring that the price which is used for calculating the government take is a fair and reasonable one. The lack of other gas sales prices to benchmark against and the level of tariffs charged by the owners of the links in the chain between the export point and the price paid for the gas in the final market, makes this difficult.

In an LNG project, for example, the FoB price is commonly used for calculating tax in the midstream or integrated projects. This is supposed to be the price paid by the end user, net of deductions for the transportation, regasification and marketing of the gas. Both the final market price and the level of deductions significantly impacts the FoB value, so government has a strong motive to ensure that all of these are fair. This creates difficult challenges.

The first issue is establishing that the final market price compares with similar sales by other producers into similar markets. Most gas export sales are under long-term (20–30 years) contracts, and the terms of sales agreements reflect numerous factors. The gas price in any period is normally derived from a base price agreed at the time of signing the contract and reflective of markets at the time, then linked by formulae which refer to the prevailing prices of competing fuels, inflation and other indices. Price floors and ceilings are often included.

Shifts in bargaining power and market conditions over time mean that the price being paid for gas under one agreement may be significantly different from that under another. These prices are also only rarely reported, so it is difficult to ascertain if the price in any particular contract is significantly higher or lower than is being paid for gas from other sources. In these situations, governments can refer to the few published gas prices that exist, with the most well known being the Henry Hub spot price in the US. In Europe, the most established spot price index is the National Balancing Point (NBP) in the UK.

Where the final destination is expected to be a market which does have reported gas prices, the sales agreement will often take the reported price as the basis for the FoB price, less deductions and any additional indexation factors. Thus, sales to the US could reference Henry Hub, with the FoB price increasing or decreasing as that price changes. The more directly the sales price is associated with a widely reported spot price, the more transparent the agreement can be seen to be and the more likely it is that the FoB price is fair.

The government of the producing country should also be concerned with the level of deductions being made from the final price to cover the costs of getting the gas to the market. An FOB price derived from the final market in the US, for example, might be expressed as follows:

$$\text{FoB Price} = \text{Henry Hub Price} \times (100 - (A + B + C))\% - (X + Y + Z), \text{ where}$$

- A = volumes lost in liquefaction process.
- B = volumes lost in regasification process.
- C = volumes lost in pipeline to Henry Hub/market.
- X = shipping tariff from export point to receiving terminal.
- Y = tariff for regasification.
- Z = pipeline tariff from regasification plant to Henry Hub/market.

An array of factors influence the levels of tariffs which are charged by the owners of the shipping, regasification and pipeline links in the chain. These include the availability of alternative suppliers of the services and facilities, distances involved, operating and capital costs of the facilities and the rates of return included in the owners' tariff calculations (which may be regulated but normally are not).

The same companies may own more than one of these links and have an interest in moving economic rent to the lowest-taxed link. Thus, government needs to carefully monitor and benchmark each of the tariffs being deducted from the final sales price. Although this can be very difficult – and investors clearly have advantages of asymmetry of information – there is an increasing amount of data and methodologies in the public domain which can help establish benchmarks. For example, third-party tanker freight rates are publicly quoted and several pipeline companies publish existing tariff rates on their websites.

Guidelines for 'reasonable' rates of return to be included in gas processing and pipeline tariffs are established under the US Federal Energy Regulatory Commission (FERC: www.ferc.gov) and Canada's National Energy Board (NEB: www.neb.gc.ca) rulings. It remains true, however, that ensuring fees charged for handling and processing gas (outside of the producing government's jurisdiction) are fair and reasonable is a significant problem for many governments. One possible solution to this is to place the 'burden of proof' onto the producing company in a self-assessment of the FoB price received. Under this policy, the company would need to demonstrate to the government that the fees it was paying (and volume losses it incurs) are within a reasonable range for the relevant cargoes.

A final issue related to netback pricing which has emerged in recent years is that the agreed FoB price may not actually reflect the final realised price. Some companies have developed integrated LNG businesses and can make use of their presence in different markets to optimise the economic benefit from any LNG trade. For example, an LNG buyer could agree to pick up LNG cargoes from a producing country, with an agreed price formula linked to the prevailing Henry Hub gas price, with the intention that the cargoes will be sold into the US market. However, if the buyer has an opportunity to sell the cargo into a different market (e.g. Asia), then it can do so and benefit from the price upside. The producing government (and producing company) will receive none of the upside unless the LNG sales agreement specifically addresses the issue. As a result, producers are beginning to seek specific sharing mechanisms for additional price upside in new LNG agreements.

B *'In-country' costs*

The issue of fair and reasonable fees charged is also pertinent to links in the value chain within the country. Fees will be charged by infrastructure owners (IOs) to third parties (e.g. producers of small gas satellite fields (SPs)) for use of gas gathering, processing and transportation facilities. Some transport facilities – primarily major gas pipelines in North America – are owned by companies which have no economic interest in the producing fields, but it is common for the development of natural gas infrastructure to be included as part of a first phase of upstream gas field development. Tariff agreements for the use of these facilities are normally the result of commercial negotiations between the IO and SP and rates will be negotiated somewhere between the IO's incremental cost of providing the service (which may be near to zero) and the SP's opportunity cost of developing an alternative option to deliver its output to market (which would often render the development uneconomic).

In the early years of an emerging basin, the major infrastructure will normally be owned by the producers of the initial field developments and their production will use most, if not all, of the available capacity. In these circumstances the IOs can essentially offer 'take it or leave it' terms to SPs. As basins mature and the number of pipelines and other alternative routes to market increase, the SP should develop a stronger bargaining position. As production from older fields decline and capacity becomes available in processing facilities and pipelines the IO will normally be keen to share the ongoing operating costs with SPs and tariff terms will become more favourable.

Tariff agreements are expected to arise from negotiations but, to different degrees, governments retain the right to intervene if an SP complains about the rates being offered by the IO. Canada and the US have regulatory bodies which oversee tariff settlements and provide guidelines for industry to follow. In the UK the industry and government have jointly developed guidelines for infrastructure access. In Norway and several developing economies with well developed national oil companies, all gas pipelines are operated by the state and pipeline tariffs are established by government.

Processing and transportation tariff arrangements are normally based on an SP securing a certain amount of capacity, often with an additional element based on actual throughput. This may be modified by 'use or pay' terms, which oblige the SP to pay a fee on the basis of a certain amount of throughput, regardless of how much production is actually sent to the facilities. Additionally, the SP may seek 'firm', i.e. guaranteed, or 'interruptible' access to the facilities, with lower tariff rates for the latter arrangement. Both parties will assess the risks of capacity and production volumes being available when negotiating the terms. Other agreements will provide for an 'all in' single rate, but in most cases the actual rate agreed will normally be calculated with some reference to the IO's operating and capital costs.

The 'operating fee' is normally established to share the ongoing operating costs of the infrastructure, according to each party's share of total throughput. The 'capital charge' is supposed to enable the IO to recover costs and make a return on equity/capital employed, and agreement on what is a reasonable return is one of the most likely sources of breakdown in negotiations between the parties. Some governments have issued guidelines on what is regarded as a 'reasonable' return on equity. IOs are not obliged to use these in negotiations, but if a case goes in front of the regulatory body, a significant departure from the return rate (without good cause) could be deemed unsupportable.

Fiscal terms can influence tariffs sought by IOs and the tariffs can impact fiscal revenues. Third party tariff income is normally either taxable or reduces tax allowances, which means that IOs seeking a net income must build the effective tax rate into their calculations. Where IOs are subject to different royalty or tax rates, this can create a competitive advantage for the IO with the lower tax rate as it can charge a lower fee to generate the same net after-tax income.

Similarly, because of the deductibility of tariffs, governments need to ensure that the tariffs charged are not being manipulated to achieve tax minimisation. The opportunity for this will be most apparent when the IO and SP have different tax rates and if a company has an economic interest in both the IO and SP.

C Subsidised prices or fiscal revenues?

In most developing countries, domestic energy prices are regulated and the resulting low prices available make these projects relatively unattractive to producers. In many countries, the inability of local consumers to pay anything like the international market prices for gas has traditionally meant that developing gas for domestic use has been considered uneconomic by investors, who are mostly interested in exporting gas to the more lucrative markets in North America, Europe, Japan and Korea.

The increase in energy prices between 2002 and mid 2008 has slowly been reflected in increasing domestic prices in developing countries, and interest in local projects is growing among producers, not least because of the surge in costs associated with exporting gas, whether by long-distance pipeline or LNG. With a strong political desire in most countries to expand local gas utilisation, the more the economic differential between domestic and export sales is reduced, the more attractive local projects will become. However, the transition from the current price structure in most developing countries to one comparable to that prevailing in the main consumer countries will take time.

In the meantime, to encourage development of gas supplies for domestic utilisation, governments are beginning to require gas producers pursuing export projects to include a component of domestic gas utilisation. For example, a new LNG project may require producers to also provide feedstock to a local power plant, as part of the overall development. Without the domestic commitment, the export project will not be approved. Thus, producers are obliged to supply the local market, although they will tend to keep their involvement in supplying gas to buyers as far upstream as possible.

Where prices are below the costs of production, the only way investors can be persuaded to develop the gas is if the government provides a subsidy – either explicitly or implicitly through some form of consolidation with oil production. Nigeria, for example, got around a similar economic impasse by allowing oil producers to consolidate the capital costs of gas utilisation projects to be recovered from oil revenues, thus attracting 85 per cent tax relief, while allowing any operating profits to be taxed under standard corporate tax rules, at a 30 per cent rate. Under certain circumstances, the tax generated from the production would be less than the tax relief allowed up front – an implicit subsidy for the oil producers. Investors claim that without this fiscal incentive, local gas prices – including the feedgas price the Nigerian LNG ('NLNG') project pays – are not high enough to enable economic development of the reserves. There has been much debate over the fiscal rules for gas projects in Nigeria in the past few years, but a new fiscal regime has yet to emerge (3Q 2008).

Where there is a significant divergence between domestic and export prices for gas, governments can either incentivise domestic projects through lower taxation or explicit subsidies to producers. Alternatively, they can reduce the economic attractiveness of export projects by levying an export duty on production. This can reduce the netback price to equate to the price available in the domestic market. There are a number of countries which impose such duties on oil exports, but only a small number apply export duties to gas, notably Argentina and Russia.

5 Conclusions

The government's pricing, NOC equity position and fiscal policies for natural gas projects must be developed simultaneously. If the existing upstream and downstream fiscal regimes are different – which is normal – the transfer price between the upstream and midstream operations becomes crucial. Under arm's-length agreements between upstream and midstream operations, market forces should dictate an appropriate price. If ownership of the two operations is the same, however, a proxy transfer price needs to be established. Alternatively, a separate tax regime could be developed for an integrated gas project, with the combined upstream and midstream operations treated as the taxable entity.

Just as it does for oil, governments need to closely monitor and benchmark final market prices, interim transfer prices and charges in each link of the value chain to ensure that taxable income is fairly calculated. In particular, government and producers should aim to share in realised market prices which are greater than expected, and this needs to be addressed in gas sales agreements. Unlike oil, however, the availability of market data on such sales is limited and often held confidential under long-term gas sales agreements, suggesting that the 'burden of proof' should rest with the taxpayer.

A high liquids content in a natural gas project significantly enhances its profitability and can enable producers to charge a lower price for gas. This can make the difference between a gas project being economically viable or not. When the liquids are liable to a high tax rate (e.g. oil tax rates), this economic benefit can be neutralised for investors. It is, therefore, important to consider how condensate is treated under differentiated fiscal terms, as this can influence the pace of development of the gas industry.

Gas projects may require more attractive fiscal terms than oil projects as a result of lower profitability, caused by lower energy equivalent prices; higher transportation costs; and longer, flatter production profiles. Fiscal terms which are progressive and linked to project profitability could apply to both oil and gas and the level of government take will automatically be lower from less profitable projects.

Acknowledgements

My thanks to Rich Ruggiero for the insightful comments he made in his discussion of the slides presented in Washington. During the conversion of that presentation to this chapter, the content has benefited enormously from the observations of Philip Daniel, Michael Keen and Charles McPherson of the IMF. My thanks also go to Andrew Pearson and Gavin Law of Wood Mackenzie's Gas and Power team for their guidance throughout the preparation of the paper.

Notes

1 Government take = Sum of all royalties, taxes, profit share, etc., expressed as a percentage of the pre-take cash flow or NPV. Country take = Government take + NOC equity cash flow.
2 'Associated' gas normally refers to gas which is produced in conjunction with oil but where oil production is the primary focus of the project. 'Non-associated' gas normally refers to fields/reservoirs which contain mostly gas reserves, although associated liquids such as condensate may be present as well.

Part III

Special topics

7 Evaluating fiscal regimes for resource projects

An example from oil development

Philip Daniel, Brenton Goldsworthy,
Wojciech Maliszewski, Diego Mesa Puyo, and
Alistair Watson

1 Introduction

The unprecedented rises in the internationally traded prices of crude oil and natural gas (petroleum) between 2002 and 2008, and the sudden fall after July of 2008, have concentrated attention once again on how petroleum revenues are shared between owners of the resource in the ground (usually governments) and the companies that extract the petroleum. A large portion of world production is undertaken by companies owned by the governments that also own the resource – in a group of countries representing over 30 percent of world output (including, for example, Iraq, Kuwait, Mexico, and Saudi Arabia) production is exclusively undertaken by national oil companies (NOCs) or even by the government itself. Among member states of the OECD, on the other hand, production by NOCs is now much less common. Across most of the world, the pattern falls somewhere in between – often with the NOC participating alongside private investors in extraction under petroleum rights granted by the government. In these cases, the NOC participation terms are part of the overall fiscal scheme (from the viewpoint of a private investor), and the NOC's net revenues form part of consolidated public sector revenues.

In the mining sector, exclusively state-owned production is less prevalent, though still important (in China and in Chile, for example, as well as many former Soviet Union countries). This chapter is concerned with circumstances in which petroleum or minerals are developed with at least part of the capital provided by private investors, so that those investors participate in both the risks and rewards.

The strong rise in prices for petroleum and mineral commodities occurred against great uncertainty (see Figure 7.1 for petroleum). Forecasters and forward markets have had a poor record of anticipating market developments. Fiscal regimes designed in earlier times, especially those with little built-in responsiveness to price, came under strain, leading to renegotiation of agreements or unilateral imposition of new terms by governments.[1] The price boom also caused a surge in demand for inputs to petroleum and mining production – whether

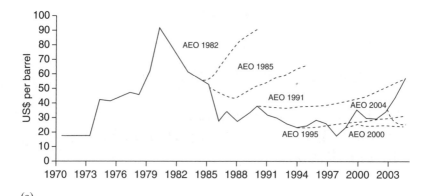

(a)

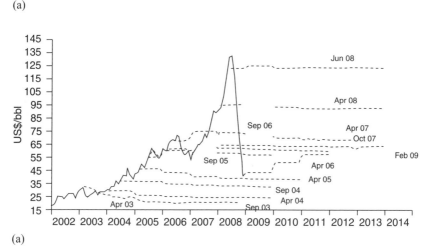

(a)

Figure 7.1 Uncertainty in prices and price forecasts (sources: US Department of Energy, Annual Energy Outlook (1982, 1985, 1991, 1995, 2000 and 2004); and IMF World Economic Outlook).

Notes

Charts are revised versions of Figure 2.3 in Ossowski *et al.* (2008).

* The solid lines are spot oil prices. The dashed lines are EIA price forecasts (top chart) and future prices (bottom chart).

** West Texas Intermediate (WTI) crude oil.

specialized skills, plant and equipment, or supplies – which sharply drove up the costs of exploration, development, and production. For petroleum, it also caused a revival of exploration interest in areas thought previously to bear a relatively lower probability of success, and in recovery from high cost and technically challenging locations or sources – deep water and oil sands, for example. Earlier generations of petroleum fiscal regimes designed either from forecasts of field profitability, or with reliance on field size and rates of production as a proxy for potential economic return, have not worked well in the face of such change in market conditions. Mining regimes limited to a low royalty and corporate income tax also came under strain.

This chapter outlines evaluation criteria and a modeling approach that can be used to analyze fiscal regimes for the petroleum and mining sectors from the perspective of a host government. We illustrate with the case of the impact of fiscal regimes at the point of the decision to develop a petroleum discovery. This is the core of evaluation of fiscal regimes, upon which evaluation at other decision margins (exploration, re-investment, abandonment) can be built. The basic approach to exploration evaluation (estimation of expected monetary value, or EMV) requires assignment of probabilities to an unsuccessful outcome and a variety of possible discoveries. The economics of the discovery cases will be like the development project cases studied here. The approach will be similar for mining projects – illustration is left for a subsequent paper.[2]

For many host governments, a key objective is attraction of exploration investment. Hence their interest in international comparisons. International comparison of fiscal regimes, however, has to interact with other factors – above all, the "prospectivity" (combined geological attractiveness and location) of an area. This paper makes no attempt at comparisons of prospectivity (at which oil companies themselves and consultants to the industry are expert, while staff of the IMF are not), except to the extent that differences in fiscal regimes may imply differences in prospectivity. Significant differences from country to country in the results of their fiscal regimes (for governments and investors) using identical project examples need to be explained by something – prospectivity as a combination of geological risk, physical location, and political risk being the most likely. If they emerge, and are not explained, then an initial case for revision of a fiscal regime can be made.[3]

We outline, first, criteria that can be used to evaluate minerals taxation systems and, second, indicators that can be used in a practical project modeling framework to assess the regime against the criteria. Although much of the approach draws from standard procedures used by practitioners in the evaluation of petroleum projects and fiscal regimes for resources,[4] this chapter tries to relate these to concepts employed in wider analysis of tax systems and their incentive effects.

The task is different from, but a variant of, the process of project evaluation for investment decision-making by companies.[5] In particular, a government will typically have objectives for the efficiency of revenue-raising, preferences concerning the risk profile of outcomes, and about timing or delay in revenues, as well as objectives that it may hold in common with investors for a regime that maximizes investment and output over time. In this chapter, the core building block for decision-making is analyzed – the profile of a petroleum project during development and production – from which a probability distribution of differing outcomes can be constructed to guide exploration decisions. The decision process itself works in the opposite direction (from exploration to development and production), with the higher risks usually at the earlier points, but each stage requires an assessment of the end and intermediate points.[6]

The application of the criteria and indicators is illustrated using a simulation for "Mozambique." The chapter does not replicate any particular contract or field for that country, but uses the model exploration and production concession contract with possible bid or negotiated parameters added by the authors. The circumstances of a country such as Mozambique recur elsewhere: one major petroleum project is already operating, there are further discoveries but, as yet, no further development decisions, and exploration interest is significant but possibly not sufficient to permit an auction process to work properly. After considering fiscal regime issues for this "Mozambique," the chapter locates the possible outcome in international comparisons. As with all such exercises, these have limitations and need to be carefully interpreted, taking account of things they do not show. An investment decision in any country will be determined by much more than a mechanical comparison of the effect of a fiscal regime on investor returns, simulating an identical field across a number of regimes.[7]

2 Evaluating resource taxation systems

A Criteria used in evaluating resource taxation systems

Resource taxation systems can be quantitatively evaluated for their neutrality, revenue-raising potential, risk to government (stability and timing of government revenue), effects on investor perceptions of risk, and their adaptability and progressivity.[8]

Neutrality

Neutrality in public finance usage means that a tax instrument (or regime) causes the least possible unintended disturbance to private economic decisions that would be made in the absence of tax. A neutral tax is one that does not change marginal decisions about investment, production, or trade that would have been made in the absence of tax. There will be instances where the imposition of tax can enhance economic efficiency, by correcting for externalities that arise when private and social interests diverge – that is, when there is market failure. For example, governments may use tax policy to reduce environmental pollution when the market, left to itself, would have polluted in excess of a socially optimal amount.

Neutrality in taxation of mining and petroleum activities means that a tax does not, of itself, alter the order in which projects including exploration are undertaken; nor does it alter the speed of extraction, decisions about reinvestment, or the decision to abandon a petroleum field, or close a mine.

Revenue-raising potential

The presence of natural resource rents makes resource industries major potential contributors to government revenues. Governments seek to tax as much of available resource rent as is compatible with the desired rate of investment in exploration and development, and of production. In most jurisdictions,[9] the government is the owner of the rights to mineral deposits in the ground. Thus, in addition to ensuring the resource sector makes its due contribution to public revenues in the same manner as other industries (through general taxation), fiscal arrangements are usually designed to secure a reward for ownership to the government. Government will usually receive a payment for this resource, separate from the regular income tax. This additional payment should be no greater than the value of resource rent – a return to the government as the resource owner which will not alter the behavior of the firm.[10] In this discussion, we abstract from the debate about whether resource rent should be broken down into components that include pure rent in the Ricardian sense, and the "user cost" or Hotelling rent – in the sense of the opportunity cost of exploiting a mineral deposit today rather than at some point in the future (for discussion see Boadway and Keen, Chapter 2). The evaluation techniques described here are capable of encompassing both views: effective tax rates can be computed including the effect of a resource payment, or with resource payments treated as part of project costs.

Neutrality itself will be relevant to revenue-raising capacity across a country's mineral endowment as a whole. Efficient allocation of mineral investment implies higher real generation of rent over time, and thus greater taxable capacity.

The effect of the tax system upon the investor's perception of risk will also affect its revenue-raising capacity. If the fiscal terms tend to promote contract stability, or reduce the dispersion of expected outcomes, or avoid enhancing the prospect of negative returns then the size of taxable rent may be increased. Defining rent as the surplus over all necessary costs of extraction, including the minimum returns to capital needed to induce investment in the first place, the reduction of risk will reduce the premium for risk attached to the required minimum returns.

Revenue-raising capacity will also vary with the maximum marginal rate of tax[11] that can be levied on an additional dollar of income or cash flow, and still remain consistent with incentives to continued productive efficiency. It will not usually be feasible to aim to tax 100 percent of rent because there are problems of accurate estimation, possible presence of quasi-rents, and the need for sufficient incentive to continued efficient operation.

Finally, the adaptability of the tax system to the realized profit of a project will also determine its capacity to raise revenue. This is also the progressivity criterion, discussed below.

Risk to government

With given risk preferences on the part of government and investors, it should, in principle, be possible to apportion risks and expected returns in an efficient manner for an individual project. Gains may be made where the parties are prepared to trade mean expected value for risk.[12] The preferences of the government will vary with its underlying fiscal position, access to capital markets, the extent of its portfolio of present and prospective resource projects, and the size of a project relative to the overall economy.

Stability and timing of resource revenue is an important consideration for the design of the tax system where there is high government exposure to this volatile source of revenue. In principle, welfare will be maximized where a government can maintain a sustainable fiscal position and, using access to capital markets, mitigate the domestic effects of mineral revenue volatility. Even where this is not always possible, those governments with a diverse portfolio of mineral assets are likely to be better able to withstand volume and price fluctuations than a government dependent, for example, on just one or two large projects. Moreover, a medium-term macroeconomic framework, buttressed by a savings strategy for resource revenues, could be preferable as a stabilizer to a sub-optimal tax system.

For those with large resource tax revenues, weak fiscal positions and limited access to capital markets, or with a very restricted portfolio of projects, a stable revenue stream throughout the life of the project may be desirable – even if it results in some diminution of total revenues over time. The more a government prefers such stability, the more it will favor a fiscal regime weighted towards fiscal instruments such as royalties that are related to total volume or value of minerals produced, and less towards taxes based on profits or cash flow.

A risk-averse party will attach greater weight to outcomes falling below the mean of the probability distribution of expected outcomes,[13] whereas a risk-neutral party will attach the same weight to all outcomes whatever their location along the probability distribution. The usual (though not always correct) assumption is that companies are risk averse, while governments are risk neutral. For a risk-neutral government, the variance of expected outcomes will be a reasonable measure of risk. A risk-averse government may seek to reduce that variance, foregoing the prospect of exceptional revenues to reduce the risk of very poor outcomes. If it is argued that the opportunity cost to government of exploiting the particular resource is low, then companies and governments would face significantly different profiles of potential outcomes – government would face the chance of a sub-optimal gain, while companies face risk of absolute financial loss.

The risk of deferral of government revenue is subject to the same considerations.[14]

Effects on investor perceptions of risk

Reduction of risks perceived by investors may reduce the required rate of return and raise the amount of rent available for collection. Risks faced by resource investors include: substantial initial investment exposure before revenues are generated and the possibility of a long payback period to recover this investment; uncertain commodity prices; and the political risk of unilateral alteration of fiscal terms by governments, or even – at the extreme – outright expropriation.[15]

Subjective expectations will play an important part in the determination of mineral rent – taken to mean the value of the product of a resource minus all the necessary costs of production, including the minimum return to capital that is require ex ante to induce the investment. Under uncertainty, expected return will be an assessment of the probability distribution of returns after tax. The supply price of capital to a project will be a convenient summary measure of the probability distribution, loosely termed the "rate of return," required by the least demanding investor. Because this is a subjective assessment, government can influence it by measures to increase the security of investment, accelerate the recovery of investment (payback), and reduce the likelihood of those negative outcomes that add greater weight to the investor's perception of risk.

Assuming resource companies to be risk averse, they will attach greater weight to outcomes falling below the mean of a probability distribution of expected outcomes. In analyzing resource taxation problems, however, it can be argued that, in practice, investors associate risk with failure to attain a target rate of return.[16] If so, the greater the value of outcomes below the target the greater the risk, and then risk can be measured as the expected value of outcomes with negative present value, discounting at the supply price of investment.

The assumption of risk aversion on the part of investors is very likely to hold where a significant part of the contribution to total investment funds is made by "bankers." This will occur where the finance for a project is not wholly a balance sheet liability of sponsoring companies, but where project lending is provided by financial institutions relying not on the guarantee of the sponsors (at least after completion) but on the cash flows and assets of the specific project.[17] Although "bankers" providing such finance may charge an interest rate margin above the cost of credit guaranteed by the sponsor companies, they still do not (usually) participate in the potential for equity-type returns when a project is especially successful. For a project financed in this way, therefore, the providers of capital as a collective have a strong preference ex ante for the avoidance of negative outcomes. In loan calculations, this will be expressed as a requirement for the project to meet certain financial ratios, especially a debt cover ratio (ratio of free cash flow after taxes to obligations for principal and interest payments on debt).

The contribution of any tax regime to expectations of stability in contract terms will be difficult to measure. The closest proxy is likely to be some measure of the responsiveness of the fiscal regimes to changed circumstances in output prices, costs, or volumes of production.

Adaptability and progressivity

The adaptability of the tax system to realized profit will have a strong bearing on revenue-raising capacity, especially when the tax system is of general application across projects. Taking the realized profit, or "profitability," as the combined outcome of costs, output prices, and output volumes, the adaptability of the system will also influence investor perceptions of risk. A system that responds flexibly to changes in circumstances may be perceived as more stable.

Depending upon the parameters set, it may also be less likely to increase risk, since it will take relatively less in conditions of low, or no, realized profit.

Adaptability can be measured by indicators of progressivity (discussed below), where progressivity means that a tax regime will yield a rising present value of government revenue as the pre-tax rate of return on a project increases. Conversely, a regressive regime will bear heavily on projects of low profitability, and the government share will decrease as intrinsic profitability rises.

Interaction among criteria

There are unavoidable trade-offs between neutrality, revenue-raising capacity, the risk and timing of the receipt of revenue, and the adaptability or progressivity of a fiscal system. A fiscal regime that is less reliant on income taxation and more on royalties will generate a relatively more stable and timely revenue stream, while imposition of import duties will yield a revenue stream during the investment phase. However, import duties will increase the cost of investment, and royalties may raise the marginal cost of extraction – discouraging development, at the margin, of otherwise economic projects or remaining resources. Similarly, an increase in the tax rate applicable to existing projects may raise revenue potential, but it will deter future investment (and, in the long run, reduce revenue). Administrative considerations are also important (see Chapter 11 by Calder). For example, a royalty based on a transparent price formula may be easier to administer and monitor than a resource rent tax.[18]

These trade-offs and administrative considerations call for political judgment – a unique best policy cannot be proposed.

B Indicators for measuring the evaluation criteria

Indicators for evaluating the economics of the project

The evaluation of a mineral taxation system from the investor's standpoint requires the assessment of before- and after-tax economics of the project. This section examines a number of alternative methods for doing this that incorporate uncertainty and an investor's assessment of risk.

NPV and variations of the discounted cash flow method

SINGLE DISCOUNTED CASH FLOW

The discounted cash flow (DCF) method is the traditional approach used by investors to calculate a project's net present value (NPV). In this approach, the expected values of future cash flows are discounted using a risk adjusted discount rate (RADR), or "hurdle" rate. If the cash flows are known with certainty, the discount rate only needs to account for the opportunity cost of capital to the firm – a "risk free" cost of capital. However, if the cash flows are uncertain (the usual case), the discount rate will equal the sum of the cost of capital and the premium that is required to compensate the investor for risk. In resource projects, those risks can be project-specific and country-specific. A typical approach begins with the principle that the hurdle rate should equal the firm's cost of capital (see Appendix II for an approach to estimation of the cost of capital). This will reflect the firm's financial leverage, after-tax borrowing costs, and expected return on equity. Calculations are typically performed, first, on an all equity basis, so that financial leverage can be then be separately evaluated as a means to optimize returns to the firm's equity. For individual project appraisal, the hurdle rate might consist of the cost of capital, plus a premium for technical and market risks in the project (including price risks), and a premium for sovereign risk related to the country in which the project is located. Hurdle rates for initial project screening are often uniform, and set by corporate policy.

The risk-adjusted DCF method has been criticized for not properly accounting for cash flow uncertainty. In addition to the practical difficulty in choosing a risk-adjusted rate, the DCF method has been criticized for applying a single discount rate to both revenue and expenditure cash flows. Many argue that revenues and expenditures should instead be discounted separately, using rates that reflect the riskiness of each cash flow component.[19] Further, the use of a single discount rate assumes that the risk structure is stationary, which may not be the case, especially for long-life mining projects where risk tends to decline as the project develops.[20]

Comparison of internal rates of return (IRR) is a variant of the DCF method. The IRR is the discount rate that equates the NPV of a project to zero. A common investment rule is to accept an investment project if the opportunity cost of capital (equivalent to the hurdle rate) is less than the IRR – in which case the NPV would be positive. There are, however, a number of additional pitfalls in using the IRR (Brealey and Myers, 2005). These include the possibility of there not being a unique IRR, inability to account for an opportunity cost of capital (and, hence, discount rate) that varies over time and difficulty in ranking projects where the initial outlay is different.[21]

SENSITIVITY ANALYSIS

Sensitivity analysis is often used to provide the investor with an assessment of the range and distribution of likely outcomes in the DCF method. The base case, and reference point for further analysis, is the NPV generated by estimating the expected value of each variable used in the DCF calculation. Investors will also be interested in the best and worst cases. These can be generated by using values of those variables with uncertain future values that lie at the extremes of a probability distribution. Additional scenarios can also be run to isolate the impact of each source of uncertainty. For example, the effect of different commodity prices can be analyzed by holding input costs and other uncertain variables constant. A key limitation of this approach is that it gives little insight into the relative likelihood of different outcomes, and provides no guideline for hurdle rate adjustments after incorporating uncertainty (provided that the hurdle rate is properly risk-adjusted under the base case, using the same rate in an alternative scenario may lead to double counting of risk).

An alternative approach to accounting for risk is to discount certainty-equivalent cash flows using the risk-free interest rate. The certainty-equivalent cash flow is the amount that would make the investor indifferent between having that amount for certain or maintaining the rights to the uncertain cash flows from the project. In other words, the certainty equivalent approach adjusts for risks in the estimates of the cash flows, not through adjusting the discount rate. Financial market information can often be used to construct certainty-equivalent cash flows for resource projects. This method is easy to apply, however, only when price variability is the single source of uncertainty, and even then, difficult assumptions need to be made about forward prices beyond the maturity for which they are available (Grinblatt and Titman, 2002).

This approach involves defining a probability distribution for each project variable that is uncertain, and sampling from these distributions the cash flow for each period. After large numbers of samples, an estimate of the probability distribution of project NPV can be made. A number of useful summary statistics can then be calculated, including the expected NPV, standard deviation of NPV, and the probability of the NPV being less than a chosen threshold. Simplifying assumptions have typically been needed to make the model computationally tractable,[22] and most commonly involve assuming that some variables are deterministic and those that are stochastic are normally and independently distributed.[23] To the extent that these assumptions are not valid, the estimated NPV distribution will deviate from the true (unknown) distribution. In principle, if all uncertainty is properly taken into account in the Monte Carlo simulation, the hurdle rate can be set at the cost of capital, with all risks reflected in the distribution of the NPV. The distribution of outcomes from the simulations can be used as an input to decision making directly, or summary statistics can be constructed, reflecting investors' attitude toward risk. Since accounting for all the project uncertainty is difficult, some risks may still need to be reflected in the hurdle rate rather than directly in the simulated cash flow.

Incorporating managerial flexibility

A major criticism of DCF methods outlined so far is that they ignore managerial flexibility. Specifically, they implicitly assume that managers are passive once the binary decision on whether to invest has been made, regardless of how future events unfold (Smith and McCardle, 1998). In reality, however, managers respond to developments in output prices and other uncertain variables by expanding or abandoning production, or by varying the firm's output mix or its production methods (Slade, 2001). In some cases, managers may also have the option to wait before committing to invest. Options such as these are valuable and so the DCF method will understate the NPV of those projects that afford managerial flexibility.[24]

The decision tree approach (Box 7.1) improves upon the previous methods by reflecting investors' decisions over time in an uncertain environment. Decision trees outline the available options embedded in projects. They also take into account uncertainty in important variables by attaching probabilities to discrete outcomes. The decision tree has nodes which represent points of uncertainty (e.g. unknown commodity price) or decision (e.g. continue or suspend production), and branches which represent a range of possible alternatives at each node (e.g. commodity price is high or low). The project is valued at the end of each branch by discounting the cash flows arising along that branch. Similarly, the probability of an individual outcome can be determined by multiplying the probabilities at nodes along the branch. Thus, the method provides a range of possible project outcomes, and informs the investor of the relative merits of various decisions. The main advantage of decision trees is that they explicitly account for different managerial responses. They require, however, that probabilities be determined at each node. Moreover, the decision tree method has even more difficulty in incorporating correlation between variables (Galli *et al.* 1999), and can quickly become very complex and intractably large unless limiting simplifying assumptions are made (Smith and McCardle, 1998).

The real option method incorporates the value of managerial flexibility by recognizing that the methodology to value financial options can also be applied to value real assets. A basic call option gives the buyer the right, but not the obligation, to buy a security at a specified price in the future. Similarly, an investor can purchase the rights to undertake an investment project: the underlying asset is the present value of expected net cash flows from the project; the exercise price of the option is the required investment outlay; and the term of the option is the period for which the firm has the rights to the project. A similar framework can be applied to analyze other real options such as the flexibility to change levels of production in response to price movements. The real option method, however, is difficult to apply in practice, and requires a number of simplifying assumptions. These assumptions typically include that the commodity price is the only source of risk. In addition, the results are sensitive to the stochastic process that the commodity price is assumed to follow.

In view of some of the complications of the decision tree and real options methods, they are not further pursued in this paper, although the modeling approach explored in this paper can be extended to incorporate the decision tree method.[25] In particular, a specific case of the decision tree is the assessment of expected monetary value (EMV) in the assessment of exploration economics. The quantitative appraisal in this paper is confined to decision-making at the development margin, but the project modeling apparatus can be straightforwardly adapted for the analysis of the effect of fiscal regimes on exploration decisions, using EMV analysis (see Box 7.1, and Appendix III).

Box 7.1 Using the modeling framework to evaluate choice of exploration location

Investors will seek to identify countries which provide the highest return on exploration investment measured on a risked, after tax basis – simply expressed as expected NPV per dollar of expenditure. This can be comparatively evaluated by calculating Expected Monetary Value (EMV) for a range of potential countries or jurisdictions. The evaluation of a development project, set out in this paper, is a key building block for calculating EMV.

The EMV equals the sum of: the probability of unsuccessful exploration multiplied by expected after tax NPV loss from failed exploration costs, and the probability of each type of successful discovery multiplied by the expected after tax positive NPV from successful projects. The relative probability of each outcome would require a geological and technical assessment. (See Appendix III for a more formal treatment.)

The after-tax NPV loss from failed exploration would comprise:

- Expected costs for carrying out an appropriate exploration program up to the point where either a discovery, or a decision to pull out, would be made.
- Reduction of this exploration cost by any tax benefit, to the extent that the investor is able to claim a tax deduction against other operations in that country, if any exist.

The expected NPV of a successful discovery, and EMV, could be calculated using a decision tree taking into account: the type and size of projects arising from a discovery, given that country's geological setting, and history of other developments; the relative probability of each potential project; expected after tax NPV for each potential project, preferably taking into account specific local circumstances and cost structures.

While computationally much more intensive, the same range of analytical tools presented elsewhere in this chapter can be applied to the portfolio of potential projects, rather than a single project. In addition, the expected EMV per dollar of exploration investment would provide a useful comparative statistic (arguably the single most relevant to an investor).

EMV decision tree example:

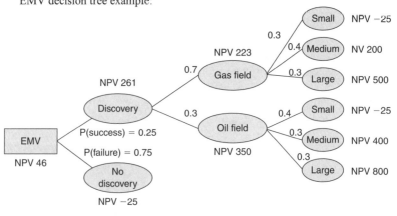

Indicators summarizing features of the fiscal regime

We begin with consideration of indicators commonly used in general analysis of taxation, and then consider how these can be applied in the specific context of petroleum and mining.

AVERAGE EFFECTIVE TAX RATE

With mobile capital, neutrality of the tax system can be interpreted with respect to the decision on where to invest, and the decision on how much to invest.[26] For a given investment, without other locational differences, the discrete choice between two or more mutually exclusive locations depends on the average effective tax rate (AETR) – how much tax a firm will pay on an average investment. It can be proxied by the ratio of tax collections to a measure of the tax base, using either national accounts and other aggregate data (Mendoza *et al.* 1994) or financial statement information (Collins and Shackelford, 1995). However, these measures have been criticized because they are backward looking in that they reflect taxes levied on income generated by past investment decisions. In response to such criticisms, Devereux and Griffith (2003) developed a framework for a forward-looking AETR. A forward-looking AETR is familiar in resource industries, calculated as the ratio of the NPV of tax payments to the NPV of the pre-tax net cash flow from a project that generates a return greater than that from a marginal investment.

MARGINAL EFFECTIVE TAX RATE

The location decision, however, depends upon evaluation of the optimal investment in each possible country, which will vary with the marginal effective tax rate (METR). The METR is the ratio of the difference between the pre- and post-tax rate of return, for a marginal investment, to the pre-tax return (see Appendix I for a more formal treatment).

The size of this "tax wedge" depends on a number of factors, in addition to the rate of tax on profit. The real after-tax rate of return on investment is affected by the tax treatment of the financing of the firm, and tax depreciation provisions. Inflation assumptions affect the calculation in that inflation erodes the value of future tax depreciation allowances, or losses carried forward, but increases the value of future interest deductions arising from debt financing. Indirect taxes, particularly import duties, may also be important, as will specific investment tax incentives, such as tax holidays, and the tax treatment of inventories. For investments that are domestically financed, the METR may also be affected by the personal income tax regime through its impact on the after-tax rate of return to saving. For example, the tax system may make a distinction between interest, dividends and capital gains, introducing distortions into an individual's choice of savings vehicle, or it may influence inter-temporal consumption preferences.

Application to resource projects

Some re-interpretation is required to apply these measures to the evaluation of resource taxation systems.

For all practical purposes, the interaction with personal income tax systems can be ignored. In the circumstances of petroleum investment in developing countries, the bulk of the inflow is from overseas and only the return at the corporate level needs to be considered.[27]

The investment decision concerns a resource whose dimensions are initially estimated and whose location is fixed,[28] and for which the techniques and scale of production are also largely fixed (with little or no substitutability among factors of production). The METR therefore may not serve as a prime determinant of the initial scale of investment at the individual project level. If we conceive of petroleum investment in a country over time, over the whole of its possible petroleum deposits, then the METR would be an indicator of the deviation between the optimum level of investment to extract available resources, and the investment that will be forthcoming with a given fiscal regime. During the extraction phase, it may also indicate which incremental investments are viable, and thus influence the proportion of the resource ultimately recovered.

The METR can be viewed as an indicator of the neutrality or otherwise of the fiscal regime. Where there is a large tax-induced wedge between before and after-tax rates of return, then the range of otherwise feasible projects that can be developed will be narrowed. The ordering of projects may also be changed if the fiscal regime produces varying METR results for projects with differing cost and production profiles.[29]

A less formal expression of this concept (which we illustrate below) is estimation of the output price (strictly, a price path) at which a particular project will generate a post-tax rate of return that will just induce investment – a "breakeven" price. An alternative is the minimum size of resource required for viability, with given techniques and prices.

Given the fixed location of deposits, the METR applied to a petroleum project can be compared across countries. Ideally, it should be calculated separately for each fiscal regime with a field example appropriate to that regime, or at least to the country's circumstances. Most international comparisons (including ours) examine the effects of different fiscal regimes on a suite of typical field examples, so that fiscal differences alone are captured.

The literature on estimating METRs is extensive, with differences in the scope of tax treatment incorporated and assumptions made.[30] Most studies only include direct taxes in the METR calculations because indirect taxes, in particular withholding taxes on payments for inputs and import duties, often come with a complex structure of multiple rates and exemptions, making their impact on a particular project difficult to determine.[31]

The AETR – better known as "government take" in the petroleum sector – is a familiar measure used in international comparison of fiscal regimes. It compares the share of petroleum rent taken by government across countries: the "government take" at a rate (or range of rates) of discount designed to simulate the risk adjusted return required ex ante by investors.

A major limitation of most AETR and METR estimates is that they ignore risk. In most cases, calculations are based on the assumption that all non-tax factors are the same in each jurisdiction being analyzed, including a common discount rate in NPV calculations. Such an approach ignores differences in risks across jurisdictions – both sovereign (political and regulatory stability, and reliability of infrastructure) and geological (uncertain reserve quantity and grade) – which may lead to erroneous country-attractiveness rankings. The previous section explored this issue with respect to the method of discounting.[32]

Stability and timing of government revenue

The stability and timing of government revenue can be assessed by analyzing the profile of estimated tax payments. Different tax regimes will create different tax profiles (a) through the effect on the timing of investment and production by altering incentives (non-neutrality), and (b) because different tax instruments will give rise to different profiles for a given pattern of depletion of mineral deposits. Stability can be assessed by calculating the variance in NPV of government cash flow, while timing can be assessed by constructing various summary measures, such as the proportion of the cash flow received in the first *n* years of the project.

C Summary of indicators

This section summarizes indicators discussed above and used in numerical examples below. Monte Carlo simulations are conducted to account for the effect of oil price uncertainty. The distribution of outcomes is measured both by summary statistics and by graphical representation of the cumulative probability distribution of outputs. Since the investor's expected return depends on the investor's attitude to risk, when applicable we consider both risk neutral and risk-averse cases: (a) where equal weight is assigned to positive and negative outcomes, and (b) where the investor is solely concerned to minimize negative outcomes (those below the assumed target rate of return). The risk-averse investor is interested not only in the probability of below target returns, but also in the relative expected value of possible negative outcomes. In particular, we are interested in the tax-induced expected negative present value: the pre-tax negative present values are subtracted from the post-tax negative present values generated under each regime.

Measures of impact of the fiscal regime upon investors

The present value of net cash flows (NPV) at a variety of discount rates, reflecting non-price risks as discussed above. Where this is calculated as the mean of a probability distribution, it will portray the likely ranking of regimes or projects by investors who weigh the probability of gains and losses equally (risk neutral), on the assumption that all other influences on the investment decision are equivalent.

The expected rate of return (IRR) on total funds outlaid in a discounted cash flow calculation, where "total funds" means equity, debt, and retained earnings expended on project investment. In accounting terms, this return on total funds comprises operating profit less capital expenditure, change in working capital, and taxes. Interest is not deducted, except in tax calculations, so interest must be covered by positive cash flow (and is thus part of the expected return).

Average and marginal effective tax rates as discussed earlier.

Breakeven price required to achieve a target rate of return.

Payback period (in years) for recovery in real terms of initial investment outlay.

Dispersion of expected IRR is the coefficient of variation of the IRR in a probability distribution of multiple outcomes.

Expected risk index is measured as the expected value of tax-induced below target outcomes in a probability distribution of multiple outcomes, in relation to a benchmark regime.

Additional measures of the impact of the fiscal regime upon government

Time profile of government revenue represents graphically the magnitude and timing of revenues, which can be easily compared from one case to another.

The tax (state) share of total benefits. The AETR is equivalent to the familiar notion of "government take," or state (plus national resource company) share of the present value of net cash flows to total funds outlaid at a given discount rate (for example, NPV15), otherwise termed "net benefits." When showing this as the state share of resource rent the plotting of the line in cases of increasing profitability usually shows a declining state share as pretax net present value rises, until very high rates of pretax return are simulated. This occurs because, where the investor bears the whole of initial capital outlay, the investor share of NPV at first rises rapidly with project profitability, until higher profitability triggers progressive elements in the fiscal regime sufficient to cause a relative increase in the government share. The effect of royalty, or minimum production shares, or income tax with long depreciation periods, is significant as a proportion of net cash flow when pretax returns are low but falls as pretax returns rise. Virtually all fiscal schemes therefore appear regressive when graphed in this way, and the progressive properties of the instruments within the fiscal regime are obscured.

It is therefore useful, in addition, to plot the state share of "total benefits" – revenues minus operating costs and replacement capital expenditure after start-up, expressed at a selected discount rate. The denominator in the share calculation therefore does not have initial investment costs deducted. These total benefits represent the cash generated by the project that is available to reward the providers of capital (to service both debt and equity, representing the initial capital outlays) and to meet all fiscal impositions, including state production shares and returns to concessional state participation. By this measure, the relative progressivity of the fiscal regime, and of each element within it can be more clearly shown. The shape of the curve also provides another indicator of the extent to which the fiscal regime is likely to impede recovery of initial capital outlays.

The state share of "rent" is a graph of the AETR calculated for a range of present value outcomes, at a discount rate assumed to represent the investor's minimum required rate of return.

Variance of government revenue measured as the coefficient of variation of the present value of government revenues from a probability distribution of outcomes.

This measures the dispersion of possible outcomes, and is a measure of risk to government (government may prefer a narrower range of potential outcomes).

Expected yield index is measured as the mean NPV of government receipts, from a probability distribution of multiple outcomes, set in relation to the figure for a benchmark regime.

Government share of total benefits in the first n *years of project operation* measures, when compared across cases, change in the timing of government revenue. In this analysis the period is ten years, but could easily be any other desired period.

Finally, it is possible numerically to illustrate some trade-offs in fiscal regime design by comparing the effect of changes as between the government's *expected yield index* and the investor's *expected risk index*. It is also possible to estimate an implied "*prospectivity gap*," on certain assumptions, as perceived by a risk-neutral or a risk-averse investor, meaning the advantage or disadvantage to the investor demonstrated by one fiscal regime when compared with another, using the same simulated project and price scenarios. As discussed earlier, prospectivity here means a combination of geological risk, physical location, and political risk. If this advantage or disadvantage is significant, then the first hypothesis to investigate is whether the fiscal regime differs as a direct consequence of differing perceptions of prospectivity. If it does not, then there is a case for revision of the fiscal regime (or for discovery of new parameters by offering prospects at auction). Table 7.1 contains a summary of criteria and indicators.

3 Evaluation of economics of fiscal terms and alternative regime

This section evaluates the economic terms for potential petroleum operations in "Mozambique" using three simulated oil fields (see Chapter 4 by Nakhle, for detailed treatment of alternative types of petroleum fiscal terms). Stylized fiscal terms ("current terms"), working within the 2007 model EPCC of "Mozambique," are evaluated in terms of neutrality, revenue-raising potential, risk to the government, adaptability, and progressivity, as discussed earlier in this paper. The "current terms" are then compared against a hypothetical alternative fiscal package to illustrate potential benefits from regime refinements. Finally, the "current" and alternative terms are set in an international context, with an estimate of the "prospectivity gap" implied by the fiscal regimes.

A General assumptions

Geology and operating costs

The simulated oil field examples are: (i) a medium-large onshore field, (ii) a medium offshore shallow water (< 200 m) field, (iii) and a large deep water field (1500 m). All exploration and appraisal,[33] development, and operating costs reflect actual cost levels in the upstream industry.[34] Table 7.2 lists projects and their costs.

Table 7.1 Evaluation criteria and indicators

Evaluation criterion	Key indicators	Type of sample or output
Neutrality	Average effective tax rate (government take in profitable case)	Single case, international comparisons
	Marginal effective tax rate (wedge between pre and post tax IRR, as % of pretax)	Single case at investor's discount rate
	Breakeven price	Price just yielding investor's discount rate
Revenue Raising Capacity	Time profile of revenue	Single case, graph
	Share of rent to government	Range of cases, graph
	Tax share of total benefits	Range of cases, graph
Adaptability/Progressivity Risk to Government	Variance of NPV of revenues (coefficient of variation)	Probability distribution of cases
	Proportion of revenues in first *n* years	Single case (or mean of distribution)
Investor Perceptions of Risk	Dispersion of expected IRR (Coefficient of variation of IRR)	Probability distribution of cases
	Probability of below-target returns	Probability distribution of cases
	Value of negative returns	Probability distribution of cases
	Cumulative probability distribution of outcomes	Probability distribution of cases, graph
Relating Revenue Yield to Investor Risk	Compare expected yield index with expected risk index	Probability distribution of cases
"Prospectivity Gap"	Present value to equalize mean PV to investor	Probability distribution of cases
	Present value to equalize PV of negative returns	Probability distribution of cases

Oil prices

The simulation of potential revenue generated by the projects uses World Economic Outlook (WEO) price projections at end-February 2009. These extend until 2014, where prices significantly compared to 2008 levels (Figure 7.2), and a constant price in real terms is assumed thereafter.

In Monte Carlo simulations we account for uncertainty surrounding future oil prices by assuming that oil prices follow a stochastic stationary first-order autoregressive (AR(1)) process. Details of the estimation of the parameters of this process are described in Box 7.2. The hurdle rate in NPV calculations below is still adjusted upwards to take account of other, non-price risks.

Table 7.2 Project examples

Onshore Oil Project

Oil production	million bbl	100
Oil production	years	17
Finding and development costs	$ per bbl	5.5
Operating costs	$ per bbl	4.4
Decommissioning costs	$ millions	20

Shallow Water Oil Project

Oil production	million bbl	151
Oil production	years	18
Finding and development costs	$ per bbl	13.6
Operating costs	$ per bbl	6.8
Decommissioning costs	$ millions	80

Deep Water Oil Project

Oil production	million bbl	1,000
Oil production	years	21
Finding and development costs	$ per bbl	11.8
Operating costs	$ per bbl	4.8
Decommissioning costs	$ millions	1,000

Hurdle rate

Cost of capital estimates for integrated petroleum companies and petroleum producers in the US in 2008 seemed to lie in a range of 8 to 9 percent in nominal terms.[35] An appropriate "project" margin over this may be 3 to 4 percentage points, bringing this discount rate conveniently close to 12.5 percent nominal or

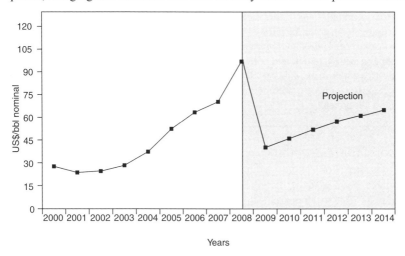

Figure 7.2 WEO oil price projection (as of February 2009).

Box 7.2 Oil price simulation

This box explains the autoregressive model (i.e. the price today helps predict the price tomorrow) used to generate the stochastic oil price simulations used in the chapter.

Data used

The original data used are the annual simple average of three oil spot prices: Dated Brent, West Texas Intermediate, and the Dubai Fateh published in the WEO between 1960 and 2008. These prices were adjusted annually for US inflation, using 2008 as the base year, and then normalized by taking natural logarithms.

Autoregressive (AR) model

It is assumed that real oil prices follow an autoregressive process given by

$$y_t = \alpha + \beta \, y_{t-1} + e_t \tag{1}$$

where y_t is the oil price in real terms defined above, α and β are parameters relating the current price to its past value, and e_t is a stochastic error term distributed normally with zero mean and variance σ^2. If $|\beta| < 1$, $\alpha/(1 - \beta)$ is the mean of y_t, to which y_t will tend to revert in the long run. Parameters of the model are estimated by OLS, yielding the following estimated equation:

$$y_t = 0.25 + 0.94 \, y_{t-1} + e_t \text{ where } e_t \sim N(0, 0.26) \tag{2}$$

Stochastic simulations

In stochastic simulations, future oil prices are generated recursively using equation (2), starting again from the latest available price level (an average price of US$95/bbl was used for 2008), and with error terms randomly generated (using a normal distribution with parameters reported in (2)). Additionally, lower (US$20/bbl) and upper (US$200/bbl) bounds on oil prices are imposed to avoid extreme values. This exercise is repeated multiple times to construct a range of possible outcomes for future oil prices.

10 percent in real terms. What then is the appropriate discount rate for an activity outside the investor's home country, incorporating country risk? On dollar denominated bond spreads, the additional margin is probably somewhere in the range of negligible to 10 percent, implying that a "worst case" discount rate (from a government viewpoint) would be 20 percent in real terms, with a "best case" at 10 percent real. In line with earlier discussion, this paper uses a hurdle rate above the minimum to account for non-price risks. The effects of varying this rate upwards, and the discount rate for government downwards, are also illustrated.

A Economics of "current terms" and alternative package

Current terms

The "current terms" applied in "Mozambique" are summarized in Table 7.3.

Revenue-raising capacity

TIME PROFILE OF REVENUE

The revenue pattern over the cycle of the projects mainly reflects the production profile. The onshore and shallow water fields have similar profiles, both reach peak production rates early in the life of the project with a subsequent steady decline in production. The deep water project also has high initial production, but reaches its peak production level later in time. While all three petroleum projects have substantial revenue potential, the magnitude will depend on price dynamics. The main source of government revenue, under the current fiscal regime, would be the share of profit oil, followed by corporate income tax (CIT) and royalty. Table 7.4 summarizes the main economic results for the three oil projects under the "current terms." All results, including revenue and rates of return are measured in real terms unless otherwise noted. The AETR is measured

Table 7.3 Simulated "current terms"[+]

Royalty	10%
Cost Recovery Limit	65%
R-factor based profit petroleum sharing*	
R-factor <1	10%
1< R-factor <2	20%
2< R-factor <3	30%
3< R-factor <4	40%
R-factor > 4	50%
CIT rate	32%
Dividend and interest withholding tax (WT)	20%**
State equity participation	10%***

Notes
+   The fiscal terms are assumptions by the authors, set in the framework of the Model Contract EPCC of 2005 and 2007 published by the Mozambique National Petroleum Institute for its 2007 Licensing Round (www.inp-mz.com).
*   The R-factor is the "payback ratio". An R-factor = 1 indicates that costs and revenues of the contractor are equal (i.e. undiscounted real net cash flow = 0).
** For modeling purposes it is assumed that: (i) 50% of development costs are financed through debt, repayable ten years after production starts with an interest rate of LIBOR + 1%; and (ii) all investor cash flows after repayment of income tax and debt are remitted as dividends, on which withholding tax is charged. In practice, however, the investor can reinvest profits, or arrange activities in a way that reduces dividend withholding taxes.
*** State equity participation is assumed to be carried during exploration (repayable), but no premium is charged for the option to participate in a commercial discovery. This is concessional participation (in comparison with the terms that a private party would face), and the net proceeds to the state are treated as part of the fiscal take.

Table 7.4 Summary results for the "current terms"

	"Mozambique" "current" fiscal regime		
	Onshore	Shallow water	Deep water
Project pre-tax real IRR	92%	56%	31%
Post-tax real IRR to contractor	70%	45%	22%
Project pre-tax NPV at 10% ($mm)	1,869	2,852	12,145
Contractor NPV at 10% ($mm)	561	919	3,193
Payback period at 10% (years from start of production)	2.1	3.0	6.0
Government revenue NPV at 10% ($mm)	1,331	2,055	9,582
Government take (AETR) at 10%	71%	72%	79%
Project pre-tax NPV at 15% ($mm)	1,259	2,083	6,586
Contractor NPV at 15% ($mm)	384	675	1,427
Payback period at 15% (years from start of production)	2.2	3.2	7.0
Government revenue NPV at 15% ($mm)	908	1,596	6,062
Government take (AETR) at 15%	72%	77%	92%
Project pre-tax NPV at 20% ($mm)	875	1,525	3,323
Contractor NPV at 20% ($mm)	269	489	349
Payback period at 20% (years from start of production)	2.3	3.4	9.6
Government revenue NPV at 20% ($mm)	645	1,264	3,976
Government take (AETR) at 20%	74%	83%	120%

as the ratio of the NPV of tax payments[36] to the NPV of the pre-tax net cash flow from the project at a given discount rate. The AETR represents the "government take" from net cash flow.

The onshore field has the highest pre-tax profitability because of the combination of a high initial production with the lowest development and operating costs per barrel among the three projects. In contrast, because of its capital cost structure and a more evenly distributed production profile, the deep water field is significantly less profitable than the other two projects.[37]

The government take in the deep water project is higher than in the two other projects when using a rate of discount of 10 percent or higher. As the rate of discount increases, the difference in government take between the deep water field and the other two projects widens significantly, especially when compared to the onshore project. This result is explained by the combined effect of the royalty, the cost recovery limit, and the time value of money. The deep water project takes at least three times as much time to recover costs as the onshore field, and twice the time of the shallow water field (see payback periods above). Therefore, as the rate of discount increases, pre-tax positive cash flow, which occurs much later in the deep water project, is discounted proportionately more than in the onshore and shallow water projects. Thus, at higher discount rates pre-tax NPV falls at a faster rate in the deep water project, while in all cases early government revenues from royalty payments and first tiers of profit oil will be discounted proportionally. The same pattern

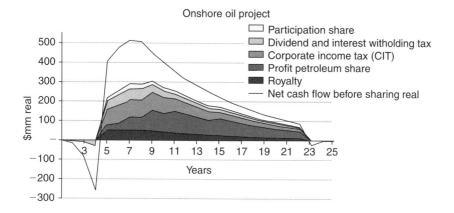

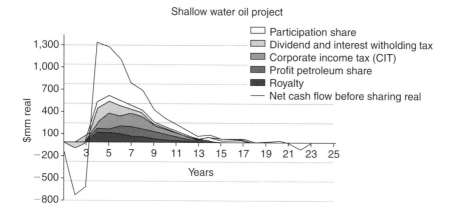

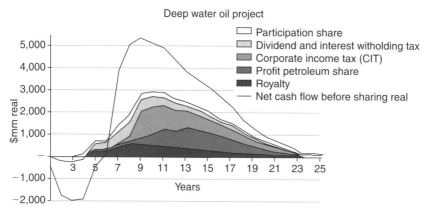

Figure 7.3 Time path of gross revenues and government revenues under "current terms" (WEO prices).

is observable when comparing the onshore field to the shallow water project, which requires approximately one year more to recover costs. The government is initially assumed to have the same discount rate as the company of 15 percent in real terms.

GOVERNMENT SHARE OF RENT

The AETR is also used to examine the share of "rent" captured for government by the fiscal regime at different levels of profitability. Figure 7.4 illustrates the AETR over a range of pre-tax cash flow, for the each field, at a discount rate of 15 percent.

Over the illustrated range of outcomes, the share of rent falls as the pre-tax present value of cash flows rises. Where the taxation share is above the horizontal axis, the government takes more than 100 percent of "rent" and the investor's ex post return will be below the supply price of capital. Under conditions of certainty, investors would not undertake the project in these cases.

B Introducing the alternative package

Although the alternative parameters illustrated here perform relatively well for all three projects, the terms could if necessary differ (for example, within a block-by-block bidding mechanism) to reflect the specific characteristics of different types of oil fields.[38] The rate of return scheme, however, adjusts well to variations in circumstances, and lessens the need for such differentiation. The alternative package keeps the "current" royalty rate in "Mozambique," to secure early revenues for the government, but increases the cost recovery limit to 90 percent – implying an effective royalty of 12.25 percent.[39] In addition it introduces a rate of return based production sharing mechanism, in place of sharing by a scale of the R-factor, and decreases the rate of interest and dividend withholding tax (WT) to rates common in recent bilateral double taxation treaties.[40]

Table 7.5 Alternative package (%)

Royalty	10
Cost Recovery Limit	90
IRR profit petroleum sharing (nominal ROR)	
IRR < 15%	25
15% < IRR < 20%	35
20% < IRR < 25%	45
25% < IRR < 30%	55
30% < IRR < 35%	65
35% < IRR < 40%	75
IRR > 40%	85
CIT rate	32
Dividend and interest WT	10
State equity participation	10

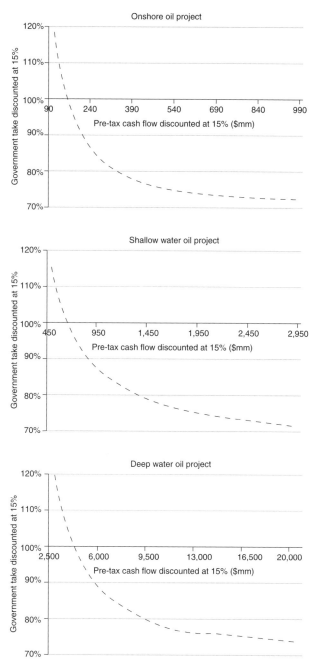

Figure 7.4 AETR over a range of pre-tax cash flows discounted at 15 percent.

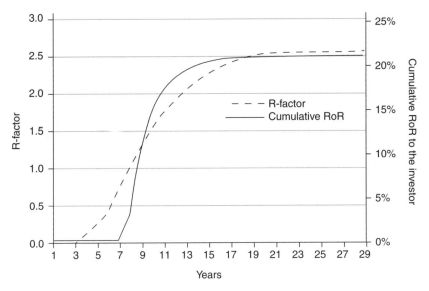

Figure 7.5 R-factor and cumulative IRR to the investor for the deep water oil project.

The key difference between the rate of return and the R-factor mechanisms is that the rate of return scheme takes into account the time value of money, while the R-factor scheme does not. Figure 7.5 illustrates this important difference under the deep water oil project. Cumulative IRR grows at a faster rate than the R-factor, and approaches its maximum more quickly than the R-factor, creating scope for the government share in the scale to increase more rapidly, without adversely affecting investor outcomes – assuming appropriate IRR tiers and profit oil shares are applied.

Figure 7.6 illustrates the revenue-raising superiority of the alternative package over the "current terms" for the onshore and shallow water oil field projects. The government revenue profile for the deep water oil field project is very similar under the "current" and alternative terms. The alternative package yields more revenue to the government than the "current terms" in the later years of the project, when costs have been recovered and profits are rising. Conversely, the "current terms" take more than the alternative package in the earlier years of the project life.

Neutrality

AETR, BREAKEVEN PRICE AND METR

Along with the AETR, the resource price at which a particular project will generate a post-tax IRR that will just induce investment (i.e. the breakeven price), and the METR at that price are also evaluated under the two regimes. The AETR, discounted at 15 percent and using the WEO prices, is significantly

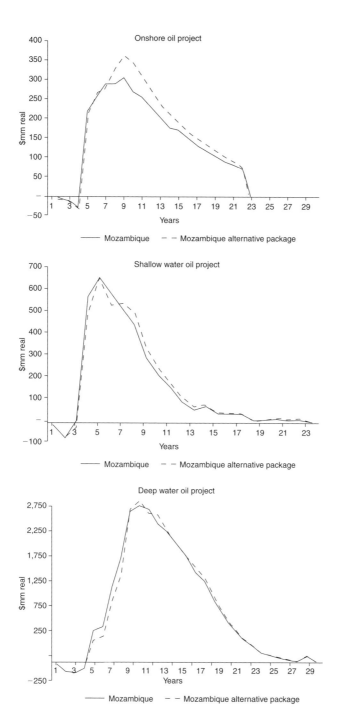

Figure 7.6 Government revenues: alternative package vs "current terms" (WEO prices).

higher under the alternative package than under the "current terms" for the onshore project, which is the most profitable of the three projects. In the shallow water project, the AETR is virtually the same under both regimes, while in the deep water project, which has the lowest profitability level, the "current terms" yield a slightly higher AETR than the alternative package. In addition, when estimating the oil price at which each project will generate a post-tax IRR of 15 percent and the corresponding METR at those prices, the alternative package fares consistently better than the "current terms" for all three projects. Table 7.6 compares the AETR discounted at 15 percent at WEO prices, the price required to generate a post-tax IRR of 15 percent and the METR at those prices between the two regimes for each oil field project. The alternative regime therefore appears to improve the trade-off between revenue-raising and investor risk (and would thus come closer to neutrality) but this result is dependent upon the price assumption used for the revenue-raising indicator.

Progressivity

The progressivity of a fiscal regime can also be examined by comparing the government share of project total benefits[41] over a range of pre-tax IRR. In Figure 7.7, the variation in pre-tax IRR (i.e. project profitability) is generated solely by varying oil prices. The share of total benefits represents the real NPV of government's revenues over the project life as a percentage of the real NPV of pre-tax total benefits.

A more progressive regime gives some relief to investors for projects with low rates of return, while allowing the government to increase its share of

Table 7.6 AETR, breakeven price, and METR

Onshore Oil Project	AETR at 15% (WEO prices) (%)	Price required to achieve 15% post-tax IRR ($/bbl)	METR at 15% post-tax IRR (%)
Alternative package	80	20	44
"Mozambique"	72	21	49
Shallow Water Oil Project	AETR at 15% (WEO prices) (%)	Price required to achieve 15% post-tax IRR ($/bbl)	METR at 15% post-tax IRR (%)
Alternative package	75	34	47
"Mozambique"	76	37	55
Deep Water Oil Project	AETR at 15% (WEO prices) (%)	Price required to achieve 15% post-tax IRR ($/bbl)	METR at 15% post-tax IRR (%)
Alternative package	87	49	43
"Mozambique"	92	52	47

revenue when the investment is highly profitable. Thus, a more progressive regime could attract investment for marginal projects (increasing government revenue over time), just as a heavy early fiscal burden on a project could deter investment altogether. The share of government revenues to total benefits over a range of pre-tax IRR is used, in Figure 7.7, to illustrate differences in progressivity between the alternative and "current" regimes.

Figure 7.7 shows that the "current terms" tend to take relatively more from projects at lower levels of profitability. At the margin of viability (toward the left hand side of the graphs) the "current terms" place a heavier burden than the alternative package in each one of the projects. The alternative fiscal package lowers the government share for projects at low levels of profitability, improving "Mozambique" attractiveness for investment in exploration, while ensuring a significant government share for highly profitable commercial discoveries (right hand side of the graph).

Risk to government

Table 7.7 compares the expected tax payments, their coefficient of variation (CV),[42] and the government share of net benefits in the first ten years of the project, at a discount rate of 15 percent. These results are calculated from the stochastic price simulations described in Box 7.3.

The alternative regime has generally a higher expected mean government NPV for the three oil projects. In terms of capturing early revenues, the alternative regime takes a higher share of net benefits than the "current terms" during the first ten years of the onshore project. In the shallow water project, both regimes take approximately the same proportion of net benefits early in the life of the project, while in the deep water field the "current terms" take a slightly higher share of net benefits during the first ten years. These results are consistent with the progressivity measures illustrated above. For example, in the deep water field, which takes more time to recover costs, the burden of the alternative regime in the first ten years of the project is somewhat less heavy on investors than the "current terms." As the pre-tax NPV of the project increases, however, this small difference in early government take of net benefits will be more than compensated later in the life of the project under the alternative package.

Finally, when evaluating the dispersion of government revenues between the two regimes, the CV of government revenue slightly increases under the alternative package for all projects. However, it is important to note that there are two offsetting effects affecting the CV of government revenue from the introduction of the alternative package. First, the wider range of government profit petroleum share in the alternative package should increase the CV when compared to the "current terms" (i.e. the alternative package has a higher standard deviation of government revenues). Second, the level of government profit petroleum share is higher in the alternative package, thus, as the pre-tax NPV of the project increases the mean government NPV will also increase, reducing the

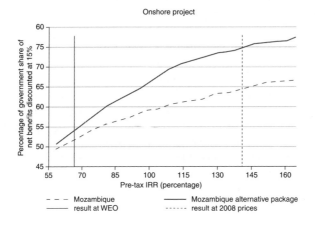

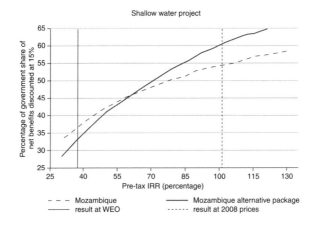

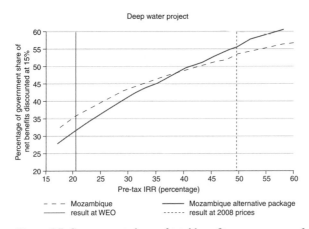

Figure 7.7 Government share of total benefits over a range of pre-tax IRR.

Table 7.7 Mean government NPV, CV, and early share of total benefits

Onshore Oil Project	Mean Government NPV at 15% ($mm)	CV at 15% (%)	Government share of net benefits at 15% during first ten years (%)
Alternative package	1,324	62	40
"Mozambique"	1,173	58	37

Shallow Water Oil Project	Mean Government NPV at 15% ($mm)	CV at 15% (%)	Government share of net benefits at 15% during first ten years (%)
Alternative package	2,253	70	35
"Mozambique"	2,141	62	36

Deep Water Oil Project	Mean Government NPV at 15% ($mm)	CV at 15% (%)	Government share of net benefits at 15% during first ten years (%)
Alternative package	8,889	74	12
"Mozambique"	8,728	66	14

CV of government revenue relative to "current terms." In the three projects evaluated here the increase in mean government NPV appears to be lower than the increase in the standard deviation of government revenues, resulting from the introduction of the alternative package. Thus, the first effect dominates, increasing the CV relative to the "current terms" for all projects.

Investor perceptions of risk

Investors' perception of risks between the two regimes is evaluated by analyzing (i) the mean expected post-tax IRR to the investor and the CV of investor returns, and (ii) the cumulative probability distribution of post-tax NPV, discounted at 15 percent under each project. Table 7.8 portrays the mean expected post-tax IRR and the CV of post-tax IRR for each project. While the mean expected post-tax IRR is very similar between the two regimes, the dispersion of returns to investors is reduced under the alternative package.

The lines in Figure 7.8 show the cumulative probability distribution of the post-tax results under both fiscal regimes. All except the deep water project show a relatively low value of expected negative outcomes; this value is smaller under the alternative regime. The cumulative distribution can also be read to show the relative progressivity of the regimes. A fiscal regime designed to maximize the government's share of rent over a project life would have a low state share until the pre tax NPV of the project becomes positive, and would then increase rapidly to capture the majority of the economic rent created by the project. This pattern is better described by the alternative package than by the "current terms."

Table 7.8 Mean expected post-tax IRR and CV

	Onshore Project		Shallow Water Project		Deep Water Project	
	Mean expected post-tax IRR (%)	CV of IRR (%)	Mean expected post-tax IRR (%)	CV of IRR (%)	Mean expected post-tax IRR (%)	CV of IRR (%)
Alternative package	51	33	33	40	21	42
"Mozambique"	57	39	33	49	20	49

In order to benchmark the "current terms" and the alternative package against international comparators, we evaluate the results from applying other countries' fiscal regimes to the deep water oil project. International comparators include deep water petroleum producers and potential producers (i.e. countries with significant exploration activity) from Africa and elsewhere. Table 7.9 lists the international comparators in descending order of petroleum daily production as of 2007. The fiscal regimes of these countries are summarized in Appendix IV. Four features of the fiscal regimes are compared: (i) the overall tax burden (measured by AETR and breakeven price); (ii) the risks to the government; (iii) how the regime affects perceived risks for investing in the country; and (iv) the "prospectivity gap" implied by each regime.

AETR and breakeven price

Figure 7.9 shows the AETR, discounted at 15 and 20 percent, for the "current terms" and alternative package against 15 international comparators, using WEO price projections; and the price required to achieve a post-tax IRR of 15 percent (i.e. breakeven price). The results suggest that the alternative package captures a greater share of net cash flow than fiscal regimes in other countries with high activity in deep water exploration, such as Ghana, Madagascar, Colombia, and Timor-Leste. By the same token, the alternative regime requires a lower price to achieve a post-tax hurdle rate of 15 percent than most of the countries just mentioned (with the exception of Ghana and Timor-Leste), and other medium and large oil producers such as Angola, Cameroon, and Norway. A higher reported price indicates that a higher pre-tax IRR is needed to offset the effect of a heavier fiscal burden to achieve the targeted after-tax return. Fiscal regimes with lower breakeven prices, such as the alternative package, represent a lower risk for investors, and may be less likely to deter exploration activities, especially in capital intensive environments such as deep water prospects.

Risk to government and comparison with investor risk

The risk to government revenue is analyzed by evaluating (i) the expected government receipts and (ii) the CV of those government receipts as a percentage of

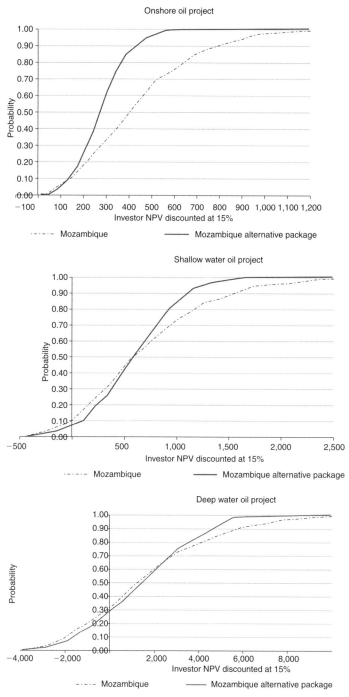

Figure 7.8 Cumulative probabilities of post-tax NPV, discounted at 15 percent.

Table 7.9 Comparator countries for analysis

	Country	Fiscal regime	Oil production 2007 ('000 bpd)	Exploration Activity
African Comparators				
1	Nigeria	PSC	2,350	Offshore and onshore (less interest onshore due to recent militant unrest)
2	Angola	PSC	1,769	Offshore and onshore
3	Eq. Guinea	PSC	400	Offshore and onshore
4	Cameroon	PSC	83	Offshore and onshore
5	Mauritania	PSC	24	Offshore and onshore
6	Ghana	PSC	6	Offshore
7	Madagascar	PSC	0	Offshore and onshore
8	Mozambique	PSC	0	Offshore and onshore
9	Namibia	Tax & Royalty	0	Offshore and onshore
10	Sierra Leone	PSC	0	Offshore and onshore
Non-African Comparators				
1	Norway	Tax & Royalty	2,270	Offshore
2	UK	Tax & Royalty	1,498	Onshore and offshore
3	Colombia	Tax & Royalty	531	Offshore and onshore
4	Australia	CIT and RRT	468	Onshore and offshore
5	Timor-Leste	PSC	79	Offshore
6	Peru	Tax & Royalty	77	Onshore and offshore (not deep water)

Sources: Energy Information Administration: World Crude Oil Production (including lease condensate) as of August 22, 2008; IMF staff.

a baseline case, which is the "current terms" in "Mozambique." We compare these with an expected risk index for investors, where again "current terms" in "Mozambique" is our baseline case.

Table 7.10 shows that the alternative regime would produce a small improvement in mean expected government receipts. On the other hand, when compared to the "current terms" in "Mozambique," there is a large decrease in the expected risk index for investors – likely, as intended, to make the deep water play in the country more attractive.

Investors' perception of risk

An investor may be reluctant to accept possible returns below a required rate or may perceive high dispersion of expected outcomes as a strong risk factor. In order to assess the effect of the tax system on returns under a range of different price scenarios, a probability distribution of returns for a range of stochastically simulated oil prices was evaluated. Table 7.11 reports the mean expected post-tax IRR, CV of IRR, and the probability of tax-induced returns below 15 percent for the investor, where "current terms" in Mozambique is our baseline case (i.e. Mozambique = 100). The countries are tabulated in

Average effective tax rate discounted at 15 percent (WFO prices)

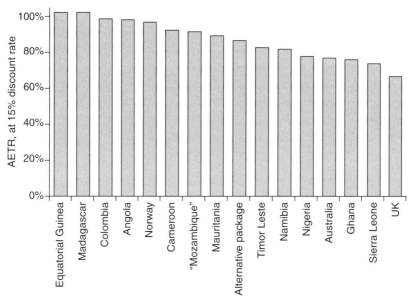

Price required to achieve 15 percent after tax real rate of return

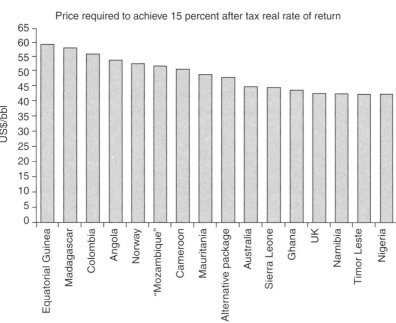

Figure 7.9 AETR and breakeven price.

Table 7.10 Index of revenue stability and yield, with expected risk index

	Deep Water Oil Project		
	Expected government receipts discounted at 15% (Mozambique =100)	Investor expected risk index (at 15% discount rate) (Mozambique =100)	Coefficient of variation of government receipts (Mozambique =100)
UK	72	52	95
Sierra Leone	77	64	91
Nigeria	88	38	110
Ghana	89	56	108
Australia	84	52	102
Timor Leste	95	24	117
Mauritania	97	70	102
Namibia	103	41	121
Alternative package	101	74	111
Cameroon	104	63	108
"Mozambique"	100	100	100
Madagascar	105	165	87
Colombia	104	130	92
Norway	108	100	103
Angola	115	87	110
Equatorial Guinea	113	128	99

descending order of the expected mean post-tax IRR. The alternative package increases the mean expected return to investors when compared to the "current terms" in "Mozambique." In an international context, the alternative package sits in the mid section of the ranking. This indicates that, on average, investments under the alternative terms will yield returns higher than the same investments under almost half of the fiscal terms in the comparator countries. The probability of generating returns below 15 percent is also in the mid level of the sample. In conclusion, the alternative package would improve the mean expected post-tax IRR for investment in "Mozambique" while reducing the risk of negative outcomes. This will be an attractive advantage for investors considering investments in countries with high petroleum potential in deep water environments, but yet without a significant commercial discovery of that kind.

"Prospectivity gap"

Objective measurement of the value assigned by investors to their perception of prospectivity risk can only be approached by an indirect route. It is possible to suggest what the value assigned to prospectivity risk (geology and location)

Table 7.11 Mean expected post-tax IRR, CV, and probability of returns below 15%

Deep Water Oil Project	Mean expected IRR (%)	Coefficient of variation of IRR (%)	Probability of expected return below 15% (%)
Project pre-tax	35	43	7
After-Tax	Mozambique = 100		Tax-related – Mozambique = 100
UK	131	97	52
Sierra Leone	121	96	64
Nigeria	118	82	38
Ghana	116	87	56
Australia	114	87	52
Timor Leste	111	77	24
Mauritania	106	95	70
Namibia	103	63	41
Alternative package	102	86	74
Cameroon	101	93	63
"Mozambique"	100	100	100
Madagascar	90	112	165
Colombia	89	95	130
Norway	88	90	100
Angola	83	78	87
Equatorial Guinea	83	104	128

would have to be in a particular country, given equal project risk, to equalize the attractiveness of the project under the different tax regimes surveyed. Table 7.12 reports: (i) the excess over lowest mean expected NPV to investor, at a rate of discount of 15 percent; and (ii) the excess over lowest expected negative NPV to investor, again at 15 percent discount rate.

According to the first column of Table 7.12, if the attractiveness of the investment is to be equal as between "Mozambique" and Equatorial Guinea, the investor would have to assess prospectivity risk to be higher in "Mozambique," to the extent that an addition to expected NPV of $941 million is required. This is the relative addition to mean expected NPV on total funds currently provided by the "current terms" in Mozambique. Under the alternative package, this difference narrows to $837 million. Alternatively, if prospectivity is viewed as equal between, say, Nigeria and the UK, then the UK "sacrifices" just under $1.3 bn of potential mean expected receipts in this deep water case.

In the second column of Table 7.12, prospectivity risk is measured as the change in tax-induced expected negative NPV to investor necessary to equalize the expected value of negative returns among countries. Thus if the fiscal regimes are correctly specified, an investor will tolerate almost $69 million of total additional negative expected returns for a project located in Mozambique as

Table 7.12 Prospectivity gap

	Deep Water Oil Project	
	Excess (shortfall) over benchmark mean expected NPV15 to investor ($mm)	Excess (shortfall) over benchmark expected negative NPV15 to investor ($mm)
UK	3,374	34
Sierra Leone	2,895	48
Nigeria	2,015	(564)
Ghana	1,963	(89)
Australia	2,187	(327)
Timor Leste	1,271	(1,026)
Mauritania	1,256	(455)
Namibia	777	(276)
Alternative package	837	(134)
Cameroon	721	(968)
Mozambique	941	69
Madagascar	613	949
Colombia	695	383
Norway	349	(0.5)
Angola	(207)	(488)
Equatorial Guinea	–	–

compared to one located in Equatorial Guinea. Conversely, under the alternative package that same investor in Mozambique will perceive a reduction of about $134 million in total negative expected returns for the same project located in Equatorial Guinea. Alternatively, an investor will tolerate $949 million of total additional negative expected returns for a project located in Madagascar compared to one located in Equatorial Guinea.

It is necessary to point out immediately that these figures cannot be taken as real prospectivity differences. They do, however, invite examination of significant differences in fiscal regimes. Such differences point up the value of auctions in discovering investors' real assessments of relative prospectivity.

Varying the discount rates

If the company's discount rate is set at 20 percent while the government's remains at 15 percent, or if the government's rate is reduced to 10 percent, the broad conclusions from this choice of alternative regimes are not altered (Appendix V). In general, the lower the discount rate of government, relative to that of the company, the more the trade-off between investor risk and government yield can be improved by targeting tax at high rates on realized rents (returns in excess of the investor's discount rate).

4 Conclusions

This chapter has attempted to set out evaluation criteria, and attach indicators or measures to them. The indicators are intended to be relatively easily calculated and interpreted. The aim is to provide a framework for numerical analysis of risk and reward trade-offs, as an aid to judgment in setting and revising fiscal regimes.

The paper shows how fiscal regimes can be assessed to pose questions about their relationship to both prospectivity and government objectives, as well as investor perceptions of risk. Mechanisms to adjust fiscal regimes (generally applicable legislation, standard contract terms, or auctions) are a separate policy question.

Appendix I The marginal effective tax rate

The standard approach to estimating the METR is to consider an investment project that just earns the required after-tax rate of return – a marginal investment – and to calculate the impact of tax on the cost of capital. Without taxes, a profit-maximizing firm will invest to the point where the marginal product of capital is just equal to the cost of using that capital. Thus, while the required before-tax rate of return on a marginal investment is not directly observable, we can infer it by measuring the user cost of capital. Algebraically, the following condition must be satisfied:

$$R = \left[\beta i + (1-\beta)\rho\right] - \pi + \delta$$

where R is the return on investment (or marginal product of capital) and the cost of capital is comprised of: (i) the market rate of interest on debt financing, i, weighted by the proportion of investment financed by debt, β; (ii) the cost of equity, ρ, similarly weighted; (iii) the expected inflation rate, π; and, (4) real economic depreciation, δ.

With taxes, the firm undertakes the same optimization procedure but on an after-tax basis, giving rise to the following condition:

$$R(1-u) = \left\{\left[\beta i(1-u) + (1-\beta)\rho\right] - \pi + \delta\right\}(1-Z)$$

where u is the corporate tax rate and Z is the depreciation allowance for taxation purposes. Note that the above expression assumes that debt financing is tax deductible but equity is not. At the after-tax equilibrium, there is a difference between this before-tax rate of return to investment and the after-tax real rate of return to savers (= r_n). This tax wedge represents the tax revenue collected by government on the marginal investment, and when expressed as a proportion of the before-tax rate of return yields the METR:

$$METR = \frac{(R-\delta) - r_n}{(R-\delta)}$$

Appendix II The cost of capital

The capital asset pricing model (CAPM) is often used to estimate the cost of equity. The CAPM is based on the principle that equity holders will be compensated, in the form of a higher expected return, for holding non-diversifiable risk (also called systematic or market risk) but not for holding diversifiable risk (non-systematic or private risk). This is because equity holders can costlessly eliminate diversifiable risk by investing in a range of stocks (diversification is most effective the greater the negative correlation between individual stocks).[44] The optimal diversified portfolio will include every traded asset and the non-diversifiable risk of an individual stock will equal the contribution of that stock to the risk of the market portfolio. The CAPM for a stock can be expressed as:

$$E(R_j) = R_f + \beta(R_m - R_f)$$

where: $E(R_j)$ is the required return on the firm's equity; the risk premium $(R_m - R_f)$ is comprised of the expected return to the optimal market portfolio, R_m, and the risk free rate, R_f; and beta, β, is the correlation between the return on the firm's equity and that of the market,

$$\beta = \frac{\mathrm{cov}(R_j, R_m)}{\mathrm{var}(R_m)}.$$

The risk premium is most commonly estimated using historical data on the market return and the risk-free return. Limitations of this approach include the implicit assumptions that the risk aversion of investors has not changed, nor has the riskiness of the market portfolio. The risk premium can also be estimated by the implied premium in the stock price. However, this too has limitations, including that the model and inputs used to calculated the expected return on the market must be correct, and it implicitly assumes that the market is correctly valued. The standard procedure for estimating betas is to regress returns of an individual stock against market returns

$$R_j = a + bR_m$$

where the slope of the regression, b, is the estimate of beta. Estimated betas will not be good estimates of the true betas if the market portfolio is not properly defined or if the standard error of the estimate is large.

There are a number of problems in applying the CAPM to estimate the cost of capital for an individual resource project. The estimated beta reflects the entire company. Thus, this approach is only valid to the extent that the company's risk profile is the same as that of the individual project being evaluated (Brealey and Myers, 1991). Moreover, a number of the CAPM assumptions, such as returns being normally distributed and jointly normal with the returns of the market portfolio, may be satisfied at the company level, but are likely to be invalid when applied to mining projects (Smith and McCardle, 1998). A better approach is to estimate a beta based on firms or price indices that are similar in risk to the project. However, this tends to be difficult to do in practice, and will necessitate considerable judgment, including on classifying risks as either diversifiable or non-diversifiable.

A further complication is that the CAPM estimate of the RADR may not reflect all relevant risks. The appropriate RADR for an individual mining project includes a premium for the mineral project risk (commodity price, input cost, and geological risks) and a premium for country risk. The CAPM estimate will need to be supplemented by an additional premium to the extent that it does not fully reflect all these risks. In many cases, it may even be necessary to use an alternative approach all together, such as relying on industry practice (Smith, 1998) or identifying each source of uncertainty and assessing (often qualitatively) a risk premium for each factor (Smith, 2000). Country risk (e.g. political and regulatory factors) could be added to the discount rate in order to accurately rank the attractiveness of country tax systems for a given investment project. Measures of country risk can be obtained from risk rating services,[45] banks, or yields on government bonds.[46] However, it may not be straightforward to obtain a country risk figure expressed as an interest rate that can simply be added to the CAPM derived risk premium.

As noted in the text: (i) because economic analysis is usually applied to a project with a successful outcome, not all systematic risks are taken into account in economic analysis; (ii) a resource company must make enough profit on successful projects to compensate for unsuccessful ones – particularly relevant in petroleum where there is low probability of success at the exploration stage.

Appendix III Exploration risk analysis

There are three general steps in petroleum exploration risk analysis:[47]

1   *A scientific (geological) risk assessment* based on a geological concept. This will involve (i) estimating the probability of hydrocarbons presence; (ii) the type(s), distribution, and volume of the hydrocarbons; and (iii) the likelihood of being able to produce the hydrocarbons. In calculating a first estimate of the probability of finding hydrocarbons, geologists initially estimate the probabilities of several geological factors,[48] and then multiply these probabilities as described below:

$$P_F = P_R \times P_S \times P_{HC} \times P_T \tag{1}$$ [49]

where P_F is the probability of a successful finding, P_R is the probability of existence of a reservoir, P_S is the probability of existence of a structure, P_{HC} is the probability of hydrocarbon charge being present, and P_T is the probability of the trap sealing hydrocarbons.

2   *Engineering design study.* Assuming that the first step provides preliminary estimates of a possible production profile over time, including production rates and timing of production, an approximation of the cost of the facilities required to extract the hydrocarbons and the value of total operating costs could be calculated. It is important to note that since this preliminary engineering study is made before drilling all factors involved in the study would also have an uncertainty component.

3   *Economic analysis.* Once the engineering design phase is completed, an economic analysis could be conducted taking into account the expected cost of capital (i.e. discount rate), anticipated contract terms, development and operating costs, and product prices.

After these three steps are completed investors interested in hydrocarbon exploration would have an idea of the probability of a successful finding, the potential costs of undertaking the project, and the potential economic gains of a successful finding, as well as some uncertainty estimates of each step.

Decision analysis

With the information compiled from completing the three steps described above, an investor would face two options:

1   *Decide not to drill,* in which case the total pre-drilling costs will be absorbed by the investor, or
2   *Decide to drill.* After the decision to drill has been made there are three possible outcomes:

   a   Successful drilling with economically attractive hydrocarbons found,
   b   Unsuccessful drilling indicating subcommercial hydrocarbons found or a dry hole (i.e. no presence of hydrocarbons), or
   c   Incomplete evaluation results, which will not resolve the uncertainty about the presence of commercially available hydrocarbons (i.e. junked hole).

Finally, a post-drilling review should be performed to compare the estimated parameters with the real outcomes. Whether the drilling is a failure or a success the post-drilling information would serve to update the original geological concept, the reserve assessment, and the risk estimates, thus providing valuable information for current and future exploration risk.

Expected monetary value (EMV)[50]

Once the probability of a successful finding, P_F, has been established, based on a geological concept (see step one above), expected monetary value can be calculated based on a decision diagram and the outcomes from steps two and three above, as follows:

$$E_1 = P_F \times V + (1 - P_F) \times C \tag{2}$$

Where P_F is the probability of a successful finding, V is the net present value of the economic gains from a successful finding, $(1 - P_F)$ is the probability of an unsuccessful project, and C is the present value of all exploration costs of an unsuccessful finding, including lease bonuses and surface fees.

A positive value of E_1 would indicate that $P_F \times V > (1 - P_F) \times C$, and therefore the project should be undertaken.

In addition, an investor would also be interested in some measurement of risk (i.e. volatility) of the expected value, E_1, calculated above. From the second moment of the project value, defined as $E_2 = P_F \times V^2 + (1 - P_F) \times C^2$, its variance could be calculated as follows:

$$\sigma^2 = E_2 - E_1^2 \equiv (V + C)^2 \times [P_F \times (1 - P_F)] \tag{3}$$

Using (2) and (3) we can now calculate the coefficient of variation (CV) of the expected value, E_1.

$$CV = \sigma / E_1 \equiv \sigma /(V + C) \times [P_F \times (1 - P_F)]^{1/2} \times [P_F \times V + (1 - P_F) \times C] \tag{4}$$

The CV indicates the volatility of the estimated mean value E_1 relative to the fluctuations around the mean. A relatively low volatility (i.e. $CV < 1$) would imply that low levels of uncertainty about the expected value, while a high volatility level (i.e. $CV > 1$) indicates significant uncertainty about the expected value.

In general, investors would seek projects that yield high values of E_1 with low volatility levels.

Prudent risk taking and the minimum probability of success[51]

Prudent risk taking is a method that complements the EMV approach. Prudent risk taking uses the minimum probability of success, along with the EMV, to decide whether a project is worth developing. The minimum probability of success is calculated as the ratio of exploration costs to the net present value of a successful finding:

$$P_M = C/V \tag{5}[52]$$

Where P_M is the minimum acceptable probability of success, C is the present value of all exploration costs as defined above, and V is the net present value of a successful finding.

According to the prudent risk taking approach, a project would only be worth developing if the value of E_1 is positive and the probability of a successful finding is greater than the minimum probability of success (i.e. $P_F > P_M$). This approach is clearly more conservative than the EMV alone.

Appendix IV

Table 7.13 Summary of fiscal regimes*

	Angola offshore	Angola onshore	Cameroon	Equatorial Guinea	Ghana	Madagascar onshore	Madagascar offshore	Mauritania	"Mozambique"	Namibia
Royalty	–	–	–	Min 13%, Max 16%	12.5%	Min 8%, Max 20%	Min 8%, Max 20%	–	10%	5%
Basis	–	–	–	daily production rate	flat	daily production rate	daily production rate	–	flat	flat
Cost recovery limit	50%–65% (with uplift)	50%–65% (with uplift)	60%	70%	–	60%	65%	70%	65%	–
Profit share	Min 30%, Max 90%	Min 35%, Max 90%	Min 20%, Max 70%	Min 10%, Max 60%	Min 12%, Max 28%	Min 20%, Max 70%	Min 20%, Max 70%	Min 20%, Max 50%	Min 10%, Max 50%	–
Basis	ROR	cumulative production	R-factor	cumulative production	ROR	daily production rate	daily production rate	daily production rate	R-factor	–
CIT	50%	50%	40%	35%	30%	–	–	30%	32%	35%
ROR taxes	–	–	–	–	–	–	–	–	–	3 tiers Min 303%, Max 50%
State participation	15%	15%	25%	15%	10% and 3.75% (optional)	–	–	18%	10%	–
	State interest carried during exploration (exploration costs repayable)	State interest carried during exploration (exploration costs repayable)	State interest carried during exploration (exploration costs repayable)	State interest carried during exploration (exploration costs repayable)	10% state interest—is carried during exploration and development (neither costs are repayable) 3.75% state interest is carried during exploration only (exploration costs are not repayable)			State interest carried during exploration (exploration costs repayable)	State interest carried during exploration (exploration costs repayable at Libor +1%)	

	Nigeria onshore	Nigeria offshore	Nigeria deep water	Sierra Leone	Australia	Timor-Leste	Colombia	Peru	Norway	UK
Royalty	10%	10%	–	10%	–	5%	Min 8%, Max 25%	Min 5%, Max 20%	–	–
Basis	flat	flat	–	flat	–	flat	daily production rate	daily production rate	–	–
Cost recovery limit	100% (with uplift)	100% (with uplift)	100% (with uplift)	–	–	100% (with uplift)	–	–	–	–
Profit share	Min 52%, Max 60%	Min 60%, Max 65%	Min 20%, Max 50%	–	–	40%	–	–	–	–
Basis	daily production rate	daily production rate	cumulative production	–	–	fixed	–	–	–	–
Tax	50% (tax allowance on development costs)	50% (tax allowance on development costs)	50% (tax allowance on development costs)	37.5%	30%	30%	33%	30%	CIT 28%, ST 50%; Special Tax (ST) is same as for CIT plus 30% uplift on investment	CIT 30%, SC 20%; Supplementary Charge is additional charge of 20% on company's ring fence profits excluding finance costs
ROR taxes	–	–	–	–	1 tier 40%	1 tier 22.5%	–	–	–	–
State participation	–	–	–	–	–	20% State interest carried during exploration (exploration costs not repayable)	–	–	–	–

Note
*Colombia has a high price duty (up to 30% rate), which is triggered once cumulative production reaches 5 mmbbl and when prices are above US$34.77/bbl. There is also an exploitation duty of US$0.1068 per bbl.

Appendix V Discount rate sensitivities

Table 7.14 presents the AETR for each project at WEO prices, discounted at 10, 15, and 20 percent; and the price required to achieve a post-tax IRR of 10, 15, and 20 percent along with the METR at those prices.

Table 7.15 shows the mean expected government NPV, CV, and share of total benefits in the first ten years of the project, discounted at rates of 10 and 15 percent for all projects.

Table 7.14 AETR, breakeven price and METR, at various discount rates

Onshore Oil Project

	AETR at 10% (WEO prices) (%)	Price required to achieve a 10% post-tax IRR	METR at 10% post-tax IRR (%)
Alternative Package	79	16	48
"Mozambique"	71	17	54

	AETR at 15% (WEO prices) (%)	Price required to achieve a 15% post-tax IRR	METR at 15% post-tax IRR (%)
Alternative Package	80	20	44
"Mozambique"	72	21	49

	AETR at 20% (WEO prices) (%)	Price required to achieve a 20% post-tax IRR	METR at 20% post-tax IRR (%)
Alternative Package	81	24	43
"Mozambique"	74	25	47

Shallow Water Oil Project

	AETR at 10% (WEO prices) (%)	Price required to achieve a 10% post-tax IRR	METR at 10% post-tax IRR (%)
Alternative Package	72	29	52
"Mozambique"	72	32	61

	AETR at 15% (WEO prices) (%)	Price required to achieve a 15% post-tax IRR	METR at 15% post-tax Irr (%)
Alternative Package	75	34	47
"Mozambique"	76	37	55

	AETR at 20% (WEO prices) (%)	Price required to achieve a 20% post-tax IRR	METR at 20% post-tax IRR (%)
Alternative Package	81	40	46
"Mozambique"	83	43	52

Deep Water Oil Project

	AETR at 10% (WEO prices) (%)	Price required to achieve a 10% post-tax IRR	METR at 10% post-tax IRR (%)
Alternative Package	76	37	52
"Mozambique"	79	40	46

	AETR at 15% (WEO prices) (%)	Price required to achieve a 15% post-tax IRR	METR at 15% post-tax IRR (%)
Alternative Package	87	49	43
"Mozambique"	92	52	47

	AETR at 20% (WEO prices) (%)	Price required to achieve a 20% post-tax IRR	METR at 20% post-tax IRR (%)
Alternative Package	111	63	42
"Mozambique"	120	66	44

Table 7.15 Government NPV, CV and early share of total benefits

Onshore Oil Project

	Mean Government NPV at 10% ($mm)	CV of Government revenues at 10% (%)	Government share of total benefits at 10% during first 10 years (%)
Alternative Package	1,878	59	36
"Mozambique"	1,657	56	34

	Mean Government NPV at 20% ($mm)	CV of Government revenues at 20% (%)	Government share of total benefits at 20% during first 10 years (%)
Alternative Package	962	64	42
"Mozambique"	855	60	40

Table 7.15 Continued

Shallow Water Oil Project

	Mean Government NPV at 10% ($mm)	CV of Government revenues at 10% (%)	Government share of total benefits at 10% during first 10 years (%)
Alternative Package	2,933	73	34
"Mozambique"	2,759	64	35

	Mean Government NPV at 20% ($mm)	CV of Government revenues at 20% (%)	Government share of total benefits at 20% during first 10 years (%)
Alternative Package	1,853	72	36
"Mozambique"	1,769	64	37

Deep Water Oil Project

	Mean Government NPV at 10% ($mm)	CV of Government revenues at 10% (%)	Government share of total benefits at 10% during first 10 years (%)
Alternative Package	13,724	70	11
"Mozambique"	13,381	63	13

	Mean Government NPV at 20% ($mm)	CV of Government revenues at 20% (%)	Government share of total benefits at 20% during first 10 years (%)
Alternative Package	5,593	80	13
"Mozambique"	5,539	71	16

Finally, Table 7.16 presents the mean expected post-tax IRR, CV of IRR, and the probability of returns below 10 and 20 percent for the investors.

Table 7.16 Mean expected post-tax IRR, CV, and probability of returns below 10 and 20%

Onshore Oil Project	Mean expected post-tax IRR (%)	CV of IRR (%)	Probability of returns below 10%	Probability of returns below 20%
Alternative Package	51	34	0	0.4
"Mozambique"	56	40	0	2

Shallow Water Oil Project	Mean expected post-tax IRR (%)	CV of IRR (%)	Probability of returns below 10%	Probability of returns below 20%
Alternative Package	34	40	0.6	16
"Mozambique"	34	50	3	22

Deep Water Oil Project	Mean expected post-tax IRR (%)	CV of IRR (%)	Probability of returns below 10%	Probability of returns below 20%
Alternative Package	20	44	5	46
"Mozambique"	19	52	11	49

Acknowledgments

The authors acknowledge contributions to the development of the framework for this chapter from Charles McPherson and Paulo Medas, and helpful comments on an initial draft from Michael Keen. Valuable comments on the conference presentation were provided by Daniel Dumas and Michael Levitsky.

Notes

1 For surveys of changes in petroleum contact terms see Quiroz (2008), and Wood Mackenzie (2008).
2 See also the chapter in this volume by Hogan and Goldsworthy (2010).
3 Daniel Johnston (2003: 108), states that "Tough terms usually correlate with good rocks," and defines "prospectivity" broadly to include Adam Smith's notions of both "fertility" and "situation" in the case of land.
4 For this perspective see for example Johnston (2003, 2007), van Meurs (1981, 2002), Lerche and Mackay (1999), Garnaut and Clunies Ross (1983), Wilson (1984), Hogan (2007), Conrad *et al.* (1990), Blake and Roberts (2006).
5 For a useful recent discussion of project evaluation measures relevant to companies and governments respectively, see Tordo (2007); see also Johnston (2003).
6 See also the later discussion of decision trees.
7 The risks in international comparisons include: misinterpretation of individual fiscal regimes, differences in treatment of indirect taxes, inconsistency of ring-fencing rules, issues of incremental investments, and interaction between host country tax systems and home country systems of investing companies.

8 See Boadway and Keen (2010), Conrad *et al.* (1990), Garnaut and Clunies Ross (1983), Wilson (1984), Hogan (2006).

9 The USA is a prominent exception (except in the case of federal lands, and the off-shore continental shelf).

10 Resource rents from mining can be defined as surplus revenues net of all costs of production, including the company's required rate of return. Economic rents, more generally, are present when there is a factor of production in fixed supply, or under imperfect competition.

11 Not marginal effective tax rate (METR) in the sense discussed later.

12 See Conrad *et al.* (1990: 45).

13 See the next section for a special adaptation of this concept in resource taxation problems: it is assumed that, in practice, investors associate risk with failure to attain a target rate of return.

14 Specification of the risk preference (utility function) of any one government is beyond the scope of this paper. In practice the preference will tend to be revealed through choices between stable and variable sources of revenue, and early or later revenue, where the risk of overall reduction of revenue is greater with the risk averse choice.

15 In principle, the risks of this type in any individual project are diversified for a company that already has a significant portfolio of producing assets. This feature underpins the argument that a large oil or mining company is better able to assume certain risks than a fiscally-constrained developing country. Nevertheless, individual petroleum projects can represent a large portion of the total budgeted outlays even of major corporations.

16 See Palmer (1980), Wilson (1984).

17 The circumstances known generally as "project finance," where the debt facilities are "non-recourse" to the balance sheets of the sponsor companies. A common arrangement in resource industries has been for sponsors to provide banks with a completion guarantee for the project facilities, which falls away after a period of commissioning and successful testing. At that point, the banks have recourse only to the cash flows and assets of the project itself. "Bankers" may in turn lay off some the risks on other parties or through insurance instruments.

18 A resource rent tax is imposed only if the accumulated net cash flow is positive. The net negative cash flow is accumulated at an interest rate equal to the company's cost of capital or discount rate. Thus, a resource rent tax provides the government with a share of returns once the company earns a certain minimum rate of return. See Boadway and Keen, and Land, in this volume for a discussion on the merits of the resource rent tax and other fiscal instruments.

19 See Jacoby and Laughton (1992), Emhjellen and Alauoze (2003), and Samis *et al.* (2006).

20 See Jacoby and Laughton (1992), and Smith (1998).

21 Multiple IRRs can come about when there is a large negative cash flow at the beginning and at the end of the project's life (e.g. a mining investment that entails significant clean up costs).

22 Though modern software can manipulate a wide range of probability distributions, and explicit specification of correlation among variables, so that the computational problem has potentially diminished.

23 In analyzing petroleum projects, Bohren and Schilbred (1980) assume that operating costs are normally and independently distributed and oil prices take one of two price outcomes with equal probability. However, for petroleum and other mineral projects, output and input costs tend to be positively correlated.

24 Another criticism is that use of WACC assumes a constant corporate structure/ gearing. This may be a reasonable assumption for large multinational.

25 But see the paper by Hogan and Goldsworthy (2010), which uses certainty equivalence.

26 This distinction is also made in Devereux and Griffith (1998a, and 2003) and in the Commission of the European Communities (2001).

27 The interaction of home and host country tax systems remains important because of the foreign tax credit issue (see Mullins, 2010).

28 Knowledge about the extent of any resource will nonetheless change as it is developed.

29 For those accustomed to estimation of METR for investment in manufacturing industry, a change of assumptions is necessary. For example, it is usually assumed that immediate expensing of capital investment for corporate tax purposes results in a zero METR for equity-financed investment. This holds only if *either* the firm has current income sufficient to deduct the investment expense in full, *or* unrecovered losses can be carried forward with interest at the firm's discount rate. The first condition does not hold for the initial investment in a large petroleum project that is ring-fenced, and the second condition is a feature of only a very few petroleum tax systems (that of Norway now incorporates it).

30 King and Fullerton (1984) and Boadway *et al.* (1987) are seminal. These studies differ in a number of ways, including assumptions about the costs of debt and equity financing, and Boadway *et al.* apply the model to a small and open economy. Boadway *et al.* (1995) extended the standard model to consider firms operating under a tax holiday. See also Mintz (1990).

31 Studies that do incorporate them typically have to make simplifying assumptions. Recent empirical applications include the analysis of corporate taxes in the EU (Commission of European Communities, 2001), the Canadian and US tax systems (Ruggeri and McMullin, 2004), sectoral incentives in Zambia (FIAS, 2004), and tax incentives and investment in the Eastern Caribbean (Sosa, 2005).

32 Other limitations are that: the neoclassical model of investment behavior on which the METR is based is only one of a number of competing theories; it measures the distortion on investment through the tax system, not the actual responsiveness of the firm to the changed incentives; the financial structure of the firm is taken as given and is not endogenous to the tax provisions.

33 Exploration costs are assumed to be sunk costs. They are therefore not included as negative cash flows, but the sunk costs are included for cost recovery and tax depreciation purposes.

34 The onshore and deep water field data were provided to FAD by Wood Mackenzie. The shallow water field is part of an FAD data bank of petroleum projects.

35 From estimates by Damodaran (2008).

36 "Tax payments" are broadly defined to include royalty, state production shares and the revenues generated by concessional state equity participation in each project.

37 In practice, a serious chance of finding such profitable fields would result in bids that reduced contractor share. There is thus an implicit assumption that such terms are set in the absence of competition, or of adjustment for the effect of high price expectations in 2008.

38 As was done, for example, in the 2006 and 2008 bidding rounds in Angola, where a scheme similar to the "alternative package" is in place.

39 The effective royalty rate is the combination of any formal royalty (such as that existing in Mozambican law) with the minimum state production share implied by a minimum profit oil share (oil remaining after royalty, minus the cost oil limit).

40 Not specifically those of Mozambique. Currently, "Mozambique" has treaties to reduce WT tax rates applicable to dividend, interest and royalty payments by "Mozambican" companies to non-residents with Italy, Mauritius, Portugal, and the United Arab Emirates.

41 Total benefits mean revenues minus operating costs and replacement capital investment, i.e. the "cake" from which taxes are paid, debt is serviced and equity providers are rewarded.

238   *P. Daniel* et al.

42 The coefficient of variation is the standard deviation divided by the mean, and is a measure of the dispersion of expected returns that can be compared among different regimes or projects.

43 Angola has the lowest expected mean to investor among the sample. However, because of a variable cost recovery limit that increases after 5 years if the investor has not recovered all costs, its lowest expected negative NPV to the investor is not consistent with the lowest expected mean measure. For this reason, Equatorial Guinea, which yielded what is otherwise the least favorable for investor, is chosen as the benchmark.

44 Companies can also diversify by investing in a range of projects.

45 One example is the International Country Risk Index published by the PRS Group, Inc. Scores range from 0 to 100 and are updated monthly for 140 countries. Sub-indices are available for political, financial and economic risks.

46 In many countries, government bond markets either do not exist or are too immature for yields to provide an accurate measure of country risk.

47 The general risk analysis approach outlined in this note is based on Lerche and Mackay (1995).

48 In the early stages of a project prospectivity data would be usually limited to surface geology, gravity, aeromagnetic and seismic surveys, and historical data on previously hydrocarbon exploration activity if available.

49 The probability of a successful finding, P_F, could be further adjusted to include the probability that the successful finding would be of a certain type of hydrocarbon, the probability that successful finding would be of certain size, etc.

50 The EMV approach developed in this note is based on the risk adjusted value (RAV) formula by Cozzolino (1977 and 1978).

51 The prudent risk taking approach was originally introduced by Arps and Arps (1974).

52 This ratio is only meaningful if V>C. Otherwise the project would not even be considered.

References

Arps, J. J. and J. L. Arps (1974), "Prudent Risk Taking," *Journal of Petroleum Technology*, Vol. 26, pp. 711–716.

Blake, A., and M. Roberts (2006), "Comparing Petroleum Fiscal Regimes Under Oil Price Uncertainty," *Resources Policy*, Vol. 31, pp. 95–105.

Boadway, R., N. Bruce, K. McKenzie and J. Mintz (1987), "Marginal Effective Tax Rates for Capital in the Canadian Mining Industry," *Canadian Journal of Economics*, Vol. 20, pp. 1–16.

Boadway, R., D. Chua, and F. Flatters (1995), "Investment Incentives and the Corporate Tax System in Malaysia," in Shah, A. (ed.) *Fiscal Incentives for Investment and Innovation*, pp. 341–373 (New York: Oxford University Press).

Boadway, R. and M. Keen (2010), "Theoretical Perspectives on Resource Tax Design," in Philip Daniel, Michael Keen, and Charles McPherson (eds.) *The Taxation of Petroleum and Minerals: Principles, Problems and Practice*.

Bohren, O. and C. Schilbred (1980), "North Sea Oil Taxes and the Sharing of Risk – A Comparative Case Study," *Energy Economics*, Vol. 2, pp. 145–153.

Brealey, R. and S. Myers (2005), *Principles of Corporate Finance* (Irwin McGraw-Hill).

Collins, J. and D. Shackelford (1995), "Corporate Domicile and Average Effective Tax Rates: The Cases of Canada, Japan, the UK and USA," *International Tax and Public Finance*, Vol. 2, pp. 55–83.

Commission of the European Communities (2001), "Company Taxation in the Internal Market," SEC(2001) 1681 (Brussels, Belgium).

Conrad, R., Z. Shalizi, and J. Syme, (1990), "Issues in Evaluating Tax and Payment Arrangements for Publicly Owned Minerals," WPS 496 (Washington: World Bank).

Cozzolino, J. (1977), "A Simplified Utility Framework for the Analysis of Financial Risk," Economic Evaluation Symposium of the Society of Petroleum Engineers (Dallas, Texas).

Damodaran, A. (2008), spreadsheet, available at: http://pages.stern.nyu.edu/~adamodar/.

Devereux, M. and R. Griffith (1998), "Taxes and the Location of Production: Evidence from a Panel of US Multinationals," *Journal of Public Economics*, Vol. 68, pp. 335–367.

Devereux, M., R. Griffith, and A. Klemm (2002), "Corporate Income Tax. Reforms and Tax Competition," *Economic Policy*, Vol. 2, pp. 450–495.

Devereux, M. and R. Griffith (2003), "Evaluating Tax Policy for Location Decisions," *International Tax and Public Finance*, Vol. 10, pp. 107–126.

Emhjellen, M. and C. Alaouze (2003), "A Comparison of Discounted Cashflow and Modern Asset Pricing Methods – Project Selection and Policy Implications," *Energy Policy*, Vol. 31, pp. 1213–1220.

Foreign Investment Advisory Service (FIAS), (2004), "Zambia: Sectoral Study of the Effective Tax Burden" (Washington DC: International Finance Corporation and World Bank).

Galli, A., M. Armstrong, and B. Jehl (1999), "Comparing Three Methods for Evaluating Oil Projects: Option Pricing, Decision Trees, and Monte Carlo Simulations," *Journal of Petroleum Technology*, pp. 44–50.

Garnaut, R. and A. Clunies Ross (1975), "Uncertainty, Risk Aversion and the Taxing of Natural Resource Projects," *The Economic Journal*, Vol. 85, pp. 272–287.

—— (1983), *Taxation of Mineral Rents*, Oxford.

Grinblatt, M. and S. Titman (2002), *Financial Markets and Corporate Strategy*, second edition (McGraw-Kill Irwin).

Hogan, L. (2007), "Mineral Resource Taxation in Australia: An Assessment of Economic Policy Options," ABARE Research Report 07.01, Australian Bureau of Agricultural and Resource Economics, available at: www.abareconomics.com.

—— and B. Goldsworthy (2010), "International Minerals Taxation: Experience and Issues," in Philip Daniel, Michael Keen, and Charles McPherson (eds.) *The Taxation of Petroleum and Minerals: Principles, Problems and Practice.*

Jacoby, H. and D. Laughton (1992), "Project Evaluation: A Practical Asset Pricing Method," *Energy Journal*, Vol. 13, Issue 2, pp. 19–48.

Johnston, D. (2003), *International Exploration Economics, Risk, and Contract Analysis* (Tulsa: Pennwell).

—— (2007), "How to Evaluate the Fiscal Terms of Oil Contracts," in Humphreys, M., J. Sachs and J. Stiglitz (eds.) *Escaping the Resource Curse* (New York: Columbia University Press).

King, M. and D. Fullerton (1984), *Taxation of Income from Capital* (Chicago: University of Chicago Press).

Lerche, I. and J. Mackay (1999), *Economic Risk in Hydrocarbon Exploration* (London and San Diego: Academic Press).

Mendoza, E., A. Razin, and L. Tesar (1994), "Effective Tax Rates in Macroeconomics: Cross-Country Estimates of Tax Rates on Factor Incomes and Consumption," *Journal of Monetary Economics*, Vol. 24, pp. 297–323.

Mintz, Jack (1990), "Corporate Tax Holidays and Investments," *World Bank Economic Review*, Vol. 4, pp. 81–102 (Washington DC: World Bank).

Ossowski, R., M. Villafuerte, P. Medas, and T. Thomas (2008), *Managing the Oil Revenue Boom: The Role of Fiscal Institutions*, Occasional Paper 260 (Washington DC: International Monetary Fund).

Palmer, K. (1980), "Mineral Taxation Policies in Developing Countries: An Application of Resource Rent Tax," *IMF Staff Papers*, Vol. 27, pp. 517–542.

Quiroz, J. (2008), *Survey of Recent Contract Renegotiations and Other Changes Initiated by Producing Countries in their Oil and Gas Industries* (New York: Revenue Watch Institute).

Ruggeri, J. and J. McMullin (2004), *Canada's Fiscal Advantage* (Canada: Caledon Institute of Social Policy).

Samis, M., D. Laughton, and R. Poulin (2003), "Risk Discounting: The Fundamental Difference Between the Real Option and Discounted Cash Flow Project Valuation Methods," Kuiseb Minerals Consulting, Working Paper 2003–1.

Slade, M. (2001), "Valuing Managerial Flexibility: An Application of Real-Option Theory to Mining Investments," *Journal of Environment Economics and Management*, Vol. 41, pp. 193–233.

Smith, J. and K. McCardle (1998), "Valuing Oil Properties: Integrating Option Pricing and Decision Analysis Approaches," *Operations Research*, Vol. 46, pp. 198–217.

—— (1998), "Evaluating Income Streams: A Decision Analysis Approach," *Management Science*, Vol. 44, pp. 1690–1708.

Smith, L. (2000), "Discounted Cash Flow Analysis: Methodology and Discount Rates," Mineral Property Valuation Proceedings, Papers presented at Mining Millennium 2000 (Quebec, Canada).

Sosa, S. (2006), "Tax Incentives and Investment in the Eastern Caribbean," IMF Working Paper WP/06/23 (Washington DC: International Monetary Fund).

Tordo, S. (2007), *Fiscal Systems for Hydrocarbons: Design Issues* (Washington DC: World Bank).

US Department of Energy, Annual Energy Outlook (1982, 1985, 1991, 1995, 2000 and 2004).

Van Meurs, P. (1981), *Modern Petroleum Economics* (Calgary, Canada: Van Meurs Associates).

—— (2002), *World Fiscal Systems for Oil*, Van Meurs Associates (New York: Barrows Company).

Wilson, J. (1984), "Taxing Mineral Resource Projects: Papua New Guinea, Indonesia and the Philippines," *Resources Policy*, Vol. 10, pp. 251–262.

Wood, M. (2008), *Fiscal Storms: A Perspective from Wood Mackenzie*, available at: www.woodmac.com.

8 Resource rent taxes

A re-appraisal

Bryan C. Land

1 Introduction

The aim of a resource rent tax is to capture resource rent realized by the exploitation of a mineral or hydrocarbon deposit.[1] Resource rent is classically understood to be the surplus value generated by such exploitation over all necessary costs of production, including rewards to capital. Following this principle, a resource rent tax targets the returns made on investment that exceed the minimum reward necessary for capital to be deployed. In practice, this means that an investor enjoys relief from taxation until a satisfactory rate of return has been earned. Thereafter, profits are shared with the host government on an ex-post basis.[2]

In response to recent dramatic swings in commodity prices, resource rent taxation is topical again, having first featured prominently in discussion of resource tax policies in the 1970s. Its use was pioneered in Papua New Guinea but since then has been rather limited. Indeed, resource rent taxes retain an image of being rather exotic instruments for taxing resource projects. Their strongest proponents regard them as an indispensible part of any tax armory, while their detractors consider them inappropriate and unworkable. Economists will find that there is a lack of robust explanatory models to refer to in support of claims in favor of or against resource rent taxes (Lund 2008).

This chapter re-appraises the benefit of resource rent taxes to host governments in the light of recent commodity price cycles. The paper revisits the theoretical underpinnings of resource rent taxation, examines the design of resource rent taxes and considers revenue management and tax administration considerations associated with their use. The paper concludes by suggesting some of the conditions that may need to be in place for a resource rent tax to merit consideration as part of the fiscal regime of a resource-rich country.

2 Resource taxation amid boom and bust

Host governments of resource-rich countries face the age-old challenge of how to tax the exploitation of a heterogeneous resource base in conditions of economic uncertainty. The possibility that higher quality mineral and petroleum deposits will generate substantial resource rents, particularly at times of elevated commodity prices, leads to an interest in how the tax system can maximize the capture of resource rent for the benefit of the country while, at the same time, preserving the incentives that make investment in the risky business of finding and exploiting mineral and petroleum deposits worthwhile.

The first development of tax policy concepts with a particular focus on resource rent capture took place in the early 1970s. This was a period of high and volatile commodity prices and of assertive host governments, often of newly independent states, which sought a greater share of resource industry profits. The design of the first resource rent tax is closely associated with tax policy in newly independent Papua New Guinea. The world class Panguna gold-copper mine was much richer than predicted at the time of approval of the project by the pre-Independence Government and prices for these two commodities exploded in the early 1970s. The fiscal terms in the original negotiated agreement anticipated neither development and left the Independence Government with a low and declining share of the mineral bonanza.[3]

The conclusion reached then was that an investor would not walk away from a world-class deposit so long as it was able to recover all its costs and earn a rate of return sufficient to justify having made the investment. The fiscal terms were changed (by renegotiation) to achieve this effect.[4] Later the same principles were applied to design a fiscal regime for future resource projects in PNG – one that would seek both to attract new investment and capture a large share of any future bonanzas.[5]

The potential to generate large resource rents in the mining sector during the 1970s and in the petroleum industry in the wake of OPEC oil price hikes in 1973 and, then again in 1979, motivated several other countries to focus fiscal policies on rent capture. Several used new tax instruments modeled on a similar basis to the resource taxes pioneered in PNG. A list of resource rent taxes employed in the mining and petroleum sectors since the 1970s is shown in Table 8.1, including those that were legislated and others that were contractual.

The dramatic and unpredictable up and down fluctuation in the prices of mineral and petroleum commodities in recent years has rekindled interest in resource rent taxes. At their peak in mid-2008, prices had risen some fivefold – and for certain commodities nearly tenfold – in a matter of just three to four years. This brought about an inevitable focus upon price-driven windfall profits of producers. The subsequent price collapse, one of the sharpest ever witnessed, has provided an abrupt reminder of the highly volatile and uncertain nature of commodity markets.

During the escalation in prices many host governments found that as extractive industry earnings grew dramatically the rise in their own revenues lagged well behind. The reason for this, at least in part, was the absence of instruments to capture resource rent in many of the fiscal regimes designed in the 1980s and 1990s. In the mining industry, many governments had relied heavily upon production royalties for revenue, several having offered tax holidays (or reduced tax rates) in the depths of depression in the sector, backed by stabilization agree-

Table 8.1 Some examples of resource rent taxes

Country	Sector	Years in Force	Legislated/contractual
PNG	Petroleum	Since 1977 (frontier areas exempt)	Legislated
PNG	Mining	1978–2002	Legislated
Australia	Petroleum	Since 1984	Legislated
Ghana	Petroleum	Since 1984	Contractual
Tanzania	Petroleum	Since 1984	Contractual
Various	Petroleum	Mid-1980s	Contractual
Ghana	Mining	1985–2003	Legislated
Madagascar	Petroleum and mining	1980s	Legislated
Canada, British Columbia	Mining	Since 1990	Legislated
Namibia	Petroleum	Since 1993	Legislated
Zimbabwe	Mining	Since 1994	Legislated
Russia	Petroleum (PSAs)	Since 1994	Contractual
Angola	Petroleum	Since mid-1990s	Contractual
Azerbaijan	Petroleum	Since 1996	Contractual
Kazakhstan	Petroleum	Since mid-1990s	Contractual
Solomon Islands	Mining (gold)	Since 1999	Contractual
Timor-Leste	Petroleum	Since 2003	Legislated
Malawi	Mining	Since 2006	Legislated
Liberia	Mining	Since 2008	Legislated

ments. In some cases, where resource rent taxes had existed previously, these had either been removed from the statute book or waived. In the oil industry, the prevalence of volume-based rather than profit-based production sharing entailed limited government sharing in any price escalation. These arrangements were particularly ill-suited to the period of price escalation that ensued in the early part of the new century. Indeed, the prevailing characteristic of petroleum fiscal regimes existing at this time was regressive (Johnston 2008).[7]

It was against this background that many host governments began to increase taxes on incumbents and, with the same objective, impose tougher entry terms than those previously in place for newcomers. This process, coupled with increasing nationalizations and the denial of direct access by the private sector to valuable resource deposits, was gathering pace at the time when commodity prices began to tumble and the entire economic climate for resources investment to deteriorate.

For the most part host governments tried to re-balance existing fiscal regimes by seeking renegotiation with incumbents. Some others preferred or, instead, felt compelled to impose new terms on a "take it or leave it" basis, calculating that their enhanced bargaining strength gave them such latitude. The reaction of industry varied. Incumbents, with immovable productive assets and sunk invest-ment costs had an option to abandon their operations, or dispute their fiscal treat-ment hoping to obtain compensation, or renegotiate and settle.[8] There were examples of each of these approaches, although few investors opted to abandon sunk investments while prices remained high. When, for example, in 2007, the Government of Venezuela increased tax rates and lifted state participation to a controlling interest in the heavy oil projects of the Orinoco, ExxonMobil and ConocoPhillips opted to withdraw from existing investments and filed legal claims for restitution and compensation. Others, such as ENI, opted instead to renegotiate their financial positions while retaining a continuing commitment to their projects. In the mining sector, renegotiations in some cases yielded concessions from existing operators, such as in Tanzania.[9] For newcomers the options were greater, though in the short term, some companies would have found that, with so many host countries tightening their terms, there were perhaps few better opportunities elsewhere.

An inevitable consequence of these episodes was strained relationships between many host governments and investors. The reopening of fiscal terms may have appeared unavoidable to host governments given the structure of fiscal terms agreed in an earlier period. However, investors were bound to have reduced faith in host governments being willing to be bound by contract sanctity in the future, even if they could understand the intense pressures felt by host governments. Now, with the reversal of economic fortunes, the dynamics of host government–investor relations have changed once more and with it the options available to each side. The new preoccupation may be less on maximizing the capture of resource rents than on sustaining investor commitments to existing projects and encouraging them to sustain investment in risky exploration ventures. It is perhaps not surprising that discussion of fiscal policies seems to be shifting increasingly towards finding means of accommodating the interests of host governments and investors in times of both boom and bust.

3 Resource rent and risk

The preceding retrospective serves to emphasize some of the salient characteristic of the resource industries and the difficulties experienced in designing suitable systems to tax them. In this section, the chapter examines the theoretical underpinnings of resource rent taxation, with a focus on resource rent and risk.[10]

The classic definition of resource rent is the ex-post surplus of the total project lifetime value arising from the exploitation of a deposit, in present value terms, over the sum of all costs of exploitation, including the compensation to all factors of production.[11] The latter includes a return on capital required by the investor. Resource rent is depicted in Figure 8.1. A compensatory return on capital would consist of a basic return equivalent to the rate of interest on risk-free long-term borrowing plus a margin that the investor considers necessary to compensate for the technical, commercial and political risks associated with investment. In principle, such allowance for risk ought not to reflect company-specific considerations.

The rent potential of different resource deposits varies as a function of "quality." In the case of mineral deposits, among the key determinants of quality are ore tonnages, mineral grades, rates of recovery of ore from a deposit taking

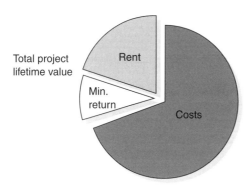

Figure 8.1 Resource rent.

into account dilution, the efficiency of ore extraction methods and the efficiency with which a saleable mineral product is obtained from the ore (e.g. metallurgical recovery rates). In the case of hydrocarbon deposits some of the key factors are the size of recoverable reserves, the quality of the oil or gas, the pressure of the reservoir and other factors affecting recoverability and the degree of processing necessary to achieve a saleable product. Further determinants of "quality" include the proximity to markets given the available technology for transporting products to markets and other aspects of the operating environment that impinge on efficiency.

The resource endowment in any country comprises a distribution of higher quality deposits and large numbers of lower quality deposits compared to the average deposit in that country. There typically exist order of magnitude differences between the highest and lowest quality deposits.[12] This is depicted in Figure 8.2 where the solid line A represents a hypothetical distribution of resource deposits by frequency along the x-axis and by rent potential along the y-axis.

The distribution is not static, however. At any point in time, prevailing prices for a resource type and the costs of producing and marketing that resource go up or down, affecting the rent potential of all deposits. Such changes are represented by the two dashed lines, one of which represents the impact of higher prices and/or lower costs and the other which represents the impact of lower prices and/or higher costs.

Ideally, the tax system should be designed with the flexibility to extract the different rents actually generated by deposits under dynamic price and cost conditions on an ex-post basis. This requires, in any individual case, that the higher the profitability of resource exploitation, the greater the share of total benefits that accrues to the host country. Where this positive correlation exists the fiscal regime is said to be progressive. The inverse of a progressive fiscal regime is a regressive fiscal regime and the difference between the two is depicted in Figure 8.3.

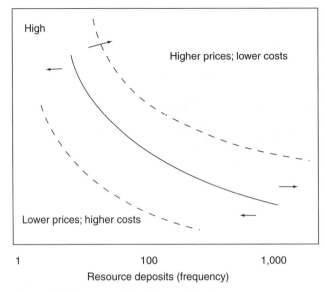

Figure 8.2 Rent potential of a hypothetical resource base.

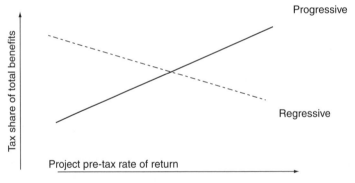

Figure 8.3 Progressive and regressive fiscal regimes (source: Daniel (2008)).

Risk aversion has an important place in the literature on resource rent. It posits that any decrease in the risk associated with an investment would, *ipso facto*, reduce the minimum return required by the investor to undertake that investment and thereby increase the resource rent potential of exploiting the deposit. The opposite would hold true as well.

In this context, the approach of the host government to taxation can affect the investor's perception of risk and, as a consequence the level of rent potential. For example, if fiscal terms were perceived to be susceptible to adverse change of an unknown magnitude on a unilateral basis, this would increase perceived risk, raise the minimum rate of return and therefore reduce rent potential. By comparison, an undertaking by the host government not to change fiscal terms, perhaps in the form of a stability agreement, might help to reduce perceived risk and therefore enhance rent potential. The experience of the last few years has shown, however, that a stability agreement that merely stabilizes an inflexible fiscal regime has little likelihood of being respected in the long run (Daniel and Sunley, Chapter 14).

The key, therefore, would seem to be to build flexibility into the tax system so that it can accommodate changes to economic circumstances that fiscal rigidity could not cope with.[13] By reducing the likelihood that a change of fiscal terms would be imposed unilaterally, such flexibility would reduce the perception of risk. It follows that the lower the compensation sought by investors for risk, the greater will be the number of projects undertaken and the greater the rent available from each. This is equivalent to an upward shift in the solid line in Figure 8.2.

4 Resource rent tax design

A Resource rent tax structure and calculation

The principles of resource rent provide the theoretical underpinnings for the design of a resource rent tax.[14] The three primary elements in the design of a typical resource rent tax are:

- specified rate(s) of return on investment that trigger the imposition of the tax;
- specified tax rate(s) imposed on net profits once the rate(s) of return has been exceeded; and
- the tax base, which is typically an individual resource project (i.e. fully ring-fenced) and allowable deductions.

A simplified example of the calculation of a resource rent tax is shown in Table 8.2, in which the threshold rate of return is set at 20 percent and the tax rate at 50 percent. All cash receipts (sales revenue and proceeds from the sale of assets) and expenses (exploration, capital and operating expenditures but not financing costs) are accounted as soon as they are incurred to derive annual net cash flow.[15] Net cash flows are compounded at the threshold rate to adjust nominal values to present values. The point at which accumulated net cash flow after compounding become positive represents the point at which a 20 percent rate of return has been achieved. The accumulation process stops at this point and subsequent positive cash flows are subject to tax at a rate of 50 percent. If in any later year the net cash flow is negative, the compounding process recommences until the accumulated value turns positive again. This situation could arise, for example, in the case of a transition from open pit to underground mining to follow a mineral deposit deeper, or the introduction of enhanced recovery wells in an ageing oil field, which in each case would require a substantial injection of new capital.

Table 8.2 The basic calculation of a resource rent tax

Year	Revenue	Total costs	Net cash flow	Adjusted NCF (a)	Tax due	After-tax NCF
1	0	100	−100	−100	0	−100
2	0	100	−100	−220	0	−100
3	0	150	−150	−414	0	−150
4	200	50	150	−347	0	−150
5	200	50	150	−266	0	−150
6	200	50	150	−169	0	−150
7	200	50	150	−53	0	−150
8	200	50	150	86	43	107
9	200	50	150	150	75	75
10	200	50	150	150	75	75
11	100	200	−100	−100	0	−100
12	300	50	250	130	65	65
13	300	50	250	250	125	125
14	300	50	250	250	125	125
15	300	50	250	250	125	125
16	300	50	250	250	125	125
17	300	50	250	250	125	125
18	100	25	75	75	38	37

Note
a Cumulative net cash flow compounded at the threshold rate of 20% until positive; thereafter annual net cash flow.

This type of arrangement can be replicated in production sharing by allocating all production to the company until full recovery of costs, plus a cost uplift corresponding to the rate of return threshold, and then allocating a share, equivalent to the tax rate, of any profit thereafter to the company.

It is also possible to emulate the fiscal effect of a resource rent tax in state equity arrangements. Where the equity is acquired by means of a loan from the investor secured against the project cash flows, the state's equity cash flow entitlement is subordinated to the loan and interest thereon. Assuming unrestricted distribution, dividend receipts (equivalent to resource rent tax receipts) will commence once the loan plus interest has been retired. The equity interest is equivalent to the rate of tax and the interest rate on the loan is equivalent to the threshold return at which resource rent tax becomes payable.

B Neutrality and efficiency

A number of surveys of resource taxes have highlighted the advantages of resource rent taxes over other instruments in terms of neutrality and efficiency (Johnson 1981, Goss 1986, Baunsgaard 2001). A well-designed resource rent tax will leave the investment decision undistorted. This will, *in principle*, enable the host government to maximize the capture of resource rent from any particular deposit without deterring investment.

In practice, there is no assurance that the threshold rate of return at which resource rent tax is triggered will correspond exactly to an investor's own minimum required rate. This is especially so if the threshold is fixed administratively and applies across the board to all resource projects, as is commonly the case. It has been argued that resource rent tax might provide an implicit subsidy to resource projects that are the most capital intensive and have longer gestation periods, owing to the effect of compounding negative net cash flows (Caragata 1989). However, this line of argument seems to imply that capital intensive resource projects with long gestation periods are avoidable or undesirable; this could hardly be the case in the resource industries.

Notwithstanding limitations that in practical terms are hard to avoid, it is generally accepted that resource rent taxes are less distorting than many other forms of tax commonly employed within the resource sector. In particular, resource rent taxes are considered to be more responsive to the underlying profitability of resource projects than a number of other taxes on profits that seek to enhance the host country tax take (McPherson and Palmer (1984), Kumar (1991)). The advantages of resource rent taxes over examples of such taxes are presented in Table 8.3, adapted from McPherson and Palmer (1984).

Many other taxes on profits are designed so that the tax rate rises as a function of one or more parameters that are proxies for profitability, such as production levels, prices, unit costs, or a combination of these. Table 8.3 illustrates two examples of these, a sliding scale tax linked to production and a sliding scale tax linked to prices. The rationale for a price-linked tax, for example, is that price movements are normally positively correlated with changes in profitability. However, this disregards the impact of potentially countervailing changes in output and costs that could reduce profitability. An approach in which the incidence of taxation is based on proxies for profitability rather than profitability itself, is an inaccurate and distorting way to capture resource rent.

As illustrated by Table 8.3, taxes in which the rate is directly linked to achieved profitability can take a number of forms. There are those in which profits are measured on an annual basis by reference, for example, to operating margins or returns on capital employed. Several countries in Africa now base their taxation of mining profits on the Variable Rate Income Tax that was first employed in South Africa. Under this scheme the rate of tax in any tax accounting period is one derived by a formula linked to the ratio of taxable income to gross income, subject to a floor rate and a top rate. There are also a number of mining agreements that contain profit taxes on a sliding scale linked to measures of return on capital, in addition to that shown illustrated in Table 8.3. This includes the Bougainville Mining Agreement of 1973 (note 5) and diamond mining agreements in Botswana and Namibia. Although more accurate in targeting resource rent than taxes based on proxies of profitability, taxes linked to profits generated in a tax accounting period (usually a year) are still not capable of targeting resource rent as accurately as a tax that is based on the cumulative profits of an investment.

The R factor, which is increasingly employed in production sharing agreements in the petroleum industry, comes quite close to the resource rent tax in

Table 8.3 Comparison of resource rent tax with other taxes on profits

Government "take" linked to	Government "take" responsive to:				
	Reserves or production	Price change	Costs	Timing of cash flows	Cost of capital
Production (daily or cumulative)	Yes	No	No	Partly	No
Example: Company share of profit oil is 50% @ low output falling to 15% @ high output (Uganda)					
Price (price caps or base prices)	No	Yes	No	Partly	No
Example: Oil profits taxed at 25% until oil price exceeds $30/bbl, thereafter rising by 0.4% for every $1/bbl > $30/bbl (Alaska, USA)					
Annual profit (profit margin or return in a tax year)	Yes	Yes	Yes	No	No
Example: Mine taxable income is taxed at the higher of 25% or 70–1500/x, where x (%) = taxable income/gross income; the higher rate applies when x > 33.3% (Botswana and Uganda; S. Africa and Namibia employ the same scheme with different values in the numerator)					
Example: Mine after-tax profits taxed at a rate of 0—15% once return on capital employed > long term bond rate + 5% (Australian mining agreement)					
R Factor (revenue: cost ratio or investment multiple)	Yes	Yes	Yes	Partly	Partly
Example: Company share of profit oil is x% @ IM < 1.5 falling to y% @ IM > 3.5, where IM = ratio of cumulative Net Income to Total Investment (India)					
Resource Rent Tax (rate of return)	Yes	Yes	Yes	Yes	Yes
Example: Petroleum after-tax cash flow taxed at 40% once the project internal rate of return exceeds the long term borrowing rate plus 5% (Australia)					

design. The R factor is a ratio measuring cumulative profits defined as cumulative revenues to cumulative costs or, as in the Indian case, cumulative net income to total investment. It is used to set the thresholds at which the share of profit oil allocated to the government increases. However the R factor is defined, its drawback is that it is not sensitive to the timing of revenues and costs (i.e. revenues and costs are not compounded annually at a discount rate, as is the case in a resource rent tax). It will therefore fail to satisfy the test of targeting resource rent as accurately as a resource rent tax.

5 Experiences in designing resource rent taxes

Having examined the principles of resource rent tax design, the chapter now examines some of the practical challenges experienced by countries in designing resource rent taxes.

A Resource rent taxes in tax system design

The capture of resource rent is an important fiscal policy objective. However, any host country must balance this objective against other fiscal objectives, including those relating to revenue management. In particular, host governments are concerned about the timing, magnitude, and volatility of revenues collected by the fiscal regime.

As a general rule governments prefer revenues that are predictable and stable. Governments also have to a greater or lesser degree a time preference for money, depending on country circumstances. The latter is represented by the discount rate on public funds. For example, the discount rate would be high in a cash-strapped developing country, or where political imperatives place an onus on short-term cash generation. A government's stance will also be influenced by the state of knowledge of the overall resource endowment. For a country in which resource exploitation is focused on a single project and future resource potential is uncertain, there may be a strong preference for short-term revenue maximization with less regard for its implications on future resource investment, coupled with a temptation to renege on any deal struck to induce investment at the outset. Such motives may be tempered in a country with a rich and diverse resource endowment that offers scope for a longer term policy perspective.

Used in isolation from any other taxes, a resource rent tax will have the following impact on revenue receipts. There will be no tax receipts from any project failing to achieve the threshold rate of return and tax receipts from any project exceeding the threshold will be delayed until an uncertain point in the future, possibly several years after the start of production. Moreover, the resource rent tax will be pro-cyclical, amplifying the revenue effects of higher and lower profitability. This will introduce heightened volatility into future revenue flows (Shukla 2008).[16]

In practice, no host government has relied on resource rent taxes on their own. Instead, resource rent taxes are combined with other taxes and charges.

Thus, in a royalty/tax regime, a resource rent tax is typically combined with royalty and corporation tax. The resource rent tax may either be used as a final tax levied on after-tax cash flows or as supplementary levy on pre-tax income, payments of which would be deductible for corporation tax purposes. The resource rent tax as first developed in PNG was applied as an "additional profits tax," levied on after-tax cash flows both for mining and petroleum. Australia's Petroleum RRT is charged before corporate income tax, however, and where the resource rent taxation approach is used to allocate profit oil, as in Angola and Ghana, sharing takes place before taxes on oil company profits (see Appendix I).

The effect of combining resource rent taxes with other taxes and charges is that some revenue is received by the host government before a project reaches the point at which resource rent tax is imposed. Experience with production sharing regimes is similar. There are very few petroleum fiscal regimes that allow full cost recovery to take place before the government receives any share of production. Royalty or a cost oil ceiling, or a combination of both, are used to assure the government of a revenue stream before the company achieves the threshold return on investment at which resource rent tax becomes payable.[17]

B Rate of return thresholds

Under resource rent taxation theory the threshold rate of return at which resource rent taxes is imposed should be no lower than the minimum return necessary for capital to be deployed. Just what that minimum should be is a matter on which the theoretical literature has reached no clear consensus. The prevailing cost of capital at any point in time can be derived from the international capital markets. However, should this cost be adjusted to take into account the characteristics of a particular investment and, if so, on what basis? The resource rent taxation literature has generally supported the idea that an investor will adjust the prevailing cost of capital to take into account expectations about the financial outcome of exploiting a specific deposit in a specific location. This is done by assigning a risk premium. In principle, the risk premium should be no higher than that required by investors on comparable investments in the host country. However, because resource deposits are few in number, vary in quality, and the returns generated vary temporally, such benchmarks are very hard to find. Surveys of investor expectations, even at a particular point in time, have demonstrated wide variation by type of investment and type of company (Johnson 1981).

Indeed, an additional complication is whether and, if so, how to cater for the particular type of company, since access to capital and the financial expectations of different sources of capital vary considerably. A cash-rich publicly quoted corporation with wide share-ownership is likely to be in a very different position from a privately held company that is dependent on venture capital financiers. Significant differences in financial expectations could also be expected to arise between a single project company and one with a diversified portfolio.

A particular challenge that the designers of resource rent taxes have to contend with is how to take into account exploration risk. Companies in the extractive industries rely on returns from a few projects to fund numerous abortive exploration ventures. The risk of drilling a dry well in the oil industry can be as high as 1-in-10 in underexplored petroleum basins and the incremental well costs are very high (i.e. investment is lumpy). Commercial viability in minerals exploration typically only follows after screening hundreds of mineral occurrences (MacKenzie and Doggett 1992).[18] Therefore, the required rate of return for an investment in exploiting a single resource deposit conceivably comprises not only a compensatory return for that particular investment but also one that would compensate for several costly exploration ventures that have returned nothing to the investor.

If exploration risk is taken into account in determining the threshold rate of return, a very high risk premium would need to be added to the basic return required by an investor in any country without proven exploration success, resulting in a very high threshold. The alternative is to relax the project-based resource rent tax ring fence to enable the costs of aborted exploration to be brought to account and recovered against revenues from a successful resource project. This would have the effect of delaying the point at which the threshold rate of return is exceeded and tax payments made.

Some examples of rate of return thresholds used in resource rent taxes are shown in Appendix I. In all cases shown, the host country has determined the threshold to be applied across the board to all qualifying investments, rather than on a project-by-project basis. In other words, the thresholds selected have inevitably been chosen to approximate required investment returns given the host government's understanding of investor expectations *on average*. The main approaches used are either to define the threshold as a fixed percentage or to define it as a fixed margin over a specified reference rate corresponding to the risk-free cost of capital, such as a bond rate or long-term debt rate, which changes annually. For the most part these are expressed in real terms.[19] The data of this sample displays a typical range of between 15 percent (Namibia) and 25 percent (Ghana) for the initial rate of return threshold.

In a number of cases, the resource rent tax is designed with an initial rate of return threshold and one or more additional thresholds at higher levels. This is particularly so among petroleum fiscal regimes that incorporate resource rent taxes (see Appendix I). This feature, coupled with the tax rates applied at each trigger point (see below), has the effect of smoothing the incremental capture of resource rent. This type of design can help to limit the possible distorting effect of applying a single threshold rate that is either too high or too low compared to the prevailing required rate of return of investors.

C Resource rent tax rates

Even assuming it were possible to fix the rate of return threshold to correspond exactly to rate of a return required by the investor, the literature on resource rent taxation is unclear in its prescription of an optimal tax rate. Although an investor will, in theory, be satisfied to obtain the minimum required return and no more, in reality, the investor is greatly interested in the tax rate that will apply on incremental returns, for a number of reasons.

Industry contends, and host governments recognize, that taxes can deter innovation and efficiency. A 100 percent resource rent tax rate would deny the investor any incremental return above the minimum required return. This approach may be justified in regulating some utility industries (e.g. power and water), where the regulator is interested in limiting the exercise of a natural monopoly to generate monopoly rents with respect to a public good. However, but for a few mineral markets in which monopoly or a high degree of cartelization exists, monopoly rents are not a primary target of resources tax policy.

A further consideration is the influence of tax rates on investor behavior. As in any fiscal regime, taxpayer behavior is influenced by marginal tax rates. If the marginal tax rate is too high it may create incentives for tax avoidance. One of the ways to do this is to spend excessively in order to avoid altogether or to defer the time at which a higher tax rate is imposed. The incentive to do so might arise when the marginal tax rate is sufficiently high to make inefficient expenditure worthwhile. Although criticism of incentives for "gold plating" are found in some of the literature on resource rent taxation, a well-designed resource rent tax will avert this outcome.

Some examples of the rates at which resource rent taxes are imposed are shown in Appendix I. The range of rates indicated by this sample, taking into account single rate versions of the tax and the starting rates of sliding-scale versions is quite wide, from a low of 10 percent in Malawi to 40 percent in Australia. Where sliding scales are used, tax rates escalate over one or more tiers, but in no case in the sample exceed 50 percent (excluding those cases in which rates are bid and could therefore surpass this level).

In those cases in which a resource rent tax operates as a charge on after-tax profits, tax rates have been set at levels that take into account the combined marginal tax rate. The Australian petroleum RRT is applied at a rate of 40 percent which, combined with a company income tax rate of 30 percent produces a marginal tax rate of 58 percent. It follows that any change in the income tax rate will modify the marginal tax rates, even if the resource rent tax rate remains the same. In order to provide stability of marginal tax rates, the Namibian additional profits tax is structured such that for any change in the income tax rate there is an automatic adjustment in the applicable resource rent tax rate (this was also the case under the former PNG additional profits tax).[20]

D Method of selecting resource rent tax parameters

In view of the issues addressed above it is important to examine how rate of return thresholds and tax rates may be set in practice. In particular, should they be set by government prescription or by some market-based process?

Prescription, especially by law, provides for equal treatment, predictability, and transparency, but offers less flexibility. The onus is placed on officials to determine appropriate terms which, if they lack suitable market information, may turn out to be inappropriate – either by deterring investment or by needlessly foregoing taxes that the investor would have paid.

The Australian approach, in which the rate of return threshold incorporates a market-determined cost of capital which is adjusted annually, offers some flexibility in setting the threshold. Those resource rent taxes for which the threshold and tax rates are prescribed in the tax legislation are the least flexible. In Namibia, for example, the Ministry had to go through Cabinet and Parliament before it was possible to offer relaxed Additional Profits Tax terms in competitive bidding for petroleum rights in the late 1990s.

Bilateral negotiation and competitive bidding offers the flexibility to tailor resource rent tax terms to market conditions. However, both may lead to multiple fiscal regimes tailored to individual projects, adding significantly to the burden of administering resource rent taxes.

Bilateral negotiation places an onus on the negotiating strength of the government to achieve a favorable outcome for the host country. A company will make the case that the high risks it assumes in exploring for and developing resources justifies a high hurdle rate for making investments, which the government negotiators may be poorly placed to disprove.

Competitive bidding offers a way to harness competition among investors to "discover" the going rate for rent capture if one or more elements of resource rent tax are biddable. While this approach might lead to multiple regimes, if the variables open to bidding are limited, the resulting administrative burden need not be significant. In Namibia, for example, although the main elements of the petroleum additional profits tax are prescribed by law, within the three-tier sliding scale, the two higher tier rates are biddable. Building on recent experience of competitive tendering of large defined mineral deposits and undercapitalized mines in Kosovo and Afghanistan, there is growing interest in an approach that would require bidders to offer a share of excess profits to the government as part of their bid. This has most recently been tested in Liberia, where world-class iron ore deposits are being auctioned. Among the criterion for a winning bid is the rate of resource rent tax offered in excess of the basic rate of 20 percent.

6 Administering resource rent taxes

A further factor to be taken into consideration in designing the fiscal regime is the administration of the regime. It is not the purpose of this paper to examine the challenges of tax administration in any depth since this topic is covered extensively elsewhere by Calder in Chapter 11. But it will be evident that any fiscal policy must take into account the likely burden that administering the fiscal regime will place on government institutions. In particular, a government needs to consider the level of human and financial resources that will be needed to ensure the efficient collection of taxes due and minimization of tax leakage. The requirement will be a function of the complexity of the fiscal regime and of individual tax instruments, and of the type of information that is needed in order to assess compliance by tax payers. In this respect, tax instruments need to be evaluated in terms of the propensity for tax avoidance by manipulating the data used to assess tax liabilities, such as the volumes and values of products sold and the costs incurred and claimed by the tax payer.

Resource rent taxes have, for the most part, the same tax filing and audit requirements as conventional income taxes. There are some differences in tax assessment that might need to be addressed by suitable additional procedures, however.

Resource rent tax is a ring-fenced tax, at least in concept.[21] A taxpayer that operates more than one taxable project under such rules would be assessed for resource rent tax on each separately. To the extent that such project ring-fencing is not also the basis for income tax assessment, tax administrators would be faced by having to make ring-fence rulings that they would not be accustomed to making. Furthermore, if the resource rent tax were a final tax on after-tax income, tax administrators would have to allocate deductions for income tax already paid among several projects separately taxable under resource rent tax. Therefore, in situations where income tax is assessed on a consolidated basis, the introduction of resource rent tax would increase the administrative burden some-what. There are, of course, many tax jurisdictions in which income tax is levied on resource projects with some degree of ring-fencing, so that this difficulty would not necessarily be new.

Resource rent tax is assessed on the basis of cumulative (multi-year) results rather than a single tax accounting period. Although tax administrators are not accustomed to this basis of tax assessment, the challenge this presents is really only a computational one. An issue that could have to be addressed, however, would be to require that full records for all relevant pre-production years that need to be brought to account are available to the tax authorities (Caragata 1989). This is most likely to be of practical relevance if a government were con-templating the application of resource rent tax to an existing mining operation. In such case it would be necessary to determine from past records a complete cash flow history on which to base the threshold for commencement of the resource rent tax liability. Indeed, this was one of the reasons cited by the Gov-ernment of Australia for imposing its petroleum RRT only on future petroleum operations when the tax was introduced in the early 1980s.

Resource rent tax is assessed on a cash flow rather than tax accounting basis. In particular, non-cash charges, like depreciation are not used. In principle, however, non-cash charges correspond to cash flows, albeit with different timing. Tax administrators might need to add procedures to be able to interpret, cross-check, and verify data presented on cash and non-cash bases.

Tax leakage safeguards for resource rent taxes (dealing with transfer pricing, allocation of overheads, expenditure verification) are no different from those needed for any other kind of profits taxation. Interest expenses are not normally an allowable deduction in a resource rent tax, so interest deduction limits under thin capitalization rulings are not required.

While not absolutely essential, the ability to administer a resource rent tax would probably benefit from an understanding, through suitable training, of the conceptual underpinnings of resource rent taxation, especially discounted cash flow, cost of risk capital, investment returns etc.

In summary, a tax office that is capable of imposing income tax on resource businesses consistently and effectively, should, with a relatively modest augmentation of skills and personnel be able to administer a resource rent tax. If a tax office does not already satisfy these conditions, then a move to resource rent taxation could represent both a significant additional administrative burden and create considerable additional risks of tax leakage.

Unfortunately, the latter scenario is the one that still prevails in many developing countries. The capacity of tax offices to carry out core functions associated with generally applicable taxes, such as income tax and VAT, is a matter that is increasingly being addressed through donor supported initiatives, such as the creation of large taxpayer units. The administration of sector specific taxes, such as resource rent taxes may, in this context, sometimes fail to attract the level of priority and commitment that is needed.

In recent experience some governments have shown a preference for levying resource taxes that are relatively easy to administer, such as windfall taxes on oil sales based on international oil price levels.[22] The attraction of such taxes is that they are simple to impose and do not require verification of profits. However, a tax that is simple to administer but is inefficient and distorting, as explained in Section 4, might not be sustainable and may need to be changed or renegotiated.

7 Tax creditability considerations

Historically, another consideration that policy makers had to take into account was whether a resource rent tax would be credited as a true tax on profits in the home country of an investor, thereby posing a risk of double taxation to the investor if this were not the case. In order for a tax payer in a home country in which profits taxation is levied on worldwide profits (as in the US) to obtain a credit against a tax already paid in a foreign country, it must show that the tax that has been paid corresponds to profits tax that would have otherwise been payable in the home country. Definitional issues that had earlier cast doubt on a tax payers' ability to do this have, for the most part, been resolved through test cases over a period of time. Creditability issues no longer appear to be a factor that would inhibit the use of a conventionally designed resource rent taxes in host countries, although it is a matter to be examined with regard to different home tax jurisdictions and any double taxation agreements in place or under negotiation (see Chapter 13 by Mullins).

8 Lessons for resource taxation

Resource taxation is a vexed issue in many resource-rich countries with disappointment at the share of profits received by host governments closely associated with resurgent resource nationalism. Recent experience of boom and bust in commodity markets has demonstrated how many resource tax systems respond weakly to changes in the economic environment.

However, resource tax systems can be made to respond better to changes in the economic environment. Experience suggests that a balanced tax system would provide the host government with reasonably predictable revenue streams throughout resource production but generate additional revenues linked to profits achieved. Sharing of profits should be sufficiently flexible to reduce temptation for future governments to change terms in boom periods – while preserving returns that compensate the investor adequately for capital employed and associated risks.

A resource rent tax is one among several available instruments for taxing profits and can be combined with one or more other tax instruments to achieve a more balanced and flexible tax system. Whether a resource rent tax is the best available instrument depends on an assessment of the revenue that can potentially be raised through it, revenue management challenges, and the administrative costs associated with its use.

A resource rent tax offers quite high potential for revenue maximization and is combined with relatively limited distortion – compared to other taxes on profits. The revenue management challenges that might be entailed by relying on a pure resource rent tax system has resulted in the combination of resource rent taxes with other fiscal instruments that provide an assurance of earlier and more predictable revenue streams. Resource rent taxes can present administrative challenges to government revenue agencies, depending on their capacity. A tax office that is capable of imposing income tax on resource businesses consistently and effectively, should, with a relatively modest augmentation of skills and personnel be able to administer a resource rent tax. If a tax office does not already satisfy these conditions, then a move to resource rent taxation could represent both a significant additional administrative burden and create considerable additional risks of tax leakage. There may also be practical limitations in trying to impose resource rent taxes on resource projects that are already in production.

The chapter has argued that the benefits of using a resource rent tax in any particular country will depend not only on its ability to extract resource rent with relative efficiency and limited distortion but also on the government's willingness to accept that its fiscal take will tend to be back-end loaded and that this form of tax will have a pro-cyclical influence on resource revenue patterns. Past experience has shown limited enthusiasm for resource rent taxes among host governments, even more so in the mining sector than in the petroleum sector. Preferences generally would appear to depend on the scale of potential resource rent at stake and the availability of public resources to achieve effective administration. However, recent experience of boom and bust in the resource industries will have demonstrated that there is a need for more balanced and flexible ways to accommodate the interests of both host governments and investors as economic circumstances change. In this respect a resource rent tax deserves serious appraisal.

Appendix I

Table 8.4 Details of resource rent taxes in selected countries

	Australia Petroleum	Timor Leste Petroleum	Ghana Petroleum	Namibia Petroleum	Angola Petroleum	Malawi Mining	PNG Mining	Ghana Mining	Liberia Mining
Name	Resource Rent Tax	Supplemental Petroleum Tax	Additional Oil Entitlement	Additional Profits Tax	Profit Oil Sharing	Resource Rent Tax	Additional Profits Tax	Additional Profits Tax	Resource Rent Tax
Single rate or sliding scale	single rate of 40%	single rate of 22.5%	sliding scale	3-tier sliding scale starting at 25%	sliding scale	10%	70% minus standard tax rate	35%	single rate 20%
IRR threshold	long-term borrowing rate (6.18% for 2008) + 5% for exploration costs/+15% for capital costs	16.5%	Varies contract by contract	15% 20% 25%	varies contract by contract	20%	20% or US Prime Rate + 12%	25%	22.5%
Legislated or contractual	legislated	legislated	contractual	legislated	contractual	legislated	legislated	legislated	legislated
Biddable	no	no	yes	2nd and 3rd tier tax rates	yes	no	no	no	yes—rate in excess of prescribed rate
Ring fence	project + abortive exploration		project			rules not yet developed	project		
Levied pre-tax or post-tax	pre-tax	post-tax*	pre-tax	post-tax	pre-tax	post-tax	post-tax	post-tax	pre-tax
Status	being imposed	being imposed	Yet to be imposed	yet to be imposed	being imposed	yet to be imposed	abolished	abolished	used in recent iron ore auction

Note
*The 22.5% rate is a net, post-tax rate.

Notes

1 As throughout the book, the term resource is used in this paper to refer to non-renewable (mineral and petroleum) resources.

2 The name "Resource Rent Tax" is currently used by the Government of Australia to label a tax that is imposed on petroleum projects and by the Government of Malawi for a tax imposed on mining projects. Tax instruments of a similar design are employed in other countries and have variously been labeled "Additional Profits Tax," "Supplementary Profits Tax," "Excess Profits Tax," etc. Resource rent tax is preferred in this paper, because of the clear connection it establishes with the target of the tax, namely "resource rent."

3 The agreement with Bougainville Copper Limited in 1969 provided for a three-year tax holiday, indefinite shielding of 20 percent of the company's income from any tax liability and generous capital allowances.

4 The renegotiated terms included an arrangement under which that part of income in any tax year that exceeded a 15 percent return on the capital base would be taxed at 70 percent compared to the then standard rate of 33 1/3 percent.

5 The PNG fiscal regime featured the "Additional Profits Tax," a resource rent tax under which the after-tax income of mines (and later oilfields) would be subject to additional taxation once a specified rate of return had been exceeded. Details are provided in Table 8.2.

6 McPherson and Palmer (1984) cite examples of rate of return based profit sharing employed in Production Sharing Contracts that had either been concluded or were under negotiation at the time in Equatorial Guinea, Guinea-Bissau, Kenya, Liberia, Pakistan, Senegal, and Somalia.

7 A fiscal regime is said to be regressive when the host government share of profits of a moderately profitable resource project is lower than that of a highly profitable resource project on a lifetime basis.

8 In March 2006 China imposed a special upstream tax levy on oil companies at rates of between 20 percent and 40 percent, linked to oil prices in excess of $40/barrel of oil, prompting ConocoPhillips to invoke the international arbitration clause in its production sharing agreement (www.MarketWatch.com). In December 2006 Algeria promulgated regulations imposing a windfall tax on production values exceeding US$30/barrel of oil, prompting Anadarko to make a charge against profits pending the outcome of negotiations or international arbitration (www.BusinessWire.com).

9 In Tanzania, a number of gold mining companies agreed in 2007 to forgo the benefit of a 15 percent annual investment allowances on unredeemed capital, thereby bringing forward the likely date at which income tax would start being paid (*Financial Times*, October 1, 2007).

10 The theoretical underpinnings for RRT were to be developed in a wealth of economic writing, exemplified by the work of Garnaut and Clunies Ross. Their 1975 publication "Uncertainty, Risk Aversion and the Taxing of Natural Resource Projects" is still widely regarded as the primary source in this area.

11 Costs are expenditures on all inputs necessary to bring a mineral or petroleum deposit into production and exploit it until closure. In the literature these are limited to direct costs and do not include externalities (e.g. environmental and social), the costs of which are borne by others (including the State). A debated point is whether to include among direct costs any expenditures associated with failed exploration (see the discussion in Section 5B).

12 In the petroleum sector, a super-giant Saudi oilfield is capable of generating significant volumes of crude oil over a sustained period under its own pressure drive, resulting in very low extraction costs per barrel of oil. The same barrel of oil is recovered from a Canadian oil-sand operation after excavation and energy-intensive processing for an extraction cost as high as ten times that of a Saudi operation. In the mining

sector, such order of magnitude differences are uncommon, nonetheless, mineral grade variation, coupled with varying mineralogical conditions, can be significant. A special case, however, is that of diamonds in which different quality diamonds can be present in a single diamond pipe, with rare finds being thousands of times more valuable that the average carat value of diamond production.

13 As Johnston (2008) points out, "built-in" flexibility has become the test for fiscal regime stability in a recent comparison of petroleum fiscal regimes conducted by oil-industry consultants Wood McKenzie.

14 In Chapter 2, Boadway and Keen explore in considerable depth the theoretical principles of resource taxation, including close examination of the Garnaut–Clunies Ross resource rent tax.

15 Capital expenditures of the company are written off in the year incurred whether this takes place before or after the start of production.

16 Shukla (2008) cites the results of models used to determine the volatility co-efficient for revenues generated by seven different tax instruments or combinations of instruments. The lowest co-efficient is for a unit royalty on its own, whereas the highest co-efficient is for a resource rent tax on its own.

17 One of the criticisms leveled against the production sharing contracts negotiated in Russia in the early 1990s is that they allow all oil (net of a modest royalty) to be allocated to the oil company to recover costs plus an uplift equivalent to the rate of return specified at which profit sharing commences. As the capital costs of developing oilfields in Sakhalin have escalated, the Russian authorities have become increasingly disillusioned with production sharing contracts structured on this basis.

18 MacKenzie and Doggett (1992) concluded that only 1 to 2 percent of all identified mineral occurrences turn out to be commercially exploitable based on empirical studies of past exploration in Australia and Canada.

19 If the threshold is expressed in nominal terms, the incidence of RRT would be affected by inflationary conditions.

20 In the PNG mining Additional Profits Tax the APT rate was defined as the 70-n where n was the company income tax rate.

21 In practice, RRT can be applied on a non-ring-fenced basis or partly ring-fenced basis. The case of Australia's petroleum RRT was cited earlier in the paper.

22 Examples of price-linked windfall taxes are the Alaskan tax on oil profits which is 25 percent until the oil price reaches $30/barrel and thereafter increases by 0.4 percent for every $1 rise in the oil price.

References

Baunsgaard, Thomas (2001), *A Primer on Mineral Taxation*, IMF Working Paper No. 5 (Washington DC: International Monetary Fund).

Boadway, Robin and M. Keen (2010) "Theoretical Perspectives on Resource Tax Design," in Philip Daniel, Michael Keen, and Charles McPherson (eds.) *The Taxation of Petroleum and Minerals: Principles, Problems and Practice.*

Caragata, Patrick (1989), *Resource Pricing: Rent Recovery Options for New Zealand's Energy and Minerals Industries*, Ministry of Energy (Wellington, New Zealand).

Daniel, Philip (2008), *Taxation and Revenue Sharing*, paper presented at the World Mines Ministries Forum, March 2008 (Toronto, Canada).

―― and E. Sunley (2010), "Contractual Assurances of Fiscal Stability," in Philip Daniel, Michael Keen, and Charles McPherson (eds.) *The Taxation of Petroleum and Minerals: Principles, Problems and Practice.*

Garnaut, Ross and A. C. Ross (1975), "Uncertainty, Risk Aversion and the Taxing of Natural Resource Projects," *Economic Journal*, Vol. 85, pp. 272–287.

—— (1983), *Taxation of Mineral Rents* (Oxford: Clarendon Press).

Goss, C. (1986), *Petroleum and Mining Taxation: Handbook on a Method for Equitable Sharing of Profits and Risk*, Energy Paper No. 19, Joint Energy Programme, Policy Studies Institute and Royal Institute for International Affairs (London: Gower Press).

Hogan, Lindsay (2007) "Mineral Resources Taxation in Australia: An Economic Assessment of Policy Options," *Abare Research Report*, No. 07.1, Commonwealth of Australia.

Johnson, C. (1981), "Taking the Take But Not The Risk," *Materials and Society*, Vol. 5, No. 4.

Johnston, Daniel (2008), "Changing Fiscal Landscape," *Journal of World Energy Law and Business*, Vol. 1, No.1.

Kumar, Raj (1991), "Taxation for a Cyclical Industry," *Resources Policy*, Vol. 17, pp. 133–148, available at: www.sciencedirect.com/science/article/B6VBM-45BC52G-37/2/507d972223e6a863363eaf87d0674b76.

Land, Bryan (1995), "The Rate of Return Approach to Progressive Profit Sharing in Mining," in Otto, J. (ed.) *The Taxation of Mineral Enterprises* (Kluwer Press).

Lund, Diderik (2008), "Rent Taxation for Nonrenewable Resources," Memorandum No. 1/2009, Department of Economics (Norway: University of Oslo).

MacKenzie, Brian and M. Doggett (1992), *The Economics of Mineral Deposits in Australia*, CRS and Australian Mineral Foundation (Kingston, Canada).

McPherson, Charles. and K. Palmer (1984), "New Approaches to Profit Sharing in Developing Countries," *Oil and Gas Journal*.

Shukla, G. P. (2008), "*Mining Taxation and Legal Framework*," paper presented at the World Bank, April 2008 (Washington D.C.: World Bank).

Sunley, Emil, T. Baunsgaard, and D. Simard (2002), "Revenues from the Oil and Gas Sector: Issues and Country Experiences," IMF Post-conference draft, June 8, 2002 (Washington DC: International Monetary Fund).

9 State participation in the natural resource sectors

Evolution, issues and outlook

Charles McPherson

1 Introduction

In one form or another, state participation has featured importantly in the development of petroleum and mining sectors worldwide over the past 40 to 50 years. While enthusiasm for state participation in these sectors has waxed and waned, it has proved a durable phenomenon, particularly in resource-rich developing countries and countries in economic transition, and there are signs that its popularity is reviving today, encouraged by the surge in commodity prices experienced over the past several years.

This chapter reviews the evolution of state participation, the variety of forms it has taken, the drivers behind participation and the issues arising, and policy responses. It concludes with a summary of selected country experiences and comments on the outlook for the future.

For purposes of this chapter, state participation is rather broadly defined to comprise a range of options from 100 percent equity participation, through partial or carried equity arrangements, to equity participation without financial obligation.

2 Evolution of state participation

Petroleum and mineral resources have long been viewed as having special strategic significance in the countries in which they are found in abundance. They were among the sectors identified by Lenin as the "commanding heights" of the economy and as such, sectors that the state must control. In a large number of countries this control has been exercised by direct state participation.

In petroleum, the movement toward direct participation began as early as the 1920s and 1930s with the formation of the first national oil companies (NOCs), Argentina's Yacimientos Petrolíferos Fiscales (YPF) and Mexico's Petróleos Mexicanos (PEMEX). It was in the 1970s, however, that the movement really gained traction on the back of a rising tide of nationalism worldwide and a growing belief in the merits of state ownership. The Organization of Petroleum Exporting Countries (OPEC) was formed at that time and very quickly experienced dramatic success in wresting substantial control and revenues from the private sector international oil companies (IOCs). The number of NOCs proliferated rapidly and with them came a rapid growth in state intervention, to the exclusion of the private sector in some countries, or, more commonly, through continued participation with the IOCs on significantly revised terms.

A great deal was expected of participation, and initially, while the industry was awash with cash, it all seemed possible. However, the oil price collapses experienced in the mid-1980s and 1990s exposed serious cracks in the model and caused a re-think of the role and organization of the NOCs and a revision of their terms of engagement in their petroleum sectors. Some NOCs disappeared or had their roles reduced, others were subjected to wide-ranging internal reviews and reforms.[1] State participation has, nevertheless, remained very much a fact of life in petroleum producing countries, and the decisions of recent country arrivals on the petroleum scene to provide for NOCs and participation, together with the aggressive re-assertion of the state's role in the petroleum sector in other countries, suggests that it is here to stay.[2]

The International Monetary Fund (IMF) has identified 41 countries as currently or potentially petroleum-rich.[3] As shown in Table 9.1, 33 of these have provided for direct state participation under various formulas and to varying degrees. The table understates the incidence of state participation in the oil and gas sectors in that it lists only those countries already counted as petroleum-rich. Many other countries whose petroleum resources are of less current significance have also provided for participation.

Statistics on control of global petroleum resources are perhaps even more telling than the numbers on incidence when it comes to illustrating the continuing significance of state participation in the sector. NOCs control 90 percent of world oil reserves and account for over 70 percent of production.[4] And 25 of the world's top 50 oil companies are NOCs.[5]

The mining story is similar. Emerging from the colonial period in the late 1960s, many countries in mineral-rich Africa identified ownership of mineral resources and of resulting revenues with their new-found sovereignty.[6] National mining companies (NMCs) were created, and ownership and direct sector participation were achieved either through nationalization of foreign-owned mining companies or their assets, or through NMC majority partnerships in various forms with the private sector. In Latin America, mining countries with a longer history of independence, fueled by the same nationalist sentiment, a resentment of perceived US dominance in the region, and sympathy for socialist economic philosophies, also established NMCs and through them sought control over their mining sectors. Zambia, Chile, and Venezuela provided high profile examples of these early trends.

By the 1980s and early 1990s disenchantment with the NMC experience had set in. Economic performance had been poor, the global mining and minerals environment had changed dramatically, a long-term trend toward lower prices was expected, and the break-up of the Soviet Union had discredited central planning in many socialist states. Lower state participation shares became common and greater emphasis was placed on creating investment frameworks attractive to the private sector either investing alone or in joint ventures with the NMC

Table 9.1 State participation in petroleum-rich countries

Country	Participation	Country	Participation
Algeria	51% CI	Oman	
Angola	20%/variable CI	Qatar	65%
Azerbaijan	20%/variable CI	Russia	Minority to 100%
Bahrain	None	Saudi Arabia	100%
Brunei Darusalam	50%	Sudan	
Cameroon	50% CI	Syria	
Colombia		Trinidad and Tobago	None
Congo, Rep. of		Turkmenistan	None
Ecuador	None	United Arab Emirates	60%–100%
Equatorial Guinea	15% CI	Uzbekistan	50%
Gabon	15% CI	Venezuela	60%–100% WI
Indonesia	10%	Vietnam	15% CI
Iran	100%	Yemen	None
Iraq	100%		
Kazakhstan	50%/variable CI	Bolivia*	
Kuwait	100%	Brazil*	Variable
Libya		Chad*	10%
Mexico	100%	Mauritania*	10%/variable CI
Nigeria	50+%	Sao Tome and Principe*	None
Norway (SDFI)	20%–56%WI	Timor-Leste*	20% CI
		Ghana*	10%F/variable CI
		Uganda*	20% CI

Sources: IMF Guide on Resource Revenue Transparency (2007); Sunley (2002); IMF staff. Countries with asterisk have potentially large medium- and long-term petroleum revenue. CI signifies carried interest. WI working or paying interest. F signifies "free" equity.

under a variety of new partnership arrangements. There have been very few outright reversals of nationalizations,[7] however, and state participation in mining, through outright ownership or share participation, either on a mandatory basis or through the exercise of option rights, remains common practice, at least on the books, particularly in Africa. Table 9.2 illustrates the incidence of state participation in 18 minerals-rich developing countries.

As was the case with oil, other countries, not yet qualifying as minerals-rich, and so not included in the table, have also opted for state participation in their mining sectors.[8]

3 Forms of state participation

As suggested above, governments embraced state participation in their natural resource sectors in a variety of forms, depending on their objectives, their circumstances and issues encountered. Before turning to consideration of these objectives and issues in Sections 4 and 5, this section will briefly review the most common forms of participation.[9] Under all forms, except the "free" equity form, the most

Table 9.2 State participation in minerals-rich countries

Country	State participation	Country	State participation
Botswana	Diamonds negotiable WI other minerals	Mauritania	
Chile	None	Mongolia	10% Local/50% Govt
Dem. Republic of Congo	5% F/Negotiated equity shares 15%–51%	Namibia	None
Ghana	10% F/20% WI	Papua New Guinea	30% WI/Not all mines
Guinea	15% F	Peru	None
Indonesia	None	Sierra Leone	10% F/30% WI
Jordan		South Africa	15% Black Ownership
Kyrgyz Republic	Variable WI 15%–66%	Uzbekistan	
Liberia	15% F/Mittal only. Law specifies 10%	Zambia	Minority Interests

Source: IMF Guide on Resource Revenue Transparency (2007); Otto (2000); IMF and World Bank staff.

common vehicle for state participation is the NOC or NMC, collectively referred to here as national resource companies (NRCs). In some countries, however, the state has exercised sector participation without the intermediation of the NRC.

Full equity participation

Possibilities under this heading include the state either: a) going ahead with investments on its own through its NOC or SME, but without private sector involvement; or b) investing *pari passu* with the private sector from the start of operations by acquiring either a majority or minority interest in an incorporated joint enterprise or a participation share in an unincorporated joint venture.[10]

The best examples of the first possibility are found in the Middle Eastern oil producing countries. Mexico, whose constitution explicitly excludes private participation in petroleum, provides another example. While relatively rare in numbers, these examples are clearly very important in terms of volumes of oil.

Examples of the second option can be found in both the petroleum and mining sectors, although joint enterprise participation is relatively more common in the mining sector while the unincorporated joint venture route is more typical of oil.[11]

Carried equity participation

Carried equity participation may take several forms. The most frequently encountered is the partial carry, usually in the context of a state/private investor unincorporated joint venture. Under this approach, the private investor "carries" or pays the way of its NRC partner through the early stages of a project – exploration, appraisal, and possibly even development – after which, the NRC spends *pari passu* with the private investor, as under full equity participation. The private investor may or may not be compensated for the funds advanced on behalf of the state, and, where compensation does occur, it may be with or without interest reflecting the time value of money, and/or an "uplift"[12] in recognition of the risks incurred on the state's behalf. A full carry occurs where all costs are borne by the private investor and compensation including interest and/or an uplift is paid out of the project itself.

"Free" equity participation

So-called "free" equity participation is a simple grant of an equity interest directly to the state without any financial obligation or compensation to the private investor. Once a feature in mining, where it was sometimes regarded as a payment for the right to exploit the mineral resource, and is still "on the books" in many countries, it is now found only rarely in new agreements.[13]

Production sharing

Production sharing is a popular form of state participation in oil prospective or producing developing countries. Production sharing is similar to "free" equity participation in that it provides the state with an equity share income after cost recovery by the private investor, without any offsetting financial obligation. In contrast to "free" equity, however, production sharing involves the state, represented by its NOC, actively in operations as a commercial party, a regulator and a fiscal agent. As the state's representative, the NOC participates with private investors in the conduct of operations, as it does under full and carried interest equity arrangements. At the same time, however, the NOC oversees those operations from a regulator's point of view[14] and takes responsibility for assessing, collecting and commercializing the production share due to the state and remitting proceeds to the state.

Production sharing is often combined with some form of equity participation by the NOC either on a 100 percent basis or a carried interest basis.

4 Objectives of state participation

The drivers or objectives of state participation in the oil, gas and mining sectors fall under two general headings – non-economic, and commercial and fiscal.

A Non-economic objectives

Non-economic objectives were, and are still today, extremely important. They are both symbolic and practical.

On the symbolic side, the NRCs have been presented as national champions. As suggested above, their participation in the resource sectors was regarded as essential for protection of sovereignty and the national interest. Founded in fact or not, it would be hard to underestimate the emotional appeal of the NOCs and NMCs in this role, past and present.

On the practical side, state participation was expected to regulate, or rein in, the behavior of private sector investors in the national interest, to build national capacity in the resource sector through the transfer of managerial and technical skills and information from the private sector, and, whether explicitly stated or not, to address a wide range of development goals outside the resource sectors. Specific objectives under these several headings included, but were not confined to, job creation, the promotion of local content in petroleum operations, provision of social and physical infrastructure, regional development, and, not least, and especially in the case of petroleum, income transfers through supply of products at subsidized prices.[15]

B *Commercial and fiscal objectives*

The commercial or fiscal objectives of state participation in the resource sectors were, and are, more straightforward than the non-economic objectives. They are focused on the maximization of revenues flowing to the state from these sectors.

In the first instance, NRC participation was and is expected to generate additional revenues for the state in the form of commercial profits and resulting taxes and dividends, emulating and eventually displacing the private investors in this role.

Second, participation was and is expected to obtain a higher share of sector revenues for the state either through recovery of a share of the fiscal benefits "given away" to the private sector in favorable deals or through capture of a major share of the rents generated by profitable projects and, most visibly, and recently, attributable to the stunning increases in prices for oil and minerals.

Over time, most countries qualified the straightforward revenue maximization objective by taking into account other classic fiscal objectives, such as containment of exposure to risk, and the need to compete with regimes in other countries to attract investor interest.

How these several non-economic, commercial and fiscal objectives relate to the various possible forms of participation is part of the discussion in the next two sections.

5 Issues arising from state participation

Experience with state participation in the resource sectors has identified a number of issues, at both economy-wide and sector-specific levels.

A *Governance*

One of the most important issues posed by state participation at the economy-wide level relates to governance. The tendency of resource wealth to undermine governance in resource-rich countries or to exacerbate pre-existing weaknesses in governance is well documented and has been widely discussed.[16] Unfortunately, more often than not, state participation in the resource sectors has been a contributing factor. With access to significant financial flows and exercising considerable influence over economic activity both inside and outside the resource sectors, the NRCs were natural targets for control by elites who commonly flew the flag of protection of sovereignty and national interest yet who were, in fact, interested in pursuing their own political and personal agendas. In doing so, they had every interest in making sure that the operations of the NRCs were non-transparent, in politicizing their management, in promoting a lack of clarity with respect to the roles and responsibilities of the NRCs and related ministries and agencies, and in ensuring dependency of the NRCs on the elites for funding and other operational prerequisites. The resulting capture of the NRCs encouraged erosion of governance at the economy-wide level, with negative consequences for economic and social development and political stability. Of course, this abuse of participation need not be, and has not proved inevitable. Political context is critical in determining outcomes.[17]

B Macroeconomic management

Closely related to the issue of governance is the issue of macroeconomic management, both on the expenditure side and the revenue side. On the expenditure side, the assignment to NRCs of a long list of non-sector specific tasks raises serious risks. While understandable in one respect, NRCs having access to funds and, in relative terms, management skills, in other respects this practice is bound to create problems. In the first place, NRCs, beyond the possible cash and debatable managerial advantages, do not have real comparative strengths in addressing these issues. Second, many of these tasks when the NRC does take them on are conducted off-budget. Quasi-fiscal activities, especially when they are as significant as those commonly assigned to NRCs, prejudice effective macroeconomic and budget management and make forward planning exceptionally difficult. On the revenue side, given the notorious opacity of NRC operations, the substitution of revenue shares from equity participation for tax revenue and/or assignment of fiscal agency roles to the NRCs can be particularly damaging, resulting in weakened accountability and revenue losses. Whether or not the funds attributable to state participation actually go to the budget will depend upon the fiscal (tax and dividend) regime applied to the NRC, on the clear definition of any fiscal agent roles, and, importantly, on their enforcement.

C Funding

Funding state participation presents a third set of issues at the economy-wide level.

Funding of state participation can be problematic. The resource sectors generate a lot of cash, but they are also very cash-hungry. Funding significant participation draws resources away from other urgent budget priorities, jeopardizing overall development objectives, and creating social and political tensions. It may also run counter to macroeconomic and fiscal policies designed to protect the economy of a resource-rich country from Dutch Disease[18] by investing in the growth of non-resource sectors. Putting more eggs back into the resource basket does not help in this regard. Nigeria's experience over the last several years, considerable reform efforts notwithstanding, dramatically illustrates the dilemma. Figure 9.1 contrasts sharply the budgetary allocations made to the Nigerian National Oil Company (NNPC) to fund its own operations and its share of "cash calls" from its private sector joint venture partners with allocations to competing sectors, including critical social sectors such as education, health and housing, physical infrastructure such as roads, and construction and agriculture.[19]

The funding issue is particularly worthy of debate because, under appropriate fiscal and legal conditions, resource-rich countries should be able to replace state funding with private sector investment. This would not only relieve tensions over budget allocations, but also avoid putting public funds at risk. Even where exploration risks are side-stepped through partial carries of the type described above, risks remaining at the development stage can be substantial and, not

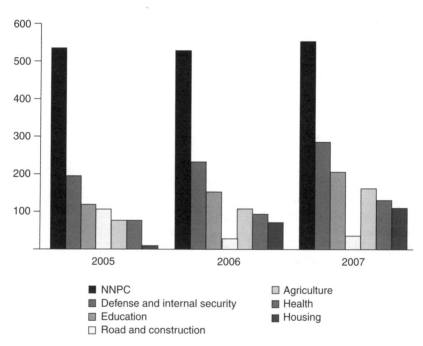

Figure 9.1 Competing budgetary allocations in Nigeria, FYs 2005–2007 (billions of Naira) (source: Central Bank of Nigeria and IMF staff estimates).

Note
Funding for social programs and infrastructure is for federal spending (current and capital) only. An unknown amount of funding also occurs at the state level.

unreasonably, many have questioned the appropriateness of exposing public funds to such risks.

A counter-argument to the case made for withdrawal of state participation on an equity funding basis and its replacement by private sector funding is that withdrawal of state equity funding will reduce state revenues. While equity participation may result in higher revenues to the state than taxation alone might provide, the gains are likely to be small, particularly where modern efficient fiscal systems are applied, as Figure 9.2 suggests. Each bar shows the discounted value of the fiscal revenues received from a hypothetical oil development project under the fiscal regimes for each of the six countries shown, together with the after tax return to state equity participation at the indicated level. The latter represents assumed revenue gain attributable to participation. While the charts show this to be an overall revenue gain, albeit small, the gain may be overstated. To the extent that equity participation has a fiscal equivalent, as it does under carried interest formulations. Its introduction may require offsetting adjustments to other fiscal terms in order to maintain investor interest.[20]

Figure 9.2 illustrates the argument for efficient taxation as an alternative to participation for oil. The argument is weaker for mining where to date fiscal regimes have been less successful in capturing rent. Figure 9.3 compares government take from a hypothetical oil project in three oil producing countries to take from a hypothetical copper project in three mining countries. The government take achieved through the fiscal regime is typically significantly higher for oil than for mining.

The potentially substantial financial demands of participation raise issues at the sector as well as the economy-wide level. Serious debate over budget allocations often leaves the NRC short of funds to meet project "cash calls" from its

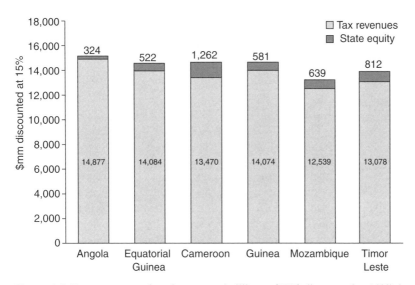

Figure 9.2 Tax revenues and equity returns (millions of US$ discounted at 15%) (source: DMF staff estimates).

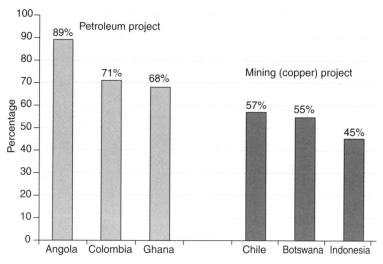

Figure 9.3 Government take from oil and mining projects compared (in %, based on cash flows discounted at 15%) (source: IMF staff estimates).

private sector partner, delaying project implementation, deferring revenue, and reducing project value. Where this is a real possibility, as it frequently is, the state may find the potential revenue gains from participation versus the no-participation, tax-only case erased by the induced delay. Efficient taxation, without participation, can produce more revenue for the state than state participation where participation results in even a one year delay in project start-up. Figure 9.4 illustrates the issue for a hypothetical oil development project in Angola. The bars on the left show the discounted value of total fiscal revenues including equity returns from the 15 percent participation of Sonangol, Angola's NOC. Should difficulties in meeting Sonangol's funding obligations delay project start-up by one year the value of Angola's fiscal revenues inclusive of its equity return would fall significantly relative to the no delay case and even relative to the no equity, no delay case shown on the right. It is probably fair to say that the no equity 100 percent private investor case, for the reasons discussed above, is less likely to result in delay.

While the Angola case is hypothetical, meeting cash calls has been a very real and persistent problem in Nigeria, where NNPC's inability to come up with funds has frequently delayed projects. The response has been to convert NNPC's full equity obligation into a carried equity interest with NNPC's private partners lending NNPC the cash to meet its obligations and being repaid out of NNPC's share with interest. NNPC has entered into such arrangements, on one occasion or another, with nearly all the major private sector operators in Nigeria. Unfortunately, these so-called "alternative finance" deals are confidential, making it very difficult to assess the cost and risk exposure to Nigeria.

A number of countries, Angola among them, have sought to avoid the funding delay risk by arranging non-recourse project finance, together with their private

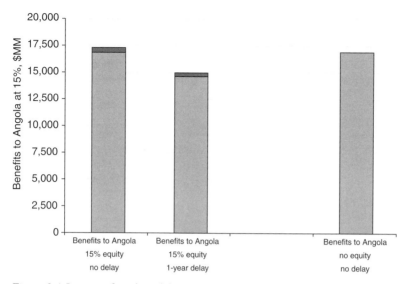

Figure 9.4 Impact of project delays on state revenues, Angola (millions of US$ discounted at 15%) (source: IMF staff estimates).

sector partners. This is not always possible but where it does occur and the finance is truly non-recourse and cannot be regarded as sovereign debt, it has the additional advantage of reducing fiscal risk.

D Commercial efficiency

With few exceptions, NRCs to date have not scored well on commercial efficiency or profitability. Obstacles to improved performance are traceable to the other issues identified in this paper. An overall context of weak governance, pervasive government interference, lack of transparency and accountability, and the extensive assignment of non-commercial tasks are systemic factors. Underfunding or erratic funding also play a major role. Where state participation excludes or limits competition that, too, can be expected to adversely affect performance. Competition is considered a major driver of efficiency.

E Conflicts of interest

Conflicts of interest arise when the NRC participant finds itself simultaneously cast in the role of partner to a private investor, or indeed acting on its own commercial interest, and of a regulator and/or fiscal agent. As noted above, this is especially common under production sharing.[21] Wearing its commercial hat, the NOC or NMC may take positions which are opposite to those expected of a protector of the state's interest. That this risk exists is made obvious when private investors, normally ambivalent about state participation, are found to favor modest participation on the grounds that its NOC or NMC partner is likely to protect its (the private investor's) operational or fiscal interests vis-à-vis the state's.

F Sector responsibilities and institutional capacity

A further concern raised by the formal assignment or practical assumption of regulatory or fiscal functions to or by the NRC is that the NRC too often soon usurps the authority of the government ministry which is nominally and ought actually to be in charge – the sector ministry or the ministry of finance. In doing so, it will also erode any institutional capacity those ministries might have established or hoped to establish, attracting and retaining essential talent through higher salaries and access to greater influence. This tendency is all part and parcel of the overall governance issue.

NRCs being typically closer to or partnered with private investors are better placed than ministries or government agencies to take advantage of private sector contractual obligations to provide training and otherwise assist in the transfer of managerial and technical skills. The same may be the case with respect to the provision of technical, operational, and financial information. While this is in part appropriate, it acts to further strengthen the NRCs relative to those oversight ministries and agencies. Legal and contractual provisions can be written, and usually are, to extend these obligations to ministries and agencies as well, but to be effective the ministries and agencies need to have been assigned, in practice as well as legislation, the authority and the staffing that creates an incentive to take advantage of the obligations.

6 Policy responses

It is difficult to take exception to many of the objectives set out in Section 3. However, as the preceding discussion suggests, there is reason to question the appropriateness of participation as the delivery mechanism, certainly as it has been practiced to date.

Over the past several years, a number of positive policy responses to the specific issues raised by state participation have been discernible:

* A greater reliance on, or confidence in, well structured laws and regulations as alternatives to direct participation. Ownership is no longer viewed as essential to protection of the national interest. Of course, laws and regulations can be abused as well, but on accountability and transparency grounds they are generally preferable to participation.[22]
* Increased clarity on roles and responsibilities of government ministries and agencies charged with sector oversight. The trend towards transferring non-commercial, quasi-fiscal activities and regulatory or fiscal functions from NRCs back to appropriate ministries or independent agencies, thus removing obstacles to commercial efficiency and reducing or eliminating the

potential for conflicts of interest, has been particularly important in this regard. This re-assignment of roles is typically paralleled by efforts to build capacity in the receiving ministries and agencies.

- A global movement in support of greater transparency and accountability in natural resource sectors in which transparency of NRC operations and finances features prominently. Credible audits and regular public reporting and other assurances of integrity are heavily emphasized.[23] Macroeconomic management concerns have increasingly stressed the importance of transparency in the resource sectors and, in particular, the explicit recognition in budgets and planning documents of the financial and fiscal costs and risks associated with state participation.
- An increased effort on the part of private sector investors to provide assurances and evidence of accountability.
- A more cautious approach towards exercise of state participation options and a trend towards lower levels of maximum participation. In some cases, the state has wholly or partially withdrawn from sector participation. Elsewhere an increased emphasis on forms of participation which reduce state exposure to funding obligations, e.g. carried interests, non-recourse finance and/or production sharing, can be observed. At the same time many countries have provided more space for private sector participation and competition.
- Increased sophistication in resource tax design, and a growing recognition of the advantages of efficient taxation over equity participation as a means of raising revenue.

It should be emphasized that these are not universal or consistent trends. There is no shortage of exceptions, however. Both are reflected in the selection of country experiences contained in Section 7.

7 Selected country experiences

The summaries given below each illustrate a variety of experiences with state participation. Norway's experience, and that of its neighbor Denmark, are widely viewed as best practice, but, as the examples show, that view is not universal.

Norway[24]

Norway's first petroleum licensing rounds were conducted in the 1960s. No state participation was involved at first, but awards soon after entailed a net profits interest for the state, minority state interest and then, following the creation of Statoil, Norway's NOC, in 1972, majority participation. It is noteworthy that all through this period, Norway consciously encouraged participation by the foreign private sector, on the grounds of expected benefits from competition, risk sharing, and the transfer of technology and petroleum management skills.

In its early days, Statoil was granted preferential status in the sector. Its initial 50 percent interest increased to a 51 percent majority on commercial discovery and was carried through the exploration phase by the private partners. In some licenses there was provision for a higher initial share and/or progressive participation as a function of production. Statoil developed rapidly as a commercial enterprise. From the outset commercial efficiency was Statoil's primary objective. The institutional structure of the sector was very clear. The sector ministry was in charge of policy, reporting to the Storting or Parliament, the Norwegian Petroleum Directorate was established to provide technical and regulatory oversight, while Statoil occupied itself with commercial operations. This approach, and all major subsequent policies affecting the state's role in the sector, were subject to extended public discussion and debate, affording key stakeholders an opportunity to make their views known.

In the 1980s Norway's sector policies evolved further, based on Statoil's demonstrated commercial strengths, an appreciation of the benefits of privatization and the influence of European Union initiatives on competition. In 1985, Statoil's portfolio was split in two, part remaining with Statoil and part going to a new vehicle of participation called the State Direct Financial Interest (SDFI). All vestiges of Statoil's preferred status were removed and Statoil became a normal commercial company competing with other companies on the same terms. The exploration carried interest was abolished. No non-commercial operations were assigned to Statoil. In 2001 Statoil was partially privatized. The state continued to hold an 80.8 percent interest in Statoil, but without Board participation and without interference in the company's operations.[25] The SDFI was set up to hold the state's direct participation in licences. The SDFI was initially managed on behalf of the state by Statoil, but management was later passed to Petoro, which was established as a non-profit state owned agency. While some of the participation interests inherited by Petoro were as high as 56 percent, a more modest level of 20 percent has become the norm in current licence rounds. The SDFI's revenues and expenditures are included in the government's budget and the implications of state participation are explained in the budget documents, identifying any associated fiscal risks. The SDFI's budget is approved by the Storting on an annual basis in the context of debate on overall budget priorities.

The Norwegian political, social, and economic context – a long tradition of good governance, transparency and public debate, sound economy, and a high level of education and skill – suggest that its experience is not easily transferable, yet it is clearly reflected in the aspirations of a number of developing countries, exemplified by the three discussed below.

Denmark

Before turning to those countries, it is worth noting the very close parallels between the Norwegian approach and that adopted by it close neighbor, Denmark. Current arrangements in Denmark call for the state to hold a mandatory 20 percent working interest (no carry) in all licences. The state interest is held by the Danish North Sea Fund. Separately, DONG, the Danish NOC, can hold an interest in any licence on the same basis as a private investor. DONG itself is scheduled for partial privatization.

The next three countries – Brazil, Colombia, and Indonesia – have all made significant progress over the past several years towards the best practice exemplified by Norway and Denmark.

Brazil[26]

The early history of Brazil's petroleum sector was strongly nationalistic. The popular phrase "O Petroleo e Nostro" – the oil is ours – supported Petrobras, Brazil's NOC, in a monopolistic role and invited extensive government interference in the petroleum sector.

By 1995, however, the country's deepening financial crisis and a growing global interest in privatization led to fundamental and sweeping reforms in the Brazilian economy and society. As part of this, Petrobras' monopoly was ended in 1997 and opened up to foreign private participation and competition. Petrobras could either compete with other companies on the same footing or partner with them in joint ventures. Petrobras was partially privatized, reducing the state interest to 51 percent, and the company was subjected to the same fiscal regime as the private companies. On top of taxes Petrobras pays a 25 percent dividend to its owners, public and private. All regulatory functions which had previously been the responsibility of Petrobras were transferred to a new independent agency, the Agencia National de Petróleo (ANP). Petrobras received no subsidies and was not assigned any non-commercial activities.

Petrobras is now incorporated in the state budget process and its investment and operating plans are subjected to rigorous scrutiny. A high degree of transparency applies not only to the overall budget process but also to Petrobras in particular, which must conform to not only the disclosure requirements of its own code of conduct, but also those of the stock exchanges on which it is listed. Responding to critics of his privatization reforms, then President Cardoso noted that the soft budget constraints and opaque accounting which had previously applied to Petrobras had essentially privatized the company in a different way, sheltering the transfer of its economic benefits to privileged groups in the Brazilian society – managers, employees, and political patrons.

Since 1997, Petrobras has flourished, doubling its oil production in 10 years. Debate over participation has re-opened, however, following in the footsteps of two enormous oil discoveries offshore.[27] At the core of the debate is the appropriate division of expenditure and revenue. If Petrobras participates in development of these finds under existing arrangements it will be exposed to massive funding obligations, and further it is felt by many that private shareholders should not benefit to the extent current arrangements would allow, and finally that fiscal returns to government from the anticipated development projects are too low. Possible policy responses now under consideration in Brazil include raising taxes and royalties, addressing the revenue issues, or establishing a new 100 percent government-owned company, allowing it to enter into production sharing contracts with private investors over the new highly prospective areas. The latter would relieve Petrobras and the state of funding obligations, while retaining a considerable measure of control and adding to tax and royalty revenues through the production share.

Colombia

As has been the case with the Scandinavian neighbors, Norway and Denmark, Colombia and Brazil have shared similar petroleum sector participation experiences. Colombia's NOC, Ecopetrol, was created as early as 1951. It combined the role of regulator, administrator, and investor. It entered into a limited number of 50/50 contracts with foreign oil companies on a preferential or concessional basis, being carried through to commercial discovery.

Change came later than in Brazil, but was ushered in 2003 in response to economic difficulties and the need to attract foreign investment to reverse rapid production declines. Contract terms were improved, and institutional structures were overhauled. Ecopetrol remained at first a 100 percent state-owned company but its regulatory and administrative roles were transferred to the Ministry of Mines and Energy to be implemented through a new government agency, the National Hydrocarbons Agency (ANH). Ecopetrol's exploration carry was dropped, and it is expected to perform as any other company. In late 2007, a 10 percent stake in Ecopetrol was sold to the public and was oversubscribed. A further 10 percent will be offered in 2008.

Indonesia

The third important oil producer in this trio of recent reformers is Indonesia.

In the 1950s and 1960s, very quickly after independence, Indonesia moved to assert control over its oil and gas sector. This was done through government-owned companies and tougher terms, and culminated in the creation of Pertamina in 1970. The law establishing Pertamina set out its duties which included significant obligations to act as an agent of government, including licensing, procurement, supply of the domestic market, etc.

The PSC, an Indonesian innovation, was introduced at that time, emphasizing participation in management, training, and technology transfer, but also creating large regulatory roles for Pertamina, related to approvals of procurement and costs, cost control, collection, and marketing of the government's production share and key operational decisions.

Initially, Pertamina had a degree of independence from government, but it soon came under the control of ruling elites and was treated as a "cash cow" for channeling funds to those elites and/or their pet projects. The company's portfolio expanded to include golf courses, aircraft, ships, foreign property holdings, and hospitals. The powerful cost approval process and local content rules were abused to steer business towards political bosses and their cronies. One of the most onerous responsibilities assigned to Pertamina was to assist in the so-called national unity effort by distributing petroleum products at substantially subsidized prices. As a consequence of these pressures, Pertamina became involved with massive corruption and took its eye off the ball of efficient performance in the petroleum sector. A 1999 audit of Pertamina by PricewaterhouseCoopers identified losses of $2 billion annually in corruption, waste, and inefficiency. Funds leakages from Pertamina had several sources. Pertamina's direct role in revenue collection often siphoned off cash before it made it to the Indonesian Central Bank. Pertamina's own operations were notoriously inefficient.

As long as prices were high, Pertamina's corruption and inefficiencies were affordable. There was enough money for everyone – "all boats were rising." The collapse of prices, first in the mid-1980s and then again in the mid-1990s, however, forced a serious re-think of the state's and Pertamina's roles. In the late 1990s, increasing dissatisfaction with the corruption and waste, and the Asian financial crisis, gave the technocrats in government – the "Berkeley Mafia" – an upper hand in the management of Indonesia's affairs. Helped by the end of censorship, and increased public awareness of abuses, a new Oil and Gas Law was passed in 2001. Pertamina's previous special status under law was abolished. The company's regulatory and administrative functions were transferred to a new agency MIGAS, inside the Ministry of Energy and Mines. Government production shares were forwarded directly to the Indonesian Central Bank bypassing Pertamina. Contracting and revenue accounting were all to be made more transparent and accessible to the public. Financial flows related to Pertamina's remaining exploration and production operations were to be subjected to the same standards as applied to the IOCs in their PSCs.

Pertamina's experience contains important lessons for other NOCs and governments placing similar demands on their participation in the petroleum sector. The next three countries – Venezuela, Bolivia and Russia – which might be characterized as returning resource nationalists, are perhaps cases in point.

Venezuela[28]

Venezuela first nationalized its oil industry in 1975. All rights to hydrocarbons were vested in the state. The Ministry of Energy and Mines was made responsible for sector policy and oversight and PDVSA was established as the NOC with a monopoly over petroleum operations to implement policy on the Ministry's behalf. PDVSA's President and Board were appointed by the President of Venezuela. Taxes and royalties from PDVSA were to be used for the economic and social development of the country while PDVSA itself was to focus on development of the oil and gas sector. The participation of foreign or private investors required Congressional approval and was not welcomed.

By the 1990s the country's economic position remained poor and it became evident that if PDVSA would not be able on its own to undertake the investments required to grow the oil sector and provide the revenues needed for development. This led to the introduction of the "Apertura Petrolera," an initiative which provided more favorable terms to investors and opened new areas for private sector participation. PDVSA retained operational control but reduced its financial exposure to less then 50 percent. The initiative was generally regarded as a success. New private sector investment increased reserve additions and reversed the downward trend in production. Production increased from two million barrels per day to 3.4 million barrels per day.

The benefits of oil were not widely distributed, however, and poverty remained pervasive, providing an opening for the populist politician Hugo Chavez who was elected President of Venezuela in 1998 by a significant margin. Chavez was highly critical of the "Apertura," charging that it was too generous to the foreign companies and had eroded Venezuelan control. His conflict with PDVSA led to an oil industry strike in 2002. Chavez responded by firing 25 percent of PDVSA's work force which was largely professional, and their replacement at a senior level by political allies with little or no petroleum expertise. Under Chavez's subsequent nationalization policy taxes and royalties were increased by a large margin, Venezuela's stake in joint ventures was increased from 20 percent to 60 percent, and the state took over ownership of some 30 small oil fields.

When Chavez came to the Presidency the price of oil was $7.50 per barrel. The dramatic price increase which followed funded a massive expansion of state spending on social and physical infrastructure. A high percentage of this spending depended on revenues from taxes and royalties on PDVSA, however a significant percentage was also channeled through PDVSA directly. PDVSA was regarded as more efficient than government bureaucracy but equally important was the fact that channeling funds through the NOC made it easier to target favored recipients and gave the Presidency and executive branch a competitive advantage over Congress in the control of funds. PDVSA's social spending in 2006 was over $13 billion, up from $7 billion in 2005.[29] Spending on social programs, including product price subsidies, was 40 percent more than spending on oil and gas operations. The scale of this spending led some to question PDVSA's finances. These have proved difficult to assess, however, since PDVSA has released no audited accounts since 2005. PDVSA is borrowing heavily. Foreign investment dropped by 55 percent in 2006, and production is estimated to have declined to 2.3 million barrels per day. Costs are high in Venezuela because of the maturity of a number of producing oil fields and the challenges of producing the heavy oil from Venezuela's Orinoco Belt region.

Venezuela may represent an extreme example of the response of many oil-rich countries to the oil price boom. As a result of the dramatic increase in oil prices, most have been able to record overall budget surpluses At the same time many are significantly increasing the size of their non-oil spending and non-oil deficits, exposing several of them to serious fiscal risks should the oil price drop sharply.[30]

Bolivia

In the mid-1990s, Bolivia, like Venezuela, responding to poor performance in its oil sector and an urgent need for new investment, embarked on a privatization and liberalization program. The country's NOC, YPFB, was partially privatized in 1994, and a new Hydrocarbons Law was passed in 1996 which improved terms for private investors and allowed them to enter into Risk Service Contracts with YPFB which granted them ownership and free disposition of oil at the wellhead.

Investment in the sector surged, but by the mid-2000s growing discontent surfaced among indigenous people over perceived inequities in revenue sharing and a perceived return to the days of foreign domination. A national referendum in 2004 showed a majority in favor of state ownership. In 2005, a new Hydrocarbons Law reclaimed wellhead ownership of all production and called for conversion of existing contracts to new forms deemed more acceptable from a national point of view. YPFB was re-nationalized.[31] A newly elected populist President, Evo Morales, launched a campaign of resource nationalism under the slogan that "hydrocarbon wealth must go back to the people," and issued a Nationalization Decree in 2006 setting a time limit for contract renegotiation.

The process was slowed by the evident lack of institutional capacity at YPFB and by funding shortfalls, but by late 2007 all foreign operators had signed new Operations Contracts with YPFB. Similar in structure to PSCs, but with sharing expressed in revenue rather than production terms, these put the state squarely back in the sector.[32] YPFB is responsible for collecting revenues owed government and for the marketing of all production and for a wide range of approvals. It is too early to assess results. A statement by President Morales, however, harkens back to a classic challenge for state participation. Morales called for a restructured YPFB that would be "efficient and socially controlled."

Russia

After break-up of the Soviet Union and years of central planning, the Russian economy went through a period during the 1990s of rapid privatization. This occurred without the benefit of the coherent or defined legal and fiscal structure and handed the oil sector over to a few so-called oligarchs. Foreign capital was at first courted but few major deals resulted. The transfer of major national assets to the oligarchs generated deep resentment.

Under a new President, Vladimir Putin, the state began to re-assert itself in the energy sector and state-owned or influenced oil and gas companies have been obtaining controlling interests in previously foreign-led projects. Further state presence or control of critical export facilities has grown rapidly, while private projects have met with obstacles put up by state-owned enterprises and/or government agencies.[33]

The "new frontier" that appeared to have been opened up in the 1990s gave way to revived centralist and nationalist policies. President Putin has explicitly stated that Russia's vast natural resources should be used to rebuild the country's world prestige and status. The political elite has entrenched itself in the oil and gas industrial complex and recent developments in the oil sector appear to be driven by political rather than economic considerations.[34] This has been the case not only internally but also internationally where Russia has become a major player as an exporter and as an investor.

An alternative response to the excesses of the early privatizations might have been to put in place a proper legal and fiscal framework, including appropriate oversight, and continue to encourage private sector participation with or without direct state participation. Russia claims that this is still its approach, but actions seem to suggest otherwise. It remains to be seen whether the direction Russia has taken will be sustainable or will bring back some of the problems of its past.

The next two countries reviewed, Saudi Arabia and Mexico, have both opted to run their petroleum sectors through wholly-owned state monopolies.

Saudi Arabia[35]

The Saudi approach to the nationalization was very different from that of other countries. Saudi Arabia's oil and gas sector had been run for years by a consortium of major IOCs, the Arabian American oil Company, or Aramco. Nationalization of Aramco in the 1970s was gradual and non-acrimonious. Saudi Aramco, the NOC, replaced Aramco, but many of the Aramco companies continued as advisers to Saudi Aramco ensuring continuity of management strengths and technical skills.

Policies since nationalization have been similarly unique. Under strict instructions from the king, the new Aramco has been left very much to itself on operational matters. Aramco reports to the Supreme Petroleum Council, a body made up of senior government ministers, but the Council's approvals are largely perfunctory except in major policy or strategic issues such as production levels. This history has resulted in a high degree of professionalism and internal accountability in the company. Saudi Aramco's budgets and operations are scrutinized carefully within the company and higher levels of government within the context of a running 5-year economic planning horizon.

The major concern with the approach Saudi Arabia has taken towards participation in its oil sector relates to the external availability of critical financial and other data. Internal transparency exists but external transparency on key topics is non-existent.

There has been only one internal challenge to Saudi Aramco's monopoly. That occurred during the late 1990s and early 2000s when focused re-opening of the oil and gas sector was considered with a view primarily to providing a competition or bench-marking check on Aramco's operational performance and commercial efficiency. While IOC interest in the initiative was understandably high, it died without results after protracted negotiations.

Mexico

In contrast to Saudi Arabia's experience, the nationalization of Mexico's petroleum sector in 1938, provoked by a deep resentment of foreign domination, was dramatic and very confrontational. Foreign assets were taken over by PEMEX, the NOC, which became and remains an extraordinarily important national symbol. PEMEX's monopoly position was enshrined by constitutional provisions which rule out private participation in the petroleum sector.

Over the years, PEMEX also became highly politicized and political interference was the rule rather than the exception. Corruption, inefficiency, and waste were rumored to be rife. At the same time draconian taxes made PEMEX highly dependent on non-transparent negotiations with government for funding of its operational and investment budgets.

In recent years, it has become very evident that a major crisis is looming in the sector, with significant implications for the economy overall, given that oil accounts for some 30 percent of budget revenues. Reserves and production have begun to decline rapidly and without new investment Mexico could cease to be a net exporter of oil within the next 5 years. Investment requirements to reverse this trend, however, are enormous as are technical challenges, since new reserves will have to come mostly from frontier deep water areas in the Gulf of Mexico. These prospects have brought a number of positive changes. Mexico's government which took office in late 2006 is committed to a major reform of the country's energy sector, which is expected to include a package of fiscal, governance, and budgetary reforms for PEMEX designed to enhance performance and the ability to raise finance and ultimately grant greater operational and budgetary independence within existing constitutional constraints.

This review closes with selected experiences of two important mining countries, Zambia and Chile.

Zambia

In the mid-1990s Zambia retreated from nationalist, state-ownership agenda for its mining sector and launched with new legislation a program of privatization. Various divisions of its NMC, Zambia Consolidated Copper Mines (ZCCM), were sold to private investors over the period 1997 to 2000, and ZCCM was converted from an operating company to an investment holding company, ZCCM-IH, with a minority interest in most successor companies, typically in the 10–20 percent range. The Government, through its 87.6 percent interest in ZCCM-IH thus holds an equity interest in the same mines.

When ZCCM was privatized, the price of copper was depressed, with no certainty as to when or by how much it might recover. One way for Zambia to share in any potential future upside profitability as a result of a price recovery was to take a passive equity interest in the new mining companies. This equity interest, which was granted as part of the purchase price for the mines, took two forms. The first was a free carried interest, and the second a carried interest repayable with interest out of ZCCM-IH's income from the equity stake concerned.[36] In addition to the equity interest, Price Participation Agreements (PPAs) were signed which provided ZCCM-IH with a share of revenues earned above an agreed price threshold. Each of these mechanisms had an approximate fiscal equivalent had they been paid to Government rather than ZCCM-IH. The free carried interest equates to a dividend withholding tax and the reimbursable carry resembles a resource rent tax. The PPAs were similar to price-related royalties. The approach represented a classic use of participation to share in rents or windfalls without changing the existing tax regime.

Unfortunately, significant price increases in copper notwithstanding, the detailed conditions of these equity participation formulas are such that the Government has seen only negligible revenues from them. This is attributable partly to the fact that payments are triggered by the declaration of a dividend by the mining companies, which they have successfully avoided by reinvesting earnings, and partly to ZCCM-IH's costs and liabilities which have limited any pass-through to Government. As a result of the failure of these schemes to deliver an increased revenue share, the Government announced its intent to "explore the scope for raising the taxation of mining" and in fact acted to increase taxes and royalties. The very recent collapse in prices proved these increases to be unsustainable and they have been withdrawn.

Chile

Chile has a long mining history which was for years dominated by foreign firms mostly from the United States. In the 1950s, the government began to assert more authority over the mines through taxes and the creation of a Copper Department to oversee and participate in mining operations. The process of "Chileanization" began in earnest in 1966 when legislation was passed to create mixed societies with foreign companies under which the state would own 51 percent of the deposit and take a direct role in the production and commercialization of copper.

In 1971, a constitutional amendment nationalized all major mines "as demanded by the national interest and in exercise of the sovereign and inalienable rights of the state to freely use its wealth and natural resources." The Corporation National de Cobre de Chile (Codelco) was formed by decree in 1976 to take charge of the state's mining interests. Codelco is the world's largest copper mine and is one of Chile's largest companies accounting for 5 percent of GDP, 25 percent of exports and 17 percent of the budget. It is 100 percent state-owned and its Board is named by the President of Chile.

Codelco has benefited from the policies applied in general to Chile's state-owned enterprises. These include limited government interference, and a high degree of transparency. Its operational flexibility is hindered at times by the required transfer of close to all of its income to the state in the form of taxes, royalties, and dividends. Ten percent of its export income is earmarked for Chile's military. The tight rein on Codelco's revenues facilitates government control. Chile's Minister of Mines has been quoted as saying: "Codelco is an unsubstitutable resource that is necessary to the Chilean Government to fund its social programs."

Lately Codelco's future has become a matter of public debate. Costs are rising, output is falling, and the resources required to make needed investments are substantial. The company is increasingly challenged in global markets by smaller, more agile mining companies' mergers and growth. This has led to calls for Codelco's privatization. So far, the Government's response has been draft legislation to improve Codelco's governance and make it more efficient and competitive.

Codelco may in many ways be a model in adopting a number of the elements of best practice in its own operations and in its relations with Government. That said, the core issues of state participation are ever present – demands on funds, tensions between commercial and social functions, efficiency.

8 Conclusion

State participation in the oil, gas and mining sectors of resource-rich countries has been, and is likely to remain, a globally significant phenomenon. In its various forms, it has raised serious issues and has too often been abused. These issues and abuses are now well recognized. Where they persist, their continuation is surely in good part due to a political economy that tolerates or even encourages them. Where governments have a serious commitment to reform and development, policy responses to the challenges of state participation have been positive and a growing body of best practice is emerging. In most countries, policy responses are likely to stop well short of full withdrawal of the state from the resource sectors, but those responses can be expected to not only significantly reduce the risks of adverse consequences, but also substantially increase the likelihood of achieving looked-for benefits. Policies focused on enhanced governance – clarity of roles and responsibilities, transparency, accountability – and the active scrutiny and support of all stakeholders, domestic and global, will be central to the process.

Acknowledgments

This chapter was prepared for the FAD conference on Natural Resource Taxation, held in Washington, DC September 25 to 26, 2008. The chapter complements and extends a previous paper by the author on a similar topic (McPherson 2003). Comments and suggestions from Philip Daniel, Michael Keen, Brenton Goldsworthy, Bryan Land, Honoré Leleuch and Gordon Barrows, and support from Diego Mesa Puyo in preparing exhibits, are gratefully acknowledged. The views expressed are the author's only and do not necessarily represent the position or policy of the IMF.

Notes

1 The United Kingdom abolished its NOC. Norway, Brazil, Colombia, Indonesia, and Algeria are among those that significantly revised the roles assigned to their NOCs. See Section 7 for a discussion of these and other examples.
2 Relative newcomers with established or planned NOCs include Timor-Leste, Mauritania, Ghana, and Uganda. Major oil producing states recently expanding their direct intervention in their oil and gas sectors include Venezuela, Bolivia, and Russia.

3 IMF (2007), Appendix I. Countries are considered petroleum or minerals-rich (Table 9.2) on the basis of the following criteria: (1) an average share of petroleum and/or mineral fiscal revenues of at least 25 percent during the period 2000–2005; or (2) an average share of petroleum or mineral export proceeds in total export proceeds of at least 25 percent. Norway is the only developed country meeting these criteria (petroleum).

4 BP Statistical Review (2008).

5 Petroleum Intelligence Weekly (2000).

6 Radetzki (1985, 1990) and Garnaut and Clunies Ross (1983) are early and excellent references on national mining companies.

7 Zambia, the Democratic Republic of the Congo, and Ghana provide examples.

8 NMCs, however, do not show the dominant control over mineral resources that NOCs have in the oil sector, reflecting the stronger push-back to state ownership during the industry's lean years.

9 See Daniel (1995) for a comprehensive discussion of forms of participation and their fiscal equivalence.

10 For clarity, the state in this case has less than a 100 percent share but both spends and receives revenue in full proportion to the share it has.

11 This is partly due to a history of fewer cases of successful unincorporated joint ventures in mining.

12 The "uplift" is an agreed multiple of carried costs. Where recovery of interest on carried costs is explicitly allowed for, the uplift relates only to compensation for risk. Where interest cost recovery is not explicitly provided for, the uplift is expected to cover both interest and risk.

13 Ghana's petroleum and mining agreements both feature free equity interests. Recent petroleum agreements have retained this feature.

14 Selected ongoing reform programs, e.g. in Ghana and Nigeria, are transferring the regulatory role from the NOC to an independent regulatory agency to avoid conflicts of interest.

15 Many of these assigned roles are quasi-fiscal in nature, i.e. they properly belong with government. Transferring them to the NRC allows the executive branch to get around budget constraints. See discussion on issues of macroeconomic management in Section 5B, and on Venezuela in Section 7, for a prominent example of this practice.

16 See Karl (1997), McPherson (2004) and Humphreys (2007).

17 See Eifert et al. (2003) and Ossowski et al. (2008). Both provide convincing evidence on the importance of political economy and institutional contexts in predicting success in the management of resource revenues.

18 Dutch Disease refers to the appreciation in real exchange rate of the resource rich country which erodes the competiveness of non-resource tradeable commodities and as a result the diversity of the country's economic base.

19 While the social rate of return on investment in these sectors might be expected to be as high or higher than the return on investments in the oil sector, weaknesses in governance and institutional capacity may produce lower returns. This has led some to support favorable allocations to the oil sector. Restructuring of oil sector financing arrangements in Nigeria, specifically the incorporation of joint ventures between the NOC and private investors, may obviate the need for calls on the budget in the future.

20 Daniel (1995).

21 It is by no means exclusive to production sharing, however. The same situation is frequently found in Latin America without production sharing.

22 See IMF (2007) for an extended review of policy recommendations on resource sector governance, many of which are reflected in the policy responses listed here.

23 The Extractive Industries Transparency Initiative (EITI) has played a central role, supported by a number of civil society and bilateral government initiatives (www.

eitransparency.org). See also www.revenuewatch.org and www.publishwhatyoupay.org.
24 See Al Kasim (2006).
25 In 2007 Statoil merged with another Norwegian oil company Norsk Hydro. The government's stake in the merged company fell to 62.5 percent.
26 See Lewis (2007).
27 See New York Times (2009).
28 See Energy Information Administration (2007) for an overview of Venezuela's policies. Also Rosenberg (2007).
29 Rosenberg (2007).
30 See Ossowski *et al.* (2008).
31 The re-nationalization involved YPFB taking 51 percent of the elements of YPFB previously spun off and "capitalized" under the privatization program.
32 The 44 Operations Contracts involve no risk outlays by YPFB. More recent terms require 60/40 YPFB-majority-owned companies to be the contractor; exploration risk stays with the private party, but YPFB takes development risk.
33 See Energy Information Administration (2008).
34 See Helm (2006).
35 See Marcel (2006) and World Bank (2007).
36 Available only up to completion of an agreed development program.

References

Al-Kasim, Farouk (2006), *Managing Petroleum Resources: The Norwegian Model*, (Oxford: Oxford Institute of Energy Studies).

Bearing Point Inc. (2003), "Options for Developing a Long-Term Sustainable Iraqi Oil Industry," study prepared for USAID.

Baunsgaard, Thomas (2001), "A Primer on Minerals Taxation," IMF Working Paper 01/139 (Washington DC: International Monetary Fund).

British Petroleum Statistical Review of World Energy (2009), available at: www.bp.com/productlanding.do?categoryId=6929&contentId=7044622.

Daniel, Philip (1995), "Evaluating State Participation in Mineral Projects: Equity, Infrastructure and Taxation," in James Otto (ed.) *Taxation of Mineral Enterprises* (London: Graham & Trotman).

Eifert, Benn, Alan Gelb, and Nils Bjorn Tallroth (2003), "The Political Economy of Fiscal Policy and Economic Management in Oil-Exporting Countries," in Jeff M. Davis *et al.* (eds.) *Fiscal Policy Formulation and Implementation in Oil Producing Countries* (Washington DC: International Monetary Fund).

Energy Information Administration (2007), Country Analysis Briefs, Venezuela.

Garnaut and Clunies Ross (1983), *Taxation of Mineral Rents*, Ch. 5 (Oxford: Clarendon Press).

Hehm, Dieter (2006), "Russia's Energy Policy: Politics or Economics?" *Open Democracy News Analysis*, available at www.opendemocracy.net.

Humphreys, Macarton, Jeffrey Sachs, and Joseph Stiglitz, eds. (2007), *Escaping the Resource Curse* (New York: Columbia University Press).

International Monetary Fund (2007), *Guide on Resource Revenue Transparency*, available at: www.imf.org/external/np/fad/trans/guide.htm (Washington DC).

Karl, Terry Lynn (1997), *The Pandora of Plenty: Oil Booms and Petrostates* (Berkeley: University of California Press).

Lewis, Steven (2004), *Critical Issues in Brazils Energy Sector* (Houston: Baker Institute for Public Policy).

Marcel, Valerie (2006), *Oil Titans: National Oil Companies in the Middle East* (London: Royal Institute of International Affairs).

McPherson, Charles (2003), "National Oil Companies: Evolution, Issues, Outlook," in J.M. Davis *et al.* (eds.) *Fiscal Policy Formulation and Implementation in Oil Producing Countries* (Washington DC: International Monetary Fund).

——— (2004), *Petroleum Revenue Management in Developing Countries* (Oil and Gas Energy Law).

Naito, Koh, Felix Remy, and John Williams (2001), *Review of Legal and Fiscal Frameworks for Exploration and Mining* (London: Mining Journal Books).

New York Times (2009), "Brazil Seeks More Control of Oil Beneath Its Seas," August 18, available at: www.nytimes.com.

Ossowski, Rolando, Mauricio Villafuerte, Paolo Medas, and Theo Thomas (2008), "Managing the Oil Revenue Boom: The Role of Fiscal Institutions," IMF Occasional Paper 260 (Washington DC: International Monetary Fund).

Otto, James, Maria Luisa Batarseh, and John Cordes (2000), "Global Mining and Taxation Comparative Study" (Golden Colorado: Colorado School of Mines).

Petroleum Intelligence Weekly (2000), PIN's Top 50: *How the Firms Stack Up*.

Radetzki, Marian (1990), *A Guide to Primary Commodities in the World Economy*, Chapter 7 (Oxford: Basil Blackwell).

——— (1985), *State Mineral Enterprises: an investigation into their impact on international mineral markets*. Resources for the future and the Pennsylvania State University, in cooperation with the International Institute for Applied Systems Analysis Resources for the Future (Washington DC: Johns Hopkins University Press).

Rosenberg, Tina (2007), "The Perils of Petrocracy," *New York Times*, November 4, available at: www.nytimes.com/2007/11/04/magazine/04oil-t.html.

Stevens, Paul (2003), "National Oil Companies: Good or Bad? A Literature Survey" (Washington DC: World Bank Workshop).

World Bank (2008), *Implementing the Extractive Industries Transparency Initiative: Lessons from the Field* (Washington DC).

10 How best to auction natural resources

Peter Cramton

1 Introduction

This chapter examines the design of auctions for natural resources, such as oil and mineral rights, focusing especially on issues faced in developing countries. Of course, auctions are not the only approach to assigning oil and mineral rights. Rights are sometimes assigned via informal processes, such as first-come-first-served, or other formal processes, such as beauty contests (an administrative process). The advantage of an auction is that it is a competitive and transparent method of assignment, which if well designed, can maximize revenues for the developing country.

Whether an auction is feasible depends in large part on the quality of the resources. When the quality is high, as in the case of known proven reserves, then it is easy to attract bidders to compete in the offering. Prospective bidders anticipate that the participation costs will be covered by the expected profits from participation. In situations where the quality of the resources is not high, such as exploration rights for speculative prospects, then attracting bidders may be difficult, especially if the country does not have a good reputation from prior sales. In the case of poor resources, what may be needed is not an auction to determine the best terms for resource exploitation, but a reverse auction to identify the companies that are willing to offer quality exploration services at minimum cost to the government. In this chapter, I focus on settings where the resources are of sufficiently high quality that attracting bids from oil and mining companies is not a problem.

Careful auction design is essential to achieving the country's goals. Indeed, design and process issues are even more important with developing countries, given their weaker administrative capacity and perhaps greater vulnerability to corruption and collusion. In general, it is necessary to tailor the design to the particular setting. Still there are a number of useful insights we can draw from recent auction theory and practice, both in oil rights auctions and in other sectors. For ease of exposition, I use oil rights auctions as my leading example, but nearly all of the design issues are the same if the country is auctioning other natural resources.

Fortunately, the use of effective auction designs is well within the grasp of developing countries. With the help of experts, these auctions can be designed and implemented in short order.

The first step is defining the product: the term of the license, the lot size, royalties, and tax obligations. An important part of the product definition is the identification of what terms are biddable and what terms are fixed. Next a number of basic design issues must be resolved: sequential vs. simultaneous sale (with lots sold either one after another or all at once), dynamic vs. static auction (using either an ascending auction process or a single sealed-bid), the information policy (what bidders know when they place their bids), and reserve prices (the minimum selling prices). Collusion and corruption also must be addressed.

The structure of bidder preferences is an important input in the design choice. The items for sale – the right to explore and develop natural resources on a particular geographic lot – are sometimes substitutes and sometimes complements. Bidders' values are interdependent, since each bidder has private information, such as from surveys and seismic tests, that is relevant in determining the largely common value of the lot, based on the net value of the extracted resource. This preference structure suggests, it will be argued below, that some version of a simultaneous ascending auction is best, since this will promote efficient pricing and packaging of the lots.

In this chapter I consider a number of alternative auction formats.

At one extreme is the first-price sealed-bid auction used in the US for offshore leases. The bidders simultaneously submit bids for each desired lot. Each lot is awarded to the highest bidder at the winning bid price. This simple format is suitable for marginal lots with nearly additive value structures (that is, the value of a package is equal to the sum of the values of the individual lots) and small value interdependencies across bidders. It also may mitigate collusion.

At the other extreme is the package clock auction (Ausubel *et al.* 2006, Cramton 2009). As explained below, this is a version of the simultaneous ascending auction often used in the auction of radio spectrum. The package clock auction is a method of auctioning many related items over multiple bidding rounds, allowing bids on packages of items. The auction begins with a clock stage. The auctioneer names a price for each lot and the bidders respond with the set of lots they desire at the specified prices. Prices increase on lots with more than one bid. This process continues until there are no lots with multiple bids. At this point there is a supplementary round in which bidders express values for any desired packages of lots. An efficient assignment of lots is found based on the supplementary bids and all the bids in the clock stage. Prices are determined from the competition among the submitted bids.

The package clock auction encourages effective price discovery in the clock stage and the supplementary round promotes an efficient assignment and competitive revenues. Although this approach may appear complex, it is actually simpler for bidders than common alternatives. The price discovery (the development of prices over many bidding rounds) reduces guesswork and focuses the bidders' attention on the relevant part of the price space. Then the supplementary round gives the bidders a means to further express package preferences and fine-tune the assignment of lots. The approach is well suited for high quality prospects, with complex value structures depending on the particular package of lots won as well as the private information of other bidders.

Still other designs between these two extremes are appropriate when the bidder preferences are not so complex that package bidding is essential and not so simple as additive values. Just as a fisherman tailors his equipment to the desired catch, an auction designer must tailor the auction format to the structure of bidder preferences and other aspects of the setting.

I begin with some motivating insights from auction theory and practice (Section 2). Then, in Section 3, I consider bidder preferences and some of the basic design issues in natural resource auctions. Section 4 addresses problems specific to developing countries. Sections 5 and 6 examine the experience with oil rights auctions and auctions in other sectors. Section 7 presents the package clock auction. Section 8 considers a number of alternative auction formats and makes recommendations based on the particular setting.

2 Motivating insights from auction theory and practice

A Why auction?

Auctions allocate and price scarce resources in settings of uncertainty. Every auction asks and answers the basic questions: who should get the items and at what prices? Auctions are a competitive, formal, and transparent method of assignment. Clear rules are established for the auction process. Transparency benefits both the bidders and the country. It mitigates potential corruption and encourages competition through a fair and open process.

A primary advantage of an auction is its tendency to assign the lots to those best able to use them. This is accomplished by competition among the bidders. Those companies with the highest estimates of value for the lots likely are willing to bid higher than the others, and hence tend to win the lots. There are several subtleties, which are addressed below, that limit the efficiency of auctions. Still, a well-designed auction is apt to perform well with respect to both efficiency and revenues.

Informal processes, such as negotiation on a first-come-first-served basis, lack transparency and are vulnerable to favoritism and corruption, which undermines competition. The reduced competition inherent in an informal process reduces both the efficiency of the assignment and the country's revenues. Informal processes also tend to be more vulnerable to expropriation, further discouraging competition.

A common alternative to an auction, especially in mining, is strict first-come-first-served without discretion and without negotiation. In this case, the terms of revenue sharing are part of the tax code, although this would appear to be vulnerable to change and hence expropriation.

Another alternative to auctions is an administrative process, often called beauty contests, in which resource companies present plans for exploration and development according to a formal process. This approach may be more flexible than auctions, but it makes the assignment less transparent and more vulnerable to favoritism and corruption.[1]

B How much competition is enough?

Auctions rely on competition to assign and price scarce resources. Competition is often limited as a result of significant participation costs. This is especially true when auctioning natural resources, since it is quite costly to estimate the value of a particular opportunity. Companies may decline to participate if they fear that more than four companies are apt to compete in the bidding. To motivate costly information acquisition, the country may have an initial stage, which identifies a short-list of the most qualified bidders.

In situations where there are only a few bidders, then the auction design should reflect this. This is accomplished with greater reliance on reserve prices and sealed-bid mechanisms. In all cases, the country should attempt to minimize participation costs. A clear and complete information memorandum, detailing the opportunity, is an important step in this process.

C Does auction design matter?

One of the most important results of auction theory is the revenue equivalence theorem: under particular assumptions, the four standard methods for auctioning a single item (first-price sealed-bid, second-price sealed-bid, English ascending, and Dutch descending) all result in the same expected revenue for the seller, and indeed maximize revenues among all trading mechanisms when the seller sets an appropriate reserve price (McAfee *et al.* 1987). From this, one might conclude that auction design is of little importance – that all standard auctions perform well. This, however, is the wrong conclusion.

The assumptions required for the revenue equivalence theorem are quite special: auctioning a single item, independent private values (this term being explained later), risk neutral bidders, an exogenous number of bidders, no collusion or corruption, and symmetric bidders (the bidders appear identical aside from their private information). In practice none of these assumptions holds: many related items are for sale; bidder values depend at least in part on value estimates of other bidders and these estimates are correlated; bidders care about risk; bidder participation decisions are of paramount importance; there are ex ante differences among the bidders (e.g. some are large and some are small); and mitigating collusion and corruption are important. Each of these features impacts the performance of alternative auction designs. A good auction design must tailor the design to the particular setting.

D Objective

The first step of auction design is to identify the objectives of the auction. I assume here that revenue maximization is the overriding objective. The country seeks to get as much revenue as possible over the long term from its oil and mineral resources, appropriately discounting future revenues. Certainly, there are other objectives, such as the timing of the revenues and country employment and investment, but revenue is the main objective.

Regardless of the objective it is important the auction have a clear and unambiguous method of translating bids into winners and terms. Ideally bids can be made one dimensional by fixing all but one term (e.g. bonus bid or production share), or by creating a scoring function with which to evaluate multi-dimensional bids (the scoring function determines a single-dimensional score given a vector of biddable terms).

E Product definition

The second step is product definition – what is being sold. There are two key elements: 1) the contract terms of the license (duration, royalties, tax obligations) and the identification of biddable terms, and 2) the geographic scope of the lots. Lots are generally defined as rectangular blocks or tracts, as specified by a pair of longitude and latitude coordinates within what is known as a graticulation system. The appropriate size of the lots depends on the quality of the prospect. More promising regions support smaller lots. In the US, lots are nominated by the oil companies. This is a sensible approach in most cases because it guarantees at least some interest in the auctioned lots.

F Auction process

To promote transparency, the auction process must be specified well in advance of the tender. The process should be open to all companies on a nondiscriminatory basis. The process begins with a public advertisement of the tender. The procedure for awarding a lot is described, including bidder qualification procedures and the auction rules.

A clear and complete statement of the auction process is essential to bidder participation. The country should be committed to the process. Finally, the process should allow for and encourage input from the resource companies. At a minimum this would include the nomination of lots, but allowing comments on all aspects of the rule making is generally worthwhile. Bidder participation and bids are enhanced if legitimate bidder concerns and preferences are addressed.

Today it is a simple matter to conduct the auction over the internet. This is especially desirable if a dynamic auction is used. Expert auction services are easily procured through a competitive bid request for proposals process. There are several well-developed commercial auction platforms suitable for auctioning natural resources over the internet. An internet auction reduces bidder participation costs, which increases both auction competition and auction revenues. Moreover, internet auctions can be completed without additional delay. The bottleneck typically is the administrative process, rather than the auction design and implementation.

3 Bidder preferences and auction design

A The structure of bidder preferences

Before considering design issues, it is helpful to think first about the bidders' preferences. There are three standard valuation models: private values, common values, and interdependent values. *Private values* assumes each bidder's value does not depend on the private information of the other bidders. *Common values* assumes packages of items have the same value to all bidders; these values are unknown, and bidders' estimates of the common value reflect that uncertainty together with their own private information and that of other bidders. *Interdependent values* is a general valuation function in which each bidder's value of a package depends on his private information as well as the private information of the other bidders, these values being unknown.[2]

The oil rights setting (as well as that of other natural resources) is the textbook example of common values. All companies value the oil at about the same level (the world price of oil), but there is enormous uncertainty about the quantity of oil and the cost of extracting it. Before bidding, each company estimates these uncertainties from geological surveys, seismic tests, and analysis of petroleum engineers. Yet each company would like to have the private information of the other bidders to further reduce uncertainty. The common value depends not just on the bidder's estimate of value, but on all the other estimates. In practice, there are also some private value elements – the company's exploration and development capacity, its reserves, its expertise in the particular type of prospect, its ability to manage exploration and political risks – but these elements typically are of secondary importance. Thus, the oil rights setting has interdependent values with strong common value elements. Most other natural resources have similar preference structures.

An important feature of the common values model is the *winner's curse*. This is the insight that winning an item in an auction is bad news about the item's value,[3] because winning implies that no other bidder was willing to bid as much for the item. Hence, it is likely that the winner's estimate of value is an overestimate. Since a bidder's bid is only relevant in the event that the bidder wins, the bidder should condition the bid on the negative information winning conveys about value. Bidders that fail to condition their bids on the bad news winning conveys suffer from the winner's curse in the sense that they often pay more for an item than it is worth. In natural resource auctions, adjusting bids in light of the winner's curse is a key element of strategy. In contrast, in private values auctions, there is no winner's curse: each bidder knows its value and that value does not depend on the values of the others.

Thus far we have focused on how package values depend on private information. A second important dimension is the structure of package values. How does the bidder value a package of lots?

The simplest valuation model is *additive values*: the value of a package is the sum of the values of the individual lots. In natural resource auctions, additive values is a good first approximation. The primary determinant of value is the quantity of oil, and the quantity of oil in a package of lots is the sum of the quantities in each lot.

Values may also be subadditive or superadditive.

With *subadditive values*, the value of a package is less than the sum of the individual values. One source of subadditive values is capacity constraints on exploration and refining. Additional lots have less value if the company lacks the resources to efficiently exploit that value. Another source is risk, holding many lots within the same region where values are highly correlated is riskier than holding a few lots in each of many dispersed regions. Values for substitute goods are subadditive.

With *superadditive values*, the value of a package is greater than the sum of the individual values. Superadditive values is the case of complements or synergies. One source of complements is exploration and production efficiencies that arise from holding many neighboring lots. Traditional economies of scale may arise in drilling from sharing staff and equipment. A more subtle form of complements comes from more efficient exploration. For example, if two neighboring lots are owned by different companies, each may have an incentive to free ride on the exploration efforts of the other – waiting to see if the other's drilling is successful. As a result, the exploration of both tracts may be inefficiently delayed. Hendricks and Porter (1996) provide both a theoretical model and empirical support for this behavior in the US offshore oil lease auctions. If instead, the two lots are held by the same company, there is no information externality and the lots are explored efficiently. A related synergy comes from the common pool problem, in which neighboring lots are drawing oil from the same pool. When the lots are held by the same company, the exploitation of the pool is efficient; whereas, with separately held lots, the companies would need to negotiate a unitization agreement to coordinate the development. Ideally, lots are defined to avoid this problem, but the country may not have sufficient information to avoid it entirely.

In the natural resource setting, additive values may be a good first approximation. Nonetheless, complements (superadditive) and substitutes (subadditive) likely are important in at least some applications. If this is the case, then the auction design needs to allow for efficient packaging. Otherwise, if values are largely additive, then packaging issues can be safely ignored, resulting in a much simpler auction design.

B Basic design issues

I now address several key issues of auction design in the natural resource setting.

With sufficient competition, open ascending bidding is better than a single sealed bid

An essential advantage of open bidding is that the bidding process reveals information about valuations. This information promotes the efficient assignment of lots, since bidders can condition their bids on more information.

Moreover, since bidders' private information likely is positively correlated, open bidding may raise auction revenues (Milgrom and Weber 1982). Intuitively, bidders are able to bid more aggressively in an open auction, since they have better information about the item's value. The open bidding reveals information about the other bidders' estimates of value. This information reduces the bidder's uncertainty about value, and thus mitigates the winner's curse – the possibility of paying more than the value of the item. Thus, bidders are able to bid more aggressively, and this translates into high revenues for the seller.

The advantage of a sealed-bid design is that it is less susceptible to collusion (Milgrom 1987). Open bidding allows bidders to signal through their bids and establish tacit agreements. With open bidding, these tacit agreements can be enforced, since a bidder can immediately punish another that has deviated from the collusive agreement. Signaling and punishments are not possible with a single sealed bid.

A second advantage of sealed bidding is that it may yield higher revenues when there are ex ante differences among the bidders (Maskin and Riley 2000, Klemperer 2002). This is especially the case if the bidders are risk averse and have independent private values. In a sealed-bid auction, a strong bidder can guarantee victory only by placing a high bid. In an open auction, the strong bidder never needs to bid higher than the second-highest value; that is, the point at which all of the weaker bidders dropped out.

In natural resource auctions, an open auction probably is best, provided the design adequately addresses potential collusion. The reason is that values have a strong common value element. The exception to this recommendation is drainage lots (ones adjoining developed tracts) in which one bidder has much better information about value.

Simultaneous open bidding is better than sequential auctions

A frequent source of debate is whether items should be sold in sequence or simultaneously. A disadvantage of sequential auctions is that they limit information available to bidders and limit how the bidders can respond to information. With sequential auctions, bidders must guess what prices will be in future auctions when determining bids in the current auction. Incorrect guesses may result in an inefficient assignment. A sequential auction also eliminates many strategies. A bidder cannot switch back to an earlier item if prices go too high in a later auction. Bidders are likely to regret having purchased early at high prices, or not having purchased early at low prices. The guesswork about future auction outcomes makes strategies in sequential auctions complex, and the outcomes less efficient. Nonetheless, some amount of sequencing may be desirable to avoid having too much riding on a single auction event at a single time. Both government and companies may face less risk with some sequencing.

In a simultaneous ascending auction, a large collection of related items is up for auction at the same time. Hence, the bidders get information about prices on all the items as the auction proceeds. Bidders can switch among items based on this information. Hence, there is less of a need to anticipate where prices are likely to go. Moreover, the auction generates market prices. Similar items sell for similar prices. Bidders do not regret having bought too early or too late.

Proponents of sequential auctions argue that the relevant information for the bidders is the final prices and assignments. They argue that simultaneous auctions do not reveal final outcomes until the auction is over. In contrast, the sequential auction gives final information about prices and assignments for all prior auctions. This final information may be more useful to bidders than the preliminary information revealed in a simultaneous auction.

Supporters of sequential auctions also point out that the great flexibility of a simultaneous auction makes it more susceptible to collusive strategies. Since nothing is assigned until the end in a simultaneous auction, bidders can punish aggressive bidding by raising the bids on those items desired by the aggressive bidder. In a sequential auction, collusion is more difficult. A bidder that is supposed to win a later item at a low price is vulnerable to competition from another that won an earlier item at a low price. The early winner no longer has an incentive to hold back in the later auctions.

In natural resource auctions, the virtues of the simultaneous auction – greater information release and greater bidder flexibility in responding to information – would improve efficiency. So long as collusion is addressed a simultaneous sale is preferred.

Package bidding should be considered

Another design issue is whether to accept package bids – bids for a particular package of lots – or only accept bids on individual lots. Package bidding is desirable when a bidder's value of a lot depends on what other lots it wins, because values are not additive. Package bidding also has advantages when bidders have budget constraints or other constraints that depend on the package of lots won, such as minimum size constraints. Then bidders may prefer being able to bid on a combination of lots, rather than having to place a number of individual bids (bids on individual lots). With a package bid, the bidder either gets the entire combination or nothing. There is no possibility that the bidder will end up winning just some of what it needs.

With individual bids, bidding for a synergistic combination is risky. The bidder may fail to acquire key pieces of the desired combination, but pay prices based on the synergistic gain. Alternatively, the bidder may be forced to bid beyond its valuation in order to secure the synergies and reduce its loss from being stuck with some low-value lots. This is the exposure problem. Individual bidding exposes bidders seeking synergistic combinations to aggregation risk.

Not allowing package bids can create inefficiencies. For example, suppose there are two bidders for two adjacent parking spaces. One bidder with a car and a trailer requires both spaces. She values the two spots together at $100 and a single spot is worth nothing; the spots are perfect complements. The second bidder has a car, but no trailer. Either spot is worth $75, as is the pair; the spots are perfect substitutes. Note that the efficient outcome is for the first bidder to get both spots for a social gain of $100, rather than $75 if the second bidder gets a spot. Yet any attempt by the first bidder to win the spaces is foolhardy. The first bidder would have to pay at least $150 for the spaces, since the second bidder will bid up to $75 for either one. Alternatively, if the first bidder drops out early, she will "win" one lot, losing an amount equal to her highest bid. The only equilibrium is for the second bidder to win a single spot by placing the minimum bid. The outcome is inefficient, and fails to generate revenue. In contrast if package bids are allowed, then the outcome is efficient. The first bidder wins both spots with a bid of $75 for both spots.

This example is extreme to illustrate the exposure problem. The inefficiency involves large bidder-specific complementarities and a lack of competition. In natural resource auctions, the complementarities are less extreme and the competition likely is greater.

Unfortunately, allowing package bids creates other problems. Package bids may favor bidders seeking large aggregations due to a variant of the free-rider problem, called the threshold problem. Continuing with the last example, suppose that there is a third bidder who values either spot at $40. Then the efficient outcome is for the individual bidders to win both spots for a social gain of $75 + 40 = 115. But this outcome may not occur when values are privately known. Suppose that the second and third bidders have placed individual bids of $35 on the two lots, but these bids are topped by a package bid of $90 from the first bidder. Each bidder hopes that the other will bid higher to top the package bid. The second bidder has an incentive to understate his willingness to push the bidding higher. He may refrain from bidding, counting on the third bidder to break the threshold of $90. Since the third bidder cannot come through, the auction ends with the first bidder winning both spaces for $90.

A second problem with allowing package bids is complexity. If all combinations are allowed, even identifying the revenue maximizing assignment is a difficult integer programing problem when there are many bidders and items. Nonetheless, our understanding of and experience with package auctions has advanced considerably in recent years (Cramton *et al.*, 2006). I therefore consider package bids as a viable option. Whether package bids are desirable will depend on the details of the setting.

Reserve prices

Reserve prices in natural resource auctions have two main purposes: 1) to guarantee substantial revenue in auctions where competition is weak but the reserve is met, and 2) to limit the incentive for – and the impact of – collusive bidding. Reserve prices mitigate collusive bidding by reducing the maximum gain of the collusive bidding. Setting reserve prices for natural resource auctions is difficult given the enormous uncertainty of values. The approach taken in the US is to have a low minimum bid that applies to all lots, and then accept or reject winning bids ex post. Thus, the reserve price is secret and can depend on the observed bidding behavior.

Bonus bid, royalties, and production sharing

Natural resource auctions, especially for oil and gas rights, commonly involve bonus bids and either royalties or production sharing. The bonus bid or signature bonus is the payment determined in auction for the right to explore and develop the lot during the license period. If exploitable reserves are found, the license is renewed for a nominal fee as long as development continues. The royalty is the share of the oil and gas revenues that goes to the government. Royalty rates vary country to country and even within countries. For example, in the US offshore oil lease auctions, the royalty rate is 1/6; whereas, the onshore rate typically is 1/8. The motivation for royalties is to have the oil company payment more closely reflect ex post realized value. This reduces the risk of the oil company. The disadvantage of royalties is that like a tax it distorts investment decisions. A larger royalty rate reduces the incentive for the oil company to invest in exploration and development activities. In contrast, the signature bonus is a sunk cost after the auction and does not distort subsequent investments. In a setting where there is no uncertainty about values, then only a bonus bid is needed (a zero royalty rate); in a setting where exploration and development are costless, then a 100 percent royalty rate is optimal. In practice, natural resource auctions have large uncertainty about values as well as large exploration and development costs. Thus, an intermediate rate is generally best.

Production sharing contracts attempt to further reduce oil company risk and better manage investment incentives by specifying the terms of cost sharing and profit sharing throughout exploration and development.[4] The contract can allow the oil company to recover exploration and development capital costs (in whole or in part) before the country shares in the revenues. Then the government's profit share increases with the success of the project, allowing the terms to handle both marginal and windfall economics. The contracts often are made immune to tax changes by having the government counterparty, typically the national oil company, liable for all taxes. Work programs specify a lower bound on exploration effort. This is an important constraint on more marginal lots, where high government profit shares might otherwise discourage exploration.

With production sharing contracts, it is common for bidding to be over the government's highest profit share, rather than the signature bonus. Thus, bidders compete on their willingness to share profits in the most favorable circumstances. This approach, used recently in Libya and Venezuela, reduces oil company risk without upsetting development incentives, since the bid share only applies for lots that are highly successful. Development incentives are further maintained by having the government share in the development capital costs and the operating costs. If the government's share of development capital and operating costs is the same as its production share, then post-exploration the project essentially is a joint venture with first-best incentives for development.

4 Problems specific to developing countries

Developing countries face additional challenges in establishing an effective auction program. These include political risk, fear of expropriation, favoritism, and corruption. These issues are not unique to developing countries, but may be more pronounced. All of these challenges tend to discourage participation, reducing competition in the auction. A country must recognize that resource companies seek out the most desirable opportunities for auction participation.

The strongest indicator of success of the auction program is robust competition. The geological prospect of the region is a primary factor in attracting resource companies, but political, legal, and process factors are also important. Unfortunately, there is little a country can do in the short term to reduce political risks. Over the medium term, the country can pass laws and create other institutions that provide the ground rules for resource exploration and development, and support long-term investment. Legal risks can be further reduced through choice of contract law.

Fear of expropriation or adverse renegotiation can be mitigated somewhat through the cash flow structure of the contract terms. For example, a pure bonus bid system (zero royalty) is problematic in light of expropriation risks. This would force the oil company to sink most funds upfront, making the company vulnerable to expropriation. Even developed countries, such as the UK and the US, have a tendency to adjust tax rates to capture a larger share of "windfall" profits. As a result, companies heavily discount bonus bids. Some reliance on royalties or production sharing is better, since these payments are not due until after revenues or profits have been received by the oil company. Another option is share bidding in which oil companies offer equity shares in the venture (the highest offered share wins the lot). In this case the country and the oil company are partners. Each makes investments and reaps rewards according to its share. This approach further shifts risks from the oil companies to the country. More importantly, it aligns the interests of the company and the country, reducing expropriation risks.

Favoritism and corruption are addressed in the auction process. A transparent, nondiscriminatory process is the key to mitigating favoritism and corruption. Independent third-party auction managers can help as well. Likewise, a trustee observing and commenting on all aspects of the auction process can further reduce the possibility of corruption. This step is common of auctions in a regulatory setting.

Developing countries may have strong preferences or constraints with respect to cash flows, especially if they have limited access to world capital markets. For example, a country may be unable to make upfront outlays and may have strong preferences for early payments. Such a country, however, must recognize that too much focus on early revenues may greatly reduce total revenues, especially in an environment where renegotiation risk is high; that is, where the company fears that terms may deteriorate in the event early investments prove successful. For this reason countries often are better off with production sharing contracts

with small upfront payments and large government shares in the event of successful finds.

5 Experience with oil rights auctions

Oil rights have been auctioned in many countries throughout the world. The
United States, Russia, Venezuela, Brazil, and Libya are examples.

A The US experience

The most studied program is the US offshore oil lease auctions. Porter (1995)
provides a survey of this work and is the basis for this discussion. These auctions
began in 1954. The product auctioned is a lease granting the right to explore and
develop a particular tract for a period of five years (US auctions use the terms
'lease' and 'tract', rather than 'license' and 'lot'). If oil is found and developed,
the lease is renewed for a nominal fee as long as production continues. The
process begins with the oil companies nominating tracts for auction. The government then makes a list of tracts to be auctioned. The auction, in its most common
form, is a simultaneous first-price sealed-bid cash auction. Each bidder simultaneously submits a dollar bid on each of the tracts it desires. The bid must meet or
exceed the minimum bid, which is stated as a dollar amount per acre. The per-
acre minimum depends only on the type of tract. A tract is either awarded to the
high bidder or all bids on the tract are rejected; thus, the reserve price is secret
and determined after the bids are observed by the government. A winning bidder
pays its bid, which is referred to as the bonus. In addition, the company pays a
royalty of 1/6 of revenues for any oil extracted. Bidders are allowed to bid
jointly; however, after 1975, none of the top-eight oil companies could combine
in a joint bid with another top-eight company.

Tracts are of three types. Wildcat tracts are new offerings that are not adjacent to developed tracts; drainage tracts, as mentioned, are adjacent to developed
tracts; and development tracts are a reoffering. There is an important economic
difference between wildcat tracts and drainage tracts. With a drainage tract,
bidders holding leases on adjacent tracts may have a much better estimate of
value than those without adjacent tracts. Thus, the drainage tract sales may have
large asymmetries among the bidders; whereas in the wildcat sales bidders are
more symmetric. This difference has important implications for both bidding
behavior and auction design.

From 1954 to 1990, there were 98 auctions. On average, 125 leases were sold
per auction. Eight percent of the high bids were rejected. The auctions raised
$282 billion from bonus bids and $202 billion from royalties (2009 dollars).
Hendricks *at al.* (1987) estimate from ex post price and quantity data that the
government share of rent was 77 percent with the oil companies receiving 23
percent.

Porter (1995) concludes that the US auction program in many respects is well
designed. Certainly the government is getting the lion's share of the value. On

drainage tracts informed bidders (those with leases on adjacent tracts), reap informational rents. The government could consider using a higher royalty rate on these tracts to the extent that the informational rents are not capitalized in the earlier wildcat sales.

One potentially troubling feature of the US offshore program is the use of the simultaneous first-price sealed-bid format. This is easy for the government to implement, but poses challenges to bidders, which may reduce efficiency and revenues. In particular, the format prevents the bidders from expressing preferences for packages of tracts and it provides no price discovery. In addition, a bidder's budget constraints or other package-based constraints either cannot be satisfied or can only be satisfied by greatly distorting one's bids.

Onshore auctions in the US are conducted at the state level. These auctions often are done as sequential open outcry auctions: each tract is sold in sequence using an English auction. This approach allows for some price discovery and better handles budget constraints, but it still forces bidders to guess auction prices for leases sold later.

B Experience outside the US

Unfortunately, there is little publicly available information about oil rights auctions in developing countries, and little research on the topic. Sunley *et al.* (2002) provide a study of government revenue sources from oil and gas in developing countries. Typically, countries employ a number of revenue methods: bonus bids, royalties, production sharing, income taxes, and state equity. Not surprisingly, the terms vary widely across countries, reflecting at least in part differences in political risks and geological uncertainty. A reasonable conclusion is that auctions are a desirable method of allocating the rights among companies, but multiple revenue sources should be used to best manage risks and incentives.

Recent auctions conducted in an environment of high oil prices have been highly competitive, especially in regions with known reserves. For example, in the Libyan auction of 15 lots on 29 January 2005, some lots received as many as 15 bids.

Johnston (2005) examines the contract terms and bidding in the 2005 Libyan auction. This case study offers insights into modern contract terms and bidder competition in a major auction of excellent prospects during a period of high price expectations. The 15 lots were offered in a simultaneous sealed-bid auction, in which oil companies bid a production share and a signature bonus for each desired lot. Each lot was awarded to the company with the highest production share (share of gross revenues going to the government). In the event of a tie, the signature bonus was used as a tie breaker.

The contract terms fully specify the split of revenues and costs between the government and the oil company. For example, on lot 54, the winning production share was 87.6 percent. This means that the government gets 87.6 percent of the gross revenues, for which it pays none of the exploration costs, 50 percent of the development capital, and 87.6 percent of the operating costs. The oil company uses the remaining 12.4 percent of the gross revenues to recover its costs (100 percent of exploration costs, 50 percent of development capital, and 12.4 percent of operating costs). Once these costs are recovered from the 12.4 percent, the excess ("profit oil") is split between the government and the oil company according to a sliding scale based on a revenue/cost index. The government's share of this excess increases from 10 percent to 50 percent as the company's cumulative revenue/cost index increases from 1.5 to 3. Under these terms, the initial upfront capital expense is limited to the exploration cost and a modest signature bonus. Since development capital costs are split 50–50, the high production share does mean that some profitable fields may go undeveloped. However, once development capital is sunk, the 87.6–12.4 split of operating costs results in first-best incentives for extraction.

Competition in the Libyan round was intense with an average of 7 bidders per lot. The winning production shares ranged from 61.1 to 89.2 percent with a mean of 80.5 percent. The government take (share of project profits) depends on the assumptions one makes on costs and revenues. Johnston (2005) estimates the government take to range from 77.0–97.7 percent with a mean of 89.9 percent, well above the 80 percent that is more typically captured for good prospects or the 77 percent realized in the US auctions before 1990.

The 1996 Venezuela auction of 10 lots had similar contract terms and also was highly successful. There were some important differences. The ten lots were offered in sequence. Also to maintain better development incentives, the production share bids were capped at 50 percent. First, the bidders bid production shares, and then in the event of a tie (e.g. two or more bid 50 percent) the bidders bid signature bonuses to break the tie. This resulted in large signature bonuses for desirable lots, shifting risk to the winning oil companies. However, the Venezuela terms were more favorable than the Libya terms with respect to cost recovery, so it is unclear which terms were riskier. Indeed, the government take estimate of 92 percent remains a landmark figure (Johnston 2005).

Although negotiated rather than auctioned, the Kashagan production sharing agreement in Kazakhstan demonstrates the flexibility of these contracts for providing risk sharing and investment incentives (Johnston and Johnston 2001). The Kashagan contract terms were unusual in allowing the oil company to recover costs and a return on investment before the government shares much in gross revenues. Then the government take increases to a maximum of 94 percent after high cumulative production. Such terms reduce oil company risk and fears of expropriation. In contrast, the US approach with bonus bids and a small royalty implies a significantly smaller government take.

6 Recent experience with auctions in other industries

Over the last ten years there has been a great advance in the development of methods for auctioning many related items. Innovative auction designs have been proposed and applied to allocation problems in several industries. The auction of radio spectrum is one important example, but these methods have been adopted in several industries, such as energy and transportation.

A Simultaneous ascending auction

The simultaneous ascending auction is one of the most successful methods for auctioning many related items. It was first introduced in US spectrum auctions in July 1994, and later used in dozens of spectrum auctions worldwide, resulting in revenues in excess of $200 billion.

The simultaneous ascending auction is a natural generalization of the English auction when selling many items. The key features are that all the items are up for auction at the same time, each with a price associated with it, and the bidders can bid on any of the items. The bidding continues until no bidder is willing to raise the bid on any of the items. Then the auction ends with each bidder winning the items on which it has the high bid, and paying its bid for any items won.

The reason for the success of this simple procedure is the excellent price discovery it affords. As the auction progresses bidders see the tentative price information and condition subsequent bids on this new information. Over the course of the auction, bidders are able to develop a sense of what the final prices are likely to be, and can adjust their purchases in response to this price information. To the extent price information is sufficiently good and the bidders retain sufficient flexibility to shift toward their best package, the exposure problem is mitigated – bidders are able to piece together a desirable package of items, despite the constraint of bidding on individual items rather than packages. Moreover, the price information helps the bidders focus their valuation efforts in the relevant range of the price space.

Auctions have become the preferred method of assigning spectrum and most have been simultaneous ascending auctions. (See Cramton 1997 and Milgrom 2004 for a history of the auctions.) There is now substantial evidence that this auction design has been successful (Cramton 1997, McAfee and McMillan 1996). Revenues often have exceeded industry and government estimates. The simultaneous ascending auction may be partially responsible for the large revenues. By revealing information in the auction process, bidder uncertainty is reduced, and the bidders safely can bid more aggressively. Also, revenues may increase to the extent the design enables bidders to piece together more efficient packages of items.

Despite the general success, the simultaneous ascending auctions have experienced a few problems from which one can draw important lessons (Cramton and Schwartz 2002). One basic problem is the simultaneous ascending auction's vulnerability to revenue-reducing strategies in situations where competition is weak. Bidders have an incentive to reduce their demands in order to keep prices low, and to use bid signaling strategies to coordinate on a split of the items.

A second problem in the early US auctions arose from overly generous installment payment terms for small businesses. This led to speculative bidding. Winning prices were well above subsequent market prices, and most firms defaulted on the installments and went into bankruptcy. The end result was that substantial portions of the mobile wireless capacity lay fallow for nearly ten years. Some 3G auctions in Europe (notably the UK and German auctions) also ended at prices well in excess of subsequent market prices. However, the European auctions did not allow installment payments, so the outcome was simply a wealth transfer from the shareholders of the telecommunications companies to the taxpayers.

B Simultaneous clock auction

A variation of the simultaneous ascending auction is the simultaneous clock auction. The critical difference is that bidders simply respond with quantities desired at prices specified by the auctioneer. Clock auctions are especially effective in auctioning many divisible goods, like electricity, but the approach also works well for indivisible items like oil lots. There is a clock for each item indicating its tentative price. Bidders express the lots desired at the current prices. For those lots with excess demand the price is raised and bidders again express their desired lots at the new prices. This process continues until supply just equals demand. The tentative prices and assignments then become final.

If we assume no market power and bidding is continuous, then the clock auction is efficient with prices equal to the competitive equilibrium (Ausubel and Cramton 2004).

Discrete, rather than continuous rounds, means that issues of bid increments, ties, and rationing are important. This complication is best handled by allowing bidders in each round to express an exit bid – the bidder's maximum willingness to pay – whenever they drop a lot. Since preferences for intermediate prices can be expressed, the efficiency loss associated with the discrete increment is less, so the auctioneer can choose a larger bid increment, resulting in a faster and less costly auction process.

A second practical consideration is market power. Although some auction settings approximate the ideal of perfect competition, most do not. In the US oil auctions, especially in recent years when more marginal tracts have been offered, it is common for tracts to receive one or zero bids. In such a setting, tacit collusion is a real concern with the dynamic auction. The chosen information policy can help mitigate this possibility. By controlling the information that the bidders receive after each round of the auction, the auctioneer can enhance the desirable properties of price and assignment discovery, while limiting the scope for collusive bidding. In the clock auction, this is done by only reporting the total quantity demanded for each lot, rather than all the bids and bidder identities, as is commonly done in the simultaneous ascending auction.

Clock auctions have been used with great success in many countries to auction electricity, gas, pollution allowances, and radio spectrum. Participants value the simplicity and price discovery of the auction.

C Details matter

Not all auctions are successful. The most common source of failure is a lack of participation. Sometimes this is because what is being sold has little value. Other times the lack of competition is the result of a poor auction process, for example the product is ill-defined, the marketing is inadequate, or the political risks are too great. Recognition of the needs of the bidders is critical in getting participation. An important lesson is that careful planning and design are essential to maximizing results. These efforts can translate into billions of dollars in higher revenues.

7 A practical package auction

In this section, I describe a practical method for auctioning many related items, which allows package bids – the package clock auction (Ausubel *et al.* 2006, Cramton 2009). This method is suitable for oil and mineral rights auctions, especially in situations where packaging issues are important. For example, different bidders combine lots in different ways, and business plans depend on the package of lots won. Then, I describe variations in situations where packaging issues are less important. All methods are described with oil or mineral rights auctions in mind. The items sold are licenses to explore and develop specified geographic lots. The bidder expresses quantities of either 0 or 1 for each lot offered.

The package clock auction begins with a clock stage and concludes with a supplementary round.

The clock stage is an iterative auction procedure in which the auctioneer announces prices, one for each of the lots being sold. The bidders then indicate the lots desired at the current prices. Prices for lots with excess demand then increase, and the bidders again express quantities at the new prices. This process is repeated until there are no lots with excess demand.

Following the clock stage, the bidders submit supplementary bids. The supplementary bids are either improvements to clock bids or bids on additional packages that were not bid on in the clock stage.

Once the clock and supplementary bids are collected, the auction system takes all these bids and performs a series of optimizations to determine the value maximizing assignment, and the prices to be paid by each winner.

A Clock stage

The clock stage has several important benefits. First, it is simple for the bidders. At each round, the bidder simply expresses the set of lots desired at the current prices. Additive pricing means that it is trivial to evaluate the cost of any package – it is just the sum of the prices for the selected lots. Limiting the bidders' information to a reporting of the excess demand for each item removes much strategizing. Complex bid signaling and collusive strategies are eliminated, as the bidders cannot see individual bids, but only aggregate information. Second, the clock stage produces highly useable price discovery, because of the item prices. With each bidding round, the bidders get a better understanding of the likely prices for relevant packages. This is essential information in guiding the bidders' decision making. Bidders are able to focus their valuation efforts on the most relevant portion of the price space. As a result, the valuation efforts are more productive. Bidder participation costs fall and efficiency improves.

There are several design choices that will improve the performance of the clock stage, when packaging issues are important. Good choices can avoid the exposure problem, improve price discovery, and handle discrete rounds.

Avoiding the exposure problem

To avoid the exposure problem, bids in the clock stage are package bids. The bidder wins the entire package or nothing.

The disadvantage of this rule is that the clock stage may end with a substantial number of unsold lots. However, this undersell will be resolved in the supplementary round.

Improving price discovery

In auctions with more than a few items, the sheer number of packages that a bidder might buy makes it impossible for bidders to determine all their values in advance. Bidders adapt to this problem by focusing most of their attention on the packages that are likely to be valuable relative to their forecast prices. A common heuristic device to forecast package prices is to estimate the prices of individual items and combine these with the corresponding quantities to estimate the likely package price. Clock auctions with individual prices assist bidders in this *price discovery* process.

Price discovery is undermined to the extent that bidders misrepresent their demands early in the auction. One possibility is that bidders will choose to underbid in the clock stage, hiding as a "snake in the grass" to conceal their true interests from their opponents. To limit this form of insincere bidding, the US Federal Communications Commission (FCC) introduced an activity rule, discussed in a moment, and similar activity rules have since become standard in both clock auctions and simultaneous ascending auctions. In its most typical form, a bidder desiring large quantities at the end of the auction must have bid for quantities at least as large early in the auction, when prices are lower.

A common activity rule in clock auctions is monotonicity in quantity for each lot. As prices rise, quantities cannot increase. Bidders must bid in a way that is consistent with a weakly downward sloping demand curve for each lot. This works well when auctioning a single product, but is overly restrictive when there are many different products. If the products are substitutes, it is natural for a bidder to want to shift quantity from one product to another as prices change, effectively arbitraging the price differences between substitute products. This lot-by-lot rule is sometimes referred to as "no switching," since the bidder cannot switch from one lot to another.

A weaker activity requirement is a monotonicity of a bidder's *aggregate* quantity. This allows flexibility in switching among lots. This aggregate monotonicity, rather than lot-by-lot monotonicity, is the basis for the FCC's activity rule. A weakness of this rule is that it assumes that quantities are readily compa-rable. Oil lots, however, are not comparable. For example, the area of the lot is a poor measure of quantity.

Ausubel *et al.* (2006) and Cramton (2009) propose alternative activity rules, based on revealed preference ideas of standard consumer theory, that do not require any aggregate quantity measure. Straightforward bidding – bidding on the most profitable package in every round – will always satisfy these revealed-preference activity rules. The rules prevent bidders from shifting to packages that are relatively more expensive.

Handling discrete rounds

As described above, discrete bidding rounds are handled with exit bids, enabling the bidder to express quantity reductions at intermediate prices. This allows the use of much larger bid increments without much loss in efficiency. In this way, the auctioneer can better control the pace of the auction, which is important here given the large uncertainty in lot values.

B Supplementary round

The supplementary round is a final sealed-bid opportunity for the bidder to improve its bids on packages bid on in the clock stage as well as submit bids on additional packages. Day and Raghavan (2007) and Day and Cramton (2008) provide a practical method to implement the supplementary round. For further details of the pricing rule and activity rule see Cramton (2009).

C The package clock auction

The package clock auction begins with a clock stage for price discovery and concludes with the supplementary round to promote efficiency.

Why include the clock stage?

The clock stage provides price discovery that bidders can use to guide their cal-culations in the complex package auction. At each round, bidders are faced with the simple and familiar problem of expressing demands at specified prices. Moreover, because there is no exposure problem, bidders can bid for synergistic gains without fear. Prices then adjust in response to excess demand. As the bidding continues, bidders get a better understanding of what they may win and where their best opportunities lie.

The case for the clock stage relies on the idea that it is costly for bidders to determine their preferences. The clock stage, by providing tentative price information, helps focus a bidder's decision problem. Rather than consider all possibilities from the outset, the bidder can instead focus on cases that are important given the tentative price and assignment information. Rather than simply decide whether to buy at a given price, the bidder must decide which lots to buy. The number of possibilities grows exponentially with the number of lots. Price discovery can play an extremely valuable role in guiding the bidder through the valuation process.

Price discovery in the clock stage makes bidding in the supplementary round vastly simpler. Without the clock stage, bidders would be forced either to determine values for all possible packages or to make uninformed guesses about which packages were likely to be most attractive. My experience with dozens of bidders suggests that the second outcome is much more likely; determining the values of exponentially many packages becomes quickly impractical with even a modest number of items for sale. Using the clock stage to make informed guesses about prices, bidders can focus their decision making on the most relevant packages. The bidders see that they do not need to consider the vast majority of options, because the options are excluded by the prices established in the clock stage. The bidders also get a sense of what packages are most promising, and how their demands fit in the aggregate with those of the other bidders.

In competitive auctions where the items are substitutes and competition is strong, we can expect the clock stage to do most of the work in establishing prices and assignments – the supplementary round would play a limited role. When competition is weak, demand reduction may lead the clock stage to end prematurely, but this problem is corrected in the supplementary round, which eliminates incentives for demand reduction. If the clock auction gives the bidders a good idea of likely package prices, then expressing a simple approximate valuation in the supplementary round is made easier.

Why include the supplementary round?

The main advantage of the supplementary round is that it pushes the outcome toward efficiency by collecting bids for additional packages and improvements of clock bids.

A natural concern with the supplementary round is that it may discourage bidding in the clock stage. The activity rule that operates between the clock stage and supplementary round is essential in mitigating this possibility. Bidders bid aggressively in the clock stage, knowing that a failure to do so will limit their options in the supplementary round.

D Implementation issues

We briefly discuss three important implementation issues.

Confidentiality of values

One practical issue with the supplementary round is confidentiality of values. Bidders may be hesitant to bid true values in the supplementary round, fearing that the auctioneer would somehow manipulate the prices with a "seller shill" to push prices all the way to the bidders' reported values. Steps need to be taken to assure that this cannot happen. A highly transparent auction process helps to assure that the auction rules are followed. Auction software can be tested and certified to be consistent with the auction rules. At the end of the auction, the auctioneer can report all the bids. The bidders can then confirm that the outcome was consistent with the rules. In addition, there is no reason that the auctioneer needs to be given access to the high values. Only the computer need know.

Price increments in the clock stage

When auctioning many items, one must take care in defining the price adjustment process. This is especially true when some goods are complements. Intuitively, the clock stage performs best when each item clears at roughly the same time. This gives the bidders the best opportunity to make use of the price information in the dynamic process. Thus, the goal should be to come up with a price adjustment process that reflects relative values as well as excess demand.

One simple approach is to build the relative value information into the initial starting prices. Then use a percentage increase, based on the extent of excess demand. For example, the percentage increment could vary linearly with the excess demand, subject to a lower and upper limit.

Expression of supplementary bids

Even with the benefit of the price discovery in the clock stage, expressing a valuation function in the supplementary round may be difficult. When many items are being sold, the bidder will need a tool to facilitate translating preferences into values. The best tool will depend on the circumstances.

At a minimum, the tool will allow an additive valuation function. The bidder submits its maximum willingness to pay for each lot. The value of a package is then found by adding up the values on each lot in the package. This additive model ignores all value interdependencies across lots; it assumes that the value for one lot is independent of what other lots are won. Although globally (across a wide range of packages) this might be a bad assumption, locally (across a narrow range of packages) this might be a reasonable approximation, especially in the setting of oil rights. Hence, provided the clock stage has taken us close to the equilibrium, so the supplementary round is only doing some fine-tuning of the clock outcome, then such a simplistic tool may perform reasonably well. And of course it performs very well when bidders actually have additive values.

The bidders' business plans are a useful guide to determine how best to structure the valuation tool in a particular setting. Business plans are an expression of value to investors. Although the details of the business plans are not available to the auctioneer, one can construct a useful valuation tool from understanding the basic structure of these business plans.

8 Alternative auction formats and recommendations

It is not possible to specify one "best" design – the best approach depends on the setting. The package clock auction as described above is an excellent choice in settings where packaging issues are important. It has been used in recent spectrum auctions in the UK and the Netherlands. In other settings, variations are worth considering. The variations depend on how four issues are handled.

1 Clock bidding

    a Package bids.
    b Individual lot bids.
    c None.

2 Activity rule

    a Revealed preference.
    b Lot-by-lot monotonicity.

3 Supplementary bids

    a Package bids.
    b Individual lot bids.
    c None.

4 Pricing in supplementary round

    a Bidder-optimal core (a winner pays the smallest amount that respects competitive constraints coming from the other bids; in the case of a single lot, this is the second-highest bid).
    b Pay-as-bid (a winner pays its bid).

With clock bidding for packages, bidders are allowed to drop a lot whose price did not increase, so long as the price did increase for another lot. Also the prices increase along the line segment from the start-of-round prices to the end-of-round prices. In contrast, with clock bidding on individual lots, a bidder cannot drop a lot when the price does not increase, and the price path is not constrained to move along the line segment from the start-of-round prices to the end-of-round prices. For example, the price of one lot may move all the way to the end-of-round price, while another lot stops increasing halfway between the start and end price as a result of a drop by one or more bidders.

The standard package clock auction is defined by the first option (a) for each issue: clock bidding for packages with the revealed preference activity rule, followed by a supplementary round with package bids and bidder-optimal core pricing. This is a sensible choice when packaging issues are important as well as value interdependencies and price discovery. This approach is the most difficult to implement, but accommodates the richest set of bidder valuations.

At the other extreme is the US offshore approach, which is simultaneous sealbid for individual lots with pay-as-bid pricing (1c, 3b, 4b). This approach makes sense if there are no packaging issues (for example, additive values), little value interdependencies, weak competition, and potentially large asymmetries among the bidders. Although this method is easy to implement, it is problematic for bidders unless values are additive.

Another variation, close to the US approach, has clock bidding on individual lots, a lot-by-lot activity rule, and no supplementary round (1b, 2b, 3c). This effectively is a simultaneous ascending auction version of the US approach. This is sensible in settings where packaging is of only minor importance (nearly additive values), but value interdependencies makes price discovery important. This approach also works best when competition is not too weak and bidder asymmetries are not too large.

A similar variation, close to the US spectrum auctions is clock bidding on individual lots, a revealed preference activity rule, and no supplementary round (1b, 2a, 3c). This would work well when there are moderate packaging issues and value interdependencies. The approach has good price discovery and does allow bidders to piece together desirable packages of lots. The format improves on the US spectrum auctions in two respects. Tacit collusion is mitigated with the use of clocks and only reporting excess demand, rather than all bids. Efficient packaging is facilitated with the revealed preference activity rule. This method is easy to implement and yet accommodates a richer set of valuations.

A final variation, related to the Anglo-Dutch format (Klemperer 2002), has clock bidding on individual lots, a revealed preference activity rule, and a supplementary round with individual lot bids and pay-as-bid pricing (1b, 2a, 3b, 4b). However, in this variation, the price clock stops when demand falls to two on the lot, so there is still excess demand. The excess demand is then resolved in the simultaneous pay-as-bid supplementary round. This approach is well-suited to situations where packaging is of minor importance (nearly additive values), but value interdependencies make price discovery valuable, and competition is weak with potentially large bidder asymmetries. The approach enjoys some of the price discovery benefits of the dynamic methods, but handles weak competition and bidder asymmetries better than the approach without a last-and-final round.

The approaches are summarized in Table 10.1.

For settings where there are sets of lots with substantially different value structures, it makes sense to use different formats with different sets of lots. For example, a country may have 12 wildcat tracts that are excellent prospects, 36 drainage tracts that are good to excellent prospects, and 200 tracts that are marginal prospects. The excellent prospects could be done as a standard package clock, the drainage lots as an Anglo-Dutch, and the marginal prospects as a first-price sealed-bid. With this approach the package clock auction is not complicated by the great number of drainage and marginal lots. Moreover, the drainage lots may have large asymmetries among the bidders as a result of private drilling information from neighboring lots. The Anglo-Dutch design handles these asymmetries well. Finally, additive values is probably a good assumption on marginal prospects and in any event the economic loss from the less efficient first-price sealed-bid approach is not great when auctioning marginal lots. Alternatively,

Table 10.1 Alternative auction approaches

Auction format	Ideal setting	Features
First-Price Sealed-Bid		
Simultaneous sealed-bid	Private values	Easiest to implement
Pay-as-bid pricing	Additive values	No price discovery
		Handles weak competition
		Handles bidder asymmetries
Anglo-Dutch Clock		
Clock individual bids	Mostly private values	Harder to implement
(stops with demand = 2)	Nearly additive values	Some price discovery
Revealed preference		Handles weak competition
activity rule		Handles bidder asymmetries
Supplementary with		
individual bids		
Pay-as-bid pricing		
Clock No Switching		
Clock individual bids	Interdependent values	Easy to implement
Lot-by-lot activity	(both private and common	Good price discovery with
rule	values)	nearly additive values
	Nearly additive values	Handles production shares
Clock with Switching		
Clock individual bids	Interdependent values	Harder to implement
Revealed preference	(both private and common	Very good price discovery
activity rule	values)	
No final supplementary	Substitutes and mild	
round	complements	
Package clock		
Clock package bids	Interdependent values	Hardest to implement
Revealed preference	(both private and common	Excellent price discovery
activity rule	values)	Excellent efficiency
Supplementary bids	Complex structure of	Competitive revenues
Bidder-optimal core pricing	substitutes and	
	complements	

since implementing three different formats is probably too much, the country could split the lots into two sets: those with high prospects and those with low prospects. The first-price sealed-bid format could be used for the low-prospect tracts and one of the dynamic formats could be used for the high-prospect tracts.

A Some simple examples

Much of the discussion has been focused on more complex settings where a country has many lots to auction and the bidders are interested in packages of lots. Here I consider some simple examples involving a single lot and therefore no packaging issues, such as a single offshore prospect, privatization of an existing mining facility, or rehabilitation of a mining project. In each of these cases there is a single partially known prospect. The two main approaches are either a sealed-bid first-price auction or an ascending auction. The sealed-bid approach is preferable in situations where there is weak competition (one or two bidders) or the bidders are highly asymmetric (there are large differences among the bidders). An ascending auction is preferable in situations where competition is strong and differences among the bidders are not large. With both formats a reserve price should be set to protect the country from the possibility of little competition. In addition, competition should be encouraged by reducing participation costs as much as possible.

B Libya and Venezuela reconsidered

Although the 2005 Libya auction and 1996 Venezuela auction were successful, I do believe they could be improved. The Libya auction, using simultaneous sealed-bids, prevented both price discovery and efficient packaging. The Venezuela auction, using sequential sealed-bids, allowed only minimal price discovery and packaging. In both auctions, competition was anticipated to be strong. Values included both private and common elements, although the common elements were more important. Values probably were nearly additive, although bidders likely faced budget and risk constraints given the size of the commitment.

In such a setting, a simultaneous clock auction is desirable, and especially simple given the small number of lots. Bids would be over the production share. In the case of Venezuela, I would drop the 50 percent cap on production share and adjust the terms so that the government shares in the development capital expense, thereby improving the development incentives without limiting the production share. A lot-by-lot activity rule (no switching) is desirable given the bidding is on production shares. Under this rule, once a bidder stops bidding on a lot, the bidder cannot return to the lot at higher production shares. This simple rule allows price discovery and some degree of packaging.

9 Conclusion

Auctions are a desirable method of assigning and pricing scarce natural resources. A well-designed auction encourages participation through a transparent competitive process. The design promotes both an efficient assignment of the rights and competitive revenues for the seller.

I find that a variety of auction formats are suitable for auctioning natural resources. The best auction format depends on the particular setting, especially the structure of bidder preferences and the degree of competition. When bidders have additive values and competition is weak, a simultaneous first-price sealed-bid auction may be best, especially if the lots are marginal prospects (relatively low value). When bidders have nearly additive values and competition is stronger, then one of the clock auctions should be considered. This approach will improve price discovery and reduce bidder uncertainty, improving efficiency and revenues. Finally, for high-value lots in which packaging issues are important (bidders care about the particular package of lots won), a package clock auction is appropriate. The package clock auction has excellent price discovery and handles complex bidder preferences involving substitutes and complements. The package clock auction does well on both efficiency and revenue grounds.

Regardless of the auction format, a critical element of the design is defining what is being sold. Possibilities include bonus bids, royalty rates, and/or production shares. These contract terms determine the allocation of risk between country and company, the cash flows over time, and the incentives for exploration and development. Bidding on production shares, rather than bonuses, typically increases government take by reducing company risk and fears of expropriation.

Notes

1 It has, however, worked well in environments (such as the Norwegian continental shelf) where other features of the institutional context militate against corruption.
2 Formally, index bidders by $i = 1,\ldots, n$, and let S be any subset (or package) of the items up for auction. With private values, bidder i's value for the package S is given by $v_i(S)$. With common values, bidders have only estimates $v(S, s, t_1,\ldots, t_n)$ of the value to each, where, s is the state of the world (reflecting common uncertainty) and t_i is bidder i's private information (with the common value increasing in each bidder's estimate t_i). With interdependent values, each bidder i only has estimates of the value $v_i(S, s, t_1,\ldots, t_n)$, this being increasing in t_i and weakly increasing in the others' estimates $t_j, j \neq i$.
3 In the sense that $E(v_i \mid i \text{ wins}) < E(v_i)$, where v_i is bidder i's uncertain value.
4 For further elaboration and discussion, see, for instance, in Nakhle (2009).

References

Ausubel, Lawrence M. and Peter Cramton (2002), "Demand Reduction and Inefficiency in Multi-Unit Auctions," Working Paper No. 9607, Department of Economics, University of Maryland.
—— (2004), "Auctioning Many Divisible Goods," *Journal of the European Economic Association*, Vol. 2, pp. 480–493.
Ausubel, Lawrence M., Peter Cramton, and Paul Milgrom (2006), "The Clock-Proxy Auction: A Practical Combinatorial Auction Design," in Peter Cramton, Yoav Shoham, and Richard Steinberg (eds.) *Combinatorial Auctions*, Chapter 5, pp. 115–138 (MIT Press).
Ausubel, Lawrence M. and Paul Milgrom (2002), "Ascending Auctions with Package Bidding," *Frontiers of Theoretical Economics*, Vol. 1, pp. 1–45, available at: www.bepress.com/bejte/frontiers/vol1/iss1/art1.
Compte, Olivier and Philippe Jehiel (2002), "Auctions and Information Acquisition: Sealed-bid or Dynamic Formats?" Working Paper, CERAS-ENPC, available at: www.enpc.fr/ceras/jehiel/ascendRand.pdf.
Cramton, Peter (1997), "The FCC Spectrum Auctions: An Early Assessment," *Journal of Economics and Management Strategy*, Vol. 6, pp. 431–495.
—— (2007), "How Best to Auction Oil Rights," in Macartan Humphreys, Jeffrey D. Sachs and Joseph E. Stiglitz (eds.) *Escaping the Resource Curse*, Chapter 5, pp. 114–151, New York: Columbia University Press.

—— (2009), "Spectrum Auction Design," Working Paper, Department of Economics, University of Maryland.

—— and Jesse Schwartz (2002), "Collusive Bidding in the FCC Spectrum Auctions," *Contributions to Economic Analysis and Policy*, Vol. 1, available at: www.bepress.com/bejeap/contributions/vol1/iss1/art11.

——, Yoav Shoham, and Richard Steinberg (2006), *Combinatorial Auctions* (Cambridge: MIT Press).

Day, Robert and Peter Cramton (2008), "The Quadratic Core-Selecting Payment Rule for Combinatorial Auctions," Working Paper, in the series *Papers of Peter Cramton* No. 08qcspr, Department of Economics, University of Maryland.

—— and S. Raghavan (2007), "Fair Payments for Efficient Allocations in Public Sector Combinatorial Auctions," *Management Science*, Vol. 53, pp. 1389–1406.

Hendricks, Kenneth and Robert H. Porter (1996), "The Timing and Incidence of Exploratory Drilling on Offshore Wildcat Tracts," *American Economic Review*, Vol. 86, pp. 388–407.

Hendricks, Kenneth, Robert H. Porter, and Bryan Boudreau (1987), "Information, Returns, and Bidding Behavior in OCS Auctions: 1954–1969," *Journal of Industrial Economics*, Vol. 35, pp. 517–542.

Johnston, Daniel (2005), "Tough Terms—No Surprises: Libya EPSA IV License Round–29 January 2005," White Paper, Daniel Johnston & Co.

—— and David Johnston (2001), "Kashagan and Tengiz – Castor and Pollux," White Paper, Daniel Johnston & Co.

Klemperer, Paul (2002), "What Really Matters in Auction Design," *Journal of Economic Perspectives*, Vol. 16, 169–189.

Maskin, Eric and John Riley (2000), "Asymmetric Auctions," *Review of Economic Studies*, Vol. 67, pp. 439–454.

McAfee, R. Preston and John McMillan (1987), "Auctions and Bidding," *Journal of Economic Literature*, Vol. 25, pp. 699–738.

—— and John McMillan (1996), "Analyzing the Airwaves Auction," *Journal of Economic Perspectives*, Vol. 10, pp. 159–176.

Milgrom, Paul (1987), "Auction Theory," in Truman Bewley (ed.) *Advances in Economic Theory – Fifth World Congress* (England: Cambridge University Press).

—— (2004), *Putting Auction Theory to Work* (England: Cambridge University Press).

—— and Robert J. Weber (1982), "A Theory of Auctions and Competitive Bidding," *Econometrica*, Vol. 50, pp. 1089–1122.

Nakhle, Carole (2010), "Petroleum Fiscal Regimes: Evolution and Challenges," in Philip Daniel, Michael Keen, and Charles McPherson (eds.) *The Taxation of Petroleum and Minerals: Principles, Problems and Practice*.

Parkes, David C. and Lyle H. Ungar (2000), "Iterative Combinatorial Auctions: Theory and Practice," Proceedings of 17th National Conference on Artificial Intelligence (AAAI-00), pp. 74–81.

Porter, Robert H. (1995), "The Role of Information in US Offshore Oil and Gas Lease Auctions," *Econometrica*, Vol. 63, pp. 1–28.

Sunley, Emil M., Thomas Baunsgaard, and Dominique Simard (2002), "Revenue from the Oil and Gas Sector: Issues and Country Experience," IMF Conference Paper (Washington DC: International Monetary Fund).

Part IV

Implementation

11 Resource tax administration

The implications of alternative policy choices

Jack Calder

1 Introduction

This chapter analyses the administrative challenges presented by different resource tax instruments. It concludes that all tax bases commonly used for resource taxation present significant administrative challenges. Progressive profit-based taxes[1] can present greater challenges than others. Importantly, however, the capacity required to meet those challenges in a well-designed progressive profit-based resource tax regime can be quite limited, and is often exaggerated. Certainly the potential difficulties need not rule out adoption by a developing country with poor administrative capacity if, as is often the case, the country's resource industry is concentrated in the hands of a relatively small number of large companies. In any case, the apparent simplicity of alternatives to such regimes is often, in practice, deceptive.

The conclusion that administrative difficulty need not rule out a progressive profit-based resource tax regime is subject to two important provisos, namely that within such a regime, so far as is possible: policy is simplified and made workable, and administrative procedures and institutional capacity and governance strengthened.

In practice these provisos are often not met. This chapter does not discuss strengthening of administrative procedures and institutional capacity (which are discussed in Chapter 12 by Calder). But it discusses ways in which policy might be simplified to minimize administrative complexity. It briefly discusses practical and political obstacles. Finally it discusses the role of tax administrators in the formulation of resource tax policy.

2 Types of resource tax base and challenges they present

Resource tax policy means the design of the rules governing resource taxes. These rules may be found either in tax legislation or in licence agreements. There are two different types of tax rule: (1) those that determine who pays tax, on what (the tax base), and at what rate, and (2) those that set out the administrative procedures to be followed. The design of administrative procedures is itself a matter of choice and policy, but the term tax policy is more commonly used to describe the design of the tax base and rates, and it is in that sense that policy is discussed in this chapter.[2]

There are various types of resource tax base, and some present greater administrative challenges than others. To mention some of the most common:

- *Bonuses* payable when exploration and production licence agreements are signed (or on some later event such as commercial discovery) are the simplest of all. They require a single payment on the happening of a clearly defined event, with no on-going administration. (Of course, awarding licences in a way that achieves the best possible negotiated terms and avoids the risks of collusion and corruption requires the design of sound administrative procedures, and raises many important and complex issues.[3] These are not, however, generally thought of as a tax administration issues, and are not discussed in this chapter.)[4] Bonuses, being paid up-front, are obviously not responsive to later unforeseen changes in profitability or prospects, so large bonuses may lead to re-negotiation of the resource tax regime, thus indirectly creating administrative complication later.
- *Specific (volume-based) taxes* ($x per barrel or tonne, for instance) are the simplest on-going tax. This is not to say that they are without difficulty. Establishing the volume of production is essentially a physical process – installing, maintaining and testing meters to measure production quantities, analysing the quality of production, monitoring production flows to ensure there is no scope for illegal extraction or theft. These processes are sometimes described as physical audit. They are highly technical and also require complex equipment. Analysing production can be particularly difficult with mining extraction, where tax authorities typically face the challenge of having to determine the mineral content of large piles of rocks being exported for processing. This requires considerable expertise both in mineralogy and sampling techniques, as well as sensitive and expensive measuring equipment.
- *Ad valorem (value-based) taxes* (y% of gross revenue, for example) are the next simplest tax. Value is volume times price, so the difficulties of establishing price are added to those of establishing volume. The huge volatility of natural resource prices increases the scope for error and manipulation. Reliance on realized sale prices presents major risks. The main problem is transfer pricing between connected parties. Connected party transactions are common in resource industries, which are often carried out by vertically integrated company groups engaged in downstream as well as upstream operations. Resource production is normally subject to a high tax regime, so the risk of these transactions being mis-priced in order to transfer profits to a lower tax regime is significant, and can arise with not just cross border but also domestic transactions. Establishing market values is often easier for natural resources than for other industries since prices of internationally traded physical commodities are generally quoted on international exchanges and by international pricing services such as Platt's. (For other industries it is often necessary to value non-traded services or intellectual property). But prices may not be quoted for rarer minerals, and even for common ones pricing can still present difficulties because of variations in

quality, or because there is no access to international markets (often the case for gas,[5] and sometimes even for oil where pipeline capacity is limited) and a limited domestic market from which to establish comparable uncontrolled prices. Even where parties are not connected, there are risks of artificial and manipulative pricing, for example where overseas energy markets are subject to government regulation, or where the terms of contracts between unconnected buyers are affected by undisclosed separate contracts. Use of different pricing bases also presents problems.[6] Use of financial instruments to hedge against (or speculate on) commodity or currency price movements can be a further complicating issue (and discussed further in Appendix I).

- *Profit-based taxes* add significant additional complications. Profits are essentially revenues less costs. Establishing revenues involves not only all the difficulties of valuing production but the difficulties of valuing other revenues that might be included, such as ancillary income, financial income, gains on disposal of licence interests, etc. It also involves all the difficulties of establishing costs. For example:

  - Applying different depreciation rates and categorizing costs for that purpose;
  - Applying "uplift"[7] (where relevant) and categorizing costs for that purpose;
  - Accounting issues on timing of cost recognition, including the treatment of stocks, and of provisions and reserves (abandonment provisions are a particularly important feature of resource production accounting);
  - Allocation of cost, and ring-fencing[8] issues – difficult generally, and particularly difficult where widely different tax rules and rates apply to linked operations such as oil and gas production;
  - Applying cost recovery limits;
  - Transfer pricing of costs;
  - Treatment of finance costs. This includes the problem of thin capitalization,[9] and may be complicated by finance leasing,[10] currency gains and losses, and use of financial instruments to hedge against interest and exchange rate movements on borrowings;[11]
  - Applying cost control rules and mechanisms;
  - Applying other specific limits on deductibility;
  - Links to other cost regulation (where tax deduction depends on adherence to non-tax regulations, e.g. on employment policy);
  - The treatment of cost offsets, e.g. compensation receipts, insurance recoveries;
  - The treatment of losses.

- *Rent capture mechanisms* of various kinds (as reviewed in Land (2010) and, for minerals, Otto *et al.* (2006)) modify volume, value or profits-based taxes in ways intended to capture a larger share of rent.[12] Sometimes the modification may simplify the underlying tax (for example, an excess profits tax could have simpler or more restrictive rules for finance costs than the normal profits tax)[13] but more often the modification adds complexity, and may also magnify the difficulty of the underlying tax (for example, a profits-based rent capture mechanism increases sensitivity to misallocation of cost). Some rent capture mechanisms are less complex than others, but the least complex (for example, oil royalties with a rate that varies with water depth) may be the least effective at capturing rent. To meet their intended purpose some rent capture mechanisms, such as excess profits taxes or rate of return-based production sharing, ought to apply to cumulative results over the life of production, which adds slightly to their administrative complexity.

*   *State commercial participation* is not strictly a tax, but limits on government commercial risk may make it tax-like. It poses some administrative challenges similar to those of tax administration, for example the need for reliable and transparent accounting, as well as commercial and business challenges (though these will be reduced to the extent that the government merely acts as a sleeping partner). State commercial participation may involve service or "buy back" contracts with international oil companies (where the company has no equity interest but merely receives a fee). Oversight of such contracts presents some challenges similar to those faced in administering profits taxes (for example, monitoring and controlling costs).

It can be seen that the above types of resource tax form an ascending ladder of administrative complexity, with each new step adding a further level of complexity to the previous level, and with a particularly large increase at the step from value-based to profit-based taxes.[14]

Resource production companies are also subject to normal business taxes, such as VAT, import and export duties, income tax on non-production activities, and withholding taxes. These taxes normally apply in the same way as to other companies, so they do not normally raise policy or administrative issues peculiar to resource production. They are therefore not directly relevant to the subject of this chapter, but two points are worth mentioning:

*   Resource production companies typically become entitled to large VAT repayments (since almost all of their output is exported, and hence zero-rated), and these present particular administrative difficulties (discussed in Chapter 3 on resource tax administration);
*   Payments to service contractors are a particularly important feature of resource production, and withholding taxes on those payments present significant administrative problems in their own right, discussed at Appendix II.

3 Administrative difficulty not to rule out progressive profit-based regime

If administrative considerations are ignored, resource tax policy should be determined entirely by the government's wider policy aims. The main objective will generally be to strike the best balance between, on the one hand, maximizing government revenue and, on the other, providing a competitive enough regime to encourage development of resources in accordance with overall economic and resource management policy. A further but possibly secondary objective may be to secure early and assured resource revenues, thus reducing government risk.

It is sometimes argued that these objectives are difficult to achieve with a tax regime based wholly or mainly on production taxes such as royalties. A low royalty rate encourages investment when prices are low, but gives the government a poor return when prices are high; a high rate gives the government a good return when prices are high, but discourages investment when prices are (or are expected to be) low. Similar arguments apply to very simple profits taxes. The desired objectives can generally best be fulfilled by a mainly profit-based tax regime incorporating an effective rent capture mechanism, with a limited role for royalties or cost recovery limits to reduce government risk and provide assurance of early revenues.

Apart from these theoretical arguments, practical international tax considerations may also point in the same direction. If international companies pay mainly production taxes, they are likely to be subject to profits taxes in their home country, since production taxes are not creditable. Taxing rights are thus in effect shared with the overseas country, reducing the tax the resource producing country can impose without creating disincentives. Profits taxes, on the other hand, can be designed to be creditable against home country tax under double tax provisions, giving the resource-producing country sole taxing rights. (Government share of profit oil may not itself be a creditable tax, so resource-producing countries normally impose income tax on the contractor's share of production to ensure that taxing rights do not pass overseas).

But, as explained, profits taxes and sophisticated rent capture mechanisms present complex administrative problems. Their complexity and difficulty of calculation make them less transparent than other taxes and thus increase opportunities for corruption and bureaucratic rent-seeking. Administrative considerations must be taken into account in designing a tax regime. It is no use having a theoretically perfect regime that is in practice impossible to administer. On the other hand the administrative tail must not wag the policy dog. The aim is not to avoid administrative difficulty for its own sake, but only so far as that difficulty makes the government's policy objectives impossible to meet in practice.

The argument that resource taxation should be based mainly on progressive profits taxes is not without controversy, and this chapter does not aim to take sides on the issue (discussed more fully in Boadway and Keen (2010) and Land (2010)). Instead it merely addresses the question: *If* a progressive profit-based resource tax regime (i.e. one based mainly on profits taxes and effective rent capture mechanisms) is considered to meet a government's broad policy objectives more effectively than the alternatives, should the difficulty of administering such a regime nevertheless discourage governments with poor administrative capacity and governance from adopting it? And if so, what levels of capacity and governance are required before such a regime should be adopted?

Clearly it is difficult to generalize. Where, at one extreme, a resource industry consists of a small number of major sophisticated investors producing minerals with high but volatile unit prices from a small number of hugely profitable projects, then the case for such a regime may be stronger, and the administrative challenges it presents less demanding – for taxpayers and governments – than where it consists of a large number of small unsophisticated businesses producing low value bulk commodities at steady prices from numerous small, low profit operations.

This is no doubt one of the reasons that mining tax regimes tend in practice to be more oriented than oil tax regimes towards production taxes:[15] in some countries mineral production is carried out by a relatively large number of players, some of whose operations, particularly before the commodity boom, were not necessarily very profitable. But in other countries the mining industry is highly profitable and concentrated in a few hands, as the oil industry usually is. One of the main reasons for the greater production tax orientation in those countries may be simply that their tax regimes are older and came into existence when economic theories of tax design were less well developed.

This chapter is mainly focused on the situation where resource production is dominated by a small number of highly profitable companies. There is a strong case for arguing that *if* a progressive profit-based resource tax regime has significant policy advantages, then *all* such countries, no matter how poor their levels of capacity and governance, should be capable of developing the capacity needed to administer such a regime to the standard required to achieve those advantages. The standard required is not necessarily perfection. If the policy advantages are significant then an imperfectly administered progressive profit-based regime may meet the government's objectives more effectively than a regime based mainly on simpler taxes, however well administered. In other words the policy benefits such a regime may outweigh the administrative benefits of the simpler alternatives. The question therefore is not whether a developing country can develop the capacity to administer a progressive profit-based regime perfectly, but whether it can develop the capacity to administer it effectively.

Say that the government of a developing country concludes that in most likely scenarios a progressive profit-based regime will, if administered to the standards prevalent in developed countries, result in significantly higher investment and a significantly higher tax take than a regime based mainly on production taxes. The argument that it should nevertheless adopt the latter kind of regime must rest on the proposition that the additional capacity required for effective administration of a progressive profit-based regime cannot be acquired at any cost, or at least not at a cost (including opportunity cost) significantly less than the likely benefit. Just how credible is that proposition, given the scale of resource tax revenues in most resource-rich countries, and the small number of companies whose tax has to be administered? Just how expensive can a good tax auditor be? Can the cost really be so significant relative to the tax involved? The capacity demands of a progressive profit-based resource tax regime can in fact be quite limited, and are often exaggerated.

But this argument does not just have to be settled on the basis of theory. The test case is Angola: a poor country, ravaged by years of civil war, generally perceived as having extremely poor capacity and governance, which nevertheless adopted what is regarded as one of the most progressive and sophisticated resource tax bases, rate of return-based production sharing. Angolan oil tax administration is far from perfect: it has many serious defects. It also has strengths, and continues to be strengthened, though it has a long way to go. The important point is that, taken in the round and despite all its serious administrative weaknesses, Angola's progressive profit-based oil tax regime broadly achieves the intended policy objectives and is generally considered, by international standards, to be reasonably effective. If Angola can achieve this, can it really be beyond other countries?

A second leg to the argument that limited administrative capacity should not be a barrier to adoption of progressive profit-based taxes is that in practice the administrative simplicity of tax regimes based mainly on production taxes is often deceptive. Even their original design tends to be complicated by multiple royalty rates for different minerals and different project areas, often with complex, discretionary provisions built in to cope with adjustments to costs or prices. Then, despite these complications, such regimes are often destabilized by later resource price volatility, with new taxes being introduced, or bells and whistles added to existing taxes, to make them responsive to changing economic environments.[16] These changes create an administratively complex patchwork of taxes, and may also offer opportunities for corruption since they are often based on administrative discretion or informal memoranda of understanding. They also increase perceived investor risk. So as well as being less fitted to meet government policy objectives in theory, this kind of regime may in practice be administratively more complex and less transparent than a progressive profits-based regime built on one or two complex but uniform, flexible and stable taxes.

Of course the fact that even countries with poor general administrative capacity *should* be capable of effective administration of a progressive profit-based tax resource tax regime is no guarantee that they *will* be. That depends on them taking the steps necessary to strengthen administrative procedures and institutional capacity. Often there is a lack of political will to do this. (But without this political will it is likely that *any* tax regime will be badly administered).

It also depends on them having a *workable* progressive profit-based resource tax regime. Often, administrative capacity is inadequate not so much because this kind of regime has been adopted as because it has been poorly designed.

4 Scope for simplification within progressive profits-based tax regime

Clearly if countries adopt a progressive profit-based regime, they should do as much as they reasonably can to simplify administration within that overall framework. It may be possible to do this in ways that carry no significant policy cost.

A Consolidate tax sub-regimes

One source of complexity in many countries is the existence of several different resource tax regimes. Often this is for the reasons discussed earlier, that simple tax regimes have been progressively complicated to make them more responsive to changes in the economic environment. Sometimes it reflects changes of tax policy and fashion. For example it is not uncommon to find a traditional tax and royalty regime applying to original resource concessions, and PSAs applying to later ones, with different negotiated fiscal parameters and production sharing rules in later PSAs from those in earlier ones. Bringing these different sub-regimes more closely into line would simplify administration.

B Use standardized contracts

If tax policy requires different licence areas to be taxed in different ways, the resulting complexity will be greatly reduced by the use of standardized contracts or concession regimes, with a limited number of variable parameters.

C Use familiar industry and accounting concepts

The use of familiar and internationally established industry concepts – for example in the categorization of tax deductible costs – will also simplify administration. Commercial accounting principles may not provide a sufficiently reliable measure of profit, but there are administrative advantages to using them as the starting point, with modifications only where required to provide greater clarity and uniformity or incorporate specific policy objectives.

D Reduce the number of taxes

Another source of complexity is the existence of numerous different resource taxes. To some extent this may be unavoidable. For example, a single tax combining a charge on profits with a royalty on production might not qualify for double tax relief against overseas profits taxes, so royalty has to be a separate tax. And production sharing might have to be combined with a separate income tax, again to ensure there is no overseas tax (as explained earlier).

But often there is a whole zoo of minor additional taxes, such as education tax, surface rental, tariffs, and so on, with little apparent policy justification: often a minor adjustment to the rates of the main resource taxes would generate as much revenue as all these minor taxes combined. Sometimes the intention is to hypothecate these taxes to a particular purpose. But it is questionable whether meeting, say, education expenditure from a possibly volatile tax has clear policy advantages over meeting it from a planned central budget. These minor taxes are often individually simple to administer, but their overall effect is to complicate the tax regime.

Regional taxes (for example, taxes charged by states operating within a federal structure) are often an issue, especially because of the highly uneven geographic distribution of resource production in many countries. Sharing of resource tax revenues with sub-national governments may be desirable on policy grounds, but it is administratively much simpler if this is done by distributing a centrally administered tax via the central budget, rather than allowing sub-national governments to administer their own separate taxes, and it can also be argued that this is preferable for policy reasons.[17]

E   Coordinate rules for different taxes

Reducing the number of taxes, where possible, will simplify administration. Where it is not possible, the complexity resulting from having several resource taxes can be reduced by:

- Using common building blocks in their design. For example, the measure of production for royalty purposes can be the same as its measure for income tax purposes. In a combined production sharing and income tax regime, the measure of profit oil and of income tax profit often differs (for example, interest may be allowed as a deduction in calculating income tax profit but not profit oil) but even if not identical, the measures should at least capable of straightforward reconciliation.[18]
- Minimizing the number of government agencies responsible for them.
- Coordinating their administrative rules. For example it may be possible to bring different taxes together in a single tax return so that they are subject to common filing rules. And if different taxes use common building blocks, common audit and disputes resolution procedures may be possible.

F   Simplify particular provisions

In many countries particular provisions of resource tax legislation present more than their fair share of administrative difficulty, and there is often scope to reduce that difficulty by simplifying those provisions. The following are examples of approaches taken by some countries to simplifying the treatment of problematic issues:

- Pricing of production on the basis of benchmark prices may be a cruder but simpler and more transparent method than pricing it on the basis of actual sales subject to transfer pricing rules.
- Differences in the tax treatment of different cost categories (for example, different rates of depreciation or uplift on exploration, development and production costs) are a major source of complexity. Reducing these differences may result in a less sophisticated measure of profit, but may be simpler and more transparent.[19] Allowing immediate write-off of costs more widely may reduce government cash flow, but this can possibly be compensated for by adjusting royalty rates or cost recovery limits.

- Allowing interest deductions based on standard rules (for example limiting eligible debt to 50 per cent of development costs less production income, or applying earnings stripping limits) may be cruder than allowing interest based on individual assessments of what companies could borrow in the open market, but again may be simpler and more transparent.
- Placing reasonable limits[20] on deductible costs paid for goods and services from associated companies may be cruder than allowing full deduction but restricting costs to market value, but again may be simpler and more transparent.
- The treatment of currency gains and losses is often seen as problematic. International accounting standards now provide generally consistent rules, but may not apply in a particular country, or may not form the basis for a particular tax. Where, as is often the case, resources and major contracts for costs are priced in US dollars, and companies prepare their accounts in dollars, the incidence of exchange differences in tax computations will generally be minimized if companies are also allowed to account in dollars for tax purposes.
- Taxation of capital gains on disposal of licence interests can add numerous complications and uncertainties to resource taxation, but some approaches are simpler and more transparent than others.[21]

Some simplifying measures of the above kind involve departures from taxing companies on the basis of their actual profits. Foreign tax credit for resource taxes may require them to be based on profits, and there is a risk that any such departures will lead to loss of tax credit. It is difficult to be specific about this, because the law in the overseas country is often unclear on this issue (and the line taken by the overseas tax authority may differ from the one taken by the courts). But generally, if the departure from actual profits has a marginal overall effect, or is narrowly targeted on tax avoidance, or is mainly to clarify something that would otherwise be uncertain, there is a reasonable chance that the tax will remain creditable.

Simplifying measures of this kind undoubtedly introduce rough edges into the tax system, and quite apart from causing foreign tax credit problems these may make administration more, not less, difficult. For example:

- Formulas to cap costs can become arbitrary and unrealistic, distorting decisions and generating avoidance and pressure for negotiated concessions. If deductible costs cease to bear any relation to real costs, foreign tax credit is also jeopardized.
- Some countries allow uplift on certain categories of cost instead of allowing a deduction of finance costs. This can increase disputes about cost categorization, and the combination of uplift and high tax rates can reduce companies' incentive to control costs, and even create "gold plating" incentives, where for each dollar spent a company saves more than a dollar in tax.[22] Tax administrators must then try to identify and disallow unnecessary expenditure, which can involve complex and opaque negotiations. Non-recognition of finance costs may also jeopardize foreign tax credit.[23]

Striking the best balance between administrative simplicity and transparency on the one hand and optimal policy objectives on the other is not straightforward. Many developing countries have individual resource taxes that are admirably simple and straightforward from an administrative viewpoint, but have a resource tax regime that is too complex overall, because of the number of different taxes and the number of different sub-regimes applying to different licence areas. (But considering the extravagant complexity and obscurity of the tax regimes of some developed countries, there should certainly be no assumption that they are any better at striking the right balance).

5 Resource tax and resource management

Links between resource taxation and resource management add considerably to administrative complexity. By resource management is meant the management and control of resource operations. All countries regulate resource operations to some degree. They designate licence areas, negotiate and issue licence agreements, agree and monitor work programs, impose health and safety rules, set out obligations to protect the environment, for example, by removing oil installations at the end of production, and so on. This regulation is normally the responsibility of a sector ministry, but in PSA regimes it is usually shared with the national resource company (NRC).

In most developed countries, there is little connection between resource management and resource tax administration, but in developing countries there is often a close connection. This is clearest in PSA regimes, where companies must have their budgets and costs approved by the NRC or sector ministry on a day-to-day basis. Approval might be withheld for a range of operational reasons, for example, technical objections, commercial objections, environmental objections, employment policy objections, objections about lack of local content and so on. Whatever the reason, costs not approved are non-recoverable for the purpose of calculating profit oil. Often this means they are not deductible for the purpose of income tax on the contractor's share of profit oil either. Operational requirements are also more likely to be built into developing countries' traditional tax and royalty regimes. For example, costs may not be deductible if they are not in accordance with employment laws, insurance requirements, environmental regulations and so on. More generally, tax legislation may require costs to be "necessarily" incurred.

A simplified way of describing this difference of approach is to say that in some countries the job of the tax authorities is to tax the production or profits companies *actually* achieve, while in others the job is to tax the production or profits they *ought* to achieve. A major factor behind the second approach is a concern that resource production companies, left to themselves, cannot be relied upon to control costs. This concern may be justified if the tax regime contains inadequate cost containment incentives or even "gold plating" incentives.

What is certain is that building resource management objectives into resource tax legislation makes tax administration much more complex and demanding. It is hard enough to find people able to interpret tax laws and audit tax returns effectively, let alone able to tell oil companies how to run an oilfield. Tax administration can be made simpler and more transparent if tax design contains adequate cost containment incentives, and fiscal and resource management regulatory functions are then kept separate.

6 Practical obstacles to policy simplification

The foregoing discussion of tax policy and administration may seem somewhat academic, given that resource rich countries already have resource tax regimes in place. (Indeed countries often have resource tax regimes in place before resources are even discovered). These tax regimes may be sub-optimal, but in practice may be difficult to modify even to eliminate major policy flaws, let alone to simplify administration. Re-negotiation of contracts or introduction of new tax legislation may face practical or political obstacles. Any change of tax base creates losers, who will object to the change. The existing tax regime may be frozen by stabilization clauses (the pros and cons of such arrangements are discussed in Daniel and Sunley (2010)). Even where the granting of new concessions creates an opportunity to change the rules, the advantages to be gained from doing so may be outweighed by the disadvantages of creating yet another distinct sub-regime.

What this means is that there are often severe practical limits on the scope for amending tax policy to simplify tax administration. As is so often the case, the best way to reach the desired destination is "don't start from here," but starting from anywhere else is impossible. That said, new tax resource tax regimes do come into existence, and existing ones are often not quite as stable in reality as they are in theory. And even within an existing regime companies may be willing to accept changes that make the law clearer, simpler and more uniform, if introduced with proper warning and consultation. Companies, after all, have an interest in stabilization of tax, but they have no interest in the stability of unpredictable and inconsistent tax administration. Some of the simplifications suggested earlier relate to the administrative framework rather than to tax policy. Even these may require extensive changes to legislation and licence agreements, which countries may be reluctant to contemplate, but in general changes to the administrative framework are less sensitive than changes to the tax base, and less likely to be challenged under stabilization clauses, particularly where they benefit companies as well as the government.

So opportunities to re-design tax so as to improve administrative simplicity and transparency may arise, and should be taken. An important part of any tax administration reform programme should be a detailed review of resource tax legislation to identify sources of avoidable administrative difficulty.

7 Policy role of tax administrators

There are clear arguments against combining the tax policy and administrative functions. Tax administrators are not best qualified to develop resource tax policy so as to reflect the government's overall economic and resource management policies. They may also face a conflict of interest, and, whether for honourable or self-interested motives, give excessive weight to administrative considerations in formulating policy. Combining policy and administration may also increase the risk of inappropriate political interference in administration.

Tax administrators should, however, be involved in the process of tax design, particularly on its practical aspects. They are best placed to advise on the practical implications of new tax policy, and to identify areas where existing policy is failing to achieve its desired objectives, perhaps because of loopholes or uncertainties in the law. Many issues that countries identify as causing problems for tax administration essentially result from such policy failings. Often there is scope to resolve them by administrative means, but sometimes what is needed is a change in the law. But where administrative departments have no effective tax policy advisory function these detailed issues are not brought to the attention of ministers. There may be a presumption (on the part of ministers and companies as well the administration itself) that stabilization clauses rule out changes in the law anyway. But where the tax base is being eroded by the exploitation of loopholes or ambiguities in the law, governments must be ready to change the law, whatever stabilization clauses may be in place (a risk that companies should be aware of). So tax authorities should be encouraged and given the resources to carry out a limited policy advisory function.

Long range revenue forecasting and scenario building are essential to policy formulation, and tools such as economic models may be developed for this purpose. This is primarily a matter for tax policy makers rather than tax administrators. But again it is appropriate for tax administrators to play some part in this, since their work provides information helpful for forecasting, and they also need to understand and be able to account for any major discrepancies between forecast and actual revenues.

8 Conclusion

Weaknesses in administrative capacity should not prevent countries from adopting what they see as the best resource tax policy framework. But within such a framework they need to design policy so as to make administration simple and transparent as possible. There may be practical and political obstacles to achieving this, particularly where a resource tax regime is already established, but political will, constructive dialogue with companies, and development within tax administration of a strong tax policy advisory function may allow some of these difficulties to be overcome.

Appendix I Taxation of hedging instruments

Many resource tax administrations report particular difficulty with the tax treatment of hedging instruments. (These instruments can of course also be used for speculation).

Companies can hedge receivables or payables. Examples of the latter include hedging against interest or exchange rate movements on borrowings. Insurance contracts can also be considered as a type of hedging. For simplicity, however, this appendix focuses on hedging against commodity or currency price movements relating to resource revenues. There are many types of hedging instrument, but in general they are based either on a forward contract (which obliges both parties to deal at a future date at a set price) or an option (which gives one party the right to deal with the other at a future date at a set price). Instruments of the latter type raise more complex accounting issues. Again for simplicity, this note considers the issues by reference to the former type of instrument.

International companies often carry out hedging operations through their head office management company, since it has a complete picture of group companies' overall net exposure to risks, and can hedge them more efficiently. But sometimes local companies may be allowed to hedge their own risks, perhaps because it is considered more tax efficient.

The basic problem often faced by tax administrators is a lack of clear policy on these instruments. Tax law often contains no specific provisions about them, and their treatment under general tax provisions may be unclear. Sometimes this uncertainty just relates to timing of recognition of gains and losses. International accounting standards have in recent years developed more consistent treatment of these instruments, but that is of little help if the tax concerned is not based on commercial accounting principles, or if international standards do not apply in the country concerned. Sometimes there is a more fundamental uncertainty as to whether tax law provides for gains and losses on these instruments to be recognized at all. The lack of a clear policy direction makes it difficult for administrators to decide how to attempt to resolve these uncertainties.

Even where a particular treatment can reasonably be inferred from general tax provisions, tax authorities are often uneasy about whether it is appropriate or consistent with policy intentions. In some cases this unease may reflect the fact that different taxes appear to treat hedging in different ways. For example, it may be clear that hedging transactions cannot be recognized for the purposes of royalties or production sharing, but that they *can* be recognized for the purposes of company profits tax. Of course, different taxes do not have to be consistent, but the absence of any clear policy reason for the inconsistency inevitably raises doubts about whether it is intended. Another possible inconsistency is between the treatment of a forward sale (where a company sells nickel in June, say, for delivery at the end of December) and of a spot sale hedged by a separate forward contract (where, say, a company sells nickel on the spot market in December, which it had hedged by a separate forward contract with a third party in June). These two transactions may be economically equivalent, but in some countries tax law may apply to them differently. Again this inconsistency may raise doubts about the underlying policy intention. There may also be concerns that companies can somehow exploit such inconsistencies to avoid tax. Indeed tax authorities may be generally uneasy about the tax avoidance potential of these instruments, and this may be amplified by their lack of knowledge or understanding of them.

To the extent that this is a policy issue, it strictly falls outside the scope of this chapter. But it is the sort of technical policy issue with which tax administrators have to grapple and on which they are commonly expected to advise. The appropriate advice may, however, depend on a number of factors.

One factor that may influence thinking is a perception that resource companies can consistently "beat the market" when using hedging instruments. If they can, the government might fear that they can use their forecasting skills to avoid tax. For example if a company "knew" that oil prices would rise more than the market expected, it could generate a loss by hedging in (high tax) country A against the price going down, but generate a corresponding profit by betting in (foreign tax haven) country B that the price would go up. It would seem quite unlikely that resource companies can consistently beat the market in this way, but some government officials and ministers may think otherwise.

A more important issue is whether the treatment of these instruments is consistent with the broad underlying policy objectives of the country's resource tax regime. Broadly the policy options for these instruments are:

1 Recognize all gains and losses for tax purposes;
2 Disregard all gains and losses;
3 Tax gains but disallow losses;
4 Recognize some gains and losses, but not others.

In most developed countries the broad aim of company tax policy is to tax companies on the commercial profits they actually make (so long as derived entirely on an arm's length basis) and not on the basis of some artificial construct created by tax law. The emergence of more consistent accounting standards has reinforced this trend. Option 1 is consistent with that policy, since hedging transactions form part of a company's profit. But even in those countries there are often major exceptions to following commercial accounting principles for tax, and these often become a focus of tax planning and avoidance. Because of concerns about use of financial instruments for tax planning, countries adopting option 1 generally buttress it with some sort of anti-avoidance provision. Companies would probably prefer option 1 (assuming that the option of allowing losses and not taxing gains is unavailable!).

With natural resources, however, governments tend, particularly in the developing world, to see production companies primarily as instruments in the execution of the national resource exploitation policy, and resource tax as the price they pay for the privilege of being selected as such an instrument. Taxing them on their actual profits might be seen as a good idea if it promotes the government's resource management policy, but is not a tax policy objective in itself; and in practice, in various ways, tax is charged without regard to actual profits. (For example, royalties and cost recovery limits produce tax irrespective of profits, ring-fencing rules exclude costs not related to resource production, and a whole range of other costs are disregarded as not in line with resource management objectives). Governments with this sort of outlook are unlikely to be persuaded that the fact that hedging transactions form part of companies' actual profits is in itself a good reason to recognize them for tax purposes. And they may have positive reasons for not recognizing them. The fact that their tax regimes depart so far from commercial profit criteria may be seen as increasing the risk of such instruments being used for tax avoidance and arbitrage. Governments may be uncertain how far such fears are justified, but may be unwilling to take the risk. They may have little confidence in any anti-avoidance restriction or their capacity to enforce it.

Even if not used for tax avoidance, a more basic objection these governments might have is that tax recognition of hedging transactions would fundamentally weaken their control over resource management policy. In effect resource revenues would come to be determined not by actual prices in world markets, but by company decisions on hedging those prices. The extent of hedging would, moreover, be arbitrary as far as the government was concerned, since it would depend on the extent to which particular companies chose to hedge, and, in the case of international companies, the extent to which they did so through the local company. Governments might feel that, rather than subject themselves to such vagaries, they should adopt option 2 and then decide for themselves whether and how far to hedge their exposure to oil and currency prices, in the light of their own economic plans and risk management priorities.

Option 3 – tax gains but disallow losses – obviously gives governments the best of both worlds. Companies would object to it on basic grounds of unfairness, and on that basis it might seem that no government would adopt it. In some countries, however, it may be the reality, if their profits taxes apply to companies' gross revenues, broadly defined, but give deductions for specifically defined costs, which do not include hedging losses (perhaps for the simple reason that no-one gave any thought to such things at the time when the law was framed). For practical purposes option 3 would soon morph into option 2, at least for international companies, since they would ensure that any hedging operations were carried out elsewhere (perhaps after having their fingers burnt in the meantime).

Option 4 – recognize some hedging transactions but not others – may currently prevail de facto in some countries, without any deliberate policy choice on the matter, simply because, as explained above, tax law recognizes them for the purpose of some taxes and not others. Alternatively, countries could actively choose this option because they wanted to distinguish transactions on some other basis – for example, to recognize genuine hedging transactions for the purpose of resource taxes, but not speculative transactions; or to recognize commodity price hedging but not currency hedging; or to recognize hedging transactions within defined limits but not beyond. Any such option is likely to be much more complex than the other options.

If hedging transactions cause tax administrations problems, it may be that what is needed is for them to identify examples and use them to initiate a policy discussion with ministers and companies, to establish clearly which of these options will be adopted as the way forward.

Appendix II Payments to subcontractors

A large part of the value of production is paid to service contractors. Understandably governments want to tax this activity (though it might conflict with their desire to build up their own service industries).

Service contractors should be taxed on their actual profits, but ensuring that they pay local business profits taxes can be administratively difficult, because they are often in the country temporarily and may have no permanent office. So governments often apply a simple but crude withholding tax (WHT) to the companies that pay service contractors.

Ideally contractors should be able to offset any WHT deducted from their receipts against their liability to local business profits tax. For contractors compliant with local business tax obligations, the WHT essentially becomes a payment on account of that tax. It is a final tax only for contractors not complying with local business tax obligations. An essential element of this arrangement is that where the WHT deducted exceeds the final business tax liability, the excess should be repaid. (In practice tax repayment procedures in developing countries are often very poor.)

In order to tax service contractors, it may be necessary to legislate to extend the normal geographic range of business taxes to include offshore areas.

The definition of the scope of the services to which WHT applies can raise a number of technical issues (for example, distinguishing service payments from lease rentals, agency fees, etc) to be considered in the course of tax audit. (WHT may, however, apply to lease rentals, etc, as well).

Service companies often demand payment on net of tax terms. Resource production companies then gross up the payment. The result is that the WHT becomes an additional company cost deducted in calculating their resource tax. With a 10 per cent WHT rate, a net payment of $90 is grossed up to $100. With a 60 per cent resource tax rate, the net cost of the $10 WHT to the resource company is $4, and $6 is in effect recouped from the government. But if service companies obtain tax credit for WHT suffered, resource companies may be able to resist net of tax arrangements or alternatively negotiate lower prices.

Taxation of service contractors raises various international tax issues. The normal rule in double taxation agreements (DTAs) is that a country can tax business activities of foreign taxpayers only if carried on through a permanent establishment. In some DTAs this requirement is disapplied to resource industry services. Clearly it is best for resource-producing countries if their DTAs are of this kind. In some cases this might require re-negotiation of DTAs. Many developing countries do not have a wide range of DTAs. Where DTAs do not exist companies may well be able to obtain double tax relief in their home jurisdiction in practice, and if the home country insists on their having a permanent establishment in the developing country to obtain double tax relief, setting up such a permanent establishment may be relatively straightforward.

It can be difficult in practice to establish where services are performed, and this too may require careful audit. Services may be performed partly in the country and partly abroad. If WHT is not to be easily avoided it will have to apply to such cases. How business profits taxes apply to such cases will depend on the precise wording of the legislation. Companies may split contracts to provide separate payment for services performed abroad and services performed locally, and the tax authorities will have to determine whether these are genuinely separate services, and if so, whether the allocation of price between them is reasonable.

Some developing countries have attempted to extend the scope of their taxes on services to include services performed wholly overseas – for example the overseas construction of a rig sold to an oil production company, or administrative and technical services provided by head office management companies. This is contrary to all the normal principles of international taxation. The overseas country in which the services are performed will reasonably regard those principles as giving it primary taxing rights over them, and will therefore not allow double tax relief for taxes charged elsewhere. The service company will therefore suffer double taxation, and may well recoup the additional cost from the production company.

In some cases it may be doubtful whether the country's legislation allows the scope of the WHT to be extended in this way. But withholding taxes are not normally covered by PSA arbitration procedures, and companies may have no confidence in their ability to obtain a fair ruling under tax appeals procedures. In other cases it may be clear that the legislation does indeed provide for taxation of services performed wholly overseas.

This is sometimes described as a difficult issue, but there is no difficulty in judging the rights and wrongs of it. The developing country may resent so much of its resource revenues being used to pay for services performed overseas, but that provides no justification for taxing those services. If the shoe were on the other foot, and an overseas country decided to tax companies' resource production activities in the developing country because it resented the high cost of those resources, there would be howls of outrage. The situation is no different.

It may be difficult in practice for companies to do anything about this. In some cases they may resort to avoidance – for example, buying equipment through an intermediary rather than direct from a construction company – but in other cases that may not be possible. They are unlikely to be able to persuade their home government to take retaliatory action against the developing country. (In some ways the developing country's action presents the same problems as asymmetric guerrilla warfare.) Service companies will insist on net of tax arrangements or higher prices, so that most of the additional tax cost is effectively recouped from the government, but that may take time, and some of the additional cost will stick with resource production companies. In the longer term they will need to take account of this issue in negotiating licence agreements, and either obtain assurances of adherence to accepted principles of international taxation, or factor the additional tax cost into their bids.

Acknowledgements

I am grateful to David Kloeden, Michael Keen, Charles McPherson and other participants at an IMF seminar in July 2008 for helpful comments and suggestions.

Notes

1 By a "progressive profit-based tax" is here meant a profit tax levied at a rate that increases with the level of profit or profitability.
2 The choice between a traditional tax/royalty regime and a Production Sharing Agreement (PSA) regime is not a matter of tax policy in that sense, because, as has often been pointed out, similar tax bases can be designed under either regime. At the risk of oversimplification, the choice between these types of regime is essentially a choice between different administrative frameworks.
3 See for instance Chapter 10 by Cramton.
4 Tax administration requirements should be a factor taken into account in evaluating licence bids. It should be important, for example, that bidders have strong internal anti-corruption policies; are subject to anti-corruption laws in their home state; have strong administrative systems and controls; use international accounting standards; and require group companies to trade with each other on arm's length terms. Awarding licences to a single company rather than a consortium may seem an administrative simplification but the lack of oversight by commercial partners may actually increase administrative risk.
5 See Kellas (2010) for a detailed discussion of gas pricing.
6 Ring-fenced resource taxes are generally intended to tax resource production at its value at a specified delivery point (for example a tanker inlet) less costs limited to those required to get it to that point. If, as is sometimes the case, a pricing basis other than FOB (free on board) is used – for example CIF (Cost Insurance Freight) – this effectively brings non-ring-fenced costs into account, and an adjustment (up or down depending on the exact nature of the pricing basis used) may be required.
7 Uplift means increase of actual costs by a fixed percentage for tax deduction purposes.
8 Ring-fencing may apply to resource production generally (that is, with revenues and/ or costs arising from a company's non-production activities excluded in calculating its resource tax liability) or to particular areas (where resource taxes for each area must be calculated separately). Complications are increased where these different kinds of ring-fencing apply to different taxes within a regime.
9 Thin capitalization is the excessive financing of business by debt rather than equity so as to exploit tax deductibility of interest.
10 A finance lease is an instrument that in substance is a loan financed asset purchase, but in legal form is an asset rental. International accounting standards recognize the substance and treat part of the lease rental as interest. If this is not followed for tax, finance leases can be used to circumvent tax restrictions on interest deductibility. (And if it is not followed for the purpose of PSA rules they can be used to avoid ownership of production assets passing to the state).
11 Appendix I contains a detailed discussion of the taxation of hedging instruments.
12 The term rent is used in this chapter to mean excess profits.
13 Interest deductibility is generally a requirement for income tax to be creditable against foreign tax. So long as income tax credit eliminates liability to foreign tax, there is no need for other taxes to be designed so as to be creditable.
14 Various hybrid taxes blur the distinction between value and profits-based tax. For example royalty may be calculated on production less certain defined costs – not

enough to make it a true profits tax, but enough to ensure that it is not simply related to production value either.

15 Otto *et al.* (2006) provide an excellent and comprehensive summary of mining royalty regimes.

16 Most oil-producing countries have found it necessary to modify their tax regimes in recent years so as to capture more of the rent generated by high oil prices (Angola and Norway being two of the rare exceptions).

17 Sub-national taxes are less common for oil than other minerals. They are an important feature of some industrialized countries (e.g. Canada and Australia) and some Asian countries (e.g. Malaysia and Indonesia) but are not so common in sub-Saharan Africa.

18 PSA cost recovery limits are a major source of discrepancy between profit oil and income tax. Unusually, Indonesia decided to allow 100 per cent cost recovery to eliminate this discrepancy.

19 In the UK, for example, all oil company costs are now immediately written off. This is a departure from the accountancy principle of matching costs with revenues, but is a major simplification.

20 For example PSAs usually impose narrow limits on the goods and services that can be provided by associates and the charges that can be made for them.

21 The simplest and fairest way to incorporate licence disposals into profits taxes is to give symmetrical treatment to buyer and seller, but this produces little if any additional tax. An alternative simple approach, also producing no tax, is simply to disregard proceeds and costs of licence disposals for tax purposes. Some regimes provide for asymmetrical treatment (where the seller is taxed on the proceeds but the buyer's ability to deduct the cost is limited). This may produce additional overnment revenues, but results in profits being taxed on an unrealistic basis, distorting investment decisions and encouraging complex tax planning and avoidance.

22 Cases where a dollar spent saves a large part of a dollar in tax are common, but cases where it actually saves more than a dollar are very rare (taxation of Nigerian natural gas providing one example).

23 It is understood, however, that the UK's Petroleum Revenue Tax is accepted as creditable in the US on the grounds that uplift is a proxy for interest.

References

Boadway, Robin and Michael Keen (2010), "Theoretical Perspectives on Resource Tax Design," in Philip Daniel, Michael Keen and Charles McPherson (eds) *The Taxation of Petroleum and Minerals: Principles, Problems and Practice.*

Calder, Jack (2010), "Resource Tax Administration: Functions, Procedures and Institutions", in Philip Daniel, Michael Keen and Charles McPherson (eds) *The Taxation of Petroleum and Minerals: Principles, Problems and Practice.*

Cramton, Peter (2010), "How Best to Auction Natural Resources," in Philip Daniel, Michael Keen and Charles McPherson (eds) *The Taxation of Petroleum and Minerals: Principles, Problems and Practice.*

Daniel, Philip, and Emil M. Sunley (2010), "Contractual Assurances of Fiscal Stability," forthcoming in Philip Daniel, Michael Keen and Charles McPherson (eds) *The Taxation of Petroleum and Minerals: Principles, Problems and Practice.*

Kellas, Graham (2010), "Natural Gas: Experience and Issues," in Philip Daniel, Michael Keen and Charles McPherson (eds) *The Taxation of Petroleum and Minerals: Principles, Problems and Practice.*

Land, Bryan (2010), "Resource Rent Taxes: A Re-appraisal," in Philip Daniel, Michael

Keen and Charles McPherson (eds) *The Taxation of Petroleum and Minerals: Principles, Problems and Practice*.

Otto, James, Craig Andrews, Fred Cawood, Michael Doggett, Pietro Guj, Frank Stermole, John Stermole and John Tilton (2006), *Mining Royalties* (Washington DC: World Bank).

12 Resource tax administration

Functions, procedures and institutions

Jack Calder

1 Introduction

Bad resource tax administration is not the biggest risk faced by resource-rich countries. Badly designed resource tax policy and mismanaged expenditure of resource revenues, for example, have probably been far more damaging. But bad resource tax administration is still a significant risk, both in its own right – incompetence and corruption can cause serious damage to government revenues and reputations, and serious problems for investors – and because it magnifies other major risks: for example, resource revenues are more likely to be wasted or misappropriated if tax administrators do not properly account for them, and poor administrative capacity can lead to bad tax policy choices.

Natural resources are often found in developing countries, and often dominate those countries' economies. Such countries commonly suffer from weak general administrative capacity and governance, which are exposed to huge additional pressures by the scale and complexity of resource taxation. Many struggle to meet this challenge, and urgently need to strengthen their resource tax administration. The scale of the challenge must be recognized, but it should not be exaggerated. Resource production is a complex industry, but so are all major international industries, and administering taxes on resource production companies is not inherently more difficult than on other large international businesses. Indeed some features of the industry make (or should make) tax administration less difficult, and if countries could get the simple things right they could often achieve significant improvements. But this requires the political will to make the necessary reforms, and, for reasons discussed later, that is often missing.

This chapter discusses resource tax administration issues relating to:

- Functions and procedures (routine and non-routine).
- Institutions (organization, capacity and governance).

In each of these areas it identifies general problems and weaknesses, and puts forward ideas for administrative reform and strengthening.

Badly designed resource tax policy can be a major contributor to weak tax administration. The interaction of resource tax policy and administration is not discussed here, but is covered in Chapter 11.

Generalizations are dangerous (this being one of the few exceptions). Inevitably some readers will find that some of the issues identified do not feature in their countries, or conversely that some of the issues they do face are not identified. Some of the suggestions for improvement may not be appropriate to their case. There can be no universal guidelines for tax administration of an industrial sector: the right approach where a sector consists of 100 taxpayers paying $100m each will be fundamentally different from where it consists of one million taxpayers paying $1,000 each. This chapter focuses mainly on the situation where resource production dominates an economy and is carried out by a small number of companies relative to the general taxpayer population. Many of the suggestions it makes are predicated on those two assumptions (and many would be identical for any other identifiable small group of taxpayers dominating an economy). These assumptions do very often hold true in the case of oil, and quite often in the case of other minerals, but where they do not, some of the suggestions may not be valid.

2 Administrative functions and procedures

The rules governing administrative functions should be clearly set out in tax legislation and license agreements, and should comprehensively describe the rights and obligations of both taxpayers and the tax authorities.

A Self assessment

There has been a widespread tendency in recent decades for governments to adopt self assessment as the basis for tax administration. Under self assessment, taxpayers are required to assess their own tax on the basis of published tax rules, and then pay it on the due date without receiving an assessment or tax demand from the government. Self assessment is usually associated with an approach summed up as "process now, audit later."

Self assessment has clear advantages for the government. It transfers virtually all routine administration to taxpayers, and also requires their full participation in the non-routine task of applying complex tax law. Small taxpayers may lack the technical and administrative capacity to shoulder these burdens, but they are not generally a problem for large resource production companies.[1] Self assessment frees up government resource for more difficult, non-routine functions. The clear separation of the functions of assessment and audit reduces opportunities for collusion. Self assessment also requires the government to make tax rules clear, public, unambiguous and non-discretionary.

So self assessment increases transparency and reduces demands on administrative capacity. It is therefore a good basis for resource tax administration. Many resource tax regimes have adopted the key feature of self assessment, namely the requirement (reinforced by sanctions) to pay tax on the due date without the need for a government assessment. But some such countries could further improve the simplicity and transparency of administration by embracing self assessment more fully, for example by eliminating some remaining requirements for administrative intervention in tax calculations, and removing the need for tax authorities to make a formal assessment where no amendment to the company's figures is required.

An objection sometimes made against self assessment is that it is all well and good for countries with sophisticated and compliant resource production companies concerned to maintain their good reputation; but not for countries where companies with little concern for either reputation or standards have an important presence in the resource production industry.[2] The implication is that self assessment weakens the government's ability to deal with such companies, but there is no reason why that should be the case in a well-designed self assessment regime. Such a regime reinforces taxpayer obligations with strong penalties to deter non-compliance, and allows the tax authorities to assume assessment and collection functions quickly and forcefully wherever companies, despite those penalties, fail to comply. Of course tax authorities do need to be ready to take vigorous enforcement and penalty action where that is necessary, but that is the case in any tax regime, and the advantage of self assessment is that the need for administrative intervention is limited to the non-compliant minority. The tax authorities also need the capacity for effective audit of resource companies' self assessment tax returns, but self assessment should not significantly increase the audit burden, since audit of large company tax returns is something they already ought to be doing anyway.

Although self assessment is now common in resource tax regimes, production sharing does not generally follow self assessment principles, since companies have to submit budgets and costs for government approval on a continuous basis in order for costs to be recoverable. For most costs the rules allow approval to be assumed if no objection is received within a certain time, so the extent of administrative intervention by the government may be limited in practice, but even so it is generally very far from being a "process now, audit later" approach.

B Routine functions

It is helpful to divide tax administration into routine and non-routine functions. Routine (or clerical) functions are about the mechanics of gathering tax. Non-routine (or technical) functions, discussed later, are about ensuring tax is quantified correctly.

Routine functions are:

- registering taxpayers;
- processing tax returns;
- issuing tax assessments; and
- collecting tax.

These functions, routine in themselves, can be problematic when dealing with a large taxpayer population. Typically, many taxpayers fail to:

- make themselves known to the tax authorities; and/or
- file tax returns; and/or
- pay tax due.

Managing these risks presents significant administrative challenges for any tax authority.

Such challenges will arise in resource tax administration in countries where mining is carried out by numerous small businesses. But in most countries resource production, and particularly oil production, is carried out by a small number of large companies. Identifying these companies presents no difficulties, and the majority are generally compliant with routine obligations to submit tax returns and pay tax, especially if these are backed by a robust penalty regime.

C Possible model for routine assessment and collection

In developed countries assessment and collection are administered along the following lines.[3] Within the tax department as a whole responsibility for assessing different taxes is assigned to particular offices – for example oil taxes are assigned to an oil tax office. These offices have control systems, supported by IT, to monitor receipt of tax returns. If taxpayers do not submit self assessment returns on time, then the tax office has to charge penalties and, if the failure continues, issue assessments. Particular staff in these offices have the job of recording assessed – including self assessed – taxes for which their office is responsible, as well as any amendments resulting from audit or appeals. Assessment data such as type of tax, type of payment due (e.g. instalment or final payment), tax year, due date and amount, are extracted from tax returns[4] and other documents, and entered into a taxpayer account record held on a departmental IT network. (In some cases taxpayers submit data electronically). This account record therefore shows all the taxes assessed by different offices on each company, but the system can also be interrogated to produce aggregate data on assessed taxes, by type of tax, year, etc.

Assessment staff cannot enter details of payments into the system. That is the responsibility of staff working in separate accounts offices. These staff collect payments received, but large companies generally make payments direct into a nominated bank account by electronic transfer, identifying themselves by a unique tax reference. They are not required to give the bank details of what taxes they are paying. The bank notifies the collector of payments received from each company on a daily basis. The collector's job is to record these payments on the company's account record. Payments are allocated against taxes assessed in the order in which they become due.[5] The collector cannot enter tax charges on the record, but can enter a charge for interest (calculated automatically) where any tax is unpaid at the due date. Collection staff are responsible for enforcing payment if taxes continue to be unpaid. The taxpayer account record can be interrogated to produce data on taxes paid – and unpaid – by individual companies, and also aggregate data. So the system allows analyses of tax revenues to be produced on a tax assessed (accruals) basis, and a tax paid (cash) basis. Taxpayers are given regular updates on their account record, and can also access it, on a read-only basis, with a secure password via the internet.

Procedures for tax repayments are similar in principle, with some additional security procedures.

The system described is quite massive where applied to an entire taxpayer population. But there is no reason why a separate system on these principles should not be set up just to deal with resource production companies. All it would have to do in a typical resource tax regime is record the taxes assessed on and paid by a few dozen companies, so a small system used by just a few staff would be all that was required.

In short, for compliant taxpayers routine assessment and collection are essentially accounting functions:

- create taxpayer accounts;
- debit taxes due (as shown on returns, assessments and amendments);
- credit payments received.

D Problems with routine administration in developing countries

Poor control and management of tax assessments and payments

In principle, then, routine administration of resource taxes should in most countries be much simpler than routine administration of other taxes. But it causes problems in some countries. It is not likely that poor routine administration results in large amounts of resource tax going unpaid in these countries, particularly if a self assessment regime is in place. The problem is more the tax authorities' failure to account properly for taxes assessed and collected. Accurate and reliable accounting for the huge resource tax revenues that tax agencies assess and collect is clearly essential in itself, especially in a poor governance environment, and is also an essential first step towards proper accounting for the government's expenditure of those revenues.

Among the factors that complicate routine resource tax administration are:

- Too many different resource taxes, often with their own individual, uncoordinated sets of rules for returns, assessments and payments of tax.
- Complex filing and payment regimes for each tax. It is common for royalties to be assessed on a quarterly basis, but in some countries mining royalties are assessed monthly or even more frequently. Short deadlines for submitting returns result in adjustments to returns and payments, causing further paperwork and complication. Profits taxes are usually assessed annually, but typically companies might have to submit a provisional tax return

before the tax year, four quarterly tax returns during the year and a final annual tax return after the year end, and pay tax in 12 monthly instalments during the year with a final thirteenth payment (or overpayment claim) when they submit their annual return. All this can result in a huge amount of paperwork. For royalties a possible simplification is to reduce the number of assessment periods and payment dates – for example by moving to annual assessment and tax payable in four instalments. For annual taxes, in-year instalments could be required on a quarterly rather than a monthly basis. (Moving from quarterly to monthly payment dates would have an adverse effect on government cash flow, so quarterly payment dates might have to be adjusted to compensate).

- Too many different agencies responsible for different taxes, often with poor levels of cooperation. When no single agency is responsible for resource taxes, companies have to give the collector analyses of each payment in order to account to each agency for its tax, and this greatly increases the paperwork.
- Poorly qualified and managed staff.
- Poor procedures, including poor form design, making extraction of assessment data difficult – indeed assessments may not be separately recorded at all.
- Poor IT support and management information systems. A particular problem is that there is often no IT network. Transmission of data between different agencies with tax responsibilities (for example, the tax department, the oil ministry and the National Resource Company (NRC)), between these agencies and the bank, and between collection and assessment staff within each agency, therefore involves huge amounts of paper shuffling, which is often done badly. Extraction of aggregate management information from all this paper is difficult.
- Failure to make any single agency or person responsible for recording aggregate resource taxes.

A further problem in some Production Sharing Agreement (PSA) regimes is that the NRC withholds government revenues (whether proceeds from disposal of government oil or tax due on the NRC's commercial participations) to meet regulatory costs and quasi-government expenditure, without accounting properly for these deductions, making it difficult in turn for the tax authorities to account properly for assessment and payment of tax.

Poor management of risk of late tax payment

Another common problem area is failure to manage the risk of late payment of tax. There is more to in-year returns and instalments than simply processing them. The reason they are required is that governments want resource taxes to be paid during the tax year, and not after it. For annual taxes there are essentially two methods for calculating in-year instalments:

- They can be based on the actual results of a particular period within the tax year – for example the profits made each quarter year.
- They can be based on equal instalments of the estimated annual tax.

The second method is most frequently used for income tax. Where tax is paid in kind, for example where the NRC takes physical delivery of government profit oil under a PSA, the first method generally has to be adopted. The government cannot, for example, take one quarter of estimated annual oil production in the first quarter of the year if no production actually occurs in that quarter. Countries often use a mixture of these methods for different annual taxes.

Whichever method is used, there is a risk that companies will calculate instalments wrongly. Forecasting annual tax can be difficult, because of uncertainty about future costs, sale prices and production levels. Calculating tax on results for a particular period can also be difficult, since the tax rate for the period may depend on annual results, such as the level of cumulative production. Late payment of tax is a second order risk compared with non-payment, which results if tax is understated in a final tax return. It nevertheless carries a cost to the government, and the tax authorities need to control that risk. Many countries aim to do this by charging penalties, or penalty interest, if companies underpay tax during the year, but this can be difficult to police. First, there is the sheer volume of paperwork generated by the weaknesses discussed earlier. Second, where instalments are based on actual results, audit of periodic returns is needed to establish inaccuracies, but for most tax authorities auditing annual returns is a big enough challenge, let alone auditing in-year ones. Third, penalties are normally chargeable only if a company is at fault, so if it has underestimated its instalments it has to be established that its estimate was unreasonable at the time it was made. This can be difficult, and companies normally resist penalties strongly. The upshot is that there is often no effective monitoring of the risk of late tax payment.

A better approach is simply to charge interest at a commercial rate on a no-fault basis if instalments are underpaid. If companies have to pay tax in four equal instalments, for example, one quarter of the final annual tax is simply compared with each instalment paid, and interest is charged on any underpayment from the date the instalment was originally due. Countries using this approach generally also repay interest, but at a lower rate, on overpaid instalments. Many developing countries do not routinely charge interest on tax paid late.[6] Calculating interest might seem administratively challenging, but with computerization it need not be, and any additional complexity is outweighed by the advantages achieved. The government is effectively protected from loss through delayed payment, without the need for companies to produce detailed quarterly returns – at most a simple notification of the instalment paid is required – and without the need for tax authorities to check them or to establish fault on the company's part. A criticism sometimes made is that it is unfair to charge companies interest when accurate prediction of instalments due is impossible. That criticism is misconceived. What is unfair is if companies who manage to estimate their instalments accurately are financially disadvantaged compared with ones who underestimate them, and that is precisely what happens where interest is *not* charged.

Where instalments are based on actual results, underpayments cannot be established simply from the final annual tax return in the way suggested above (unless the return requires analysis of results by period), so some audit of in-year returns remains necessary. But it is important not to use excessive resources on this, and limited sample checking, to establish the extent of the risk and to control it, is the best approach. If underpayments are established, penalties can be charged where companies are clearly at fault, but again this can be difficult to establish, and here too it is simpler and more effective to charge interest on a no-fault basis, reserving penalties for extreme cases. This also allows a coordinated approach to the collection of different taxes with different instalment bases.

Poor management of tax repayments

A further problem with routine administration in many developing countries is an inability to cope with tax repayments. This may partly be cultural: governments just cannot see large companies as recipients rather than as payers. It may be because of fears of fraud or embezzlement if tax administrators are given the right to repay tax. It may be because of lack of government funds or sclerotic budgetary processes for authorization of government expenditure. Whatever the reasons, there are often virtually no established procedures for making direct tax repayments, though there are often procedures under which companies can offset tax overpayments against future payments. Resource companies generally do have future tax liabilities against which overpayments can be set, but in some situations this might not be possible. For example, as resource production comes to an end there may be heavy abandonment costs and little revenue, so there may be no tax for later periods. There may even be losses or changes to cumulative rates of return that give rise to repayment claims. Another important and more common example is that there may be regular claims to substantial VAT repayments because resource industry inputs are subject to VAT but outputs (to the very large extent that they are exported) are zero-rated. In some countries resource industry inputs are exempted from VAT simply because of the inability to handle repayments. This is a pragmatic solution to the problem, but can cause further problems in turn.

Why poor routine administration matters

Do the weaknesses in routine administration discussed above matter, given that substantial amounts are probably not going unpaid, and at worst some tax may be being paid late? Yes, they do. "Probably" just isn't good enough, and proper accounting for resource taxes is an absolutely basic and essential administrative task. Another reason is that cumbersome, badly run, paper-based systems use scarce administrative resource, create confusion, and divert management attention from more important issues.

The important thing is that fixing these systems should be eminently *do-able*. After all, controlling, monitoring and recording the taxes assessed on and paid by a few dozen companies should not require rocket science. But doing it would be an important starting point, and indeed could go a long way, towards creating a sense of professionalism within the tax authority, and improving its national and international reputation.

E   Non-routine functions

Non-routine functions directly related to resource tax administration – meaning ones that involve the exercise of complex technical judgment – are: valuation of oil or other resources; tax audit, and dispute resolution and appeals. There are other important non-routine administrative functions not directly related to the assessment and collection of tax, of which the most vital are: advising on tax policy (as discussed in Chapter 11); providing guidance and advice to taxpayers, and; preparing reports and accounts. These last two functions are discussed later.

Valuation of oil or mineral resources

The value of oil or mineral resources produced needs to be established for both production and profits taxes, and involves functions separate from tax audit. The value of production is essentially volume × price.

As discussed in Chapter 11, physical audit procedures to establish the volume of production are often highly technical and require complex equipment. They have to be carried out continuously, not just as a year end exercise. The risks can be significant, so it is vital to perform these functions well.

Pricing may also be carried out as a separate process from audit. It is a process by which tax authorities determine in advance what prices companies must use for valuing their production when calculating their taxes. This advance pricing procedure is adopted because of the prevalence of transfer pricing risks and other pricing risks in the resource industry, as discussed in Chapter 11. Pricing of production is clearly crucial, and presents significant risks.

Different countries use different approaches to pricing. Some require market value to be used only for non-arm's length transactions – the difficulty is then how to spot these and how to establish the market value. Others require *all* transactions to be based on market value: for instance, all production in a quarter may be valued at average market value for that quarter. In theory this removes the need to identify non-arm's length transactions.

There are different approaches to establishing market value. Some countries base it on the average value of arm's length sales (this means they have to spot non-arm's length sales after all, and also presents the risk of companies manipulating the average).[7] Others base it on benchmark prices quoted on international exchanges or publications like Platt's Oilgram: the problem is to identify suitable benchmarks and make necessary adjustments. Others use a combination of these methods. The use of benchmark pricing is likely to be the most straight-forward and transparent method, but is appropriate only if there is a genuine relationship between the benchmark and the true market value.

Where prices cannot be based on benchmark prices (and for some commodities such as gas, that may not be possible) it is important that companies should be required to self assess on the basis of arm's length prices. The onus should be on them to identify non-arm's length transactions, to price them on arm's length terms, and to keep records to justify the prices used – and they should be liable to penalties if they fail to do so.

Pricing can sometimes involve quite complex formulae if combinations of methods have to be used, and there may be scope for differences in the way these are applied. It is important that the application of these formulae is clearly determined by the government agency responsible, and communicated both to companies and to tax auditors.

In some countries the tax authorities take the lead in proposing prices; in others companies put forward proposals along with supporting evidence, which the tax authorities choose to accept or amend. Usually there are provisions for arbitration, often involving international experts rather than local courts, in cases of dispute.

This is a difficult and complex area requiring technical expertise and system-atic information-gathering. Identifying and challenging artificial pricing is diffi-cult for most developing countries. Companies generally have an information advantage. National tax administrations would benefit greatly from greater pricing transparency by other administrations: often prices in other countries in the region, which could serve as useful benchmarks, are not made public.

Under an oil PSA, the NRC generally takes physical delivery of the govern-ment share of profit oil, disposes of it and remits the proceeds to the government.[8] Whichever basis is used to value this oil, the amount actually received by the government is the amount realized by the NRC. Disposal of oil requires signific-ant levels of specialist expertise, both in managing physical stocks and in market-ing. It presents significant further challenges to administration, and risks to the government, since the NRC or marketer may dispose of the oil at less than true market price through corruption or incompetence. It may be possible to reduce this risk by setting up arrangements under which the NRC and commercial com-panies compete against each other in the marketing of government oil. Govern-ments should – but often do not – account openly and transparently for differences between the market value of government profit oil and the amounts actually realized by the NRC. Where the NRC does market government oil this allows it to acquire information and expertise needed for oil pricing, and for that reason it may be considered appropriate to make the NRC responsible for that function. But because of the risks mentioned it may be a better idea to make a government department responsible for that function *and* for auditing the NRC's performance in achieving true market prices on disposal of government profit oil.

Although physical audit and resource pricing are separate functions from tax audit, it is important that tax auditors check that the volumes and prices established by those procedures are indeed reflected in companies' tax returns. (Adjustments in respect of unsold stocks or under or overliftings[9] may be required).

Tax audit

Audit of resource tax returns is clearly important. If resource taxes are clear and well-designed (admittedly a big if), the scope for error should not be exceptional. But in any tax regime there is always some scope for error, for differences of interpretation and for unacceptable tax manipulation at the margin, and even marginal errors can involve very large amounts of money where resource tax is concerned. And of course, if resource taxes are *not* clear and well designed, as is too often the case, the scope for error is all the greater.[10]

Tax audit often suffers from one of two, and largely contrasting, faults: It is weak and ineffective, or it is aggressive and unfair, with inadequate protection for taxpayers from unreasonable audit demands, tax adjustments and penalties.

The first fault is probably more common, and may be seen by governments as presenting the greater risk. Resource production companies are not inherently more likely than other companies to understate their tax – indeed because their position in developing countries is often vulnerable, it can be extremely risky for them to engage in wholesale tax evasion or avoidance, even assuming company policy allowed it. Often company policy actually reduces tax risks to the government. For example, many international companies set profit maximization management goals for their subsidiaries, which make abusive transfer pricing less likely. Even so, if governments leave an open door, some companies will soon walk through it, and commercial competition will then cause others to follow. Without effective tax audit, the government may suffer huge and increasing loss of revenue. Companies, on the other hand, may derive a short-term gain from exploiting a weak audit regime. But they should realize that in the longer term this may come back to bite them, since it may eventually lead to the development of more aggressive and unfair auditing, unwelcome fiscal changes, and the loss of reputation as a good investor.

Aggressive and unfair auditing is clearly a problem for companies, but governments may consider that it presents a gain for them. Again this is short-sighted. Aggressive and unfair audit regimes are a major discouragement to investment, and also encourage tax avoidance. They also foster corruption, which may cost the government much more than the apparent gain. Corruption is clearly a major risk in resource tax audit, which can involve massive sums, large margins and considerable complexity. An auditor may be bribed to turn a blind eye to a small percentage adjustment (but a large absolute sum) and detecting that this has happened may be virtually impossible. An aggressive and unfair audit regime greatly increases the risk of corruption, since even companies that would never normally consider paying bribes may feel compelled to do so if it is the only means of warding off excessive and unreasonable tax demands, and from there it is but a short step to paying bribes to reduce their tax to less than the amount due.

Tax audit and information powers should be clearly set out in tax legislation or production agreements. Normally these powers are extensive, often backed by harsh penalties for non-cooperation. This is generally appropriate, but there should also be safeguards for taxpayers. The key safeguard is effective rights of appeal against audit adjustments and penalties, but audit powers should themselves be reasonable and subject to limits, with rights of appeal against unreasonable demands. It is often good practice to explain in published guidance or codes how audit powers will be exercised and what safeguards are available to taxpayers. On the other hand there should be no restrictions that make effective audit of resource production companies impossible.[11]

The first step towards an effective tax audit programme is a well-designed tax return. The tax return and supporting information should include information needed for preliminary risk analysis. The return itself should be in a standard format, which should be published, so that companies can prepare it themselves and do not require government-prepared forms. It should so far as possible make use of information companies keep for their own purposes. When returned by the taxpayer, it should be accompanied by commercial accounts, which should be reconciled with the tax calculation. Where license areas or parts of them are ring-fenced, separate returns will be required for each, but even where that is not the case it will still generally be useful to have results analysed by area, for reasons explained at the end of the next paragraph. Where possible, different resource taxes should be consolidated in a single return, and the different calculations reconciled. Submission of tax returns in electronic format may ensure that complex calculations (such as rate of return) are correct, and may also assist risk analysis, by facilitating comparison across different concession areas or reconciliation of global and individual company results for particular concessions. (It also assists routine administration). It is good practice to consult fully with resource companies on the design of tax returns.

An important point where oil production is concerned is that it is normal for a consortium of companies acting in a joint venture to bid for oil licenses (primarily as a means of spreading risk). The rights and obligations of the partners are set out in a joint operating agreement. One of the companies is appointed as operator. It carries out operations and allocates costs to its joint venture partners. The joint operating agreement contains detailed accounting rules that the operator must follow. For example, they spell out how costs are to be categorized, and place tight limits on payment of costs to associated companies. Joint operating agreements follow a fairly standard format from country to country. The rules are therefore well understood and consistently applied. Many of the rules are relevant for tax purposes, and if they are built into tax policy and information requirements, the common understanding and consistency of application can bolster tax compliance. Operating companies can expect criticism and claims for redress from their partners if they fail to follow the rules, and if the failure results in unexpected tax liabilities, the reaction will be all the stronger. These rules need to be understood and taken into account by tax auditors. Focussing the tax audit on the operator, and then checking that the costs allocated by the operator to its non-operator partners are correctly reflected in their tax returns, may be a more efficient and cost effective approach than auditing all the partner companies equally.

PSAs are closely modelled on joint operating agreements, and contain similar accounting rules, with similar benefits.

These agreements result in oil companies being subject to more audit than normal – as well as internal audit and the annual commercial audit, they are audited by joint venture partners under the terms of joint operating agreements, and by the NRC under the terms of the PSA. The NRC audit is discussed in more detail later. The joint venture audit provides some assurance to the tax authorities. For example partners will use it to check that excessive costs are not being paid to the operator or its associates. It may not remove the need for a tax audit, since the interests of joint venture partners are aligned with those of the tax authorities only to a limited degree, but its importance should not be under-estimated. A further point about these other audits is that they increase the need to ensure that tax audits are not more burdensome than necessary. Even oil companies do not have unlimited administrative capacity to meet audit demands, particularly in developing countries.

The mining industry is not characterized by joint ventures and standard joint operating agreements such as are common in the oil industry, and therefore does not benefit from the same degree of international consistency in tax accounting and oversight by joint venture companies. Audit of royalty regimes by a sector ministry, common in the mining industry, may present further problems. Royalty returns are usually required quarterly or even more frequently, so more audits are required than for annual taxes, and of smaller amounts. Royalty returns are not based on annual accounts, so companies have to prepare and present separate records, which have not been subject to commercial audit. The results of the audit then have to be passed to the income tax auditors and compared with the income tax return – a procedure often poorly managed, but required if duplication of audit is to be avoided. Compared with a single comprehensive annual tax audit, this is not an efficient way of doing things.

Different countries take different approaches to annual tax audit. At one extreme, some opt for full coverage of taxpayers, with comprehensive field audits[12] in every case. This is often combined with a formal approach, with advance notice of the audit and a formal report on its conclusion. Other countries take a varied approach, combining full field audits of selected companies with limited desk audits of others. And others (possibly after a first year systems audit) rely primarily on a mixture of desk audit and selective records examination. This is often combined with a less formal approach. The choice of approach may depend in part on which the tax authorities find most productive in practice. But for larger companies, annual audit is advisable because of the large amount of tax at risk, and for the very largest, particularly if they are concession operators, the annual audit should be comprehensive and detailed.

Whichever approach is taken, the success of tax audit largely comes down to the skill and capacity of the auditor. Although desk audit may not be the best approach, one skilful auditor intelligently analysing the risks presented by the tax regime, asking pertinent questions and examining well-chosen records from his desk can achieve more than a whole army of field auditors going unintelligently through the motions. Field audits are generally more effective if auditors make a preliminary analysis of particular tax risks, decide which ones to focus on, and identify the kinds of records and tests needed to examine those risks, rather than simply turn up with a vague idea of looking at nearly everything.

This sort of preliminary planning and analysis should also allow auditors to limit the number of records to be examined and give companies advance notice of at least some of those records, some of which it might be possible to provide before any field visit. Such steps improve the efficiency of the audit process and make it easier for companies to cooperate.

Most of the challenges posed by resource tax audit are similar to those posed by tax audit in any other major industry. Of course there are various specific technical issues that commonly arise in resource tax audit and some of these are complex, but not necessarily more complex than specific technical issues arising in other industries.

Very large adjustments can arise from resource tax audits. It is important that any proposed audit adjustments, and the reasons for them, are clearly explained to taxpayers. Sometimes this is done in a formal audit report, which can be helpful. It is also important that adjustments should as far as possible be agreed in the course of the audit, and the legislation should allow time for this. Otherwise it puts an impossible burden on formal dispute resolution procedures. Although the auditor's job is primarily to establish facts and apply the law in accordance with the evidence, negotiation on audit issues inevitably sometimes involves matters that are not entirely clear cut. This presents obvious corruption risks, so it is important that auditors are subject to control and oversight. Records should be kept of the issues discussed and of the outcome, and in cases involving large amounts there should be consultation, again recorded, with managers not directly involved in the audit.

In some countries it is not the practice to charge either interest or penalties on tax increases established by the tax audit (though power to do so may exist). This means in effect that the government loses money and companies have an incentive to understate tax. Interest should invariably be charged, whether or not the understatement is attributable to fault by the company – otherwise companies that calculate their tax wrongly are advantaged over those that calculate it correctly. Penalties are an essential feature of any self assessment regime. They should be charged[13] where omissions result from negligence (i.e. any failure by responsible company personnel to exercise reasonable care) or fraud, and should vary with the gravity of the offence and amount of tax put at risk. Culpability may be difficult to establish, and companies may strongly resist penalties, but the threat, even if carried out only occasionally, has major deterrent value. It is important, however, that penalty criteria are clearly defined and that there are effective appeal procedures against unreasonable charges, so that the threat cannot be used aggressively and unfairly.[14]

Audit adjustments, and any interest and penalties, should be charged, collected and separately accounted for in the same way as normal taxes. They should also be analysed to assist future risk analysis and taxpayer education.

Because of the large amounts involved, an effective tax audit regime can often repay the costs of audit – indeed the costs of running the entire tax system – many times over. Some tax administrations fund audit salaries and costs out of audit adjustments, and some provide bonuses or rewards for auditors on the basis of audit adjustments. An objection to this is that the main reasons for large audit adjustments are often poor tax design (such as unclear or over-complex provisions), poor levels of voluntary compliance, and aggressive and unfair audit practices, none of which it is appropriate to reward or encourage. It is true that the skill and effort of tax auditor may also be an important factor, and for that reason many administrations dismiss the above objection. But in countries where taxpayer safeguards are poor, there is a strong risk of encouraging over-aggressive audit, with all the disadvantages outlined above. In some countries resource companies are required to directly fund the cost of the tax audit. Given the corruption risks already present, it seems ill-advised for governments to *impose* a requirement on companies to give payments to tax auditors.

PSA regimes raise particular audit issues, especially where a NRC acts for the government. As a taxpayer, it should account to the government for the proceeds of disposal of government profit oil, and may also be subject to taxes on its commercial participation. Best practice is for it to be required to make tax returns to the finance ministry in the same way as other companies. In some countries the NRC accounts to the sector ministry, which thus has a much greater audit role, which it may lack the accounting expertise to carry out. Audit of NRCs is often poor in practice whichever agency it accounts to. NRCs are often powerful organizations under limited ministerial control, with poor standards of accounting, and it can be difficult to enforce tax obligations on them. Often there is a basic uncertainty over whether it is even appropriate to do so, because the NRC is regarded primarily as a government agency, indeed as a superior government agency, rather than as a taxpayer.[15]

Another issue is that the year end audit of the accounting records of the contractor companies under the terms of the PSA (often known as the "cost recovery audit") is, in effect, a tax audit, but it is often the responsibility of the NRC or another agency reporting to the sector ministry. There is inevitably a huge overlap between the cost recovery audit and the income tax audit, and in mixed production sharing/income tax regimes this can result in duplication of audit effort and lack of clarity about who has ultimate responsibility for the tax audit function. In some countries the tax department may in effect leave it to the NRC or sector ministry, but they may not have the required expertise. In addition if the NRC is responsible for the audit and also has a commercial role, there will be a conflict of interest, and the NRC may pose as big a risk to government revenues as contractor companies. In other countries, the NRC or sector ministry and the tax department carry out separate audits, often simultaneously, with no communication between them. Obviously the best approach is to try and coordinate the tax and cost recovery audit in some way, and produce a coherent result, but that is rarely done in practice. Possibilities to consider include:

- Some sort of joint audit by the tax department and NRC or sector ministry.
- Focusing the audit of each agency on different issues: for example the NRC/ sector ministry could focus more on operational issues and on whether approval procedures had been correctly followed, and the tax department more on accounting issues.
- If separate audits are carried out, there should at least be a requirement that audit reports are exchanged and that each set of auditors meet during the planning and execution stages of their audits to exchange details of their audit plans and emerging findings.
- If the NRC or sector ministry uses a commercial auditor, it could incorporate a training requirement for tax department staff in the terms of the contract. Those staff would then participate in the cost recovery audit, which would let them see what issues had already been covered, and also provide the wider benefit of exposure to best audit practice in a commercial accounting firm.

Another approach is for the tax agency reporting to the finance ministry to assume responsibility for audit of the calculation of profit oil. This avoids duplication and problems of poor accountability and conflict of interest on the part of the NRC, but it may be difficult to reconcile with the terms of the PSA. It can also cause practical difficulties for companies when tax authorities disturb the existing understanding with the NRC as to how PSA provisions should be applied. The change of approach might concern matters of interpretation (such as how particular costs are dealt with) or of practice (such as how rigorously procedures for approval of costs should be followed). These problems will be lessened if the tax authorities provide written guidance on their interpretation of tax law and discuss it with companies beforehand.

Dispute resolution/appeals

It is important that most disputes are resolved by agreement in the course of the audit, or in subsequent discussion or negotiation on the audit findings. Resolving disputes by formal litigation is extremely resource-intensive and usually very slow, and judicial institutions may be unable to cope with a large volume of cases. Successful negotiation depends upon there being reasonable clarity in the law, and adequate input from effective negotiators well trained in the law. Where these conditions are met, the need for formal arbitration may be quite rare. But some cases may require it, either because agreement is impossible or because negotiations are stretched out for an unreasonable time.

Unresolved disputes may concern matters of fact or matters of law or a combination of the two. In either case taxpayers should have formal rights of appeal, and there should be clear and open procedures for this.

Many countries have tax tribunals functioning at a level below the court. These tend to be slightly less formal, and can decide points of fact as well as law. But they may not be seen as competent to decide complex resource tax disputes, and they may also not be seen as impartial or even-handed in their procedures, particularly if chaired by finance ministry officials. Also there is a risk of corruption where large sums are involved. Appeals to the court are usually possible but often only on points of law, so there may be no impartial arbitration on points of fact. On the other hand it can involve lengthy and cumbersome procedures if points of fact need to be decided by courts. Often there are doubts about the competence, impartiality and integrity of the courts too.

PSAs attempt to get round these difficulties by providing for expert international arbitration. Of course this only helps companies if the government accepts the results of any arbitration, which does not always happen. It also creates possible uncertainty over jurisdiction – who would prevail if the courts reached different conclusions on income tax from those reached by international arbitrators on profit oil? There might be some scope for integrating the tax appeals procedures and the PSA arbitration procedures. For example, the PSA procedure could be built into the law on tax appeals. Alternatively, if tax appeals are first heard by a finance ministry tribunal, it might be possible to agree as a matter of practice that international experts of the kind provided for by the PSA should be appointed to that tribunal, where this was formally requested by the appellant.

As well as competent and impartial judicial institutions, there is a need for the tax authorities to have the legal skills for effective presentation of their case. Again, as with audit, good dispute resolution is mainly a question of administrative capacity.

3 Institutions

A Organization

Centralized or dispersed administration

For most industries other than natural resources, tax administration is the responsibility of a tax department or departments reporting to the finance ministry. Some countries (for example the UK) adopt exactly the same approach for resource tax administration.

In other countries the sector ministry and/or the NRC have responsibilities for resource tax administration. A fairly typical arrangement in a traditional tax and royalty regime is that profits taxes are the responsibility of a tax department reporting to the finance ministry and royalties the responsibility of the sector ministry. In PSA regimes, government profit oil is generally the responsibility of the NRC (though sometimes it is the sector ministry), and income tax the responsibility of the tax department. But there are many variations. Regional or state taxes may be administered separately from central or federal taxes. With minor taxes such as education taxes, surface rental and so on, the allocation of administrative responsibility varies from country to country.

One reason why the sector ministry tends to be involved in resource tax administration is that physical audit, especially in the mining industry, requires technical expertise, for example in mineralogy, which is more likely to be found in the sector ministry than the finance ministry. The fact that the sector ministry is heavily involved in the day-to-day physical regulation of resource operations also makes it a natural (though not inevitable)[16] candidate for physical audit functions. Once it is responsible for physical audit, making it responsible for volume and value-based taxes may then seem a logical next step. Companies may prefer a single point of contact in government, and may prefer the sector ministry to administer tax because they have to deal with the sector ministry anyway, and may feel that it has a better understanding of their business. Another factor is that in some countries the sector ministry is part of a larger economic development ministry, which may be more powerful than the finance ministry. But tax departments reporting to finance ministries generally have more expertise in administering profit-based taxes, so even where the sector ministry is heavily involved in tax administration these taxes tend to end up with them.

Spreading administration between different agencies is sometimes argued to have theoretical advantages, the main one being that if no one office controls the whole tax procedure, it reduces the risks of serious error and collusion. But it also has disadvantages, such as:

- complexity;
- more regulators for companies to deal with;
- duplication of work;
- lack of clarity about responsibilities;
- lack of accountability;
- uncoordinated management, systems and procedures.

Complexity often begets further complexity, with new coordinating agencies set up to oversee existing agencies.

The risk that over-centralization will create opportunities for corruption and collusion may be greater in countries where general civil service standards are poor and controls lax. That said, in many developing countries over-dispersal of resource tax administration seems to present greater risks than over-concentration. Organizational complexity results in downright disorganization. It may actually increase the risks of error and of corruption, because nobody can see the big picture, and efforts to strengthen standards and accountability are dissipated among several departments rather than focused on a single compact administrative unit. In practice the best course is generally to minimize the number of agencies responsible for resource taxes, and within each agency centralize administration within a specialized office (as discussed below). Where tax administration is concentrated within a department reporting to the finance ministry, this means that companies will have separate points of contact on resource management and fiscal regulation. But companies have to cope with this in many countries, and do so quite easily where responsibilities are clearly defined and fiscal regulators adequately trained in the nature of the industry.

But the dangers of such a centralized approach must be recognized. Any centralized administration risks falling under the control of a corrupt politician or official, who may seek to fill it with people prepared to milk the system on his or her behalf. So this approach must be backed up by effective measures to strengthen transparency and control.

It is probably a mistake to think that administration is spread over different agencies in developing countries because of any theoretical analysis of the advantages and disadvantages. Natural resources are the big thing in those countries: everyone wants a piece of the action, so the division of responsibilities may owe more to ministerial in-fighting than anything else. A further political factor is that in highly decentralized federal states, local states may have extensive administrative autonomy, which they are reluctant to surrender to federal government. So dispersal of resource tax administration is often the political reality, and strong vested interests, and mutual mistrust between government institutions, can make organizational simplification difficult to achieve in practice. This difficulty is increased by the fact that it may be impossible to achieve without changes to contracts or tax law or even constitutional law.

Cooperation between agencies

Where administration does remain dispersed between different agencies, the question is how to minimize the disadvantages. The important thing is to try and improve cooperation, which is often poor in practice. Somebody has to make this happen. However desirable cooperation between government agencies might be, it does not just occur spontaneously. What is more likely to occur spontaneously is that they ignore each other. (They may even act against each other). If agencies do not cooperate, it may require someone with authority over both of them to intervene. Unfortunately the combination of political power and an interest in tax administration is rare – and presidents may prefer keeping their ministers sweet to banging their heads together.

An essential first step in improving cooperation is to review and clarify exactly each agency's responsibilities. This review should be used to examine the scope for removing duplication and overlap of functions, and for streamlining and consolidating procedures, for example by consolidating tax returns or setting up consolidated collection and banking arrangements. Procedures for exchange of information must be put in place, perhaps even set out in legislation, and then made part of staff job descriptions. Co-location of parts of different agencies specializing in resource tax might be a good way of improving cooperation – for example sector ministry staff responsible for royalties might be located in the same office as finance ministry staff responsible for resource profits taxes. Further ways of improving cooperation and breaking down barriers include regular interchange of personnel and temporary secondments (which might need steps to equalize pay and conditions) and joint training. High level joint committees can be useful, but by themselves are not enough.

NRC involvement in tax administration raises particular problems for cooperation. In some countries (such as Brazil, Algeria and Indonesia) governments have stripped NRCs of their fiscal and operational regulatory roles, leaving them to operate entirely as commercial companies – but these are the exception rather than the rule. Where NRCs do play a role in tax regulation, this can, as discussed earlier, create duplication of function and uncertainty about final responsibility. So cooperation between the NRC and tax agency is vital. But it is often poor in practice, for various reasons, including differences of culture, status and ministerial sponsor. The relationship is made more problematic, where, as is normally the case, the NRC is a commercial taxpayer – indeed often the biggest taxpayer in the country – as well as a fellow regulator. If the NRC's role is limited to regulation and it has no commercial equity interest, this may make cooperation easier to achieve in practice.[17]

Organization within tax agency

Within individual departments, it is generally considered best practice to concentrate resource tax administration in a specialized office. This might be free standing or might be a sub-division of another office, for example a large taxpayer office (LTO). This should depend on the size of the resource sector relative to other large business. If other large business taxes are insignificant relative to resource taxes, the pay and grading of resource tax administration, and its place in the management hierarchy, should reflect its much greater importance, and that may be difficult to achieve if the resource tax office is merely a part of the LTO.

Practices differ on whether the specialized office takes responsibility for production companies' non-resource taxes, such as withholding taxes, VAT or downstream taxes. There are arguments for and against. The advantage of doing so is that it provides companies with a one-stop shop, gives staff a better overview of the company's affairs, and makes accounting for resource company revenues more straightforward. The disadvantage is that these other taxes might distract attention from the main business of resource taxation, and they might in any case be better administered by offices that specialize in them.

In developing countries where general tax administration capacity is poor, the case for bringing everything to do with resource companies into the specialized office is much stronger. As discussed later, the aim should be to make the specialized office a centre for administrative excellence, so it will generally be able to administer non-resource taxes better than other offices, and to this advantage of stronger capacity will be added the advantages brought by consolidated administration. For example the problem of VAT repayments may be easier to solve where VAT is administered by a resource tax office with common accounting and banking systems, of the kind discussed earlier, for *all* resource company taxes. VAT repayable would be credited to the company account record, and companies would effectively recover it by offset against resource tax liabilities.

A further issue to consider is whether the resource tax office should be responsible for taxation of contractors to the resource industry. In many developing countries payments to contractors are subject to withholding taxes, and there seems a good case for the resource tax office to be responsible for these taxes when paid by resource companies.[18] The general arguments for this set out in the foregoing paragraphs are strengthened by the fact that these taxes are likely to be a major source of government revenue, so, as with resource taxes, a high standard of administration is vital. It is far less clear, however, that the resource tax office should be responsible for administering the taxation of service contractors themselves.[19] If service contractors are subject to a special resource industry tax, then there is a case for the resource tax office administering that tax, but not if it would result in the resource tax office dealing with small, low yielding cases. And if, as is more generally the case, they are subject to general industry taxes, it is probably best to leave them to non-specialist offices. Otherwise the resource tax office may find itself dealing not only with field service contractors but also catering companies, transport companies, office suppliers and the like, which would be a waste of its specialist expertise and a distraction from its main task.

Separate non-civil service agency for resource tax administration?

It is sometimes argued that a separate unit outside the normal civil service structure should be set up to take control of the entire resource tax administration function. This would have the potential benefits of centralization already discussed (but also the potential risks). The other claimed advantage is that it would free resource tax administration from the capacity limitations of the civil service, such as inefficiency, inadequate pay scales, and an over-bureaucratic, perhaps corrupt, culture, and improve transparency and accountability.

In the past two decades, many countries have, on the strength of such claimed advantages, established semi-autonomous revenue authorities, separate from traditional civil service departments, to take responsibility for general tax administration. Kidd and Crandall (2006) point out that such revenue authorities have theoretical disadvantages as well as advantages, and that the evidence that they are more successful than other forms of organization in practice remains inconclusive. Similar theoretical and practical doubts may apply to the argument for establishing a semi-autonomous agency with specific responsibility for resource tax administration (which would operate not only outside traditional civil service departments but also outside any semi-autonomous revenue authority).

NRCs provide a practical example of an administrative unit outside the normal civil service structure with responsibilities for resource taxation and management. They often do have better focus and capacity than government ministries, but ministerial control over NRCs is often weak, and their transparency and accountability poor. Their example certainly does not strengthen the argument that a separate non-civil service unit will inevitably improve resource tax administration.

Whichever agency administers resource taxes must ultimately remain accountable to government ministers, so will essentially remain a civil service department, whether semi-autonomous or not. The primary issue is the need for a more centralized and coordinated approach, as well as a step change in transparency and professionalism, whether this occurs within an existing civil service structure or not. As a practical matter it may be easier to persuade governments to try and achieve these changes in a specialist unit inside an existing department or agency, rather than by setting up some new structure, which may be politically controversial and require major legislative change. Retaining the unit within an existing department will also enable it to function as a role model and centre of administrative excellence to be extended eventually to the rest of the tax administration.

B Administrative capacity

Limited extent of resource tax capacity requirements

It is obvious that resource taxation presents a challenge to administrative capacity, especially in developing countries, many of which struggle with routine functions, let alone technical and professional functions. The huge imbalance in expertise between taxpayers and tax administrators makes effective fiscal control difficult. But it is important not to exaggerate the challenge. The requirements for effective resource tax administration are good, qualified, motivated staff, adequately paid, well trained, properly managed, supplied with adequate accommodation and resources, particularly IT, and given an adequate delegated budget and authority to do their job. These requirements may be difficult, but they are not unique to resource tax administration, and indeed it should be easier to meet them in the case of resource tax administration than in the case of general tax administration.

Staff numbers

There is no simple guide to the number of staff required for resource tax administration, since it depends on a number of factors, such as the scale of the sector, the number of taxpayers, the number and complexity of taxes, the number of agencies involved, the extent of computerization, and so on. But in most countries the number required is quite small,[20] and the emphasis should be more on quality than numbers. It is difficult for developing countries to find thousands of good people to run a large tax department, but finding the small number needed for resource taxation should be much more manageable.

Remuneration costs

Salaries of resource administration staff in developing countries are often completely inadequate. The salary levels needed to attract staff of the calibre needed and to discourage inappropriate taxpayer influence are generally much higher than civil service norms, a problem that is generally aggravated by competition from resource companies (often themselves under pressure to employ indigenous staff). It is possible to compensate to some degree for salaries that do not match industry levels by emphasizing the national importance of the work, but salaries need to be reasonable to make this message credible. Governments often fail to recognize the need to reward resource tax administrators with higher pay and grading than other tax staff, to reflect the greater importance of their work and the greater competition for their expertise.[21] Even if they do, the position of the resource tax office within the departmental hierarchy may make this difficult to achieve in practice. Changes to departmental structure may be required to overcome such problems. If these political obstacles can be overcome, then paying good salaries to, say, 50 resource tax administrators would not be at all expensive relative to resource revenues – indeed since they would be more likely to do a good job it would probably *increase* government revenues.

Recruitment practices

But of course it is no use paying high salaries to people who are not up to the job. Existing staff are often inadequate. Paying them the rate appropriate for the job would be futile – they need to be replaced. But recruitment policy is often poor, and nepotism common. Resource tax offices often have no control or influence over appointments, but are dependent on bureaucratic and unresponsive civil service personnel departments. Recruitment practices need to be strengthened, but this should be manageable for the small number of staff required.

Staff training

Another thing that is often lacking is any systematic staff training or guidance. Training for routine administrators should not be difficult, since they are essentially data entry clerks. Training resource tax auditors and managers is much more demanding, but is obviously essential. It needs to provide a thorough grounding in resource industry operations and accounting, in national resource tax legislation and the issues it presents, in audit powers and techniques, and in the use of any IT available to support audit activity. Suitably qualified people may have some of this grounding already, and if they need more it should be possible to provide it by buying in outside assistance and also by setting aside resources for in-house development of training materials. It is good practice to gather guidance on resource tax law and procedures into a resource tax manual or handbook, which can also, as discussed later, be used as a means of publicizing the government's application of law and practice to the industry. The preparation of such a manual, even with external assistance, need not be prohibitively expensive.[22]

Performance management

Something else often lacking is any effective management of staff performance. There is no setting of targets or objectives, no monitoring of performance, no annual reporting, and no mechanisms for rewarding good achievement or getting rid of poor performers. Unfortunately, this is not a problem governments can just throw money at: often it needs a fundamental change of culture. But again to create this change in a small resource tax office should not be impossible. If this change is successfully achieved, it can then serve as a model for progressive adoption of improved practices by the remainder of the administration.

Information technology

IT support is in theory not essential for resource tax administration, but in practice it is a necessity because it can help in all sorts of ways. IT makes it easier to control and execute routine functions; to monitor activities and establish audit trails; to gather management information and account for assessment and collection. It thus simplifies administration and improves transparency, reducing risks of corruption. IT manipulation and analysis of data from tax returns and other sources can also strengthen audit risk analysis. In developing countries staff often do not have enough computers or adequate IT systems. A further common problem is the absence of a functioning computer network – and creating a network is all the more difficult if resource taxes are administered by several organizations located in separate offices using incompatible software systems. But if that problem can be solved, the difficulty of providing effective IT support for resource taxation should not be exaggerated.

Of course IT can be expensive – large developed countries spend hundreds of millions of dollars annually on it. (And it still doesn't work!) But that is to build and maintain systems used by tens of thousands of staff to deal with millions of taxpayers. A computer network and IT system to be used by a few dozen people for controlling and recording routine tax administration for a small number of resource production companies need not be complex or expensive. Standard off-the-shelf spreadsheet and database software, with strengthened security features, may do the job perfectly adequately. The cost of such a system might be only in the tens of thousands of dollars. Of course if a government has already succeeded in developing an effective integrated tax administration system (ITAS) for general tax administration, it can be adapted for resource tax. But if not, it makes more sense to concentrate on the manageable task of building a dedicated IT system for resource tax administration, and then use that as the pilot for an ITAS – with additional functionality as needed – that can in due course be rolled out across the wider administration as funding and capacity permit.

Facilities

Adequate facilities and accommodation boost morale and increase effectiveness, but are often missing. Again it should not be expensive or difficult to provide these for a small resource tax office.

Funding

Funding arrangements for resource tax administration are often inadequate. Core funding should come from a secure budget line. Complementary funding for specific purposes may be obtainable from loans, credits, donor grants, and so on. Even where funding is adequate in theory, actual spending is often stymied by turgid, bureaucratic budgetary procedures. Sometimes governments circumvent these self-created problems by allowing tax departments to retain tax revenues to meet administrative costs, but if that practice is adopted it needs to be accompanied by appropriate accounting procedures, which, as discussed later, are often absent.

Need to focus capacity strengthening on resource taxation

Many of the weaknesses discussed above are typical of tax departments in developing countries. Of course it would be quite untrue to say that they are all corrupt, incompetent, underpaid, poorly trained, badly equipped and accommodated, mismanaged and bureaucratic. Some have made great progress in strengthening capacity. But in many resource-rich countries tax departments do suffer from these weaknesses, or at least some of them.

It is not easy to turn round a large tax department with all these weaknesses, especially if there is not the money to do it. But when major natural resources are discovered, that is not the problem the government faces. Its problem is that it needs a small number of people to collect a huge amount of revenue from a tiny number of companies. Despite the fact that doing this well should be a more manageable task than running a large tax department, governments often appear constrained by the standards of their existing tax administration. But if resource taxes provide the majority of their revenues, strengthening resource tax administration must be the government's absolute priority. If governments focus on that task, then at least some the problems of strengthening capacity may be manageable, given the limited staff and other requirements. If, on the contrary, governments treat resource tax administration as just another part of general tax administration, the problems of strengthening capacity will be much less manageable. This is not to say that governments should abandon efforts to strengthen general tax administration – but if they tie the strengthening of resource tax administration to that wider objective, it will be less likely to happen in practice.

So on the assumption that improving standards of resource tax administration is an urgent requirement, whereas improving standards of general tax administration is a long-term and intractable task, governments need to be prepared to fund, staff and manage resource tax offices in a completely different way from other tax offices.[23] Can they do this within the structure of an existing department? It should not be impossible, but it certainly needs a readiness to make major changes, including possibly a fundamental departmental restructuring. Otherwise they need to consider the option of a separate unit outside the existing structure, as discussed earlier.

As discussed by McPherson in Chapter 9, governments of resource rich countries often concentrate capacity building on their NRCs, which enjoy better staffing, salaries, training, facilities and funding than civil service departments. This can lead to institutional capacity in civil service departments being weakened or hollowed out rather than strengthened. Strong capacity in the NRC could in theory enable the requirements of resource tax administration to be met, but that would depend on the NRC being solely responsible for it, subject to strong ministerial control, fully accountable and transparent, and not subject to conflict of interest arising from its commercial involvement in the resource industry. In practice these conditions are generally not met. Strengthening of capacity in the NRC is therefore no substitute for, and may even detract from, strengthening of resource tax administrative capacity in government departments.

Outsourcing

A solution to capacity constraints adopted by some governments is to outsource resource tax administration to private firms and consultancies. Outsourcing some services – for example legal representation in arbitration proceedings – is common in developed as well as developing countries, but wholesale outsourcing of core tax functions is not common in developed countries. In developing countries PSA dispute resolution and audit are usually outsourced, but government departments are less likely to outsource functions. Some countries have gone much further than others.[24]

Although outsourcing is a way of addressing capacity shortages, the real motivation may be that governments are unwilling to disturb existing departmental practices and structures. For example, they may see difficulty in paying private sector salaries or implementing a hire and fire culture for resource tax administrators within a civil service department, but be content for consultants to do this.

Countries do not generally see outsourcing as an ideal permanent solution. No doubt an economic argument could be advanced that the international and homogenous character of the resource production industry gives specialized international consultants and professional firms a comparative advantage in administrative functions such as audit and price determination, whereas the comparative advantage of national tax authorities lies in less specialized areas. But most countries regard it as more appropriate and desirable for resource tax administration to be carried out by government agencies, and resort to outsourcing as a temporary solution, to fill gaps in administrative capacity and standards in the short-to-medium term, and provide systems and skills transfer to develop the government's own capacity in the longer term. Contracting out is therefore accompanied by obligations to employ local staff and/or provide training and twinning opportunities.

There is no doubt that use of international consultants and professional firms can sometimes improve standards of administration, in terms of both efficiency and integrity, and also transfer valuable skills. It may also provide reassurance to foreign investors. In some areas, such as commodity pricing or mineralogical analysis, it may be difficult to develop local expertise to match that of specialist international firms. If governments find themselves unable in practice to achieve the capacity strengthening that outsourcing would provide, then theoretical arguments against outsourcing should not be allowed to prevail.

But in practice outsourcing is not always a success either. The standards of service delivered by professional firms can be very variable, and it can be difficult to exercise the necessary oversight over their work. Their links with resource companies may cause conflicts of interest. The cost of outsourcing can be extravagant. In effect governments may move from paying civil service salaries that are uncompetitive even by local standards, to paying top international consultancy rates plus expensive travel and subsistence costs plus a hefty profit margin, without ever exploring whether a solution between these two extremes would give better value for money. Often the desired transfer of skills does not take actually place, perhaps because of lack of commitment by the consultants, but often because, in the absence of civil service reform, the civil servants who are the supposed recipients of those skills do not have the capacity to absorb them. There is also a risk of corruption in the outsourcing process itself, with kickbacks, mutual back scratching between consultants and senior civil servants, and the local employment obligation translating simply into an even better paid sinecure for the chief secretary's not very bright nephew. Some countries, having experimented unsuccessfully with outsourcing of the tax audit function to professional firms, have reverted to in-house audit.[25]

C Governance

The IMF *Manual on Fiscal Transparency*[26] and *Guide on Resource Revenue Transparency*[27] are concerned not just with tax administration but also with wider issues such as formation of resource tax policy and management of expenditure of resource revenues. But many of the principles outlined have particular relevance to tax administration. Three of the key themes are clarity of roles and responsibilities, public availability of information, and assurances of integrity.

Clarity of roles and responsibilities

Two important aspects of clarity of roles and responsibilities are, first, the need to assign distinct roles to institutions so as to avoid confusion and conflict of interest (a general concern in relation to state participation, as McPherson stresses in Chapter 9), and second the need for an explicit basis for taxation, so that tax administrators do not carry out their job in a discretionary and non-transparent fashion.

In dealing with natural resources the government should draw a clear separation between policy, regulatory, and commercial roles. For resource regimes, Figure 12.1 illustrates an organization of roles and responsibilities that meets the principles set out in the guide.

As explained earlier, in many developing countries the tax regime is designed to achieve resource management objectives, and the sector ministry often plays a part in tax administration, for example by collecting royalties, so even if roles are separated as shown in the diagram, some overlap may remain within the regulatory role.

Turning to resource tax law, this needs to be well organized, accessible, clear and understandable. Countries often have several resource taxes, and sometimes rules vary from one license area to another, so to achieve these aims it is best to use standard contracts, with a limited number of variable parameters, and to set out the standard rules in consolidated legislation. And of course, all the rules, standard or not, need to be published. In many countries license terms are kept secret. Generally the terms leak out to the industry very quickly, so in effect it is only the people – sometimes including even those in the tax office! – who are kept in the dark.[28]

Simplification of resource tax legislation has already been discussed. Resource tax legislation often confers considerable discretion on tax officials, in which case it needs to be reviewed to make it more objective and specific and remove discretions. Changing to a self assessment regime can act as a catalyst for this, because self assessment requires the rules to be clear enough to allow companies to calculate their own tax. But it is difficult to include every detail of policy and practice in tax legislation without making it too long,

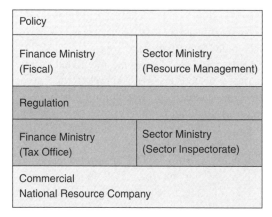

Policy	
Finance Ministry (Fiscal)	Sector Ministry (Resource Management)
Regulation	
Finance Ministry (Tax Office)	Sector Ministry (Sector Inspectorate)
Commercial National Resource Company	

Figure 12.1 Separation of roles.

complex and inflexible. So legislation needs to be backed up by publication of authoritative administrative guidance setting out how any remaining discretions will be exercised and how general principles in tax law will be interpreted and applied in practice. As discussed earlier, some countries prepare a regularly updated resource tax manual as the main resource tax training document for staff, and this may also be published (possibly with limited omissions) as the main form of guidance for the industry. Companies may not agree with departmental interpretations set out in such publications, but will often put up with them so long as they are properly explained and do not come as a nasty surprise.

The industry should be consulted both on changes to legislation and on changes to the guidance. Often this can best be done through an industry representative body. Governments of developing countries sometimes treat such bodies with suspicion, but the existence of a forum for regular dialogue between the resource industry and tax authorities, including those responsible for administration as well as policy, has many advantages.

Companies may also seek guidance on particular issues, or even binding rulings. The need for this should be limited if tax legislation has been made clear and objective. It can raise quite difficult issues – tax authorities will not want to be sucked into complex tax planning exercises, for example – and may also place an excessive strain on resources. But within limits the authorities should respond to reasonable requests.

Clear and explicit legislation achieves nothing if tax auditors are then free to misapply and misinterpret it. So companies must be given clear explanations of audit adjustments and have effective rights of appeal against them. It is impossible to overstate the importance of access to honest, competent and impartial arbitration – it is the bedrock of fair tax administration. If a country's own judicial systems cannot provide this, they must either be strengthened or replaced by international arbitration by reputable experts.

PSA regimes raise particular transparency issues. In the literature they are often presented as just a different way of achieving the same policy objectives as can be achieved by a traditional tax regime. The choice may be neutral where policy is concerned, but it is generally not neutral where transparency is concerned. PSAs do have the advantage discussed elsewhere of incorporating clear and internationally established rules. But: PSA terms are often kept secret; PSA contracts are full of administrative discretions, with approval for transactions having to be obtained at every turn; standards of accounting by NRCs are often poor, and; there is a fundamental conflict and confusion of roles where the NRC is involved in policy, regulatory and commercial activity, as is generally the case.

Concern about these conflicts has led some countries in recent years to remove NRCs' policy and regulatory functions. This requires a major, though not necessarily complex, revision of the tax regime. Essentially the NRC's responsibilities under the PSA are assumed by a non-commercial government agency, and the NRC then interacts with commercial companies under a joint operating agreement as a commercial company and not as a state regulator.[29]

Public availability of information

Under this theme a key issue is the need for resource tax administrators to report publicly on their performance, and in particular to account for their assessment and collection of resource tax revenues. They are not responsible for preparing government accounts and explaining the relationship of resource revenues to government budgets, but their limited accounting role is crucial to that process.

Failure to account properly for resource tax revenues is common. Audits under the Extractive Industry Transparency Initiative (EITI)[30] and similar exercises in various countries have established that, even with huge effort, governments cannot provide basic reliable aggregate data on resource revenues.[31] This is one of the most serious and damaging weaknesses in resource tax administration. It means that the government has not taken even the first step towards properly managing and accounting for the expenditure of public funds. It has a huge impact on the government's reputation and the confidence that international observers and their own people have in it.

As explained earlier, computerized records of resource taxes assessed and collected should be maintained, which are capable of being interrogated to produce comprehensive accounting data on a cash and accruals basis. It is helpful if all resource revenues are paid into a single nominated bank account. This should be swept daily into a treasury account, sometimes known as a consolidated fund, held with the central bank.[32] The treasury account should be controlled by the government's chief accounting officer, who should obtain from the tax authority details of transfers of funds to this account and reconcile them with central bank records on a daily basis. The tax authority should be responsible for preparing comprehensive accounts of taxes assessed, collected and paid to the treasury account. In practice, because of the spreading of administrative functions, often there is no single tax authority responsible for producing comprehensive accounts of resource revenues, and someone has to be made responsible for this.

The central bank should not play any direct role in tax administration. In some developing countries it carries out tax reporting and accounting functions simply because there is no tax authority responsible for aggregate resource revenue accounting. But one thing that is essential is that its accounting systems and those of the tax authorities should be capable of being reconciled. A particular issue that often complicates this is that resource production companies generally account and pay their taxes in dollars. At some stage revenues need to be translated into local currency before being reported in national accounts, and it is important that exchange differences should be clearly and consistently handled.

The tax authority must also account for the costs of tax administration. Some countries allow retentions of taxes collected to cover the administrative costs of ministries and/or the NRC. Often these are expressed in percentage terms, and, with the increase in resource prices and resource tax take to mid-2008, reached astronomic levels, far in excess of any amount that could legitimately be spent on administration. But there is often no accounting for these costs at all.

An annual report containing a consolidated account of resource tax revenues and administration costs should be published by the tax authorities in a clear and comprehensible format. This report should also describe the department's progress in performing its key functions and meeting its key objectives. There is no practicable single performance indicator for a tax department, but it should be able to demonstrate that all declared resource taxes have been assessed and collected on time, and give an account of the progress and outcomes of its valuation, audit and dispute resolution programs.

Assurances of integrity

Administration should be organized to minimize opportunities for collusion, but without making organization too complex. For example, audit staff should not be involved in routine assessment and collection. Audit managers not directly involved in the audit should oversee major audit decisions. There should be teams working on audits and other activities. There does need to be continuity in functions such as audit, but there should be periodic changes of allocation every few years. Administrative appeals and reviews should be carried out by staff not responsible for the decisions being reviewed, and of course there should be a right of appeal to a wholly independent body. IT should be used to provide audit trails, allowing identification of the officer who entered data on the system, which should be cross-referenced to the source document.

Whether or not governments have a general anti-corruption program, tax departments should have one of their own. Tax officials should be subject to ethical codes, preferably backed by severe anti-corruption legislation, which should be rigorously enforced.

Resource tax administration is so important and presents such major risks that auditors should be crawling all over it. Audit should cover all agencies involved in resource tax administration, including the NRC. Each agency should have an internal audit office, with published procedures open to review. A national audit body independent of the executive government should audit annual accounts of resource tax revenues and costs, and should also periodically review administrative systems for controlling major risks. Its reports should be submitted to the legislature, and published. In practice there is often no effective audit, or no audit at all, of resource tax administration, even though internal audit and national audit offices may in theory exist. Where these offices do exist their capacity is often poor. In that case, efforts should be made to improve their capacity, and until a reasonable standard is achieved independent professional accountants should be employed.

Audit of how a tax authority carries out its functions and controls particular tax risks may be more challenging than audit of its annual accounts, as it may require detailed understanding of resource tax law and practice. Obviously the audit cannot involve a re-audit of resource companies' tax returns, but it should involve examination of the tax authority's audit systems and selective review of audit papers. In reviewing tax audit files an area that it is often useful to focus on is reconciliation between companies' commercial accounts and their tax returns. Public companies generally like to maximize their commercial profits but minimize their tax, so comparison of their commercial and tax profits can be instructive.

As well as adherence to standards set out in the IMF's *Manual on Fiscal Transparency* and *Guide on Resource Revenue Transparency*, participation in EITI should be helpful. In many cases weaknesses in government accounting systems have made the reconciliation of company payments and government revenues a difficult task. But if accounting is improved in the ways discussed in this chapter, the EITI comparison should become straightforward, allowing attention to pass to more important issues, such as whether resource tax policy and the expenditure of resource revenues are being properly managed and controlled.[33]

Wider civil society should play a role in monitoring the accounts and activities of resource tax administrators, and EITI rightly places emphasis on this. But tax authorities are normally primarily answerable to government ministers, who should in turn be answerable to the legislature. It is important to strengthen understanding of the requirements for good administration in parliament as well as civil society.

Tax administration should be legally protected from direct political interference. This is often one of the objectives behind the creation of a semi-autonomous revenue authority, though how effective such a measure is in practice will ultimately remain dependent on the politics and governance of the country concerned.

4 Politics of resource tax administration reform

Obstacles to reform of resource tax administration

This chapter has tried to make clear the inherent difficulty of some aspects of resource tax administration, and the pressure that the large amounts of money involved can place on weak administrative capacity and standards. On the other hand, however, resource tax administration requires very few people to do it, costs little relative to resource tax revenues, and should be capable of being tightly managed and controlled. Some aspects such as routine assessment and collection should be relatively easy. The poor reputation many administrations have is often based not so much on their failure to do the difficult things as on their failure to do the easy things, like accounting for taxes assessed and collected. How difficult can it be just to count up the taxes assessed and paid each year by a few dozen companies?

When strong resource tax administration is so clearly essential, why do governments fail to achieve it? Are there political obstacles to reform? One possibility is that governments resist reforms because they are mismanaging and even embezzling resource revenues, and it is not in their interests to be held accountable. There is less pressure from their people for them to administer resource revenues efficiently and transparently, because these revenues are collected from large companies, who do not vote, or riot in the streets, and are usually foreign anyway. Once the money is rolling in, they may be able to ignore external pressure for reform, and may be able to buy off domestic pressure. An effective political opposition with a strong interest in reform can be a key driver of change, but often does not exist. Such governments may be interested in strengthening resource tax administration so far as necessary to get the money in (for example by strengthening audit), but not interested in strengthening transparency.

Governments may also be reluctant to reform administration in ways they see as strengthening the position of resource production companies. There is often considerable mistrust of these companies. Governments may think they already use their wealth and expertise to exploit the country's administrative weaknesses. They may see fairer and less arbitrary application of tax rules as weakening, not strengthening, administration. Governments who feel that they obtained a bad deal in negotiating their resource tax regime, perhaps because they did so under the stress of civil war or other political or financial upheaval, perhaps simply because the extent and profitability of the resource sector were unknown, may see aggressive and unfair administration as a means of redress. Companies are vulnerable once they have committed large investments to a country. Governments may wish to exploit this vulnerability, but, to avoid the legal risk of tearing up agreements, attempt to impose new terms by the back door of unfair administration, despite all the risks this presents: corruption, breakdown of the rule of law, discouragement of investment. Companies may in turn react by adopting aggressive tax planning and avoidance strategies, creating a vicious circle of mutual mistrust. The story may end with the company losing its investment entirely.

Undoubtedly there are cases in which governments deliberately resist reform of resource tax administration for such reasons. But sometimes politicians who genuinely want resource taxes to be administered in an efficient, transparent and fair way may be in the ascendant. Even then, however, reform may not proceed, because they cannot cut their way through the complex web of practical, historical and legal obstacles, entrenched sectional and local interests, political turf wars, institutional lethargy and general resistance to change. Reform may require extensive changes to legislation, the re-design of procedures, the shaking up of institutional organization and relations, the reform of institutional structures and practices, and stepping on the toes of some powerful people. So governments may genuinely want reform – but not quite enough to overcome so many problems. They can achieve it only if they make it a priority, and are ready to take the difficult actions necessary. This needs leadership: somebody needs to have the interest, the incentive and the power to take the lead and make it happen.

The technical assistance role

What can institutions like the IMF do? It has to be recognized that their efforts will be constrained by the sort of government they are dealing with. The minister earnestly discussing reform across the table may have large foreign bank accounts, properties and yachts funded by corrupt tax administration. Whatever reform is agreed in principle, he or she will want to ensure that these are not affected. Reform that might serve to boost the minister's personal flow of funds may be adopted; reform that threatens to stem it may be adopted in theory but will be frustrated in practice.

Suppose though that there is a genuine will to reform. A major role for the IMF and similar institutions is to help countries diagnose the health of their resource tax administration, and identify the cures necessary. With administration, this requires detailed study of what countries do, not what they say they do (which is often very different). Even with detailed study, it will often be very difficult to get to the bottom of what is going on – corrupt practices, for example, will be well concealed. From countries' own points of view, what they need is not generic theories of resource tax administration delivered from on high (like this chapter!), but an assessment of their own particular problems, taking account of the peculiarities of their own resource tax legislation, their own institutions, their own needs. Far-reaching change may be needed, but there needs to be recognition of the practicalities and political realities of getting from here to there.

Any assessment and recommendations ought to be agreed government-wide. For understandable reasons, IMF assistance may be focussed on the finance ministry, and it may well be that strengthening the finance ministry's role in resource tax administration is a key plank of any reform program. But often reform depends on cooperation with, and improvement of, other agencies, such as the sector ministry, the NRC, the justice department, the central bank, the accountant general. They all need to be involved. More effective appeal procedures or more effective audit of tax departments, for example, may be essential to any reform of administration, but recommending these improvements achieves nothing if the finance ministry just shrugs them off as the responsibility of some other department. Often different providers of technical assistance work with different parts of government, and better cooperation between these agencies might produce a more coherent and wide-ranging reform.

One possibility that has been suggested is the development of a scorecard for assessing resource tax administration, with scores for different criteria to provide quantified benchmark comparisons between different countries. Such scorecards can be problematic, because the assessment of the chosen criteria can be highly subjective, and quantified measures of this kind can often lead to distortion of effort and attempts to game the system. A more limited but perhaps more useful tool might be the development of a standard approach to assessment of resource tax administration. This is important because if key elements (again, such as effective appeal procedures or effective external audit of tax departments) are missing, it might nullify any reform project. Domestic and international observers need to be able to identify such evidence of lack of true commitment. Standard IMF-sponsored fiscal transparency audits, based on the principles set out in the manual and guide discussed earlier, could perhaps be developed for the more limited field of resource tax administration.

Following assessment, short-term expert technical assistance and training may be required to implement some of the recommendations. This is often best provided by personnel in other tax administrations directly involved in the same kind of work. Flying visits to tax offices in foreign capitals can be a nice way to see the world, but more extensive (and intensive) assistance provided at home is likely to be more useful in practice. Among countries, Norway, Canada, South Africa, and Australia have developed active foreign assistance programs, and no doubt other governments with relevant experience could be persuaded to do more.

When countries first discover new resources, as, for example, in Ghana or Uganda, they are often determined to avoid the notorious past failures of other resource tax regimes, and very receptive to advice as to how to do this. They will, of course, want to develop their own ideas, but focusing technical assistance on such countries at this crucial stage of their development may be particularly rewarding.

Finally, resource companies should be an important source of technical assistance. Like governments, they have an interest in good tax administration, and they are the main repository of technical expertise. In many countries they do offer training and other assistance, but there is often seen to be a conflict of interest, both in the sense that they have competing interests in the interpretation and application of tax law, and also in the sense that they have competing interests in recruiting the best tax administration staff. Despite this, companies can make a useful contribution in countries where they operate. But it might also be helpful to establish systems under which companies sent staff on short-term secondments to provide technical assistance to tax administrations in countries in which they were not active. This would provide a challenging development opportunity for staff, and help to foster mutual understanding between companies and tax administrations. (And companies might welcome the opportunity to ensure that competitor companies in other countries are not enjoying unfair tax advantages).

5 Conclusion

Political obstacles to resource tax administration reform clearly exist, but where there is a will there should be a way. International organizations, foreign governments and the resource industry itself can help countries along that way, but the first and most important requirement is the political will to make the journey.

Acknowledgements

I am grateful to David Kloeden, Charles McPherson, Keith Tucker and other participants at an IMF seminar in July 2008 for helpful comments and suggestions.

Notes

1 In some countries small mining businesses play an important part in the mining industry. Self assessment may present more problems for them, and like other small businesses they may need more government intervention.

2 Singling out particular examples might be invidious, but as a general point countries
affected by civil war may attract, and be more willing to grant resource concessions
to, companies of this kind.

3 The description here is based on UK practice, which is assumed to be typical.

4 Tax returns generally contain a lot of other data not required for routine processing
but intended to help taxpayers calculate their tax or to assist the tax audit function.
Capturing this data as part of routine processing makes the task much more difficult,
and if the system cannot cope, or is not designed to handle this type of data, it should
be left to tax auditors to review it separately. Tax return data requirements for audit
purposes are discussed later.

5 This is by no means a universal feature of developed country tax regimes (and there
may be exceptions to it in the UK) but it is a key step towards simplification of routine
administration.

6 It is possible that some countries have religious objections to charging interest on tax
paid late, and are therefore obliged to rely on penalties.

7 For example, if prices had risen during a quarter, companies could make sales only to
connected parties in the last month of the quarter, so that no arm's length sales at
these higher prices would be taken into account in calculating the average. This may
to some extent be countered by a requirement, common under such arrangements, that
arm's length sales account for a minimum percentage of actual sales.

8 The NRC may contract this function out to a private marketing company, and agreements usually also provide that partner companies can be required to do it, but in most
cases the NRC itself carries out the disposal.

9 It may be impractical to share each oil lifting among joint venture partners exactly in
accordance with their entitlement, so some partners may temporarily "overlift" and
others "underlift" relative to their entitlement. For tax purposes, they must use a consistent basis (whether entitlement or liftings) for reporting share of production, otherwise some may fall out of account.

10 For example Russian transfer pricing legislation is not clear or well designed, and in
the case of Yukos reportedly gave rise to huge audit adjustments.

11 In Azerbaijan, for example, the time allowed for tax audit is exceptionally short and is
a barrier to effective audit.

12 "Field audit" denotes the practice of carrying out audit activity mainly at the business
premises. (It does not mean audit of an oil field.)

13 Some PSAs contain no penalty provisions at all, possibly because of the greater
emphasis on advance approval rather than post transaction audit.

14 Negotiation of penalties to take account of factors such as the gravity of the offence
does, however, present obvious risks of corruption, and, no doubt influenced by this
risk, some countries – for example Uganda – apply the same standard penalty to *all*
tax understatements.

15 McPherson in Chapter 9 reviews experience and the conclusions to be drawn in this
and other aspects of state participation in petroleum and hard minerals activity.

16 In Ghana, responsibility has initially been allocated to the Customs and Excise department – another agency whose work involves day-to-day oversight of physical
transactions.

17 In practice it would be extremely unusual for a NRC to be limited entirely to a regulatory role.

18 See Chapter 11, Appendix II for further discussion of these taxes.

19 In general, where large companies withhold tax – for example, employment taxes –

from a large number of taxpayers, it makes sense for an LTO or specialized office to be responsible for administration of the withholding tax, but local offices to be responsible for taxation of the recipients. This requires efficient procedures for dissemination of details of tax withheld to local offices.

20 The UK, with a more complex than normal oil sector, with many small fields and minor companies, uses around 50 people to administer oil taxes.

21 This can be a contentious issue. Obviously the object of the exercise is to attract better quality administrators to the resource tax office – staff who are not better quality should not enjoy higher pay and grading simply because they happen to work in a resource tax office. But the rationale for attracting better quality staff is not that the work is necessarily more demanding, it is that it is more important to do it well. Taxing, say, a bank may be as demanding as taxing an oil company, but that does not mean its pay and grading should be the same. That would send the market signal that the government was equally keen to attract scarce talent to either job – but if the oil company pays ten or 20 times as much tax as the bank (quite feasible, with higher profitability and tax rates), and if better quality administration increases the tax paid (otherwise why even discuss it?), that would be an inappropriate signal to send.

22 Angola, for example, will reportedly soon publish a comprehensive oil tax manual.

23 The same rationale applies to capacity building for administration of any other sector that dominates an economy. In non-resource-rich countries it will usually apply to a general LTO.

24 For example Angola has, for some time now, outsourced most of its oil valuation, audit and legal work, and a few years ago it effectively outsourced its routine tax administration too.

25 Tanzania considers that it improved its resource tax audit by bringing it in-house and giving auditors intensive training with assistance provided by the Canadian government.

26 Available at:www.imf.org/external/np/fad/trans/index.htm.

27 Available at: www.imf.org/external/np/pp/2007/eng/101907g.pdf.

28 Timor-Leste provides a notable exception to the normal obsession with secrecy. Its government has enacted legislation requiring the terms of all PSAs to be made public, with no concern that this will weaken its negotiating position.

29 This approach has been adopted by Indonesia, which was an early pioneer of PSA regimes.

30 This initiative was originally sponsored by the UK Department for International Development, and has been adopted by a large number of countries. It focuses on publishing and reconciling resource taxes paid by companies and those received by the government.

31 In some cases the figures for tax receipts can be reasonably reconciled with company payments, but the figures do not reconcile with those showing up in the budget. This suggests a problem outside the scope of tax administration, but proper publication of tax figures might prevent, or reduce the likelihood of, that problem occurring.

32 This chapter does not consider any special requirements arising where a country has a special Petroleum Fund.

33 In April 2008 the World Bank and other partners launched the EITI++ initiative to cover such wider issues.

References

Calder, Jack (2010), "Administrative Challenges from Resource Tax Policy and Administration," in Philip Daniel, Michael Keen and Charles McPherson (eds) *The Taxation of Petroleum and Minerals: Principles, Problems and Practice*.

Kidd, Maureen and Bill Crandall (2006), "Revenue Authorities: Issues and Problems In Evaluating Their Success," IMF Working Paper WP/06/240 (Washington DC: International Monetary Fund).

McPherson, Charles (2010), "State Participation in the Natural Resource Sectors: Evolution, Issues and Outlook," in Philip Daniel, Michael Keen and Charles McPherson (eds) *The Taxation of Petroleum and Minerals: Principles, Problems and Practice*.

Otto, James, Craig Andrews, Fred Cawood, Michael Doggett, Pietro Guj, Frank Stermole, John Stermole and John Tilton (2006), *Mining Royalties* (Washington DC: World Bank).

13 International tax issues for the resources sector

Peter Mullins

1 Introduction

As a result of the globalization of economic activity, international tax issues have become an increasingly important consideration not only for foreign investors, but also for governments in designing their tax systems. This is especially the case for the resources sector where many firms operating in that sector, particularly in developing countries, are likely to be foreign multinational firms. While a country's domestic resource tax regime is obviously important, the effects of that regime and its attractiveness to investors can be enhanced or undermined by the tax rules applying to international transactions. Therefore, governments need to consider international tax issues in tax policy design to ensure the resource tax regime is competitive and attractive to foreign investors, and at the same time, will ensure that the state, as resource owner, receives the intended share of the economic rents from the natural resources. This latter objective includes ensuring the revenue is not unnecessarily eroded through aggressive tax planning.[1]

In designing a resource tax regime, governments also need to be aware of recent international trends in corporate taxation, such as corporate tax competition and the new corporate income tax (CIT) regimes being implemented in some countries. These trends may affect a country's attractiveness to investors, may influence the way an investment in a resource project is best structured, and also could affect the revenue yield for the government. The trends – in particular the recent CIT innovations – may also provide lessons in designing resource tax regimes, as several of these innovations have been in the direction of rent taxation which has been the focus of much of the debate on resource tax design. While much attention is given to CIT issues, design issues relating to other taxes such as labor taxes, VAT and other indirect taxes are also important.

This chapter considers these international tax issues. Section 2 discusses recent international corporate tax trends. Section 3 considers a number of key international tax issues for resource companies, including the important issues of double taxation and transfer pricing. Also considered are other CIT design issues, labor taxes and indirect taxes. Section 4 concludes.

2 International corporate tax trends and resource taxation

The most obvious international trend in CIT in recent years has been the significant decline in CIT rates. In many countries this decline has been accompanied by a broadening of the tax base, including (at least in higher income countries) reducing the level of tax incentives.[2] A more recent development has been the new CIT regimes such as the allowance for corporate equity (ACE). This section discusses those trends and considers whether they have any implications for resource taxation.

A Corporate tax competition

A steady decline in statutory CIT rates has been obvious across most regions, suggesting evidence of tax competition. For example, the average CIT rate in OECD countries has decreased from 36 percent in 1997 to 27.8 percent in 2007, while EU countries have experienced an even more significant decline, with the average rate falling from 35.5 to 24.2 percent during the same period.[3] Resource rich countries also appear to have followed this trend. For example, Keen and Mansour (2008) show that in Sub-Saharan Africa, for the period 1980 to 2005, the average CIT rates for resource rich countries declined (from 40 to 35.4 percent) but by slightly less than the average decline for the region (40.4 percent to 33.2 percent).

The main motive for tax competition appears to be to attract internationally mobile capital. It could be argued that resource rich countries may be less concerned with tax competition as the natural resources are location specific, so that the mobility of capital argument for tax competition is less relevant. If this is the case, then it would be expected that CIT rates may be higher in resource-rich countries, with a smaller reduction in CIT rates over time. However, it may be that countries compete even in the taxation of natural resources for other reasons, such as: the scarcity in the managerial and technical skills in resource extraction (Osmundsen, 2005); scarcity in available finance for resource projects; or imperfect competition.[4]

Despite the international trend to reduce CIT rates, corporate tax revenues have not necessarily fallen.[5] For many countries, CIT revenues as a share of GDP have broadly remained unchanged. In the OECD, corporate tax revenues as a share of GDP actually increased from 2.8 percent of GDP in 1995 to 3.7 percent of GDP in 2005.[6] The trend in developing countries has also been to reduce rates but it appears that corporate tax revenues have fallen, suggesting that tax bases have not been broadened sufficiently to offset the rate reductions.[7] Keen and Mansour (2008) suggest that, at least for Sub-Saharan Africa, including for resource rich countries, the trend may be more positive. The outcome for resource rich countries is not unexpected given the commodity price boom in recent years.

For CIT revenue as a share of GDP to have remained broadly unchanged in many countries it must be that the reduction in rates has been offset by an expansion of the tax base. Reasons given for the expansion include: a reduction in tax incentives; improved tax administration; increases in corporate profits as a share of GDP; increased volatility of corporate profits coupled with the asymmetric treatment of losses (tax being due when profits are positive, but no rebate being paid when they are negative);[8] and a shift to incorporation as CIT rates are reduced relative to rates of personal taxation. The last argument is less likely the case for resource rich countries, at least in the resources sector, as it would be expected that most participants in the sector would be incorporated due to the size and nature of the operations in the sector. While the sector is likely to have been affected by the winding back of general tax incentives, it will usually continue to be entitled to some sector specific incentives due to the size and importance of the sector, and often its political influence. For example, when Australia reviewed its business tax regime in the late 1990s it reduced the CIT rate and broadened the tax base by removing accelerated depreciation, including for assets used in the resources sector. However, it continued to retain the special immediate write-off of exploration and prospecting expenditure.

The reduction in CIT rates, and the potential for loss of revenues, appears to strengthen the case for resource rent taxes in resource rich countries. Resource rent taxes may provide a way of exploiting any lesser intensity of tax competition in the resource sector. In any case, the revenue impact of a reduction in CIT rates may be blunted as, with given royalties or resource rent tax, a reduction of CIT should increase the range of projects that crosses any hurdle rate for investors, potentially yielding more resource taxes to the government.

There are a number of benefits from combining a reduction in statutory CIT rates with base-broadening, including lowering the marginal tax rate (although the extent of this will depend on the country's fiscal situation), improving economic efficiency – due to a more efficient allocation of resources as a consequence of removing distortions created by incentives – and reducing complexity in the tax system. Despite these benefits, there are concerns with tax competition and the potential 'race to the bottom' – that is, one country's cut in the tax rate or reduction in the tax base (by an increase in tax incentives, for instance) makes others worse off (due to a loss of revenue, investment and/or profits) so that other countries respond, resulting in tax rates which are too low and/or tax bases too narrow in terms of the collective interest. This is especially a concern for developing countries, where fiscal mobilization is often a priority (emphasizing the importance of revenue from the resources sector).

Regional coordination

The concerns with tax competition suggest that some form of international cooperation on a regional basis could reduce the pressure for tax concessions, including in the resources sector. Regions, such as the EU and more recently the Central American countries, have moved in the direction of cooperation through codes of conduct, treaties, or simply notifying other members of current and new incentives. The main purpose of this coordination is usually to reduce harmful tax competition within the region. While resource rich countries may be less willing to cooperate due to the location specific nature of the resources, there could still be benefits in cooperation.[9] A recent example of coordination in the mining area is the common mining code being developed in the West African Economic and Monetary Union.

In developing regional cooperation there are three key issues to consider: (i) the set of countries which may be willing to enter into a coordination agreement; (ii) the form of coordination; and (iii) the coverage of any agreement. Ideally it would be best if all resource rich countries could participate; otherwise there is a risk that a non-participating country could reduce the effect of coordination by offering a more favorable regime compared to that offered by the countries cooperating. The coordination could take a number of forms, such as a non-binding code of conduct or a binding regional treaty. The experience in the EU, and more recently in Central America, is that binding commitments are likely to be more effective. In the EU the binding state aid rules are widely considered to be more effective than the non-binding code of conduct, while in Central America a treaty commitment has been considered necessary. The coordination agreement could cover issues such as tax rates, incentives, non-discrimination of foreign investors, and transparency.

B New CIT regimes

A more recent development in the design of the CIT is that countries have been considering more fundamental restructuring of the CIT, some of which move towards the taxation of rents, a topic which is of interest to policymakers concerned with the resources sector. These new regimes include:

Allowance for corporate equity (ACE)[10]

The ACE, which has been adopted in Belgium (and was used in Croatia from 1994 to 2001), is an attempt both to eliminate the arbitrary discrimination between debt and equity finance, and move the CIT closer to a pure profit tax. Under the ACE, a corporation can deduct against CIT not only interest paid on its debt but also a notional return on its equity, calculated using an interest rate that theory suggested be set at something approximating a risk-free nominal rate (Belgium uses the ten-year government bond rate as a proxy).[11] There are a number of advantages of an ACE compared to a standard CIT, including: (i) ensuring neutrality for financing choices, as firms will be indifferent between debt and equity finance in terms of their CIT implications; (ii) neutrality to investment, whatever depreciation scheme is adopted,[12] as no tax is charged on marginal projects – for such projects the after-tax return should match the pre-tax return; and (iii) the system is not affected by inflation, as any increase in monetary profits that is due to inflation will be offset by a higher notional return, as the notional interest rate will also be higher as a result of inflation. There are two main disadvantages of the ACE: (i) due to the narrower tax base, the CIT rate may need to be higher in order to collect the same amount of revenue, which could be harmful in the presence of tax competition; and (ii) there is doubt as to whether some countries will allow double tax relief for tax payments under the ACE (although this has not been the experience in countries which have adopted the ACE – see the discussion on foreign tax credits later in this section).[13]

Zero-rate CIT on retained earnings

The zero-rate CIT has been adopted in Estonia, which repealed the standard CIT in favor of taxing only dividend distributions. This model has attracted interest from other countries, especially in Eastern Europe and Central Asia. Under the zero-rate CIT, retained earnings are not taxed, while the company is taxed at 21 percent on the amount of dividend distributions (regarded by Estonia as a CIT). Dividends paid to residents are not subject to further tax while dividends paid to non-residents are subject to a withholding tax at a rate that depends on whether or not a double taxation agreement is in place. While in principle the system is attractive in its simplicity and efficiency, and in treating debt and equity financing broadly uniformly, there are concerns with the system including: (i) the zero-rate CIT is not fully compatible with the EU Parent-Subsidiary Directive, and Estonia has been asked by the European Commission (EC) to change the system as of 2009;[14] (ii) it may create new distortions, such as lock-in effects for corporate profits;[15] (iii) there are questions as to whether foreign parent companies can credit the tax under pre-existing double taxation agreements; and (iv) most importantly, a move to such a system could well involve a significant revenue loss.[16]

Restrictions on interest deductibility

These restrictions have been adopted (for example, by Denmark, Germany and Canada) with the objective of limiting interest deductibility of corporations. The policy objective is similar to the ACE in that instead of treating dividends like interest, at least a portion of interest is treated like dividends. The measures introduced in Denmark and Canada were aimed at tax planning techniques using debt financing relating to foreign subsidiaries, while in Germany the measure was partly aimed at stimulating the use of equity.[17]

The impact of these new regimes on taxpayers in the resources sector is likely to be similar to that on other taxpayers. The neutral treatment of debt and equity under each of the regimes may lead to a shift towards greater use of equity financing, although the resources sector appears to be less reliant on debt financing than other industry sectors. For example, the debt to equity ratio of mining companies (other than oil, gas and coal) in Canada in 2003 was 52.9 percent which was much lower than the all industry average of 92.1 percent. The average debt to equity ratio for the oil and gas extraction and coal mining companies, at 100.4 percent was similar to the all industry average.[18] A similar outcome arises in the United States where the debt to equity ratio of most companies in the sector is below the all industry average. For example, the average debt to equity ratio in 2003 for coal companies (97 percent), metals and mining companies (73 percent) and petroleum companies (83 percent) was below the all industry average of 108 percent, however, the ratio for natural gas companies was higher at 181 percent.[19] The generally lower debt to equity ratio for the resources sector may reflect debt holders' lower tolerance of risk than equity holders, considering that resources, which are the main assets of the company, are not good collateral because of price volatility. It may also reflect concerns with the ability to fully claim deductions for interest due to loss carry forward limitations or the some-times project specific basis of resource taxation.

In the case of the ACE, investors in the resources sector may seek a separate notional interest rate for the sector to take account of the higher risk (and there-fore the higher required rate of return) of resource projects. However, if the aim of the ACE is to avoid distorting investor's decisions (both financing and invest-ment) then a single rate is appropriate, and there is a strong argument for using a risk-free rate.[20] In any case, adoption of different notional interest rates for dif-ferent sectors could be unnecessarily complex.

The adoption of a zero-rate CIT on retained earnings in a resource rich country may have the advantage of encouraging resource companies to retain profits and, hence, reinvest in the country, in particular in further developing the resources sector. This reinvestment may not always be efficient as it could lead to a lock-in of profits which could be better used elsewhere in the economy.

From an international tax perspective, questions arise as to the foreign tax credit implications of the ACE and zero-rate CIT (there is a more detailed dis-cussion of foreign tax credits in the next section). It appears that despite the tax base for the ACE being different to the tax base for the standard CIT, countries are likely to accept taxes paid under the ACE as creditable. Investors into Belgium, and previously Croatia, do not appear to have had any difficulties in obtaining credits for taxes paid under the ACE. Similarly, it appears that inves-tors into Estonia have been able to claim credits for Estonia's tax at the corpor-ate level on dividends paid: there is an apparent acceptance by other countries that the tax is a tax on profits, rather than a withholding tax on dividends, and therefore may be treated as an underlying corporate tax for crediting purposes. This means that a company in another country receiving dividends may be enti-tled to a tax credit for both withholding taxes on the dividends as well as the tax paid by the company in Estonia on the dividend. A concern with the zero-rate CIT on retained earnings is that, if a country only imposes the usual dividend withholding taxes without the tax at the corporate level on dividends, there could be treaty implications. Some double tax treaties have 'subject to tax' clauses which essentially require that double tax relief will be provided on dividends received in the residence country on the condition that the profits in the source country are subject to CIT. Therefore, in the case where the source country does not tax the profits but only imposes a withholding tax on payment of the divi-dend, the residence country could deny double tax relief. Estonia appears to have overcome this concern by successfully arguing that its tax is a tax on profits imposed on distribution, rather than simply a dividend withholding tax. However, if the zero-rate CIT was designed to simply tax dividends in the share-holders' hands, relying solely on withholding taxes, then this may cause a problem.

3 Selected international tax issues for resource companies

This section discusses a number of international tax policy design issues which are important to consider in designing a resource tax regime.

A Double taxation (foreign tax credits)

Probably the most important international tax issue is the treatment of foreign tax credits. It is usually accepted that the country in which profits are derived (the *source country*) has the first right of taxation on that income, although the source country may forgo that tax for its own policy purposes or under a double tax treaty (this would be rare for rents from natural resources). Countries in which the tax-payer resides (the *residence country*) have two broad choices for taxing foreign source income earned by their residents: the worldwide tax system and the territo-rial tax system.[21] Under *worldwide (or residence) taxation*, foreign source income earned abroad is taxed in the taxpayer's country of residence. A tax credit (known as a foreign tax credit) may be given for income taxes levied in the source country, usually up to the amount of domestic tax on the income (since foreign income could be taxed at a different rate in the source country). Under *territorial taxation* – based on the source principle of taxation and sometimes referred to as the *exemp-tion system* – foreign source income is exempt from tax in the taxpayer's country of residence and, therefore, is taxed only in the source country.[22]

In practice, no country has a pure worldwide system or a pure territorial system. Countries with a worldwide tax system often have elements of a territorial system – in particular, deferral of tax on certain foreign source income until it is repatri-ated to the country of residence. Countries with a territorial system often impose limitations on access to the exemption so that foreign source income falling outside those limitations is taxed in the country of residence. For example, to prevent tax avoidance, the exemption usually does not apply to passive income such as, inter-est, rent, royalties and portfolio dividends. Also, countries applying a territorial system usually only allow an exemption if the resident company holds a signific-ant (non-portfolio) interest in the foreign company and may not exempt 100 percent of the foreign income. A more accurate description of countries would be those with a predominantly worldwide tax system and those with a predomi-nantly territorial tax system. Table 13.1 lists countries which have a predominantly worldwide system or predominantly territorial system.[23]

As many resource companies are multinational companies, and it is usual for resource companies to be taxed in the producing (source) country, the treatment of foreign source income in their residence countries is important. In particular, companies which are residents of countries with worldwide taxation (such as the

Table 13.1 International tax systems for dividends received by corporate taxpayers, 2008

Predominantly worldwide system	Predominantly territorial system
Ireland	Australia
Japan	Austria
United Kingdom*	Belgium
United States	Canada
	Denmark
	Finland
	France
	Germany
	Italy
	Luxembourg
	Netherlands
	Portugal
	Spain
	Sweden

Note
* The UK government announced in November 2008 that it intends to move to a territorial system from 2009 for large and medium size businesses.

United States, United Kingdom and Japan), will be taxed in their home country on resource profits and therefore may be subject to higher tax payments in their home country, or may even be subject to double taxation, unless foreign tax credits are available for taxes paid in the source country. The clear implication is that if the taxes in the source country are not creditable then investing in the source country is unlikely to be attractive for investors from countries with a worldwide system.

Whether or not a tax is creditable depends on the particular tax law in the residence country and on any double tax treaties in place (unless the territorial system applies). However, a tax paid in the producing country that in nature resembles a home country income tax (for example, is on net income rather than – like a royalty – gross income) is most likely to qualify for a tax credit. Some specialized mineral taxes, such as a resource rent tax and in particular payments under a production sharing agreement, may be deemed to differ in nature from a standard corporate tax and, therefore, could face difficulties in qualifying for a tax credit. Some developed countries such as Australia, Canada, the United Kingdom and the United States, offer credit for some of these types of taxes, but often with restrictions and sometimes only under a double tax agreement (see Box 13.1 for a discussion of the law in the United States). The treatment of these taxes can be clarified by making it clear in a double tax treaty that such taxes are covered by the treaty (for example, the UK treaties often refer to its petroleum revenue tax and the Australian treaties often refer to its petroleum resource rent tax and include it as a tax on income).

The crediting of taxes on foreign source income also has tax rate setting implications for a resource rich country. If a source country offers a low CIT or resource rent tax rate and the investor is from a country with a worldwide

Box 13.1 United States crediting of resource taxes

Section 901 of the Internal Revenue Code allows a credit against US income tax for the amount of any income, war profits or excess profits tax paid to a foreign country. The regulations (see Regs. 1.901–2 and 1.901–2A) provide that a foreign levy is a creditable income tax if: (i) it is a tax; and (ii) the 'predominant character' of that foreign levy is that of an income tax in the United States. A foreign levy is considered to be a tax if it is a compulsory payment pursuant to the authority of a foreign country to levy taxes. There are three requirements that a foreign levy must satisfy to qualify as an income tax:

- Realization: the tax is imposed on or after an event that would result in the realization of income under the Internal Revenue Code.
- Gross receipts: the tax is imposed on gross receipts which are not greater than fair market value.
- Net income: the base of the tax is computed by reducing gross receipts by the recovery of significant costs and expenses reasonably attributable to the gross receipts.

However, a foreign levy is not a tax if the payer receives, directly or indirectly, a specific economic benefit from the foreign country (the payer is referred to in the law as a 'dual capacity taxpayer' – that is, the payer is making a payment in their capacity as both taxpayer and acquirer of an economic benefit). An economic benefit includes a right to use, acquire or extract resources (such as government-owned petroleum). These regulations appear to address two broad concerns: (i) as the state often both grants the mineral right and levies income taxes, the high tax rates on some oil and gas profits could partly represent payment for the grant of the mineral rights: and (ii) the foreign government may be disguising royalty payments as taxes so that the companies can claim foreign tax credits for the royalties.

In order to determine which portion of the payment is for an economic benefit and which is similar to an income tax, the regulations set out a safe harbor formula which limits the credit available to the amount of tax that would have been paid in the foreign country by a non-dual capacity taxpayer. Any excess tax is deductible rather than creditable (similar to the tax treatment of royalties).

In addition to these rules there are further special crediting rules (under section 907) which apply to two types of foreign income from natural resources:

- Foreign oil related income (FORI), which is income from processing, transporting, distributing or selling oil and gas (and/or its primary products) and income from disposal of assets used in those activities; and
- Foreign oil and gas extraction income (FOGEI), which is income from the extraction of oil and gas and from the disposal of assets used in the extraction activities.

In the case of FORI, the foreign tax credit is reduced to the extent that the credit relates to tax which is materially greater than the tax that would be imposed by the foreign country on income which is not FORI. The excess is deductible. The foreign tax credit for FOGEI is limited to the U.S. CIT rate with any excess able to be carried over to other years. These provisions could apply where, for example, a resource rich country imposes a differentially higher CIT rate on oil or gas activities.

system, then there is essentially a transfer of revenue from the source country government to a foreign government. Therefore, a resource rich country could set the rate at a level sufficient to soak up the foreign tax credits in the residence country.[24] However, if a significant investor country, such as the United Kingdom or United States, moved to a territorial system this could make it more difficult to protect high tax rates and hence could have a significant impact on tax rates and tax revenues in resource rich countries.

Similarly, if the source country offers a tax incentive to resource companies (such as a tax holiday), that concession may be undone in the residence country if it has a worldwide system, unless the two countries have a double tax agreement that allows for tax sparing – that is, a form of double tax relief where the effect of a tax incentive provided by the source country is preserved in the residence country (Japan allows tax sparing in some treaties while the United States does not). In contrast, if the investor is from a country with a territorial system, then generally no further tax will be paid in the residence country irrespective of the tax rate (or tax incentives) provided by the source country. An exception would be if the residence country imposes conditions on the exemption, such as the profits not being derived in a tax haven.

A source country can also assist in maximizing the foreign tax credit in the residence country by ensuring that any offsetting of one domestic tax against another domestic tax is done in a way that does not reduce whichever of those domestic taxes is creditable in the residence country. For example, a source country may be indifferent if a tax on royalty is creditable against a CIT or vice versa. However, for a foreign investor, the CIT is more likely to be creditable in the residence country and therefore they would prefer the CIT to be creditable against the royalty in the source country. Of course, more certainty can be provided by clearly separating royalties and income taxes.

Double tax treaties

As mentioned previously, double tax agreements can play an important role in determining the taxing rights of the source country as well as avoiding double taxation. These agreements may contain special provisions relating to the resources sector. The usual purpose of these provisions is to ensure source taxing rights on income from the exploration for, or exploitation of, natural resources. Resource rich OECD countries such as Australia, the United Kingdom, Norway and Denmark have such provisions. This is usually achieved through expanding the general definition of a 'permanent establishment' in the treaty to include activities for the exploration and exploitation of natural resources, in addition to the usual coverage of a mine, gas or oil well, a quarry, or any other place of extraction of natural resources. A 'permanent establishment' arises where a business has an enduring presence in the source country, so that the source country has the taxing rights on the profits of that business. The other provisions of a double tax treaty which may include reference to natural resources include: as mentioned previously, the taxes subject to a treaty may specifically include resource taxes to ensure those taxes are covered for double tax purposes; and, immovable property (for purposes of treaty articles relating to income or capital gains from such property, including shares in companies the assets of which are primarily immovable property) will normally include rights to work natural resources.

Another factor to consider in negotiating tax treaties is the level of withholding taxes. A country may negotiate different withholding taxes, such as for royalties, for different treaty partners. This variation in rates may pose problems for developing countries in negotiating with investors in the resources sector who may seek to force down withholding tax rates in resource agreements to the lowest rate available in the host country's treaties. A better approach is to try to limit the variation in withholding rates. In any case, developing countries may have little to gain from setting low withholding tax rates on income sourced in their country, as the withholding tax can be a back-up defense for transfer pricing and any reciprocal low rates in the other country are likely to be of little benefit due to the probable limited income flows from that country.

The withholding tax concerns raise the question as to whether it is beneficial for resource rich countries, especially developing countries, to enter into double tax treaties. On balance, the benefits of double tax treaties in determining taxing rights and avoiding double tax are likely to outweigh the withholding tax concerns.[25] Interestingly, the experience of resource rich countries in entering into double tax treaties varies. For example, Kazakhstan has a fairly extensive treaty network for a developing country, with 39 treaties, while countries such as Venezuela and Saudi Arabia[26] have less than 10 double tax treaties. A similar difference arises for resource rich countries in the OECD, with Canada and Norway each having over 80 treaties while Australia has less than 50. This evidence suggests that, while investors in the resource sector may pursue governments to enter into double tax treaties in order to provide tax stability and to ensure creditability of taxes, other factors may be more important, such as political pressures and negotiating capacity.

B Transfer pricing and other anti-avoidance rules

One of the key challenges for all governments is how to protect the revenue base in the face of aggressive tax planning. Multinational companies, including in the resources sector, are often at the forefront of this tax planning. Governments across the world have responded to this challenge by introducing rules to limit the impact of aggressive tax planning, such as abusive transfer pricing, thin capitalization and controlled foreign corporation rules.

Transfer pricing

By a transfer price is simply meant the price or value charged in transactions between related parties. Abusive transfer pricing is when these prices are misstated in order to shift the apparent source of profits to the taxpayer or jurisdiction which provides the most advantageous tax outcome. A taxpayer seeks to minimize income and maximize deductions in high-tax jurisdictions and vice-versa in low tax jurisdictions. While the usual concern relates to transactions across countries, abusive transfer pricing can also arise domestically between companies that face different marginal CIT rates, either because they are subject to different statutory rates (as a consequence, for example, of special incentive regimes, or as is sometimes the case of resource companies, for which the tax rate may be higher) or because of differing loss positions. Transfer pricing is an issue for all multinational companies, and no less so for the resources sector. While for some (though by no means all) resources there may be a readily available world market price for the tangible product flows, establishing such a price for many other transactions, such as those involving intangibles and services, is likely to be more difficult. Governments are concerned that abusive transfer pricing may erode the tax base, while investors are concerned with certainty of the tax treatment of their cross-border transactions.

There are many opportunities for abusive transfer pricing in the resources sector. For example, extraction or production, refining, marketing and distribution of the resource could arise in a number of different tax jurisdictions. Other examples of abusive transfer pricing in the resources sector include: claiming excessive fees for managerial and technical services shared by a company's international operations; licensing of intellectual property in low tax jurisdictions; and providing capital goods and machinery in leasing arrangements at above-market costs.

Abusive transfer pricing is often difficult to detect and prevent. Despite these difficulties, as a minimum the tax law should provide that transactions between related parties should be on an arm's length basis – that is, the transfer price is that which truly independent parties would reasonably have expected to pay. Taxpayers should be obliged to declare and justify pricing for related party transactions. The burden of proof for prices should be with the taxpayer, not the state. As mentioned previously, an arm's length price may be readily available for the tangible resource product flows, but for many other transactions, in particular those involving intangibles and services, it is difficult to establish arm's length prices. This is particularly the case with very complex organizational structures which involve multiple firms in different jurisdictions. This uncertainty can lead to disputes between taxpayers and the tax authorities, which can be a disincentive for investors, and create an administrative burden for tax administrators. The uncertainty can be partly alleviated by ensuring there are clear, transparent and fair mechanisms for dispute resolution available to taxpayers.

To overcome these concerns it is useful to establish a clear sequence of alternatives. For example, the OECD has a set of transfer pricing guidelines, which consider country specific circumstances and describe a sequence of acceptable methods for setting transfer prices (see Box 13.2). The advantage of these rules is that they establish an internationally accepted basis for determining arm's length prices. While developing countries may find it difficult to implement these laws, the OECD does offer assistance (mainly through regional training workshops) to developing countries to help them implement and administer the rules in a broadly standard way, while reflecting the country's particular circumstances.

Box 13.2 OECD transfer pricing guidelines

The OECD Guidelines, *OECD Transfer Pricing Guidelines for Multinational Enterprises and Tax Administrations*, set out two broad categories of transfer pricing methods: the traditional transaction methods and the transactional profits methods.

The *traditional transaction methods* are preferred by the OECD as they are most direct, although under the guidelines the taxpayer must choose the method which gives the best estimate of the arm's length price. The traditional transaction methods include: (i) comparable uncontrolled price (CUP) – comparing the price for a transaction to third party dealings in a comparable uncontrolled transaction in similar circumstances; (ii) resale price – ascertaining a price based on the goods or services provided together with a normal profit margin in a transaction with an unrelated third party; and (iii) cost plus method – ascertaining a price based on the costs incurred by the supplier plus a mark up taking account of the functions performed and the market conditions.

The *transactional profits methods* consider the profits that arise from related party transactions. and include: (i) profit split method – considering the value of each party's contribution to the profit; (ii) transactional net margin method – considering the net profit margin relative to an appropriate base (such as costs, sales, assets).

Another measure to reduce the potential for tax avoidance through related party transactions and to provide certainty for both taxpayers and tax administrators is the use of advanced pricing agreements (APAs). An APA is an agreement between the authorities and taxpayer as to the transfer prices, or methodology, that will be accepted in some future transaction(s). These are now used by many countries, and can be especially useful in the resources sector due to the substantial investment involved in resources projects and the significant revenue implications for the authorities. One concern for the resource sector could be the usual three- to five-year time period for APAs, which is unlikely to be long enough to cover long-term resource contracts. However, some countries allow longer time periods depending on the taxpayer's circumstances, while most countries also provide a process for renewing APAs which is less onerous than the original APA process.[27] In any case, a longer term APA may be disadvantageous to a taxpayer if there are changes in the critical assumptions on which the APA is based.[28]

APAs can also be used in determining prices for domestic transactions. For example, the petroleum resource rent tax laws in Australia were recently updated to allow the Commissioner of Taxation, with the agreement of the taxpayer, to determine the gas transfer price in the case of an integrated gas-to-liquids project. A more recent international development has been the negotiation of bilateral and multilateral APAs.[29]

Monitoring transfer prices and negotiating APAs requires specialized skills which are often scarce in the tax administrations of developing countries. One option for overcoming these limitations is for regional cooperation in negotiating APAs or at least agreeing on the methodology to be used by countries within a region. This may help provide certainty for taxpayers and partly alleviate the limitations posed by the skills gap.

Thin capitalization

Thin capitalization is a situation in which the owner(s) of a corporation, either directly or through related entities, provide it with an artificially large amount of capital by way of debt rather than equity. While there may be commercial reasons for financing a project with a large amount of debt, governments and revenue authorities are concerned that this can provide significant tax savings because, unlike dividends, interest payments reduce the corporate tax base. The extent of the savings will depend on such features of the tax system as capital gains tax rules, withholding taxes, and the treatment of dividends. For example, debt finance is more tax advantageous than equity in a country which double taxes corporate profits (at the corporate level, and again on payment of the dividend), the CIT rate is relatively high, or where opportunities for a double deduction for cross-border debt may be available (for example, Canada has recently proposed limiting a practice where complex cross-border transactions were used to 'double dip' interest deductions.)[30]

The response of many countries to thin capitalization has been to design rules that limit the amount of interest deductions where the ratio of debt to equity is, in the authority's view, excessive. These rules may deny interest deductions if the substance of the debt arrangement is to reduce tax, although the usual approach is to legislate a specific test debt to equity ratio. Any single test debt to equity ratio will do rough justice to some companies, since reliance on debt naturally varies across different activities. Specifying sectoral rates such as for the resources sector, however, will only add to complexity and provide another source of dispute. The international practice is for test debt to equity ratios to range between around 1.5:1 and 4:1 (for example, Netherlands, Spain, Hungary, Australia and Japan use a 3:1 ratio, the United States uses a similar ratio as an administrative guide, while the ratio in France is 1.5:1). These ratios are usually based on average debt and equity over a year. As mentioned previously, some countries have adopted further interest restrictions which complement the thin capitalization rules in denying interest deductions relative to earnings.

Controlled Foreign Corporations (CFCs)

CFC rules are intended to combat the sheltering of profits in companies resident in low-tax or no-tax jurisdictions. They usually apply to companies located in low tax jurisdictions and controlled by a resident shareholder, their essential feature being that they attribute a portion of the income accrued in such companies to that resident shareholder, irrespective of repatriation of the income. Generally, only passive income (such as dividends, interest, rent and royalties) fall within the scope of CFC legislation, not active income (such as from genuine activity in the low-tax country). CFC rules can also have implications for a source country which may set its tax rates at such a low level that it triggers CFC provisions in another country. This could lead to a transfer of revenue from the source country government to a foreign government and may also make the country less attractive to foreign investors.

For many companies operating in the resources sector it is unlikely that CFC rules will apply to their resource activities as the multinational company will clearly be conducting genuine business activities in the source country. However, CFC rules could apply if the resource company tries to avoid home tax by parking the profits in another jurisdiction to delay repatriation. There may also be cases where a tax administration may conclude that certain related activities are treated in a similar way to passive income. For example, see Box 13.3 for a discussion of special US Subpart F rules (the US CFC rules) which apply to US oil companies.

Box 13.3 Special US subpart F rules for oil companies

US oil companies can be required to include as currently taxable income certain foreign base company oil related income earned by their foreign subsidiaries including: income derived outside the United States from the processing of minerals extracted from oil or gas wells into their primary products; the transportation, distribution, or sale of such minerals or primary products; the disposition of assets used by the taxpayer in such a trade or business; and the performance of any related services. The rules do not apply if the income is derived in the same country in which the resources are extracted or used. The rules also only apply to large producers, which are defined as companies producing more than 1,000 barrels per day. The effect of these rules is that the profits will be taxed in the United States when they are derived, even if the profits are not repatriated to the United States. These rules were introduced in 1982 because the US Congress was concerned that US oil companies paid little or no US tax on the high revenue of their foreign subsidiaries. Congress determined that multinational oil companies earned significant revenues from activities performed after the oil had been extracted, (such as the transporting, refining, trading and retail sales of the petroleum) and that the fungible nature of oil (oil from different locations being readily substituted) and the complex structures involved suited tax haven type operations.[31]

International cooperation – information exchange

One of the most effective ways of combating international tax evasion is by effective exchange of information between tax authorities.[32] This exchange of information is especially important in monitoring the activities of multinational companies. Double tax agreements typically contain provision for information exchange, although often with various restrictions, such as the absence of an obligation to provide information that the tax authorities do not routinely acquire. Over the last few years both the OECD and the EU have taken major steps to strengthen international information exchange, as part of their wider efforts to counter harmful tax practices. For example, the OECD revised the exchange of information article (Article 26) of its Model Income Tax Treaty in order to specifically provide that the obligation of national governments to exchange information must override bank secrecy and other confidentiality laws. Exchange of information is important in dealing with the resources sector where there are many complex cross-border transactions between related parties.

C Cross border fields

Resource fields sometimes cross international borders (for example, between Norway and the United Kingdom, Australia and Timor-Leste, and Kuwait and Iraq). While these cross border fields raise political and jurisdictional issues, they also raise revenue issues. In particular, how the income from the resources is to be taxed in each of the source countries. To provide certainty for investors and reduce disputes between countries it is preferable for the countries to negotiate an agreement or treaty covering issues of cooperation such as infrastructure, licenses, access, dispute resolution, as well as the taxing rights of each country. If there is more than one field it may be preferable to have a single agreement covering the relevant area (for example, the UK and Norway have a treaty which covers all fields which straddle the UK-Norway North Sea Continental Shelf). A double tax treaty between the countries could also support the general cooperation agreement.

In deciding on a taxing regime, there are essentially two broad options:

- Apply a single taxing regime to the field, with each country receiving a share of the determined tax revenue (for instance, a percentage of royalties equivalent to each country's share of the field). While this provides taxpayers with some certainty, it requires cooperation between the participant countries' tax administrations and limits each country's ability to adjust the taxation of the field to align it with the taxation of resources solely within its borders.
- Each country might apply its own tax laws to its share of the profits, which would have to be split between the countries. While this option preserves each country's sovereignty with regard to tax regimes, it is likely to be more complicated for taxpayers and may deter investors who have to deal with the different regimes.

The latter option is likely to be more acceptable to governments. However, to operate effectively it will require a clear agreement between the relevant countries, setting out each country's rights and obligations.

D Other CIT design issues

There are other CIT design issues with international implications which may influence foreign investors' location choices.

Ring-fencing

One CIT design measure which may be imposed by a country is ring-fencing – that is, a limitation on consolidation of income and deductions for tax purposes across different activities, or different projects, undertaken by the same taxpayer. There are benefits for a government in ring-fencing as it can ensure government revenue where a company undertakes a series of projects and may wish to deduct exploration or development expenditures from each new project against the income of projects that are already generating taxable income. However, ring-fencing may hamper companies undertaking further exploration and development activities due to the inability to claim deductions for such activities on new projects. It may also encourage tax planning if the ring-fenced tax regime is more onerous than the standard tax regime. For example, locating lower-taxed downstream activities outside the ring fence, including in another jurisdiction, or transfer pricing to shift profits outside the ring fence or costs inside the ring fence. Another concern with ring-fencing is that it can be especially complex where one tax (such as a resource rent tax) is ring-fenced but another tax (such as the CIT) is not. If a government imposes ring-fencing then it is important to have provisions to cover the transfer pricing and other aggressive tax planning concerns.

Corporate reorganizations

Another CIT design issue likely to be of interest to foreign investors is the resource country's tax rules for corporate reorganizations (often involving mergers and acquisitions), including capital gains tax rules (for both shareholders and the company assets). Foreign investors may want to acquire a domestic company or restructure existing companies undertaking resource activities in a country. These corporate reorganizations are a common practice in business and are undertaken for a number of reasons including: economies of scale or scope; diversifying or expanding lines of business or markets; exiting businesses and inefficient structures; changing management structures; altering the balance or diversity of shareholder control; and improving tax outcomes. While many of these reorganizations are limited to companies resident in one jurisdiction, cross-border corporate reorganizations continue to increase with globalization. Many factors need to be considered in a corporate reorganization, such as regulatory issues, transactional costs, financial reporting requirements, and tax issues. Many countries provide special rules for corporate reorganizations to limit the taxable events that would otherwise arise on a corporate reorganization. For example, in most tax systems gains in value that accrue on most types of property are taxed on a realization basis (no matter the form of consideration). Absent a special arrangement, the transfer of an asset or the exchange of stock under a reorganization would therefore be a taxable event. If the asset was a depreciable asset, in most cases the 'new' owner would recommence depreciation based on the consideration for the asset. Also, tax attributes, such as losses, may no longer be available. Such tax outcomes seem inappropriate for a reorganization where there may be no change in the underlying ownership or use of the assets, and are likely to impede an efficient restructure.

It is for these reasons that many countries provide rules for tax neutral reorganizations. The broad objective of these rules is to find a balance between three important considerations: (i) removing tax impediments to restructuring, which may be important as an economy develops to meet the pressures of the global economy; (ii) ensuring that gains are taxed when a restructuring is used to enable companies and their shareholders to effectively realize the gains; and (iii) ensuring reorganizations are not used for tax avoidance. To achieve these broad objectives, three conditions are usually necessary for a tax neutral treatment of a corporate reorganization: (i) the ownership of the surviving companies is substantially the same as that of the predecessors; (ii) the assets, and hence business activities, of the surviving companies are substantially the same as that of the predecessors; and (iii) the reorganization has a genuine business purpose. If resource rich countries wish to achieve the broad objectives, they should seek to introduce rules to facilitate tax neutral reorganizations.[33]

A related issue is the tax treatment of the disposal of an interest in a resource project, when the disposal occurs offshore. For example, a foreign resident may wholly own a foreign company which, in turn, wholly owns a resident company undertaking a resource project. The foreign resident may dispose of the underlying ownership of the project by selling the interest in the foreign company. If the transaction had arisen in the source country, any gain may have been taxed in that country. However, as the transactions occurred offshore, the gain will arise in a foreign country. Rules can be developed to overcome this by essentially taxing gains on the disposal of a significant indirect interest in such property in the source country. These rules could be supported in treaties by giving the source country the taxing right on such gains.[34] However, such rules usually require the tax authorities being able to both identify the offshore transaction and trace the ultimate ownership of the companies, which can be difficult even for developed countries with sophisticated tax administrations.

Special zones

Another design issue for governments to consider is special zones. These go under many names – export processing zones, special economic zones, and free trade zones – and are usually designed to encourage exports and/or domestic processing (including in the resources sector) and also to attract labor intensive industries. These zones differ widely, including in the nature of any special tax treatment they offer. This is sometimes substantial, and may include partial or full exemptions for both direct and indirect taxes.

There are concerns with these zones, including: (i) they are prone to tax abuse – even though these zones are usually designed to ensure incentives only apply to exported goods and services, it is often difficult to ensure there is no leakage to the domestic market, while abusive transfer pricing is also possible; and,

(ii) potential violation of WTO rules (at least if subsidies or direct tax exemptions are provided, and except for least developed countries, which have a carve out). If tax incentives are to be provided in these zones then they should be restricted to customs and (though not to be recommended) indirect tax exemptions, so as to limit the revenue risk. It is also recommended that such zones be designated areas which are closely monitored, which suggests that such zones are not appropriate for upstream activities.

E Labor taxes

While the focus of this chapter has been on international corporate tax issues, it is worth briefly mentioning the personal tax issues relating to expatriates. Some countries provide tax incentives to workers in the resources sector to attract foreign labor. These incentives often take the form of reduced, or even zero, personal income taxes for expatriates. The objective is usually to attract labor because of the scarcity of managerial or technical skills (see the earlier comment in Section 2A that this could also be a reason for resource tax competition) and/or the reluctance of the local workers to undertake the work.

While these incentives can be effective in attracting workers, they may raise equity issues due to the different treatment of local and expatriate workers, and potentially inhibit the development of local expertise. Even if the earnings are exempt or taxed at a low rate in the source country, moreover, they may not always be exempt in the expatriate's residence country. The usual practice, in domestic law and in double tax treaties, is that the source country has the sole taxing right for salary and wage income. However, some countries may have as a condition that if an employee derives income in another country and that income is exempt then it is taxable in the residence country. This could limit the attractiveness of the source country exemption.

F Indirect taxes

Indirect taxes, such as customs duties and VAT, are also important to consider in the design of a resource tax regime. In principle, the resource sector should be treated in a similar way to other sectors. In practice, however, the resource sector is often treated differently because of the size and nature of its operations, or as a fiscal incentive to attract foreign investment.

Value added tax (VAT)

In resource rich countries, most, if not all, the output from the resources sector will be exported. Under a destination-based VAT (that is, the total tax paid on a good or service is determined by the rate levied in the jurisdiction of its final sale) it is usual to zero-rate exports (that is, no VAT is imposed on the supply of the goods or services and a credit is given for VAT on inputs). The effect of zero-rating is that exporters will be entitled to ongoing refunds for tax credits for inputs, including investment goods, which could be significant for taxpayers in the resources sector due to their very large investment needs. It may be difficult, especially in developing countries, to pay refunds in a timely fashion given that administrative capacity is often weak. In that case, the VAT becomes, in effect, an export tax. An export tax is not usually a preferred policy option, though it might in principle be appropriate if a country has power in the world market for some resource or cannot effectively tax income directly.[35] This situation with refunds is further exacerbated by the size of the VAT refunds, particularly during periods with large investment requirements.

The response adopted by many countries to this problem is to provide VAT exemptions for imported capital goods and sometimes imported inputs for the resources sector. This approach is not considered good tax policy as such exemptions are prone to abuse, complicate administration, and of course, may cost revenue which often has to be recouped from elsewhere in the tax system. Moreover, exempting imported capital goods could create a pro-import bias which could lead to a similar treatment being sought for domestic suppliers to projects (so as not to discriminate between domestic and foreign suppliers), which can be especially problematic due to the potential scope for domestic firms to evade VAT. However, if the capacity of the tax administration is not sufficient to adequately administer a refund-based system, then a specific sector exemption for capital goods may be necessary. Such an exemption should be limited to capital goods which are specific to the sector and preferably not available in, or resalable into, the domestic market. The exemption could be further project or time limited (for example, ceasing at the commencement of commercial production).

Customs duties

While import duties are becoming a less significant source of revenue for most countries due to trade liberalization, many countries, especially developing countries, still impose such duties – with potential implications for the resources sector. Like the VAT, the most significant impact for the resources sector will be felt through imported capital goods. Resource companies, which are looking to make a substantial investment, are likely to seek import duty exemptions for the capital equipment they need. Such exemptions can also be sought as a way to minimize dealings with customs officials: foreign companies with substantial import needs can be a target for corrupt behavior. The practice of some countries to deal with this issue is to exempt specialized equipment, such as for exploration and development, from import duties. If this is to apply, and assuming a country wants to continue to protect its import duty base, then the exemption could be limited to capital goods not available in the domestic market and further restricted by requiring the equipment be re-exported after its use (assuming the equipment is still usable). Project or time limitations could also apply.

Export duties are also becoming less significant, and in fact, many countries have now removed them altogether in order to facilitate trade. If exporters (actual or potential) are to take advantage of the greater opportunities provided by easier access to export markets (especially with the growing number of trade agreements), it is important that these opportunities not be vitiated by domestic policies (including tax policies) that impair exporters' international competitiveness. Despite the general move away from export taxes, they continue to be levied by some countries on natural resources (often timber, but sometimes minerals or oil) in the absence of alternative forms of taxes, or as a means to tax windfall gains, and/or encourage domestic processing. While the natural resources taxed by export duties are usually timber, some countries, such as Malaysia, Russia, Ghana and South Africa, impose export taxes on non-renewable mineral and energy resources. Unless there is some clear scope to exploit power in world markets – in which they can in theory raise national welfare, though only at the cost of others – the preferred tax policy is to remove export taxes, and develop an appropriate domestic tax on economic rents from natural resources to ensure the government's fair share of those rents, and, if a government wants to favor domestic processing, deploy a production subsidy that is both better targeted to that aim and more transparent.

4 Conclusions

In designing a resource tax regime it is clear that international tax issues must be considered if the regime is to be attractive to investors and at the same time ensure the government receives its intended share of revenue. Resource rich countries will want to ensure their right to taxation of the rents yet limit the potential for double taxation of profits derived by multinationals. This can be achieved by ensuring that domestic taxes are similar in nature to resource taxes levied in other countries, and also through negotiating double tax treaties which give recognition to the source country's right to taxation and also clarify that income-based resource taxes are covered by the treaty so as to ensure crediting.

Due to the complexity of transactions in the resources sector and the potential for tax planning, it is important to ensure the tax law has provisions to protect the revenue through transfer pricing and thin capitalization provisions which the authorities are able to be administer effectively. Certainty can also be provided to taxpayers, as well as the revenue authorities, through the use of APAs. The scope for regional cooperation should also be considered. There are also a number of broader tax design issues for the government to consider, embracing the CIT, labor taxes and indirect taxes, which can affect foreign investors' location choices. Most of these issues are not unique to the resources sector, but are of interest to foreign investors in other sectors.

Finally, in designing the tax system it is important to be aware of international tax trends. The resource sector is affected by the rise of international corporate tax competition and new CIT regimes. Even though natural resources are location specific, it is important for resource rich countries to monitor international tax trends.

Acknowledgments

I am grateful to Alan Fischl, Emil Sunley and conference participants for comments and suggestions. Views and errors are mine alone, and should not be attributed to the Australian Tax Office.

Notes

1 The administration of the tax laws in a country can also affect its attractiveness to foreign investors. For a discussion of issues relating to resource tax administration see Chapter 11 by Calder.

2 Devereux *et al.* (2002) discuss developments in corporate taxation, including the impact of tax rate reductions and base broadening on effective tax rates.

3 Based on a survey of CIT rates in KPMG (2007).

4 Boadway and Keen discuss these and other possible reasons for such competition in Chapter 2.

5 Prior, at least, to the crisis that began in 2008.

6 Based on data from OECD (2007).

7 For a discussion of these trends see Keen and Simone (2004).

8 Auerbach (2007) argues that this is what happened in the United States in recent years.

9 Although in Chapter 2 Boadway and Keen suggest that, as the reasons for tax competition are not fully understood, the case for coordination is less clear (for example, if downward pressure on tax rates reflects imperfections in market competition, than coordination is likely to be inferior to reducing these imperfections).

10 The use of an ACE as a tax base for taxing resource rents, and the proper choice of notional interest rate, is discussed further in Chapter 2.

11 Burggraeve *et al.* (2008) study the macroeconomic and fiscal impact of the Belgium ACE.

12 Faster depreciation, for example, reduces shareholder equity and hence future notional interest deductions – the two canceling out in present value terms.

13 For a fuller discussion of the ACE see Klemm (2007), and also see Keen and King (2002) for a discussion of the ACE in Croatia.

14 The EU Parent-Subsidiary Directive has two main objectives: (i) eliminating tax obstacles for profit distributions between groups of companies in the EU by removing withholding taxes on payments of dividends between associated companies in different member states; and (ii) preventing double taxation of parent companies on the profits of their subsidiaries (the exemption of the distributions is often known as the 'participation exemption'). In the case of Estonia's CIT regime the question was whether the tax on distributions imposed under the regime is a tax on profits which happens to be imposed at the time of distribution (which is Estonia's argument) or is a withholding tax on dividends which is subject to the Directive. The EC consider it is equivalent to a dividend withholding tax and therefore that Estonia's CIT regime is not in compliance with the Directive.

15 Some would argue, however, that the rate of tax applied to dividends should have no effect on payout decisions (so long as that rate is not expected to change): the tax must either be paid now if profits are distributed or later if they are retained and distributions made later, so that the tax is simply unavoidable.

16 Lehis *et al.* (2008), provide an overview of the Estonian CIT system in particular its compatibility with EU law.

17 The German reform disallows a tax deduction for net interest expense that exceeds 30 percent of earnings before interest, tax, depreciation and amortization where the net interest expense exceeds €1 million. In Denmark interest expenses are restricted by

two cumulative rules: (i) net financing expenses exceeding DKK 20 million are deductible up to a cap equal to the combined value of 6.5 percent of the tax base of Danish assets and 20 percent of the value of foreign subsidiaries; and (ii) a maximum interest deduction of 80 percent of earnings before interest and tax. The restrictions in Canada are explained in the later discussion on thin capitalization.

18 Based on data from Statistics Canada.

19 Based on information from the Capital Structure database at Stern NYU which is available on the web at: http://pages.stern.nyu.edu/~adamodar/.

20 Drawing on Bond and Devereux (2003), Boadway and Keen argue in Chapter 2 that in principle the appropriate level for the notional rate is that of a risk-free return.

21 A resident of a country in the case of an individual is normally determined by the person's usual place of abode. In the case of companies, residence can depend on factors such as place of incorporation, or place of management and control. Also, a company with a permanent establishment in the source country (that is, a business with an enduring presence in the source country) is usually treated like a resident.

22 For a discussion of the arguments for and against the territorial system see Mullins (2006), which discusses the debate in the United States on whether to introduce a territorial system.

23 Countries may also have a worldwide system in their law, but the practice may be different due to the administrative difficulty in taxing residents on their worldwide incomes, for example, owing to a lack of information (often because of lack of information sharing with other countries).

24 Care needs to be taken to ensure the tax is not limited to countries which offer foreign tax credits, as the United States have a 'soak-up' rule which denies a credit if the source country's tax is dependent on whether the residence country offers a foreign tax credit.

25 It is worth noting that another benefit for developing countries in negotiating double tax treaties is their positive impact on foreign direct investment (FDI). Neumayer (2006) provides evidence that double tax treaties increase the flow of FDI to middle-income developing countries.

26 In Saudi Arabia, non-resident companies investing in the country are subject to tax, while Saudi resident companies are exempt.

27 In the United States 30 percent of APAs executed in 2007 were for a period greater than five years. Also, the average time to complete an APA renewal was 25.5 months, compared to 38.2 months for new APAs (Internal Revenue Service (2008)).

28 Although it may be transparent to publish APAs, this would not be the usual practice due to privacy concerns around protecting taxpayer information as well as taxpayer reluctance to release what may be sensitive commercial information. However, one option is to publish optional safe harbour APAs which can help ensure that taxpayers in certain industries are treated in a similar manner.

29 For example, of APAs executed in the United States between 1991 and 2007, 350 were unilateral, 413 were bilateral and ten were multilateral (Internal Revenue Service (2008)).

30 These transactions sought to obtain two deductions for the same financing expense. Under the arrangements a deduction was claimed in both Canada and abroad (often in a low tax jurisdiction), even though in some cases the income from the investment may not be taxable in Canada if the foreign country has a tax treaty with Canada. It was also possible to arbitrage differences between Canadian and US tax rules to obtain a similar outcome. For a fuller explanation of the so-called 'double-dip' see the press release of the Canadian Minister of Finance on May 14, 2007 (Press Release 2007–041).

31 For a discussion of the history of the Subpart F rules, see Office of Tax Policy (2000).

32 See Keen and Ligthart (2006) for an overview of information exchange including a review of the key economic, legal and practical concepts, and issues bearing on the

analysis and implementation of information exchange, and an account of recent policy initiatives and emerging theoretical insights. For a discussion of the merits and limits of information exchange see Tanzi and Zee (2001).

33 For a more detailed discussion on designing rules for the tax treatment of corporate reorganizations see Vanistendael (1998).

34 For example, Article 13 of the OECD Model Tax Convention provides that gains derived by foreign residents may be taxed in the source country if the gains arose from the alienation of shares deriving more than 50 percent of their value from immovable property situated in the source country.

35 See Harrison and Krelove (2005) for a discussion of VAT refunds and how countries have attempted to deal with VAT refund concerns.

References

Auerbach, Alan J. (2007), 'Why Have Corporate Tax Revenues Declined? Another Look,' *CESifo Economic Studies* (Munich: CESifo).

Boadway, Robin and Michael Keen (2010), 'Theoretical Perspectives on Resource Tax Design,' in Philip Daniel, Michael Keen, and Charles McPherson (eds.) *The Taxation of Petroleum and Minerals: Principles, Problems and Practice.*

Bond, Stephen R. and Michael P. Devereux (2003), 'Generalised R-Based and S-Based Taxes Under Uncertainty,' *Journal of Public Economics*, Vol. 87, pp. 1291–1311.

Burggraeve, K., P. Jeanfils, K. Van Cauter and L. Van Meensel (2008), 'Macroeconomic and Fiscal Impact of the Risk Capital Allowance,' *Economic Review*, National Bank of Belgium, pp. 7–47, (Brussels, Belgium).

Calder, Jack (2010), 'Resource Tax Administration: The Implications of Alternative Policy Choices,' in Philip Daniel, Michael Keen, and Charles McPherson (eds.) *The Taxation of Petroleum and Minerals: Principles, Problems and Practice.*

Commission of the European Union Countries (2001), 'Company Taxation in the Internal Market,' Commission Staff Report COM (2001) 582 (Brussels, Belgium).

Devereux, Michael P., Rachel Griffith and Alexander Klemm (2002), 'Corporate Income Tax Reforms and International Tax Competition,' *Economic Policy*, Vol. 17–35, pp. 451–495.

Harrison, Graham and Russell Krelove (2005), 'VAT Refunds: A Review of Country Experience,' IMF Working Paper 05/218 (Washington DC: International Monetary Fund).

Lehis, Lasse, Inga Klauson, Helen Pahapill and Erki Uustalu (2008), 'Compatibility of the Estonian Corporate Income Tax System with the Community Law,' *INTERTAX*, Vol. 36, Issue 8/9, pp. 389–399.

Keen, Michael and John King (2002), 'The Croatian Profit Tax: An ACE in Practice,' *Fiscal Studies*, Vol. 23, pp. 401–18.

Keen, Michael and Ligthart, Jenny E. (2006), 'Information Sharing and International Taxation: A Primer,' *International Tax and Public Finance*, Vol. 13, pp. 81–110.

Keen, Michael and Mario Mansour (2008), 'Revenue Mobilization in Sub-Saharan Africa: Key Challenges from Globalization,' paper presented at the conference, 'Globalization and Revenue Mobilization' (Abuja, Nigeria).

Keen, Michael and Alejandro Simone (2004), 'Tax Policy in Developing Countries: Some Lessons from the 1990s, and Some Challenges Ahead,' in Sanjeev Gupta, Ben Clements, and Gabriela Inchauste (eds.) *Helping Countries Develop: The Role of the Fiscal Policy*, pp. 302–352 (Washington DC: International Monetary Fund).

Klemm, Alexander (2007), 'Allowances for Corporate Equity in Practice,' *CESifo Economic Studies*, Vol. 53, 2/2007, pp. 229–262.

KPMG (2007), *Corporate and Indirect Tax Rate Survey 2007*.

Lehis, Lasse, Inga Klauson, Helen Pahapill and Erki Uustalu (2008), 'Compatibility of the Estonian Corporate Income Tax System with the Community Law,' *INTERTAX*, Vol. 36, Issue 8/9, pp. 389–399.

Mullins, Peter (2006), 'Moving to Territoriality? Implications for the US and the Rest of the World,' *Tax Notes International*, Vol. 43 (10), 2006, pp. 839–853.

Neumayer, Eric (2006), 'Do Double Tax Treaties Increase Foreign Direct Investment to Developing Countries?' *The Journal of Development Studies*, Vol. 43, pp. 1501–19.

Organisation for Economic Co-operation and Development (2007), *Revenue Statistics, 1965–2006* (OECD: Paris).

Office of Tax Policy (2000), 'The Deferral of Income Earned Through US Controlled Foreign Corporations: A Policy Study' (Washington DC: Department of Treasury).

Osmundsen, Petter (2005), 'Optimal Petroleum Taxation Subject to Mobility and Information Constraints,' in Solveig Glomsrød and Petter Osmundsen (eds.) *Petroleum Industry Regulation within Stable States*, pp. 12–25 (Ashgate: Aldershot).

Tanzi, Vito and Howell H. Zee (2001), 'Can Information Exchange be Effective in Taxing Cross-Border Income Flows,' in Krister Andersson, Peter Melz, and Christer Silfverberg (eds.) *Modern Issues in the Law of International Taxation* (Kluwer Law International).

United States, Internal Revenue Service (2008), 'Announcement and Report Concerning Advance Pricing Agreements' (Washington DC: Internal Revenue Service).

Vanistendael, Frans (1998), 'Taxation of Corporate Reorganizations,' in Victor Thuronyi (ed.) *Tax Law Design and Drafting*, Vol. 2 (Washington DC: International Monetary Fund).

Part V
Stability and credibility

14 Contractual assurances of fiscal stability

Philip Daniel and Emil M. Sunley

Introduction

Mining and petroleum agreements governing the exploration and development of natural resources frequently include contractual assurances of stability. These stability clauses are intended as legally binding commitments by the host country's government. The commitment may be for an initial period of years or for the length of the agreement. They may cover a broad-range of host country laws or be limited to fiscal laws or even certain provisions in the fiscal laws, such as tax and royalty rates. This chapter primarily addresses contractual assurances of fiscal stability.[1] "Fiscal stability" here means stability and predictability in the taxation, production-sharing, pricing, or state participation rules that govern the division of proceeds from a resource project.[2]

Fiscal stability clauses are generally justified by: (1) the large size and the sunken nature of the initial investment, and (2) often a long period required to recover investment and earn a reasonable return, taken together with (3) a lack of credibility on behalf of the host country to abstain from changing the fiscal rules – possibly singling out high rent petroleum or mining operations – once the investment is sunk (the "time inconsistency problem").

It can be argued that the need for a fiscal stability clause is less compelling under certain conditions: a history of sound fiscal management, statutory and effective corporate tax rates in line with international rates, low tariff rates and non-imposition of taxes that distort investment and production decisions (e.g. asset taxes, excises on machinery), non-discrimination between domestic and foreign investors, a low level of corruption, a transparent tax policy process, and a reasonably efficient tax administration. Adaptability and progressivity in the fiscal regime may also serve as an alternative. There may also be other forms of intervention that reduce risk to investors (subsidies, infrastructure provision, perhaps even state equity shares). Fiscal stability clauses are more common in mining and petroleum agreements negotiated by developing or transition countries than in those negotiated by developed countries. Some developing countries with a significant petroleum sector, including Angola and Nigeria, and most developed countries, including Norway and the United Kingdom, do not grant fiscal stability clauses in their petroleum agreements.[3]

This chapter focuses on *contractual* assurances because these have emerged as the instrument of choice in preference to attempts to *legislate* for fiscal stability (Brown 1990, Cameron 2006). Although, in principle, it is feasible to have constitutional devices to constrain the freedom of a legislature to enact new laws, in practice this is rare in the fiscal arena. What parliaments enact parliaments may undo. For this reason, attempts to provide in law that a tax regime is immutable, or to guarantee the stability of contractual fiscal terms by converting the contract into law, are usually seen as insufficient in themselves. Governments may, however, bind themselves by contract to compensate (or exempt or indemnify) an investor, if changes to an agreed fiscal regime, or components of it, are made by law or otherwise. For this to be effective, it is necessary that the government has a clear power in law to make such a contract, that there is an acceptable mechanism for adjudicating an alleged breach (usually international arbitration), and that any award made as a result of the breach of the contract is enforceable. Enforceability commonly requires that, in respect of the particular contract, the government has waived the right to rely on immunity against such proceedings or awards that its sovereign status usually provides.[4]

Such contractual assurances take various forms. The most common are: (1) those that provide for exemption from or compensation for any specified fiscal change, and (2) those that provide for some form of "rebalancing" of contract terms to deal with a tax-induced change in the expected benefits to a party. There are very few known cases where alleged breaches of such assurances have been brought to arbitration or litigation, raising important questions about the real function of such assurances. In earlier times, however, many cases were brought by companies about actions by governments that were alleged to amount to expropriation. Legal review of fiscal stability clauses has therefore tended to proceed by analogy with these earlier circumstances.[5]

A Mining and petroleum fiscal regimes

The government, as resource owner, has a valuable asset in the ground. This asset – crude oil, natural gas, or hard minerals – can only be exploited once. To convert this asset into financial resources, the government may use various fiscal instruments that will attract investment as well as secure a reasonable share of economic rent for the government.[6] The government can collect revenue from the resource sector by a variety of tax and non-tax instruments. Most countries collect the government share of economic rent either through a tax/royalty regime or a production sharing arrangement.[7] Both types of fiscal regimes include production-based and profit-based levies. There may also be bonus payments and annual rental payments, but these are less important. In some countries, the government participates more directly in project development as a shareholder.

A tax/royalty regime may involve three levies: (1) a royalty to secure a minimum payment, (2) the regular income tax, and (3) an additional tax, such as a resource rent tax, to capture a larger share of the profits of the most profitable projects.

Under a production sharing arrangement there usually is an explicit royalty payment. In addition, the parties agree that the contractor will meet the exploration and development costs in return for a share of any production that may result. The contractor will have no right to be paid in the event that discovery and development does not occur. In principle, the government retains and disposes of its own share of petroleum or minerals extracted, though joint-marketing arrangements may be made with the contractor.

The mechanics of production sharing in principle are quite straightforward. The production sharing contract (PSC) will usually specify a portion of total production, which can be retained by the contractor to recover costs ("cost oil"). The remaining oil (including any surplus of cost oil over the amount needed for cost recovery) is termed "profit oil" and is divided between the government and the contractor according to some formula set out in the PSC.

A petroleum or mining agreement under a tax/royalty regime, a production sharing regime, or a hybrid of both may include a fiscal stability clause – the focus of this chapter. Whether or not a natural resource agreement includes a fiscal stability clause, a robust fiscal regime will more likely ensure fiscal stability and reduce the pressure to renegotiate agreements. A robust fiscal regime is one that produces a reasonable sharing of risk and the economic rents between the governments and investors over a wide range of outcomes where prices, costs, and the quality of any discoveries are uncertain. In general, a robust fiscal regime ensures that the government's share of revenue increases when the natural resource project is highly profitable. A robust fiscal regime is therefore adaptable and progressive.

There is not one optimal fiscal regime suitable for all resource projects in all countries. Countries differ, most importantly in regard to exploration, development, and production costs; the size and quality of natural resource deposits; and investor perception of commercial and political risk. Ultimately, there is a market test for each country's fiscal regime – can the country attract investment in its petroleum or mining sectors? If not, the fiscal regime may be inappropriate.

B Why should companies want – and governments grant – fiscal stability assurances?

Fiscal stability assurances are a possible answer to what is known as the time inconsistency (or dynamic inconsistency) problem in government policies. The problem occurs when a government announces a policy in advance (such as a tax regime), but after the fact finds it welfare-increasing to go back on the commitment implied by the policy.[8] Although the reversal of the commitment might provide the greatest welfare over a short time horizon, the cost comes in perceptions that the government reneges on its promises, and has lost credibility. Future social welfare will then be reduced because the government can adopt only those policies that do not require it to have credibility. When "time-inconsistent" actions, such as a unilateral tax change, are an issue, then rules rather than discretionary policy making produce a better outcome. When discretionary policy is maintained, there may be under-investment: companies become reluctant to invest where the weakness of their bargaining position, once investment is sunk, may be exploited. Fiscal stability assurances are one variety of "rules" that are used to overcome this problem.

Fear of future tax rises can produce sub-optimal investment decisions at each of the margins of exploration, development, and production. Petroleum and mining are both highly capital intensive, so that the risk of failure to go forward with investment in projects at the development stage has especially damaging effects. A credible commitment not to change tax terms once investment has been committed should, in principle, raise the level of investment. This applies both at the level of the country as a whole, for securing the optimal level of exploration and development investment overall, and within an individual project where incremental investment decisions can be made as production proceeds.[9]

Despite desirability of commitment to tax stability on these grounds, it is difficult to achieve. First, the full life-cycle of a petroleum or mining project can be very long, and that of a petroleum or mineral province as a whole much longer. A typical planning horizon for the production phase of a large petroleum field might be 20 to 25 years, after an exploration and development phase that might have taken ten years. A few large mines still operate around the world that are more than 100 years old;[10] among modern developments, productive lives in excess of 25 years are common.[11] These horizons are far longer than the life expectancy of most governments.[12] Governments may be able to make commitments of their own, but cannot bind the legislative competence of the state in future. Contractual assurances of fiscal stability represent efforts to navigate around this feature.

Second, it may be difficult for fiscal arrangements to envisage all possible economic outcomes. Pressures may arise from investors (in adverse circumstances) and from governments (when projects yield returns above expectations) for changes in terms. In addition, the substantial sunk and immobile capital element in a project makes it effectively impossible for investors to switch to other locations in the face of an adverse change in fiscal terms. One of the tasks in design of fiscal regimes is to improve their adaptability and progressivity, subject to an appropriate apportionment of risks, so that the probability of contract stability is raised.

Assurances of fiscal stability made by governments have features in common with other institutional devices designed to promote wider fiscal discipline. They may not be quite what they seem. A strict reading of the relevant legal texts may raise questions about the power of the government to make the assurance, about the construction and arbitration of a dispute under its provisions, or about the enforcement of any award. These questions, however, may not cover the underlying purposes of parties to an agreement.

Recent discussion of fiscal institutions and fiscal rules has suggested three hypotheses about the effectiveness of arrangements made to promote fiscal discipline (Debrun and Kumar, 2008). By analogy, these are useful in interpreting the operation of fiscal stability assurances.[13]

The first is the "commitment" hypothesis: the presumption that, by entering into a fiscal stability agreement, governments have given themselves incentives to abide by a set of fiscal terms, seen as appropriate prior to the investment commitment. Alternatively, this hypothesis can encompass the attempt of one arm of government to bind the actions of another, or of a present government to bind the actions of a future one, in the belief that the public interest is thereby served.

The second is the "signaling" hypothesis. In this case, the "signal" is to other potential investors in the resource sector, first, that the government has a serious commitment to stability of fiscal terms, and, second, that if a project runs into difficulty it is not the result of government fiscal impositions. Alternatively, the "signal" could be interpreted as a signal of underlying competence, where the government is less likely to arrive in circumstances that it will need to turn to heavy resource taxes. On this interpretation, willingness to offer a fiscal stability assurance is part of the promotion of an attractive investment climate.

The third is the "smokescreen" hypothesis. This relates to the transparency of fiscal impositions on a project. A fiscal stability assurance could be constructed so that it remains in place, but when adherence to its full terms becomes too costly, governments "cheat" by use of devices not covered by the assurance. This hypothesis would explain efforts by companies to make such contractual assurances increasingly watertight. It would also pose challenges to attempts to restrict the scope of such assurances.[14]

Each of these will have a counterpart in company assumptions about the purpose and usefulness of a fiscal stability assurance. If companies believe they are a "commitment" device, they are likely to value the assurances, even if a company has no serious intention of invoking dispute proceedings under the assurance. If companies see them only as "signaling" devices (unless only competent governments are believed to signal), or still worse as a "smokescreen," then they are likely to find them less valuable.

The case for fiscal stability clauses lies in the large size of the investment, long period required to recover investment and earn a return, and lack of host country credibility. Fiscal stability clauses, however, may not be in the best interest of the shareholders. Let us assume that fiscal stability clauses reduce fiscal risk. This reduction in risk may come at the price of a lower take for the contractor all other things equal. Instead of laying off the fiscal risk through a fiscal stability clause, the shareholders might be better off if the contractors accepted fiscal risk in exchange for a lower government take. The argument would hold if shareholders can adequately diversify their fiscal risk.

In a few cases, governments have explicitly charged an "insurance premium" for a fiscal stability assurance. Examples are more common in mining than in petroleum. In the case of mining, Peru charges a 2 percent premium on the income tax rate where the investor takes a stability assurance.[15] Chile for many years offered a corporate income tax rate guaranteed for ten years, but at a rate significantly higher then the general corporate income tax rate. Papua New

Guinea introduced a premium on the income tax rate for the same purpose in 2002.

The difficulty with this argument (and with the insurance premium) is that the differential position of investors with and without fiscal stability assurances becomes a "license" for governments to change terms for those not protected. The contribution of a fiscal stability assurance to the overall credibility of the government's commitment to maintain a tax regime over a long period may thus be undermined.

C Fiscal stability in context

Stability of contract terms and the legal basis for a resource project encompasses more than fiscal stability alone. Peter Cameron describes the general notion of "stabilization" as "all of the mechanisms, contractual or otherwise, which aim to subject the contract provisions to specific economic and legal conditions which the parties considered appropriate at the time that the contract was concluded" (Cameron, 2006).

A fiscal stability clause is a contractual guarantee included in petroleum or mining agreement. In reviewing an agreement, the first question to be asked is whether the fiscal stability provision was granted and approved with full legal authority. The authority for a government to negotiate resource agreements is usually included in a country's petroleum or mining law, and this law may also include the authority for the government to include a fiscal stability clause in an agreement.

Some agreements contain fiscal provisions inconsistent with the country's fiscal laws. In general, negotiated agreements – i.e. contracts – cannot override a country's enacted legislation. Adding a fiscal stability clause to a contract with fiscal provisions inconsistent with enacted legislation may give the contractor some rights under the contract, but it does not cure the inconsistency between the contract and the enacted legislation. When contract provisions are inconsistent with enacted legislation, the contract may be submitted to parliament for approval, which would give the contract the force of law. This approach has been used in Liberia, Sierra Leone and other countries.

Fiscal stability clauses are not always neatly packaged and they need to be read in the context of other provisions in the mining or petroleum agreement, the relevant laws of the country, bilateral tax treaties and bilateral investment treaties. First, fiscal stability may be enhanced by domestic legislation – the mining or petroleum law, the investment law, the company law, (and contractual assurances) ensuring national treatment,[16] non-discrimination,[17] and arbitration of disputes. Contracts sometimes provide for renegotiation of terms if both parties agree. Some contracts also include "most-favored contractor" clauses, which provide that the contractor will be eligible for any benefits granted another contractor under a future agreement.

Second, there are two primary purposes of bilateral income tax treaties: (1) to mitigate double taxation of income and (2) to provide mutual assistance in combating tax avoidance and evasion. With respect to the first purpose, income tax treaties divide the taxing jurisdiction between the two countries that are party to the treaty and they usually include an article on the elimination of double taxation when a source of income is subject to tax in both contracting states. Treaties limit the right of a contracting state to tax capital gains, other than gains from immoveable property (real estate), realized by a resident – an individual or a company – of the other contracting state.[18] Treaties also provide for reduction in withholding taxes on dividends and interest income sourced in one contracting state and paid to a resident of the other contracting state.

Third, bilateral investment treaties set terms and conditions for foreign direct investment by residents from one contracting state in the other contracting state. These treaties usually include a number of guarantees – fair and equitable treatment, protections from expropriation, free transfers. They also allow for recourse to international arbitration. These guarantees, of course, may also be included in a country's investment law.

D Two formulations of the fiscal stability clause

In contracts, there are, in general, two formulations of the fiscal stability clause. Under the frozen law formulation, the laws in force when the agreement is signed are frozen for the life of the contract or for a period of years. In Liberia, the Amended Mittal Mineral Development Agreement[19] provides an example of the frozen law formulation:

> ... the CONCESSIONAIRE and its Associates shall be subject to taxation under the provisions of the Minerals and Mining Law and the Code and all regulations, orders and decrees promulgated thereunder, all interpretations (written or oral) thereof and all methods of implementation and administration thereof by any agency or instrumentality of the GOVERNMENT (the Code and all such regulations, interpretations and methods of implementation and administration collectively, the "Tax Corpus"), in each case as in effect as of the date of this Agreement.... For the avoidance of doubt, any amendments, additions, revisions, modifications or other changes to the Tax Corpus made after the Amendment Effective Date shall not be applicable to the CONCESSIONAIRE. Furthermore, any future amendment, additions, revisions, modifications or other changes to any Law (other than the Tax Corpus) applicable to the CONCESSIONAIRE or the Operations that would have the effect of imposing an additional or higher tax, duty, custom, royalty or similar charge on the CONCESSIONAIRE will not apply to the CONCESSIONAIRE to the extent it would require the CONCESSIONAIRE to pay such additional tax, duty, royalty or charge.

Under the agree-to-negotiate formulation, the parties to the contract agree to negotiate in good faith to maintain economic equilibrium if there are any adverse changes in the laws (or regulations). The Kurdistan Region model production-sharing agreement[20] provides an example of the agree-to-negotiate formulation:

> 43.2 The obligations of the CONTRACTOR resulting from this Contract shall not be aggravated by the GOVERNMENT and the general and overall equilibrium between the Parties under this Contract shall not be affected in a substantial and lasting manner.

> 43.3 The GOVERNMENT guarantees to the CONTRACTOR, for the entire duration of this Contract, that it will maintain the stability of the fiscal and economic conditions of this Contract, as they result from this Contract and as they result from the laws and regulations in force on the date of signature of this Contract. The CONTRACTOR has entered into this Contract on the basis of the legal, fiscal and economic framework prevailing at the Effective Date. If, at any time after the Effective Date, there is any change in the legal, fiscal and/or economic framework under the Kurdistan Region Law or other Law applicable in the Kurdistan Region which detrimentally affects the CONTRACTOR, the terms and conditions of the Contract shall be altered so as to restore the CONTRACTOR to the same overall economic position as that which CONTRACTOR would have been in, had no such change in the legal, fiscal and/or economic framework occurred.

> 43.4 If the CONTRACTOR believes that its economic position has been detrimentally affected as provided in Article 43.3, upon the CONTRACTOR's written request, the Parties shall meet to agree on any necessary measures or making any appropriate amendments to the terms of this Contract with a view to re-establishing the economic equilibrium between the Parties and restoring the CONTRACTOR to the position it was in prior to the occurrence of the change having such detrimental effect. Should the Parties be unable to agree on the merit of amending this Contract and/or on any amendments to be made to this Contract within ninety (90) days of CONTRACTOR's request (or such other period as may be agreed by the Parties), the CONTRACTOR may refer the matter in dispute to arbitration as provided in Article 42.1.

> 43.5 Without prejudice to the generality of the foregoing, the CONTRACTOR shall be entitled to request the benefit of any future changes to the petroleum legislation or any other legislation complementing, amending or replacing it.

Agree-to-negotiate fiscal stability clauses are more common than frozen law clauses, particularly in recent years.[21] Unless the clause is specified in great detail it may not be worth much. Under most resource agreements, the parties can by mutual agreement always agree to amend the agreement and thus an agree-to-negotiate fiscal stability clause may not add much protection for the contractor.

Under production-sharing agreements, the contractors usually pay income tax on their share of production, in part, because the contractors want an income tax in the host country that will be creditable against the income tax liability in the home country.[22] Some production sharing agreements provide that the income tax will be paid out of the government's share of production, and under these agreements the government's share of production would be higher, all other things equal (as there is no separate income tax payment). A significant advantage of this approach is that the contractors have fiscal stability with respect to the income tax – any future changes in the tax rules would affect only the allocation of the government's share between tax and non-tax oil. This option for achieving fiscal stability, which is not very widespread, is not discussed further in this chapter.

When tax laws are changed, existing projects or investments are often "grandfathered"; that is, exempted from the new rules. Grandfathering prevents retroactivity and ensures transitional equity, or so it is said. Grandfathering can also provide a kind of fiscal stability.

In general, when countries change their capital recovery rules making them less generous, the costs of investments that have already been made would be allowed to be recovered under the old rules. Similarly, if a country repeals its provisions for tax holidays, investments that currently are enjoying tax holidays would be grandfathered as long as they continue to meet any prior conditions. The repeal of tax holidays would only apply to new investments. Similarly, if a country repeals tax exemption for interest on government bonds, existing bondholders would usually be grandfathered, as they otherwise would incur a capital loss. However, if the general tax rate is increased, the tax rate on income from prior investments would not be grandfathered. Changing the tax rate that applies to income earned in the future (even from prior investments) is not viewed as a retroactive tax change and therefore grandfathering is not appropriate. Thus the general practice of grandfathering certain tax changes affecting prior investments does not provide fiscal stability for all tax changes and thus is more limited than the fiscal stability clauses included in petroleum and mining agreements.[23]

E Issues

Fiscal stability clauses raise a number of practical issues: (1) unsustainable benefits, (2) the frozen or reference law, (3) the offsetting change, (4) the one-way bet, and (5) fiscal stability as an option.

Unsustainable benefits

Fiscal stability, by locking in domestic laws as of the date the mining or petroleum agreement is signed, may provide contractors with unsustainable benefits, when there is significant change in circumstances or when the locked-in law is defective. The laws, of course, can be amended, but the amendments will not apply to existing contracts covered by the typical fiscal stability clause, unless the clauses are somehow rescinded, or there is voluntary agreement that amended arrangements will apply. We illustrate with a couple of examples.

Zambia

Mining Development Agreements were made from 1997 onwards in the context of privatization of the state-owned copper mines (Zambia Consolidated Copper Mines, ZCCM). At the time, the country was desperate for investment after a long period of decline at ZCCM, and with metal prices low. In exchange for substantial commitments to redevelop mines, investors acquiring assets were given fiscal terms that included a royalty rate of 0.6 percent, an income tax rate of 25 percent, privileges on withholding taxes and customs duties, in addition to the existing provisions of law on expensing of exploration and development capital expenditure.[24] Their obligations to share profits with the legacy ZCCM (through equity shares and price participation arrangements) were constrained by dividend distribution limits and lifetime maxima.

The agreements were successful in stimulating substantial reinvestment in the mines, despite the withdrawal of one major investor (apparently taking substantial losses) in 2002, just prior to the start of the recent commodity price boom. By 2006–2007, however, the growth of mine production and exports was so fast, with world prices reaching record levels, that the government's revenue take appeared paltry by comparison. The government acted first to revise the fiscal regime for new projects in 2007, and then in 2008 it amended the Mines and Minerals act to invalidate all existing Mining Development Agreements – thus also invalidating, under Zambian Law, the fiscal stability assurances. A new fiscal regime, containing a price-related windfall tax and a variable income tax, was introduced for the whole mining sector.[25]

At the time of writing, no legal challenge to the government's actions was apparent. These fiscal stability assurances were accompanied by international arbitration and a waiver of sovereign immunity.

Tanzania

In 1997–1998, Tanzania introduced a new Mining Act (1998), and amended its Income Tax Act to provide a new fiscal regime for the mining sector. The sector was moribund, though with numerous discoveries from prior exploration, so the new law aimed at jump starting mine development decisions by offering improved security of tenure and generous fiscal terms.[26] The package was successful in encouraging mine development: some four new mines were developed prior to the first amendments of the scheme in 2001, with many more in subsequent years, and Tanzania is now the third largest gold producer in Africa (after South Africa and Ghana), from zero formal production in 1997. It was not successful, however, in generating substantial revenues for the government from these new mines.

Among other incentives, the law provided an additional (annual) capital allowance of 15 percent of unredeemed development capital expenditure (i.e.

development capital expenditure that has not been offset against profits that would otherwise be subject to tax).[27] A similar provision (at 12 percent) existed in South Africa for gold mining capital expenditure.[28] This provision transformed the regular income tax into a modified resource rent tax (RRT),[29] assuming the 15 percent additional allowance approximates the contractor's opportunity cost of capital.

The 15 percent additional allowance applied to all unredeemed development costs. This led to a double dip. If all unredeemed capital costs are debt financed at 10 percent, no tax would be payable until the project has earned a 25 percent internal rate of return before tax and interest expense – a 10 percent return to pay the interest on the borrowed funds and an additional 15 percent return to cover the additional allowance.

Prevention of this outcome required that the 15 percent uplift would not apply to unredeemed capital expenditure which is debt financed. Alternatively, the law could have provided a denial of interest expense on debt used to finance assets subject to the additional capital allowance. The mining tax change also predated a reform of the liberal interest deduction provisions of the general Income Tax Act. Nevertheless, the law was clear: unredeemed development capital expenditure (uplifted by 15 percent) is offset each year against "gains or profits chargeable to tax," which would be after interest expense is deducted.

Because of high leverage and low operating margins, these companies paid no income tax for a significant period. This position became unsustainable – especially when gold prices began to rise – once it became clear that Tanzania was to attract significant amounts of foreign investment to the mining sector.

In 2001, the 15 percent additional capital allowance (together with certain other incentives) was repealed for companies entering into a mining Development Agreement after July 1, 2001. Existing mines were grandfathered. When the new Income Tax Act of 2004 was adopted – a complete rewrite of the Income Tax Act of 1973 – there was a general "grandfathering" rule for companies that have binding agreements with the government. In 2007, companies with fiscal stability assurances protecting the capital allowance, were reported to have agreed to forego the capital allowance in future and to have made significant payments of past tax that would have been due in the absence of the allowance (ICMM, 2009).

Mongolia

The discovery of the Oyu Tolgoi copper/gold deposit by Ivanhoe Mines in 2001 brought international attention to the Mongolian mining sector. When this deposit is developed, the resulting mine could be one of the largest copper mines in the world. To this end, the government in 2007 negotiated an Investment Agreement with Ivanhoe, and its partner Rio Tinto,[30] The government submitted the agreement to Parliament for approval, as the agreement overrode current law in a number of respects. Without taking action on the agreement, Parliament passed it back to the government. Negotiations are stalled at the time of writing.

The Oyu Tolgoi Investment Agreement that was submitted to Parliament contained the frozen law approach to fiscal stability for a long list of taxes and fees, including the dog tax and inheritance and gift taxes.[31] A major problem would have been that current income tax law is defective and would have conferred unintended benefits on the investor.[32] For example, the law's provision relating to transfer pricing between related parties only covers a parent/subsidiary relationship. Thus, transactions between two companies controlled by a third company would not come under the income tax law's definition of a related party. If this defect is not corrected, mining companies would be able to shift profits by using transactions between "related companies" that fall outside the income tax law's restrictive definition of related party. The income tax provision relating to excess use of debt (thin capitalization) is also too restrictive as it applies only to related parties narrowly defined. There are other ambiguities in the provision.

The frozen or reference law

When a petroleum or mining agreement contains a fiscal stability clause, problems may arise in determining just what the fiscal laws were when the agreement was signed. During the effective period of the stability clause, the laws will be amended, possibly several times a year. They may be totally redrafted. By the twentieth year of the contract, there is likely to be no one in the tax administration who remembers the fine points of the tax laws that applied 20 years ago. If the tax administration is dealing with a number of resource contracts signed over a period of years, contracts signed at different times, even during the same year, will be administered under a different set of fiscal laws, complicating tax administration.

The frozen or reference law for purposes of fiscal stability usually includes not just the actual law but all regulations, interpretations (which may or may not be publicly available), and all methods of implementation and administration.[33] Determining the "law" years ago can be a daunting task, though the companies benefiting are likely to maintain careful records.

Timor-Leste (formerly, East Timor) provides an example of the problems of determining frozen law. Before 1999, contractors in the "Zone of Cooperation" in the Timor Sea[34] were taxed in accordance with a treaty under both Australian and Indonesian law, with tax assessable under each reduced, in effect, by 50 percent to reflect the attribution of petroleum in the area. After Indonesia relinquished control of East Timor in 1999, the United Nations Transitional Administration in East Timor (UNTAET), acting on behalf of East Timor, agreed that the contractors would be taxed under East Timor's law but incorporating Indonesian law, frozen as of October 25, 1999. Although new petroleum fiscal legislation and other tax laws have been enacted since the restoration of independence in 2002, specific exclusions were made for four pre-existing production sharing contract areas such that the frozen Indonesian law would apply. In the case of the one major project in what is now the joint development area (90 percent of petroleum attributable to Timor-Leste, 10 percent to Australia), the frozen Indonesian law is supplemented by a specific Timor-Leste tax law for the project, and by a tax stability agreement. In common with all projects in the joint area, taxation is also subject to the double taxation code under the Timor Sea Treaty. The tax stability agreement "freezes" the whole package as at January 1, 2002, but is a two-way street, as discussed below.

The offsetting change

When a fiscal stability clause requires the parties to the natural resource agreement to negotiate terms so as to restore the economic position of the contractor, there may be troubles reaching an agreement. These agree-to-negotiate stability clauses presume that the effect of the change in the fiscal terms can be appraised and an offsetting change agreed to. If there is no uncertainty about costs and revenues and agreement on an appropriate discount rate, the effect of the change in the fiscal terms may be quantifiable. Under these conditions, an increase in the income tax rate could be offset by a reduction in the royalty rate, but the changed fiscal regime would have different economic effects at the margin. Moreover, with uncertainty as to costs and revenues, the offsetting change that would be appropriate under one set of assumptions would likely be too generous or not generous enough under a different set of assumptions.

One possible approach would be for the parties each year ex post to determine the offsetting adjustment, possibly a payment from the state to the contractor – that is, use retrospective adjustments to restore the contractor's economic position. This would require calculating pro forma tax returns under current law and old law each year. This would involve considerable administrative burden on the contractor and the government.

One-way bet

The fiscal stability clauses in many mining and petroleum agreements are asymmetric: protecting the contractor from adverse changes to the fiscal terms but passing on benefits of reductions in tax rates or other changes beneficial to the contractor, such as more liberal rules for cost recovery. If fiscal stability is a one-way bet and the government later wants to reduce tax rates and broaden the tax base, the company protected by the stability agreement will be entitled to the reduced rates but may not be subject to the provisions that broaden the tax base.[35] This can make future tax reform very difficult, especially if large contractors are protected by stability agreements that entitle them to all beneficial tax changes. Conferring future beneficial tax benefits on these contractors would provide them with a windfall. If a contractor wants a fiscal stability agreement, it would be reasonable for stability to be a two-way bet, which would be the case when the contractor is protected from unfavorable changes in the law and does benefit from favorable changes.

Of course, when the fiscal stability clause is a two-way bet, the government could, by statute, grant contractors the benefit of any new tax concessions, including rate reductions. Given changes in economic circumstances, this may be appropriate public policy.

As mentioned above, the Timor-Leste fiscal stability agreement for Bayu-Undan fixes tax parameters in both directions – the contractor does not benefit from tax reductions. This probably works well where the fiscal regime is in any case flexible, with strong reliance on profit and cash flow bases.

Fiscal stability is an option

When originally introduced in 1980, Chile's Foreign Investment Law (Decree Law 600) provided various investor protections and guarantees, including fiscal stability for ten years (extended to 20 years for investments exceeding US$50 million). In exchange for the guaranteed protection from changes in the income tax law, the investor was required to pay a combined corporate income tax and dividend withholding tax of 42 percent, excluding the specific mining tax. The general rate applicable on corporate profits and remittances at the time was 35 percent – 7 percentage points lower. An investor could waive fiscal stability but only one time. These arrangements have since been amended (Chile, Foreign Investment Committee, 2005), but a fiscal stability option remains available.

Mining companies have generally opted for fiscal stability and the higher tax rate in the early years of the project when the project is producing tax losses and before any profits are remitted. However, once the project begins to produce taxable profits, companies waive fiscal stability and take their chances that the generally applicable tax rate on profits and remittances will not be increased to a rate above 42 percent. Nonetheless, during the start up phase, the option for fiscal stability is an important guarantee for the investor.

The pattern of events in Tanzania and Zambia lends some support to this idea. Although, in retrospect, the fiscal regimes granted to mining in those countries proved too favorable to investors to be politically sustainable when circumstances changed, the initial packages did succeed in promoting the desired increase in investment. These packages consisted of both the favorable fiscal regimes and the contractual assurance of fiscal stability. A substantial expansion of the tax base in the mineral sector occurred. Tanzania first revised terms for subsequent investors – a standard procedure in petroleum producing countries when risks are reduced and prospectivity[36] is improved – and then implemented measures agreed by consensus to increase its take from existing mines. Zambia acted in a more radical fashion by legislating a revised regime without undertaking prior renegotiations.

In both these cases, the fiscal stability assurance initially acted as a "signaling" device, but it was not necessarily tenable through the originally specified term. Whether or not a government's actions in changing a fiscal regime, despite a fiscal stability assurance, prove acceptable may be a function of (1) the rapidity with which an investor has recovered initial outlays, with an acceptable rate of return, while the assurance is valid, and (2) the likelihood that, thereafter and under changed or unpredictable fiscal terms, established investors can continue to anticipate sufficient incremental returns.

These possibilities are inconsistent with a strict interpretation of *pacta sunt servanda* but they are consistent with some of the possible motivations for fiscal stability assurances sketched earlier in this chapter.

F Invoking a fiscal stability clause

There are few examples where the fiscal stability clause has been invoked in arbitration or court proceedings. The Duke Energy case, concerning a power project in Peru is an exception: "an investment dispute arising out of the imposition of taxes," where the tribunal found for the company, in part, because of the validity of a stability agreement.[37] Otherwise most of the case law cited seems to come from older cases about alleged expropriation (Cameron, 2006). One reason examples are difficult to come by is that invoking the fiscal stability clause in an agreement is the "nuclear option." Embarking on this path will lead to an irretrievable breakdown in relations between the host government and the contractors.[38] This is not an outcome that any party wants. This suggests that the real benefit of a fiscal stability clause may be to sow the seed of doubt in the host government that it might be invoked and thereby promote appropriate behavior.

G Contract renegotiation

Recent sources identify more than 30 countries that have revised their petroleum contracts or petroleum fiscal systems since 1999.[39] Wood Mackenzie (2008) identifies 28 countries where governments or national oil companies have changed terms for petroleum to increase their share of profits or government take. Most of these changes have occurred since oil prices began to rise again in 2002. The story is similar in the mining industry, though perhaps with fewer countries making changes.[40]

In some of these cases, fiscal stability assurance were included in agreements – illustrating that they do not necessarily prevent renegotiation, or unilateral action by governments, when circumstances are perceived to have changed. Cameron (2009, forthcoming) points out, however, that the absence of a fiscal stability assurance may make arbitrators less willing to rule in favor of companies where they allege that a fiscal change represents a breach of previously made commitments.[41]

Contract renegotiation appears to have occurred mainly where fiscal regimes in place did not contain instruments that could respond with adequate adaptability and progressivity to changed circumstances. In recent years, of course, this has usually meant adaptation in favor of governments; in the 1990s, on the other hand, the required adaptability was often in the direction of granting benefits to investors.

The cases of changes of terms also include some where the manner of change was consistent with the government's prior commitment to investors who entered before the change. Once risk was perceived to be reduced, tougher terms were offered. One means for achieving this is by including items among the fiscal terms in the criteria for bids at licensing rounds. Angola, for example, in its deep water licensing rounds of recent years, has used both bidding for bonuses and a rate-of-return production sharing scheme that responds well to changes of circumstances.

Conclusion

Fiscal stability clauses are common and may reduce investor risk and create a more favourable investment climate and thereby ensure that the government receives a larger share of the rents from the natural resource project, all other things being equal. On the other hand, if companies accept fiscal risk, all other things equal, they may receive a larger share of the rents from the project. Fiscal stability clauses can be problematical, leading to disputes between the government and the contractor. They are not a panacea for a poorly designed fiscal regime or for weak governance.

It is not obvious that a fiscal stability assurance ultimately constrains a government when the protected terms become clearly untenable, whether by reason of changed economic circumstances, errors in regime design, or simply a change of political direction. Nevertheless, the "seed of doubt" that the assurance will be invoked may well preserve a fiscal regime applicable to a contract for longer than would otherwise have been the case.

Countries that want to include a fiscal stability clause in their mining and petroleum agreements may want to consider a time-limited provision that would cover the capital recovery rules, the income and withholding tax rates, royalty rates, and a maximum rate on import duties. However, any tax law change that affects businesses generally (e.g. a change in the thin capitalization rules) and that does not discriminate against the petroleum or mining sectors would apply. Companies would also be able to rely on non-discrimination provisions and other protections in domestic law and investment and income tax treaties. The risk with such an alternative is that the "smokescreen" motivation comes into play.

A fiscal stability assurance, in the long run, is unlikely to be a substitute for a credible overall commitment by a government to maintenance of predictability in its fiscal regime. This predictability may not only mean fixed parameters, but also an anticipated process, or set of criteria, by which a government may modify a regime when circumstances require. The government's ability to make such a commitment is affected by the public perception of the appropriateness of a fiscal regime for securing a reward to the state on behalf of the population as resource owner.

Acknowledgments

The authors acknowledge, without implicating, Peter Cameron for guidance on legal issues, and Michael Keen and Joseph Bell for helpful comments.

Notes

1 Stability clauses have been used to insulate investors from having to implement new environmental and social laws. See International Finance Corporation (2008).
2 Thus the chapter is not concerned with fiscal stabilization in a macroeconomic sense.
3 Both Norway and the UK have fiscal regimes for North Sea petroleum projects that include the regular income tax and an additional tax to capture a share of the economic rents of the most profitable projects. The UK has changed its regime more frequently than Norway, and now applies two different regimes depending when the oil field was developed. Royalty was abolished in the UK in 2003. The Norwegian regime has been more stable although the royalty rates were changed from 10 percent to 8 and 16 percent in 1972; lifted for new fields in 1987; and later phased out. (See Nakhle (2008).)
4 A typical contract provision would state that:

> the Government on behalf of the Republic hereby irrevocably waives any right to rely on sovereign immunity in respect of arbitral proceedings...and further waives claim to immunity [from enforcement proceedings] and [from execution of any award against property or assets of Government that are used for a commercial purpose].

5 Cameron (2006) and Cameron (2010, forthcoming) provide a comprehensive survey, see also Bernardini (2008).
6 Countries may also establish state-owned companies to explore and develop natural resource deposits. This alternative is outside the scope of this chapter which addresses fiscal stability clauses in petroleum and mining agreements between governments (or state-owned companies) and private investors.
7 Production-sharing arrangements are far less common for hard minerals than for petroleum.
8 This description of the problem draws on a note by Eric le Borgne (2006); the problem has been widely recognized since the work of Kydland and Prescott (1977) in the field of commitments to monetary policy.
9 For an extended discussion of these points, upon which we have drawn, see Osmundsen (2010).
10 For example, the Ashanti GoldFields underground mine in Ghana.
11 Examples include the Freeport McMoran copper mine in West Papua, Indonesia, Escondida (and other mines) in Chile, El Cuajone and Toquepala in Peru, Bingham Canyon in Utah, US.
12 An interesting exception is Botswana, where continuity of party rule by democratic election has accompanied substantial continuity of mineral contract arrangements.
13 These are not precise reformulations of the hypotheses set out by Debrun and Kumar, but possible views of fiscal stability assurances suggested by their wider analysis of fiscal institutions and rules.
14 A frequent recommendation in FAD technical assistance.
15 Peru offers stability assurances under its general legislation, and a broader legal stability assurance under its mining legislation.
16 National treatment provides that domestic and foreign investors can make investment in a country on the same terms.
17 Non-discrimination provides that there will be no discrimination between foreign investors from different countries.
18 Some treaties provide that gains derived by a resident of a Contracting State from the alienation of shares deriving more than 50 percent of their value directly or indirectly from immovable property situated in the other Contracting State may be taxed in that other State.
19 The Mineral Development Agreement between the Government of the Republic of

422   *P. Daniel and E.M. Sunley*

Liberia and Mittal Steel Holdings N.V. dated August 17, 2005, and the Amendment thereto dated December 28, 2006.

20 See: www.macleoddixon.com/documents/Draft_Kudrdistan_Region_Production_ Sharing_Contrct_June 2007.pdf, last accessed: June 12, 2008.

21 However, as most mining and petroleum agreements are confidential, it is not possible to quantify trends in the use of fiscal stability clauses.

22 The United States and the United Kingdom (until 2009) are home countries that tax world-wide income of their resident companies. In general, when distributions are remitted from a foreign subsidiary to a parent company in the United States or the United Kingdom, the parent company includes the dividend and the underlying corporate tax and any withholding tax on the dividend in taxable income. The parent company then is able to claim a foreign tax credit for the income and withholding tax paid in the host country up to the amount of home country's tax on the foreign source income. Under US tax rules, a foreign income tax paid out of the government's share will only qualify for the foreign tax credit if certain technical conditions are met.

23 Professor Michael Graetz has argued that grandfathering is economically inefficient although he does favor some phased-in relief. See Graetz (1977). This seminal article by Professor Graetz has generated a rich literature on grandfathering and other forms of transitional relief.

24 The revisions to legislated fiscal terms appear to have been sufficiently controversial that they were specifically backed by a retrospective amendment to the Mines and Minerals Act of 2002. The amendment, now repealed, provided that the development agreement "may contain provisions which notwithstanding the provisions of any law or regulation shall be binding on the Republic...."

25 The government subsequently removed the windfall tax in its budget of 2009.

26 Both Tanzania and Zambia exemplified an international pattern at the time. It should be recalled not only that the price of gold had fallen from a high of $500 per oz in late 1987 to close below $300 at the end of 1997, but also that the country was recently emerging from an extended period during which expropriations of both foreign and national businesses had been widespread.

27 Not including exploration capital expenditure.

28 See Van Blerck (1992), 13.3 to 13.12.

29 A RRT is imposed only if the accumulated cash flow from the project is positive. The net negative cash flow (in the early years) is accumulated at an interest rate that, in theory, is equal to the contractor's opportunity cost of capital adjusted for risk. RRTs have been levied in Australia and Papua New Guinea, but in addition to the regular income tax not as a replacement for it.

30 For a copy of the agreement, see www.openforum.mn/index.php?coid=1835&cid=329, last accessed: June 5, 2008.

31 To our knowledge, companies do not pay inheritance and gift taxes.

32 There are other provisions that need liberalizing. For example, the loss carryover period is limited to two years.

33 See the Mittal agreement quoted earlier.

34 The 1972 treaty between Australia and Indonesia establishing a seabed boundary between the two countries left a gap in the boundary in the Timor Sea, known then as the "Timor Gap." This gap occurred because any seabed boundary between East Timor and Australia would have had to be established by Australia and Portugal. In 1975, Indonesia invaded East Timor. In 1989, Australia and Indonesia bilaterally concluded the Timor Gap Treaty in which they permitted the exploration and exploitation of petroleum resources in the area of disputed sovereignty.

35 Depending on the exact wording of the fiscal stability clause, a company protected by an agree-to-negotiate stability clause may only be able to negotiate an offsetting change if a package of changes leaves the company in an adverse economic position. However, the Kurdistan model agreement, cited above, would allow the contractor to

request the benefit of any future changes. In effect the contractor could cherry pick a balanced tax reform package combining, say, lower tax rates with less favorable capital recovery rules.

36 "Prospectivity" means the likelihood of making a petroleum discovery, and then also the likelihood that any discovery can be commercially developed.

37 Duke Energy International Peru Investments No. 1 Ltd v Peru, ICSID Case No. ARB/03/28, IIC 30 (2006).

38 See, for example, Louis T. Wells and Rafiq Ahmed (2006).

39 Wood Mackenzie (2008), Quiroz (2008).

40 At least eight cases are known to the authors, covering: Chile, DR Congo, Guinea, Liberia, Mongolia, Peru, Tanzania, and Zambia.

41 Citing the 2007 ICSID award in Parkerings-Compagniet AS v. Lithuania, ICSID Case No. ARB/05/8, IIC 302 (2007), dispatched September 11, 2007.

References

Bernardini, Piero (2008), "Stabilization and Adaptation in Oil and Gas Agreements," *Journal of World Energy Law and Business*, Vol. 1, pp. 98–112.

Brown, Roland (1990), "Contract Stability in the Petroleum Industry," *CTC Reporter* No. 29, pp. 56–60 (New York: United Nations).

Cameron, Peter D. (2006), *Stabilisation in Investment Contracts and Changes of Rules in Host Countries: Tools for Oil and Gas Investors*, final report for Association of International Petroleum Negotiators (AIPN), available at: www.aipn.org.

—— (2010), forthcoming, *International Energy Investment Law: The Pursuit of Stability* (Oxford).

Chile, Foreign Investment Committee (2005), available at: www.cinver.cl/index/plantilla2.asp?id_seccion=1&id_subsecciones=140.

Debrun, Xavier and Manmohan S. Kumar (2008), "Fiscal Rules, Fiscal Councils and all that: Commitment Devices, Signaling Tools or Smokescreens?" in *Fiscal Policy: Current Issues and Challenges*, Proceedings of the 9th Banca d'Italia Workshop on Public Finance (Rome: Banca d'Italia).

Graetz, Michael (1977), "Legal Transitions: The Case of Retroactivity in Income Tax Revision," No. 126, *University of Pennsylvania Law Review*.

International Council on Metals and Minerals (ICMM) (2009), *Minerals Taxation Regimes: A review of issues and challenges in their design and application*, ICMM and Commonwealth Secretariat (London, United Kingdom).

International Finance Corporation (2008), "Stabilization Clauses and Human Rights," draft, *Research project conducted for IFC and United Nations Special Representative to the Secretary General on Business and Human Rights*, March No. 118.

Kydland, Finn E. and Edward C. Prescott (1977), "Rules Rather Than Discretion: The Inconsistency of Optimal Plans," *The Journal of Political Economy*, Vol. 85, pp. 473–492.

Le Borgne, Eric (2006), "Windfall Taxes," *Tax Issues Papers (TIPS)* (Washington DC: International Monetary Fund).

Nakhle, Carole (2008), "Can the North Sea Still Save Europe," *OPEC Energy Review*, Vol. 32, Issue 2, pp. 123–138, available at: http://ssrn.com/abstract=1209254 or DOI: 10.1111/j.1753-0237.2008.00146.x.

Osmundsen, Petter (2010), "Time Consistency in Petroleum Taxation – The Case of Norway," in Philip Daniel, Michael Keen, and Charles McPherson (eds.) *The Taxation of Petroleum and Minerals: Principles, Problems and Practice*.

Quiroz, Juan Carlos (2008), *Survey of Recent Contract Renegotiations and Other Changes Initiated by Producing Countries in Their Oil and Gas Industries*, draft, Revenue Watch Institute.

Van Blerck, Marius (1992), *Mining Tax in South Africa*, Taxfax CC (Rivonia, South Africa).

Wells, Louis T. and Rafiq Ahmed (2006), *Making Foreign Investment Safe: Property Rights and National Sovereignty*, Oxford University Press.

Wood Mackenzie (2008), Note on *Fiscal Storms*, available at: www.woodmackenzie.com (London: Wood Mackenzie).

15 Time consistency in petroleum taxation

Lessons from Norway

Petter Osmundsen

1 Introduction

Operating as they do in some of the world's more unpredictable and unstable countries, petroleum companies face considerable political risk. A hot topic in the energy sector at present is the expropriation of investment by host states. According to Erkan (2008), direct expropriation has been rather exceptional over the past two decades and has been replaced by indirect (creeping and regulatory) expropriation.

The question of the ability and willingness of governments to commit themselves to a fixed policy is relevant to a number of aspects of economic policy. It is particularly important in relation to industry's long-term frame conditions.

Many central banks conduct monetary policy in accordance with a fixed rule, typically the stabilisation of inflation. Kydland and Prescott (1977) were awarded the Nobel Prize for economic sciences in 2004 for demonstrating how the effects of expectations about future economic policy can give rise to a *time consistency problem.* If economic policymakers are unable to commit in advance to a specific decision-making rule, they will often fail to implement the most desirable policy later on. Kydland and Prescott's results offered a common explanation for events which, until then, had been interpreted as separate policy failures – when economies become trapped in high inflation, for instance, even though price stability is the stated objective of monetary policy. This research shifted the practical discussion of economic policy away from isolated policy measures towards the institutions of policymaking, a shift which has largely influenced the reforms of central banks and the design of monetary policy in many countries over the past decade. The concept of time consistency in planning is general, however, and also applies to taxation of natural resource industries like petroleum and mining.

In so far as it is feasible, commitment is also a desirable quality in petroleum taxation. The major challenge in attracting petroleum investments is the high frontloading of investments. After petroleum companies have made large irreversible investments in production and distribution facilities, a government can achieve a short-term gain by increasing taxes above the level which the companies were led to expect when development began. The problem facing the government, however, is that oil companies may expect this type of tax behaviour. Thus, it is important to apply a dynamic economic analysis in this case, taking account of companies' expectations about a government's future tax policy. An unexpected tax increase is likely to lead to an upgrading of company expectations about the taxation of future developments. Moreover, an opportunistic and state-contingent tax policy – e.g. a scheme where taxes change in response to oil price changes – will increase uncertainty about the future level of rates. Companies will then face political as well as technical and financial risk: political risk in terms not only of dramatic changes in tax and regulatory regimes, but also of relatively minor deviations from announced policies. After upgrading both the expected size of, and the uncertainty around, the future tax burden, companies will be less interested in participating in future licences. It is also reasonable to suppose that they will change their attitude to existing fields towards adoption of a more short-term approach. The emphasis will shift towards faster pay-back at the expense of long-term reservoir utilisation. Taken together, these considerations may well – for reasonable discount rates – reduce future tax revenues by a greater amount than the short-term gain.

Special conditions in the petroleum industry which inhibit credible commitment are discussed in Section 2. Section 3 applies existing literature on the commitment issue (principal-agent theory and signalling games) to the petroleum industry. Efforts are made in Section 4 to characterise Norwegian along the commitment-opportunism dimension, and opportunities available to the government to commit itself to a fixed tax policy on the Norwegian continental shelf (NCS) are discussed. Except for Section 3, which is technical (and can be skipped), the chapter is written to accessible to a broad group of readers. It is also written so that readers may skip Section 3.

2 Special conditions in the petroleum industry

Credible commitment on future tax policy is generally important in providing the right investment incentives. Fears of future tax rises can yield welfare losses as a result of under-investment. In this context, and taking Norway as an example, under-investment can take two forms: (1) the overall development of the NCS might fall below an optimal pace of production and (2) spending on individual fields could be below the desirable level – in other words, the balance between investment and operation expenditure is sub-optimal. Welfare (deadweight) losses from distortions in the form of under-investment represent a particularly important problem in a capital-intensive industry such as petroleum production. An additional problem for recovery of non-renewable resources is that the absence of a credible tax policy can also yield losses in the real economy by distorting production decisions. An example of the latter is that absence of credibility could lead to faster extraction and thereby sub-optimum reservoir management and a low recovery factor (i.e. a lower fraction of the overall reserves will be extracted). For simplicity, the discussion below focuses on the problem of under-investment (the problem of speeded-up production is analogous). The relative size of the problems of under-investment and sup-optimal reservoir drainage will depend on the level of monitoring and control by the resource authorities. Sub-optimal reservoir drainage can to some extent be detected by the resource authorities. Under-investment is perhaps less detectable, as some of the investment options may not be known to the government. The problems associated with the lack of credible commitment by the government with respect to taxation is similar to the problem created by weak property rights, which the empirical work of Bohn and Deacon (2000) shows can slow oil extraction.

Several features of the petroleum industry make it particularly difficult for a government to achieve credible commitment where taxation is concerned. One obvious problem is the long time frame for both individual fields and overall activity. Exploration operations are time-consuming, field development takes several years, and a reservoir may produce petroleum for more than three decades. The planning horizon for an individual field is accordingly very long. Moreover, expectations of new discoveries mean that the time frame for the industry as a whole is substantially longer. This lengthy planning horizon for both government and companies means that dynamic aspects are more important than in most other industries.

Other relevant considerations are rents in the petroleum sector that can be high, and the lock-in of major investments, which make it particularly tempting for governments to secure short-term gains through unanticipated tax increases. Capital spending on production installations and transport systems account for the bulk of costs on the NCS. These are tailored facilities with a little value in any alternative use.[1] After specific and irreversible investments have been made on the NCS, the government could impose high taxes without suffering appreciable static deadweight losses: the tax base is relatively inelastic. However, such a policy would incur a dynamic welfare loss through changed expectations by the companies about the government's future tax policy.

Another aspect of the commitment issue is that the government is limited to incomplete contracts. Full commitment would mean complete long-term contracts. Long-term commitment is constrained by institutional conditions, as discussed below. Complete contracts would have to specify tax rates for all possible future conditions. All future renegotiations of the tax system would then be unnecessary, as the tax contracts would contain conditions regulating cases of both extremely low and extremely high oil prices, extreme variations in resource potential, extreme cost variations; and different combinations of all those contingencies. In practice, however, the petroleum industry is characterised by a high level of economic and technological complexity. So it would be impossible to conceive of all future outcomes relating to costs, technology, reserve estimates and prices, and, even if it were no, such extensive contracts would also involve substantial transaction costs.

A problem related to incomplete contracts is that a great many petroleum tax instruments have been developed by the government over the years. Even if central rates were fixed, ex post rises in the tax burden could be achieved by adjusting one or several other factors which are significant for assessed taxes. One example could be changes to tax-free allowances. New rules could also be adopted on which expenses are deductible. Such deductions include many estimated costs and non-standard input factors which have no established market price. These are often delivered by companies in the same group. It is difficult to develop clear rules in advance for such discretionary deductions. Companies also run the risk that the government will introduce new types of taxation in the future to supplement existing forms. All sorts of environmental taxes are a case in point.

In many instances fiscal stability agreements are entered into, to improve the government's commitment. For a thorough discussion of such agreements, see Chapter 14 by Daniel and Sunley. These type of agreements, which often were in place, did not prevent a number of host countries to raise petroleum taxes when oil prices increased dramatically last year. This was done in various ways. Some countries simply violated the fiscal stability agreements. Others circumvented these incomplete contracts by imposing additional types of taxes (and thus adding to the complexity of the tax system) or by disallowing expenditures in the tax accounts. However, 2008 was indeed a special year, and stability clauses may be fruitful under less extreme price variations. See also Chapter 2 for Boadway and Keen's for discussion of a range of devices for addressing time consistency issues.

An important institutional constraint on the government's opportunities for credible commitment in tax policy is provided by the constitutional principle that today's elected representatives cannot bind a future Storting (parliament). This issue is common for all forms of taxation, but is perhaps particularly important for the petroleum sector because of the size of the government's tax take and the long-term nature of the business. The petroleum sector is so significant for the Norwegian economy that making very strong commitments on the future taxation of this industry could be a matter of democratic concern, even though they might enjoy broad support in today's Storting. Whereas the Constitution is an obstacle to effective long-term commitment in petroleum taxation, it could potentially also prevent ad hoc tax changes. One institutional arrangement proposed in Norway to enhance the government's credibility in terms of commitment is to use the constitution. The idea is that a constitutional provision will effectively commit the authorities since amending the constitution is time consuming and requires a qualified majority in the Storting. However, the long planning horizon required in the petroleum industry means that a four-year process to amend the constitution will not be much help. Nor will the requirement for a qualified majority necessarily be any great assistance because of the temptation to secure a high tax take in the short term.

In addition to the provisions of the constitutions, the government will also face political constraints on possible attempts to establish a credible committed petroleum tax regime. A relevant consideration in this context is that Norwegian voters dislike big profits and high dividends at private petroleum companies (perhaps particularly when these are foreign-owned), which give the impression that a national natural resource which belongs to the community is under-taxed.

The government accordingly faces problems in committing itself in a credible way not to introduce extraordinary taxation when times are particularly good. An underlying media reality is that, as oil prices and the US dollar exchange rate against the Norwegian krone rise, it will be tempting for journalists to assert that private interests and foreigners are capturing an excessive share of Norway's petroleum wealth. The fact that the same investors lose money in bad times is not such an interesting subject to write about.

These features of political constraints are by no means unique to the Norwegian petroleum sector – which has a very favourable score on indices of political risk. They apply generally to petroleum and mining countries.

3 Commitment and the taxation of non-renewable natural resources

This section use established models from game theory and regulation theory to illustrate and explore the problem of commitment faced by the government on the NCS.[2]

A Repeated game

The Norwegian government has chosen a policy of gradual recovery for the country's petroleum reserves, and very largely the same companies submit applications in each licensing round. The licensing process can therefore be regarded as being close to a repeated game. The first best tax policy will be for the government to commit to a fixed approach. After the companies have made specific and irreversible investments in period one, however, the government will have incentives to raise taxation in period two. This is because its assumed goal of maximising welfare means that it wishes to secure a given tax take with a minimum of distortions, and taxing irreversible investments does not cause (static) deadweight losses. The problem with the commitment solution is thus that it is not renegotiation proof (that is, not 'subgame perfect'). Because the government will wish to re-optimise in period two, the first best tax policy – which involves commitment – is not credible (that is, not dynamically inconsistent).[3] As a result, the companies will not regard the government's attempts at commitment as credible, and will expect it to behave opportunistically in each period. Given these expectations, this is then also the best approach for the government. The equilibrium which arises in such simple models for repeated games is characterised by under-investment on the NCS.

To reduce the problem of under-investment, the government will want to commit itself in a credible way to a reasonable level of taxation. In principle, this can be achieved by developing a reputation for sticking to a non-confiscatory tax rule or by creating institutional arrangements which penalise the authorities if they depart from such a rule. Reputation or institutional arrangements can be a partial substitute for long-term state-contingent contracts and reduce to some extent the problem of under-investment.

As discussed above, the effect of institutional arrangements is limited. To all intents and purposes, therefore, the government will have to concentrate on reputational effects in a possible attempt to create a credible commitment to the petroleum tax regime.

Simple models for repeated games predict an opportunistic tax policy with the absence of credible opportunities for commitment. Taking this to its logical conclusion could mean, for example, nationalisation of locked-in investment made by foreign companies on the NCS. Since Norway has an open economy and is an integrated member of the international community, the companies will generally not regard this as likely in Norway. In particular not in the petroleum industry, where the tax system has been particularly stable. Although the Norwegian government is not expected to implement drastic nationalisation measures, and so has greater credibility than politically unstable countries with a smaller degree of international integration – or countries where nationalistic aspects are more dominant than pragmatic rent collection – it will still be necessary to build a reputation for abstaining from more drastic measures which provide an ex post increase in the tax burden.

In analysing the dynamic taxation problem, I will consider two categories of games: those with complete and incomplete information about what type of tax collector the Norwegian government is. The latter is by definition free to re-optimise in each period – in other words, credible commitment is basically regarded as unattainable.[4]

In a game with complete information, the companies are assumed to know the government's goal: to capture the largest possible share of the petroleum rent while simultaneously taking account of the fact that the tax system will affect the size of this rent. In a simple model with a finite time frame (T periods), sub-optimum investment will be unavoidable in the equilibrium state. The explanation is as follows. The government's policy in period T cannot affect future tax revenues. Period T is therefore in reality a one-period game, and the government will choose the dominant strategy with high ex post taxation. The petroleum companies, who are assumed to have complete information, will foresee the government's strategy in period T. As a result, equilibrium in period T-1 will not influence the future. The government will again choose high ex post taxation (this is the 'dominant strategy')[5] and through backward induction equilibrium is characterised by high taxation and sub-optimum investment in each period.

In a model with an infinite time frame,[6] the under-investment problem can be reduced by adopting suitable 'trigger strategies.' (A trigger strategy is a class of strategies employed in a repeated non-cooperative game. A player utilising a trigger strategy initially cooperates but punishes the opponent if a certain level of defection (i.e. the trigger) is observed). Characterised by the following expectations, it is possible to achieve a sequentially rational equilibrium without under-investment. The companies expect a reasonable level of taxation if this has been observed earlier. Should the government deviate from that pattern of behaviour, heavy taxation is expected for the following *n* periods. The government will not now choose the dominant one-period policy of heavy taxation, since the gain in the present period is not sufficiently large to offset the loss of tax revenues as a consequence of under-investment in the following *n* periods.

Consider now the case in which companies may have incomplete information about the government's preferences over petroleum taxation. That could be the case with a change of government, for instance. By observing actual tax policy over time, however, the companies will form a picture of the government's priorities. A simple framework for analysing the under-investment problem in this case is a finite time-frame one in which the government is one of two possible types – weak or tough – and companies have incomplete information about which type it is. The weak type will give the companies a reasonable return in each period, while the tough prefers a ruthless pursuit of revenues. In the final period, it is pointless for the government to develop a reputation as a reasonable tax collector. The tough type will accordingly opt for high taxes. Earlier in the game, however, the tough type will have an incentive to pass itself off as weak in order to encourage investment on the NCS. This imitation strategy involves imposing a reasonable tax burden and thereby building a reputation as a reasonable tax collector. A high level of taxation would yield high revenues in the short term, and thereby an immediate efficiency gain in that taxes which cause distortions in other sectors could be reduced. This short-term gain must be balanced against the long-term cost of under-investment as a consequence of revealing that the government is a tough type. If the government has a good reputation at the start of the signalling game and is a patient player, it might be willing to accept a short-term loss of tax revenues in order to build and entrench a reputation.

B Dynamic regulation models

Petroleum regulation not only needs to account for repeated interaction between government and agent, but also account for the dynamics inherent in the resource constraint, as petroleum resources are exhaustible. Regulation theory presumes asymmetric information between the various parties in a contractual relationship. Through their activities, the companies acquire private information – in other words, information not directly available to the government (hence the asymmetric information): examples include development and operating costs, reservoir estimates by the companies, and their required rates of return.

Private information would not represent a problem if it were possible to ask the companies for relevant data and expect a truthful report. However their assumed efforts to maximise shareholder return could give company representatives incentives to report strategically. That means not reporting their best estimate at different stages of the life cycle of the petroleum field (such as resource estimates at the licensing stage and cost reports at the production stage), but selecting the outcome which will serve the company best. Strategic reporting should not be understood as deceit or illegal behaviour. Petroleum operations are highly complex, both financially and technologically. Companies accordingly often operate without exact costs or reservoir sizes, but rather with qualified estimates of these. The data and measurement methods to be used can be open to discussion, and cannot usually be unable to relate to an objective truth. In these circumstances, the companies can opt not to report their best estimates but rather to act strategically by drawing on the datasets and measurement methods which best serve their interests. Legislation and regulations for the petroleum sector often contain formulations such as 'best estimate', but breaches of such provisions are generally impossible to prove.

Asymmetric information is a genuine problem in most taxation and regulatory circumstances, but a number of special aspects of the petroleum industry mean that the government's information problem is greater here than in other sectors: a) because of the petroleum rent, the *incentives* for strategic reporting are greater on the NCS, and b) a vertically integrated multinational petroleum company has greater *opportunities* for such behaviour.[7] State participation and national oil companies can in part be seen as means for weakening the information asymmetries.[8]

To illustrate the problem associated with private information in the petroleum sector, first assume that the government has the same information as the companies (symmetric information). It will then be in a position to capture the whole petroleum rent without causing distortions in company dispositions. In other words, it will be able to levy a tax of 100 per cent on the net cash flow or financial profit, and this will be the optimal level of taxation. In reality, the tax system we observe is not like that.[9] At the same time, we see that a substantial staff has been built up in the petroleum tax office and the Norwegian Petroleum Directorate in part with the aim of checking company reporting of financial and technical data. In other words, the assumption of symmetric information is unrealistic. Tackling the information imbalance is one of the biggest challenges facing the resource management authorities.

The problem of asymmetric information in the petroleum industry is analysed by Osmundsen (2005, 1998, 1995). It is argued there that the tax regime on the NCS has emerged to a much greater extent than on land as the result of a bargaining game between the companies and the government. This game is analysed within the framework of principal-agent theory (also known as regulation or incentive theory.)[10] Petroleum deposits on the NCS are a collective resource which belongs to the whole community. In administering this resource, the Ministry of Petroleum and Energy acts as a principal on behalf of the Norwegian population. The petroleum companies are agents who are awarded production rights. In exchange, they pay taxes which benefit the community. The challenge for the government is to devise a tax and licensing system which collects a large proportion of the petroleum rent for the community while simultaneously giving the agents incentives to pursue exploration, development and production in an optimal manner from the principal's perspective.

According to regulation theory, credible commitment is a great advantage. This is because an inability to make commitments reduces the government's opportunities to secure the revelation of the private information held by the companies, or means that such revelation will be costly for the government in the form of a lower level of taxation.[11] The explanation lies in what is called the 'ratchet effect.'

On the basis of private information, companies with low recovery costs (reflecting high productivity or large petroleum reserves) will secure an information rent. This is because, instead of reporting their real costs, they can choose to pretend to be (imitate) a high-cost producer, for example, by means of strategic transfer pricing. This will yield an economic rent on the basis of the efficient company's absolute cost advantage. In a static model, the optimum under reasonable assumptions will be characterised by revelation of their true type by each firm (a 'separating equilibrium.') This means different tax packages for different types of firms, where the dimensions of tax packages are licence fees and royalties. The low-cost company will be indifferent to whether it chooses revelation or imitation, and receives an information rent equal to the economic rent of the imitation strategy. In the transition to a dynamic model, however, a low-cost producer will fear that revealing information at the start of the game will mean heavier taxation and the elimination of the information rent in all future periods – this is the ratchet effect. If the government lacks opportunities to make credible commitments, the companies will therefore be unwilling to reveal their private information today. It is generally the case that a principal achieves the maximum welfare if able to make credible commitments. This is because the commitment can be regarded as an extra means for bargaining. The opportunity set is widened, since commitment makes it possible to duplicate every contract which could be concluded without a credible commitment, so welfare increases.

Because of the ratchet effect, a general outcome in regulation theory is that the optimal approach for the principal – if it has credibility – will be to commit not to take advantage of the information revealed in the first period. This emerges from a model by Baron and Besanko (1984), where the private information parameter is not correlated over time and which shows that the optimal approach with commitment is to repeat the static (one-period) contract in each period. However, this model has limited relevance for the petroleum sector because it does not include the dynamics, mentioned above, relating to physical values.

A more realistic approach in dynamic models for the production of non-renewable natural resources is for private information parameters to be correlated over time. Possible examples of private information parameters include the company's efficiency and quality, or the size of the reservoir, and it is reasonable to assume that this information has a similar impact on production costs in the various periods.[12] As discussed in Section 2, it is also reasonable to assume that the government will lack credibility in any attempt to lock tax policy completely for the whole planning horizon.

Laffont and Tirole (1988) show that it is difficult to achieve clear results of regulatory problems in models with no commitment and correlated information parameters. This is again because of the ratchet effect. Since the government cannot commit itself to abstain from collecting the whole information rent after information is revealed in the first period, the company – in order to have adequate incentives to reveal its information – must be given a high information rent in the first period to compensate for future loss of profit. It could now be optimum for a company with poor efficiency or reserves to imitate a low-cost operator in period one and terminate its operations in period two when a more demanding contract is offered. The incentive constraint[13] now binds in both directions, and not only upwards as in the static model or in one with commitment or independent information parameters. This gives very complex equilibrium properties. That applies to an even greater extent to petroleum regulation because of the additional dynamics provided by the resource constraint – high production in period one yields reduced reservoir pressure and thereby higher production costs in period two. As a result of this reserve effect, production costs are inter-temporally correlated.

Two articles model dynamic regulation of non-renewable natural resources under asymmetric information on production costs, and find unique equilibrium by making simplified assumptions which eliminate the ratchet effect. In an article on mine operation, Gaudet *et al.* (1995) assume uncorrelated information parameters – in other words, information on production costs in period two is assumed to be the same as when the contract is concluded. This simplification allows them to analyse the case without credible commitment. In the other model, Osmundsen (1998) assumes credible commitment in order to be able to analyse a dynamic regulation problem in the petroleum industry with correlated information parameters. These two works also differ with regarded to modelling the inter-temporal effects which follow from resource taxation. While Gaudet *et al.* impose a resource constraint which binds for certain parameter values, Osmundsen introduces a reserve-dependent and asymptomatic cost function (production costs decline with rising residual reserves, and move towards infinity as the resource base contracts towards zero) which implies that the resource constraint does not bind.[14] This realistic assumption substantially simplifies the analysis.

Both models yield the result that, because information is asymmetric, the optimal approach is to distort (relative to solutions with symmetric information) both the overall scope and the pace of production in order to tax a larger proportion of the economic rent. In the case with commitment, this deviates from the well-established result that the optimum solution for the principal is to repeat the static contract – in other words, to distort overall production but not the production profile: see Baron and Besanko (1984). The reason why it is optimal to distort the production decision is as follows: the difference in information rent for two companies with differing efficiencies is provided for a given quantity by the absolute cost difference for the relatively more efficient company. Assuming that not only average but also marginal costs decline with greater efficiency, we see that the relative cost difference and thereby the information rent is rising in quantity. As a consequence, the government can reduce the information rent for the companies (increase the tax rate on the economic rent) by reducing the quantity. The gain from reducing the information rent must be balanced against the loss incurred from sub-optimum production adjustments (distortions in overall quantity and production tempo).[15]

When we add the inter-temporal coupling of production costs owing to the resource constraint, it would not be optimal to repeat the static contract even with symmetric information. Moreover, in order to improve tax opportunities under asymmetric information, the optimal approach is to distort the production tempo because of type-dependent dynamics in production costs. Osmundsen (1998) assumes that the reserve effect is type-dependent – a reduction in production costs as a result of an increased holding of resources is greater for inefficient producers than for efficient ones. In other words, the level of efficiency and the residual holding are substitutes (dynamic single crossing property).

Under certain circumstances, the models proposed by Gaudet *et al.* and Osmundsen deviate with respect to the sign on the distortion in production pace. With a binding resource constraint in Gaudet *et al.* (1995), it would be optimal for a set of company types to increase their pace of production. In Osmundsen (1998), however, the optimal approach is to reduce the pace of production for all types except from the most efficient. Gaudet *et al.* find that it could also be optimal to distort the production decision for the company with the lowest costs.

A two-period production model implies that tax paid at the beginning of period one is a function of the production level in both periods – in other words, that we have a three-dimensional tax function. Through a generalisation of Laffont and Tirole (1986), Osmundsen (1998) shows that the optimum inter-temporal contract can be implemented with a menu of tangent planes generated by licence fees and royalty for each period. That is, the companies get a menu of license fees and royalties to choose from, and by their choice they reveal their true cost type. These types of self selection mechanisms are seldom used, however, probably due to their complexity. Note that traditional theory on resource taxation advises against production-distorting royalty. This theory, which assumes symmetric information, prescribes neutral taxation.[16] With asymmetric information, however, we are in a next-best situation where a distorting tax could be optimal, as the distortion of the companies' production decision alleviates the information problem.

4 The Norwegian model for resource management and taxation[17]

Norway has a discretionary licensing system. A regulatory framework has been established whereby oil companies have ideas and carry out the technical work necessary to recover the resources, but their activities also require approval from the authorities. Such approval is needed at all stages, from exploration drilling through plans for development and operation to decommissioning proposals for fields.

The government receives significant revenues from the petroleum industry, with 31 per cent of its total income deriving from this sector in 2007. According to the revised national planning budget for 2008, the estimated value of remaining petroleum reserves on the NCS is NOK 3,790 billion in 2008 money. The government receives a large share of the value created through:

- taxation of oil and gas activities,
- royalties and fees,
- direct ownership in fields on the Norwegian continental shelf (through the State's Direct Financial Interest),
- dividends from its shareholdings in the StatoilHydro oil company.[18]

Petroleum taxation is based on the Norwegian rules for ordinary corporation tax. Owing to the extraordinary profitability associated with production of Norwegian petroleum resources, a special tax is also levied on income from these activities. The ordinary tax rate is 28 per cent, the same as for land-based activities, while the special tax rate on top of this is 50 per cent. When calculating taxable income for both ordinary and special taxes, an investment is subject to depreciation on a linear basis over six years from the date it was made. Companies may deduct all relevant expenses for exploration, research and development, net finance, operation, decommissioning and so forth. Consolidation between fields is permitted.

In order to shield normal return from the special tax, an extra deduction – the uplift – is allowed in the calculation base for special tax. This amounts to 30 per cent of investment (7.5 per cent per annum for four years from the year the investment was made). The uplift is designed so that the marginal tax on cost (in net present value terms) is equal to the marginal tax of income. Companies which are not in a tax position may carry forward their losses and the uplift with interest. An application may also be made for a refund of the fiscal value of exploration costs in the company's tax return.

The petroleum tax system has been designed to provide neutrality, so that an investment project which is profitable for an investor before tax will also be profitable after tax. This makes it possible to harmonise the desire to secure significant revenues for the community with the requirement to provide sufficient post-tax profitability for the companies.

5 Government commitment opportunities and today's Norwegian practice

As discussed in Section 2, a number of special conditions in the petroleum industry make it difficult for the government to commit to a fixed tax policy on the NCS. Nor do any international institutional relations exist which could solve the problem. Section 3 discussed, on the basis of the theory of repeated games, whether the government could achieve an effective commitment through reputational effects. A common denominator of repeated game models is that they depend on the government being a patient player if it is to overcome the problem of under-investment fully. A sitting government may perhaps be patient while in office, but the length of that stay is uncertain. Because of the long planning horizon on the NCS, the period a government is in office – even if its re-election is expected – will probably be short relative to the relevant time frame for petroleum investment.

However, the economic models which have been reviewed cover only the extreme points: where possible, the principal will want to make a full commitment in tax policy; if not, it will want to conduct a fully opportunistic policy – in other words, confiscatory taxes will be levied on irreversible and specific investments. Reality will undoubtedly lie somewhere between these extremes, and variations in policy can be seen between different resource-owning countries.

A pragmatic interpretation of the economic theory of commitment could be that the highest possible consistency over time in taxation is desirable, even where full commitment is not possible. Future taxation of an individual field should therefore be as predictable as possible, and efforts should be made to avoid frequent ad hoc changes in the tax regime. Similarly, efforts should be made to avoid ratchet effects.

The large scale of private investment and the substantial number of new licence applications indicate that the Norwegian government has succeeded in establishing a credible commitment to a reasonable level of taxation for the petroleum industry. It can hardly be claimed today that overall investments are too low – the level of activity is at record levels, first of all by massive investments to increase production from the existing fields (increased oil recovery). The investment levels are still high into 2009. Determining whether unexpected tax changes might have prompted selective under-investment or speeded-up production on individual fields is more difficult. Exploration activity, which provides the best indicator of confidence in future frame conditions, has been weak for a number of years, and new stand-alone developments are few. As always, it is difficult here to distinguish between the effect of fiscal terms and company assessments of the prospectivity of the NCS in a more mature phase. It would in any event be relevant to ask whether the same development and production could have been achieved – but with a higher tax take – if a greater degree of commitment in tax policy could have been established.

Norwegian petroleum tax policy has been entirely stable in recent years, despite the dramatic rise in the oil price. That contrasts with most other producer countries, even ones like the UK, where we have seen several considerable ad hoc tax increases. The stability of Norwegian frame conditions must accordingly be regarded as an important element underlying the fact that the country has succeeded in maintaining the level of activity on the NCS – with an unchanged level of taxation – even though the prospectivity (i.e. the amount, quality and extraction costs of oil and gas in the remaining reservoirs) of parts of these waters has declined. In today's economic setting, stable frame conditions will represent an important competitive edge for the NCS. The new system of cash refunds for the fiscal value of exploration costs in company tax returns has proved effective in attracting new players to the NCS. This is because the capital required for making a commitment in Norway has been substantially reduced in that the government directly refunds around three-quarters of exploration expenditures, i.e. the companies do not have to be in a tax-paying position to receive the government's part of the investment. For a sector which is currently very concerned with reserve replacement, this system can yield good additions to reserves in relation to the effective capital outlay. The Norwegian framework also allows companies to book the entire reserves in a field, unlike the position in countries with production sharing agreements where only cost and profit oil can be booked.

6 Changes to tax policy over time

Norway's earlier petroleum tax policy was to tailor taxes and licence requirements to prevailing economic conditions in the industry – in other words, to adapt the tax system to developments in costs, technology, proven recoverable reserves, foreign exchange rates and petroleum prices so as to ensure operators some reasonable level of profitability. The policy of tailoring the tax system could give the impression of being a political rule which effectively commits the government on petroleum taxation. This is not entirely the case, since the policy is discretionary and accordingly does not represent a complete state-contingent contract. The purpose of this implicit contract is to attract new investment. Since the price of petroleum measured in Norwegian kroner has the highest volatility among these economic factors and moreover represents a systematic risk, tax changes have typically occurred in the event of price rises (tax increases in 1975 and 1980) and reductions (tax cuts in 1986); all of them applying both to existing and new projects. However, each of these tax revisions has also taken account of changes in costs and technology as well as new estimates of recoverable reserves; on a sector basis.

Lund (1999) argues that the most important reason why tailoring the tax system is necessary is that it is not fully neutral. In cases of neutrality, the tax base will be identical with the petroleum rent, and will therefore exercise no distorting effects on development and operational decisions. A non-neutral system produces distortions, and these become more serious when prices fall. An important example of this in the previous Norwegian petroleum tax system was the non-linearity provided by incomplete tax deductions for losses. The latter can be carried forward, but are not compensated for the alternative cost of the capital. This is a particular problem in the petroleum industry because of the long time lag between exploration and the start to production. If the company fails to reach a taxable position, losses could never be deducted.

Another reason for choosing a tailored tax system is the political constraints imposed by voter dislike of large profits and high dividends at private petroleum companies. That places effective constraints on how much risk the government can transfer to the companies. A full commitment in tax policy would probably have meant high profits and dividends for the private companies in good times. To avoid this, the tax system is tailored in such a way that company profits are more evened-out: that is, after-tax profits do not surge when oil prices increase, but this is balanced by cushioning them when prices fall. This gives the impression of efficient taxation. However, a substantial proportion of the risk is transferred to the government.[19]

The earlier petroleum tax regime on the NCS resembles the equitable mechanism described in Baron (1989). This mechanism lies between full commitment and pure opportunism. In Baron's model, the private company is free to withdraw from the business relationship in each period, and the government is unable to commit to a fixed future policy. The parties conclude a voluntary agreement, whereby the company renounces the right to withdraw from the business relationship, and the principal in return places restrictions on its opportunism. Because of major irreversible and specific investments on the NCS, the companies do not have opportunities for withdrawing from the business. Instead, they can refuse to participate in new licensing rounds. Until the NCS has been completely developed, the government will therefore have an incentive to limit its opportunism.

The equitable mechanism can represent an opportunity in conditions where full commitment in the form of fully state-contingent contracts is not possible. It is worth noting that this mechanism does not entirely resolve the commitment problem, since it requires that the principal is in a position to give credible guarantees on non-negative profits to the companies after they have revealed their information on costs and reservoirs, or after an irreversible and specific investment has been made. Baron's response to this is to assume that the equitable mechanism takes the form of a written contract between the parties (in effect a fiscal stability agreement), and that procedural demands and legal precedence limit the government's opportunities to change this ex post. This could be relevant in our context, since procedural requirements in Norwegian law protect companies on the NCS from arbitrary and opportunistic action by the regulator. However, key elements in the regulation of the petroleum sector do not take the form of explicit legal contracts, but are instead implicit contracts between the ministry and the industry. Rather than binding legal agreements, Norway's international obligations can protect the companies to some extent against arbitrary treatment. Similarly, the threat of diplomatic problems and economic penalties from other countries can have a disciplinary effect on tax policy towards foreign companies.

The controversial issue of asymmetric treatment of old and new fields with regard to royalty is relevant to the discussion on commitment. As noted by Lund (1999), a negative royalty was introduced in the 1986–87 tax reform following a drop in the price of petroleum. However, this applied only to licences with a development plan approved after January 1986. That is an asymmetry; the tax increases of 1975 and 1980 (which were implemented in the wake of price increases), in contrast, embraced all fields. This asymmetry recalls the ratchet effects described in Section 3, and can be regarded as an opportunistic policy – high tax on irrevocable investments. This practice undermines the credibility of the government's implicit tax contract. The problem is that tax changes are made on an ad hoc basis. If progressivity is an important goal for the government, it would be better from that perspective to construct a clearly defined and stable progressive tax system.

Lund (1999) concludes that this asymmetric tax policy will, all other factors being equal, reduce the interest of the companies in new licences. In order to maintain the level of investment, the government must reduce its required tax take. It would have been possible to maintain a higher level of taxes if the government had avoided a reputation for asymmetric taxation. I support that conclusion, and would add that credibility in taxation is becoming ever more important as the number of fields remaining to be developed falls.

The principle of uniform taxation of all fields, old and new, which was established in Proposition no. 12 (1991–1992) to the Odelsting division of the Storting can be regarded as an attempt to secure a reputation for non-discrimination.[20] It must be emphasised that the problem of time-inconsistent taxation does not lie in the fact that different tax levels are assessed for *different* fields, but that taxation of the *individual* field is not consistent over time – in other words, that the tax system responds asymmetrically to price rises and falls over the production period. Taxes are increased when prices rise, but not reduced to the same degree when they fall. A lack of neutrality in the tax system would eventually necessitate a lower effective tax rate in order to secure the development of marginal fields. If the tax take from existing profitable fields is simultaneously to be protected, a system of differentiated field taxation would emerge.[21] It is worth noting that making a credible commitment to equality of effective taxation of profitable and marginal fields can create the opposite of the ratchet effect. Through such a commitment, the companies would expect the government to reduce the tax burden in future in order to secure the development of marginal fields. With equal treatment, this would also apply to very profitable fields which are already in production. We could then get a position where the effective tax burden is higher in the development phase than during production – in other words, that development expenses are deductible from a higher rate of tax than is later levied on operating revenues. That could yield a socio-economic loss in the form of over-investment on the NCS.

A development has taken place in the Norwegian petroleum tax system over the past decade, away from an approach tailored to the prevailing oil price and towards a fixed regime independent of that price. This trend towards a greater degree of commitment in frame conditions coincides with shifts towards an even more neutral tax system, which reduces the need for tax adjustments when oil prices move. Among the modifications which have yielded greater neutrality are the ability to carry losses forward with a risk free interest rate, opportunities for transferring tax-related losses when winding up companies, and direct payment of the government's share of exploration costs (by tax refund).[22]

7 Conclusion

Although a number of special factors make commitment difficult in petroleum taxation, a certain degree of credibility can be achieved through practising stable and reasonable levels of taxes over time. An important reason why the Norwegian government has so far achieved credibility is that the desire to secure the development of a substantial number of new fields has had a disciplinary effect on the taxation of producing fields. As the NCS matures, with fewer new fields in line for development, the government will depend on a reputation as a predictable and reasonable tax collector to avoid under-investment. The signs are that the Norwegian government has succeeded in building a reputation for consistent field taxation over time. However, such a reputation is easily lost, and thus the Norwegian government continuously needs to take tax credibility into account in tax decisions. According to contract theory, a commitment of this kind – providing it is regarded as credible by the companies – will yield a higher tax take from the petroleum sector. Norwegian petroleum taxation has been very stable in recent years despite sharp oil price rises. Frequent tax increases in other resource-owning countries have thereby enhanced the competitiveness of the NCS.

One could say that Norway originally made an implicit promise to the oil industry concerning a reasonable level of taxation. This was achieved by adjusting tax rates at regular intervals and tailoring them to the industry's overall economic position. In other words, there was commitment in tax policy even though the level of taxation varied over time. The important consideration in this context is that the tax changes follow a specific rule and are symmetrical. If they are asymmetrical – in that taxes rise more readily with higher prices than they fall with lower prices – the implicit promise to the industry will have been broken. There have been few such breaches in Norwegian oil history. The problem with many of the tax changes seen recently in a number of producer countries is that they do not follow a specific rule and are perceived in a number of cases as arbitrary. Importantly, credibility is not necessarily at odds with progressive taxation, as long as the progressive elements are part of the initial tax contract. Actually, it might even help credibility in political economy settings, as discussed and illustrated in Chapter 2 by Boadway and Keen. However, progressivity may in some cases have detrimental incentive effects.

Over the past decade, Norway has shifted to a policy of absolute commitment, where the tax system is unchanging. This has been made possible by changes which ensure that the regime is neutral. Changes to the tax system in response to distortions caused by the same system are thereby avoided. However, a number of industry participants and external analysts believe that the Norwegian government will have to reduce taxes if the oil price falls to a sufficiently low level.

Generally speaking, an underlying cause of frequent ad hoc changes in petroleum taxation is a distorting tax system which needs to be adjusted when the oil price moves substantially. Another reason for the lack of commitment and credibility in petroleum taxation may have been that this regime is governed by relatively short-term considerations, with great weight given to the tax take in the present budget year or in the government's period of office. A third cause of tax adjustments could be various national considerations which override pragmatic evaluations concerning the maximisation of the tax take from the petroleum sector.

On a general basis, the conclusion is that petroleum tax should be shaped in a long-term perspective with the emphasis on credibility and predictability. However, this does not mean that all the elements in the Norwegian petroleum tax regime are suitable for all types of producer countries. Norway's petroleum taxation has changed over time on a couple of significant points. The system has become more neutral, for instance by tax refunds of exploration costs. As a consequence, the Norwegian government has steadily accepted more risk, which can be seen as a logical consequence of higher wealth. This calls for considerable financial strength, which not all producer countries possess. When operations began on the NCS, the Norwegian government utilised mechanisms such as carried interest and the sliding scale, which reduced its capital requirements and exposure to risk. The Norwegian model is also based on many detailed and discretionary contracts between the regulatory authorities and the oil companies on such issues as the determination of licence awards, norm prices[23] deductible expenses and production permits. This makes very heavy demands on the expertise and integrity of the government administration. If such expertise and integrity are not fully present, simpler and more transparent administrative models would be preferable.

Acknowledgements

I would express my thanks for rewarding conversations with and comments on the chapter itself from Michael Keen and a number of key specialists in the oil sector.

Notes

1 If removal costs are taken into account, the alternative value could be negative.
2 The focus will be on the problem of commitment in the taxation of non-renewable resources. A broader treatment of the credibility issue in economic policy is provided by Persson and Tabellini (1990).
3 This concept derives from macroeconomics. See Kydland and Prescott (1977).
4 For an introduction to game theory, with the emphasis on applications, see Gibbons (1992).
5 In game theory, dominance (also called strategic dominance) occurs when one strategy is better than any other strategy for one player, no matter how that player's opponents may play.
6 Strictly speaking, the game between the government and the petroleum companies will not have an infinite time frame, since petroleum is a scarce non-renewable resource. An infinite time frame can nevertheless be defended by assuming a stochastic end date for operations on the NCS: this is a reasonable given that exploration yields the discovery of additional reserves, and production experience leads to revision of estimated reserve in existing fields.
7 For more details, see Olsen and Osmundsen (2001, 2003) and Osmundsen *et al.* (1998).
8 Though of course they can also bring their own difficulties: see for instance Chapter 9 by McPherson.
9 One reason is that such an accurate handling of costs of revenue is not possible so that the tax system exactly collects the resource rent, e.g. with incomplete cost deductions the calculated rent is not exact – it actually includes the return to some variable factor.
10 For a good overview of this subject, see Laffont and Tirole (1993).
11 I will concentrate in the following on the extreme cases of no commitment and fully credible commitment. An intermediate case covered in regulation theory is a con-

dition with long-term committed contracts, in which the parties are unable to undertake not to renegotiate. Problems with access to information also often arise in this case. See Laffont and Tirole (1993).

12 The case of independent cost parameters can be descriptive of a regulation position where the private information relates to factor prices, which are independent over time.

13 The incentive constraint ensures that the company reports truthfully. In the static model, a high-cost producer must not have a (strict) gain from pretending that it has low costs in order to secure lower tax: the incentive constraint is then said to bind upwards. As noted, dynamic models with no commitment and correlated information parameters can also bind downwards – in other words, low-cost producers can have incentives to imitate high-cost ones.

14 We will see an interior solution due to strongly increasing costs. The proportion of the resource base pumped up from the reservoir is normally 20–60 per cent. It is technically possible to improve recovery even further, but this will be very expensive.

15 The optimal approach is to distort the production decision to the point where the expected marginal deadweight loss from the distortion corresponds to the expected reduction in marginal deadweight loss in other sectors of the economy which is made possible by increased tax revenues from the production of natural resources.

16 See, for example, Garnaut and Ross (1975). Land discusses experience with rent taxes in Chapter 8.

17 This section is based on Facts 2008 – the Norwegian petroleum sector by the Ministry of Petroleum and Energy and the Norwegian Petroleum Directorate.

18 StatoilHydro is an international oil company in which the Norwegian state holds the majority of the shares.

19 Optimal risk sharing between government and companies under financial, information and political constraints is an important subject which deserves closer study.

20 Despite this statement on uniformity, the differential treatment of fields developed before and after 1 January 1986 remains. On the other hand, no new asymmetries have been proposed.

21 Such variation has already been introduced by allowing the State's Direct Financial Interest to vary from field to field.

22 See Bjerkedal and Johnsen (2005).

23 Administratively fixed prices – to avoid transfer pricing.

References

Baron, David P. (1989), 'Design of Regulatory Mechanisms and Institutions,' in Richard Schmalensee and R. D. Willig (eds) *Handbook of Industrial Organisation*, Vol. 2 (Amsterdam: North Holland).

Baron, David P. and David Besanko (1984), 'Regulation and Information in a Continuing Relationship,' *Information Economics and Policy*, Vol. 1, pp. 267–302.

Bjerkedal, Nina and Torgeir Johnsen (2005), 'The Petroleum Tax System Revisited,' in Solveig Glomsrød and Petter Osmundsen (eds) *Petroleum Industry Regulation within Stable States. Recent Economic Analysis of Incentives in Petroleum Production and Wealth Management* (Ashgate Studies in Environmental and Natural Resource Economics: Ashgate Publishers).

Boadway, Robin and Michael Keen (2010), 'Theoretical Perspectives on Resource Tax Design,' in Philip Daniel, Michael Keen and Charles McPherson (eds) *The Taxation of Petroleum and Minerals: Principles, Problems and Practice.*

Bohn, Henning and Robert T. Deacon (2000), 'Ownership Risk, Investment, and the Use of Natural Resources,' *American Economic Review*, Vol. 90, pp. 526–549.

Daniel, Philip and Emil Sunley (2010), 'Contractual Assurances of Fiscal Stability,' in Philip Daniel, Michael Keen and Charles McPherson (eds) *The Taxation of Petroleum and Minerals: Principles, Problems and Practice.*

Erkan, M. (2008), 'A Way of Mitigating Political Risks: Contractual Devices,' Papers and Proceedings, 31st IAEE Annual International Conference, Istanbul, June 18–20.

Garnaut, Ross and Anthony C. Ross (1975), 'Uncertainty, Risk Aversion, and the Taxing of Natural Resource Projects,' *Economic Journal*, Vol. 85, pp. 272–287.

Gaudet, Gérard, Pierre Lasserre and NgoVan Long (1995), 'Optimal Resource Royalties with Unknown and Temporally Independent Extraction Cost Structures,' *International Economic Review*, Vol. 36, pp. 715–749.

Gibbons, Robert (1992), *A Primer in Game Theory* (Harvester Wheatsheaf).

Kydland Finn E. and Edward C. Prescott (1977), 'Rules Rather than Discretion: The Inconsistency of Optimal Plans,' *Journal of Political Economy*, Vol. 85, pp. 473–491.

Laffont, Jean-Jacques and Jean Tirole (1993), *A Theory of Incentives in Procurement and Regulation* (Massachusetts: MIT Press).

—— (1988), 'The Dynamics of Incentive Contracts,' *Econometrica*, Vol. 56, pp. 1153–1175.

—— (1986), 'Using Cost Observation To Regulate Firms,' *Journal of Political Economy*, Vol. 94, pp. 614–641.

Land, Bryan (2010), 'Resource Rent Taxes: A Re-appraisal,' in Philip Daniel, Michael Keen, and Charles McPherson (eds) *The Taxation of Petroleum and Minerals: Principles, Problems and Practice.*

Lund, D. (1999), 'Taxation and Regulation of an Exhaustible Natural Resource: The Case of the Norwegian Petroleum,' in E. Figueroa (ed.) *Economic Rents and Environmental Management in Mining and Natural Resource Sectors* (Santiago/Edmonton: Univ. Chile/Univ. Alberta).

McPherson, Charles (2010), 'State Participation in the Natural Resources Sectors: Evolution, Issues and Outlook,' in Philip Daniel, Michael Keen and Charles McPherson (eds) *The Taxation of Petroleum and Minerals: Principles, Problems and Practice.*

Ministry of Petroleum and Energy and The Norwegian Petroleum Directorate (2008), available at: www.petrofacts.no.

Olsen, Trond E. and Petter Osmundsen (2003), 'Spillovers and International Competition for Investments,' *Journal of International Economics*, Vol. 59, pp. 211–238.

—— (2001), 'Strategic Tax Competition: Implications of National Ownership,' *Journal of Public Economics*, Vol. 81, pp. 253–277.

Osmundsen, Petter (2005), 'Optimal Petroleum Taxation – Subject to Mobility and Information Constraints,'" in Solveig Glomsrød and Petter Osmundsen (eds) *Petroleum Industry Regulation within Stable States. Recent Economic Analysis of Incentives in Petroleum Production and Wealth Management* (Ashgate: Ashgate Studies in Environmental and Natural Resource Economics).

—— (1998), 'Dynamic Taxation of Non-Renewable Natural Resources Under Asymmetric Information About Reserves,' *Canadian Journal of Economics*, Vol. 31, 4, pp. 933–951.

—— (1995), 'Taxation of Petroleum Companies Possessing Private Information,' *Resource and Energy Economics*, Vol. 17, pp. 357–377.

——, Kåre Petter Hagen and Guttorm Schjelderup (1998), 'Internationally Mobile Firms and Tax Policy,' *Journal of International Economics*, Vol. 45, 1, pp. 97–113.

Proposition No. 12, (1991–92) to the Odelsting, 'Om lov om endring i lov av 13. juni 1975 nr. 35 om skattlegging av undersjøiske petroleumsforekomster m.v.'

Persson, Torsten and Guido Tabellini (1990), *Macroeconomic Policy, Credibility and Politics* (Harwood Academic Publishers).

Index

Page numbers in *italic* refer to tables. Page numbers in **bold** refer to figures.

abandonment costs 109
accelerated depreciation 96
activity rules 307, 308, 309, 311, 312, 314
ad valorem royalties 29, 53, 127, 132, 140–3
ad valorem (value-based) taxes 320–1
additional profits tax 125–6, 254, 255
administration and compliance costs 134–5, 140, 142
administrative capacity 361–6
administrative functions and procedures 341–56
advance petroleum revenue tax (APRT) 111
advance pricing procedure 348
advanced pricing agreements (APAs) 390–1
Afghanistan 255
Africa 76, 83–4
agree-to-negotiate formulation 411–12, 417
Algeria 110, 175
Allowance for Corporate Equity (ACE) 32–3, 35, 63, 381–2, 383
Anglo-Dutch clock bidding 312
Angola 106–8, 174–5, 252, 325
anti-corruption programs 370
arm's-length prices 167, 171, 183, 348, 349, 389, 390
ascending auctions 41
assurances of integrity 370–1
asymmetric information: and auctions 53, 62, 81; in contractual relationships 431; and low-income countries 77; in petroleum industry 431–5; and resource tax design 23–4, 53–6; and royalties 63, 81

auctions 40–2; approaches *313*; and asymmetric information 53, 62, 81; and competition 291, 292, 295–6, 300; for natural resources 289–315; packaged approach, China 84; for price discovery 81
audit adjustments 353, 354
audit powers 351
audits of tax administration 370–1
Australia 108, 109, 139, 374, 388; North West Shelf LNG 174; petroleum resource rent tax (PRRT) 252, 254, 255, 256, 390; residual price mechanism (RPM) 171–2
average effective tax rate (AETR) 45–6, 47–9, 60, 199, 200–1, 218, **221**

barriers to new entry 43
beauty contests 41, 291–2
Belgium 381, 383
benchmark prices 348–9
bid variables 42
bidder asymmetries 301, 312, 314
bidder competition 291
bidder-optimal core 311
bidder preferences 290, 294–9
bilateral income tax treaties 410–11
bilateral investment treaties 411
bilateral negotiation 255
blocks of resources 41, 42
Bolivia 109, 127, 128, 280–1
bonus bids 299, 300
bonuses 42, 97, 320
booking of reserves 113
borrowing, low-income countries 77, 79, 82–3
borrowing costs 39, 195

Botswana 129, 249
Brazil, state participation 277–8
breakeven prices 170–1, 174, 200, 202,
    218, **221**
Brown Tax 32, 33, 35, 131, 137
business taxes 322, 335
buyback agreements 103–4, 117

Canada 374, 382, 388
capacity strengthening, resource taxation
    364–5
capacity to invest 79
capital allowance 172
capital asset pricing model (CAPM) 226–7
capital costs 172
capital gains 328, 411
capital scarcity 77
carried equity participation 266–7
carried interest 40, 132, 139, 267
cash calls 271, 272
cash flow-based rent taxes 35, 63–4
cash flow equivalent tax schemes 33, 36
cash rebates 131, 138
cash subsidies, investments 57
Central America 380, 381
central banks 78, 369, 425
centralized tax administration 356–8
certainty equivalent approach 143–4
certainty-equivalent cash flows 196
certainty-equivalent discount rate 50
certainty equivalent value (CEV) 143, 144,
    145, 148, 149
Chad 78
charges 42–3
Chile 125, 127, 128, 284–5, 409, 418
China 83–4, 129
CIT *see* corporate income tax
clock bidding 311, 312
clock stage, auctions 290, 306–9, 310
code of conduct, regional 380, 381
collusion 41, 81, 296, 297, 298, 306, 369
Colombia 278
commercial and fiscal objectives, state
    participation 268
commercial efficiency, NRCs 273
commitment device 59
commitment hypothesis 409
commitment technologies 78, 80, 84
commodity prices 82, 83, 241, 242
common values, auctions 294
competitive bidding, resource rent 255
concessionary regimes 93, 94–5, 97, 105,
    112
condensate 175

confidentiality of values 309–10
conflicts of interest 273–4
consumption scarcity 77
contract renegotiation, and fiscal stability
    assurances 419–20
contractual assurances of fiscal stability
    405–20
contractual regimes 93, 98–104
Controlled Foreign Corporations (CFCs)
    391–2
copper mining 125–6, 283–5, 414, 415–16
copper prices 20, **21**, 125, 126, 283, 284
corporate income tax (CIT) 43–4, 60, 96,
    99, 101, 108, 127, 131; CIT design
    393–6; international trends 378, 379–84;
    and mining 127, *128*, 131, 189; and
    natural gas 169; and petroleum 96; rates
    379, 380, 386; regimes 381–4; revenues
    379–80
corporate profits 380
corporate reorganizations 394–5
corporate tax competition 379–81
corporation tax (CT) 96, 110, 111, 252
corrective taxes 42
corruption 81, 291, 300, 350, 357, 366
cost of capital 195, 226–7, 252
cost oil 39, 99, 100, 407
cost-plus price 171–2
cost recovery 99–100, 101–2, 252, 267
cost recovery audit 354–5
country risk, minerals 124
country take **172**
credible commitment 426–35
Croatia 381, 383
cross border fields 393
customs and excise duties 127, 397–8

deadweight losses 426, 427, 429
debt to equity ratio 382–3, 391
decision analysis, of exploration 228
decision tree approach 197–8
Democratic Republic of Congo 128
Denmark 276–7, 382
depleting natural assets 75, 76, 77, 78
depletion allowances 43
depreciable assets 32
depreciation rates 37
developing countries: and auctions 289,
    300–1; and progressive profit taxes 323,
    324–9; and tax administration 344–8
development phase and costs 16, 17, 28,
    46, 103–4, 135
development tracts 296, 301
differentiation across projects 25

differentiation of royalties 29
direct state participation 263, 264, 265, 274
direct tax instruments 129
discount rates: and AETR 46; and NPV
    195, 201; and rent taxes 35, 36; and
    resource tax design 25, 49–51
discounted cash flow (DCF) 194–6
discovery bonuses 97
discovery process, low-income countries
    76, 80–1
discrete bidding rounds 305, 307, 308
dispute resolution, audits 355–6
distortions 24, 29, 31, 63, 431, 432
dividend distributions 382
dividend withholding tax 210, 284, 383,
    384, 411, 418
dividends 382, 383, *385*, 391
domestic market obligation (DMO) 101
domestic prices, natural gas 182
double tax relief 326, 335, 336, 382, 383
double taxation 257, 323, 336, 384–8,
    410–11
double taxation agreements (DTAs) 22,
    257, 335, 382, 383, 392
double taxation treaties 210, 383, 387–8
drainage tracts 296, 301, 302
drilling, decision analysis 228
Dutch Disease 270
dynamic regulation models 431–5

earmarking: resource revenues 77, 78;
    spending from borrowing 83; tax
    revenues 43
economic efficiency 132–3, 380
economic profits 31–2, 37
economic rent 15, 135, **136**, 138, 143,
    166–7, 406
Ecuador 109
effective tax rates 45–9, 191, 202
efficiency, resource rent tax 248–51
efficiency losses 28–9, 132, 140, 141
energy prices 182
engineering design studies 228
English auctions 302, 304
enhanced oil recovery (EOR) 100, 103
equity financing 382
equity interest 172, 173, 248, 267
equity participation 40, 127
equity returns **271**
Estonia 382, 383
ethical codes, tax officials 370
European Union 380, 381, 393
European Union Parent-Subsidiary
    Directive 382

excess profits taxes 80, 131
exemption system 384
exhaustibility 25–7
expected monetary value (EMV) 197, 198,
    228–9
expected net present value (ENPV) 143,
    144
expected rate of return 202
expected risk index 202
expected yield index 203
exploration: costs 16, 17, 28, 96, 135; and
    investment 82, 198; phase 16, 28, 46;
    risk 252–3; risk analysis 227–9
export duties 397–8
export prices, natural gas 178–80, 182
export taxes 31, 42, 397
exposure problem 297, 298, 304, 307, 308
expropriation 58, 115, 300, 425
extraction path 28
extraction phase and costs 16, 17, 25, 46,
    81
extraction rights 81, 83–4
Extractive Industries Transparency
    Initiative (EITI) 129, 369, 371

favoritism 291, 292, 300
finance ministries 274, 354, 355, 356,
    357–8, 373
first-come-first-served negotiation, mining
    291
first-price sealed-bid auctions 290, 301,
    302, 312–13, 314
fiscal accounts 27
fiscal arrangements 93–104
fiscal constitution 78
fiscal instruments in mineral taxation
    124–5, 129–35
fiscal loss 134
fiscal regimes: design 105–9; mining and
    petroleum 406–7; for resource projects
    187–225
fiscal revenues 181, 182
fiscal ring fences 173, 174
fiscal risk 114, 409, 420
fiscal stability 114–15
fiscal stability agreements 428
fiscal stability clauses 58, 405–20, 428
Manual on Fiscal Transparency 366, 371
flexibility: in integrated budgets 78; rent
    collection 133; in tax system 115, 245,
    247
foreign direct investment 128, 411
foreign financial assets 79, 82
foreign investment 19

foreign levy 386
foreign oil and gas extraction income (FOGEI) 386
foreign oil related income (FORI) 386
foreign-owned firms 22, 23
foreign tax credits 44, 101, 328, 383, 384–8
forward contracts 332
forward-looking AETR 199
free equity participation 267
Free on Board (FoB) price 173, 176, 178, 179, 180
frozen law formulation 411, 412, 416–17
full equity participation 266
funding: of state participation 269–73; for tax administration 364
Future Generations Fund model 78, 79
future tax policy 56, 58, 408, 426, 427

gas *see* natural gas
gas transfer price (GTP) 171, 174
geared royalties 81–2
geological risk assessment 227
geological uncertainties 81
geology 19–20, 23, 62
Germany 382
Ghana 127, 128, 252
gold mining 39, 414–15
gold plating incentives 254, 328
governance 14, 57, 129, 268–9, 366–71
government: and borrowing 82–3; credible commitment 76–7, 426–7, 428, 429; and discount rates 49–51; and equity holdings 40; and fiscal regime 202–3, 406; and fiscal stability assurances 407–10, 420; and investors 15, 19, 35, 56–8, 244; policy, oil 90–104; regulation 166, 171, 174, 321; reputation and investment 57–8; and resource tax reform 371–2; revenue 17–19, 41–2, 201, 251; and risk 52, 133, 191–2, 215–17, 218–20; share of total benefits 203, *217*; sovereign rights, oil 112; state-run operations 53; and tax base 15
government take: and AETR 200–1; and fiscal design 105, 106; mining 271, **272**; natural gas 178; oil 271, **272**; and risk sharing 116; and transfer pricing 170–1
graduated price-based windfall tax 132
grandfathering 413
gross royalty 95–6
Guide on Resource Revenue Transparency 366, 371
Guyana 127

hedging instruments, taxation of 331–4
Henry Hub spot price (US) 179
high-income countries 77–80
hold up problem 15
host governments and investors 24
Hotelling rent 16, 25, 191
hurdle rate 194, 195, 196, 205–6

import duties 44, 397
in-country costs, natural gas 180–1
incentive constraint 434
incentive regimes 76
incentives: for investors 15; for tax setting 24
income tax audit 354–5
incomplete contracts 427–8
independent power projects (IPP) 167
indirect taxation 129, 396–8
individual lot bids 297, 311, 312
Indonesia 128, 278–9
industrial linkages 19
industry costs 141
inflation 381
information exchange between tax authorities 392–3
information powers 351
information rent 433, 434
infrastructure owners (IOs) 180–1
infrastructure provision 42, 83–4
institutional capacity 274
institutions: robustness of 76; and tax audits 356–71
intangible assets 32
integrated budgets 77–9
integrated projects, natural gas 167, **168**, 171, 173–4
integrated tax administration system (ITAS) 363
integrity of tax administration 370–1
interdependent values, auctions 294
interest: charges for tax underpaid 346, 347; deductibility against corporation tax 382–4; deductions 33, 199, 256, 328, 391; expense 96, 99, 108, 256; paid on debt 32; rates, signature bonuses 82; rates, world 79, 82
internal audits 352, 370
internal rates of return (IRR) 195, 202
international arbitration, tax audits 356
international considerations for tax 22–3
international corporate tax trends 379–84
international investment agreements 58
International Monetary Fund (IMF) 264, 366, 371, 373, 374

International Oil Companies *see* IOCs
international tax: competition and
  coordination 60–2, 380–1; and
  government policy 323, 335; issues
  378–98
intertemporal trade 51, 52
investment: costs 16; in development 46,
  47, 48; in extraction process 76–7;
  incentives 100, 127, 299, 426; and pace
  of exploration 82
investor risk, perception of 132, 192–3,
  217–18, 220–2, 246
investors: and discount rates 49, 51; and
  resource projects 15
IOC–NOC cooperation 90, 91, 92–3
IOCs: and Angola 106, 107; and buyback
  agreements 104; and contractual
  regimes 98; and PSCs 99, 115, 116; and
  risk 116–17; and service contracts 118;
  and state participation 264
Iran 118
IRR-based sliding scale for profit oil 106
IT support for tax administration 363

Jamaica 127
joint operating agreements 351–2
joint ventures 19, 22, 127, 351

Kazakhstan 129, 303, 388
Kosovo 255
Kurdistan 411–12
Kuwait 104

labor taxes 396
large taxpayer office (LTO) 359
late payment of tax 345–7
lease bonuses 97
legal assurance, future tax policy 58
legal risks 300
Liberia 129, 255, 411
Libya 299, 302–3, 314
license agreements 319, 320, 329
license areas 326, 329
licenses, auctions 290, 293, 306
liquefied natural gas (LNG) 163, 164, 165,
  167, 168
loans from public agencies 82
long-term government bond rate (LTBR)
  139, 144
loss-offset 43, 138, 139
losses 36, 43
lot-by-lot monotonicity 307, 311, 312, 314
low-income countries 62, 75–85
low tax jurisdictions 391

macroeconomic management 269, 275
Malaysian LNG (MLNG) project 169–70,
  172
managerial flexibility 196–7
marginal benefit 25
marginal cost 25, 46
marginal effective tax rates (METRs)
  46–9, 199, 200, 201, 225
marginal tax rate 38, 39, 191, 254, 380
market power 24, 305
market value 348–9
Mexico 91, 282–3
midstream taxation, natural gas 169–74,
  183
mineral exports 122, *123*
mineral fiscal regimes 123–9
mineral prices **124**, 125, 127, 128–9
mineral taxation 122–59; selected
  countries *150–9*; simulations 143–9
minerals-rich countries 265, *266*
minimum tax 53
mining agreements 405, 407, 410, 416,
  420
mining industry, tax audits 352
mining tax regimes 324
mixed system, mineral taxation 142–**3**
mobile capital 199, 379
monetary policy 425
Mongolia 129, 415–16
monopoly 84, 90, 93
monopoly rents 254
monotonicity 307
Monte Carlo simulations 196, 201
"Mozambique" simulation 203–24
multinational companies 22–3, 384–5,
  389, 392
multiple fiscal regimes 255

Namibia 128, 249, 255
national audit offices 370
National Balancing Point (NBP), UK
  179
National Energy Board (NEB), Canada
  179
national mining companies (NMCs) 265
National Oil Companies *see* NOCs
national resource companies (NRCs): and
  governance 269; policy and regulatory
  functions 359, 368; and PSA regimes
  329, 345; as regulator 273, 274, 359,
  368; and state participation 266–8; and
  tax administration 356, 359, 360–1, 365;
  and tax audits 354–5
nationalization, mining 126, 127, 243

natural gas: comparison with oil taxation
174–6; domestic demand 165, 166, 182;
exports 163, 165; and oil prices 176–7;
pricing and taxation 178–82; pricing
policies 170; production profiles 177–**8**;
resources and demand 163–5; risks
166–7; sales agreements 183; taxation
169–78; value chain 165–9
natural gas liquids (NGLs) 175
negative lifetime rents 36
negative tax liabilities 57
net cash flow, resource rent tax 247
net cash flow under contractual systems
101–2
net present value (NPV) 143, 144, 194–6,
198, 201
netback prices 171–2, 180
Netherlands 311
neutrality 132, 190, 191, 194, 212–14,
248–51
Nigeria 78, 79, 174, 182, 270, 272
Nigerian National Oil Company (NNPC)
270, 272
no switching rule 307, 314
NOC equity 172, 173
NOCs 90, 91, 103–4, 172, 187, 263–4
non-civil service agencies, tax
administration 360–1
non-discrimination provisions 405, 410,
420, 440
non-distorting tax 16, 38, 63
non-economic objectives, state
participation 267–8
non-recourse project finance 272–3
non-routine functions, tax administration
342, 348–56
non-tax instruments 129
non-tax revenues 27
nonlinear royalty 55
normal profits 80
North Sea 112
North West Shelf LNG, Australia 174
Norway: concessionary regimes 108, 113;
double taxation treaties 388; fiscal
stability 114; petroleum taxation 109,
426–42; Snøhvit LNG 173–4; state
participation 275–6
Norwegian continental shelf (NCS) 426–7,
429–30, 432, 436–7, 438–9
Norwegian model 85, 435–6, 442

obsolescing bargain 15
OECD: and information exchange 393;
and transfer pricing 389–90

OECD countries 76, 78, 80, 85, 92, 187
offsetting change, fiscal stability clauses
417
offshore auctions, US 302
oil industry 89–90
oil prices **20**, 109–12, 114, 127, 176, **177**,
205, 206
oil producing strategies 91–3
oil production profiles 177–**8**
oil rights, auctions 289, 294, 301–3
oil taxation, comparison with natural gas
174–6
Oil Taxation Act 1975 110
Okpai IPP, Nigeria 174
onshore auctions, US 302
OPEC quota restrictions 113
open bidding 295–6
opportunity costs 30
optimal tax design 53–5
Organization of Petroleum Exporting
Countries (OPEC) 127, 263
output-based royalties 132, 133, 134, 140–2
output prices 20, 200
outsourcing of tax administration 365–6
ownership of oil resources 112

package bids, auctions 297–8, 311
package clock auction 290, 306–10, 311
package values, auction lots 294–5
packaged contract 84
paid equity 132, 134
Papua New Guinea 125–6, 127, 128, 241,
242, 252, 409–10
pay-as-bid 311
pay on behalf PSCs 101
payback 75, 96, 109, 124, 202
payback ratio 100, 131
penalties: self assessment 342, 343, 353;
underpayment of tax 346, 347
permanent establishment 387
permanent income hypothesis 79
Peru 127, 128, 419
petroleum agreements 405, 407, 410, 416,
420
petroleum fiscal regimes 89–119
Petroleum Profits Tax (PPT) rate 174
petroleum rent 432
petroleum rent tax (PRT) 111
petroleum resource rent tax (PRRT) 109,
171, 252, 254, 255
petroleum-rich countries 264–5
petroleum taxation 425–42
physical audit procedures 302, 348, 349,
357

policy makers 23–4, 49
policy responses, state participation 274–5
political interference, and tax administration 371
political pressure 58, 59–60, 78
political risks 21, 40, 49, 300, 425
politics of resource tax administration reform 371–4
positive lifetime rents 36
poverty, in resource-rich countries 83, 129
premature closure of operations 28
present value-equivalent rent taxes 33–5, 36, 37
price boom (2002–2008) 129, 187, **188**
price discovery 41, 290, 304, 306, 307–9
price-linked tax 249
price regulation 176, 181
price shocks (1970s) 127–8
price uncertainty 20
pricing of production 348–9
private competition, mining 125
private information: auctions 294, 296; in petroleum sector 431, 432, 433
private ownership, oil 90, 91, 92, 93, 112–13, 187
private sector investment 268, 270, 271, 275
private values, auctions 294
privatization, mining 126, 128
producers, selection of 40–1
product definition, auctions 290, 293
production bonuses 97, 101
production costs 25, 135
production profiles, gas and oil 177–**8**
production sharing 39, 248, 267, 300, 342
production sharing agreements (PSAs) 39, 98; and fiscal stability 413; and national resource companies (NRCs) 329, 345; and tax audits 352, 354–5, 356; transparency issues 368
production sharing contracts (PSCs) 98, 99–101, 105–6, 107, 115, 299, 407
production taxes 324
profit-based royalties 29–30, 127, 131, 132, 133, 134
profit-based taxes 321
profit oil 39, 99, 100–1, 106, 355, 356, 407
profit-shifting 44, 59, 60
profit taxes 249, *250*
progressive fiscal regime 245, **246**
progressive profit taxes 323, 324–9
progressive rent tax 38, 66
progressivity 37–9, 48–9, 52, 58–60, 194, 214–15

project-based approach, tax design 24–5
project delays 272, **273**
project profitability: minerals 143–9; natural gas 176, 183
project risk 133
property rights 31, 42
proportional tax 38
prospecting process 80–1
prospectivity gap 203, 222–4
PSA regimes 329, 345, 356
public availability of information 369–70
public funds at risk 270–1
punishment strategy for investors 57
punishments, auctions 296

Qatar 173
quality of resource deposits 244–5, 289
quasi-rents 16–17, 28, 31, 38, 58, 66

R-based cash flow tax 32
R-factors 100, 131, 210, 212, 249, 251
RasGas LNG, Qatar 173
ratchet effect 433, 434, 437, 439, 440
rate of return (ROR) 100
rate of return scheme 210, 212
rate of return thresholds 247, 252–3
rationing schemes 40–1
R&D expenses 17
real assets 197
real option method 197
reference law 416–17
regional cooperation and coordination 380–1, 391
regional taxes 326–7
regional treaties 380, 381
regressive fiscal regime 194, 243, 245, **246**
regulation: government 166, 171, 174, 321; of resource operations 329, 357
regulation theory 429, 431, 432, 433
regulatory framework 91, 93, 104, 114, 116, 119, 435
renegotiation: adverse 300; in mining 125, 126, 243, 244
rent-based taxes 31–7, 55, 56, 63, 131, 137–9
rent capture mechanisms 321–2
rent collection 133
rent extraction 16, 23
rent potential 246–7
rents 80, 427
repeated game 429–31
reserve prices, auctions 298–9
residual price mechanism (RPM) 171–2
resource constraint 431, 434, 435

resource extraction 25, 26–7, 76–7
resource management 329–30
resource price movements **20–1**
resource projects, fiscal regimes 187–225
resource rent tax (RRT) 33, 241–59;
    administration 255–7, 258; and cash
    flow-based rent taxes 63–4; design
    247–55; as fiscal instrument 131; and
    mineral taxation 138–9, 142–3;
    parameters 254–5; rates 253–4; and tax
    competition 380
resource rents 123, 135–6, 138, 191, 244–7
resource revenue accounting 369–70
resource revenue transparency 129
resource revenues 17–19
resource-rich countries 17–19
resource stock depletion 25
resource tax administration 319–36,
    340–74; assessment of 373–4; reform
    371–4; tax administrators 330–1, 332
resource tax base 319–22
resource tax design 13–66
resource tax legislation 329, 330, 367–8
resource tax offices 359–60
resource tax regimes 45–9
resource tax returns 350, 351
resource taxation: boom and bust 241–4;
    low-income countries 75–85; and
    resource management 329–30; systems
    190–203
retained earnings 382, 383
revealed preference activity rule 211, 308,
    312
revenue equivalence theorem 41, 292
revenue management 251, 258
revenue-raising 40, 190–1, 193, 194, 207–10
rights of appeal, tax audits 351, 355
rights to exploit natural resources 40–1,
    289
ring-fencing: and CIT design 43, 394; and
    integrated natural gas projects 173, 174;
    oil and gas activities 97–8; of taxes 256
risk adjusted discount rate (RADR) 194
risk-averse government 192
risk-averse owners, natural gas 167
risk-averse (RA) private investors 135,
    136, 137, 138, 140, 144, 193, 246
risk-free interest rate 36, 138, 139, 144,
    196, 383
risk-free investment 144
risk-free rate of return 135
risk-neutral government 192
risk-neutral (RN) private investors 136,
    137, 138, 142, **143**, 144

risk premium 135, 136, 137, 138, 139, 140,
    143, 144, 252, 253
risk service contracts 98–9, 102–4, 112,
    117
risk sharing 51–3, 115–17
risks: mining sector 123–4; natural gas
    166–7
roles and responsibilities, tax
    administration 366–8
ROR systems 100
routine functions, tax administration 342–8
royalties 27–31; and asymmetric
    information 53–6, 63; and auctions 299,
    300; and corporate income tax (CIT) 44;
    and excess profits taxes 80; geared 81–2;
    gross 95–6; and PSC regimes 99, 100;
    role of 30–1
royalty rates, minerals 124, 125
Royalty/Tax Systems 95
Russia 105–6, 281–2

S-based cash flow tax 32
sales taxes 127
Saudi Arabia 91, 282, 388
sealed bid 41, 290, 296
sector ministries 274, 329, 352, 354, 355,
    356–7, 367
sector responsibilities 274
sector-specific charges 42–3
sector-specific profit taxes 39
sectoral tax design 15
segmented projects, natural gas 167, **168**,
    173
self assessment regime 341–2, 353, 367
semi-autonomous agencies, tax
    administration 360, 371
sensitivity analysis 195–6
sequential auctions 296–7, 302
service contractors, payments 322, 335–6,
    360
service contracts 98, 99, 102–4
shadow price 25
share bidding 300
signaling, auctions 296, 306
signaling hypothesis 409
signature bonuses 42, 82, 97, 101, 106,
    299
simplification: of progressive profits-based
    tax regime 325–9; of tax administration
    330
simulations, mineral taxation 143–9
simultaneous ascending auctions 304–5,
    312
simultaneous auctions 296–7, 302

simultaneous clock auctions 305
sliding scale, royalty rate 96, 127, 132, 141, 142
smokescreen hypothesis 409, 420
smuggling 60
Snøhvit LNG, Norway 173–4
social optimality 28
South Africa 129, 249, 374
sovereign risk 37, 63, 132–3, 140, 141
special petroleum tax (SPT) 96–7, 109
special zones 395–6
specific royalties 29, 132, 142
specific (volume-based) taxes 320
spillovers 19
spot markets 167, 176
SPs 180–1
stabilization clauses 330
staff, tax administration 361–3
standard taxes, resource sector 43–5
standardized contracts 326
state commercial participation 322
state equity 132, 133, 248, 271
state ownership: gas reserves 165; mining 127, 128, 187; oil 90
state participation: mining 125, 126, 128; natural resources 263–85; objectives 267–8; policy responses 274–5
state share of rent 203, 207
subadditive values, auctions 295
subcontractors, payments 322, 335–6
subsidised prices, natural gas 181–2
substantial rents 15–17
substitute goods 295
sunk costs 14–15, 16, 28
superadditive values, auctions 295
supplementary bids 310, 311
supplementary petroleum duty (SPD) 111
supplementary round, auctions 290, 306, 308, 309, 310, 311, 312
Suriname 127
synergies 295

Tanzania 414–15, 418
tariffs 24, 44, 179, 180–1
tax administration *see* resource tax administration
tax appeals 355–6
tax assessment 343–4, 369
tax audit 349–55, 366, 368
tax authorities 329, 331, 332, 342–3, 369–71
tax avoidance 22
tax base 15, 31–7, 247, 319–22, 379, 380
tax collection 343–4, 369

tax competition 23, 60–2, 379–81
tax creditability considerations 257
tax credits 37
tax holidays 242, 413
tax incentives 96, 379, 380, 387
tax instruments 27–49
tax legislation 115, 319, 327, 329, 330
tax neutral reorganizations 395
tax policy 319–36
tax rates 37–9, 105, 108, 138, 247
tax refunds 36
tax regimes 15
tax regulation 359
tax reliefs 36, 37, 97, 108, 116
tax repayments 344, 347
tax returns 350, 351
tax revenue 17–19, **271**
tax/royalty regime 406, 407
tax rules 19, 22, 57, 319
tax (state) share of total benefits 202
tax sub-regimes, consolidation 326
tax systems: design 251–2; international considerations 22–3
tax take 45–6, 105, 106, 108
tax tribunals 356
tax underpayment 346, 347
tax wedges 46, 199
taxes on profits 249, *250*
technical assistance and resource tax reform 373–4
technical assistance contracts (TACs) 103
territorial taxation 384–5, 387
thin capitalization 391
threshold rates 38, 138–9, 247
time consistency: and fiscal stability 407–8; in petroleum taxation 425–42; and resource extraction 77; and resource tax design 15, 56–60, 62, 64–6
time profile of government revenue 202, 207–10
Timor-Leste 416–17, 418
tracts 301
transfer pricing 43, 60, 170, 172, 173, 183, 388–93
transparency 129, 275, 291, 293, 368
treasury account 369
trigger strategies 430
two-way bet 417–18

UK 105, 108, 109, 311
UK Continental Shelf (UKCS) 92, 106, 108, **110**
UK petroleum fiscal regime 110–12
uncertainty 19–22, 31, 36, 46, 51, 52

under-investment 426–7, 429, 430, 431,
    436, 437, 441
understatement of tax 346, 350, 353
unsustainable benefits, fiscal stability
    clauses 413–16
upstream taxation, natural gas 169–74, 183
uranium prices 20, **21**
US 109, 386
US Federal Communications Commission
    (FCC) 307
US Federal Energy Regulatory
    Commission (FERC) 179
US Gulf of Mexico (GoM) 92, 105
US offshore oil lease auctions 301–2, 311
US subpart F rules, oil companies 392
user fees 42

valuation of oil or mineral resources
    348–50
value chain, natural gas 165–9
variable costs 15
variance of government revenue 203

VAT 44–5, 127, 322, 347, 396–7
Venezuela 109, 127, 279–80, 299, 303,
    314

WAEMU (West African Economic and
    Monetary Union) 61
welfare losses 426, 427
wildcat tracts 301, 302
windfall tax, mining 126, 129
winner's curse 294, 296
withholding taxes 22, 127, 322, 335–6,
    388
workers, risks 22
world capital markets 79
world prices 22, 24
worldwide taxation 384–5, 387

Yemen LNG 173

Zambia 126, 128, 129, 283–4, 414, 418
zero-rate CIT on retained earnings 382,
    383, 384